THE DUCHY OF NOVGOROD

Lovat

Dvina

Volokolamsk

OF MOSCOW

Varmia

Kaluga

Oka

Ryazan

Dnieper

Dorogobuzyaz

Tula

Orsha

Berezina

Mslivlavls

nsk

ich

Gomel

Chernigov

Desna

Voronezh

Pripet

Don

Doniets

THE GREAT HORDE

Kiev

Zhitomir

Pereyaslav

Dnieper

Braclav

Bug

HY

A

RY

TARTAR KHANATE OF THE CRIMEA

Sea of Azov

Review copy £31.95

2702 ① £ 2

A | -

FOREWORD
TO THE PAST

FOREWORD TO THE PAST

A Cultural History of the Baltic People

ENDRE BOJTÁR

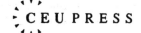
CEU PRESS

Central European University Press

First published in Hungarian as *Bevezetés a baltisztikába* by Osiris,
Budapest, 1997

English edition published in 1999 by
Central European University Press

Október 6. utca 12
H-1051 Budapest
Hungary

400 West 59th Street
New York, NY 10019
USA

Translated by Szilvia Rédey and Michael Webb

Distributed in the United Kingdom and Western Europe by
Plymbridge Distributors Ltd., Estover Road, Plymouth, PL6 7PZ, United Kingdom

ISBN 963-9116-42-4

Library of Congress Cataloging in Publication Data
A CIP catalog record for this book is available upon request

Printed in Hungary by Akadémiai Nyomda Kft.

CONTENTS

PART FIVE
CONCLUSION
OWN AND ALIEN IN HISTORY   343

FOREWORD TO THE ENGLISH EDITION

This book is, for the most part, an unchanged version of my book *Bevezetés a baltisztikába: A balti kultúra a régiségben* [Introduction to Baltic Studies: Baltic culture in Antiquity] which appeared in Hungary in 1997. In places I felt marginal modifications and extensions were necessary—only, however, to the extent of a few sentences, or at most, some paragraphs. I omitted references of purely Hungarian concern, but I added a number of works that I came across after the Hungarian edition was published. These include Arnold 1967, Boockmann 1992, Dubonis 1997, Gudavičius 1998, Kahle 1986, Nowak 1983, Pistohlkors 1994, Schaudinn 1937, and Schlesinger 1975.

There were two issues I felt I needed to amend to more forcibly represent my standpoint. One is the question of ethnogenetics. I sought to counterbalance my lack of expertise by referring to a number of studies which might help the orientation of the reader. These include Cavalli-Sforza–Cavalli-Sforza 1995, Haeseler – Sajantila – Pääbo 1996, Häusler 1997, Julku 1997, Niskanen 1997, Pääbo 1995, Sajantila et al. 1996, Sajantila–Pääbo 1995, and Villems et al. 1997. The other question—more important with regard to the book's topic—concerns the emergence of the state structure of the Grand Duchy of Lithuania in the Middle Ages, and the related problem of the Leitis people. The highly significant studies published by J. Kazlauskas 1995 and A. Dubonis 1998 on these issues have opened new perspectives in the research of Baltic ethnonyms.

Endre Bojtár

Budapest, June 1999

ABBREVIATIONS

acc.	accusative		instr.	instrumental
adj.	adjective		Latv.	Latvian
adv.	adverb		Lith.	Lithuanian
CHS.	Church Slavonic		nom.	nominative
Cz.	Czech		OEng.	Old English
Dan.	Danish		OGer.	Old German
dat.	dative		OHG	Old High German
Engl.	English		OLat.	Old Latin
ESlav.	East Slavic		OPol.	Old Polish
Finn.	Finnish		OSlav.	Old Slavic
FP	Finno-Permic		PFU	proto-Finno-Ugric
Fr.	French		PIE	proto-Indo-European
FU	Finno-Ugric		pl.	plural
gen.	genitive		Polab.	Polabian
Ger.	German		Pruss.	Prussian
Gk.	Greek		Russ.	Russian
Gmn.	Germanic		Sem.	Semitic
Goth.	Gothic		sing.	singular
Hitt.	Hittite		Toch.	Tocharian
IE.	Indo-European		Umbr.	Umbrian
Ill	Illyrian		Ved.	Vedic
imp.	imperative		Ven.	Venetic
inf.	infinitive		voc.	vocative

LIST OF MAPS AND FIGURES

"Nur einige Sagen, wie fremde Boten aus einer andern Welt, kommen aus dem Dunkel dieser ältesten Zeiten zu uns herüber."

(Johannes Voigt, Geschichte Preussens)

"Like alien delegates from another world, out of the darkness of those ancient times, only a few legends reach us."

PART ONE

INTRODUCTION

CHAPTER 1

THE CONCEPT OF BALTIC STUDIES

This work was the first Hungarian publication in the discipline described by the term 'Baltic studies' or 'Baltology'. In fact it was the first work to survey this field systematically in Hungarian. This is not a value judgement (originality is no guarantee of quality), it is simply an observation of fact. As far as I know, Oszvald Szemerényi, the excellent Indo-Europeanist of Hungarian origin, is the only exception. In two of his studies, neither of which was written in Hungarian and only one of which was published in Hungary, he included the Baltic languages in his comparative examinations (Szemerényi 1948, 1957). Still, these works hardly provide sufficient grounds for us to talk about Hungarian Baltology.[1] My earlier books in this area can be categorised as both educational and popularising in their intention and character (Bojtár 1985, 1989, 1990). The genre of this current study was decisively determined by its being the first of its ilk. As J. Gy. Szilágyi succinctly put it, it is not glazed with "the sauce of textbook knowledge" (Szilágyi 1994, 70) but consists mostly of such 'sauce'.[2]

In a narrow sense Baltology[3] deals with languages that are related genetically to each other and form a separate family within the Indo-European linguistic group, such as the East Baltic Latvian, Lithuanian, the extinct West Baltic (Old)

---

[1] According to his own criteria, Szemerényi would only qualify as a Hungarian as the author of his first study—the published version (Szemerényi 1948) of his lecture in 1944—because at one point he obviously considered the Polish J. Rozwadowski and the Latvian J. Endzelīns Russian researchers for the reason that at the time of their work before the First World War they were Russian citizens.

[2] The absence of a serious Baltic study in Hungarian was my incentive to stop working on this book for years or decades longer, despite its serious gaps and weaknesses (my weaknesses!), but I let it out of my hands in the hope that this work, though not, to use Horace's famous words, a "memorial longer lasting than bronze", will aid scholars coming after me.

[3] Affinity for language suggests that it should be 'Baltology' (Baltologist) following the pattern of 'Byzantinology' ('Byzantinologist') and not 'Baltistic' ('Baltist') following the pattern of 'Anglistic' ('Anglist'). The latter case is used in Latvian and Lithuanian, although the term 'Baltic philology' is applied more often. In this work I shall most often refer to the field as Baltic studies.

Prussian, and a few other less significant extinct languages or dialects. In the wider sense of the term Baltic studies examine the culture of these languages and peoples. The first part of this work will attempt to describe the history of the peoples whose languages these were. Periods will be discussed in greater detail where, alongside archaeology, linguistics played a significant role in the discoveries that fall between the Indo-European primordial fog and the beginning of historical times. The work will also offer an outline of the history of these peoples up to modern times. The second part constitutes an introduction to Baltic studies in the strict sense of the term—it will provide an external history followed by a description of the languages themselves (along the lines of earlier handbooks, e.g. Šmits 1936; Endzelīns 1945; Kabelka 1982). The third part will then elaborate on the culture (that is, other forms of consciousness) identified with or constructed around mythology in the ancient history of the Baltic peoples. This convoluted phraseology presages the problematic nature of the various forms of 'Baltic' consciousness that lie beyond language, an issue which I shall return to later.

The Hungarian term 'régiség' is roughly equivalent to the English term 'antiquity', the French *antiquités*, or even more so the German *Altertum*, the Russian *drevnost'*, the Czech *starožitnosti*, and the Polish *starożitności*.[4] 'Antiquity' can, however (especially the Hungarian term *antikvitás*), evoke associations with ancient Greece and Rome. 'Prehistory' is also a problematic term because what kind of prehistory would, in some respects, extend as far as the twentieth century. Nonetheless, this book principally focuses on the times before history.

The word 'antiquity' also refers to the scholarly studies of nineteenth-century polymaths on that period, no matter how long its duration. Debates in the fields of German and Slavic studies centre on the appearance and roles of the Slavic peoples in Europe. The debate opened with the *Slovanské starožitnosti* [Slavic antiquities], a two-volume work by Šafařik, a romantic mixture of imagery and fantasy of over a thousand pages (Šafařik 1837). K. Müllenhoff responded to this with five volumes which were no less muddled (*Deutsche Altertumskunde*, 1870–1900). G. Krek's misleadingly titled textbook *Einleitung in die slawische Literaturgeschichte*, which strove to assert that the Slavs were indigenous to Europe, has been left in undeserved obscurity to the present day (Krek 1887). L. Niederle's new work responds to K. Müllenhof's studies and reaches into the twentieth century. *Slovanské starožitnosti* [Slavic studies of antiquity], a nearly two thousand page work, remains valid in much of its detail (Niederle 1902–1911, I–III). Only Polish scholars have accomplished anything comparable, though in a somewhat simpler way, a collective work forming a lexicon (*Słownik starożytności słowiańskich*, 1–7—A handbook of Slavic antiquity, 1961–1982).

---

[4] Here, I will dismiss the notion that, as J. Hampl pointed it out, this term for antiquity cannot be applied for a definite historical period anywhere in western traditions (Hampl 1967, 306).

The cut-off point of these works is the eleventh and twelfth centuries (Labuda 1960–75/III, 10 ff.); likewise the *Reallexikon der indogermanischen Altertums-kunde* (ed. Schrader 1901) or the *Reallexicon der germanischen Altertumskunde* (ed. Hoops 1911–1919).

I will return to the question of how far back Baltic (Latvian and Lithuanian) antiquity reaches.

CHAPTER 2

THE ORIGINS AND MEANING
OF THE TERM 'BALTIC'

Over time at least four types of meaning have been associated with the term 'Baltic', often overlapping with each other to the extent that they sometimes become inseparable from one another. Such usage lies in the domains of geography, linguistics (philology), ethnicity, and politics.[1] The primary usage was presumably geographical.[2]

According to a rather widespread but erroneous belief the term *mare Balticum*, 'Baltic Sea' is directly connected with Latv. *balt/s, -a*, Lith. *balt/as, -a* 'white'. The idea can be found in textbooks as old as Šafařik's (Šafařik's 1837, 364) and also in more recent ones like Halecki (Halecki 1995, 14). In fact, the term for Baltic Sea (Latv. *Baltijas jūra*, Lith. *Baltijos jūra* or more rarely *Baltija*) does not originate from the Latv. and Lith. *balta jūra* 'a white sea' or Latv. *Bālta jūra*, Lith. *Baltoji jūra* 'White sea', nor does contemporary usage link one to the other. However, as we shall see, according to some, they may after all be etymologically related.

The term *mare Balticum* is an artificial construction. None of the peoples who lived in the region in historic times called themselves 'Baltic', nor did they refer to the sea by that name, as the sources often make clear.[3]

---

[1] For the most detail see Inno, 1979 (with bibliography); Kabelka 1982, 8–14; Zinkevičius 1984, 130–147; and Sabaliauskas 1986, 28–32.

[2] G. Rauch's insistence on the geographical term led to his claim that "(Baltic peoples) in the narrow sense of that term means the Estonians and Latvians"—at least in the fourteenth century, when the Lithuanians had not yet reached the coast (Rauch 1970, 14). The excellent summary edited by G. Pistohlkors also only discusses the history of Latvia and Estonia under the title *Baltische Länder* (Pistohlkors 1994). In this book the Baltic peoples are the Latvians and the Lithuanians, while the Estonians are not.

[3] The world of antiquity only heard about the sea quite late in time, let alone about the people living there. The Roman conquest discovered around 56 AD that great waters hindered them up in the north (Spekke 1957, 59). "There is not the slightest hint of the existence of the Baltic sea" in the sources (Hennig 1944, 367) until Strabo's *Geographia* in 7 BC (discovered only after five hundred years of obscurity) and Pomponius Mela's *De Chorographia* in 44 AD. The Baltic Sea found its correct place on the map only at the beginning of the Renaissance. C. Plinius Secundus (Pliny) (23–79) calls it '*Mare Suebicum*' after the Sueb Germanic tribe; the Alexandrian Greek

Two distinct viewpoints have evolved on the origin and first occurrence of the stem *balt-*. One of these derives it from Pliny who mentions the name in three different forms (see Kiparsky 1939, 48 and subsequently Smoczyński 1988, 815). In his *Natural History* Pliny cites the second-century BC Greek geographer K. Lampsakus who believed that there was an enormous island called Balcia three days away from the Scythian shores by boat.[4] Pliny also mentioned the Greek Pytheas of Massilia (Marseille) who had allegedly sailed around the north-western shores of Europe around 330 BC. (Allegedly, because as Strabo put it, "Pytheas, has been found, upon scrutiny, to be an arch-falsifier"—Strabo I.5.3.). Pytheas referred to an enormous island Basilia, while the historian Timaeus used the term Abalus where "amber is carried in spring by currents... The inhabitants of the region use it as fuel instead of wood and sell it to the neighbouring Teutons" (Pliny XXXVII, 36). In his work circa 250 AD, almost two hundred years later, C. I. Solinus called the island Abalcia (*Collectanea rerum memorabilium* XIX, 6; Endzelīns, 1945, 354). Many scholars think that all these references—Balcia (pronounced Balkia), Abalcia, Abalus, Basilia, Balisia (presumably a misspelling)—are to an island. Others identified Abalus and Basilia with Helgoland, Balcia-Basilia with Sweden, or Balcia (Baltia) with Jütland (SSS 1/170).[5] The difficulty in identifying these is that the stem *balt-* cannot be derived linguistically from the stem *balk-*.

Ptolemy (100–160) referred to it as '*Sinus Venedicus*', i.e. Vened bay (Ptolemy *Geographia*, 150); others named it 'Sarmatian' or even 'Scythian Ocean'. Eastern Slavic sources, from the *Nestor Chronicle* onwards, called it 'Varyag' or 'Vareg (Varangian) Sea' (after the Slavic term for the Vikings), in the seventeenth century it was called 'Swedish sea'; the name 'Baltic Sea' appeared no earlier than the end of the eighteenth century. In the Middle Ages it was referred to simply as 'the sea'. Its most frequent name is '*Ostsee*', 'East Sea', appearing for the first time on a map from 1553 (Niederle 1902/I, 34), though Adam Bremensis had used this term earlier but in lower case letters as a reference to its geographical direction and not as its name. The Germans, Danes and Swedes still use this name, in preference to 'Baltic Sea'. The Finns adopted the Swedish term even though the sea is to their west. The Estonians, in accordance to their geographical location, call it the 'Western Sea', while the Livonians and the Lithuanians simply call it 'The Sea' or 'The Gulf', or often (as the writers of the nineteenth century) 'Palanga Sea', i.e. 'Žemaitian Sea'. The Latvians called it the 'Great Sea' contrasting it to the Gulf of Riga, the 'Small Sea'. Clearly, the contemporary Latvian and Lithuanian term for the Baltic Sea is a late learned borrowing.

[4] V. Pėteraitis, a Lithuanian linguist living in Canada, recently claimed that the name 'Baltia' first appeared on the navigational map of the Alexandrian librarian Eratosthenes (ca. 275–195 BC) issued in 220 (Pėteraitis 1992, 71). However, the name does not appear in any other fragment subscribed to the Greek geographer to survive elsewhere, for example, in Pliny (Berger 1880).

[5] For a summary see Hennig, 1944, 172 ff.

What does the stem *balt*- mean? On the one hand it means 'white' (cf. IE. **bhel*-
'white'). According to G. Labuda "It is a fact, proven through a large scale
comparative investigation of material, that the words 'great' and 'white', if they
denote an area or a people, refer to a place, and 'white' usually means a point on
the compass, most often the west" (Labuda in SSS 1961–82/I, 1, 255).[6] On the
other hand, and more frequently, it meant 'swamp' (Pruss. **balt*-, Lith. *bala*,
Slavic *boloto* mean 'swamp'). Words referring to watery places, generally still
waters such as swamps, marshes, and lakes, are often linked to words indicating
colours such as those of the surface of water and water plants which diffracts light
into various colours. G. Bonfante (1985) and others after him also posit an Illyrian
word **balta* that lives on in the Albanian language (*balte* 'silt, mud'). V. Toporov
showed that **balt* 'swamp' survives in many place names from the southern shores
of the Baltic down to the Mediterranean (Toporov 1975–90/I, 189), including the
Hungarian (Lake) Balaton.[7]

E. Katonova sheds fresh and extensive light on the spread of *balt*- 'swamp'
(Katonova 1985). Her starting point is the name Polesye. Segmented Po-lesye,
the name is usually interpreted as a 'forested place'. This designation, however,
is not appropriate to the area of about hundred thousand square kilometres
bordered by the Black Sea plateau, the Belarus ridge and the valley of the Dnieper
and the Bug. The main characteristic of this area is that its waters, principally its
main river the Pripet, do not have any outlets, hence there are many lakes and
swamps. For this reason it makes more sense to postulate the stem *pal*- (*pel*-, *pil*-,
pl-) as in Lith. *palios* 'great swamp, marshland, peat-swamp', and the Lat. *palus*
'swamp'), with the suffix -s (*-es, -is, -ys, -us*), along with the forms of a parallel
bal- (*bel*-, *bil*-, *bl*-). This brings us back to the 'white' equals 'swamp' idea, and
thus the words Baltic *Polesye*, *Byala-Ruś* (first found in the fourteenth century,

---

[6] In such colour symbolism (most probably from China via the Turkic peoples) the other
points of the compass are blue for east, black for north, red for south. Hence Black Russia (seen
from Kiev), or Red Russia meaning the Dniester region of Galicia.

[7] That word provides crucial evidence for a former Baltic–Illyrian–Slavic language community (*Sprachbund*) or at least close coexistence.

The name of the river Elbe also goes back to IE. **albh*- 'white'. Its oldest forms in Celtic
and Germanic are Albais, Albios, and hence Germanic Albe > Albai, Alba > Elbe, and Celtic
Aube (SSS, 3/108). The semantic shift 'white' > 'river' occurred very early and later river
names were also derived from it even when their colour was expressly described with the Elbe
(associated with the colour yellow) and the Aube, a tributary of the Seine (green) (Krahe 1962,
292). However, linguists agree that the term Illyrian (?) Albanians (*albanoi*) in Ptolemy derives
not from this stem, but from a pre-IE *alb* 'mountain, hill' (Krahe 1938, 6). This latter stem is
related to words like the Alps, the Swabian Alb, Alba Longa, Latin *albus* 'white as mountain
snow', Albion 'craggy island' (Lambertz 1949, 6).

see Kosman, 1979, 15), and *Polovec* are part of the same set, along with Russ. *Polsha* 'Poland' which is seen less as 'meadow' (*pole*) and more as 'swamp' in this view.[8]

The other explanation of the *balt* stem is more straightforward. It refers directly to the sea. Adam of Bremen (i.e. Adam Bremensis) used this expression for the first time, "the Baltic or Barbarian Sea, a day's journey from Hamburg" (Bremensis I, 60).[9] He underpinned the naming *Sinus Balticus* through the local usage which dubbed it *balticus* because it stretches out towards the East like a belt (*in modum baltei*) (Bremensis IV, 10). Thus the adjective *balticus* was derived from the noun *balteus, balteum* 'belt', by the chronicler himself. Since Latin was not the language of the local inhabitants, the people of the Jutland and Scandinavian peninsulas, there had to be a stem that sounded similar to *balt-*. The simplest solution is to derive the stem *balt-* from the Germanic *belt-* meaning 'belt, zone'. The word has survived in several Norwegian, Swedish, and Danish place names such as the two straits must have been dividing the peninsulas of Jutland and Scandinavia which in Danish are still known as the Greater and the Lesser *Baelt*.[10] Inspired by these local place names and by the image of the bay stretching out as a belt Adam Bremensis simply translated the word into Latin, and then derived the adjective *balticus* from *balteus*. J. Endzelīns' legitimate objection that "the Danish words *Belt* and *belte* come from the Latin *balteum*, therefore they could not exist at the time of the [above] mentioned Greek authors" (Endzelīns 1945, 355) means that the correlation between *Baltia* in the Greek authors and *balticus* in the work of Adam Bremensis is merely coincidental.

Of course one should take note of the conclusion of E. Fraenkel's etymological overview: "All this is uncertain" (Fraenkel 1950, 21).

Whether its basis was IE.—Baltic *balt-* 'swamp' > 'white', or Latin *balteus* 'belt', the naming sank into oblivion and cropped up only very occasionally. The reason for this was partly that the terms *Baltisches Meer*, or *Baltisk Hav* belonged

---

[8] Katonova sees a parallel between Hun. *lengyel*, Lith. *lenkas* ('Pole') and Lith. *lenke* 'low land', Lith. *lanka* 'watery meadow'. In this case, however, the traditional explanation seems more convincing: these go back to *lędzianie* or *lędzanie* (< *lęd* 'fallow land'), a tribe on the borders of the Poles and the eastern Slavs mentioned by the ninth-century Geographer of Bavaria (which the Russian chronicles refer to as *lach*, and from which the thirteenth-century *Kronika Wielkopolska* concocted the brothers Lech, Czech, and Rus, the ancestors of the Slavs) (SSS, 3/52).

[9] A. Bremensis refers to Einhard, the author of *Vita Karoli Magni* from 820 AD, which proves only that in general he used Einhard's work as his source. But not in this case, because Einhard did not name the sea: "There is a bay east of the Western Ocean... Many different peoples live there. The Danes and the Sueons, whom we call Nordmanns occupy the northern shore and all the islands along it. On the other hand, Slavs, Aisti, and many other peoples share the eastern coast, among whom the most outstanding are the Welatabs against whom the king launched an attack at that time" (Einhard, 36).

[10] The Danish stem *baelte* 'belt' is an early Latin loan, presumably via English (Laur 1972, 53).

to a scholarly register in German and Scandinavian languages and everyday usage preferred German *Ostsee*, Danish *Østersø*, Swedish *Östersjö* (Laur 1972, 61). The German *Baltisch* replaced the Latin *balticus* around 1600 and subsequently other languages adopted this German adjective.

The submerged geographical term gradually became more widely used, especially from the second half of the nineteenth century, when it slowly took on political connotations.

In the first instance, German nobles in what was Livonia began to refer to themselves using this stem. Livonia belonged to Russia from the early nineteenth century and comprised the three so-called Eastern Sea Provinces (*Ostseeprovinzen*) of *Livland, Estland,* and *Kurland*), today's Estonia and Latvia. These nobles 'neologised' a noun from Adam of Bremen's adjectival coinage (*Kunstwort*) around 1840 (Laur 1972, 63). In the final third of the nineteenth century the term 'Baltic' (Ger. *der Balte*, Latv. *baltietis*, Lith. *baltas*) excluded the local people because they were not a factor in the creation of a nation. The language of these nobles in the Baltic was German (*baltisch-deutsch*), which only they, that is the ruling class, were allowed to use.[11]

A modified version of this usage continues in historical scholarship up to the present day. In the first edition of his fundamental work in 1944 R. Wittram studied the history of the Baltic Germans—not in the least independent of his Deutschbalt national socialist commitment. Ten years later in the second edition in 1954 he shifted from an ethnic to an areal approach and discussed the history of the 'native' Estonians and Latvians, though still excluding the Lithuanians.

The word gained a contrasting political connotation after the peace negotiations in Paris in 1919. From then on it referred to the three independent states (Republics of Estonia, Latvia, and Lithuania), including the local Germans who from then on became a minority group.

Parallel to this process, the term gained currency in linguistic studies. The increased political usage contributed to increased linguistic usage, even though the latter sense of 'Baltic' differed from the former. In his work *Die Sprache der alten Preussen in ihren Überresten erläutert* (1845) F. Nesselmann a professor at Königsberg suggested that the term should be used for a distinct language

[11] In Riga, where from 1860 the official language was Russian (Russian population: 25 percent), German was regarded as the language of the aristocracy (German population: 44 percent), while Latvian remained the language of peasants (19 percent of the population), and punishment was due to any Latvian person who would 'arbitrarily' use German in an office (Semyonova 1977, 213). Within the Baltic area differences in German dialects and origins were connected to social differences, that is, as soon as somebody opened their mouth it was obvious which social strata they belonged to (Pritzwald 1952).

(sub-)family within the Indo-European group (Nesselmann 1845).[12] It took time for the suggestion to be accepted, and the earlier habit of calling all the languages of this family either Latvian or Lithuanian lingered on into the early twentieth century.[13] In 1918 the Baltic States were established and this played a significant role in the concepts of 'Baltic philology' and 'Baltic studies' becoming prevalent. The most outstanding figure of Latvian philology, J. Endzelīns rightly stated that "it has been possible to talk about Baltic philology only since about 1920, when the Latvians and the Lithuanians established their own universities where Baltic philology could be part of the syllabus" (Endzelīns 1945, 353).[14]

[12] The political sense of 'Baltic' included Latvian and Estonian. The linguistic sense embraced Latvian and Lithuanian. Thus Latvian was common to both senses. Perhaps this explains why the Latvians used *Baltija* (today meaning the Baltic Sea) derived from the term 'Baltic' up until late in the last century instead of *Latvija* which came much later and is used today. Thus, in the title of Baltijas Vēstnesis ('Baltlandic reporter'), the first newspaper in Latvian in 1869, Baltijas referred to Latvia. Similarly, in his Lāčplēsis A. Pumpurs (1841–1902) talks about the Baltic (= Latvian) gods in this first significant work of Latvian Romanticism. The national anthem, newly in use again after the Soviet era, and first sung in public at the first Latvian Song Festival in 1873, had as its first line, "God bless Baltija" (LE./14, 1344).

[13] This explains the use of the plural in the title of P. I. Keppen's book (Keppen, 1827). Others, F. Bopp for example referred to Latvian, Lithuanian, and Prussian as Latvian (Bopp, *Über die Sprache der alten Preussen in ihren verwandtschaftlichen Beziehungen*, 1853), while again others like J. Schmidt calls it Latvian, sometimes Lithuanian, and sometimes both (Schmidt, *Die Verwandtschaftsverhältnisse der indogermanischen Sprachen*, 1872). ("Baltic that is Aisti, i.e. Litvako-Latvian"—Lautenbakh 1915, XIII.) A. Mierzyński called the entire group Lithuanian while W. Mannhardt referred to them as Latvian–Prussian after the two countries at opposite ends of the region. The word *aesti* (Lith. *aisčiai*) originally came from Tacitus and many thought that it referred to a Baltic tribe, perhaps the Prussians. K. Zeuss first used the word in his book *Die Deutschen und die Nachbarstämme* (1837) as a collective term for the Baltic tribes and it was taken up later by Lithuanian scholarship. K. Būga, the founder of Lithuanian linguistics considered this term more accurate than 'Baltic' (Būga 1923, 660). After 1934 the necessity of political unity among the Baltic countries became increasingly obvious. At that point some Latvian and Lithuanian politicians intended to name the confederation of Latvia, Lithuania, and East-Prussia *Aistija* (Aistus-land).

[14] N. Nadeschdin used the geographical term to differentiate three Russian languages: Russian proper, Pontic Russian (Ukrainian), and Baltic Russian (Byelorussian) (Nadeschdin 1841). Historians and linguists of Belarus who dispute their historical past with the Lithuanians, as well as virtually all historians of language agree that Byelorussian became an independent language largely because of Baltic: first of all it was established on a Baltic substrate, then the Byelorussians were the inhabitants of the Grand Duchy of Lithuania and their territories for centuries, today's Belarus and Ukraine were called Lithuanian Rus' as opposed to the Muscovite Rus' (Bednarczuk 1984, 47).

The term has also been used idiosyncratically, in narrow or individualistic ways. Thus during the Soviet–British–French negotiations in 1939 V. Molotov excluded Lithuania from the 'Baltic states' but included Finland, Estonia, and Latvia, because the former had no common border with the Soviet Union (Sužiedėlis 1989, 21).

In conclusion, 'Baltic' has a number of meanings: in a geographical sense it refers to the people who live on the shores of the Baltic Sea, that is, those from the Baltic; in a political sense it denotes the citizens of the three Baltic States; in terms of language and linguistics it refers to the Latvian and Lithuanian languages along with various other extinct languages or dialects (from which Prussian was the most important and in which a few written records have remained, too), in this sense the Estonians and other smaller Finnish languages and peoples, for example the Livians are excluded; in an ethnic sense it takes on one of these three meanings, depending on the occasion.

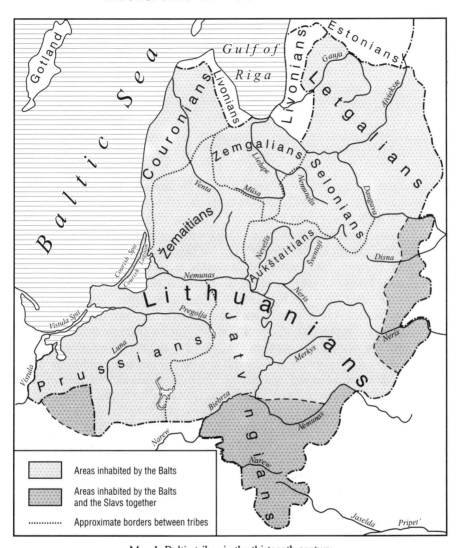

Map 1. Baltic tribes in the thirteenth century

CHAPTER 3

ENVIRONMENT

A major characteristic of the cultural history of the Baltic peoples is their isolation due to their geographical situation. On the basis of the names that became current during the Middle Ages, the Balts living along the coast of the Baltic Sea in the area from the River Vistula to Lake Ladoga were grouped in the following tribes or tribal confederations: from today's Gulf of Danzig or Gdańsk to the mouth of the River Nemunas the Prussians; eastwards from there the Sudovians (the Jatvingians) between the crook of the River Nemunas and the River Narew; the Lithuanians along the River Nemunas: the Žemaitians (Low Lithuanians) to the north-west and the Aukštaitians (High Lithuanians) to the south-east; the Couronians on the sea coast to the north-west from the Aukštaitians; the Selonians to the north-east; the Zemgalians between the Selonians and the Couronians; the Letgalians above the Selonians to the north and north-east on the right side of the River Daugava as far as the lands of the Finno-Estonians and the eastern Slavs (the Krivichi).[1] Further, the Galindian or the Golyad' tribe occupied the western, south-western, and eastern corners of the Baltic region. The Galindians who lived to the south of the Prussians were first to become extinct. The Golyad' people were mentioned several times around Moscow from as early as the twelfth century (For the Galind–Golyad' question see Part Two, Subchapter 4.7.) The Finnic tribe of the Livians occupied the eastern and western coast of the Gulf of Riga. They were not natives in Couronia (Kurland) either but from the fifth century migrated there from the south-east and the east (Johansen 1939, 304). Originally they inhabited the areas of the Upper-Volga which explains the striking similarities between the Livian and the Volga-Finnic languages as well as to the marked differences between the neighbouring Estonian and Finnic languages (Moora 1956, 122).[2]

Before the invasion of the Germanic Teutonic Knights in the thirteenth century Prussia had a hundred and seventy thousand inhabitants, a population of 4/km²; Letgale (Ger. Lettenland) had a hundred and forty-five thousand inhabitants, a population of 2.5/km²; and Lithuania a hundred and seventy thousand inhabitants

---

[1] For the sake of differentiation I shall use the names Letgalian, Letgale for the old tribe and their habitat, while for their twentieth-century form the terms Latgalian, Latgale.

[2] My hypothetical picture differs in some decisive points from this popular picture about the position of the Baltic tribes in the thirteenth century, a matter I shall return to later.

and a population of 3/km^2 (Łowmiański 1935, 22). (In comparison, Athens in its golden age had about two hundred fifty to two hundred seventy-five thousand inhabitants—Finley, 1972, 67.)

In the north, the Baltic Sea vanished into the mist of fairy tales. "So far (and here rumour speaks the truth), and so far only, does the world reach," wrote Tacitus (Tacitus 45). As Map 1 (page 13) shows, the Couronians were the only maritime people among the Balts from as late as the seventh or eighth century to the end of the first millennium. Through irrefutable linguistic arguments V. Zeps demonstrated that the entire vocabulary of the Baltic languages which is connected to fishing, water transport, and the sea in general has Livian–Estonian roots (Zeps 1962, 84–97). The name 'Kurs' ('Couronian') was not an ethnic but a geographic term which denoted the area inhabited by the people living on the coasts of today's Lithuania and Latvia, that is it meant the 'real' Baltic Couronians as well as the Livians who have almost become extinct.[3] A tribe that was involved with maritime piracy similar to that of the Vikings was mentioned in the ninth century as Couronian, while the German tradesmen who stepped ashore in the Gulf of Riga in the twelfth century refer to them as Livians. Thus it becomes clear that they

---

[3] The name of this people is perhaps < *liva* 'sand'. During history the once populous tribe went through a 'natural' assimilation as well as with several longer or shorter phases of violent absorption. This led to only a few dozen surviving Livians in Latvia by the 1970s. After the first 'national renaissance' the second happened in 1918, though according to Lukinich not without hiccups: the Livians were only allowed to put themselves down as Latvians in the 'nationality' field of their official papers, and Kaphberg, the one single protester (popular belief says he was from a princely family dating back to the twelfth century) was put into a madhouse, then later imprisoned by the Latvian authorities, to die in incarceration (Lukinich 1935, 42 ff.). Heinricus, Livonia's chronicler dates it to 1203 that bishop Theodoricus took a certain Caupo to Germany with him, "who was like a king or high lord (*rex et senior*) of the Thoreydan Livians" (Heinricus VII, 3). A probable extinction of the Livians is based on the same reason as the dying out of any tribes or peoples in general: that is the lack of any literary culture in an environment of assimilation which has been ruled by a literary culture. In 1935 there were eight Livian books: The Gospel according to Matthew in three different dialects (in east and west Livian in 1863, and its central Livian translation in 1880); five alphabet books; a singing book; and a mixed notebook (Lukinich 1935). We have to mention the journal "Livli" (the Livian), and other ethnographic and linguistic initiatives (most importantly L. Kettunen's work *Livisches Wörterbuch mit grammatischer Einleitung* published in Helsinki in 1938). Nonetheless, all these could hardly be enough to keep the Livians alive. T. Karma's recent article claims that in 1994 200 people considered themselves Livians, and that "at the time of the third national renaissance of the Livians". He believes that the development of the Livian literary language is indispensably necessary, for which there are attempts in the once more independent Latvia (Karma 1994). In another article he honestly declared that he did not know whether or not the Livian language and the Livians themselves could be saved (Karma 1994a, 27).

For the most comprehensive information about the Livians see the study collection of Estonian and Latvian scholars, Boiko 1994; in Hungarian, Domokos 1985.

lent their names to the whole of today's Latvia and Estonia (Livland) because together with the Couronians they constituted a large population and not solely because the Germans came upon them first. As the *Livonian Rhyming Chronicle* tells us, "Their tribe is large" (line 379). Consequently, they were dominant in the amalgam of tribes from the seventh or eighth century until the beginning of the thirteenth century.

From the other Baltic tribes the Lithuanians, or more precisely the Žemaitians, reached the sea only quite late, in the late eleventh century. They gained access to the coast above Klaipeda at Palanga, but with only a narrow exit. This position was determined for the six hundred years following the peace negotiations in Melnas in 1422. Although the Prussians held a one hundred and seventy kilometre stretch from the coast, their lifestyle remained mainland-bound because the ninety-six kilometre long Couronian Spit and the sixty-five kilometre long Vistula Spit (in German *Frisches Haff*, Friesian Spit) closed them off from the open sea. In reality only the Sembian peninsula[4] had direct contact with the sea but its coast was steep and unsuitable for water transport (Biskup–Labuda 1986, 32). Nonetheless, there were two settlements there which seem to have been the only ones in the entire Baltic area to show any signs of urbanisation. One of these was Truso (Pruss. Druso, Drusa > Germanised Drausen) where the Swedish and Danish roads crossed. It probably lay at the site of today's Polish Lake Drużno, south of the town of Elbląg in the eighth or ninth century.[5] The other one was Wiskiauty (Lith. Viskiautai, Ger. Wiskiauten), twenty-eight kilometres from Kaliningrad. It is an archaeological site that was established in the last century. Its richness suggests that it was a Danish–Swedish trade centre from the ninth to the early eleventh centuries (Lit. E. XXXIV, 325–327).

Some linguists and historians take a fundamentally different standpoint from archaeologists. The linguists examining water names (e.g. Gerullis 1924; Bonfante 1985, 317) along with the historian H. Łowmiański have essentially different views from the scholars whose principal discipline was archaeology (e.g. Kilian 1955, 190 ff.; Moora 1956). The first group is of the opinion that the ancestors of the eastern Balts reached the Baltic Sea very late, on the cusp of the first and second millennia AD. The latter party believes that the Balts, that is the ancestors of the Latvians and Lithuanians, already lived on the coast at the turn of the third and second millennia BC. There are roughly three thousand years between the

---

[4] The name of the forty times thirty kilometre long peninsula which is currently part of Russia, once belonged to Königsberg, and of which Kaliningrad is the centre.

[5] Pruss. *drus* 'salty spring', cf. Lithuanian *Druskininkai* or Ukrainian *Truskavec*. The location of the settlement is debated because the lake was much bigger in the ninth century, it spread as far as the town Elbląg (SSS 1/389–91).

two hypotheses, consequently the theories of the two parties vary greatly about the entire prehistory of the Baltic.[6]

The mainland was closed by impenetrable forests and swamps on all sides: the Baltic Sea area; the deep basin of the Pripet which was practically one vast swamp; and the mountain chains of the Carpathians. The Valday ridge formed an obstacle to an east–west passage with its highest point at over three hundred metres and which stretches from the spring area of the Daugava in the north to the southern shores of Lake Onega. Rivers east of the Valday water-parting ridge flow into the Black or the Caspian Sea, while those to the west rush into the Baltic Sea. Two great rivers lie to the west: the nine hundred thirty-seven kilometre long Nemunas (Russ. Nieman; Polish Niemen; Ger. Memel), and the thousand kilometre long Daugava (Ger. Düna; Latin Duna, Dune; its earliest reference is the Gothic Dyna, especially its upper section on Russian territory usually referred to as Russ. Western-Dvina; Polish Western-Dźwina). There are maps of Livonia from the seventeenth century where the marked routes are swamp wading paths, there were hardly any roads at the time (Mugurēvičs 1965, 9). The first accounts of the tracks (Ger. *Wegeberichte*; Polish *brody krzyżackie* 'Wading Paths and Passages of Crusaders') of Prussian and Lithuanian territories were given by the converted Prussian and Lithuanian 'guides' (Ger. *Leitsleute*), 'traitors' between 1384 and 1402. They mapped up areas that the Teutonic Knights wished to conquer (for some travel accounts see Mannhardt 1936, 126 ff.; Mierzyński 1892–96/II, 88 ff.; for the most reports see SRP/II, 662–711).

Weather conditions added to the inaccessibility of the Balts. Snow and ice formed just as much of an obstacle in one part of the year as thawed-out soil in the other. As a result it was practically impossible to conquer the Baltic peoples from the south, i.e. from the mainland. Some believe that this is why the great migration of the Hun invasion avoided them (Hensel 1988, 583). Attack from the sea in the north would also have been restrained. It is most likely that the Norman attempts between the seventh or eighth and the mid-eleventh centuries could have achieved only temporary and sporadic successes. They reached as little as the Sembian peninsula and the Courish territories (including the north-western parts of today's Lithuania, see Dundulis 1985, 12). For example, the Swedish Vikings only managed to gain sovereignty over the Couronians from 853 to 862, and never for any length of time (Johansen 1939, 263). The most that Denmark, the contemporaneous leading power of the eleventh and twelfth centuries, could do was to add the Sembians, the Couronians, and the Estonians to its own tax-payers.

---

[6] Probably the most characteristic representative of archaeologists who slip archaeological cultures, ethnicity, and languages in each others' places without any hesitation is M. Gimbutas (Gimbutienė). She writes about the Balts in a geographical and a linguistic sense without any differentiation.

A lightning conquest of the inner lands was a hopeless undertaking.[7] The Teutonic Knights of the thirteenth century must have realised that, too. In the initial period, each summer the 'natives' would reoccupy the territories that the Germans had won over in the winter (Urban 1989, 10). They were forced to realise that they could only slowly press inwards, step by step, by building castles from which they were able to gain control over larger and larger territories during the winters when the enemy's presence was revealed in the snow and uncovered by the thin forest.[8]

The impenetrable swamps and forests are reoccurring motifs at all levels of life in the Baltic. They explain many puzzles, for example, the archaic nature of the language which is a result of relative isolation, and also their burial rites.[9]

There is an authentic account at our disposal of the strange burial rites of the Balts, more precisely the Baltic Aesti (who were perhaps the Prussians), from as early as the ninth century. The British King, Alfred the Great, translated or commissioned a translation into Anglo-Saxon of the seven volume world history *Historiarum adversum paganos* by the Hispanic P. Orosius (around 415) between 890 and 893. It was a fundamentally important book in the Middle Ages. P. Orosius added a chorography to the front of the *Historiarum* with a geographical description of the countries and lands that came up in the seven volumes.[10] King Alfred then expanded this chorography with two accounts of travel in northern Europe (at that time Germania). One is by a Norwegian writer Ohthere, the other by the Norman-Danish or Anglo-Saxon Wulfstan, the King's delegate. Wulfstan wrote about the lands of the Aesti (later Prussia). He is, without any grounds, referred to as a tradesman (Labuda 1960, 23). He visited Truso on the southern coast of the Baltic Sea somewhere between 870 and 890 where he jotted down or dictated his accounts to his sponsor the King. This became the first detailed written de-

---

[7] This is why there is such a determining difference between the Vikings roaming in western and southern Europe and the Varangians in eastern and northern Europe: the former looted and destroyed everything from England to Sicily, while the latter carried out trade for the most part peacefully (Łowmiański 1957). B. Rybakov's main argument is this against the 'Normanists', that is that the Normans (the Vikings) could not have conquered the Kievan Rus' because they had no chance of an unexpected lightning attack due to the terrain (Rybakov 1963, 297).

[8] Even at the time of established contact routes in the thirteenth century information from Prussia took five weeks to reach the curia in Rome (Powierski 1981, 389).

[9] P. Tret'yakov highlighted that in forest areas archaeological cultures could be identified with the corresponding ethnic cultures even in the Iron Age, simply because 'foreigners' could not penetrate the territories (Tret'yakov 1962, 4).

[10] G. Labuda pointed out that an image painted by Orosius lived on about northern and eastern Europe up until the late Middle Ages, since the oldest remains of the manuscripts of the two fundamental works of the region (Tacitus' *Germania*, and Ptolemy's eight volume *Geographia*) were found only in 1454 and 1470, and published as late as 1513 and 1533 (Labuda 1975, 31–32); not to mention that, contrary to popular belief, the latter only gave instructions for making maps, but contained no actual maps (Beck 1973, 44).

scription of this part of the world. Amongst other things, he claimed: "There is a custom among the Este that after a man's death he lies indoors uncremated among his relatives and friends for a month or two. The kings and other high-ranking men remain uncremated sometimes for half a year—the more wealthy they have the longer they lie above ground in their homes. All the time that the corps lies indoors it is the custom for there to be drinking and gambling until the day on which they cremate it" (Wulfstan, 32). In his genial novel, S. T. Kondrotas, a contemporary Lithuanian writer, transfigured this custom into a mythical and symbolic element of nineteenth-century Lithuanian village life, consequently the origins of this custom never became clear (Kondrotas 1982).[11] However, J. Bobrowski gave a credible and rather simple explanation for this 'ripening of the corpse'. The excellent German writer of East-Prussian origins wrote in his novel, which is set in East-Prussia between the two World Wars: "People in this region do not lack experience. They have seen a dead body or two. Those who live in the valley know that there is no child who does not spend weeks at a time under the same roof as the corpses. Farmsteads are built on hillsides in the flood region, each with its own hill. Then, at the end of February, or in March as the ice begins to thaw, it is impossible to even step on it, it is like walking on cotton wool, it crackles a bit and is slushy, although it has no intention yet of melting. It is impossible to get anywhere by boat. At this time of the year one is cut off for five, six, or even eight weeks, there is no contact with the neighbouring farmsteads, and the village is completely inaccessible. Although, what passes for a village in this region is an utter exaggeration. Let us rather say the borough, or the post office, though none of these are of any use at this time, everyone is isolated and alone. Should someone die at this time, they will be left in the house until the spring, until the *Schaktarp* [Lith. šaktarpis 'soggy bank, the edge of the ice'—E.B.] disappears, and the thaw is over. Which is how they refer to this season. It understandably has a separate name. But should the dead body have to remain in the house, there is still no cause for concern: there is always a coffin at hand, in the corner" (Bobrowski 1966, 103).

This inaccessibility often played an important part in their fate. Perhaps the most spectacular example of this came in the mid-thirteenth century and which at the time determined the fate of the whole of Europe. Following the collapse of the Kievan Rus' it was uncertain whether its principalities and territories would belong to Lithuania or to the principality of Halicz-Volhynia. The question was resolved by the fact that the Tartars were able to reach Halicz-Volhynia while

---

[11] This is known from elsewhere, too. Jacob was unburied for seventy days—though embalmed (Genesis 50, 3). According to Wulfstan the Aestii used another method: "There is a tribe among the Este that knows how to cause cold, and this is why the dead men there lie so long and do not rot, because they keep them cold. If two containers are put out full of beer or water, they can cause one of the two to be frozen over whether it is summer or winter" (Wulfstan, in SRP 1861–74).

Lithuania was protected from them simply by distance and the swamp forests of the Polesye and Dnieper area (Lyubavskiy 1910, 28). Vladimir, Volhynia's capital town declined and became an insignificant village following the Tartar devastation in 1283, whereas Lithuania set out on the road to becoming a great power.

Examples of their inaccessibility can be shown until recent times: in the Second World War, and then later in the Soviet–Lithuanian war between 1944 and 1952, there were forests fifty or sixty kilometres from any city, from which neither German nor 'developed Soviet military engineering' could smoke out the resisting partisans.[12]

Nevertheless, it was not only military but also trade routes that bypassed the Balts until the turn of the twelfth and thirteenth centuries. They only took a small share of the trade that flowered in the tenth century which was maintained by the Arabs and the Jews between Scandinavia and southern Europe.

The South could only be reached via waterways. Two major roads crossed Eastern Europe in a north–south direction. One connected the Baltic Sea with the Adriatic, it began in the western Baltic and went along the Elbe from the Jutland peninsula. The Prussians could have accessed that route with the help of the now almost extinct (except for the Kashubs) Western-Slavic tribes (the Pomorans, the Velet-Rugians, the Obodrits, and further to the west the *Polabians*) who lived on the coast. Yet, they did not. There is very little evidence of trade on this route mainly because of the swamps and marshland which made it impossible to travel from east to west along the shores, and also because the rivers there were not transcontinental (Jażdżewski 1981, 633).

The other route went through the territories of the eastern Slavic peoples. The Balts, living between the two routes, remained isolated (Niederle 1911/III, 48). This picture is underpinned by infrequent archaeological finds, as well as by scarce references to the southern coast of the Baltic Sea in the runes of the tenth to twelfth centuries (Mel'nikova 1977, 36). The River Nemunas, springing from the middle of the mainland, was not part of this second route because there was no waterway from there onwards to the south (Łowmiański 1957, 80).[13] However, there was a watercourse from the Daugava, because its source is close to where three other rivers: the Dnieper, the Volga, and the Lovat spring. Between any of these four rivers ships or boats could be pulled through or carried across on carts on the

---

[12] Of course, forest gave protection, acted as a division line, and was an important source of food. As the Lithuanian proverb says: "You enter the forest on foot and come out with a cart" (Biržiška 1952, 103).

[13] The river Nemunas, the 'mother of Lithuanian rivers' gained its importance during the German invasion, when the Teutonic knights found the castle of Klaipeda in 1252, and advancing from there upstream they tried to fight the Žemaitians and hinder their cooperation with the Prussians.

so-called *voloks* (< Russian *voloch* 'to pull') which were deep tracks in constructed ditches.[14]

In the above, the spring area of these four rivers on the Valday ridge could be accessed via two paths. One of these set out from the Daugava that flows into the Gulf of Riga. The Baltic tribes that lived on the lower part of the river, that is the Zemgalians and the Letgalians paid taxes to Polotsk, a town from the tenth century which was built at the crossing of the Rivers Polota and Daugava and which was the 'capital' of the eastern Slavic Polochan tribe, which points at the importance of the passage.

The shortest route for the Varangian tradesmen arriving from the Swedish trade centres of Birka and Gotland led across the Daugava; finds of Arabian coinage stand as proof of that even though only small ships could have travelled there.[15] This problem made the other route, which began in the Gulf of Finland, even more significant (Arbusow 1939, 174). The most valuable export goods for the Varyag from the eastern Slavs were animal furs and slaves, female slaves in particular. Having obtained these they proceeded to the south, first on the River Neva from Lake Ladoga, then from Novgorod at Lake Ilmen on the River Volkhov, and on to the River Lovat (Dvornik 1949, 62). The Gulf of Finland won its prominence when the other eastern Slavic princes who were rivals to the prince of Polotsk intentionally made the Daugava area a 'dead corner' (*zu einem toten Winkel*). It

---

[14] Villages sprung up along the *voloks* where the inhabitants (the Volochans) had continuous work in loading and shifting cargo, towing, rope production, trade, and so on (Alekseyev 1966, 89).

[15] The question around Riga's foundation is connected to that. Heinricus mentioned the town at the year 1209 in his *Chronicon*. There were some who connected the reference *portus Livonicus* in the year 1185 to Riga, however this reference in Heinricus' chronicle proved to be an inclusion from the sixteenth century, i.e. a forgery. It is impossible to presume an early port there because bishop Albert had to establish a castle and a port to allow the Germans to harbour their large vessels, since the previous two settlements found by the Augustinian Meinhard (from Segeburg in Holstein), were only capable of receiving smaller boats (Laakmann 1939).

It seems likely that the town inherited its name from the tenth-century village, and that from the creek 'Ringa'. Its etymology is debated, there were attempts to connect it to Latin, Celtic, Livian, German, Slavic, or the Scandinavian tongue of the Vikings. Latvian linguists derived it from the Baltic **ring* 'curl, swirl'. The word cannot be Couronian, as V. Dambe claimed (Dambe 1990), because in the Couronian from -in, -en sound combinations the '-n-' did not diminish. A. Caune—reviving S. Bielenstein's (Bielenstein 1892) and V. Kiparsky's (Kiparsky 1939, 46) hypothesis—claims that the Zemgalians would have named the settlement in the tenth century as they reached the Gulf of Riga (Caune 1992). The only valid counter-argument could be that if the Zemgalians had reached the Gulf of Riga—which in itself is uncertain—then why would the Livians have been living there in the twelfth century? Heinricus called the Zemgalians the "pagan neighbours" of the Gulf of Riga (Heinricus I, 6).

is striking because trade in Tallinn, which was in Danish hands, was flourishing in spite of its location being much further north and east (Wittram 1954, 15).

Of course the geographical situation alone would not have cut the Baltic peoples off from the 'civilised world'. As we know, the civilised world discovers places for itself if there is something to be had there, be it a cheap crop or oil. However, there were neither mineral resources nor suitable circumstances for agriculture in the area. Consequently even in the twelfth century there were no towns (Moora–Ligi 1970, 22), which would be one of the signs of a civilised society. There was nothing apart from amber that would have justified the 'discovery' of the Baltic. This is how amber became the emblem of the Baltic peoples, and validates the devotion of a separate chapter to the questions around it. In discussing those, we can cast a glance into almost every corner of Baltic prehistory.[16]

[16] For the best summary concerning Baltic amber from both a humanities and a scientific perspective including an extended bibliography see, Katinas 1983; also the special issue of the Journal of Baltic Studies on "Amber" (1985/3). For the first and second centuries AD see Spekke 1957.

CHAPTER 4

AMBER AND THE AMBER ROUTE

Let me start this overview with a detour which is relevant to Baltic studies as a whole. J. Voigt presented the prehistory of Prussia, indispensable for any research of the Baltic, in a work of nine volumes. After he had taken stock of the materials concerning the amber routes he broke into a summarising sigh, "*Wahrheit und Dichtung!*" (Voigt 1827–39/1, 90). It seems that the amalgam of truth (scholarship) and poetry (fabrication) could induce similar laments for the study of any discipline that deals with the cultural history of the Baltic be it linguistics, archaeology, mythography, or ethnography.

Every scholarly examination is guided by preconceived ideas and misconceptions often barely distinguishable from each other. Anglo-Saxon 'new-critics' dubbed the latter 'fallacy' meaning a presumption that was dragged (or rather slipped) into the field of investigation from a different area, which is presented as proven or self-evident, but which is in fact an unverified piece of hypothesis.

Fallacy that is interwoven into a major part of Baltic studies is the nationalistic, or to use D. Fischer's phrase "ethnocentric" fallacy (Fischer 1970, 226).[1] (This phenomenon is apparent to the extent that a reader of little practice will easily spot the national background of the author of a given scholarly work.)

Circumstances certainly offer an explanation for the transformation of truth into poetry. These are the miserable conditions of the development and the forming of their national identity, as well as the foreign suppression that hindered the establishment and nurturing of traditions almost all the way through the history of the Balts. What R. Simon said about the Eastern Europeans in general is valid for the Balts, too: "It is possible to invent once respected ancestors to compensate for the lack of a middle class and for the distorted development of a nation (Sumerians, Huns, Dacians, Getas, Thracians). It is possible to foster daydreams about non-existent *Urheimat*s, we can create mythical, never existent popular fantasy cul-

---

[1] D. H. Fischer's amusing book takes stock of the logical misinterpretations of historians, especially those which, as the subtitle suggests, would be avoidable with logical thinking. Thus, for instance, an ethnocentric fallacy is a brief sub-case of compositional fallacies. I believe this relation to be the other way round: ideological fallacies, such as nationalism, encourage—albeit unintentionally—logical misinterpretation.

tures, and to counterbalance this multifaceted and troublesome architecture we can deny all this to the neighbouring peoples" (Simon 1996, 301). In 'the Eastern European situation' human thinking has the natural inclination to verify the authenticity of something by its age. This easily results in distorted forms. D. Kiš' aphoristic wording sounds credible: "History is written by the victors. Legends are woven by the people. Writers fantasise. Only death is certain" (Kiš 1997, 131). However, when 'the people' start writing their history—for example Baltic studies!—then initially they will write *against* the 'victors' and 'aliens' and not with the aim of 'objective' scholarly truth, most often admittedly so. Up to 1918, there were only very few works to which nationalist fallacy could not be ascribed. Even association with the Indo-European language family could be a motive for boasting, as A. Švābe's bitterly self-ironic words from 1915 demonstrate: "More and more languages were discovered that had the right to enter the family of the sacred Aryan languages, and one day it came to the Lithuanian–Latvian language. When our colleagues abroad arrived at this memorable conclusion, our local patriots and popular national romantics began to clap as if they had won some huge prize. Be happy, people of slaves and peasants, your sisters were the saints of India and the Greek muses were your patrons! Yes, the old Greeks. I understand the satisfaction: the Latvian, who was labelled a roaring beast for centuries, suddenly started to glow with happiness" (Švābe quoted in Biezais 1961, 50). For Adamovičs, the historian of religions, who examined the late Iron Age, the religion of the pagan Latvians was "the basis and content for national cognisance and pride at the same time. We can see that our ancestors stood on the peak of the culture of their time in their religious life and with their knowledge" (Adamovičs 1937, 110). The Polish–Lithuanian territorial argument was reflected back many thousands of years when the Polish archaeologist J. Kostrzewski accused M. Gimbutas (Gimbutienė), an American of Lithuanian origin, that she "due to a misinterpretation of patriotism allocated a many times larger area to the Balts" than it was in reality when she demarcated the Lithuanian *Urheimat* (Kostrzewski 1967, 14). This naturally fitted into a long series of mutual accusations. To bring an example from the other side, too, according to the excellent ethnographer J. Balys, A. Mierzyński and A. Brückner insisted on proving that the ancient Balts were barbarians because they themselves were Polish (Brückner 1929/8, 34). On another occasion a different Lithuanian folklorist blamed Brückner for his German origin, "The echt Poles of the Gloger–Brückner–Obst type" wrote Biržiška in a dismissive manner (Biržiška 1919, 114).

In 1918, with the establishment of an independent Latvia and Lithuania, an opportunity arose for coming to terms with the past with somewhat less emotion and bias involved. Summaries came to light which could have constituted a solid base for further debates.[2]

This promising development was interrupted by the Soviet invasions in 1940 and 1944. It is clear to anybody who is familiar with the Soviet system's ruthless hounding of any national independence what it means when scholars like Mikolas Letas Palmaitis changed his name from Russian to Lithuanian and together with V. Toporov stated that, after linguistic, theoretical-empirical, and cultural-histori- cal motivations it is also the moral incentives that underpin the reconstruction and resuscitation of the Prussian language (Toporov 1983, 36). "Students on Lithu- anian faculties were educated not only to be historians of literature or linguistics but also to be 'professional patriots'" (Viliūnas 1994, 15). And true, no Baltologist was able to be free of patriotic nationalist tendencies during the period of the Soviet system, independent of where they actually lived. The emigrant Baltolo- gists are a separate group within the field of Baltology which is why I, unusual though it may seem, indicate the place of abode of some of them. They were chased away from their homeland by the Soviet system or were prevented from visiting their homes, often for decades at a time. As a result it is particularly difficult for them to avoid the traps of patriotic fallacy.[3]

No matter how unbelievable it might sound the nationalistic fallacy can be caught with the questions, seemingly answerable through pure scholarly rigor and method, as to whether or not amber is amber, and if it is, where it comes from. The most common emergence of amber is on the coast of the Baltic Sea from the Latvian borders to Schleswig-Holstein and to the shores of the Jutland peninsula, and within this area it is the Sembian peninsula that is traditionally referred to as the 'Amber Coast' (Viitso 1994, 104). However, it is also true that "from an

---

[2] On the Lithuanian side there is the multi-author work edited by A. Šapoka (Šapoka 1936), and on the Latvian side the collection of studies first published in German in 1930, then in Latvian in 1932, in which eighteen authors wrote about the various 'national disciplines' and forms of consciousness (Schmidt 1930; Balodis–Šmits–Tentelis 1932).

[3] At the outset I was led purely by scholarly interest: studying the avant-garde literature of the 1910s and 1920s and with some background knowledge of the Hungarian and Slavic literary world, an idea came to me that there must have been something similar in the Baltic literatures, too. The literary historian of small countries inevitably becomes a 'factotum': I was also drawn to newer areas and eras of Baltic culture—with increasing enthusiasm. I was motivated most of all by the moral and political drive toward a nationalist or 'patriotic' fallacy. That other thing that emerged in the meantime, beyond the orientation—which is *not scholarship,* however, which is why I am trying to keep it separate from my so-called scholarly discoveries—is clearly personal: the joy of discovering a whole culture on the cusp between existence and non-exis- tence or reality and fantasy. This in-between state for me constitutes the domain of freedom. First subconsciously, then gradually more and more consciously I grew to view this, obviously due to the Balts' influence for over a quarter of a decade, as a special situation with a unique value.

archaeological viewpoint the varieties of amber of non-Baltic origin seem insignificant" (Bohnsack–Follmann 1976/2, 288). Nonetheless amber can be found elsewhere, too: in Italy, Romania, France, and Portugal. Only nationalist bias could explain the situation where "most of [those] scientists were Northern European ... [who] were eager to prove the exclusive use of Baltic amber in the ancient world" (Todd–Eichel 1974, 297).

The Finn Agricola recognised the differences between the various types of amber (succinit from the Baltic, simetit from Sicily, and rumaenit from Romania) in the sixteenth century, and in the nineteenth century the reasons behind these differences were found mostly by Otto Helm, a pharmacist from Danzig. A. Mierzyński wrote that after Schliemann had found a great quantity of amber in the graves of Mycenae from 1200 BC chemical analyses showed that there were two types of amber, "1) genuine succinus, that is, amber containing three to eight percent of succinic acid, which can be found from the German and Baltic coast to the foothills of the Central European mountains; 2) amber from outside the above area, containing very little if any succinic acid, which makes it a type of resin. This is largely characteristic of areas such as Sicily, Asia Minor, the Hispanic Santander, Northern Italy, Bohemia, or Japan. Chemically, Romanian amber has the same consistency as amber from the North, but it has a matte finish and is characterised by the many faults it contains. Amber from Galicia contains little acid and is mixed with sulphur. Finds from Spain and Southern Italy contain formic acid instead of succinic acid, and pyrogallus appears in amber from Japan. Objects made of amber found in Italy, Hallstatt, Mycenae and other non-northern places contain succinic acid in the same concentration as amber from the North, therefore it is apparent that they originated from northern countries, including the Baltic region" (Mierzyński 1892–96/I, 31–32).

Modern chemists, first of all C. W. Beck and his fellows at the University of Vassar, using the latest infrared spectrum examinations proved that amber from places other than the Baltic can also contain succinic acid. Therefore, one must be careful when speaking of the ancient amber route and amber trade, at least until the previous finds are examined using new methods.[4] However, there are chemists, for example A. Rottländer, C. Beck's German adversary and leader of the laboratory in Mainz, who claimed that even with the most modern methods at best the age of a piece of amber can be determined but by no means where it came from, so "at the moment the amber routes appear to be fictions" (Rottländer quoted in Todd–Eichel 1974, 298).

In his popularising summary G. Childe described this frequently reoccurring fiction among prehistorians: "Graves and hoards containing amber clearly mark

[4] The *Union Internationale des Sciences Préhistoriques et Protohistoriques* established a special international committee to take stock of the finds so far, with the task of creating a *Corpus Succinorum Veterum*. See Beck 1982, 1985, 1985a.

the route by which the fossil resin travelled from the coasts of Jutland towards Greece. All was carried up the Elbe as far as its junction with the Saale. Here there was a bifurcation. One route followed the Elbe into Bohemia, then crossed the Hercynian Forest to the Danube and went upstream to the mouth of the Inn. There it rejoined the alternative route up the Saale, down the Main, and across to the Danube. The combined streams went up the Inn to the Brenner Pass and then, after an easy porterage down the Adige to vanish in the Adriatic, or crossing the Apennines, to be shipped to the Aeolian Islands and so to Greece (...) Sammland amber probably joined that from Jutland on the Saale" (Childe 1958, 162–163).

From the passage it becomes apparent that talk about amber trade is chiefly based on the richness of the Celts, i.e. upon 'western' finds. Most likely the expression 'amber route' spread following J. M. Navarro's study in 1925 *Prehistoric Routes between Northern Europe and Italy Defined by the Amber Trade*, though the term was also used in the last century. The term struck a cord with other famous routes of luxury trade always important to the actual trader such as silk route or spice route. They lent some scholarly and at the same time mysterious overtones to the subject matter.

There was always something mysterious in the material itself. The first mention is in runic tablets from Assyria in the tenth century BC, but several finds stand proof that it was known and used in Denmark from the Mesolithic times and in the Eastern Baltic from the Neolithic Age (Hensel 1988, 53). However, what it was used for is still debated. There are theories that it fulfilled mythical and cultic functions besides being an ornament. Nonetheless, in the east Baltic between the Bronze Age and the thirteenth or fourteenth centuries exclusively amber, mostly pearl shaped, was discovered placed next to dead bodies in graves. No artefacts used as ornaments have ever been found for which there are relatively as many examples from the earlier Neolithic period (Vaitkauskienė 1992). What the meaning of these amulets placed in graves could be can only be a matter of guesswork. The oldest traces on sea shores, from the eighth or seventh millennia BC, were found near Hamburg. In the eastern Baltic area the first amber products were found from around 4000–3500 BC, in the surroundings of Moscow from the second millennium, in western Europe from the Hallstatt-culture between 1000 and 500 BC, in Mycenae from 1600 BC, and in Rome from 900 BC. Following Pliny (Pliny XXXVII, 51), S. Grunau, a sixteenth-century monk, wrote in his chronicle: "Amber crushed into small pieces and mixed with barley water cures urine constriction, and breaks urinary stones; if it is mixed with camomile and rubbed around the ribs stabbing pains stop; *item* amber mixed with rose and rubbed on the head ceases dizziness; *item* wearing lighter amber protects from alcohol poisoning; *item* amber mixed in a little hemp-oil, gives a good varnish for protecting painted pictures" (Grunau I, 51).

In the ancient world the source of mystery around amber was thought to be related to its connection to the Sun. Its Greek name of unknown etymology was *electron*, first mentioned in *Odyssey*. It seems to stand in relation with the *elector* used for the shining Sun in the *Iliad* (Hughes-Brock 1985, 260). W. Gilbert, a British doctor at court in the seventeenth century, made our term 'electricity' from *electron* (Spekke 1957, 4). In Greek mythology amber is mentioned together with horses, the Sun, and the God Apollo. All of them come up together in a poem by the Roman poet Ovid in one of the stories in *Metamorphoses* written between 1 AD and 8 AD: Phaethon, the son of the Sun (Phoebus Apollo) and a terrestrial being, Queen Clymene borrowed his father's fiery heavenly cart drawn by four horses. The horses went wild and Phaethon dies an instant death falling from the skies. In their sorrow the Heliads, his elder sisters and the daughters of the Sun turned into poplar and from under their bark "...their tears still / Flow on, and oozing from the new-made boughs / Drip and are hardened in the sun to form / Amber and then the clear stream catches them / And carries them for Roman brides to wear" (Ovid, 35, lines 363–366).[5]

After the collapse of the Roman Empire the demand for amber decreased for several centuries. Trade towards Aquileia and Massilia, the two amber-processing centres, stopped as a result of the war with the Markomanns in the second century. The war had its peak between 70 AD and 160 AD (Wielowiejski 1982, 269), so much so that Heliogabalus, the Roman Emperor in the early third century, complained that he could not decorate the pillar hall of his palace with amber (Pasquinucci 1982, 273). It seems that in the early Middle Ages it was used only in medicine and to cense (instead of incense), however at the beginning of the thirteenth century it gained favour again. We know this because the Teutonic Order who conquered the Prussians strictly retained the right to exploit amber which became a Prussian state monopoly from 1642. Unauthorised people were not allowed to walk any shores where the sea washed out amber, and fishermen had

---

[5] Amber had two different names in Latin: *sucinum* and *glaesum* (from Germanic language). Ovid, however, used the Greek term here, which G. Devecseri translated into Hungarian as ámbra. This is not simply a mistranslation, but the misemployment of two things—with a long standing tradition. It is public knowledge (today) that amber is fossilised Tertiary pine resin, while ambergris is an odorous, grey, waxy material formed in the intestines of sperm of whales. The knowledge regarding the vegetal origin of amber—which Ovid's story speaks of—was unknown for a long time. Pliny, the most significant authority of the ancients also made it clear that "amber is formed of a liquid seeping from the interior of a species of pine ... The exudation is hardened by frost or perhaps by moderate heat, or else by the sea ... Even our forebears believed it to be a 'sucus', or exudation from a tree, and so named it 'sucinum'" (Pliny XXXVII, 42–43). Several other ideas circulated. Servius, the second-century historian, for example, claimed that amber is ambergris that hardens in sea water. Later this confusion of the two materials resulted in the identification of the two terms: several languages use the Persian-Arabic word (with Middle Latin mediation) (Mikkola 1937, 34) for both matters, only differentiating them with the adjectives 'grey' or 'yellow', for example English *yellow amber*, French *ambre jaune*, Italian *ambra gialla* 'amber'; and *ambergris, ambre gris, ambra*.

to pledge a so-called amber-oath every three years according to which they would hand any amber that was caught over to the State.

The use of amber for decorative and artistic purposes gained momentum with the Renaissance. The most famous artefact was created by two masters from Danzig in 1709. It was a vast mosaic of a series of enormous sheets of smooth and carved amber alternately covering the entire wall surface of a room. The first Prussian King, Friedrich Wilhelm I, ordered it for the palace in Potsdam, which, however, seven years later the King gave to the Russian Czar Peter I as a present. The room was built into the halls of the Winter Palace in Petersburg until 1755, when it was transported to the newly finished summer residency of the ruler, to Tsarskoye Selo, today's Pushkino. New inlays, skirting boards of precious stones, and pieces of amber were added to it. It became a kind of museum of amber and stayed there for nearly 200 years. In 1944–45 the Germans packed it all up into boxes and took it to a secret place, and since then no one has heard any more about it.

For a long time amber was simply fished for, as the above mentioned Grunau recorded: "It [amber] can be seen glittering and floating in the water in the night, but the bigger pieces lie at the bottom. When the north wind starts blowing all the peasants from the area come to the shore and throw themselves after those at the bottom, naked and with nets in their hands. A peasant then receives a net-full of salt for each net-full of amber. And many peasants drown in the water in the process of this fishing" (Grunau I, 49).

Later it was mined from the strata that once lay under sea water. The first mine opened on Sembia in 1658. Large scale mining only began in 1860 when the Stantien-Becker company was established on the Courish Spit and Sembia. It soon became the state *Königliche Bernstein Werke Königsberg* (Royal Bernstein company, Königsberg). They offered their amber collection of matchless value to the University of Königsberg which, along with the university, fell victim to fire in the Second World War. Before the First World War the company mined an average of four hundred thousand kilograms of amber a year. Between 1860 and 1950 ninety-nine percent of the exploited raw material came from the richest sites: Sembia and the Courish Spit (Lit. E. VII, 259 ff.). Today the annual production of amber is six to eight hundred kilograms in Lithuania, and one to two hundred kilograms in Latvia.

It becomes obvious that in historic times and especially in the nineteenth and twentieth centuries amber constituted a Baltic property. The question remains whether or not this situation could be projected back into prehistoric times. From the second half of the nineteenth century the richest finds turned up from the following places: around Gdańsk (Danzig) and Wrocław; Sembia; the Courish Spit (from near a village called Juodkrantė); Palanga; the Latvian Sarnate; and recently after the 1960s from about two hundred kilometres off the Latvian shores the lake side of Lubana north of Daugava—and all of this originated from the

Neolithic and Copper Ages (Loze 1969, 1979, 1980). (Traces far from the sea point toward processing or transit trading centres such as Lake Lubana or Wrocław.)

Is there a direct continuity between the Modern and the Neolithic Times? Again one of the fundamental questions of prehistory crops up: whether or not the Balts were natives on the shores of the Baltic Sea, or were immigrants in the Middle Ages.

The two correlating written sources which connected amber to the ethnicity of the Baltic Sea for the first time suggest the latter to be the case. Tacitus wrote about the Aestians in *Germania* which he finished in 98 AD "...they ransack the sea also, and are the only German people who gather in the shallows and on the shore itself the amber, which they call in their tongue 'glaesum'. Nor have they, being barbarians, inquired or learned what substance or process produces it: nay, it lay there long among the rest of the flotsam and jetsam of the sea until Roman luxury gave it fame. To the natives it is useless: it is gathered crude; is forwarded to Rome unshaped: they are astonished to be paid for it" (Tacitus 45).[6] It is obvious that Tacitus thought that the Aestians were a Germanic tribe because he placed them after the tribe of the Suions within the borders of Suebia, a territory that was inhabited by the Germanic peoples. Only after that did he mention the three tribes (the Peucinus, the Venedus, and the Fennus) where he was uncertain of their Germanic or Sarmatian origins (Bonfante 1985, 317).[7] Pliny once unambiguously noted, "it [amber] is conveyed by the Germans mostly into the province of Pannonia" (Pliny XXXVII, 43). Tacitus' theory is also shown from the usage of the Germanic word *glaesum*.[8] It seems strange that the Balts would not have referred to their most important product with their own word. J. Endzelīns' counter-argument is rather crooked. He believed that the Balts used a foreign word in their trade proceedings with foreigners which would not exclude the possibility

[6] A. Spekke, the Latvian historian who lived in Sweden, believed that such a depressing opinion of the Aestians (whom he considers Baltic as an obvious fact, though it is far from sure) could only have developed in Tacitus from the strong influence of a mediating person. "Quite clearly we are dealing here with some shrewd mediator who had an interest in vilifying the 'amber procedures' in order to promote himself. How and why this is so, we can no longer tell. It seems to me—and I shall be willingly responsible for this hypothesis—that here we have come across one of the 'approaches' so common in Baltic history which extend through the unhappy history of these people like a crimson thread: namely, a tendency to accept the foreign point of view and to attribute to the Balts all the derogatory reports made by their enemies, strangers who have endeavoured to oppress and exploit them, and whom they have so fiercely resisted" (Spekke 1957, 86).

[7] Indirectly G. Gerullis, the German linguist of Lithuanian origin (perhaps the most sober Baltologist) said the same when considering the Galindians and the Sudocians, mentioned by Ptolemy, the first Baltic tribes we know by name (Gerullis 1921, 44).

[8] Old English *glaer* 'amber'; Old Norwegian *glaesa* 'offer a sacrifice or express adoration with some glittering object'; and from here with a transposition of meaning > 'something glittering': Danish *glar*, Ger. *Glas* 'glass' (Bonfante 1985, 317).

that they also had their own word for it (Endzelīns 1944, 6). This cannot stand because Pliny referred to a geographical location with the Germanic word, too—the amber islands (*insulae glaesiae, Glaesaria*) (Pliny IV, 97, 103, XXXVII, 42), and it is practically out of the question that the Balts would not use their own word for these—if they lived there, that is.

The Baltic terms for amber are the following: Lith. *gintaras* (dialectal *gentaras*); Latv. *dzintars, dzitars*; Pruss. *gentars* (although that is to some extent a reconstructed form, see Toporov 1975–90/II, 211). Their etymology is yet to be deciphered (the Russ. *jantar* is a later transmission from the Baltic language, see Zinkevičius 1984–94/I, 163). It is related to the Hungarian word *gyanta* 'resin', which is "a loan-word in Hungarian, but neither its direct source nor its direct transmitter is sufficiently clear" (Benkő 1967, 1120). V. Voigt gave a good summary of the problem, although there he only considered the probabilities of a Balto-Finno-Ugrian encounter connected to the coast, describing the views of B. Larin and J. Mikkola (Voigt 1971). In his later article he wrote about a Baltic-Hungarian convergence at the Dnieper–Dniester between the third to fifth centuries, at which point the Hungarians would have borrowed the Baltic word (Voigt 1980, 80). It is also possible that the Baltic tribes came into contact with the Hungarians only a few hundred years later through trade with the Khazars.[9]

However, the most likely theory is that the Baltic and Finno-Ugrian tribes met in the Oka basin near the Volga and the Kama in the mid or early second millennium BC. In this case the word is one of the strongest pieces of evidence for the location of one of the Baltic's *Urheimats*. *Jarndar*, the Mari word for 'transparent, glassy', and *jandar* the Chuvash word for 'glassy, glass pot' point toward that—notice that it is the same shift in meaning as *glaesum > Glas*! ("The word does not give a Baltic impression and is obviously borrowed, even if from ever so early times, from a language which the amber traders spoke"—J. Mikkola 1938, 35). Whether the Balts took over the word from the Finns or the Hungarians, or the other way round, the procedure happened in the (pine)forest zone and when much later the Balts reached the sea they simply transferred the name *gyanta* (resin) learned previously to a similar material seen there (for example that lets out the same scent when burning), i.e. amber.

Another document is nearly half a millennium younger than Tacitus' notes. It also connected the amber of the Baltic Sea to ethnicity and again to the Aestians. There is a letter of response to the Aestians from Theoderich the Great, King of the eastern Goths (Ostrogoths) written in Ravenna, the then city of the Emperors

---

[9] "It cannot be considered unexpected that the Hungarian term for 'amber' resembles the Baltic name, if we take into account the unique situation of Pannonia that it owed to its role as a transit region on the amber route" (Toporov 1975–90/II, 215). This statement does not stand, given that it was in the first and second centuries that Pannonia played this role—at a time when the Magyars were nowhere to be seen in the region.

(493–526 AD). It is now in the archives of the Roman Flavius Cassiodorus (485–578 AD) or Senator, as he was actually called (Wattenbach–Levison 1952–63/1, 74). Completely out of the blue an Aestian delegate visited the proconsul of the eastern Roman Emperor, conqueror of Italy, and handed over a set of amber as a present to him.[10] The Gothic King was uncertain of the purpose of the present. He had only heard about the existence of the 'barbarians' from the accounts of Cornelius (Tacitus) written down hundreds of years earlier. From the quill of Cassiodorus, the scholarly Roman chancellor, came the answer: "The arrival of your delegates informed us of your wish to enter into acquaintance with us. That you who live on the shores of the Ocean wish for friendly relations with us seems to us an extremely pleasant and worthy request. We are also pleased that our name has reached you at such a distance although we did not seek you out. Keep kindness in your hearts for me whom you know and whom you sought out with good wishes from an unknown land, since boldly setting out among so many peoples presumes an urgent desire. Besides wishing the same to you we hereby inform you of our grateful receipt of the gift of amber which the bearer of these words brought to us. It seems from the accounts of your delegates that this light material is washed onto your shores by the waves of the Ocean, but where it comes from is, according to their words, unknown to you despite that it is you, among all peoples, who collect it in your homeland. In the works of a certain Cornelius (Tacitus—E.B.) it is said to be sap that seeps from a tree on an island in the middle of the Ocean (*ex arboris succo*) and so it is called *succinum* which then hardens with the heat of the sun. The soft, light colored material becomes an extinguished metal which shines at times in shades of yellow and red at others glitters with a fiery light. The changing tides of the sea clean it and the waves throw it to you on the shore. We felt we had to inform you of this so that you would not believe that which is a hidden secret to you is unknown to us. Nonetheless, come to us more often in such a way opened by your love, because it is always a good thing to win the favors of rich kings who, albeit only through a humble present, will soften to a better humor and thus strive to offer greater praises. We shall pass on sundry messages through your delegates through whom we inform you that we are sending you something that shall fall close to your hearts" (Cassiodorus V, 2).

The letter has a very modern tone.[11] The civilised world with developed techniques educated the barbarians who deliver raw material which they know

[10] The Aestii took all the trouble to establish contact with their distant relatives (who had forgotten about their kins), either (?) because they carried a Germanic consciousness even in the sixth century, or they were *actually* Germanic—since after the Goths had advanced to the south-east the Germanic tribe of the Gepids stayed at the Vistula estuary for a long time (Lakatos 1973, 47).

[11] B. Schumacher's presumption that the letter was perhaps never sent, but was simply a "chancellery exercise of style" ("kanzleimässige Stilübung"), is completely unfounded (Schumacher 1958, 8).

nothing about. A certain curious puzzlement can be sensed in the letter, perhaps rooted in the frequent west–east and north–south phase delay. Maybe the Aestians intended to involve their Ostrogothic kin in "a gift-exchange characteristic to primitive and archaic societies" (Finley 1956, 87), which the 'civilised world' (here the south) was over by then. As M. Eichel put it "the exchange of valuable gifts preceded trade" (Eichel 1978, 322). In a certain period amber was also part of trade exchange. Amber found in graves in Mycenae and proven to be from the Baltic was exchanged for shells or objects decorated with shells excavated from northern graves and proven to be from the Aegean area (Renfrew 1972, 467 ff.).

Neither Tacitus' writing nor Senator Cassiodorus' letter point at a permanent route of traders with intermittent stations in between. The third mention of Baltic amber is another account of a one-off undertaking. Contrary to the two previous ones this note is not connected to one given tribe. Pliny mentioned a Roman rider (*eques Romanus*—one belonging to the order with horses, basically a tradesman) from the period of Caesar Nero who brought back so plentiful a supply "from the shores of Germania" passing through Carnuntum (in Pannonia, near where the small River Morava joined the Danube about forty kilometres from today's Vienna) to Rome that the nets used for keeping the beasts away from the parapet of the amphitheatre were knotted with pieces of amber (Pliny XXXVII, 45).

As a summary discussions about the amber trade are only possible on the basis of archaeological finds and therefore with particular care. C. Renfrew along with G. Childe are probably the most influential archaeologists of our century. What C. Renfrew said seems to be generally valid, "the amber trade between the Baltic and the Aegean in the Mycenaean period, the cornerstone of many a theory and of chronologies, may yet prove to be a myth" (Renfrew 1979, 24). The most common method of creating a myth is by slipping data from different eras on top of one another. We have several references to how much the Greeks then later the Romans liked amber. For example Homer (Homer *Odyssey* 15, 460) or as Pliny put it, "a human figurine, however small, is more expensive than a number of human beings, alive and in good health" (Pliny XXXVII, 49). It is perhaps a bit rash to draw conclusions from the above and from the value of amber in modern times, as M. Gimbutas did (Gimbutas 1991, 152). In the middle of the fourth millennium BC an Indo-European herding tribe, the people of the so-called Bell Beaker culture pushed up from Poland along the Baltic shores to the territories of the Nemunas and Narva cultures in the third millennium. This can be traced. M. Gimbutas believed that non-Indo-European ancestors of the Balts inhabited that area. She reasoned that these herders went up there because of "their quest for amber to which they attached great ideological importance" (Gimbutas 1991, 383).

Far be it from me to try to suggest that there was no amber trade. Archaeologists uncovered evidence far from the sea and the material had to reach these places somehow. Yet I believe that there is not much point in talking about amber trade from a general approach. Non-specifically we can establish simply that amber was the most important item in the north–south trade through which the far-off Balts could maintain some contact with the European centres. However, under the term 'Balts' solely the ancestors of the western Balts from along the coast (Prussians?, Couronians?) should be inferred. The territories of the eastern Baltic tribes fell in between the two north–south trade routes even if they reached as far as the sea, so the ancestors of the Latvians and Lithuanians were left out of the business.

The expression amber route is misleading in itself. There were not one but several routes depending on where they began, which stations they passed through, and who or what peoples kept them under their control.

Four starting points can be assumed from the early Bronze Age. The western route went from the Jutland peninsula on the River Rhône and Lake Geneva then onto the River Rhône (referred to as 'amber river') all the way to Marseille. It is highly likely that such 'western amber' can be found in the Wessex culture of south England. However, the Elbe also joined the Vltava and along the river near the Alps again two routes led to Bavaria and to Silesia, Saxonland, and Thüringia. Amber from Jutland could well reach southern Europe already in the early second millennium, which is indicated by the finds in Mycenae.[12]

This route that functioned from the late Neolithic period stopped in the seventh century. Trade was transferred to the second and especially the third centres that produced raw material: to Western Prussia (Vistula > Poznań > Silesia > Carnuntum > Danube > Adriatic); and to East Prussia, that is Sembia. The route starting from the Sembia peninsula is very old. It developed in the early Bronze Age, around 1300 BC. The Sembia people exchanged their raw material for bronze with the Slavs of Pomorze who then passed on the bronze products to the eastern shores of the Baltic Sea as far as Finland (Okulicz 1973, 227). They also transported it to the entire mainland forest zone of Russia that fell on the European side. According to I. Loze they did that as early as the third millennium BC (Loze 1980, 84).

Amber from Prussia could have reached southern Europe, just as western amber did. The route from Sembia led through the eastern Alps, across the Postojna pass, through northern Slovenia[13] on the river Pomente down to the Adriatic (Malinowski 1982, 113–115). Between the sixth and the third centuries BC, the intermediaries were the Veneds, then later the Celts. Due to the war against the Marckomman, trade contacts ceased with the Romans and the Balts were 'lum-

---

[12] The shipwreck found near the southern Anatolian Kas in 1982 stands as proof to this. Her rich load included amber from the Baltic. Mycenae played an intermediary role between the Near East, Crete, Sicily, and southern Italy (Renfrew 1991, 328).

[13] According to the Slovenian archaeologist F. Starc, all amber found in early Iron Age Slovenia is of course of local origin (Starc quoted in Todd–Eichel 1976, 337).

bered' with their product. There was plenty of amber to be found among Baltic relics, especially from the fifth century.

Amber from the fourth, most eastern location, the coast of Latvia could also have arrived in southern Europe. The target stations were Greek cultic places such as Dodona, Delphoi, or Olympia. The route went across the Dnieper through Scythia (Voigt 1827–39/1, 92). This path began to gain its importance from the late third century exactly at the time when the Greek colonial towns that held the trade of the route in their hands collapsed as a result of the Gothic and Hun attacks in the third and fourth centuries. As V. Katinas commented, with exemplary objectivity, the significance of this route is incomparable with the previous ones, just as it is advisable to handle the amber routes between the Baltic and southern Europe as a geographical potential rather than a historical reality (Katinas 1983, 10).

PART TWO

THE BALTIC TRIBES AND PEOPLES

CHAPTER 1

THE INDO-EUROPEAN *URHEIMAT* AND PROTO-LANGUAGE

1.1. Difficulties in writing about prehistory

The history of the Balts can be divided into two major periods: firstly, before written sources are present, that is prehistory in the strict sense; and secondly, following the appearance of written sources, that is the era beginning with the ninth century AD. The first epoch leads into the second with nearly one and a half thousand years of sporadic references to the Balts which can be encountered perhaps even as early as in the works of Herodotus.

T. Mommsen noted that, "scholarly work and the research of illiteracy [that is prehistory] would be a work field for village pastors and retired soldiers" (Mommsen quoted in Vogt 1949, 330). His malicious comment has lost its validity over the past hundred years, because in the place of amateurs serious scholars and entire research institutes in the field have been trying to cast light onto the darkness of antiquity. Nevertheless the essential and theoretical difference between writing about prehistory and history remains, which justifies a twentieth-century historian expressing their thoughts as sharply as Mommsen did, "it would be folly to believe that we can or even will be able to write a history of the Dark Age. Archaeology, comparative linguistics and comparative mythology, the testimony of contemporary documents in Syria and Egypt, for all their value, quickly reach absolute limits in the light they can throw" (Finley 1991, 24).[1]

The writings of prehistory can at best reach logical hypotheses that may fundamentally differ from each other. Using the Bible James Usher, a seventeenth-century archbishop of Armagh, is known to have calculated that God created the world in 4004 BC, with "a later 'scholar' fixing it with remarkable precision on October 23rd of that year, at nine o'clock in the morning" (Renfrew 1973, 21). Such precision is perhaps farfetched, but the other extreme also lacks gravity. Modern writing of prehistory offers a choice for the location of the Indo-European *Urheimat* among a range of hypotheses with various continents and several

---

[1] P. James enlightened the gloom of the Dark Age of Greek history between 1200 and 800 BC through an exemplary exploitation of interlinked archaeological and written sources (James 1993). However, this makes no difference to the general validity of Finley's statement. P. James had written sources at his disposal, distant, though definitely connected to the period under examination. There are no such sources in the case of the Balts.

thousand years between them. If somebody, being neither an archaeologist, an anthropologist, nor a historian of languages had to learn about the field of prehistory, they would measure with the acuity of the outsider. In addition, such a person would need to enumerate many more respected and quoted arguments to back themselves up than they would probably wish to. However, it is hard to shed the feeling, although the notion is unusual amongst scholars, that the importance of their work lies in the path they follow in answering a question, accumulating and activating an unbelievable amount of knowledge, rather than in the conclusion of their labour, the answer itself. Perhaps it also lies in playing with thoughts as the subtitle of Renfrew's book expresses; a "puzzle" that refers to his predecessor G. Childe's words, "our survey of prehistoric Europe has disclosed a fragmentary mosaic of barbaric cultures—or rather several imperfect mosaics one on the top of the other. All are so incomplete that the pieces can be fitted to make different patterns. It is often doubtful as to which mosaic an individual fragment belongs. By transposing pieces from one mosaic to another the patterns are radically altered and their whole significance is drastically changed" (Childe 1950, 330).

Prehistory writing essentially attempts to match the facts of archaeology, incorporating physical anthropology as well as the facts of the history of languages. This means that archaeology, starting out from a given area,[2] in our case the Eastern Baltic region, examines the (ancient) history of the peoples, while linguistics examines the peoples speaking Latvian and Lithuanian. (The latter once spoke a common Baltic tongue and before that a common Indo-European language.) The match can only be successful if the people living in this area knew about their ancestry, and thus developed a certain sense of continuity, that is a historic consciousness connected to that area. It is obvious that when, for example L. Kilian mentions "an eastern Baltic race and means humans among the Finns and the northern Russians, sturdy and blond" (Kilian 1982, 21), then that has nothing to do with those speaking the Baltic language.[3]

It is almost impossible to connect the concepts of 'Baltic' and 'the Balts', not just theoretically but also in practice. It is rare to come across exceptional people, like the Hungarian J. Harmatta, the Polish H. Łowmiański, the Russians V. Ivanov

---

[2] Contrary to a frequent misconception, even among archaeologists, "archaeological cultures ... do represent regions within which there was substantial conformity in a limited range of material traits ... and 'ritual' objects or monuments" and not societies (Anthony 1991, 194).

[3] Even today it is worth emphasising (or today once more) that the anthropological concept of 'species' is only an ideal and typological construction. This is just like the notion of, for example, 'the people' in the sense of a community with a genetic heritage and not a real biological generation (also Róna-Tas 1989, 6).

and V. Toporov, who are experts in all areas of prehistory, that is, who are simultaneously anthropologists, archaeologists, and linguists.[4]

Why is it then that writing about prehistory can only stumble about in a forest of often paradoxical hypotheses?

Briefly, the answer is that through the lack of written sources neither archaeology nor linguistics is able to create historical facts for themselves. Historically, only that exists which can be connected to time. For different reasons and in different ways this problem raises insoluble questions for both fields.

Such insolubility emerges from the way historical facts are created. Historical facts encompass some characteristics of a group of people or an ethnicity (geographical, racial, religious, political, etc.). These characteristics form a net that changes with time and are not simply 'there', they are evoked by a historian who allocates a characteristic feature to data that exists in its physical and natural generality (see Carr 1962, 4–5).

1.1.1. Archaeology

In themselves archaeological finds are no more than data which become historical facts through either their connection to written sources or their identification through the drawing of analogues. A series is concocted by setting the data into the context of similar finds and thus the find's "interpretation of meaning is constrained by the interpretation of context" (Hodder 1991, 5). However, there is no such thing as a natural series, because every aspect by which a series is marshalled, or where data is categorised is created by the archaeologist historian. The result is always context dependent and as such varies according to the archaeologist concerned. For the first time, or at least the most thorough, the fresh movement of the 1960s that is 'new archaeology' and its successor the so-called 'processual archaeology' faced questions that pointed further than the shovel of

---

[4] For this reason collective works uncover the Baltic ethnogenesis in a most comprehensive way: Volkaitė-Kulikauskienė 1981, 1981a, 1987, Moora 1956, Mugurēvičs 1980, Etnograficheskiye 1980, Butrimas 1990, Engel 1939.

M. Gimbutienė called attention to the many uncertainties which have another cause inherent in the history of science: archaeology and linguistics were not in synchrony with each other. The more youthful discipline of archaeology launched into an intensive study of central and eastern Europe after the Second World War which was determining for the research of Indo-Europe. However, by this point linguists had lost their faith due to the number of controversial theories, and along with the archaeologists turned to other 'more scholarly' themes. Only the last 20–25 years have brought changes and a new cooperation between linguists, archaeologists, and (unfortunately—E. B.) researchers of myths (Gimbutienė 1985, 4).

the archaeologist on ground.[5] However, there are still many, in the Central and Eastern European region, perhaps the majority, who have been barely influenced by the theoretical thinking of the new wave, if at all. They persist in the misunderstanding that, "archaeological finds, unlike the written sources of the discipline of history, are objective in themselves, in their physicality, and in being objects" (Makkay 1982, 76), or as R. Rimantienė, a leading Lithuanian archaeologist put it, "every archaeological source is real and therefore more reliable and richer than written ones" (Rimantienė 1995, 16). The material and objective nature of objects are mixed up with their existence and (scholarly) cognisance. Archaeology, that is not the discipline of the shovel but a discipline concerning humans who reveal meanings, views finds as neither objective nor subjective in themselves but rather as neutral, objects in nature. First L. Vekerdi presented the views of D. Clarke and C. Renfrew, the two leading figures of new archaeology. He wrote with appropriate certainty, "data and facts on their own are not only mute but they do not even exist in this 'virgin' manner" (Vekerdi 1976, 33). In the next stage the only thing that can be said about objects in nature, insignificant in the sense of social science or humanities, is that they were formed by human hands which, however, does not make them more objective from the perspective of social science (or archaeology). "An Etruscan tomb is nothing more than an assemblage of artifacts, despite the sophistication of technology or of the wall-paintings, so long as there is no adequate literary key to the conventions and values represented by the artifacts" (Finley 1975, 94). These empty assemblages become archaeological facts when they are set into a context. Nonetheless, this act of putting them into contexts is what eventually creates meaning, it does not draw a more objective result simply because its constituent parts are material objects.

The history of Baltic archaeology also shows how 'subjective' archaeology is in the manner described above. The range of finds uncovered and collected from the early nineteenth century were initially attributed to the Scandinavians (the view that the Scandinavian *Urheimat* was in the eastern Baltic held sway for a long time). Then, following C. Grewingk's work in the late nineteenth century, a professor from Dorpat (Tartu), the same finds were reattributed to the Finno-Ugrians. Finally, following A. Bezzenberger's book in 1897 they were ascribed to the Balts. K. Būga and later J. Endzelīns, the two respected linguists, developed a hypothesis that was built on an analysis of water names according to which the Baltic *Urheimat* lay at the upper reaches of the Dnieper, the Balts having pushed upwards toward the north-west from there edging out the Finnic peoples. In the 1940s Būga's concept underwent rigorous criticism and researchers, throwing out the baby with the bath water, returned to the autochthonous theory according to which Balts had lived in the basin of the Rivers Nemunas, upper Dnieper,

---

[5] For information about the matter which is useful not only to archaeologists see Gardin–Peebles 1992, Renfrew 1973, 10 ff., 1987, 5 ff.; 1990, 1991.

Daugava, and upper Oka, 'since time began'. In the next 20–30 years the various conceptions lived alongside each other more or less mixed to the taste of any given researcher (see Volkaitė-Kulikauskienė 1987, 24 ff.).[6]

1.1.2. Physical anthropology

Along with the other disciplines of prehistory archaeology shares the difficulties which spring from the 'subjectivity' of historical facts. In addition to this, archaeology has another strange reason for its indecisiveness which is most apparent in the physical anthropology that works with human reminiscences, a peculiar range of source materials. Physical anthropology can belong to social sciences only as part of archaeology. The history of humans does not belong to the history of forms of consciousness. A skull constitutes extant data purely in its natural generality. A human being that lived in a given territory enters (pre)history by gaining a name and social characteristics from some context and thus becomes the subject of social anthropology. "In the language of social anthropology *person* is sharply distinguished from *individual*. The individual is a living biological animal who is born, develops to maturity, grows old and dies; the person is the set of offices and roles which attach to the individual at any particular stage in his life career" (Leach 1982, 149).

The answer to the question of how much anthropology can contribute to the understanding of the prehistory of the Balts and the Baltic is 'very little, practically nothing'. C. Renfrew's summarising judgment has to be acknowledged, "at the moment it is safe to look on any supposed claims about 'racial' groups or 'racial' affinities', based on a study of skeletal materials over the past 10,000 years, with the greatest suspicion" (Renfrew 1987, 4).

---

[6] It is perhaps unnecessary to say that the aspects of the categorisation of a find are far from always scholarly, but they often become mixed up with various non-scholarly fallacies. When the most frequent nationalist slip is embraced by some form of state politics it can have tragic consequences, even the possibility of scholarly research can be endangered. W. Schmidt reported that in 1936 only the writings of scholars who believed in the northern European origins of the Indo-Europeans were published in the *Hirt-Festschrift*, and those who favoured an ancient eastern homeland were kept in silence (Schmidt 1949, 313–314). (E. Benveniste was allowed to elaborate on his views that it is linguistically impossible to place the ancient homeland in northern Europe in a way that the 'correct' standpoint was there in brackets from the pen of the editor.) The other example is from the 1980s. The Vice Rector of the Teacher Training College of Vilnius denounced one of his tutors because he taught the students that the 's' at the end of words were retained in Lithuanian, while they had been dropped in Russian. The Vice Rector was of the opinion that such a trend of poverty could not occur to the great Russian language even three or four thousand years earlier.

Processual archaeology is known to have turned to the examination of great (economic) processes because research in prehistory is deprived of the possibility of obtaining any concrete specific facts, and it must be content with the "generic individual" (Bell 1992, 42). As far as I am able to judge from my rather superficial knowledge, the new discipline called ethnogenetics or molecular anthropology can arrive at even more generic individuals than archaeology. This discipline has emerged in the past few years, and one of its leading figures, the Finn S. Pääbo says "so far we have just seen the small beginning of what someone has called the biggest archeological excavation of all time: the quest into the genome to reveal our past" (Pääbo 1995, 1142).[7] Let it be about the more traditional genetics based on the crossing of genes represented by Luigi Cavalli-Sforza, or about the research seeking the matrilineal lineage, that of 'the ancient Eve,' based on the examinations of the mitochondrion of the cells, or even that which seeks out patrilineage, that is, 'the ancient Adam,' based on the Y chromosome, the problem remains the same. On the one hand, how the examined populace is to be chosen (for example, how many groups of peoples' genetic stock have to be examined to allow us to declare that Europe was genetically uniform) and on the other hand, how data from this can be matched to social sciences (for example, genetic language family to linguistic language family), since the representatives of molecular anthropology, like the majority of natural scientists chasing the specter of objectivity, wishes to obtain an analytical method that is „free from preconceived ideas about what constitutes, for example, 'nations', 'peoples', or 'races'" (Haeseler–Sajantila–Pääbo 1996, 139).

Historians, say in the case of the Indo-Europeans, have to find an explanation of the paradox that peoples with different biological and anthropological features, such as the Swedes and the Kurds, once spoke the same language, or that this biologically and anthropologically uniform Europe has so many ethnicities and languages.

The statements of anthropology generic to whole continents also say very little to researchers of the Baltic. Anthropology lost its credibility with the Nazi research of races. In the 1960s it regained its role through the study of the ethnogenetics of the Balts, but it mainly contributed to craniology (study of skull size) and somatology (study of the build of the body). From the 1970s, mostly due to R. Denisova from Riga (Denisova 1975, 1977, 1989, 1991, 1991a) the methods of historical serology (study of blood groups), dermatology (study of the skin), and odontology (study of teeth) were also used (see Grāvere 1990, 9 ff.).

The first human appeared in the southern part of the Baltic around the tenth to the ninth millennium BC; in the northern part during the eighth millennium BC; and the more or less complete inhabitation of the area can be dated around the

---

[7] I first heard of genetic research in prehistory from the medical professor George Klein of Stockholm; he supplied me material to read and study, for which I am grateful.

seventh and sixth millennia BC (Deṇisova 1975, 16 ff.). However, these processes presumably must have taken place several thousand years later, because even the most daring estimates claim that the thaw following the Ice Age occurred around eight thousand BC (e.g. Gimbutienė 1985, 26 ff.). Only after that could the migration from southern to northern Europe have begun. The main reason for the big difference is that "radiocarbon dating... revolutionised earlier chronological concepts and extended the time frame of the Neolithic and Copper Ages by more than three millennia. This modern dating method was further refined" by dendro-chronology by five hundred to a thousand years (Gimbutas 1991, 436). The finds of the Baltic were only partly reexamined with the new methods, there is no way to use dendrochronology in the eastern Baltic at all.[8] This results in total chaos between the periods established earlier by the history of languages and archaeology, and then later by radiocarbon methods, and finally by calibrating dendro-chronology. The River Daugava was the northern limit of the Magdalenian and Swidri cultures that spread from the south and west. In the areas of Estonia and Latvia the Kunda culture developed from the previous two in the Mesolithic era during the seventh to the sixth millennia BC, while in Lithuania the Nemunas culture ruled, also affected by the Maglemose culture, and it carried on into the Neolithic era (Mugurēvičs 1993, 284 ff.). There are those who oppose this theory that emphasises continuity and refute a southern and western connection among the Baltic finds.

Nonetheless, it seems to be a general conviction that at the turn of the third and second millennia BC in today's Lithuanian and Latvian (and Estonian) territories the ancestors of the Balts (more precisely the 'Balticonians'!) appeared "whose ancient periods of ethnic history and genesis we have no clear concept of, neither do we know where they came from" (Deṇisova 1975, 5). There are two incomplete concepts, that is hypotheses, in use, often represented too definitely and sometimes with a dogmatic perseverance.

The first, propounded by the Estonian archaeologist H. Moora (1956, 1964, 1970), claims that the forest zone was populated in the fifth–fourth millennia BC from two directions, east and south. From the east, southern and western Siberia a cross-breed of the Europoid and Mongoloid races is thought to have wandered west (as far as today's Kaliningrad) and met the Europoid tribes in the Baltic area. The emergence of the ancestors of the Finnic tribes—the people of the comb-marked ceramics—came as a result of this dual effect. However, there was more to come, this time from the south. In the early second millennium the Indo-Europeans (the peoples of the Battle-Axe and the Corded Ware ceramics cultures) appeared in the basin of the Vistula, the Odera and the Elbe. On their easternmost flank were the ancestors of the Slavs and the Balts who, in search of pastures, were

---

[8] Only pine and oak are suitable for dendrochronological examinations, and only if they grew in a dry area (Rimantienė 1995, 16).

heading east and north-east, towards the middle and upper section of the Dnieper and the upper Volga. Another group of these Indo-Europeans, the ancestors of the western Balts, made their way towards the east on the shores of the sea. These groups are thought to have met the Finnic peoples after 1800 BC. Consequently, in the first millennium BC, western Lithuania and south-western Latvia saw the arrival of Baltic tribes from the west; while eastern Lithuania and south-eastern Latvia (Letgale) were populated by Baltic or Balto-Slavic tribes from the Dnieper (Moora 1956,106 ff.)

The second theory's main representative is R. Deņisova (Deņisova 1989, 1991, 1991a). Besides the depth of time and a greater emphasis on the European race she diverts from the previous theory in one significant detail. She believes that the two races could be found in the eastern Baltic as early as the Mesolithic era. These two groups were the presumably earlier and more dominant Europid race with elongated heads, high foreheads, and wide faces, and the Mongoloid type with a wide but flat face, and pressed nose. The Europid group populated not only Lithuania but also Latvia from the south and south-west, and basically originated from the eastern shores of the Mediterranean Sea. They reached as far as the Crimean peninsula and Scandinavia in the Mesolithic era, and by the Neolithic period established the Dnieper–Donieck culture. In this way they divided Central and Eastern Europe: the southern shores of the Baltic Sea and Scandinavia belonged to its western zones, whereas the middle Dnieper and the Crimea fell into its eastern parts. This meant that when the Finno-Ugrians expanding westwards arrived at the eastern Baltic they found the Europid tribes there who by then had occupied the entire area. These were people from the regions of the River Nemunas in southern Lithuania and western Belarus as well as northern Lithuania, Latvia, Estonia and the surroundings of Petersburg. A culture that was only discovered at the end of the 1950s and which Lithuanian archaeologists call Narva, while the Latvians refer to it as eastern Baltic or Abora-Lagaža culture (Deņisova 1977, 183 ff.).

Consequently, the autochthon population of the eastern Baltic differs according to different researchers: the Estonian researcher considered it to have been the Finno-Ugrians, while the Latvian votes for the Europid group that preceded the Indo-Europeans and from which the Baltic groups emerged.

Both theories, and any others formed using anthropology can be questioned and undermined with an obvious practical motivation: there are very few finds. "They that saw one piece of evidence saw none, who saw a thousand saw one" cites J. Molino with clichéd anthropological wisdom (Molino, 1992, 21). It is difficult to find anthropological and archaeological contexts even when there is something to put in an analogous order, what if there is nothing!

In her summarising monograph R. Deņisova gives an account of the data she used for her conclusions, "255 skulls from the Mesolithic, the Neolithic, and the Bronze Ages; and 13 series of 375 skulls from the first and the early second millennia" (Deṇisova 1975, 9). Six female and fourteen male skulls from the fifth and fourth millennia serve as the basis for the picture about the Mesolithic era (Deṇisova 1975, 17), and the rest must belong to the Neolithic period since R. Deṇisova herself claims that finds from the Bronze and the Early Iron Ages are totally absent (Deṇisova 1975, 14). E. Šturms was forced to declare of the finds in the eastern Baltic that they were very scarce even compared to the last two Stone Ages, and that the latest excavations could not contribute much more either (Šturms 1930, 139). J. Graudonis testified likewise "we have no anthropological finds from the territories of Latvia between 1500 BC and the first century AD" (Graudonis 1967, 5). G. Česnys, the leading Lithuanian historian anthropologist, adds that 15 male skulls represent the Narva culture from the areas of Latvia, a few pieces of bone from Lithuania, and for the Nemunas culture one solitary (!) skull stands as evidence (Volkaitė-Kulikauskienė 1987, 69).

It is clear that an enormous gap of nearly two millennia exists even in this meagre stock of materials. This is because the burial of corpses was only fashionable in two Ages widely separated from each other in time. These were the Neolithic era and—due to the Roman influence—the first few centuries AD. Otherwise the people of the Baltic cremated their dead up until the spread of Christianity as late as the thirteenth or fourteenth century (Okulicz 1973, 12).

Ultimately the fundamental and inextricable weakness of anthropology and archaeology in dealing with prehistory lies in the following: they are unable to create a continuous context, or to maintain their own subject consistently.

1.1.3. Language history

The archaeology of prehistory is incapable of reproducing history, that is a series of structures, meanings, and values concocted by humans in continuous time. Another auxiliary discipline of prehistory is the history of languages. It struggles with a different quandary: its subject is language, with the help of and along which it attempts to 'roll up' time which it is able to do because language is the only continuous form of consciousness. This continuity is derived from the double nature of language which lies in both its natural and historical or societal sides. It is a 'voiced meaning' therefore we do not need to allocate some meaning to the natural data which is there in the smallest unit of language, i.e. the linguistic sign. However, there are two problems with the continuity of language. One is that, if I may say, language is too continuous: due to its natural components, it can be traced back to the beginning of human speech. As A. Borst put it in his monumental textbook discussing comparisons of languages before linguistics, "the question of the origins of language is a question about the essence of people" (Borst 1957–63/IV, 1947). With this, we have arrived beyond 'physics', that is in the realm of metaphysics (philosophy or belief) of the given disciplinary area. We have to admit that G. Révész, the author of one of the most thorough monographs about the origins of language (Révész 1946), is right to say in his study in the conclusion to his book, "If we wish to make the idea of the *Urheimat* and ancient language to some extent plausible, then the time of prehistoric wanderings must be put into the far Ice Age, and most of all we have to presume that it is probable that the hominids who took part in these wanderings had already used the language that constitutes the likely ancient language. I believe that, even with such presumptions, the reconstruction of a proto-language cannot attain a scholarly value. The problematics of the proto-language of humanity prove to be not only indecipherable but actually nonsensical" (Révész 1942, 18).

Due to its limitless continuity each language can actually be traced back to one ancient language. For this reason many attempts were made to trace back languages in order to claim them as the *lingua adamica*: Hebrew, Phrygian,[9] Arabic, Egyptian, Syrian, Greek, Latin, Germanic, Celtic, even Hungarian, and Baltic.

The continuity of language can guide us back to more than the ancient language. Any of the many features of an ethnicity (race, place of living, religion, political and economic institution, folklore, moral, custom, occupation, identity, self-naming, etc.) can be made a historical aspect, and like a parasite on the continuity of language, can be slipped onto the language. If I wanted to be malevolent I would say that this slippage is what is termed writing about prehistory. The temptation toward slippage is so intense that it is almost impossible to resist. It is known that 'realists' and 'nominalists' stand opposed to one another in the matter of reconstructed ancient languages. 'Realists' believe that reconstructed language forms were once real (e.g. Szemerényi 1971–82/I, 28 ff.). 'Nominalists' think that the reproduced forms simply reflect correspondences among an assortment of known data (e.g. Trubetzkoy 1939). In historical questions only realists could speak up, because nominalists only acknowledge synchronic facts saying that for example the 'Indo-European' language is clearly a linguistic reconstruction. Still, the curiosity unavoidably remains: what kind of peoples spoke this ancient Indo-European language? A race, a homeland, a religion, an occupation, etc. are all sought for the linguistic reconstruction. No matter how much everybody accepts theoretically that an archaeological culture is purely an empirical category without ethnic or linguistic content, if the dogged efforts of generations connected the finds of H. Schliemann and followers to the Trojan battle sung of by

---

[9] In the case of the Phrygian language the source is Herodotus who gave an account of an interesting anthropological experiment. The first word of a pair of twins who were brought up without human words, was *bekosz* the Phrygian for 'bread' which made it obvious to the Egyptian king who had ordered the experiment that the first human spoke Phrygian. (From the above experiment G. Becanus, a sixteenth-century doctor from Antwerp, came to the conclusion that it is the people of Antwerp who speak the most ancient and thus the noblest of languages, Flemish, because the Phrygian word for 'bread' is related to the Flemish *becker* 'bread maker, baker'—Olender 1992, 14.)

Homer—practically any scholarly argument is pointless.[10] It does not help to know that, say, the first archaeological culture that can certainly be linked to the Slavs originated as late as the sixth or seventh centuries AD (Tret'yakov 1966, 190), because based on the certainty that these Slavs inevitably had ancestors, anybody with enough will could 'discover' them even thousands of years back.[11]

Like the one and only ancient language, the one and only *Urheimat* is also a question of credo. Between the Rivers Tiger and Euphrates humanity's cradle was rocking, or was it in Africa for that matter? As M. Olender writes in his excellent book, behind the search for its cradle "lies the search for a golden age shimmering on the borders of imagination and science" (Olender 1992, 8). This cradle hunt is also a blend of *Wahrheit und Dichtung* that we encounter everywhere in writing about prehistory.

Many have voiced the opinion that the artificial term *Urheimat* or 'ancient homeland' is largely unsuccessful. It suggests that a group of people can only have one *Urheimat*.[12] As S. Marstrander points out "the *Urheimat*, if at all determinable, could not be a fixed place where the 'cradle of the Indo-Europeans was rocking' but presumably a region of wanderings (*Wanderungsgebiet*)" (Marstrander 1957, 418). O. Trubachev offers the Hungarians as the only counter-example for those who are looking for a single rigid point. The Hungarians had an *Urheimat* in the Ural mountains, on the northern Caucasus, in southern Ukraine, finally between the Rivers Danube and Tisza, and they very objectively allocate the word 'original settlement' to all these activities and establishments (Trubachev 1982/4, 11). J. Harmatta opposes the use of the term because "the *Urheimat* of languages is lost in the fog of human evolution and it would be misleading to call the lands of their later prehistoric or historic expansion the *Urheimat*". Instead, he offers the somewhat stumbling expression of "old areas of settlement" (Harmatta 1972, 314). For the time being I will stick with the old term, but will use it in the plural instead of the singular, and mark areas with it that can be in some ways torn out or fenced off in the course of following the migrations of tribes and peoples. Not to mention that the term fulfils the useful function of constantly reminding us of the fictive and fairy tale like nature of the concept...

---

[10] Although there is only "a single bronze arrowhead found in Street 710 of Troy VIIa" it is used as evidence of a connection between an archaeological culture and an ethnicity (Finley 1974, 394).

[11] The reasons for this fundamental slip could be manifold. There are times when even mysticism is brought into the picture as with W. Brandenstein (Brandenstein 1962, 536), though usually much more prosaic fallacies stand in the background.

[12] For the nominalist there was no ancient homeland. "Proto-Indo-Europe, the country east of the asterisk, is a Never-Never Land less real to me than the world of the enduring cluster of motifs on which variations are struck but the prototype is a heuristic and intellectual construct" (O'Flaherty 1981, 23).

The other, and most important drawback in the continuity of language is that the changes in language that could serve as measurement of time are slow to the point where they become almost imperceptible. From among the facts of language only a few items of vocabulary can be tied to time more precisely, and those also just if sources are at our disposal. Consequently language history is only able to state anything at all about the history of a group of people speaking a given language within extremely broad time limits. For example the Slavic and Baltic languages borrowed a lot of words from each other but, with the exception of a few, it is not easy to determine when the loan happened "and it is certain that the oldest was not more than a thousand years ago" (Otkupshchikov 1984, 89). In the lack of material sources "we are undoubtedly in need of some material criteria or criteria established by historical phonetics for us to be able to reliably determine the age of a unit in a word stock" (Harmatta 1967, 215).

The history of vocabulary examined on the basis of material criteria is called linguistic and cultural history or linguistic paleontology.

There is no common word for 'sea' in the Indo-European languages, which would be proof that the peoples speaking these languages lived far from the sea. Or another example, it is well known that the idea that the *Urheimat* must be found somewhere in Asia, in the Sanskrit speaking north India held sway for a long time even after the rebuttal of the identification of the Indo-European *Urheimat* and the Biblical paradise as late as the mid-nineteenth century. Linguistic paleontology questions this presumption and does that on the basis of the 'material evidence' of the word 'camel'. The word for 'camel' in Prussian is *weloblundis*, but it used to mean mule and not camel. The Prussians borrowed the word from the Polish *wielbłąd*. The Slavic word is a very old loan from the Gothic *ulbandus*, which came through a regular chain of sound changes from the Greek *elephas*. However, the Greek word referred to the elephant and not the camel (camel was named with the word camelos—Latin *camelus*—borrowed from a Semitic language). So, the Indo-Europeans not only had no common word for the animal with humps on its back but they also mixed it up with the elephant and the mule. The truly 'ancient' Lithuanians had no word for camel up until 1642 when the language revolutionary Širvydas created the word *kupranugaris* that translates as 'one with a bumpy back'. This could not have happened had the *Urheimat* been somewhere such as Kashmir or northern India where camels are indigenous (Sabaliauskas 1986, 6). Most likely what happened was that the Indo-Europeans encountered a big unknown animal at one of their new settlements and transferred the familiar big animal's name onto it, and camel became an elephant (Gamkrelidze–Ivanov 1984/II, 525). In other cases, for a long time those who placed the Indo-European *Urheimat* in northern Europe (northern Germany, the southern part of Scandinavia, and the Baltic) tried to justify their statements with the spread of the words 'beech' *bhago* and 'salmon' *lakso*. A. Scherer correctly pointed out that the odd, isolated word could hardly be brought up as proof: corresponding forms that can be derived from *bhago* mean different trees in Latin, Greek, and Kurdish[13] (Scherer 1950, 293).

The method results in incompatible statements even if vast areas of word stocks are compared rather than a few items. For example, according to A. Scherer the 'Indo-European' terminology describing land cultivation is more or less entirely restricted to western Indo-European (not Aryan) languages (Scherer 1950, 294). At the same time in their monograph mainly based on linguistic paleontology Gamkrelidze–Ivanov state the opposite. In the fourth millennium BC the language of the Indo-Europeans of Asia Minor refers to developed agriculture and land cultivation which was underdeveloped in Central Europe and on the steppes north of the Black Sea (Gamkrelidze–Ivanov 1984). Archaeologists such as Gimbutas (1985b), Renfrew (1987), or Makkay (1991, 124) refute this theory beautifully.

All these controversies and uncertainties spring from the fundamental mistake of linguistic paleontology which considers words that can be found in more or less all (Indo-European) languages to be the same as the ancient ones, as for example E. Pulgram (Pulgram 1958, 463) or H. Kronasser (Kronasser 1959, 490) point out.

Research aimed at place names and especially names of rivers is another attempt at tying language to time.[14]

Examination of hydronymies can be undertaken using two methods, both of which are built on a presumption that hardened into dogma and thus became false: the name of a spring or a river is always 'ancient' and it does not change because one people takes it over from another. That is without mentioning those water names that Vanagas calls unmotivated or possessive names that are named after somebody or something (Vanagas 1981). Twenty-six percent of Lithuanian water names are unmotivated and they of course cannot be etymologically explained and thus connected to any ancient past.

One of the methods of studying hydronymies was developed by M. Vasmer (e.g. Vasmer 1930). From the modern state of language founded on written sources and the living language he established, what appellatives, common words, and derivation patterns construct water names in, say, the Baltic languages (bridge, swamp, bush land, white, long, etc.). Wherever he finds such words in the past, he qualifies them Baltic. This method is tempting, because a number of the water names (perhaps the majority) are indeed conservative, or at least more conserva-

[13] "In the Golden Age honey trickled from oak trees. ... Cronos was asleep in a delirium of honey—since then there was no wine—when Zeus put him in irons" (Kerényi 1971, 29). What could this oak be?

[14] In the first decades of the research of eastern Europe J. Rozwadowski, then M. Vasmer (Vasmer mainly 1941) obtained boundless praise. After the war H. Krahe and his student W. Schmid should be mentioned. Baltic place names were uncovered most comprehensively by K. Būga, then W. Schmid, along with the Russian linguists V. Toporov and O. Trubachev. For the history of the research see Toporov–Trubachev 1962, 3–13.

tive than other parts of language like words for settlements, and thus are capable of resisting even a more or less complete change of language. However, exactly this timelessness across languages makes water names unsuitable for measuring smaller periods of linguistic time. And here we are again. As K. Katičić the Croatian linguist emphasises, place names constitute a sub-system within the system of the language, and "on the basis of place names, it is impossible to draw any direct conclusions about language" (Katičić 1964, 9).

The other more speculative and thus more doubtful method was formed by H. Krahe (most elaborately in Krahe 1964). He examined the layers of European water names and did so using two theses underpinned by nothing at all. One is that the oldest layer will always be the one that (a) cannot be explained with the language of the people who currently live on the banks or shores of the given water, and/or (b) consists of a monosyllabic stem carrying a meaning (at times derived or conjugated monosyllabic words). He found that these monosyllabic water names give a system which he christened *Alteuropäisch* [Old European][15] (Krahe 1964, 13 ff.). The web of old European water names comprises waters from Scandinavia to lower Italy, and from the British Isles to the Baltic. It denotes the period of the development of the common Indo-European language which was finished by the second millennium BC. H. Krahe claims that by that time the western languages (Germanic, Celtic, Illyrian, so-called Italic group—the Latin-Faliscus, the Osk-Umber along with the Venet—Baltic, and to some extent Slavic though they still constituted a uniform old European language and further divided only later) had already dissociated from the ancient Indo-European language (Krahe 1964, 32–33). The similarities in European water names resulted from the radiation of this old European system, and not the resemblance of the common words in the later separate languages (Krahe 1964, 77).

This system of common water names logically led W. P. Schmid to presume that radiation must have started from the place where this web is the densest, and the ancient European and even more generically the Indo-European *Urheimat* must have been there. "It turned out that names belonging to such [the oldest] layers spread all over Europe in various densities and roughly as far as the River Don. Independent of whether they are in Scandinavia, the British Isles, in France, Germany, Italy, the Baltic, in the Pontus area, or Belarus they have corresponding names in the Baltic, therefore this land picture of names can be sequenced around the contemporary Baltic region in the shape of a star" (Schmid 1981, 106).

The ancient European system received much criticism, and rightly so. J. Mallory denounced W. Schmid's examples as ad hoc. For example, being unable to

---

[15] The first point essentially states that the most ancient water name is that the etymology of which is impenetrably foggy. Zeps–Rosenshield's reply to that was, "If, however, one goes by the formula 'etymological obscurity equals great age', then many Latgalian hydronyms date from the Creation" (Zeps–Rosenshield 1995, 346).

explain the Baltic river names from the Baltic languages W. P. Schmid connected those that fall into the type Indus, Indura, Indra, etc. to the Sanskrit word *indu* 'drop, drip' whose etymology is not clear itself. With H. Krahe's stems (*ar, is, ver, nar, sal,* etc.) everything as well as their opposite can be puzzled out (Mallory 1989, 276). A. Tovar's critique is more comprehensive. He demonstrates that non-Indo-European water names in the north of Europe are in majority, a fact which H. Krahe chivalrously dismisses (Tovar 1977).

J. Untermann, the author of one of the last decades' most motivating studies of the theory of language history, gives a commendable summary of the distance kept from the above methods. "There is no criteria which would help in determining who connected these names to the rivers (Untermann 1983, 148). [Therefore] every chronological statement that has no confirmation in sources with a date is sheer arbitrariness" (Untermann 1983, 153).

The conservatism of hydronymies is relative. Peoples with a new language often do not adopt old names but give new ones. The evidence is the frequent occurrence of waters where the name referring to the same water has different meanings in the different languages. For example, Daugava means 'a lot of water' in Baltic, while the Slavic name of the river (Dvina) belongs to the Iranian word family Duna, Don, Dniester, Doniec, etc. derived from IE. *dhen 'run, flow' (cf. Kiss 1978, 194). It becomes obvious that this double naming is the result of a similar proportion of the Slavic and Baltic population around the spring of the Daugava–Dvina and that their struggle against assimilation ended in a draw.

On the other hand if an area is scarcely populated or uninhabited (as presumably the eastern Baltic was before the arrival of the Balts) then the old water names could probably vanish without a trace, and the new names could consequently spread easily giving the illusion that the new group of people were aborigines there. If the exchange of these ancient conservative place names happened in scarcely populated areas then the process can take place within a single historical moment without the need for thousands of years to pass. Written sources stand as evidence that "many, if not most, Latgalian water features were renamed during the seventeenth and eighteenth centuries, following the devastation war, plague and famine" (Zeps–Rosenshield 1995, 345).

The distribution density map of Baltic water names also speaks against a necessary and general conservatism in place names.

In Map 2 we can see that, based on the traces the Balts left behind them in the form of place names, they lived in the territories of today's Latvia, Lithuania, and in the whole of Belarus, the north-western parts of Ukraine, the western areas of Russia (southern, south-western parts of Pskov and surroundings, in the regions of Smolensk and Kaluga, around Moscow, and in the governance of Tula, Bryansk, and Kursk); in the west they occupied the areas of today's Kaliningrad, and north-east Poland—all in all about eight hundred and sixty thousand square kilometres. They reached as far as the current borders of Latvia and Estonia

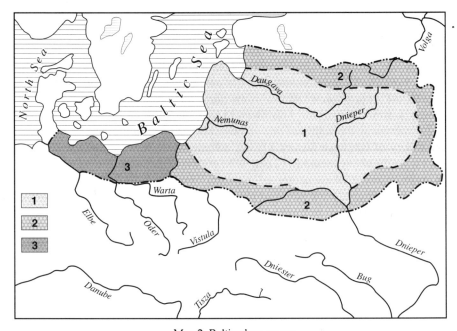

Map 2. Baltic place names
1. Frequently occurring Baltic names; 2. Infrequent Baltic names;
3. Rare and doubtful Baltic names

(Pskov) in the north, the Vistula basin in the west, the basins of the Volga and the Oka in the east, and in the south the Pripet Marshes and further on, the southern Bug.[16] However, this map only shows as much as maps usually do: location. It remains silent about time, and that the Balts would have occupied all of this enormous territory simultaneously at any point is simply delusory. This is why it is misleading to make a map timeless by tying it to time itself, as Z. Zinkevičius, a leading Lithuanian linguistic historian, does when he says that this expansion of the Balts was true of the second and first millennia BC. Of course, he does not forget to add that this population, estimated at about half a million, "occupied

[16] For a long time, primarily on account of K. Būga, the Pripet was thought to be the boundary river—serving as a sharp division—between the Slavic and Baltic tribes. However, V. Toporov and O. Trubachev discovered a number of Baltic toponyms not only on the right bank of the river, but also in the basin of the Seym and the lower Dniesna. This suggests, therefore, that (1) the Pripet was no sharp division (see also Trubachev 1968, 288); (2) the Baltic and Slavic peoples migrated in two, parallel, 'files', with the Balts in the north and the Slavs in the south (it is irrelevant at this point whether they wandered east from the north- or south-west, or towards the west from the east). The Slavs' line narrowed towards the Seym and, therefore, the Balts might have encountered the Iranian tribes living in that region—from as early as the Neolithic Age, according to Harmatta (1966a, 113).

a larger area than the concurrent Germanic or Slavic peoples, according to researchers" (Zinkevičius 1984–94/I, 151). Density shows that the Balts either arrived to or came from the more scantily populated areas. To me the first option is more logical: they spread from the south and the centre westwards to the Vistula (and beyond), eastwards to Moscow, in more and more scarcely populated rings. Denser parts are there, where they found some kind of *Urheimat* and settled for a longer period of time until they came to their current homelands. Water names communicate that the ancestors of the Latvians and the Lithuanians occupied the upper Dnieper region until as late as the first millennium AD and the first centuries of the second millennium AD. The 'most Baltic' was the basin of the Berezina, an upper Dnieper tributary (Toporov–Trubachev 1962, 235). This theory correlates to the fact, proven through archaeological finds, that the Baltic *Urheimat* stretched along a 250 kilometre long tract between the Nemunas and the Pripet (Rimantienė 1995, 43). This means on the one hand that the dense web of water names in current Latvian and Lithuanian areas developed after the end of the first millennium AD (proving that water names are not always 'very ancient'), and on the other hand that there are no firm grounds for projecting this web back to the first millennium BC, let alone the second.

The third method of linguistic history establishes the *Urheimat* on the basis of disclosure.

At the dawn of historical times there were people speaking Indo-European only in Central and Eastern Europe and the southern parts of western Asia, that is from the Black Sea to the Himalayas excluding the Arabian peninsula and Mesopotamia. In most parts of these territories Indo-Europeans were not actually aborigines: (a) In the third millennium BC in areas of India, Bangladesh, and Pakistan it was not the Indo-European cultures that flourished, and the predecessors of the Inds migrated to India from the west at the beginning of the second millennium. (b) Asian tribes lived in Iran in the third millennium BC; among these the most well known is the tribe that spoke the Elami language. (c) Asian tribes speaking Arami inhabited Armenia up to the seventh century BC. (d) The Greeks wandered into Greece in several waves. (e) Traces of non-Indo-European substratum are clear in Italy, too. (f) The Basque island that remained indicates that no Indo-European natives lived in Western Europe as far up as the Rhine. (g) Finno-Ugrian tribes were settled in the Volga basin and north Russia, several of which have survived up until now (Zinkevičius 1984–94/I, 14). The reliability of the method is shown in as much as after having excluded the above listed areas: some thought they had discovered the *Urheimat* in Northern Europe, many others in South-eastern Europe (again some at the middle and lower Danube, on the Balkan peninsula, on the steppes north of the Black Sea, along the lower Volga from where at the turn of the third and second millennium BC the Indo-European tribes, for example the Hittites, would have migrated to Asia Minor—Janiunaitė 1981). J. Harmatta, on the same grounds, placed this *Urheimat* in Proto-Asia: "From here the tribes speaking these [Indo-European] languages wandered into Central Europe through Asia Minor and the Balkan peninsula. The Caucasus and the Iranian highlands can be excluded with absolute certainty, because up to historical times and to date these two regions were occupied by non-Indo-European speaking ethnic masses" (Harmatta 1966, 247).

H. Kronasser pointed out the fundamentally equivocal nature of the method of exclusion. It can be seen this way or that way, since the territories where it is possible to prove that the Indo-Europeans were only there as migrants (mostly the three European peninsulas: the Iberian, the Italian, and the Balkan, in addition to Anatolian) cannot be disclosed *a priori* because "the native people could have already been there at an unknown earlier time" (Kronasser 1959, 484).

In order to illustrate the uncertainty of the archaeology and linguistics of prehistory it is worth glancing over some of the patterns that the puzzle entitled 'The Indo-Europeans' create. The rules of the game were set through all kinds of disciplines and methods, and it is sometimes played out in Northern Europe, at other times in Central and Southern Europe, and again at others in Asia. It is worth a glance, if only to help us "recognise the depths of our ignorance" (Renfrew 1990, XIV), and simply because variety offers beauty...

A. Scherer included 26 serious studies of the question of the Indo-European *Urheimat* and proto-language in his grandiose anthology (Scherer 1968). He began with G. Kossina's investigation which identified the archaeological culture of the so-called Corded Ware pottery with the Indo-Europeans for the first time in 1902. His choice for an *Urheimat* was in north Germany. T. Sulimirski believed that the nomadic Indo-Europeans set out from middle Asia in 2500–2000 BC and conquered first south-east, central, and north-west Europe, and from there in the second wave the whole of Europe (Sulimirski 1933, 138–40). J. Pokorny located the *Urheimat* between the Weser and the Vistula and east from that region where migration began around 2400 BC (Pokorny 1936, 213). N. S. Trubetzkoy considers the concept 'Indo-European' a purely linguistic one which cannot be connected to a location. At best it could be associated with an enormous area that stretches between the Finno-Ugrian and Caucasian languages from the North Sea to the Caspian Sea (Trubetzkoy 1939, 220–221). G. Neckel believed that the *Urheimat* was on the shores of the Black Sea because horses were domesticated there, more precisely they were domesticated there, too (Neckel 1944, 171). E. Meyer attempted to make peace between the two main viewpoints and thought that the settlement of the Indo-Europeans in the third millennium BC was to be sought after in Central Europe while the ancient Indo-European language evolved a lot earlier and probably in Asia (Meyer 1946, 281). W. Schmidt's principal argument was that Indo-Europeans brought horses into Europe in two waves. The first smaller wave introduced horses as the draught animal of Hittites, Mitannians, and Achaian battle carriages between 2000 and 1200 BC. The second and greater wave witnessed the horse-riding Indo-Germanics setting out from east and south-east conquering western Europe, and then the whole of Europe (except for Britain) on horseback between 1500 and 1000 or even 800 BC. However, horses were domesticated between the ninth and the sixth millennia BC by Turkish peoples in Turkestan, therefore both Indo-European waves had to have had their starting points there (Schmidt 1949, 314–318). A. Scherer votes for central or south Russia (Scherer 1950, 303). According to A. Nehring the best venue for a mingling of the Finno-Ugrian (Uralic) and Caucasian elements must have been at the feet of the Caucasus, east of the Caspian lowlands (Nehring 1954, 405). W. Merlingen carefully placed his vote for Romania, Bulgaria and Macedonia in an article in 1955, because there is no effective argument against them, and that is the only area where there is everything that we have to allocate to the peoples who spoke Indo-European, "land cultivation, animal husbandry, high mountains, flat lands, sea, snow in the winter, heat in the summer, wolves, bears, turtles, beach and birch trees, and a lot more—and of course wine" (Merlingen 1955–1966, 412). However, in a conclusion to the article that he wrote in 1966 he refuted his previous arguments and uttered that the question of the *Urheimat* shall never be solved in a satisfactory manner (Merlingen 1955–1966, 413). On the basis of the 'old European' water names H. Krahe places the homeland above a line drawn from the northern ranges of the Alps westwards and eastwards (Krahe 1957, 441). W. Brandenstein is of the opinion that the *Urheimat* was on the southern slopes of the Urals, and this region could only have been left after 3000–2600 BC because horses were domesticated there at that time which "played an exceptional role in the thinking of the Indo-Europeans" (Brandenstein 1962, 532–533).

1.2. The Kurgan theory (M. Gimbutas)

Marija Gimbutas' notorious study of the so-called Kurgan theory is a view amongst those where the *Urheimat* is located on the steppes of south Russia and eastern Ukraine. A little more detailed discussion must be devoted to her viewpoint because up until the early 1980s it came to be generally accepted, especially by lay opinion. This is clearly shown by the fact that the theory is included in the *Encyclopedia Britannica* and *Larousse* as *the* standpoint of archaeology. Another reason for a detailed discussion would be that in his controversial book, first published in 1973, C. Renfrew calls the author "the leading American authority of eastern Europe"[17] (Renfrew 1973, 176). Nonetheless, not least of all because

---

[17] C. Renfrew was clearly led by personal sympathy towards M. Gimbutas as they had carried out excavations together in Greece. Nobody who had personal contacts with the excellent professor could come away unaffected by her—not even the writer of these lines. Nonetheless, apart from one neutral reference (Renfrew 1979, 15), Renfrew also refuted the Kurgan theory (e.g. Renfrew 1989a, 86).

the Lithuanian-American archaeologist's book entitled *The Balts* which was published in 1963 was, and remains to date, the only work that has integrated the Balts into the prehistory of Europe and could consequently serve as a basis for reference for non-Baltologist prehistorians.[18]

M. Gimbutas elaborated the Kurgan theory gradually in several of her works, presenting details to a variety of its aspects (Gimbutas 1966, 1966a, 1970, 1971, 1985, 1985b, 1987). When in some of her books she rewrote European prehistory based on some, otherwise respectable, pacifist-feminist fallacy the story was still about the Kurgan theory, only emphasising the other side of the coin by concentrating on a non-Indo-European angle[19] (Gimbutas 1974, 1989, and the last that capped it all, 1991).

According to her theory the Indo-Europeans whose ancestors, Gimbutas believes, can be traced back to 25000 BC, established the Kurgan or barrow-burial culture along the tributary of the Volga, north of the Caspian Sea in the seventh to the sixth millennia BC and then, around the mid-fifth millennium BC, further westwards from the Black Sea (Gimbutas 1989, XIX). Here, between the regions of the lower Don and the Ural mountains they tamed the horse around 5500–5000 BC and in the following 2000–2500 years the warrior peasants of a patriarchal society used horses as a means of transport as well as in battle and thus flooded Europe (as she calls it Old Europe[20]) in four, or in other versions three waves. In this Europe (that is in the north of Europe and the eastern Baltic, too!) there was a kind of a golden age between 7500 and 3000 BC: peaceful non-Indo-European people lived there, cultivating land, law was on the side of the mother, it was a matriarchal society on all fronts led by "women as heads of clans or queen priestesses", and they worshipped the Mother God (often God of Earth). The

---

[18] Even though M. Gimbutas' book *The Balts* became less and less acceptable as its spine, the Kurgan theory, was unable to serve as a reference, it still, however, looked good in a bibliography. The book, thoroughly reworked and expanded, was published in Italian (1967), in German (1983), and in Lithuanian (Gimbutas 1985, to which edition I refer on occasions). The latter was taken hesitantly. A. Tautavičius, the leading Lithuanian archaeologist, gathered together a few outdated statements, unattended facts, unfounded conclusions, straightforward fantasies, and concluded his critique: "M. Gimbutienė's book about the Balts played a positive role abroad. It presented the beginnings of the Baltic culture and history, and partly showed the works and discoveries of Lithuania's and Latvia's archaeologists. Nevertheless, it evokes a fair bit of doubt in the careful Lithuanian reader" (Tautavičius 1986, 10).

[19] Therefore Makkay is incorrect when he states that "according to some she [M. Gimbutas] is not a follower of her own theories since 1984 " (Makkay 1991, 138). On the contrary, this woman moved around in one area of thought and was more and more convinced of being correct.

[20] M. Gimbutas was unfair when she appropriated H. Krahe's generally used term 'Old Europe' as her own. The two are not the same. The German linguist's ancient Europeans are Indo-Europeans, while the Lithuanian archaeologist's word refers to the inhabitants of the European home preceding the Indo-Europeans.

conquerors also reached the tributary of the Mediterranean, the Aegean, and the Near-East. The four waves, mixing with the encountered local substrata, brought about four versions of the Kurgan culture: Kurgan I between 4500 and 4000 BC; Kurgan II between 4000 and 3500 BC; Kurgan III between 3000 and 2500 BC; and Kurgan IV between 2500 and 1500 BC (Gimbutas 1985b, 196–200). In her last book Gimbutas spoke about three waves. Between 4300 and 3500 BC the Indo-Europeans destroyed the Varna, Karanovo, Vinča, Petreşti, Lengyel, Tisza, and Danilo-Hvar cultures; then between 3500 and 3000 BC the Cucuţeni culture. Having Indo-Europeanised Central Europe once and for all the region became the second and final *Urheimat* of the Indo-Europeans. The cultures of Baden-Ezero and the Globular Amphora, which are mixed cultures with ancient European and Kurgan elements refer to this second homeland. The third, their own (?) wave threw them towards the north-east, north-west, and south-west between 3000 and 2500 BC (Gimbutas 1991). The uniform—refuted, as we have seen—Indo-European character of the web of water names would have resulted in Central Europe becoming Indo-Europeanised. The third wave was represented by the peoples of the Corded Ware culture as the successors of the Globular Amphora culture. Among them were the ancestors of the Balts, and they Indo-Europeanised the north-western parts of Europe and middle Russia. (The ancestors of the Baltic tribes first settled between the Oder and the Vistula, and pushed into the region between the Baltic Sea and the upper Volga.) Then in the same wave in the north, the Corded Ware peoples conquered Pomorze, north-east Poland, the Mazurian lake regions, finally Sembia, and the Courish Spit. The result is the so-called Haffküsten culture ("the culture which extends along the Baltic bays, the Frisches Haff and Courish Haff"—Gimbutas 1963, 49), a hybrid product of the there en-countered non-Indo-European Narva culture, the cultures of the Globular Am-phora, and the Corded Ware culture. Around 2500–2000 BC the peoples of the Corded Ware culture edged eastwards reaching the upper Volga (evident from the Fat'janovo culture), the upper Dnieper (which is shown in the Dnieper version of the Corded Ware culture), the Pripet, and the upper Dniester (resulting in the Volynian version of the Corded Ware culture)[21] (Gimbutas 1985a, 251 ff.). The peoples of the Vučedol culture in the north-west of Yugoslavia ranged as far as the north-western parts of Greece along the Mediterranean Sea, and between 2500 and 2200 BC the culture of the Funnel-Beaker pottery arrived on the Iberian peninsula and the British Isles from central-eastern Europe.

---

[21] I think that the presumption of the Indo-European's drift from the south and the west to the north and the east contains the greatest number of elements that make sense in the entire Kurgan theory. Still it is difficult to fit it into the rest of the theory. If we take the various waves of the 'Kurgan people' (and their side and sub-waves of these, often in an opposite direction to their original) seriously then we would have to presume that for at least 2000 years the whole of Europe was the 'strolling garden' of one population, that is of the Indo-Europeans.

Between 4300 and 4000 BC the ancient European culture disintegrated in the Danube basin, but lived on in the Aegean region, the tributary of the Mediterranean, especially on the islands of Crete, Malta, and Sardinia up to 1500 BC (Gimbutas 1989, XX–XXI). Small female statues stand as evidence of and could have served the cult of the Mother Goddess, as well as the ancient European script that was present as early as the sixth millennium BC and thus is older than the scripts of the Mesopotamian Sumerian or the Harappa civilisation, and precedes the Cretan hieroglyphs and the Cyprian-Mycenaean script by several thousand years. Its language we cannot decipher because it was not Indo-European. The sacred script was used exclusively in the cult of the Goddess and never in everyday life or for state affairs. The most beautiful evidence of that are the three clay tablets with engraved symbols found at one of the sites of the Vinča culture in Tartaria. These resemble the scripts of the Aegean region, Mycenae, and Cyprus from the Bronze Age 2000 years earlier, because these latter ones survived the destruction of the Indo-Europeans without any disturbance for that long (Gimbutas 1991, 308 ff.).

Two approaches to the Kurgan theory remain, one engages in ceaseless debate while the other fails to address it at all.

The term in itself is unfortunate. It embraces various archaeological cultures so far categorised by different names under the same umbrella (adding to the above mentioned ones: the Battle-Axe and Corded Ware ceramics; Bell-Beaker pottery; the Urnfield ceramics, and the Russian Stog, Maykop, and Yamna cultures). Thus it gives the impression that on the one hand every archaeological culture connected to all Indo-European ethnicity in Europe and proto-Asia could be derived from the Kurgan culture, and on the other hand that "every barrow-burial would belong to its framework" (Harmatta 1977, 167–168).[22]

Of course, problems do not only crop up with the term alone. J. Makkay's question is rhetorical: "What historical process could serve as a parallel to an expansion that (would) last for one thousand six hundred to two thousand years, whilst hanging on to its tendencies, direction, ethnicity, and language in the same or almost the same state, all along?" (Makkay 1991, 147). There are no traces of any kind of great migration on the steppes. (According to I. D'yakonov the Indo-European languages did not wander apart, rather drifted apart— D'yakonov 1994, 38.) It is highly likely that Gimbutas' assumptions were called into life by

---

[22] The Kurgan theory can evidently thank its initial success to its offers of comprehensive explanations to a whole range of insoluble questions—occasionally without worrying about facts, and drawing its conclusions from the most varied places. Otherwise the main principles of the Kurgan theory have long ago been voiced. For example, in the Renaissance it was fashionable to place the origins of European languages in Scythia (Olender 1992, 2). Or the first edition of E. Wahle's book in 1932 'discovered' that the peaceful north and west European agricultural peoples were conquered by the Indo-Germanic warrior animal farmers who had bronze and horses by then (Wahle 1952, 60).

the memories in the subconscious of the European people and the experiences of reading about the great migration started by the Huns, then the great invasions of the sixth-century Avars, the seventh-century Bulgarians, the ninth- and tenth-century Hungarians, and the eleventh- and twelfth-century Pecheneg and Kuman peoples, and finally the 'Tartar Invasions' starting with the thirteenth century, and by no means evoked by facts. Nonetheless, as P. Anderson demonstrates, these expeditions of nomadic herder societies altered the eastern European feudalism of the Middle Ages into a type different from western European patterns, and not Prehistory or Antiquity (Anderson 1974, 218). J. Harmatta only identifies the Kurgan culture of the south Russian steppes with the ancestors of the Indo-Iranian peoples and not all of the Indo-Europeans (Harmatta 1990, 246). From an archaeological angle this culture is "the same age as the groups of the Early Bronze Age in Asia Minor or the Copper Age in the Carpathian basin, and later than the modern cultural groups of the Near-East, Asia Minor, and the other European cultures, therefore it can by no means be dated before 4000 BC and in general 3500/3000 BC" (Makkay 1991, 73).

The Kurgan theory stands neither chronologically nor, so to say, socially. Recently the majority of historians have questioned the concept that contrasts the patriarchal nomadic herder society with a matriarchal agricultural one. To any extent nomadic herding is an economic form which supplements agriculture, develops alongside it, and is insufficient without it. C. Renfrew straightforwardly states that a "nomad pastoral economy always requires the co-existence of agriculture", that is it develops after and on the sidelines of agriculture in time and location[23] (Renfrew 1987, 138).

Gimbutas based the supposed patriarchy of the Indo-Europeans and the matriarchy of the ancient Europeans on various 'facts' that are all simple misunderstandings. One is the theory of the same kinship terminology of the Indo-European languages, because "an analysis of their supposed kinship terms does nothing to confirm a theory that these hypothetical Indo-European people were 'patrilinear' or patriarchal" (Goody 1959, 91). The other one is the lack of male gods in ancient European mythology, which Gimbutas explains with a phenomenon observed in some current archaic-primitive societies, and which is termed 'virgin birth' in social anthropology. It means that the 'primitives' do not recognise the connection between copulation and birth, so men are deemed as less valuable members of society than women. E. Leach long ago demonstrated that this strange idea qualifies the social anthropologists who came to it, and not the primitives (Leach 1966). Just to add, it does not become more acceptable because it is attributed to primitives of thousands of years ago.

---

[23] At most, we can say that herding dominated agriculture in the realm of large animal farming (Róna-Tas 1983, 53), while it was the other way round in the domain of small herders, that is the so-called enclosed nomadism (Simon 1983, 130).

Lastly, the two cornerstones of Gimbutas' Old-Europe theory are typical instances of the fallacies of prehistory.

S. Piggott referring among others to P. Ucko indicated the doubtful nature of the ideas motivated by the female statues as early as 1965 (Piggott 1965, 114). P. Ucko dismissed the 'theory' in a thorough article (Ucko 1962) and then once and for all in an expansive monograph (Ucko 1968), and M. Finley could rightly term it a fairy tale (Finley 1975, 91). According to P. Ucko the female figures could be used for numerous reasons: as dolls, for initiation and magical rituals, etc., and "no evidence has been found to support the view that they represented a Fertility Goddess although some may well have been associated with a desire for children" (Ucko 1968, 444). The comparisons of various fertility goddesses or 'Venuses', at times from the Neolithic, at others the Bronze Age, then again—in the case of non-European peoples—the twentieth century, and from all corners of the globe 'only' miss the determining function of context, for example that many children are desirable in an agricultural society, while the opposite is true in a fisher–hunter community (Ucko 1962, 39).

Against the 6000 years old 'sacred script' we can say that literacy can only occur at a sufficient high level of social development. "In the case of the ancient peoples of the steppe ... [J. Harmatta put] ... the level, at which economic and social organisation opened the way or even called for the introduction of literacy" at the end of the second millennium (Harmatta 1989–90, 117)—to me even that seems too early. If this level of development is missing then scripts that emerged elsewhere could degrade to simple decoration. I think, this is what happened to the pictographic signs of the Tartaria tablets, too, which "bring up some kind of south-eastern European connection with Mesopotamia" (Kalicz 1970, 46), but what this connection was can only be a matter of guesswork. In this way C. Renfrew's skepticism, first worded in 1973, is utterly justified: "To me, the comparison made between the signs on the Tartaria tablets and those of proto-literate Sumerian carry very little weight. They are all simple pictographs, and a sign for a goat in one culture is bound to look much like the sign for a goat in another. To call these Balkan signs 'writing' is perhaps to imply that they had an independent significance of their own communicable to another person without oral contact. This I doubt" (Renfrew 1973, 186). Similarly, the systems of signs that the people of the countries of the so-called Fertile Crescent all understood perfectly well though speaking the most diverse languages cannot be seen as literacy because literacy is "pinning down speech as a system of signs" (D'yakonov 1994, 358).

The theory of the Lithuanian archaeologist[24] that is fed by her irritation with the (Indo-) European civilisation that obviously fought war after war would shed

---

[24] The so-called ecofeminists of the USA (E. Gadden, *The Once and Future Goddess*; R. Eisler, *The Chalice and the Blade*) viewed the Lithuanian archaeologist's theory as some kind of feminine prehistory, as A. Stakniené's ecstatic account tells us (Stakniené 1994, 161).

an unfavourable light on the Balts, too. To avoid this the nationalist fallacy is set into action and the following modified explanation is offered about the Balts: the Indo-European peoples or "patriarchal pastorialists" of the so-called Globular Amphora reached the eastern Baltic areas from the south "around and before 3000 BC", that is the region of the Narva culture from the fifth to the third millennia BC, where they found "a fisherman's paradise" of autochthon, non-Indo-European people" (Gimbutas 1991, 152–153). During the following one thousand five hundred to two thousand years the two cultures mingled, more precisely the newcomer Indo-Europeans assimilated the locals, but deep down "the Old European survived as an undercurrent" (Gimbutas 1991, 401). One would think that the most obvious sign of this assimilation–hybridisation is that the 'nasty' Indo-European Balts' language and culture remained. Their language yes, but not their culture—claims the Lithuanian archaeologist. Today's Balts gained their 'deep-European' culture from the female centred non-Indo-European ancient Europeans. They are the inheritors of the Narva culture, and directly so because the population of the third-millennium Latvia and Estonia survived. Their continuance is confirmed by two things. Firstly, the ancient European goddesses that can be found in Baltic mythology to date. (Contrary to this we shall see that Baltic goddesses existed exclusively in the imagination of the researchers of myths, although the great number of the female figures remaining in Latvian and Estonian folklore—not goddesses!—perhaps refer to some kind of genealogical order on the mothers' side[25]—Part Four, Subchapter 7.2.1.) Secondly, there is a "continued presence of a specific physical anthropological type" (sic!) (Gimbutas 1991).

1.3. The Asiatic *Urheimat* hypotheses

The Kurgan theory is similar to the majority of the ideas I have enumerated in that it presumes a European *Urheimat* for the Indo-Europeans. However, from the 1980s the hypotheses concerning the Asian *Urheimat* revived.

First, in a study of two parts (Gamkrelidze–Ivanov 1980, 1981), then in an imposing monograph (Gamkrelidze–Ivanov 1984) T. Gamkrelidze and V. Ivanov, both linguists, argued that the Indo-European *Urheimat* lay between the southern

---

[25] It seems that M. Gimbutas considers every European goddess (Athena, Hera, Artemis, Hekate, Minerva, Diana, the Irish Morrigan and Brigit, the Baltic Laima and Ragana, the Russian Baba Yaga, the Bask Mari, etc.) an ancient European inheritance, because there was a matriarchy in ancient Europe which is also proved by the fact that the goddesses are ancient European, which is underpinned by the matriarchy in ancient Europe ... She disapproved of G. Dumézil (who is just as 'historical' as she is), because he did not recognise the hybrid nature (ancient European woman + Indo-European man) of the Indo-European mythology coming from the above concept (Gimbutas 1989, XVIII).

part of the areas over the Caucasus and northern Mesopotamia, that is in the north of the Near East in today's eastern Turkey, southern Caucasus, and northern Iran, i.e. the immediate neighbourhood of Asia Minor. Accordingly, "ancient Indo-European civilisation belongs typologically to the ancient eastern civilisations" (Gamkrelidze–Ivanov, 1984/II, 885). They largely underpin this opinion with the reconstructed Indo-European word-stock, in which there are many that denote high mountains, cliffs, mountain flora and fauna. This means that people speaking this language could not have lived on flatlands. The names for domestic animals and cultivated plants turn attention toward Asia Minor where these animals were first domesticated, and these plants first grown. The 'Neolithic revolution', that is the spread of agriculture, and animal husbandry demanded a new type of relationship among the existing tribes. The ancient Indo-European language could serve as the means for that which probably became the *lingua franca* of the tribes from a small agricultural tribal community.

The ancestors of the Georgian and those speaking Proto-Semitic in Syria and Mesopotamia were the neighbours of the Indo-Europeans. In this way the three language families shared a language community similar to that of today's Balkan inhabitants. Another leading argument of the authors was that the palpable concentration of Indo-European languages at the dawn of historic times makes one wonder whether all the people speaking these languages had wandered into this relatively small territory. The Greek Achai, and the Luwiyan, the Hittites, and the Pali that belong to the Anatolian branch are the Indo-Iranian languages of the Mitannian empire.

T. Gamkrelidze and V. Ivanov's theory concerning the dissimilation of Indo-European unity is in accordance with the above. Their disintegration started in the fourth millennium BC at the latest (but perhaps much earlier—before the two linguists put forward their theory the beginning of their wandering apart had been estimated at around the third millennium BC). First of all, the people who spoke the old Anatolian languages (Hittites, Luwiyan, Pali) broke away, and settled in nearby Asia Minor—hence the archaic nature of their language. The Tokharian–Celtic–Italian (Italican) group of dialects emerged at roughly that time, followed somewhat later by those of the Greek–Armenian–Aryan, and the Germanic–Baltic–Slavic. The Aryan divided first to form an Indic and an Iranian branch. Some of the Iranians and the proto-Inds advanced eastward, others moved round the Caspian Sea from the east and arrived on the north shores of the Black Sea (the ancestors of the Scythians and the Osets). The predecessors of the Greeks edged westwards settling on the western shores of Asia Minor and the islands of the Aegean Sea reaching continental Greece in several waves (some of them going round the Aegean Sea by land). It seems likely that the proto-Thracians and proto-Phrygians migrated on the northern paths, too. The authors name the rest of the tribes: Celts, Italics, and the Germanic–Baltic–Slavic group as the oldest Europeans, that is 'proto-Europeans'. They also circumnavigated the Caspian Sea from the east and the north, then spent so much time on the steppes between the lower Volga and the Black Sea that the region can be seen as their second *Urheimat*. From there, after further separations, they pushed (or rather filtered) into the west toward Eastern and Central Europe, to the places where they are found in historical times.

These fresh winds from an Asian *Urheimat* were no *cause célèbre*. O. Trubachev maintains his views, because the expansion of ancient European water names can only be explained if the homeland was in Central Europe. "Basically, there is nothing in Asia Minor or Asia Major that could even remotely resemble this onomastic scenery, though obviously the ancient scriptic traditions of the Near East civilisations could also have noted something like this. A web of linked ancient Indo-European onomastic systems can only be encountered in Europe" (Trubachev 1982/5, 4). As a general counter-argument, we have seen that the system of water names is far from uniform in Europe, and what is Indo-European today comes from the simple fact that Indo-Europeans occupied and still occupy the region, and not from the ancient nature of Indo-Europeans. On the other hand the Indo-Europeans lived in their Asian *Urheimat* so very long ago when an ancient scriptic tradition that could have contributed to the survival of water names did not exist.

I. D'yakonov points out a significant dilemma in the Gamkrelidze–Ivanov theory (D'yakonov 1982). If dispersal happened through Middle Asia then some groups of people would have had to have covered such an immense distance in their journey to their historical settlements that today they would still be wandering: the Balts would have had to walk eight thousand five hundred kilometres, the Germanic peoples nine thousand five hundred kilometres, the Celts nine to ten thousand kilometres, the Italics eleven thousand kilometres. He mentions the European *Urheimat* mainly for this reason and places it between the Balkan mountains and the Carpathians. From there, probably due to overpopulation because of positive ecological and economic conditions, the Indo-Europeans spread gradually. In this way the Greeks had only to leave seven hundred and fifty kilometres behind them, the Hittites–Luwiyans a thousand kilometres to Asia Minor, the Armenians to the Euphrates one thousand five hundred kilometres, the Italics one thousand two hundred kilometres, the Celts to the *Boi*-lands (Bohemia) seven hundred and fifty kilometres and to Gallia one thousand three hundred kilometres, the Germanics to Denmark one thousand three hundred kilometres, and the Balts nine hundred kilometres to the Nemunas (D'yakonov 1982/4, 12).

C. Renfrew's theory could be seen as an amalgam of the ideas of Gamkrelidze–Ivanov and D'yakonov, though established independently from them (Renfrew 1987, in a shorter popular version 1989a). To summarise his views, the *Urheimat* was placed in south Anatolia, the Indo-Europeans arrived in southern Europe around 6500 BC, and then from the Balkans they migrated further in all directions up as far as the Russian-Ukraine steppes, where they spread agriculture because that was what Indo-Europeanised Europe.

The forerunner of the Asian *Urheimat* theories was J. Harmatta. In 1946 he drew up a proto-Asian study-hypothesis first connected to the Cimmerians (Harmatta 1953), followed by several other of his works (Harmatta 1964, 1965, 1966, 1972). Amongst others, his grounds were that "in Asia Minor the Hittites are autochthon, therefore the oldest region where the spread of Indo-European languages are palpable must be sought there" (Harmatta 1966, 246). During the Neolithic, Eneolithic and Early Bronze Age the Indo-Europeans moved from Asia Minor toward Central Europe (Harmatta 1972, 318). The fact that J. Harmatta dates the west–east division of the Indo-European languages before the Neolithic period (Harmatta 1953, 76), thus, "the divided Indo-European tribes populated a wide area by around the fourth millennium BC, which stretched from the Rhine to the Don, and from the Baltic Sea to Crete—encompassing Asia Minor" (Harmatta 1964, 41). M. Gábori's archaeological assumption is that Europe was occupied from two directions, that is from the Near East and Africa, i.e. today's 'the east' and 'the west' (Gábori 1977, 27). Based on that, J. Harmatta outlined the zones of the European language families after the Ice Age proceeding from the west toward the east: in the lower and southern part of Europe lived peoples with Ibero-Bask-Sikan languages; the mid-stream was occupied by the Indo-Europeans (who came to Europe from Asia Minor, the Balkans, and the land at the feet of the Caucasus); and the upper, northern part was inhabited by proto-Lapps and proto-Finno-Ugrians (Harmatta 1972a, 247–248).

This situation emerged in the Mesolithic, or perhaps earlier in the Upper Paleolithic periods when there was practically unlimited time for the Indo-Europeans' migration. J. Makkay gave a detailed analysis of the incompatible theories that I only mention or sometimes omit (Makkay 1991, 251). The only theory that he steadfastly adheres to is J. Harmatta's. From his work, he comes to the conclusion—without doubt elegant, though perhaps with little explanatory value— that between 5000 and 2000 BC the *Urheimat* of the Indo-Europeans can be associated with any of the various archaeological cultures in the regions from the Aegean through the Balkans to the south Russian steppes and the Baltic.

1.4. Language tree and diffusionism

It seems that in examining *Urheimat*s and their locations we are presented with an almost incomprehensible cavalcade of conflicting views. Let us make an attempt to approach the matter from the other end that is from the applied methodology.

Linguistic methods aiming at the reconstruction of the ancient Indo-European language, and archaeological methods striving to find the Indo-European *Urheimat* can be ordered into two frameworks comprising two theories each that are engaged in an eternally ongoing argument and thus a parallel can be drawn between them. In linguistics opposition between the family tree theory and the *lingua franca* theory corresponds with the conflict that exists in archaeology between the diffusionists and the evolutionists.

A. Schleicher's family tree concept, developed in the last century, presumes a common ancient language of the languages that are genetically related to each other. From that proto-language further intermittent ancient languages lead to the current languages of the given language family.[26]

Gy. László gave a very clear counter-argument in connection with the Finno-Ugrian languages: "archaeological observation of the history of settlements contradicts the former existence of a group of people of a greater number who spoke a uniform language in a relatively confined space from where they would have migrated in different directions. On the other hand, for example, the Swidri culture should be envisaged as an assembly of smaller groups scattered over a huge piece of land between central Poland and the Ural mountains... all peoples, thus each of the Finno-Ugrian peoples too, have a vast word-stock 'of unknown origin' which have nothing to do with each other, these are the so-called kinship peoples. Words that emerged 'in the separate life of a language' belong to that group, too. Could it not be possible that this vocabulary more or less existed when a primitive language evolved for communication among the tribes that were in loose contact with each other and that answered elemental, everyday questions, such as that related to body parts, and so on, that is to say that they would have referred to the simplest vocabulary with uncomplicated sentence structures and so forth simply to make themselves understood. Of course, this 'inter-linking language' took on slight variations corresponding to the distances between the peoples. Therefore there was more than one ancient language... consequently Finno-Ugrian is not an ancient state but a later formation... every distant kin language could be ancient, so we are talking about not only one language's division, rather many languages becoming closer to each other... the above presumptions show many common

---

[26] For a summary of theories of language kinship and language comparison see Róna-Tas 1978, however, this general outline does not go into Baltic studies.

features with that of Trubeckoy's, and which essentially claims that the Indo-European basic language was not but became"[27] (László 1987, 40 ff.).

The archaeological correspondence of the language tree theory is diffusionism, which is most completely put forward in G. Childe's works, most of all *The Dawn of European Civilisation* (the author continuously modified and added to the book after its first publication in 1925. I relied on the last but one version written between 1947 and 1950. The very latest was the sixth edition). The English archaeologist explains the spread of archaeological cultures—that means civilisation!—including migration, with a radiation from one centre, even though he talks about not one but three concrete historical places: Egypt, Mesopotamia, and India. He imagines "a hierarchy of urban or semi-urban communities, zoned, not only in space, but also in time and cultural level around the metropolises of Egypt, Mesopotamia and India". These provinces with "a regular series of descending grades of culture" are in contact with each other (Childe 1950, 16, 122).

For the diffusionists the most important phenomena in human culture happen once and in one place—consequently, that the occurrences are a result of divine intervention can never be ruled out!—and they diffuse from there. Of course, what diffuses is important. The most extreme representatives explain almost all 'invention' of the human world as one-off creations, except for those strictly bound to the basic instincts of humans. To date there are theologians who believe that language and the ancient language are such inventions.[28] Significant archaeologists like G. Childe and C. F. C. Hawkes think that the custom of cremating the dead spread from one centre (cf. Łowmiański 1979, 73). Others consider writing to be of the same ilk, "the alphabet is almost certainly the supreme example of cultural diffusion: all existing or recorded alphabets derive from Semitic syllabaries developed during the second millennium" (Goody–Watt 1963, 316). We can start arguing about that, since it is really possible to imagine that the invention of script was a one off act of a genius—just remember what C. Renfrew said about "the sign of the goat..." Contrary to this idea C. M. Cipolla begins his book with the words: "Writing was not a sudden invention. It developed gradually from the art of reproducing objects in one way or the other" (Cipolla 1969, 7). M. Gimbutas argues that this 'ancient European' script developed from "isolated symbols and compounds [which] seemed to have turned into morphemo-graphic (logo-syl-

---

[27] Trubeckoy's concept of course lives on in Indo-European studies. For example P. Dolukhanov expressed his thoughts with almost the same words as Gy. László: "It is probably a presumption that the ancient Indo-European language was originally of the *lingua franca* type and the means of inter-tribal communication which spread during the 'Neolithic revolution' and the following cultural and economic consolidation. This language sat on the earlier (substratum) languages while itself modifying and gradually edging those out" (Dolukhanov 1989, 52).

[28] Hampl defeated diffusionism exactly because of this mixture of belief and science (Hampl 1975a, 221).

labic) script" (Gimbutas 1991, 320). Again others talk about the diffusion of agriculture, metallurgy, tomb building, and so on and so forth.

Diametrically opposed to the above, the evolutionists consider the human race to have more or less reacted to the surrounding world due to its fundamental biological and psychological unity, conclusively humans established life spheres, cultures, civilisations in various places independent of one another. These either fell into contact with each other or they did not.[29]

---

[29] A weighty summary of the matter see Renfrew 1973, 11 ff. I refer to the ideological, and political contrasts that also appear in their world-views between the diffusionists and the evolutionists only briefly because I have no room to go into the question. Both views can have rather dangerous consequences such as racism. Diffusionism can lead to consequences that the creators of the central diffusing culture constitute a more valuable race than the people who adopt this culture (this is how G. Kossina's ancient homeland theory could be used by the Nazis to prove the superiority of the Germanic people). Evolutionism, on the other hand has the thesis that various different 'first human couples' lived in numerous places and can lead to a conclusion in which black people, or non-white races are seen as inferior to justify their slavery, as A. Hettner cites in cases in the USA where it indeed led to it (Hettner 1929, 25). It emerges from the deep elaboration of E. Leach that the contrast between the opposition of 'monogenism–polygenism' (in terms of social anthropology) is theoretically insoluble (Leach 1982, 55–85). I believe that the solution could be to keep science away from the religious and political prejudices that brought the two parties into conflict, and that it is unnecessary to extend several thousand- or million-year-old conflicts into historic times let alone into the present day.

CHAPTER 2

THE BALTIC *URHEIMAT* AND PROTO-LANGUAGE

2.1. The question of Balto-Slavic unity

What do the following opposing concepts: language tree and *lingua franca*, diffusionism and evolutionism actually mean from the perspective of Baltic prehistory?

Language tree theory can determine the branches and the medial proto-languages through the kin relationships of contemporary languages.

Closest to the Baltic branch is the Slavic.[1] A. Schlözer gave an accurate scholarly categorisation of the Baltic languages in his book entitled: *Allgemeine nordische Geschichte ... als Einleitung zur richtigeren Kenntniss aller Skandinavischen, Finnischen, Slawischen, Lettischen und Sibirischen Völker, besonders in alten und mittleren Zeiten*. He described the relationship in the following way: there is no relationship between the Slavs and the Finno-Ugrians; the Russians and the Croatians are siblings; the Slavs, the Germans, and the Greeks are third cousins; while the Latvians (the Balts) and the Slavs are second cousins. Before the appearance of the historical and comparative method this relationship was explained through the origins of the Baltic languages from the Slavic.

Many think that glottochronology is a curiosity among the history of disciplines.[2] A. Kroeber and L. Chrétien were the pioneers who tried to express the depth of the kin relations numerically. The relation between Baltic and Slavic is of a 92 proximity, while the Indo-Iranian branch, which has an indisputable common proto-language, is 91, and the distance between the Italic-Celtic branches is 87 (quotes Zhuravlev in Birnbaum 1987, 456).

Among the qualities that are only characteristic of these two branches, the correspondences within word-stocks is the most quoted. Important words are the same: Latv. and Lith. *galva*, Pruss. *galwo*, Old Slavic *glava* 'head'; Latv. *salds*, Lith. *saldus*, Old Slavic *szladъk* 'sweet'; Latv. *ezers*, Lith. *ežeras*, Pruss. *assaran*, Old Slavic *ezero* 'lake'; Latv. *zalš*, Lith. *žalias*, Pruss. *saligan*, Old Slavic *zelen* 'green'. The IE. sonoric consonants that form syllables ($\underset{.}{l}$, $\underset{.}{r}$, $\underset{.}{m}$, $\underset{.}{n}$) developed in two ways only in Baltic: il, ir, im, in, and ul, ur, um, un. From the IE. -ew became

---

[1] "For lay people the Lithuanian language could seem like a Slavic language with Latin suffixes" (Erhart 1984, 9).

[2] See for example Fodor 1961. For a more forgiving yet objective description see: Szemerényi 1971–82/II, 87–101.

-iau (IE. *lewdheyes* > Lith. *liaudis*, Slavic *ljudi*' 'people', on the other hand Ger. *Leute*). The shift in stress known as the Saussure–Fortunatov law is only discernable here (For example sing. nom. Lith. *ranka̰*, Russ. *ruka̰*, acc. *ra̰nka̰, rṵku.*) From morphology: as opposed to other languages the suffix of sing. gen. is -a; the existence of the so-called nominal (definite) adjectival forms (Lith. mažas, maža, Russ. mal, mala 'small' and mažasis, mažoji, malyj, malaja 'the small'—in Slavic languages the latter form edged out the former). In syntax double negation is common, and also genitive after negation and the predicate is instrumental.

The debate about the kin relationship between the Slavic and Baltic languages, its degree and background, is more than a hundred years old.[3] In accordance with his family tree theory A. Schleicher presumed a common Proto-Baltic–Slavic language, as a continuing branch of the Indo-European one (though many serious scholarly pens have noted that there are no Baltic–Slavic languages, only Baltic and Slavic, and perhaps there was once one singular Baltic–Slavic language). Up to the twentieth century linguists unanimously accepted the one-time existence of a Baltic–Slavic unity. From amongst them O. Szemerényi's (1948, 1957) arguments are the most persuasive, even though it seems as if he considered the sound laws, established by linguists after all, of absolute importance. Of the significant scholars Baudouin de Courtenay was the first who, in 1903, denied this unity (Bogolyubova–Jakubaitis 1959, 348). A. Meillet believes that the languages of the two branches developed from very close Indo-European dialects, and later grew parallel with each other. J. Rozwadowski differentiated three phases: common development, division, reunion. J. Endzelīns thought the other way round: after breaking away from the ancient Indo-European language the two branches developed separately, then moved nearer to each other only to become distanced again. According to V. Ivanov's and V. Toporov's theory the Proto-Slavic language must have evolved from a dialect of the Proto-Baltic language. What has been said is drawn up in Figure 1.

---

[3] For a Slavic perspective see Birnbaum 1987 and Zhuravlev in Birnbaum 1987. Judging Baltic–Slavic unity was far from clearly scholarly at all times. (Perhaps even today it is not quite pure, at a time of revived nationalism, as if one could hear from the voices of some linguists a national pride going back several thousand years...) In the famous-infamous 'imperialist poem' (*To the Slanderers of Russia*) Pushkin throws the Lithuanians and Poles into the same bag with an easy gesture "What are you clamouring about, bards of the people? Why do you threaten Russia with your curses? What has aroused you? The disturbances in Lithuania? Leave all that alone: it is a quarrel of Slavs amongst themselves, an old domestic quarrel, already weighted by fate, a question which you will not solve" (Pushkin 1964, 69). Or another example: at the end of the last century K. Valdemārs, the leading figure of the Latvian national renaissance movement, allied—perhaps with a little short-sightedness—with the czarist government against the local German powers that the Latvians and the Slavs are the children of the same family.

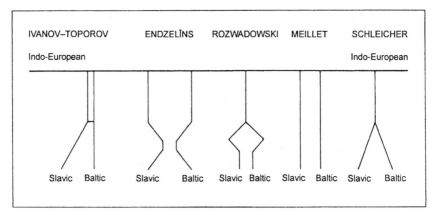

Figure 1. The Baltic–Slavic unity (Karaliūnas, 1968, 5)

From an utterly different starting point, there are some who refute that the Baltic and Slavic languages could have originated from each other (Schmid 1976, 120, Gāters 1977, 4, Trubachev 1982/4, 15).

The so-called areal linguistics enriched comparative historical examinations with new aspects based on the thesis that neighbouring languages will always develop common features. Presumably affected by that today, the majority deny the one-time presence of a Baltic–Slavic unity. H. Pohl summarised their viewpoints in a lecture in 1989. He said that only the Indo-Iranian branch could have lived on from among the Proto-Indo-European languages, and neither the Italic–Celtic nor the Baltic–Slavic can be verified on the grounds of the linguistic material available. "The so-called Baltic–Slavic unity consists of several layers that are the common inheritance, parallel development independent from each other, and the mutual effects of the neighbourhood and/or immigration" (Pohl quoted by Eckert–Bukevičiūtė–Hinze, 1994, 37). Archaeological and geographical arguments are on the side of the detractors, too. There is not really an archaeological culture that could be identified with a common Baltic–Slavic *Urheimat*.

The Germanic branch comes closest to the Baltic after that of the Slav's.[4] Linguists of the last century realised this, P. Keppen for example considered the Balts "a mixture of Slavic and Goth" (Keppen 1827, 19). It seems likely that the

---

[4] Striking examples for the relationship are the following: the Lith. '11–19' (*vienuo-lika, dvy-lika*, etc.) and the Gothic '11–12' (*ain-lif* > Ger. *elf*; *twa-lif* > *zwölf*) compound cardinal numbers, where the second part is < IE. **liqu* < **leih* 'remain, remainder'. The structure of 'one (two, etc.) remains out after ten' is shortened in the Lithuanian to 'one remains', in the Latvian to 'one after ten': *vien-pa-desmits* > *vienpadsmit, divi-pa-desmits* > *divpadsmit*, etc. (Zinkevičius 1984–94/I, 326).

Baltic–Slavic unity, or proto-language if you prefer, preceded the Baltic–Germanic–Slavic unity. W. Mańczak is of the same opinion, "There is more lexical correspondence between the Polish and Lithuanian languages than the Polish and Goth. Consequently, the Slavs have always been the neighbours of the Balts, while the Germanic peoples were originally not. It is possible that the tribes that divided the Slavs from the Germans in prehistory were called the Venet people, which would explain why the Germans have used the term 'Venedae' for the Slavs from Antiquity, while the Slavs themselves never have" (Mańczak 1984, 27).

The southern areas of Old Baltic dialects were in contact with Iranian languages such as Scythian, Sarmatian, and perhaps earlier the Thracian and the Dacian.[5]

Gamkrelidze–Ivanov recently drew up a family tree (see Figure 2) which they called a "derivational-dimensional model", probably because they were ashamed of the old fashioned, outdated family tree (Gamkrelidze–Ivanov 1984/I, 415).

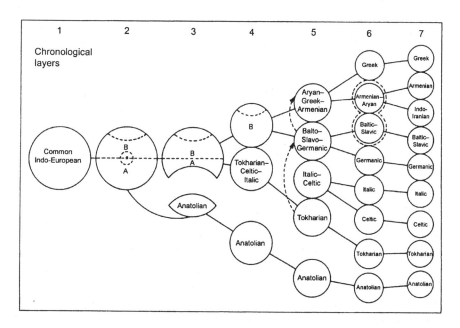

Figure 2. The Indo-European linguistic family

[5] M. Vasmer refutes this idea saying that there are no loan words in the Baltic language not even indirectly which proves that the Slavic stretch in the Pripet basin divided the south Russian Iranian tribes from the Baltic ones (Vasmer 1913, 3). However, as mentioned above, many argue against it, see e.g. Toporov–Trubachev 1962, 230, Schmid 1966, 7–9, Trubachev 1968, 274. They claim that water names stand witness to an encounter of the Balts with the Iranian tribes in the south-east in the basin of the Seym and Desna.

As mentioned earlier, first of all the Anatolian branch broke away from the Indo-European basic language, then later the Tokharian from the Tokharian–Italic–Celtic trio, and the rest further divided into Aryan–Greek–Armenian and Baltic–Slavic–Germanic dialectic groups.

2.2. The Baltic proto-language

The most significant and, if taken dogmatically, the most vulnerable point of the language tree theory is to what extent the Baltic–Slavic–Germanic, or any other branch of a language tree for that matter, uniformly formed one branch.

As Ch. Stang, a Norwegian Baltologist, explained in an article (*Einige Bemerkungen über das Verhältnis zwischen den baltischen und slawischen Sprachen*, 1939) there can be two types of units: one that was broken on an individual basis and did not come from a dialect or a society; and a unit that lies on a cultural and social foundation where there could be variations in dialects yet where the users of the language feel that they share a common tongue. These thoughts of C. Stang led E. Fraenkel to the conviction that the concept of a unity of language cannot be defined (Fraenkel 1950, 74). It is senseless to imagine an ancient language without any dialects, and whether or not the Balts and the Slavs had the feeling that they spoke the same language can hardly be determined.

Controversies can only be eased by the introduction of the notion 'isogloss'. G. Solta believes that the original Indo-European language consists of isoglosses: that is, partial correlation between certain languages (Solta 1952, 327). It is more convenient to talk about many common isoglosses and their frequent incidence instead of a language unity. Density could come through direct descent, parallel development, inter-effect, borrow-lend relationship, exchange (similarly Zhuravlev in Birnbaum 1987, 492). Of course the isogloss theory has its drawbacks, too, as it turns out from W. Porzig's work *Die Gliederung des indogermanischen Sprachgebietes* published in 1954. It takes stock of the Indo-European isoglosses and faces the difficulty of inevitable spinning around an ever-turning wheel of thoughts: we have to have preliminary ideas about the common ancient language of the languages we wish to compare in order to determine the isoglosses that contain neologies from which we can then derive the kinship of the languages compared. However this preliminary idea can only be gained from determining the isoglosses that contain neologies, and so it spins on (Hamp 1959, 179). For this very reason G. Solta says that it is more accurate to speak of Indo-Germanic dialects than of a proto-ancient language that is divided into dialects (Solta 1952, 328). A. Meillet worded this in the title of his 1908 book: *Les dialectes indoeuropéens*.

Whether or not we insert a western Old European Baltic–Slavic–Germanic, followed by a Proto-Baltic–Slavic language, it is certain that following these a Proto-(Common) Baltic branch existed. It is estimated to circa 2000–500 BC (give or take a 1000 years!). Old Baltic divided into two further areas of dialects: a core dialect formed the basis of old Lettish–Lithuanian, and a peripheral dialect which was the western proto-Baltic. Old Prussian–Jatving and the northern proto-Couronian grew out of the latter. Geographically the peripheral dialects stretched to the Baltic Sea, in the south-west and the south to the upper Vistula and the Pripet. On the right side of the Pripet old Slavs were settled. On the south-eastern periphery Balts were in contact with Iranian tribes, and also with Finno–Ugrian groups in the north-east where the Oka merges with the River Moscow. Some conclude from this that the ancestors of the eastern Balts were not engaged in direct communication with the Slavs. They were connected with them through the Baltic dialects which then left their mark on the place names in the basin of the Volga and the Oka, only to vanish later in the 'Slavic Sea'. These vanished tribes made up the bulk of the Balts, supposedly three quarters. For this reason J. Ochmański divided the Baltic languages into three rather than the usual two branches: these dialects which vanished were the eastern branch, and the central ones were the Lettish–Lithuanian languages (Ochmański 1966, 152). In a similar way, V. Sedov also differentiated between western (Prussian, Jatvingian, Galindian, Couronian, Skalvic); central (Lithuanian, Žemaitian, Aukštaitian, Latgalian, Selian, Zemgalian); and the east Balts named Dnieperians. In the latter group the only group or tribe we know of is the Goljad' (Sedov 1987, 7). Since the eastern branch disappeared it is best to stick to the traditional western–eastern division.

The peripheral old western Balts made a unit with the old Slavs, and the old Slavs broke away from this unit. Schematically we can write: Indo-European > Old Baltic > central Baltic > peripheral Baltic > Old Slavic.[6]

The old realisation is reflected in this picture that most similarities and isoglosses connect the west Baltic (Prussian–Jatvingian) and the Old Slavic languages.

According to Mažiulis the Old Baltic state looked as is illustrated in Figure 3 (Mažiulis 1981, 7).

First the west Baltic branch divided off from the Old Baltic section. We do not know exactly when, but it could not be later than around the time of Christ because perhaps Tacitus but certainly Ptolemy talk about different tribes (Aestians, Galindians, Sudovians). Archaeological finds show variations from the fifth century onwards as well: the western branch characteristically placed a grave stone on the

---

[6] For this reason Ivanov and Toporov say that a common Baltic–Slavic period preceded the Old Slavic time but the forerunner of the Old Baltic was the Indo-European original language (Ivanov–Toporov 1961).

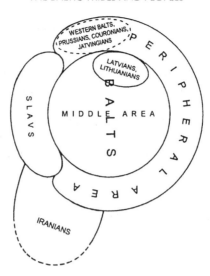

Figure 3. The evolution of the Baltic linguistic family

middle of the grave, while the eastern Latgalian–Lithuanian branch had grave heaps with Band Ware pottery.

The ancestors of the west Balts entered into contact with an unknown population encountered on the shores of the Baltic Sea, then between the second century BC and third century AD with the east Germanic tribes, for example the Gothic people, and from the third century with the west Slavs. The effect of the Vikings started to have its impact from the seventh and ninth centuries. The Prussian language is much closer to German than eastern Baltic due to the Gothic and Viking influence (Kilian 1982, 51).

The diffusion of the eastern branch ended more than a thousand years later between the fifth to seventh centuries, and perhaps began around the time of Christ (Mažiulis 1974, 122). However, to put it half a millennium (!) later is also possible (a long separation of Prussians and Latgalians–Lithuanians is the cause of the major differences between the two languages).

East Baltic tribes occupied their current territories following pressure from the Slavs. At that point they once more met the west Balts from whom they had been separated for about a thousand years. Where this encounter could have been "we cannot draw the borders even roughly" (Volkaitė-Kulikauskienė 1987, 88), because there is a continual transition between the Kurgan culture attributed to the west Balts and the Corded Ware culture clearly discernible from one thousand BC to five hundred AD. Who did the east Balts find there? According to accepted opinion they found the Finno-Ugrians. However, there are arguments to the contrary: the bulk of the scant Finnic (Estonian) loan words come from later, and were taken over through the Latvian language. Finno-Ugrian place names on current Baltic areas are also rare (Ochmański 1966).

Based on the *lingua franca* theory there is no explanation for the development of the Indo-European languages. I shall return to the theoretical inevitability of this absence. A practical argument against the theory is that the structure of the Indo-European languages is too uniform to have consisted of scattered languages from the Rhine to the Urals. The main argument is offered by the archaic nature of the Baltic languages: the Baltic language that ended up in the north shows the most similarity to the southern Sanskrit, Greek, and Latin, and that can only be explained with the presumption of a common proto-language.

2.3. The archaic nature of the Baltic languages

The archaic features of the Baltic languages make them a decisively significant part of Indo-European prehistory. Above all we are talking about the Lithuanian language here which is much more archaic than Lettish because Prussian, which would otherwise be the most archaic Baltic language, with only two thousand three hundred or so residual words no longer constitutes a full language.[7]

To give a feeling of this archaic nature the following sentence has often been quoted in Sanskrit, Greek, and Lithuanian since the seventeenth–eighteenth centuries:

God gave teeth God will give bread.
Devas adat datas, Devas dasyati dhanas.
Theos dédoke odontas, Theos dosei arton.
Dievas davė dantis, Dievas duos duonos.

The idiom is also known in Prussian:

Dewes does dantes, Dewes does geitka (quotes Mažiulis 1966–81/II, 64).

Every word is the same except for the Pruss. *geitko* 'bread' (<IE. *$g\u{u}ei$-, $g\u{u}i$- 'to live' or 'life' (Toporov 1975–90/II, 196).

[7] Not only lay people but also serious linguists mix up the question—in the enchantment of nationalist feelings—how old a language is with the one referring to how archaic it is. S. Karaliūnas gave a clear wording to the latter feature, "The Baltic languages differ from the other Indo-European languages in certain phonetic and phonological, grammatical, as well as lexical and semantic characteristics, the complexity of these forms the *specifica* of the Baltic languages. Some of these characteristics are neologisms that developed during the several centuries long independent existence of the Baltic languages, others are inherited archaisms from the ancient Indo-European past. Most of the Indo-European languages—the living ones and the ones that died out centuries ago—did not preserve these archaisms, which is why they put a higher emphasis on the specific nature of the Baltic languages" (Karaliūnas 1987, 4). So the Baltic languages are archaic, and yet rather young because we can claim the independence of the Latvian and Lithuanian languages only from the sixth–eleventh centuries AD.

The archaic nature of the Baltic languages is generally accepted.[8] Amongst other things the numbers from one to ten are often referred to as evidence:

Indo-European	Sanskrit 500 BC	Latin 100 AD	Gothic 300 AD	Old Slavic 9th century AD	Prussian 15–16th centuries AD	Latvian	Lithuanian
*oinos	ekas	unus	ains	edinъ	ains	viens	vienas
*dwo	dvau/dve	duo/duae	twai	dъva	dwai	divi/divas	du/dvi
*trejes	trayah	tres	treis	tri	no data	trīs	trys
*kwetwores	čatvarah	quattuor	fidwor	chetъri	no data	četri	keturi
*penkwe	panča	quinque	fimf	pjatъ	no data	pieci	penki
*s(v)eks	šat	sex	saihs	shestъ	no data	seši	šeši
*septm	apta	septem	sibun	semъ	no data	septiņi	septyni
*okto(u)	aštau	octo	ahtau	osimъ	no data	astoņi	aštuoni
*nevm	nava	novem	niun	devjatъ	no data	deviņi	devyni
*dēkm	dal'a	decem	taihun	desjatъ	dessimpts	desmit	dešimt[9]

The archaic features of Baltic languages were soon recognised. J. Grimm referred to Lithuanian data in 1822 (*Deutsche Grammatik*), as did F. Bopp in his expansive work in 1833 (*Vergleichende Grammatik des Sanskrit, Zend, Griechischen, Lateinischen, Lithauischen, Gothischen und Deutschen*). It will not do an Indo-Europeanist any harm to learn, at least, Lithuanian. From the summaries of the history of the discipline by A. Sabaliauskas it emerges that each significant language historian—A. Pott, A. Schleicher, A. Leskien, A. Bezzenberger, W. Thomsen, F. de Saussure, A. Meillet, J. Baudouin de Courtenay, L. Hjelmslev,

---

[8] There are a few Indo-Europeanists who feed strong doubts about the Baltic languages being more archaic than the Slavs. E. Fraenkel's sentence expresses that he believes the opposite, that is that "at times the Slavic language feels less archaic than the Baltic". So, only at times "*hin und wieder*" (Fraenkel 1950, 75). O. Trubachev, referring to A. Brückner thinks similarly. He believes that Slavic verb conjugation is definitely more archaic than that of the Baltic. According to the Muscovite linguist the Slavic branch does not originate from the peripheral dialect of the Baltic branch, and even a contact came about late around 500 BC (Trubachev 1982/4, 24). The question could be debated for ever because it is about a relationship to a *presumed* Proto-Indo-European language. To me the 'golden middle path' *aurea mediocretas* seems the most acceptable that H. E. Mayer expressed in a way that "Baltic is more conservative in phonology. Slavic is more conservative in morphology. But Baltic's more conservative phonology makes its morphology seem more conservative than Slavic's" (Mayer 1995, 67).

[9] The consonant at the beginning of the word 'nine' was originally 'n', the Pruss. *newints* 'tenth' refers to that, and 'd' replaced it analogous to the following number the 'ten' (Erhart 1984, 86).

P. Arumaa, J. Kuryłowicz, M. Vasmer, P. Ariste and so on—spoke 'Baltic' and Baltic studies were a ground pillar for their works (Sabaliauskas 1979–82, 1984).[10] The *lingua franca* idea is largely invalidated by the archaic nature of the Baltic languages. Returning to the language tree theory, many explain this archaic nature, probably most characteristic of the original Indo-European language, with an *Urheimat* in the Baltic language area. At that point they fall on the other side of the coin and in an essentially mechanical way slip linguistics in as part of prehistory writing and prehistory itself one on top of the other, thus completely mixing up two totally different layers: the scholarly layer of comparison of languages (where the focal position of the Baltic languages is indisputable) and the layer of social and historical reality (where it is at least highly probable that the Baltic languages were peripheral).

In the case of the first layer, putting the Baltic languages in the focus can answer old unsolved linguistic questions. Two of these I shall describe.

Much ink has been used in finding the third person plural verb form of the Baltic languages, following the Sanskrit and Old Greek patterns. No search is needed as soon as we accept that the Baltic form is the archaic one, because the more primitive original Indo-European language did not have separate categories for the person, time, or number of the action (Klimas 1979, 157).

The other example is connected to the isogloss of the *kentum–satem*. The Indo-European languages are known to have been divided into two groups late nineteenth century. The division was based on whether the palatal 'k' and 'g' sounds hardened into 'k' or 'g', or softened into 's' or 'z' (or 'š' or 'ž') spirant sounds. From the IE. *$kṃtóm$ 'hundred' became on the one hand the Latin *centum*, Greek *he-katón*, Gothic *hund* (h < k), Irish *cét*, and on the other hand the Avestan

---

[10] A. Meillet's utterance at the dawn of the century is well known, "they that wish to know how our ancestors talked should travel there and listen to how a Lithuanian peasant speaks" (Meillet quoted in Sabaliauskas 1986, 18). Nevertheless most researchers, such as W. Jones the Calcuttan British lawyer who discovered the kinship of the Indo-European languages in 1786, or F. Bopp who planted the comparison into scholarly grounds, chose the three dead languages Sanskrit, Ancient Greek, and Latin for the basis of their comparison, even though these show probably more 'dirt' compared to the original Indo-European language than Lithuanian. (According to the Indian S. K. Chatterji for example the Aryan peoples, the Indo-European tribes were wandering for about 700 years after they had left their ancient homeland on the south Eurasian steppes around 2100 BC, with stops in Mesopotamia, Persia, and Afghanistan. Then they settled in north India. All this of course left marks on their language, Vedian Sanskrit—Chatterji 1968). As A. Klimas the American linguist of Lithuanian origin says in the title of his article that despite all their archaic nature the Baltic languages were cornered and restricted to simple aiding and supplementary roles (Klimas 1979). The situation began to change after the Second World War, thanks to a few significant works, among which some need to be mentioned: E. Fraenkel's book (Fraenkel 1950), and his etymological dictionary (Fraenkel 1962–65); Stang's first, though incomplete, Baltic grammar book (Stang 1966); and the works of V. Ivanov, V. Toporov, and O. Trubachev among other Russian linguists.

satem, Sanskrit *šatám*, Lith. *šimtas*, Old Slavic *sъto. This way the Greek, Italic, Celtic, Germanic, and perhaps the Illyrian languages (about which we have no data) were ordered into the kentum languages, while the satem languages became the Indic, Iranian, Armenian, Albanian, Baltic, Slavic, and perhaps the Thracian and Phrygian languages (about the latter two we have no data). At the same time this grouping corresponded really well to an east–west division. The discovery of the A and B Tokharian language in Chinese Turkestan at the beginning of our century fundamentally shook the picture, and later the solution to the Hittite arrowhead writing from around the same period had similar consequences. It turned out that the most eastern and most southern languages of the Indo-European language family that had arrived in Asia Minor belonged to the kentum branch (Tokharian *känt*).

In general it is the kentum languages that were most distanced from the 'centre' as early as in prehistoric times. The Celtic language moved to the west, the Germanic to north-west, the Greek to the south, the Hittite and the Tokharian to the east and south-east. From all this W. Schmid came to the conclusion that "before the first diffusion there was no differentiation between the kentum and satem languages at all" (Schmid 1976, 118), and that "in the model the Baltic languages seem to be satemised kentum languages" (Schmid 1976, 122).[11]

2.4. The Baltic *Urheimat*

The above cannot offer a concrete reason for thinking that the central place of comparative linguistics would correlate to a geographical centre-point (in 1862 the English linguist R. Latham gave voice to the idea that, "the starting point [for research] into Sanskrit must be sought in Europe, especially in the eastern or southeastern border of the Lithuanian [language area]" (Latham in Schrader 1883, 125). Most recently F. Kortlandt compared the ancient Indo-European language to a cyclone, which began to spin on the eastern Ukrainian steppes around 4500–4000 BC throwing out individual languages from its centre, until Lithuanian remained as the last language: "The deceptive archaic character of the Lithuanian language may be compared to the calm eye of a cyclone" (Kortlandt 1990, 137). A. Senn's long familiar thesis is similar. He said that Baltic–Slavic unity existed only in the sense that these languages remained as the last Indo-European unit, after the others had dispersed (Senn 1966a, 1970). W. Schmid is the most radical representative of this language tree with a Baltic stem. He believed that the focus

[11] H. Schelesniker comes to similar results though based on other arguments. He wrote that originally the Baltic (and Slavic) languages belonged to the western Indo-European languages but underwent secondary satemisation due to eastern influence. This way they make a connecting link between the two branches (in Makkay 1991, 187–188).

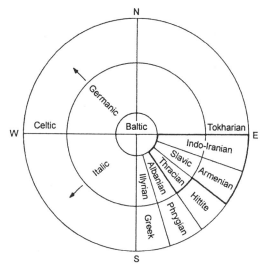

Figure 4. The splintering of the Indo-European linguistic family

of the research of Indo-European languages should be turned from south-east to north-west because that is where the web of water names is the densest (Schmid 1976, 118). His scheme explains the diffusion of the language family in time and space, as well as the kinship and contact relationships coming from the dispersal with the languages from the centre being last to leave the proto-language. (See Figure 4.)

The presumption of a Baltic *Urheimat* is unacceptable for two reasons. Firstly it leaves unanswered the question as to how and when the Indo-European tribes reached the far north, since according to the majority: "By the most modest of estimates the starting point of their [the Indo-European tribes] immigration must have fallen into the Paleolithic era" (Harmatta 1966, 247). That means they must have been there when the Baltic were still under ice, or had just begun to escape from it.

The other reason is that there is no adequate explanation for the archaic nature of the Baltic languages. Language history usually shows that changes go on most of all in the centre of a language area (unless it is geographically isolated), and that the periphery hangs on to ancient ways the most doggedly (cf. Róna-Tas 1978, 73). The archaic features of the Baltic languages can be understood most easily from precisely this: their peripheral position. The original Indo-European language, which of course was divided into dialects as any other language, developed somewhere in the south, in Asia Minor or in south-eastern Europe. From the beginning the ancestors of the Balts must have lived on the northern stretch of this language area, and during the dissipation advanced more and more to the north becoming exceedingly separated whilst they moved across and settled in uninhabited or scarcely populated territories no serious alien language affected them, consequently they could retain the original Indo-European. The following also stands by this thesis: when the Latvian language broke away from the east Baltic unity, as the last branch leaving the Indo-European stem to the north, they encountered the Finnic languages. Under their influence the Latvian language lost much of its archaic character which then remained undisturbed in Lithuanian which was free of external interference.

G. Childe seems to have faced controversies that were the result of the mentioned intermingling of layers when he writes that in the second half of the first millennium the Baltic were inhabited by "groups barely emerging from savagery in the far northern forests" (Childe 1950, 334). This is a statement of historical reality. At the same time, "the long chronology may be gratifying to the local patriotism of North Europeans" (Childe 1950, 334).[12]

Why? Because "Assuming the identity of Battle-ax folk and Indo-Europeans, it relegates the Aryan cradle to the Baltic coasts or Central Germany" (Childe 1950, 335). This is a scholarly thesis. The two theses can only result in an openly controversial admission in the last sentence of the book referring again to historical reality, "But the battle-ax itself seems older in Anatolia than in any more westerly region" (Childe 1950, 336).

Nevertheless if one does not fall into the trap of the illusory controversy emerging from the central role of language and the marginal function of culture, even then, abiding by the prescriptions of diffusionism ordered by archaeological culture, one can make an attempt to describe the passage from Indo-European to the actual Baltic languages.

Indo-Europeans scattered from their *Urheimat*s in several directions (whether it was from the Near-East, the Balkans, the basin of the mid- and lower Danube, or the steppes above the Black Sea). Among their number, the ancestors of the Slavs–Balts–Germanics, is usually identified with Corded Ware culture, a group which further divided. One part went toward the north where, during the third, second, and first millennia BC, they met with peoples of unknown 'kin' from the Narva and Nemunas cultures and were assimilated. From the Late Mesolithic period, that is from the sixth to the fifth millennium BC the Narva culture had lived in the north-eastern territories of the current three Baltic states and former Prussia, and the Nemunas culture occupied the south-western parts, both had been part of the Kunda culture in the Mesolithic period. This dynamism resulted in the *Haffküstenkultur*, or in Polish Rzucewo culture, which probably can be identified

---

[12] A separate study or pamphlet could be written about what any kind of 'local patriotism' has to do with who lived in a given territory five–six thousand years ago, and about why such a sentence is published from the ink of a scholar like Childe that observes the locals not even forgivingly but with a straightforward irony, with which prehistory writing is heaving.

with the ancient Old Slavic–Old West Baltic language and then with the Old West Baltic that broke away from the above group. The remaining group of Indo-Europeans advanced eastwards. They established the Dnieper-Daugava culture (which could be the Old Latvian–Lithuanian language) by merging with the encountered kin (Indo-European?) peoples of the Dnieper-Donieck culture in the mid-Dnieper basin. Later they met the kin (Indo-European?) peoples of the upper-Volga culture in the upper-Volga region, integrated and established the Fat'janovo culture (this could be the language of the most eastern Baltic people which later disappeared).

Several explanations can be raised against such a neat layering of archaeological cultures and languages, some of which I have already mentioned. Unfortunately a faulty outcome detracts from its authenticity, too. A. Myadzvedzeu calculated that the number of archaeological cultures by the Iron Age (eighth century BC to eighth century AD) solely on the areas of Belarus was divided into ten, but without ten independent languages to match them (Myadzvedzeu 1994, 15).[13]

However, contrary to all these problems only on the basis of these diffusionist recipes can we say anything noteworthy about the development of cultures. Evolutionism remains with the empty generalities of its encounters and the complications of the processes arising from them. It is inevitable that it should be this way. We must see that from two sets and two methods of linguistics and archaeology those within the domain of linguistics are determining, with the most emphasis being on language tree theory. I have talked about the reasons behind the prime line of linguistics: only language has continuity due to its natural and physical components. Language tree theory derives a palpable diversity from an earlier unity that is the present from the past, which makes the concept user-friendly within linguistics, as opposed to the *lingua franca* theory which thrives on the idea of an earlier diversity toward a later unity that is from the ancient past to the more recent past. The idea according to which "the individual separate languages emerged mainly with the inner shift of small communities and their occupancy on top of each other, and through relationships with outside communities with alien languages; and not primarily through changes between generation, or social and economic development" (Harmatta 1990, 245) is appealing. Nevertheless, from the participants in these processes we only really know about the one whose language emerged victorious from these encounters, and endured to the present day, or at least to the point of being recorded. For these reasons the key note of these processes, as G. Komoróczy (Komoróczy 1976, 104) or C. Renfrew (Renfrew 1989a, 86) emphasised, is the language replacement, because "languages migrated, and not peoples, even though each wandering language had

---

[13] Unless we count the dialects, too, like the authors of the work that summarises Latvia's archaeology reflecting back onto the map of the Latvian dialects of the Middle Ages to 1500–500 BC and divide the archaeological cultures correlatingly to these (Latvijas 1974, 92).

to have at least a handful of carriers" (D'yakonov, 1982/4, 18). However, we know nothing about the languages that were cast off during language replacement, they were assimilated, or vanished, or in some rare cases survived as mysterious islands like the Basque language. We can only be aware of, or have knowledge about languages ordered into language families with the help of the language tree theory. Untermann is totally justified in rehabilitating the language tree theory through argumentation using linguistic theory in his aforementioned and highly significant study, while at the same time demarcating the limits of this (the most effective theory of the principal discipline of prehistory!). "In historic times the differences between the groups of people who are proven to have spoken an Indo-Germanic language... are significant to the extent that nobody should come to the idea of bringing these languages into closer relationships with each other based on 'ethnic' criteria. In the continuity of traditions that connects those who spoke these languages with their original sub-languages and their common original proto-language as well as with those peoples speaking them, ethnic changes must also have happened (while preserving the continuity of language). The result of the processes is the diversity that can be observed later. This and only this can be read from the model that compares languages. Everything else is open, therefore all the questions remain open that refer to the periods and conditions of ethnic changes (changing places, political restructuring, reforms of religions, and the influences of neighbours). These questions can only be illuminated by historians, but they can shed light also only onto the narrow stretch between historic and prehistoric times. Beyond this stretch there is no discipline, except for linguistics, which could identify languages with peoples. Even linguistics is only able to establish *that something had happened* and cannot say anything about *what it had been*" (Untermann 1983, 155). These words are applicable to I. D'yakonov's concept, the one that sounds most acceptable to me and according to which agricultural Indo-Europeans filtered into the great territories of Eurasia while transmitting their knowledge and language to the smaller tribes living in more primitive social formations (D'yakonov 1994, 67). Which tribes these were, and what language(s) they spoke we can have only very vague ideas about.

CHAPTER 3

THE VENET(D) QUESTION

All complicity of Indo-European prehistory and all the controversies of prehistory writing is reflected in the Venet question, like 'the ocean in a drop of water.' This is not the sole reason why I have devoted a whole chapter to this problem. It lends itself to a presentation of a possible way to put together the 'Indo-European (Baltic) puzzle', which seems the most logical of all to me. A pattern which gains a variety of solutions depending on the meaning historians attribute to the little data at hand. What can be ascribed to the name of a people—an ethnicity, a language, or an (archaeological) culture? At the same time a transposition of names can go with a transposition of languages or even cultures? Perhaps it is no coincidence that in examining this question E. Hamp comes to the conclusion that "much of scientific reasoning is circular" (Hamp 1959, 179).

The uniqueness of the Venet(d) question is inherent in the fact that only the name, South Venets and North Veneds, of insoluble origin remains to us, but that this name is scattered over a huge territory.[1] G. Labuda's map (see Map 3 on next page) outlines this (Labuda in SSS 1961–82/6, 377).

The territory is divided into two areas. The northern one expanded from the British Isles (Gwyned) and Jutland (Vendsyssel), the western from the former Armorica (Normandy and Brittany with the centre of the latter being Venetia, today's Vannes), through the estuary of the Vistula, along the coast of the Baltic Sea, up to the Gulf of Finland. The southern area stretched across from Lake Boden (P. Mela called it Venetus lacus—Pauly-Wissowa's 1955, 710), through north Italy (Venedig-Venice), along both coasts of the Adriatic Sea across the Balkans and Yugoslavia to Albania. Perhaps an accidental coincidence among names, but Homer mentions a people in Asia Minor, the Paphlagons who are from the Enetai province (Homer *Iliad* II, 852), which is 'Venet-suspicious' since a few hundred years later Herodotus refers to the Enetos people twice, once as Illyrian (Herodotus I, 196) and again as the occupants along the Adriatic Sea (Herodotus

---

[1] According to the majority opinion about the Venet(d) problem (e.g. Tymieniecki 1968) the Germanics, or more precisely the Suevs, pronounced a 'd' instead of the original Adriatic 't'. Although it is not quite right because for example the Ostrogothic, i.e. "deep down" Germanic Jordanes mentions them with a 't' all three times). I shall refer to the people who lived on the Baltic Sea as Veneds and those who lived on the Adriatic coast as Venets.

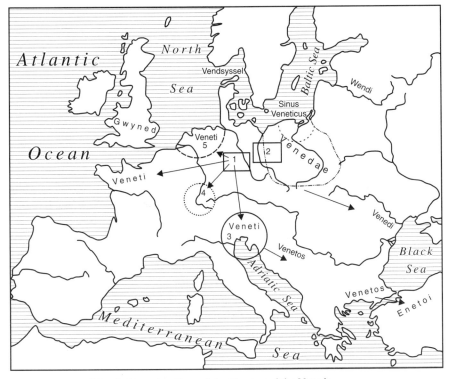

Map 3. The migrations of the Venets and the Veneds
1. The putative *Urheimat* in Thuringia; 2. The presumed *Urheimat* in Great Poland–Lausitz;
3. The Adriatic Venets; 4. The region of Lake Boden; 5. The areas of the lower Rhine

V, 9). An Illyrian = Adriatic identification became the source of many complications.[2]

The northern Veneds were first mentioned by Pliny and Tacitus, who both gained their information also from the Germans. Both place them to the east of the Vistula estuary (Pliny placed them as far as the Gulf of Finland), on the borders of Germania, and Sarmataland. Pliny calls them Venets (Pliny IV, 107) at other times Veneds (Pliny IV, 97), while Tacitus Venets (Tacitus 46). Pliny thinks they are Sarmatas, Tacitus sometimes Germans, sometimes Sarmatas. In the following century they crop up in Ptolemy's work. He wrote that "the Greater Venedae races inhabit Sarmatia along the entire Venedicus bay [Gdańsk]" where the Vistula reaches the Sarmatian Ocean (the Baltic Sea) (Ptolemy III, 5, 10). Nearly half a millennium later Jordanes' report corresponds with that: "The greater number of the Venetic people (*natio populosa*) live north of the source of the Vistula (that is

[2] H. Krahe thought that only the name of the Illyrian and Adriatic Enetos peoples are the same, but in fact they were two different tribes (Krahe 1950, 20).

the northwestern Carpathians) on endless tracts of land" (Jordanes 1960, 34 and 119). They were known by three different names in the times of the Ostrogothic bishop: Venets, Ants, and Sklavens. This is the only source which identifies the Veneds with the undoubtedly Slavic Ants and Sklavens. It is also interesting that it demarcates their habitat inland and not on the coast, because at the places where the authors of the first two centuries thought about them, that is "On the shores of the ocean, where the water of the River Vistula is swallowed by a triple estuary, there live the Vidivarius people gathered together from various tribes" (Jordanes 36). The Roman map of transport (*Tabula itineraria Peutingeriana*) serves as evidence of the duality of coast and inland that is mentioned twice.[3] The first reference (*Venadi* VIII, 1) puts them on the coast of the ocean embracing Europe from the north, while the second one (*Venadi Sarmatae* VIII, 4) east of the eastern Carpathians and the rivers flowing into the Danube and before the Dniester to the lower Danube (Niederle 1902–11/2, 123) which H. Łowmiański finds mysterious (Łowmiański 1963–70/I, 181).

Coastal and inland Slavs are also called Vened later, too. Sorbs living in upper and lower Lausitz (Lužice) are referred to as Vend, the Slovenians in Styria and Karinthia as Vind (Schuster-Šewc 1970), and those in Hungary as Vend.

The name of the coastal Veneds crops up after Jordanes, too. It is debated as to whether Wulfstan's Witland belongs there also (Wulfstan 1984, 16), in what the Germans called Widland in the Middle Ages, and many identify with the habitation of the Vidivarius peoples (cf. Skrzhinskaya in Jordanes 1960, 221). At the same place Wulfstan also talks about Vendland (Weonodlande) most likely referring to Sembia, and several place names have preserved the memories of the Veneds along the Prussian and the Lithuanian coasts. *Venet, vint-, wend-* stems in Pruss. *Venedien, Venedige*, Lith. *Wendziagola* 'borders of the Vends' (Łowmiański 1963–70/I, 61 and Ochmański 1966, 56). The Veneds crop up further to the east as well, around Riga where they escaped from Couronia (Kurland) as known from the accounts of Heinricus the chronicler, "The Wends were chased away from the River Winda in Kurland" (Heinricus X, 14). Following this Cēsis town's German name is Wenden (Mugurēvičs in Heinricus 1994, 368). The Veneds escaping from Couronia were Christened by the Germans there around Riga. It is less likely but might be true that these Veneds originating from the surroundings of the Latvian River Venta have nothing to do with the Veneds on the shores of the Vistula, but they were Baltic Finns more precisely Livs from Couronia (Mugurēvičs 1970, 298). That would mean that they did not get their name from the river but gave it to it.

---

[3] The *Tabula* is 7.5 metres of scrolls, 11 parchments, a copy of it was found in 1507, and is from the twelfth–thirteenth centuries. The age of its original is not certain. The estimations range from around the time of Christ to the ninth century. H. Łowmiański thinks it ranges "from the mid-second century to the fourth century" (Łowmiański 1963–70/I, 181).

The *Indi(ki)ja* at the beginning of the *Nestor Chronicle* points even more to the east as far as Novgorod, which E. Vilinbakhov believes to be a misspelling of *Wendia* (Vilinbakhov 1967, 308). The Veneds are in the *Nestor Chronicle*, 'without a misspelling', among the tribes of Jafet: venьdici (*Nestor Chronicle* 1950, 10). (In the 1950 edition of the *Nestor Chronicle* it was translated into Russian as 'Venetians', a rather questionable decision—206.)

The Baltic-Finn peoples also met the Veneds. Unlike the Germans they called the Russians and not the Slavs in general by names deriving from the stem 'Vened', and they still do: Finn *venaja*, Estonian *vene*, Karelian *veneä* 'Russian'.[4]

The abstruse question of who the Venets-Veneds were became even more complex when they were connected with the Illyrian problem, a complicated issue in itself. [Linked with the Illyrians J. Harmatta, just like E. Hamp, as mentioned above, in relation with the Venet-question, talks about *circulus vitiosus* (Harmatta 1967a, 232) and with full righteousness, because characteristic features must be derived from the scant remnants of the Illyrian language, based on which some of these rare linguistic remains could qualify as Illyrian, from which those features could then be derived ... and so on round and round. Thus the Vened and Illyrian question becomes an intertwining of two vicious circles.] The connection came up after Herodotus' Illyrian Enetos = Adriatic Enetos and the syllogism that if Vened = Venet and if Venet = Illyrian, then Illyrian = Vened.

The basis of the first equation is the great similarity between the proper nouns and place names, but most of all in the water names of the Baltic and the Adriatic (the most well known examples are the names of rivers that flow in the north and in the south: Odra, Dráva, Drama, Drwęca, Opawa, Notec, etc.). However, H. Łowmiański's standpoint is that this should not be enough to presume a language transposition beyond an interchange of names.[5] We do not know anything about the 'original language' of the Veneds and the Venets, and their later languages were not the same, and the Veneds oppressing the Italian population gave only their

---

[4] The conclusion can also be derived from this concept that the most north-eastern Slavic tribes, that is the Krivichs and the Slovenes of Novgorod migrated to their homeland not from the south-east but from the west from the area between the Oder and the lower Vistula (Sedov 1970). In any case there are strong arguments that claim that Novgorod was established by the western Slavs who were forced eastward at the time of the Karoling empire with the beginning of the Germanic *Drang nach Osten* (drive to east) in the eighth century. The name of the Norman (Swedish) reigning family of Novgorod-Kijev 'Ruryk (Rurik-Ryurik) means 'falcon' 'buzzard', and the falcon was the totemic animal of the western Slavic tribe the Obod(t)ritian which is also preserved in the three-branch tooth actually representing a stylised falcon in the Rurik court of arms (Vilinbakhov 1967, 58). M. Vasmer reinforces that, "J. Marquart (*Osteuropäische und ostasiatische Streifzüge* 328) stated that princes of Swedish origin ruled over the Obotritians and the Vagrians [another western Slavic tribe] in the tenth-eleventh centuries" (Vasmer 1929, 152).

[5] L. Niederle warned against considering the Armorican and the Adriatic Venets the same as the northern Veneds (Niederle 1902–11/II, 87).

names to them, and not their language which vanished into the Venet tongue. (I shall later return to the doubts about a north–south transposition of names.)[6]

Even if we accept parity between the Venet and Vened languages equality with Illyrian does not necessarily follow. Independently from each other J. Dobiáš (Dobiáš 1964, 8 ff.) and A. Tovar (Tovar 1977, 5–9) both stated that the Venets became Illyrians through, so to say, a promotion. Archaeologists were looking for 'a neat and tidy' ethnicity for the so-called Lausitz culture (1700–600 BC) and the linguists for the Old European water names. First the French pressed for the Ligurs and the Celts[7] but then German prehistorians and linguists—first of all G. Kossina, and following him J. Pokorny, and H. Krahe—made the Illyrians the 'chosen people' for the Lausitz culture and the Old European water names. However, no traces of Illyrians remain in northern Europe and a transmitter was needed which became the Veneds. Their only 'fault' was that their name was the same as the Venets. As Z. Marić put it, "the Illyrians, this small people or great tribe, lived in the region between the Rivers Drim and Vojuša from the sixth century at the latest... In the course of the Greek colonisation and the Roman conquest of the following centuries their name was transposed to a number of other tribes in the north-western parts of the Balkans, however none of the sources call any tribes living north of the Sava river 'Illyrians'. 'Illyricum' was a geographical term and 'Illyrian' the adjective derived from it which meant a person belonging to a province, a prefect or a diocese of the Illyrians... The terms were often applied to regions very far from the north-western parts of the Balkans, although this is not sufficient proof that those certain geographical regions were indeed populated by Illyrians, especially given that the meaning carried by the term 'Illyrian' also went through many changes... The borders of the Illyrian ethnicity must be sought in the north-western areas of today's Pannonia somewhere along the Danube bend" (Marić 1964, 177).[8]

[6] Of course there are standpoints on the opposite side, too. They say that the Veneds and the Venets spoke the same language even during Caesar Nero (54–68), which drives the excellent G. Labuda to a striking presumption: the Latin speaking Roman rider mentioned by Pliny went to the coast for amber to the Veneds perhaps had to use a Venet interpreter from the shores of the Po (Labuda in SSS 1961–82/6, 377).

[7] In a very thorough lexicon entry P. Melat not so long ago described the Venets as Celts (Pauly-Wissowa's 1955, 708).

[8] Scholars expanded the territory of the Illyrian people into the south, too. An extreme example of this is when the Bulgarian V. Georgiev "says the Pelasg, that is the people before the Hellas Greeks, were Illyrian. Their language would have been Indo-Germanic, a dialect of the Illyrian–Thracian language, and Etruskan was a later dialect of the latter. The Thracians and the Illyrians would have been the link between the central (Italic, Greek, Aryan) and the southern (Pelasg, Luwiy, Hittite) Indo-Germanic groups". The scholar from Zagreb only adds that "his [Georgiev's] linguistic evidence whirls in a *circulus vitiosus*". (This seems to go with the problem.) (Mayer 1957–59/I, 4–5).

Naming the Venets Illyrian is as lacking in basis as calling the Veneds Illyrian. Research was directed by the initial concept of the promotion of those languages to Illyrian and later the abandonment of the concept. H. Krahe's change of views well represents this process. In Keszthely in 1937, as a follower of Pan-Illyrism, he discussed the Venet language known through several hundred inscriptions as an Illyrian language which form the separate Illyrian branch of the Indo-European language family with the lower Italian Mesapian and the Balkan Illyrian. In 1950 he represented the point of view that the Venet language forms a separate branch in itself. In his last work he ordered the language into the Italic branch beside the Latin-Faliskus and the Osk-Umber (Krahe 1964, 33).[9] H. Krahe also presents a good example of how mechanical the slipping of the linguistic and archaeological data on top of each other was. First he realised that the Illyrian language is made up of a few so-called Mesap notices from the eastern part of lower Italy, one solitary brief notice from the Balkans, and a great number of place names and proper nouns. From this small item of linguistic material he concludes that (a) Illyrian is a kentum language and (b) its relationship to German, Latin, and Celtic languages lies in that the territory of the *Urheimat* of this language correlates solely with the Lausitz culture.

If the Italian Venets "were not of Illyrian nationality" (Dobiáš 1964, 16) then logically the Veneds should not be considered as such either. In the meantime, judgements over the Illyrian language and people also changed and after the passing of the Pan-Illyric fashion they diminished to their, so to say, real proportions.[10] If the Italic Venet and Mesap are not Illyr (though H. Krahe actually considered the latter Illyr for a long time!—Krahe 1950, 137) then what remains? Illyrian becomes one of the small languages of the Balkans that disappeared, that is one of the Paleo–Balkan languages (Zinkevičius 1984–94/I, 108 ff.). From that one solitary notice survived, a few dubious place names and proper nouns, and perhaps today's Albanian which can with difficulty be connected to these.[11] Its territory does not embrace the whole of 'Old Europe', not even the areas that the antique sources demarcate, not even the north-western part of the Balkan peninsula, but as R. Katičić convincingly proved, only the south-eastern parts and only

[9] For a summary of the debate about the characteristics of the Venet language see Szemerényi 1971–82/II, 119–120.

[10] For a most precise description of this decrease, see the meeting of the Yugoslavian linguists, archaeologists, and prehistorians in Benac 1964.

[11] Some researchers such as H. Krahe, V. Toporov, talk about an Illyrian–Baltic parallel which would be the result of the two tribes having lived together. From the previous discussions it is evident that the 'north Illyrians' i.e. the Veneds have nothing to do with the Illyrians that these researchers refer to. At best they could mean the Illyrians of the Balkans, though as J. Duridanov emphasised it the parallels must be taken with a pinch of doubt even in their case, most of all because of the dubious nature of the Illyrian data: it is hard to say what is Illyr (Duridanov 1969, 100).

proper nouns from that area can be rightfully considered Illyrian (Katičić 1964, 17). "Today the Illyrians, just like the Ligurs, are simply one people amongst many about whom we know only a little" (Tovar 1977, 9).

After forgetting about either the equality or even the kinship between Illyrian and Vened, and Illyrian and Venet, then the question arises as to what the Vened–Venet 'kin' could at least approximately have been, and closely connected to it where and when they must have lived, and from where to where they conquered the vast area where their names occur.

In the case of the Veneds the answer is twofold. As for the Veneds of the first centuries BC H. Łowmiański seems to be closest to a correct solution (Łowmiański 1963–70/I, 57–183). In a two hundred year or more debate he stood beside the Veneds being Slavs who came from the south–south-east, reached the Baltic Sea by the so-called Hallstatt C period (700–550 BC), and finished the Slavisation of the Pomorze coast (Łowmiański 1963–70/I, 94), and the Germans arriving from the north transferred the native Veneds' name onto these Slavs. The Veneds being Slavs can be stated with certainty, even though there is only one item of direct evidence for it, that is Jordanes' reference. There is a lot of circumstantial (indirect) evidence, however. To give a brief summary of these, the Veneds are uniformly said to be a great people in sources that are silent about the Slavs, in the areas where later sources place the Slavs, that is along the coast west of the Vistula estuary, east of the Sudets, north of the Carpathians, and to the lower Dnieper on the south (Łowmiański 1963–70/I, 182–183).

The Slavs were only the 'mainland' Veneds. During the first millennium the 'original' ancient Veneds occupied the coast from the Gulf of Gdańsk to the Gulf of Riga. They were gradually edged out or assimilated by the Prussian and Lithuanian tribes advancing from the east and by the Finnic tribes from the north (Łowmiański 1963–70/I, 60).

This thesis plays a decisive role in Baltic prehistory, because this is the only one that gives a feeling of who lived in the region before the Balts.

A very important note should be added to the ideas of the Polish scholar. The Veneds must have been few in number on the Baltic shores and this is why, after the appearance of the new tribes—western Slavs, Balts, Germans, and late in the first millennium the eastern Balts—they rapidly lost their language and only retained their names.

The thesis is part of H. Łowmiński's Indo-European theory, and also of Ochmański's who accepted it. It is worth casting a closer glance at it because it is probably the most comprehensive and consistent among the 'eastern' *Urheimat* theories, and because—precisely due to the Veneds—it sheds light on all the weak points of the eastern *Urheimat* theories. (At the same time, it shows that in this subject it is always the actual speaker—at this point myself—that is a hundred percent right...)

According to the Polish historian the Indo-European *Urheimat* was at the lower Volga or to the east of the river on the steppes above the Caspian Sea or the Kasakh steppes. The succeeding Old European tribes proceeded westwards from there in two waves. In the first wave during the late third millennium BC the Veneds (the people of the Corded Ware ceramics) reached Europe, so their language became "the only language which emerged from the Old European" (Łowmiański 1963–70/I, 59). The remaining disparate European languages (Celtic, Italic) were a result of a newer wave of immigration (Łowmiański 1963–70/I, 81).

The three northern European tribes moved westwards and northwards in three columns from the mid Volga and the lower Oka rivers. In the centre were the Balts, on their southern flank were the Slavs "who were in close relationship with them [the Balts]", while on their northern flank were the Germans. The southern wing advanced the quickest due to a more favourable geographical situation, so the Slavs reached their historical habitat between the Oder and the Dnieper in the mid-second millennium BC[12] (Łowmiański 1963–70/I, 91–92). After approximately 500 years of wandering the Balts in the centre, who differed from the Slavs–Germans with their Corded Ware ceramic culture (Okulicz 1973, 239), arrived around 1200 BC from near the Oka passing the Dnieper, Nemunas, and upper Daugava. In their wanderings from 1500 to 500 BC the Germans, that is, the northern wing proceeding in the least favourable circumstances found their new *Urheimat* beside the Volga and across the Gulf of Finland on the Scandinavian and Jutland peninsulas and came to the continent from there (Łowmiański 1963–70/I, 62–63). Two Old European areas were formed following the two waves of the Indo-Europeans: the northern German, and the southern Vened, the latter was later occupied by Celts, Slavs, and Balts (Łowmiański 1963–70/I, 90).

A significant point in this idea is that the ancestors of the Slavs—and obviously the western Slavs—reached the Baltic Sea at the Oder and the lower Vistula, and found the Veneds there who had arrived earlier. The transposition of names happened there and not only to the German Vened > (west) Slavic which is understandable but also to the Finn Vened > Russian (east Slavic). H. Łowmiański offers a doubtful explanation of the latter exchange in that the Finns heard from the Germans that the (west) Slavs of the Pomorze were called Vened, and later transposed that onto the eastern ones, too (Łowmiański 1963–70/I, 91). To me it seems easier to presume that much later, on the shores of the Gulf of Finland, the Finns encountered the Veneds who had by that time spoke east Slavic that is Russian since they 'as usual' had long ago lost their own language. H. Łowmiański

---

[12] Z. Goląb is of the same opinion: The north-western region between the Don and the upper Dnieper, on the north the upper Oka falls into a forest zone while the south-eastern area into a forest and steppe zone. The Old Germanics and the Old Balts pushed straight westwards across the forest, and the Old Slavs proceeded southwards. For this reason the latter developed a more advanced agriculture (Goląb 1982, 132).

adopted the theory of an early German–Baltic Finn encounter from J. Rozwa-dowski and T. Lehr-Spławiński who expanded the territory of Finnish water names as far as eastern Germany. M. Vasmer refutes that in several of his works, and said of the German–Finn encounter that, "it started not later than the first century BC" (Vasmer 1941, 83).

Another weak point in H. Łowmiański's theory is that it offers no explanation as to why the tribes coming from the east only conquered the coast so far west, and most of all as to why it was only the Slavs and not the Balts who were actually advancing north of them and closer to the sea.

So H. Łowmiański believes that the Veneds came from the east, and only their names were carried to the south. At least this idea clearly tells us where they journeyed to Europe from. The other concepts implicitly or explicitly presume that the Veneds were autochthon, i.e. the Indo-European *Urheimat* was in northern and central Europe (one can imagine G. Kossina in the background). The group of people, whether the Veneds and Venets as a whole, or ònly the Veneds or the Venets in isolation, migrated from the north to the south. H. Krahe worded this most clearly: "All of them, the Illyrians, the Italic, and the Venet have... clear connections to the Germans, that is they all came from the north... and later moved to the south" (Krahe 1950, 37). Translating this north–south movement into the language of archaeology means that the people of "the Lausitz [culture] advanced across the eastern parts of the Alps to the historical territory of the Illyrians around 1200 BC" (Mayer 1957–59/I, 4). (This became the only basis for connecting the Lausitz culture to the Illyrians and in this way, at least in scholarly studies, the Illyrians seeped into the north through the Lausitz culture.) The presumption of some 'north Illyrs' tempts even those who see most clearly. A. Mayer, a professor from Zagreb, wrote of the Illyrian language area, "besides the Roman province of Dalmacia, today's Albania, a big part of Pannonia also belonged to the core of the Illyrian region" (Mayer 1957–59/I, 8). J. Harmatta, accepting Mayer's wording, in his book review reserves the possibility that "the language of the Pannonian tribes, the Dardans and the Päons, was also Illyrian" (Harmatta 1967a, 234). However, when J. Harmatta examines where the Bronze Age *Urheimat* of the thus interpreted Illyrs was he places it, and it seems to me a moot point, in south Germany and the Alpine region. Tribes living there would have spoken Illyrian, which differed from Latin, German, and Venet. Several waves migrated from the region. First the Sikuls to Italy, then around 1300 BC the people of the barrow-burial culture, the Illyrians eastwards and then southwards along the Danube ("the first Illyr migration"). About a hundred years later the drive of the Urnfield people began on the same route towards the south-east ("the Venet migration") and finally about 750 BC people of the Hallstatt C culture expanded toward western Hungary ("the second Illyr migration") which gathered the Pannon tribes to itself (Harmatta 1967a, 234). In another study J. Harmatta places the earlier settlements (even if not the *Urheimat*) of the Venets, of these Urnfield people, to the Dunántúl

(Transdanubia in western Hungary) and east Austria from where they gradually proceeded southwards to Italy (Harmatta 1985–86, 189).

It is obvious that here archaeological cultures are mixed up with languages, and the Illyrian and the Venet once more become entangled, however J. Harmatta acknowledged their disentangling a significant research result.

As it turns out from G. Labuda's map (see p. 86) there are some who associate a north–south migration to the Veneds. T. Sulimirski places the *Urheimat* of the Veneds in Holland, part of Belgium and north-western Germany, from where some of their groups drove to the British Isles and the Jutland peninsula (the name of an island refers to that: Vendsyssel = Seeland). Around 1200 BC other groups wandered southwards to French Brittany, north-eastern parts of Italy, and further on south-eastwards across the Balkans to Asia Minor (Sulimirski 1933).[13]

Their more recent expansion began around 1000 BC and aimed for the Gdańsk coastline, and around 500 BC they occupied the whole of today's Poland giving their names to the Slavs they found and conquered there.

G. Labuda's hypothesis connects the Veneds' *Urheimat* to the north-eastern branch of the Lausitz culture, that makes it the coastline between the Vistula and the lower Oder, as well as Greater Poland and the upper and middle regions of the Oder coast. The mountain ranges of the northern Carpathians were also part of the *Urheimat*, which would correlate to the Vened mountains mentioned by Ptolemy (Ptolemy III, 5, 5). From there the Vened tribes scattered first to the south around 1000 BC, then between 600–300 BC to the south-west (Adriatic > Balkans > Asia Minor and along the upper Danube and the Rhine > Lake Boden, north Gallia > Westphalia > Britain), finally to the east, south-east. (The east Pomeranians must have been of Vened ethnicity and survived on the coast as far as Livonia, and Vened relics refer to them from between the river Prut and the lower Danube.) (Labuda in SSS 1961–82/6, 376–377).

These ideas do not offer a uniform or acceptable picture individually or together. One of the reasons for that is the persistently deep (mis)understanding that each name of a group of people has to have a separate ethnicity and archaeological culture of its own. Another reason lies in the presumption of the migration of the Veneds from the north to the south, which either avoids the question of how they reached the north completely or insists on the widely refuted standpoint that they came to be there because the Indo-European *Urheimat* was in Germany.

I believe that we can gain an uncontroversial, or at least a less controversial picture if we renew the old idea that goes back to the sixteenth century and which suggests that the Venets originated in the south, in Asia Minor. The question re-

---

[13] These directions correlate with Strabo's description, putting forward the idea that the Belgian (Celtic) "Veneti, I think, [...] settled the colony that is on the Adriatic (for about all the Celti that are in Italy migrated from the Transalpine land, just as did the Boii and Senones)..." (Strabo IV 4.1).

mains as to what their ethnicity might have been. Most of the more convincing theories, that of Harmatta's, D'yakonov's, or Renfrew's say that Europe became Indo-Europeanised from the south through the Balkans (Harmatta 1966, D'yakonov 1982, Renfrew 1987). In that case the Venets could well have been Indo-Europeans. (It would be enough to simply turn the arrows the other way round on G. Labuda's map.)[14] Nevertheless it is less likely, though not out of the question, that the Venets were Indo-Europeans, because, based on the spread of their name, they must have been a simply vast tribe whose language could hardly have disappeared without a trace so rapidly if they had reached Europe with the Indo-Europeans (recognising this controversy H. Łowmiański claimed they were the only Old Europeans that is the oldest European people).

For this reason, again following earlier concepts and not forgetting that Europe's Indo-Europeanisation as well as occupation came from the south (also Gábori 1977), it is most practical to think of the Venets as a people before the Indo-Europeans (the only bigger population whose name we know at least!). They came from the south, from or through the Balkans, and they scattered westward and eastward in the shape of a fan.[15] This would explain the dense point around the Alps, from where the Venets could spread further to the north-west, and their other group turned to the east and settled at the lower Danube and in the Carpathians. On the north, 'becoming Veneds' they could reach the Baltic Sea at

[14] If we accept a mainly south < north direction of Europe's inhabitation and Indo-Europeanisation without doubt the actual groups of people did not stay put in the one place but most likely there were wanderings here and there, and occasionally probably also in the opposite direction of their original advance of inhabitation. For example let us accept that the Slavs moved to the north-east from the south across the Balkans as far as Kasakhstan (Harmatta 1966, 247), it is proven that the Slavs populated the Balkans for the second (or who knows how manyeth) time in the first millennium BC and from the north. T. Lehr-Spławiński, one of the most reputable linguists, thinks that the Old Slavs broke away from the Indo-European community during a century long shift from the south-west to the north and to the east, then setting out from the region between the Oder, Vistula, and Bug they dispersed in all directions dividing into various branches (Lehr-Spławiński 1959, 10). This concept is obviously valid for the Veneds, too. Just because they reached their first ancient European homeland from the south to the north preceding the Indo-Europeans (or as the first most northern tribe of the Indo-Europeans) they could still have carried out southward wanderings from the north. The only problem is—as mentioned earlier this is perhaps the main problem of prehistory writing—that most of the time the 'earlier' and the 'later' cannot be determined. J. Harmatta for example considers the spread of the Indo-European languages from France to the Aral region a finished process by around 5000 BC (Harmatta 1966, 247), while D. Anthony risks the possibility, well underpinned with arguments, that the Indo-European languages did not exist before the first millennium BC in Europe (Anthony 1991, 217).

[15] The water names that can be found as far as the River Dnieper that O. Trubachev considers a west Balkan (Illyrian and Mesap) derivation point in an eastern direction (Trubachev 1968, 276).

various points, and advanced eastward along the coast. There, where they were the only inhabitants they remained longest as an individual ethnicity, perhaps until as late as the thirteenth century in a coastal stretch widening to the east. The Veneds became Slavs quickly where the western Slavs reached the coast at the Vistula estuary. Yet as a substratum people they were involved in the development of the tribes of various ethnicities (Slavic, Baltic, German, Finn) which later followed the progress of the west Balts toward the coast, and from which at least three peoples (Vidivari, Aestii, Couronians) are mentioned in sources, too. Preceding all these processes first of all the Veneds could of course have been the people of the Narva and Nemunas cultures whose ethnic origins are very unclear, and we only know for certain that "they cannot be called Indo-Europeans or Balts, they were Europids" (Rimantienė 1995, 190).

Indeed, this little is all we can state for certain. A group of people enter history by being given a name, followed by sources attaching various characteristics and features to them. The Venets–Veneds are a prime example of the way in which a people departs from history in a similar but inverted way, first losing their characteristics and features little by little until last of all their language dwindles leaving merely the name.

Their name could probably have been a collective noun similar to that of the Scythian, Sarmatian, or rather the Barbarian names, and its meaning must have referred to a characteristic of the people, for example their immigrant, emigrant, new-comer, and so on.[16] They completely lost their language and became a substrata of various Indo-European languages such as Slavic, Celtic, Italic, German, and lastly Baltic, in such a way that they left no other trace behind apart from their name.

---

[16] We can set our imagination in action: etymology so far has found the origins of the name 'Venet–Vened' in the most various domains of meanings that have been brought up. A. Bielenstein takes back the name of the River Venta to the Livonian verb *vent* 'stretch' (Bielenstein 1892, 193), J. Endzelīns (Endzelīns 1911, 358) and following him K. Būga (Būga 1923b, 546) vote for the IE. *vent(a)s* 'big' (cf. Serbian *veći*, and the Czech *více* 'more'). F. Sławski evokes the old idea that the stem of the word is the old Italic-Celtic *ven* 'love' (cf. Old Ind. *vánati* 'love'), so the Venet were people who loved and closely belonged to their tribe. Others attributed a meaning to the same stem as 'ones living in friendship' (cf. Old English *wine* 'friend'), while connecting the name with the Lith. *vanduo*, and Latin *unda* 'water' the Venets would be people living near some water. (For the various etymologies' suggestions see Łowmiański 1963–70/I, 87–88.)

I. Goldziher wrote about "migrating, wandering tribes" and that "the aspect of [these tribes] own wandering life style was one of the motifs of naming the communities, as is represented in several examples from the Kurds to the Zulus. The name *Ibhrim* 'Hebrew' is based on wandering across the most varied regions, which then means 'wanderers, migrating people, nomads'" (Goldziher 1876, 65–66). And what is our Old European or proto-European people's name hides this meaning? The Venet–Vened as the Jews of Old Europe?...

Actually... perhaps it is exactly this untraceability which tells us something. The hypothesis is growing stronger that the system of Old European hydronymies, mainly mapped out by J. Rozwadowski and H. Krahe, and here expressed with A. Tovar's critical words about H. Krahe, "is uniform not so much due to its Indo-German origins, but much more due to the fact that it developed its characteristic features over a long period of time" (Tovar 1977, 22). The Old European system is a mish-mash of Indo-European and non-Indo-European names where the previous ones are in minority. Indo-European water names are absent in eastern and southern parts of the Balkan peninsula (Łowmiański 1963–70/I, 53). Still the most striking feature is the hole which M. Vasmer called attention to (Vasmer 1929a/II, 540), and about which H. Krahe wrote: "While the Old European hydronymies are densely and richly represented in the north (Scandinavia), the entire west (also in West-Germany), the east (Baltic countries, east Prussia, Poland, etc.), and the south (including south Germany) they are strikingly scarce or completely absent in central Germany, roughly between the Rivers Elbe and Oder" (Krahe 1964, 86). Perhaps this precise area was where the Venets reached the Baltic Sea in their greatest numbers, and there in this new *Urheimat* (following the one in the Alps), they could settle undisturbed for a longer period, therefore those water names fell under their authority of name giving. It is impossible to identify them, since nothing remained of their language. At best they can be evaluated as zero morphemes in relation to the Indo-European names. Conclusively, what is not Indo-European is Venet–Vened.

The equality of the Baltic and Adriatic water names can be easily derived from the Indo-European language. There are no Indo-European–Venet water names in the north of Italy, because there the exchange of languages occurred relatively early therefore the Venets took over the Indo-European language and started talking in Indo-European–Venet. According to J. Safarewicz that meant a dialect kin with Celtic and Italic (Safarewicz 1964). In the Baltic the rest of the non-Indo-European–Veneds were forced to change their language to the Baltic language only relatively late at the end of the first millennium. Counter-intuitively, there is an absence of non-Indo-European–Vened water names in the Baltic, which can be explained with the small numbers of the Veneds. According to Heinricus' characterisation they were "a timid and poor people" (Heinricus X, 14). Consequently the later Baltic (therefore Indo-European, and as such inevitably correlating to the Adriatic and other Old European) names conceal the names that the Veneds could possibly have given.

CHAPTER 4

THE FIRST REFERENCES TO THE BALTS

The first indisputable written references to the Balts date from the ninth century AD. Almost one thousand five hundred years earlier a period begins where we can begin to realise what it is that we do not know, as opposed to the earlier 'most prehistoric' millennia about which we can be sure of absolutely nothing.

In this narrow time period that lay between prehistory in its strict sense and history, the knowledge of the writers of Antiquity about the European territory beyond the Black Sea was, to put it mildly, a little vague. They knew of the colonial towns established in a small region above the Pontus by the Greeks, but of the countries and people north and east of that they had only second or third hand, often fictional information. Each author referred to this vast area by a single name—first Scythia (Scythialand), later Sarmatia (Sarmataland)—which remained in use until the end of the Middle Ages, and only slowly gained real historical substance.

From the fifth century BC the peoples that lived there were also viewed as one, beginning with the Ionic geographer Hekataios of Miletus (ca. 550–480 BC). This may have been because these peoples were only interesting to the civilised countries from the perspectives of geography and, so to say, natural history. Since they had no history as such, every item of knowledge or information about them could be made simultaneous, shaped into a fairy tale or a myth (see also Werner 1981, 139).[1]

Herodotus (484–424 BC) is an exception[2] because he made a long journey before he described the Persian King Dareios' conquest of the Scythians in 512 BC. He travelled to Olbia, the Greek colonial town along the southern bank of the River Bug, and conducted a 'critique of sources' based on his experiences there,

---

[1] Mythologised history can be repeatedly traced through naming. J. Harmatta brought Hyperboreos (one that lives on the edge of the universe) as an example (cf. Herodotus IV, 13). The original meaning of the term was "'one that lives above the mountain', and obviously not any mountain, but above the great 'world-mountain' of the myth. This world-mountain was likely to have been the Rhipaia range" (Harmatta 1949, 4). However, once again, the Rhipaia range that Hekataios mentioned first in his now lost work could have referred to a number of places. Ptolemy said that amber came from nearby (Ptolemy III, 5, 10), and so many place it in the territories of Scandinavia or Germania, while others identify it with the Urals (SSS/1, 150).

[2] See also Harmatta 1954, 43.

which meant that he was the first to attempt to differentiate between timeless myths and 'true' stories associated with a point in time. In this way, the image of Scythia that Herodotus offers contains mixed political and geographical perspectives: he associated four groups of people (Agathyrsi, Neuri, Androphagi, Melanchlaeni) with the four by four thousand square kilometre territory ('the Scythian square') between the Danube estuary and the Sea of Azov,[3] and beyond that to the north there were only the "empty, uninhabited plains" (Herodotus IV, 17).

The Scythians broke away from the Iranian tribal federation around 700 BC. In eastern Europe in the fifth and fourth centuries BC they were succeeded by the also Iranian Sarmatian tribe (or until the third century BC Sauromatian). First they occupied the area between the rivers Don and Dnieper, later between the Dnieper and the Danube. Herodotus mentioned them east of the Don, while Strabo as being around the Danube. From the first century AD they were involved in battles against the Romans, at which point the term Scythia was exchanged for the name Sarmatia. The appearance of the Goths in the third century and the Huns in the fourth century ended their reign. Some of the Alani, their largest tribe, joined the Goths and the Hungarians and reached as far as Hispania and northern Africa; the Ossetic, their other tribe settled in the Caucasus.

Simultaneously, and after the Scythians and Sarmatians (who moved from east to west), the determining powers of eastern Europe's history were the Germanic peoples, particularly the Goths (who advanced eastward from the third century). The Goths spread out from central Sweden, and for as yet unclear reasons pushed across the isle of Gotland before they settled on the estuary of the Oder at around the time of Christ. They occupied Mazowsze along the rivers Notec and Vistula. Around the year 220 AD they reached the shore of the Black Sea, where they divided into two branches establishing strong states: the West Goths (Visigoths) west of the Dnieper, and the East Goths (Ostrogoths) east of the Dnieper.[4] The East Gothic Empire was at its peak during Hermanarich's reign (deceased 375), at which time it spread from the Black Sea to the Baltic Sea. This lies in the *Getica,* written at around 550 in Ravenna by the East Gothic Bishop Jordanes who abridged and annotated the now lost twelve volume work of Senator Cassiodorus, "Hermanarich ruled over the lands of Scythia and Germania as if it were his own" (Jordanes 1960, 120).[5]

---

[3] According to Rybakov it was seven times seven hundred square kilometres (Rybakov 1981, 225).

[4] In the Crimean there were people who spoke Gothic as late as the sixteenth century (Schmid 1981, 118).

[5] The archaeological finds appear to be different in the fifth or sixth century, and there is a resemblance between the excavated graves of the Lower Nemunas and those of South Scandinavia and Gotland. These two factors would refer to an invasion of a tribe of mixed ethnicity around the Middle Danube, the Huns, at around the end of the fifth century, which would mean that the great migration also affected the East Baltic region (Šimėnas 1992, 33; 1994, 25).

Researchers believe they have discovered the traces of a Gothic and Baltic encounter and coexistence in words with the stem *gud, for example: Gdańsk; Gdynia; sinus Codanus (meaning the Vistula spit or the Frisches Haff, as in P. Mela and Pliny, the entire Baltic Sea); in several place names of western Kurzeme; and in loan words such as Lith. gatvė 'street' (< gatwo), Latv. Vācija, Lith. Vókia, vókietis 'Germanland, German' (< the southern Scandinavian Gothic tribal name vagoth < *vaki-goth) (after K. Būga, Blese 1930, 68). 'Gothic person' is fairly commonly allocated as the original meaning to the Lith. gudas 'Belarusian person' (e.g. Schmid 1981, 120). However, it would seem more reasonable to derive the former meaning from the Pruss. gudde 'forest' (according to Fraenkel the latter ones should also come from this—Fraenkel 1950, 64), because the Goths lived west of the Lithuanians and the Prussians, later they turned far to the south, but the word always meant Ruthenian that is an inhabitant of today's Belarus and Ukraine east and south-east of the Goths (for more detail see Toporov 1975–90/II, 323–329).

The West Goths escaped from the Hun attack in 375, while the East Gothic state collapsed, and the remaining Goths were swept away with the migration that followed the Huns' fall (Labuda 1968).

The contemporaneous view of the scattered wanderings of the Goths and other Germanic tribes which preceded the 'official' migration provoked by the Huns' arrival incorporated the basin of the Black Sea, and later, under the term 'Germania,' the basin of the Baltic Sea also crept into use. At that point, the term also partly replaced the name Celtica (= Celtic-land) referring to Central and Western Europe. Poseidonios the first-century BC Greek geographer first used it, then Julius Caesar, later Strabo, and Pliny. It was fully explained in a classical sense by C. Tacitus in Germania (ca. 55–120) (Tacitus 98).[6]

In Geographia, a work containing about eight thousand geographical names, Ptolemy described the part of eastern Europe that falls between the Baltic and the Black Seas, the River Rhine and the Sea of Azov making use of the three geographical collective nouns, i.e. Scythia, Sarmatia, and Germania.[7]

---

[6] The genre of Germania has been viewed variously as a serious geographical work to a less scholarly Tendenzroman (Nagy 1932, 101). Nonetheless, it is certain that the author was governed by the concurrent preconceptions of interpretatio Romana as well as the Ionic traditions. He typologised the peoples of Germania with the set topoi of the ethnography of Antiquity, and characterised the Germanic peoples with clichés applied to the Scythians (Nagy 1932, 102 ff). For this reason J. Hampl said of Tacitus, "as an artist of style he deserves our unconditional admiration but he fails to fully comply with the demands placed upon historians either contemporaneously or currently" (Hampl 1955, 267).

[7] Ptolemy referred to the North and the Baltic Seas by one name, that is the German Sea, the eastern part of which is the Sarmatian Ocean and the southern part the Bay of Vened (Šimek 1930/I, 110). Accordingly, he placed Germania from the Rhine to the Vistula, beyond that the European Sarmataland as far as the Don, and the Asian Sarmataland between the Don and

Ptolemy was a scholar who worked 'at his desk' in Alexandria and did not check his sources in the field. This is one of the reasons why some people suspect that *Geographia* is entirely fabricated, or that the work of Marinos of Tyros, who apparently lived a hundred years earlier and to whose otherwise unknown work Ptolemy referred, is simply Ptolemy's fantasy (Beck 1973, 45). A characteristic feature of the work which indicates the degree of its authenticity is that the Vistula is the only truly existing river of the five that he assumed flew into the North Sea, the other four being distorted duplicates of the river names that advance into the Black Sea (SSS/5, 70).[8]

The probable reference to the Balts has to be deciphered from this Scythian–Sarmatian–Germanic amalgam.

It has been posited that several neighbours of the Scythians, both close and more distant, were linked to the ancestors of the Balts, for example the Geloni, the Dacians, or the Thracians, but in general these views have been discarded. Two peoples deserve more serious contemplation.

4.1. The Budini

Herodotus wrote that the Budini were a people occupying an area beyond the Tanais (the Don) and the Scythians. Their territories were covered with dense forest, they had a king, and they were the neighbours of the Neuri and the Sauromatae (Sarmatians). "The Budini, a numerous and powerful nation, all have markedly blue-grey eyes and red hair; [...] they are a pastoral people who have always lived in this part of the country (a peculiarity of theirs is eating lice) [...] The country here is forest with trees of all sorts. In the most densely wooded part there is a big lake surrounded by reedy marshland; otters and beavers are caught

---

Volga. It becomes apparent that Sarmataland came to occupy the territories of Scythia. Ptolemy simply shifted the latter a little to the East (SSS/4, 416). Throughout the Middle Ages whether they were put to the West or to the East was according to the taste of the given author. Jordanes, for example, wrote that the Vistula springing from the Sarmatian mountains (the Carpathians) divided Germania from Scythia (Jordanes 1960, 17). In *Cosmographia*, translated from the Greek by a seventh-century author dubbed 'Anonymus of Ravenna', the world was a large circle encompassed by the ocean, and peoples and countries came after each other on this circle in order of the twenty-four hours of the day; the land of the Scythians was at around 3 o'clock, meaning in the Northeast (SSS/1, 34).

[8] The unreliability of the Alexandrian scholar's data concerning the east European region has been recognised since E. Šimek's monograph written between 1930 and 1953. Given this, it is strange that in the representative work on Latvia's archaeology it is unhesitatingly stated that "the first written reports on the territories of Latvia are to be found in the works of Tacitus and Ptolemy" (Latvijas 1974, 363).

in the lake, and another sort of creature with a square face, whose skin they use for making edging for their jackets; its testicles are good for affections of the womb." All through the war against the Persians they were allied to the Scythians (Herodotus, IV, 21–22, 102, 105, 108, 109).

On the basis of this the tribe is demarcated as being on either side of the Dnieper, in Belarus, on the shores of the Baltic Sea, in Prussianland, in the areas around Lake Ilmen, and further to the East around Kursk, Voroniezh, and even Saratov. The most westerly point they are supposed to have inhabited was Galicia. (For a valuable summary of the matter and a bibliography see Rybakov 1979, 11–12.)

L. Niederle posits an explanation for this extreme disparity in views, essentially that on the basis of accounts from various travellers, Herodotus demarcated two areas as their territory. One was between the Don and the Volga, the other lay much further west in western areas of central Russia (Niederle 1902/I, 279).

Correspondingly, there are some who consider the Budini as Finno-Ugric (Permian or Votyak—for a contemporary example, Harmatta 1990, 249), others see them as Mongolian, still others link them to the Slavs or even to the Balts (of late, Deṇisova 1991a).

If the name 'Budini' was originally Slavic then it could have come from three stems: *boud* 'build', *bъd* 'guard', or *bǫd* 'tie, strengthen'—none of which seem likely to become the name of a people. On the other hand, the stem *bud-* appears in several Baltic place names which can be associated with the meaning 'damp meadow' (Toporov 1975–90/ I, 258). A Baltic origin is further supported because at the time of Herodotus it is highly likely that Baltic peoples occupied the Upper Dnieper river bank (Zinkevičius 1984, 146), particularly given that those East Balts later vanished from among the Slavs.

4.2. The Neuri

According to Herodotus the Neuri lived at the tributary of the River Hypanis (the southern Bug), west of the Borysthenes (the Dnieper). "North of them the country, so far as we know, is uninhabited." They "resemble the Scythians in their way of life" (Herodotus IV, 17). "A generation before the campaign of Darius they were forced to quit their country by snakes, which appeared all over the place in great numbers, while still more invaded them from the uninhabited region to the north, until life became so unendurable that there was nothing for them but to move out, and take up their quarters with the Budini. It appears that these people practice magic; for there is a story current amongst the Scythians and the Greeks in Scythia that once a year every Neurian turns into a wolf for a few days, and then turns back into a man again" (Herodotus IV, 105).[9]

At this point Herodotus' account is controversial: despite their flight to the Budini around 550 BC we find them in the same place at the time of Darius' conquest in 513 BC and of Herodotus (ca. 450 BC) (Herodotus IV, 125). In addition, one more settlement is named along the southern Bug besides the original: a large lake constitutes the borders of Scythia and the land of the Neuri, from which lake the Tyras (the Dniester) springs (Herodotus IV, 51).[10] H. Łowmiański thus made an utterance, unusual for him otherwise, that Herodotus should not be taken literally (Łowmiański in SSS/3, 368).

The snakes had been interpreted symbolically and 'non-literally' earlier, too. Some discovered the Germanic tribe of the Bastarns in them, and their encounter with the Neuri would have been the first Germanic–Slavic conflict (cited in Niederle 1902/I, 294). Niederle concurs that the Neuri were the first Slavic tribe of Antiquity that we can identify by name (Niederle 1902/I, 298). B. Rybakov also sees them as Slavs who unfortunately found themselves caught between the two wings of the Balts: the Baltic tribe with the snake as their totem animal crossed the Pripet and arrived on its right shore, driving away the Slavic Neuri (Rybakov 1979, 146). The latter ones are identified by Rybakov, after O. Meľnikovskaya, with the archaeological culture of Milograd of the sixth to third centuries BC[11] who fled as far as the Baltic Budini (Rybakov 1981, 536).

The presumed etymology of the name 'Neuri' also indicates their Slavic origin. It crops up in water names connected with the stems *nur > nyr > ner* 'sink', so its meaning is 'low swamp land' and 'the inhabitant of low swamp land'. In the Bug area the term *Ziemia Nurska* 'Nur-land' remained in use until historic times (Niederle 1902/I, 268).

Those who opt for a Baltic origin refer the name back to the Lith. *niaurus* 'stern' (for example Šmits in Zeids 1992, 5). The two viewpoints are reconciled in the

[9] On the basis of this O. Trubachev considers them Celts. There are numerous signs of a Celtic presence from the fifth century BC in Bohemia and also along the Danube (the Hungarian words tót 'Slovak' and mén 'stud'). The Celts who set out from Gallia toward the East became known under the Germanised name *Volcae* (Russ. *voloki*) 'wolves' (from Gallia where there was a tribe called Nervii). The Russian linguist does not believe that a werewolf belief should necessarily be inferred from Herodotus' description, but rather "the memory of their kin relationships emphasised and kept alive by rituals of the people's community", and that the Neuri were once Volcae 'wolves' (Trubachev 1982/5, 12).

[10] Popular opinion posits this large lake to be the swamps of the Pripet, which Herodotus' informants could not have reached by boat (Zinkevičius 1984–94/I, 146).

[11] W. Hensel's view is similar, he identifies the Neuri with a tribe loosely connected to the Lausitz culture from the East, which could well have been that of the Milograd (Hensel 1988, 240, 256).

hypothesis that the Neuri were a tribe that formed a Baltic–Slavic community (cited in Kiparsky 1939, 52).

The Neuri were mentioned in later sources, too. Ptolemy combined the term *Navaroi*, a literary loan from Herodotus, with *Navarum* a place name Pliny used for an area beside the Sea of Azov (Łowmiański 1964, 40); Pliny mentioned *neurre*; Ammianus Marcellinus, the fourth-century Roman historian, *neuriorum*; and in *Descriptio civitatum ad septentrionalem plagam Danubii* from circa 870 AD the so-called Geographus Bavarus (Geographer of Bavaria) referred to a tribe by the name *neriuani* (Kabelka 1982, 20–21).

Others believe that the name of the River Neris 'beaver' and the mysterious *Neroma* (*Nerova*) in the 'catalogue of peoples' of the *Nestor Chronicle* are connected to the tribe's name and refer to the Estonian *Nero-maa* 'land of the Neuri' (for these standpoints see Pašuta 1971, 247).[12]

4.3. The Aestii or Aisti

The majority of researchers hypothesises that the name Aestius, first mentioned by Tacitus in the above quoted passage about amber,[13] must refer to the Balts, or more precisely the Prussians. "To the right-hand shore of the Suebic Sea: here it [the water] washes the tribes of the Aestii; their customs and appearance are Suebic,[14] but their language is nearer British"[15] (Tacitus 45). This idea is carried

---

[12] M. Hellmann believed that *Neroma* meant the Letgalians, and came from the name of the Latvian rivulet Ner (Hellmann 1954/I, 245 ff.).

[13] Nonetheless, J. Voigt may be right (Voigt 1827–39/1, 25). The name also appears in Strabo: "...there are the Osismii (whom Pythes calls Ostimii), who live on a promontory that projects quite far out into the ocean..." (Strabo IV, 4.1.). Others gave the form *Ostiones*. The word might mean 'East (Goth)' and the promontory could be referring to the Sembian peninsula.

[14] The Sueb Sea is the Baltic Sea. The Suebi, mentioned by, among other historians, Strabo (Strabo IV, III, 4 and VII, I, 3), and Pliny (Pliny II, 170, and IV 81). They formed a strong tribal federation in the area bordered by the Elbe, the Lower Vistula, the Baltic Sea, and the Middle Danube which the Romans called Suebia (Ebert 1924/4/1, 276). The heart of the federation lay between the Middle Elbe and the Oder (Šimek 1953/IV, 197), and a contingent that crossed the Danube reached as far as Pannonia from where in the sixth century, along with the Longobardi, they advanced to Italy (Bóna 1974, 91). The other contingent, the Suevi (*suevi*, *suavi*) advanced westward and became the Swabians (Oesterley 1883, 617). There are some, for example J. Voigt, who considered both the Suebians and the Suevi to be Swedish (Voigt 1827–39/1, 51) along with the Germanic peoples collectively named the Suioni who stayed in Scandinavia (Schmidt 1941, 84). As far as I could gather this was because in the twelfth century the Swabians referred to the Suevi, as well as to the Swedes as their ancestors (Borst 1959/II, 669). R. Wenskus also regarded the identification of the Suebians as unsolved (Wenskus 1961, 255 ff.).

[15] Some thought this language Celtic, others as Germanic (Voigt 1827–39/1, 58).

into encyclopaedias, handbooks, even twentieth-century political plans (cf. Part One, Chapter 2).

After Tacitus the name vanished for several hundred years, only to reappear in the sixth century in the earlier quoted letter of Cassiodorus (*Hestis*, pl. dat.), and later in Jordanes: "...beyond their populace the Aesti live on the shores of the ocean, a totally peaceful people. To the East their neighbour is the very strong tribe of the Acatziris. By his wits and excellence [Hermanarich] subdued the tribe of the Aistius to be his subjects who live on the furthest shores of the German Sea" (Jordanes 1960, 36, 120). This would represent a vast area, as the Aca-tzirs, a Turkic tribe—that J. Voigt identified with the Khazars (Voigt 1827–39/1, 113)—occupied the lower Don.

Einhard (770–840) is the first and only(!) scholar to have used the -aist stem, "the Slavs and the Aisti live on the shores of the Eastern Sea" (*Vita Caroli Magni* XII). In the cited chorography of King Alfred Osti is written, in the second part, that of Wulfstan, Esti, Est-mere, and Eastland is used (some believe that these names do not signify the same peoples because the Slavic Osti tribe would have inherited their name from the Ostrogoths). The name then disappeared, or rather was transferred to the Estonians. In the eleventh century Adam of Bremen, citing Einhard, on one occasion denotes the littoral tribe as the Haisti (Bremen, IV, 12), while at another place he refers to today's Estonia as Aestland (Bremen IV, 17). A thirteenth-century Scandinavian runic script offers estlatum 'Estland', and aistfari 'Estonians' (Mel'nikova 1977, 201).

The linguistic, and consequently the ethnic origins of this transfer of names is debated.[16] Many think that because King Alfred's chorography referred to the same Germanic tribe as Tacitus, every variant—the anglicised *east-*, *Osti,* and the continental *Esti*—equals *aestius*, and mean 'eastern' where 'east', that is the 'right side of the Sea', is to be understood from the perspective of the Germanic sailors who roamed the water from beyond the Vistula estuary, from the Vistula Spit to the Gulf of Finland. The Germanic Aestii then gave the name to the more eastern Estonians with whom they had connections from the first century BC at the latest, and who did not have their own name because they simply referred to them-selves as *maarahvas* 'people, people of the Earth' (Endzelīns cited in Kabelka 1982, 26). The Estonians themselves only took on the name from the late nine-teenth century.

The other camp considers the Aestius, the Aestii, and the Osti as Baltic peoples. They have two counter-arguments against the explanations that omit the Balts from the picture and which, consequently, are a virtual sacrilege from the perspec-tive of local patriotism. One such counter-argument is that the Sembia where later (of course 'only' a thousand years after Tacitus) the Prussians would live, as mentioned by Wulfstan, or even Einhard, and Jordanes. Many others, for example

---

[16] For an excellent summary of the case see Labuda 1960, 51–71, and Kabelka 1982, 21–27.

Mikkola stated that Tacitus also referred to it (Mikkola 1938, 33). The transfer of names happened, as Endzelīns tells us, because the Germanic people first called the Prussians Aestii, then as they came to know them better, they realised that they called themselves Prussians, and so they transferred the name to the Estonians (Endzelīns 1945, 379). The other argument of the group was that Tacitus' *aest* could only have come from the word *east* meaning 'east' through folk etymology, while it could have been a regular development from the word *aist* (Kabelka 1982, 24), and therefore there had to be a group of people called *aistis*, an idea that (only) Einhard put forward. Attempts to explain the meaning of the *aist-* stem from the Germanic language strengthened the 'Germanic side'. The 'Prussian (Baltic) wing' gained strength when A. Gāters convincingly proved[17] that the *aist-* stem consists of the stem *au(e)* 'water' (compare it with Latv. *avots* 'water source', Sanskrit *avani* 'river', and Swedish *A* 'river') and the *-ist* derivation. Accordingly, *aist* meant 'a person living near water' (Gāters 1954). The same stem can be found in some water names, for example *Daug-ava* 'much + water', *Ab-ava*, *Bart-ava*, and there is an etymological connection to the German name of the river 'Gauja', that is 'Aa' (Bielenstein 1892, 36, 80).[18]

In conclusion, we can state that the Germanic tribe that Tacitus called Aestii encountered the Aisti (i.e. the ancestors of the Baltic Prussians), during the first millennium (sufficient data is only available to support the latter third of the millennium) when they reached the coast. Folk etymology linked the name *aist* 'person living near water' with *aest* 'east', and as such allocated it to the Estonians.[19] In this way both names carried a geographical meaning which pointed towards various ethnicities: Prussians and Couronians (Blesse 1930a, 317); Prussians and Baltic Finns (Łowmiański 1935, 7); and along with them Venedi, Germanic people, and Slavs. "Because of the importance [of this amalgam]... the Baltic Sea received its Germanic name *Ostsee* (< *Oster-see*)" (Pritsak 1982, 190).

---

[17] Though A. Gāters did not persuade everybody, for example V. Toporov expressed doubts, he basically considers the Aestii Prussians solely on the grounds of the previous argument emphasising the geographical continuity (Toporov 1975–90/I, 66).

[18] The stem also crops up in Jordanes in the forms of *Oium* and *Gepedoios* which is the Goth *Aujom* 'a country rich in water, an area watered by a river' (Jordanes 27). The Goths marked the territories of the Vistula estuary and on the shores of the Black Sea with this name (Skrzhinskaya in Jordanes 1960, 195). H. Krahe mentioned the *ab-* stem among the Old European water names meaning 'water, river', from which numerous Baltic water names are derived, for example Abava, Abuka, Abuls, Abista (Krahe 1964, 41).

[19] Since the last century the debate has continued as to whether ost/est 'east' came from the tribal name aist/aest 'person living near water', or the other way round, Germanic sailors named the tribe from the geographical point (cf. Niederle 1902–11/I, 113). A. Gāters believed that he had overcome these differences by assuming that over time the Prussian word had gone through a double transfer via the Germanic people (Gāters 1954, 246).

Describing the land of the Sarmatians in Europe, Ptolemy listed five names which (not all to the same extent) have been or are considered to be Baltic. Around Venet Bay (Gdańsk) where the Vistula reaches the Sarmata Ocean (the Baltic Sea) "the Greater Venedae races inhabit Sarmatia along the entire Venedicus bay" (Ptolemy III, 5, 10).

4.4. The Velts

The Velts (*Veltai*) were south of Venet Bay, their western neighbours were the Vends, and their eastern neighbours the Ossii (perhaps the Aisti?).

They deserve a few words because some believe them to have been Balts. They occupied the territory between the Nemunas and the Daugava, or today's southern Latvia. According to K. Müllenhoff they lived in the region of Lithuania, their name could be a metathesis of *Letuai* 'Lithuanians' (SSS/6, 365).

However, a more widespread view is that the Velts were Slavs, a part of the Vened collective noun (Niederle 1902/I, 18), being the same as the Vielets (Vjelets) who lived near the Elbe.

Ptolemy continues in the above quoted chapter, "beyond the Venets live the Gitoni [Goths] and the Finns and the Soloni. To the east from the afore mentioned live the Galindi and the Sudini and the Stavani, up to the Alani" (Ptolemy III, 5, 10).

4.5. The Stavanoi

The *Stavanoi* are a so-called *hapax legomena*, that is a name that crops up on only one solitary occasion, and is consequently open to any interpretation whatsoever. K. Müllenhoff and some other researchers associate them with the Balts, but the majority (beginning with Ch. Hartknoch, *Selectae disertationes*, 1679) consider them to have been Slavs (Okulicz 1973, 346).

H. Łowmiański asserts that the name could originally have sounded like *Sthlavanoi*, a distorted form of *Slovenoi* 'Slavs' (Łowmiański 1964, 45 ff.). This assumption is supported by Ptolemy's mention of the tribe in the region of Sarmataland, near the Alani, a pair which would have its partner in Scythia in Asia, that is the name *Suobenoi* 'Slavs' also referred to before the Alani (the Alexandrian geographer imposed order onto his fairy tales by evoking such doubles...).

4.6. The Sudini

The name, in its many variants (Sudavi, Suduvi, Sudii), certainly denoted a Baltic (Prussian) tribe. There are a number of references from the Middle Ages, accordingly I shall discuss this ethnonym later with the Prussians and the Jatvingians.

4.7. The Galindians and the Golyad's

After more than a thousand years Ptolemy's Galindians (*Galindai*) crop up again, accompanied by the Sudini-Sudavi, when P. Dusburg, the chronicler of the Teutonic Knights, described in Latin the lands and tribes the Order had conquered. He mentioned Galindia and Sudowa along with their inhabitants (*Galindite*) somewhere above the Mazurian Lakes in Poland, somewhere in southern Prussia (Dusburg, *Chronicon Prussiae*, 1326).

There were Galindians a lot further south of the settlement named by Dusburg, that is in the northern foothills of the Carpathians and the Sudeten, which signals the direction they came from. Paulus Diaconus, the historian of the Germanic Langobard tribe, referred to Golanda in his work *Historia Langobardorum* (790 AD). The Geographer of Bavaria mentioned five towns of the Golensizi somewhere in Upper Silesia (see Vilinbakhov–Engovatov 1963, 241).

For some unknown reason the Galindians set out on a great migration in all directions around the time of Christ (perhaps because the Goths caused their flight). It is possible that some of them moved to Dacia in the South with the West Goths, or perhaps westward as far as Spain's most western province, Galicia. They lost their language either among the Goths or together with them—the West Goths rapidly assimilated after the collapse of their kingdom in 711 AD, by 1000 AD the Goth language was no longer extant in Spain. In any case, the *galind-* stem is incomparably more frequent in family and place names in the Pyrenees than in the West Baltic.[20] Nonetheless, in the previous half a millennium the Galindians could also have joined other Germanic tribes such as the Heruli, the Vandals, the Burgundians, and the Langobards.

According to another hypothesis the name was carried to the Iberian peninsula by the Celts (perhaps as part of the tribe) around 700 BC, but yet another conception explains that in the tenth- or eleventh-century Arabic countries on the Mediterranean Sea, especially in Spain, there were a vast number of slaves brought over from the region of the Elbe, among whom there could easily have been Prussian–Galindians (Labuda 1960, 194).

---

[20] Bishop Prudentius Troyes (835–861) was, for example, a Spanish Galindian who immigrated with the Goths (Hellmann 1954, 33).

Although it was the second largest Prussianland after Suduvia, Dusburg spoke about Galindia (the land of Galindians) as an uninhabited forest area. This is a sign that the Galindians had ceased to exist between 1058 and 1230, they were assimilated into the tribe of the Mazuri,[21] mostly in the twelfth century when Bolesław Krzywousty attempted to conquer Pomerania and Prussianland (Łowmiański 1931, 49).

However, the Galindians can be encountered further eastward in several East Slavic sources in the form of Golyad' which has a regular correspondence to the word 'Galindian'. They were first mentioned in the *Lavrentiy Compilation of Chronicles*: Izyaslav, Prince of Kiev conquered the Golyad' in 1058. The *Ipatiy Compilation of Chronicles* (Russ. and Slavic *svod*) stated that in 1147 Sviatoslav Olegovich Prince of Rostov–Suzdal defeated the Golyad' who lived along the River Porotva. The Porotva is a tributary of the Oka near Moscow where there are a wealth of Baltic water names (among them some with a Golyad'-stem). The memory of the Golyad' has lived on into the twentieth century in folk traditions. There is the legend of a mighty giant called Golyada who could throw his hatchet as far as thirty versts from the peak of his mountain. In another version two Golyada brothers threw the hatchet to each other from opposing hills.

It is debatable as to whether there was a relationship between the Prussian Galindians and the Golyad' around Moscow, or what kind of relationship it might have been. Some think that the latter were the descendants of the Galindians who had shifted eastward. It is conceivable that a whole tribe or people might simultaneously move to a new homeland, perhaps the simplest example being that of the Langobards who left Pannonia in 568 AD and migrated to Lombardia. Others believe that the Galindians found themselves in a Russian area in the Middle Ages: many people fell captive during the battles between the Grand Duchy of Lithuania and the Russian duchies that then formed colonies. Nonetheless, this explanation is rather improbable because there is no documentation of the Russian troops ever reaching the Prussian tribes, and it would be hard to believe that the local Slavs would have forgotten their own river and spring names in order to adopt terms heard from some prisoners of war (Zinkevičius 1984–94/I, 248 ff.).

In Map 4 Toporov outlines the possible pattern of the Galindian–Golyad' migration (Toporov 1982a, 134).

The etymology of the name is clear. First J. Voigt, and later almost everyone else, derived it from the Latv. *gals*, Lith. *galas* 'border, borderland' forms, and so

---

[21] The Polish dialectical particularity known as '*mazurovat*' ('mazuration') is often explained through a Baltic substratum (Toporov 1980, 130).

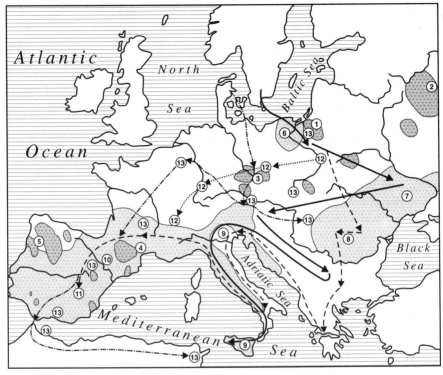

Map 4. The migrations of the Galindians and Golyad's

1. Prussian Galindia—2. Golyad's around Moscow—3. 'Galindians' in the Czech–Polish borderland—4. *Galind-* proper nouns from Saint-Sernaine (Toulouse)—5. 'Galindians' of the Pyrenees—6. Goths at the lower Vistula (100–200 BC)—7. East Goths (200–433)— 8. West Goths (200–375)—9. East Goths (433–471)—10. West Goths (from 419)— 11. West Goths (460–471)—12. Burgundians; a) first century BC to second century AD; b) third to fourth centuries; c) 410–433; d) 433–534; 13. Vandals

the name of the people meant 'people living on the borderlands' (Voigt 1827–39/1, 75).[22] Consequently, there is no point in looking for a direct relationship between the Galindians and the Golyad's the two tribes settled on the borderlands as the Balts wandered north and eastwards. It is evident that the Golyad's were the most

[22] This type of naming was in use in Baltic and other languages, for example *latgal* 'one on the borders of the Latvian people'; *zemgal* 'last among those living on the plains' 'one living at the low ends'; *marko-mann* 'one living on the borderlands' (the Gothic *marka* > Ger. *Mark* are related to the Latin *margo* 'borderland, province'); or *Ukraine* 'one on the *krain*' (< Slavic *krain* < *kraj* 'borderland').

eastern Balts.[23] It is less obvious as to whether the 'borderland location' of the Galindians was a reference to the North during their northward migration or to the western position of their settlement following their migration.

Destruction, death, and being at the end of things, were the connotations of words meaning 'one living on the borderland' as it does in Prussian, *gallan* means 'death' (Toporov 1975–90/II, 138). It seems as though, from the eastern to the western corners of Europe, the Galindians "had fulfilled the predestined fate that is reflected in their name" (Toporov 1980a, 136).

4.8. The Boruski or Borusi

Ptolemy's *hapax legomena* became the country and people's name for Borussia = Prussia and Borussen = the Prussians, still in use today. The so-called Boruskoi lived in the foothills of the Rhipaia mountains, east of the Ossii. Through the metathesis of *bor–rob* Ptolemy 'found' the *rhoboskoi* people, the Asian partner of the European tribe around the source of the Volga (Łowmiański 1964, 41).

The original 'p-' sound (compare with the Pruss. *prūsiskan* 'in Prussian') became a 'b-' in German (Bednarczuk 1982, 60). The name would probably have fallen into oblivion had Erasmus Stella (ca. 1450–1521), the scholarly–pseudo-scholarly doctor of the Duchy of Prussia, not begun to use it. In his two volume book he wrote the first Prussian prehistory (Stella, *de Borussiae Antiquitatibus*, 1498–1510). Even up to the present day the phantasmagorias carried in the work constitute one of the major sources for 'research' on myths. With this and other works E. Stella strove to win the favours of the Saxon prince Friedrich, the Grand Master of the Order of German Knights', in which he succeeded and rose as high as the post of mayor in his hometown of Zwickau. To achieve his ideological target, which was to scholarly underpin the German demands for Prussian territories, E. Stella applied everything from a distorted modernisation of names that he had read in works by the authors of Antiquity, to forging documents and concocting adventure stories—all of which led to his descendants filling libraries in the following decades.[24] As the vassal of Poland from 1466 the degraded Duchy of Prussia sought by all means to liberate itself from its depend-

---

[23] According to J. Makkay the Golyad' were around Moscow as early as the third millennium BC, then in the second millennium BC the Finno-Ugrians "reclaimed this territory from them", and in the first millennium AD the Slavs found this mixed company of Finno-Ugrian assimilated Balts' there (Makkay 1991, 217). Of course, following all that has been said about the Indo-European Baltic migration the time of the Balts' arrival is uncertain, but it is without doubt that the population in the surroundings of Moscow was Balto-Finno-Ugrian—though from when, remains a question.

[24] For E. Stella's life and work see Mannhardt 1936, 176 ff.

ency, which is why E. Stella's work was so useful to the head of state, the Grand Master.

E. Stella explained that the Ptolemaean Borusi (which became Prussen–Preussen through a shortening of their country's name 'Borussia') were a barbarian Scythian tribe who moved from the snow capped regions of the Rhipaia mountains into the lands of the Goths in the sixth century. In their new habitat, Prussianland, they intermingled with the Alani and multiplied.[25] They elected an Alan as their king whose three sons, of a Borussian mother, divided the provinces of Borussia between themselves. The unsophisticated Borussians–Prussians conquered the Germans who lived in the area and consequently, in the early thirteenth century Duke Conrad of Mazovia from a noble Saxon family, was justified in calling for the help of the Knights of the Cross. In this context E. Stella's conclusion is self-evident, ergo: this area of land is an ancestral due of the German Knights of the Cross and the Prussians were barbarian intruders in it (Jurginis 1971, 68–76).

[25] E. Stella encountered the Goths, the Alani, and the Heruli who constituted a part of the Gothic tribal federation in the works of Aeneas Sylvius Piccolomini, later Pope Pius II. It is well known that Piccolomini found Jordanes' *Getica* and published excerpts from it.

CHAPTER 5

THE BALTIC TRIBES

5.1. Power relations in the Baltic region: The Viking period

The references to the Balts at various *Urheimat* locations across the centuries are often of doubtful authenticity, those concerning the Balts furthest to the West are the more trustworthy among them. Still, together they present a foggy picture of the Balts located somewhere in the neighbourhood of, or mixed with the Venedic, Finno-Ugric, Slavic, and Germanic tribes throughout the whole period. They also depict the migrations in the millennium after the time of Christ, that is, where the legendary storms of history took them as they were swept along in hordes, especially those who had lived at the busiest cross-roads, and most of all, the Galindians.

It is wise to group the particulars of Baltic history according to the interests that moved the pens of the authors of our sources. I believe that the various regional 'millstones' (ethnic, religious, social, linguistic, etc.) can be presented in such a way that they sketch out the curve of Baltic history after the prehistoric period and, at the same time, define concepts (ethnic, territorial, public administrative, etc.) that could contribute to a better understanding of Antiquity itself.[1]

How and when did the Balts appear on the stage of European history "in the cosmos of the Middle Ages ruled by the Pope and Kaiser" (Arbusow 1939, 201)?

The quick answer as to 'how?' is that it happened in many different ways. We have to bear in mind that the last common Baltic history we can talk about is approximately one thousand, fifteen hundred, or even two thousand years ago at the time of Proto-Baltic unity. Since then, West and East Balts have walked their separate paths for long periods without encountering each other. At the end of the

---

[1] From the *more recent* historical works I shall mention the ones that I, too, have found helpful. Among them are some popularising works, as well as scholarly analyses, monographs, and collections of studies. For Latvia see Balodis 1991; Bilmanis 1951; Hellmann 1954, 1981; Kavass–Sprudzs 1972; Misiūnas–Taagepera 1983; Pistohlkors 1994; Rauch 1970; Wittram 1954. For Lithuania see Čepėnas 1977–86; Hellmann 1989, 1990; Ivinskis 1978; Jurginis–Lukšaitė 1981; Lyubavskiy 1910, Łowmiański 1931, 1983; Ochmański 1990; Šapoka 1936. For the Prussians see Boockmann 1992; Biskup–Labuda 1986; Gerlach 1978; Górski 1946; Kilian 1982; Labuda 1972; Łowmiański 1989.

For summaries presenting historical sources see Arbusow 1939; Hellmann 1981–89; Ivinskis 1986; Jablonskis 1979; Zeids 1992; Zutis 1949.

first millennium, and in the early centuries of the second, they met in the North through the Couronians who became East Balts from a West Baltic origin. Through other tribes and at other places they could have met and once more united as a 'pan-Baltic' tribe, but most of them were exterminated or assimilated before such a convergence could occur. The Prussians left their names behind them on this stage, like prompts for the Germans who would follow in the next scene, with the Latvians practically relegated to the role of 'extras' up to the twentieth century. Only the Lithuanians had a more serious role, more or less the lead role, for about two hundred years from the mid or late thirteenth century onwards. This was, however, a role which would steadily diminish in the new dramas that followed 1569 and 1795, until they, too, were demoted to the role of 'extras'.

The brief answer to the question 'when?' would be 'delayed'. Northern Europe and the central and eastern European region 'joined Europe' in the tenth and eleventh centuries. After the establishment of the German Reich in the tenth century Christian principalities and kingdoms were established one after another: the Danish (950–970); the Norwegian (1016–1030); the Swedish (1008); the Czech (915–929); the Polish (966); the Hungarian (972); and the Kievan Rus' (989). However, the Balts are missing from the enumeration.[2] This is not surprising given that the Lithuanians, the only Baltic people who existed as an independent political power at the time, adopted Christianity as late as the thirteenth century, and even then only temporarily, representing a two- or three-hundred year delay.[3] This was around 1100 at the time when "feudalism and Christianity consolidated across the whole of the new eastern and northern region" (Szűcs 1992, 26) the Lithuanians had hardly been heard of.

We can only make a strongly hypothetical depiction of society of the common features of Baltic history. Yet it seems the Balts lived in a kinship society in their early period.[4] At first kinship was indeed based on blood relationships 'in ancient times'. Later this changed, the relationship became territorial and so-called neighbourhood village communities were established. The name for the smallest territorial unit in Prussia (the only place where it is known) was the *pulka* 'plowland' (Latin *campus*) with the village at its heart. The *territorium* or *terrula* (the names are only known in Latin) 'small land' was a larger unit which comprised several *pulkas* and represented about a 1000–1500 people. Even larger units were formed from an amalgamation of *terrullas*, the habitat areas and lands (in Slavic and Latin sources *zemlya* and *terra*) of several village communities,

---

[2] Correspondingly, they are either barely mentioned in historical summaries of the region or not at all. Dvornik 1949, Halecki 1993, 1995, Sedlar 1994, and even D'yakonov's most recent summary of world history in 1994 devoted only one short paragraph to the Balts.

[3] "The Europeanisation of Lithuania went on at least until the middle of the sixteenth century" (Bumblauskas 1994, 74).

[4] Although we have no data, this seems highly likely from the analogous social development of other Indo-European peoples (Łowmiański 1949, 116).

divided by wooded borderland (Labuda 1972, 284). The foundation stone of the social structure, based on ethnicity, was originally a patrilineal relative of blood kinship, the clans then expanded through the conquest of other unrelated clans. These gradually fell into political alignment, with the tribe as its fundamental unit. Tribes are presumed to have evolved more rapidly in the first century AD,[5] while the dual processes of division and unification during the development from kinship to tribe, and later to tribal confederation went on throughout the first millennium, some believe until as late as the year 1200.

The fate of these tribes and tribal confederations developed in a diverse way depending on their geographical situation, that is, on what other powers they came into contact with, and consequently what form of state they developed—or did not develop—beyond tribal federation. As a result, outlining the external powers that determined the power relations of the Baltic region is constructive, before discussing the history of the Baltic tribes up to the thirteenth century.

In line with their geographical situation the Balts—that is the West Balts—first came into contact with the Scandinavians from the coast. When that occurred remains a matter for conjecture.[6]

The Viking conquest from the North[7] can be divided into three stages. They were traders and pirates between the seventh and the early ninth centuries.[8] This was followed by a period of plundering military expeditions led by generals and the *konnungs* (kings) up until the early tenth century. Then, after their conversion to Christianity came the missionary conquests of the Christian kings of Scandinavia, and above all the Danish king. A number of sources report on their activities.

The runic inscriptions chiefly referred to hydronyms, towns, countries, and peoples. Runes in the Alpine region which used the Etruscan alphabet appeared in the North (Bonfante 1985, 287), and a variation with twenty-four signs used by the northern Germanic tribes from the seventh century was then reduced to a script with sixteen signs. There are about three thousand five hundred such runic inscriptions, and all in all, only twenty-three report on tenth–twelfth-century eastern Europe (mostly referring to the names of Vikings who died in battle),

---

[5] Or perhaps we were only able to gather information about it from that time. Presumably the Proto-Balts also lived in tribe(s), we only have to consider their great numbers.

[6] For this compare Ellis Davidson 1976, 26.

[7] For a valuable summary on the Vikings see Gurevich 1966.

[8] As P. Hunfalvy commented "in those days maritime robbery and trade meant the same thing; if the group was weaker they exchanged goods; if they felt strong enough they snatched away the goods as well as the people with power through strength" (Hunfalvy 1871/I, 39). The original meaning of the word Hansa (later applied for the alliance in trade of countries along the coast) was 'a group of maritime bandits'. It is kept in the Polish word *chąsa* with the same meaning (Ślaski 1969, 72). Some believe that the north German word *viking* also goes back to an Old Slavic origin *vitęz* 'robber' (SSS/6, 562).

and the majority of these incriptions are connected to the eastern Slavs with only a very few that mention Lettenland, Zemgale, or Sembia (Mel'nikova 1977, 32 ff.).

The Balts are rarely mentioned in the poems or prosaic sagas of the skalds, the poets of the Middle Ages. The 'Icelandic' or 'national' sagas, just like the so-called royal sagas, offer accounts of military expeditions against the Couronians, but more prominently against the Estonians (among these sagas is S. Sturluson's (1178– 1241) famous history of Norway titled *Heimskringla*–Globe). The precise factual content of the thirteenth- and fourteenth-century sagas is even less.

The most serious source of the Viking period is the biography of Bishop Ansgar (Anskar), written by his successor Rimbert Bishop of Bremen (?–888) (Rimbert, *Vita Anskari*, 865–876). He mentions the Couronians as *Cori* at the year 853, a name which can be seen as the earliest surviving reference to a Baltic people, or at least clan. Rimbert gave the regions (*civitates*) of their territories. These were: Vredecuronia, Wende, Bihavelanc, Bandowe, Powzare, Megowa, Pilsaten, Ceclis (Rimbert 30). These are either Couronian or mixed German–Latin words.

The Icelandic sagas state that the Swedes were the lords of the Couronians, followed later by the Danes, and that at the time people in Denmark breathed the following prayer: "save us Our God from the Couronian pirates." Against this, Rimbert gives a precise account of a Danish attack in 853 and then again of a Swedish attack a year later against the Couronian fortress in Seeburg and against Apulia (Lith. Apuolė) some five days walk from the former. Seeburg is supposedly today's Grobiņa near Liepāja in Latvia, while the fortress of Apulia is likely to have been in the northern part of Lithuania near Skuodas, and as such would be the first Lithuanian word in written sources.

5.2. The Couronians

All this directs us to believe that the Couronians were not only the lords of Kurzeme–Kurland, but later the Lithuanian and Prussian coasts, and a significant proportion of today's Latvian territory as well.

Throughout the nineteenth century the Couronians were generally identified with the Livonians, for example in the following quote: "The Livonians and the closely related Couronians" (Setälä 1889, 243). Hunfalvy was of the same opinion: "no literary memory is left behind from the language of the Couronians, however, the names of their places and federations that can be found in chronicles of Henry of Latvia and others show that they spoke Livonian or Estonian" (Hunfalvy 1871/I, 59). Endzelīns' article in 1912 demonstrated that "the Couronians were not Livonians, neither were they Latvians nor Lithuanians, but a Baltic tribe that spoke a transitory dialect between Latvian and Lithuanian. Later their language was assimilated into that of the Latvians and the Lithuanians" (Endzelīns 1912/II, 441). Subsequently K. Būga called attention to the characteristic features of the Couronian tongue that were related to Prussian. V. Kiparsky had the 'last word' in his expansive monograph. He differentiated between the Baltic Couronians who occupied the southern parts of Kurland around the time of Christ, and the Baltic Sea-Finnish Livonians living in the northern territories (Kiparsky 1939, 462 ff.). The Baltic Couronians assimilated the latter group around the year 1000. P. Johansen came to a similar conclusions except that he—correctly—set the Couronian assimilation of the Livonians and the Estonians at a later point in time when the Couronians might have increased in number as a result of East Baltic tribes joining them in their migration to the Northwest (Johansen 1939). P. Johansen divided the history of the East Baltic coast into three stages: the rule of the Germanic Vikings between ca. 650 and 800; the rule of the Livonians and Estonians between ca. 800 and 1236; and the rule of the Germans after 1236 (Johansen 1939, 303 ff.). E. Blese added that from the thirteenth century the Germans ruled over the Couronians politically but linguistically they were assimilated by the Zemgalians (and in this way the Couronian language became an active element in the formation of Latvian through Zemgalian) (Blese 1937). As far as the Couronian language itself is concerned, apart from a single isogloss, it is identical to Latvian. From all of this V. Mažiulis came to the conclusion, in all probability correctly, that the Couronians were first West Balts and that later, around 500 AD, they became closer to the East Balts.

The name 'Couronian' appears in sources with a number of variations: with the 'u' or 'o' and later 'au' vowels in the stem; and (a) with the stem *kur-* (this is the Livonian variation which Scandinavian, German, and Latin sources used: Polish Kuroń, the place name Couronia; Ger. Kuren, Kurland, Kauerlant; Latin Curi, Cori, Curones, Curonienses); and (b) with the stem *kurs-* (this became the Latvian version: Latv. Kursi, Kursa, Kurzeme; Russ. Кърсь; and (c) with the stem *kurš-* (this became the Lithuanian variation: Lith. Kuršiai, Kurša—Zinkevičius 1984–94/I, 342).[9]

The Couronians fended off Christian conversion with uneven success. The Germans crushed their last uprising, fought alongside the Prussians, in 1267. From that time on their assimilation by the Latvians in the North (to the Zemgalians), and earlier and more rapidly by the Lithuanians in the south, began *en masse*. Nonetheless, G. De Lannoy, a French traveller, mentioned the Couronian language as a separate tongue as late as 1413, what is more, in 1600 M. Braudis wrote that it *"doch etlichermassen der lettischen vergleichet"* (resembles the Latvian to some extent, though is not identical to it) (Braudis cited in Salys 1958, 422). Attempts

---

[9] The etymology of the name is debated (cf. Kazlauskas 1968). It is often linked with the OSlav. word *kъrsъ* 'cleared land', or the Czech *krs* and Latv. *karslak* 'shrub, small ramose tree' (Kabelka 1982, 70).

to fix a precise point were further complicated by the fact that the people of Kurzeme–Kurland considered themselves Couronians up to the seventeenth century, and on the other hand those Latvians who lived in the territory were also said to be Couronian speakers since the mid-fourteenth century (Johansen 1939, 292).

The nationality of the inhabitants of the fishing villages along the beautiful sand bank known as the Courish Spit is debatable (Ger. *Kurische Nehrung*, Lith. *Kuršių Neringa, Nerija* or *Užmaris*). The area, 96 km long and 0.5 to 4 km wide divides the Baltic Sea from the Courish lagoon.[10] They called themselves Couronians (Latv. *kursenieki,* Lith. *kuršininkai*) although they spoke Latvian and were not the direct predecessors of the Couronians because they immigrated there from the sixteenth century, presumably from Latvian speaking Kurland which is an area divided from the Courish Spit by a narrow stretch with a few Lithuanian (Žemaitian) villages. Even in the last century A. Bielenstein complained that on the northern part of the Courish Spit occupied by Latvians (as opposed to the twenty kilometres in the South where Germans lived) the Lithuanian language slowly edged out Latvian. Church services were given in Lithuanian even in Nida (Bielenstein 1892, 3 ff.). This process became final after the Second World War.

5.3. Power relations in the Baltic region: the Slavic, Lithuanian, and German periods

The description of the attack on Apulia is the most important Baltic reference in the *Vita Anskari*, which is understandable given that the primary aim of Anskar, Rimbert, and also Adam of Bremen (their successor by more than two hundred years) was to convert the Scandinavians.[11] The Hamburg bishopric was established in 826 with precisely this in mind. When the Danes destroyed the town in 845 Ansgar moved to Bremen, from which point on the Hamburg–Bremen archbishopric was bound by a personal union. Later came the bishopric of the then Danish Lund, and the Swedish Uppsala, which only became independent in the late twelfth century.

[10] Currently the southern (western) parts of the Courish Spit belong to the province of Kaliningrad, and are inhabited by Russians who immigrated from all over the Soviet Union after 1946, while its northern (eastern) areas belong to Lithuania with a Lithuanian speaking population.

[11] Ansgar received authority from Pope Nicholas I and the German Emperor Louis the Pious (*Ludwig der Fromme*) to convert "the Swedes, the Danes, the Gotlanders, the Norwegians, the Greenlanders, the Icelanders, the Laplanders, the Slavs, and every people in the North and the East no matter what their names may be" (Rimbert, 23). And yet, we know nothing about his missionary activities among the Slavs (SSS/7, 367), and no church on Kurland was intact longer than a decade.

The hustle and bustle of conversion from the west left no intellectual traces and it ceased around the year 1000 because it shifted to the Balto-(West) Slavic lands (Balodis 1930, 116–117).[12]

From the ninth century the East Slavic expansion should be considered along-side the Vikings. Around 1000 AD the East Baltic lands belonged to the Russian Varangian, and not under Sweden or Denmark (Taube 1935, 374).

The Russian Varangians primarily occupied the Duchy of Polotsk, mentioned first in chronicles at 862 AD. It was conquered by Rogvolod, a Swedish Varangian in the late tenth century, and the dynasty was established which then engaged in a bitter hundred year war (1021–1129) with the 'Ukrainian' Kiev and the 'Russian' Novgorod, governed by the Ruriks, the other Viking dynasty.[13]

The regions within the Duchy of Polotsk were connected with each other to varying degrees. There were two fortresses with a 'semi-Duchy' between their districts which was to control trade on the Daugava. One of these was Koknese (Latin Kukenois, Ger. Kokenhusen). This *castrum ruthenicum* lay 358 kilome-tres away from Polotsk on the right bank of the Daugava. Sources first mention it at the year 1205 (Starodubets 1955). Jersika (Ger. Gerzike, Latin Gerceke), the other fortress was east of Koknese and is first mentioned as a *civitas* by Heinricus at 1209.[14]

There was a third 'semi-principality' in Lettenland that lay on the right bank of the Daugava in the North. Tālava (Lat. *Tolowa, Tholowa, Tolewe* < Finnish *tulva* 'river estuary'–Lit. E. XXXI, 293) was in the valley of the Gauja on the Estonian border and paid its taxes to the Duchy of Pskov, vassal of Novgorod.

The scarce sources and the uncertain use of words in them make it difficult to uncover these relations. There is, for example, no clear division "between [the

[12] A comparison between Rimbert's objective accounts and Adam of Bremen's fairy tale style work based on literature, primarily the *Vita Anskari* and oral reports, well represents this shift in direction. Adam of Bremen dedicated the 4th book to the countries along the Baltic Sea and to the islands beyond them. In this part he wrote about the land of the Amazons whose male children had the heads of dogs which they carried on their chests, and that the female children were gorgeous (Adam Bremensis IV, 19).

[13] Up to its heyday in the tenth century, the Polotsk duchy included the entire territory of the Krivichi tribal federation along with all the other smaller duchies such as Smolensk, Izborsk, and perhaps Pskov. The Polochani were part of these Krivichi. For the debate over the relation between the Krivichi and the Polochani cf. Alekseyev 1966, 50 ff. The Krivichi became the later Belorussian people.

[14] The etymology of both is debated. Koknese is originated from a number of languages: the Latvian (Latv. *koks* 'tree'); from the Slavic (Slavic *Kokna-nos*, where *Kokna* would be the Old Slavic name of a small tributary of the Daugava, today called Perse, and in this way the name would mean 'Kokna-promontory'); and from the German (*Koggen-naes* 'ship's bow'). The name Jersika is connected to two roots: the Slavic (*grad* 'fortress', and *jar* 'steep shore' or 'water with a strong current'); and the Old Icelandic (*gerzkr* 'viking') (Mugurēvičs in Heinricus 363, 358).

regional units of] *Grossgau, Kleingau, Burgbezirk,* or even *Dorfmark*" (Hellmann 1954, 49). What is certain is that the two principalities, which had Slavic garrisons in their central fortresses, as well as Tālava which paid a tax as a *Grossgau* district to the East Slavs in the customary manner of the time: the princes, accompanied by their armed escorts, roamed their territories between autumn and spring and lived off their dues and at the same time collected furs, wax, and honey to sell later (Iglói 1988, 9). The territory was divided into tax districts called *pagasts* (< Russ. *pogostь* < *pogostyt'* 'to be a guest somewhere for a while'), which still serve as the basis of administrative units in Latvia today. Besides this, there was a form of political division based on land (*terra*) with the unit of the *valsts* (< Slavic *volostь*) which survived in the meaning of 'state' in Latvian.

The terminology of Latvian Christianity consists mostly of Slavic loan words from the twelfth century, which is further unambiguous evidence of eastern Slavic rule, even though the eastern church conducted no missionary activities.[15]

Both as a result of the disintegration of the East Slavic principalities, and simultaneously with it, a new power appeared on the scene, namely Lithuania.

Lithuania was first mentioned in the *Annales Quedlinburgenses* by an anonymous author in 1009 in a Slavic (Russian/Polish) form as *Litua* (*Litva*). There is very little known of its rise during the eleventh and twelfth centuries. However, it seems certain that in the early thirteenth century it grew to be the significant power even beyond the Daugava, at times in alliance and at others in rivalry with the East Slavs and the Danes. Heinricus wrote that the Bishop of Riga pondered over how to liberate his young church from the Lithuanian and Ruthenian attacks in 1209, "and he remembered all those evil things that the king of Gercike together with the Lithuanians had wreaked upon the Livonians and the Latvians" (Heinricus XIII, 4).

The German conquest, the so-called *Drang nach Osten,* entered this power relation in the late twelfth century.[16]

---

[15] For this reason Heinricus wrote with contempt, "a Ruthenian mother is always sterile and childless" (Heinricus XXVIII, 4).

[16] The theory that the aggressive German drive eastwards was responsible for all the troubles of Central and Eastern Europe was conceived in the 1860s. It was conceived in opposition to Germany, and Baltic Germans in particular (also German history writing, e.g. L. Ranke). The instigators were the publicists and ideologists of Russian pan-Slavism, Russian Church historians, and Polish historians. An example is Philaret von Chernigov, one of the most respected historians of the Russian Orthodox Church, who wrote in German in one of his books as early as 1872: "In the early thirteenth century a great many landless knights who found no place in the West, at the behest of the Pope drove toward Livonia to ravage the unarmed inhabitants, or as it was referred to in those days in the West, to introduce them to Christianity. The unfortunate Livonians, Latvians, and Estonians were then baptised with fire and sword for forty years! Russland was robbed of all its littoral settlements and Eastern Christianity withered and disappeared" (Philaret cited in Kahle 1986, 16). (The last sentence identifies what really hurt

The year of 937 was a turning point in the conquest of the East-Sea Slavs and the Balts. Otto I founded Magdeburg, and in 962 Pope John XII gave its bishopric the right to establish a church district in any Slavic land (Dvornik 1949, 60). This German step into the region finalised Europe's division into a western centre and an eastern periphery, as opposed to the earlier North–South partition.[17]

The crusades were originally instigated to liberate the sepulchre of Christ in Jerusalem. The first attempts to direct them towards Eastern Europe were initiated among the Saxons and against the Vends (Sorbs), then later against the Slavs along

---

the author!) That aside, the propaganda of French, and later Anglo-Saxon diplomacy hurriedly adopted this anti-German stance, though its main proponents were Polish writers, and most of all H. Sienkiewicz (Labuda 1963, 31 ff.) who received unprecedented acclaim, both among Polish and foreign readers (see Wyka 1946). The bugbear of the *Drang nach Osten* was exaggerated most effectively by Russian bolshevism (including Sergej Eisenstein's famous–infamous film *Alexander Nevsky* which was screened before the Nazi–Soviet alliance in 1938). It received the blame for a number of other things, too: the unparalleled panic in the First World War with which one third of the Latvian population fled before the Germans, taking all their livestock and movables with them (Silzemnieks 1928, 37); or the unjustifiable and fatal trust in Stalin's Soviet-Russia. Far be it from me to refute a genuine base for fear of the German invasion in the Baltic region. Not at all. In fact, largely as a result of the German conquest entire Baltic and Slavic tribes have disappeared in the cauldron of history. From the nineteenth century aggressive German journalism and history writing retrospectively validated these conquests (H. Boockmann presents the madness of German and Polish–Russian nationalism with resigned wisdom—Boockmann 1992, 41–54). Not forgetting that even in recent times W. Hubatsch, an influential modern historian, was of the opinion that the history of the territory between the Oder and the Nemunas "should be viewed as part of German history, as geographically and historically a north-eastern German territory that belongs to German history as a whole, the shaping powers of which set out from German history"—Hubatsch 1966, 203). I believe that there is a more agreeable solution than this one-sided viewpoint or its biased contradictions (Russian historians considered Lithuanian history to be part of Western Russia's, while Polish historians saw it as a part of Poland's). It is more appropriate to treat the early centuries of Livonia's history as a more or less peaceful assimilation and as a battle fought with ever-changing alliances between Polotsk, the Lithuanians, the Swedes, the Danes, Pskov, the Poles, and the Germans. Through the opposition of Riga and the Order of Sword Bearers this struggle was also connected to the fight between the Emperor and the Pope. From these conflicts it was finally the Germans who emerged victorious in the early fourteenth century (Hellmann 1954, 19). Finally? Well, no. Only for a while, even if it was for a long while, because at least periodically it seemed that 'finally' the Russian *Drang nach Westen* [drive westwards] had triumphed. In 1561 for example, when the Livonian Order of Knights dissolved itself due to the war with Ivan the Terrible which practically destroyed Livonia; when Peter I won in Poltava in 1709; or from the third division of the Polish–Lithuanian state in 1795; or from Eastern Europe's post Second World War division to 1989 or even 1991...

[17] This shift of direction is among the most significant issues of debate in German history writing (cf. Seibt 1983, 8 ff.).

the Elbe and the Oder. In 1108 Adelgot, the archbishop of Magdeburg called the German principalities and bishoprics into battle against them. St. Bernard was the first to specifically call for a crusade. He arrived in German territories in 1147 and persuaded the Welf and Hohenstaufen dynasties to lay aside their struggle for the throne. Kaiser Hohenstaufen fought in the Sacred Land, while Henry the Lion, a Saxon prince of the Welf dynasty, launched into a holy war against the Vends and the Prussians (Urban 1975, 227).

5.4. The conquest of Livonia

The second act was played out in Livonia. Fulco, a French Cistercian who became the first Bishop of Estonia from 1167, was the leader of the mission that started out from Denmark.

As for the source materials of the history of Livonia, the Chronicle of Polotsk is the most significant from among the East Slavic chronicles, although unfortunately not a single line of it remains because in 1579 the troops of István Báthory, a Polish–Lithuanian king, took the town and completely destroyed the library and the archives of the Principality of Polotsk (Zeids 1992, 18).[18] For this reason three German chronicles serve as the only sources for the first centuries of Livonia.

The most important of the three is the *Chronicon Livoniae* cited above, written in 1225–1227 by Heinricus (Henry of Latvia, or Latvian Henry: Heinricus de Lettis, Ger. Heinrich der Lette, Latv. Latviešu Indriķis). It is subtitled *The story of the deeds of the first three bishops* and was written in the field and discusses the events between 1184 and 1227. From 1207 Heinricus gives an eyewitness account of the subjugation of the Livonians, the Letgalians, the Selonians, and the Estonians. There has been more than a hundred years of debate about whether the unknown author was of German or Latvian origin, a controversy which centres on whether the word 'de' in his name refers to an ethnic or a regional origin: that is Latvian Henry, or Henry of Latvia.[19]

---

[18] This offers insight into the general mistrust that surrounded V. Tatishchev's history of Russia published in 1773, in which the author declared that he had held the chronicles of Polotsk and Smolensk in his hands. Since then for example Alekseyev wrote, "hesitance [toward Tatishchev] has by now disappeared" (Alekseyev 1980, 16), which I can only attribute to the newly awakened Greater-Russian nationalism.

[19] A. Švābe gives an excellent summary of the debate, whilst supporting the Latvian origin argument (Švābe 1938). L. Arbusow's convincing rebuttal replied to that standpoint (Arbusow 1939, 496). Ē. Mugurēvičs gave an account of later opinions, among them the presumption of a Venedic origin (Mugurēvičs in Heinricus 24 ff.). The question is further complicated, because the original manuscript has been lost and there is uncertainty as to whether the oldest surviving copy, from the turn of the thirteenth and fourteenth centuries, was prepared from the original document (Zutis 1949, 7).

The *Livländische Reimchronik* written in High Middle German gives accounts of the period between 1143 and 1290 in 12,017 lines.[20] It is an example of the so-called *Tischbuch*, or 'table book', which was read aloud to knights during mealtimes. The only complete manuscript is from the fifteenth century. While Heinricus was a fanatical devotee of Bishop Albert and thus dealt with matters of the Church, this author, quite probably a knight himself, took sides with the Livonian Order and his principle subject was the conquest of the Couronian and Zemgalian lands.[21]

The *Chronicon Livoniae* discusses in Latin the events between 1196 and 1378, paying particular attention to the battles between the Order and the Grand Duchy of Lithuania. The author Hermann de Wartberge served under three *Landmeisters* in Riga from 1358.

Livonia's conversion was instigated from Germany and the initial step was taken when Meinhard, a monk of the Augustinian Order from Holstein, laid anchor in the Gulf of Riga accompanied by German tradesmen. After gaining permission from the Prince of Polotsk, he began to baptise the Livonians and in 1186 he became Livonia's first bishop. In 1184 he had a church raised on an island of the Daugava, some fifteen kilometres from its estuary (Heinricus called it Ger. *Holme* 'island'–Heinricus I, 7), and another in 1187 a little further from there in Ikšķile (< Estonian–Livonian *ikš/ükš* + *kila* 'solitary village, farm', Ger. Üxküll), which became the initial base of operations for the Germans. The second bishop was the Cistercian Bertold who took knights of the cross with him to aid him in his work and died in battle against the pagans in 1198. Bishop Albert von Buxhövenden (ca. 1165–1229) continued his work, and to all intents and purposes became the founder of Livonia by establishing Riga in 1201. When Albert left for home the following year to recruit further volunteers, the Cistercian Theoderich von Treiden established the Order of the Brothers of the Sword (Ger. *Schwertbrüderorden*, Lat. *Fratres militiae Christi*), the first order of knights to constitute a political power outside the Mediterranean.

The process of Livonia's conversion lasted for over a hundred years. It started out from the Gulf of Riga and was conducted with the aid of the sword. Primarily it affected the Livonians,[22] the Selonians, the Zemgalians, and those who lived in western Lettenland north and east of the Daugava (whose 'nationality' I shall return to). Livonia's eastern areas, the true Letgalians and the Couronians only came into focus after 1224. The semi-duchy of Koknese was occupied in 1207

---

[20] Also often referred to, falsely, as *Chronicle of Dietleb von Alnpeke*.

[21] There is a continuation of the *Reimchronik.* The so-called *Die jüngere livländische Reimchronik* was written after 1340 and describes the events between 1315 and 1348. No manuscript remains, there is a prose version, from the pen of J. Renner, a sixteenth-century chronicler.

[22] The Livonians paid tax to Polotsk until 1212.

and Jersika's in 1209. The concept of Livonia expanded with the conquest. It was also referred to as Maria's land after 1202 when the Pope took it under his auspices (*Terra Mariana, Terra Matris, Terra beate Virginis*), initially referring to the triangle of the lower sections of the Daugava and the Gauja, which roughly corresponds to today's Vidzeme.

Considering the land as his own *allodium* (fief) in 1207 Bishop Albert offered the land to the German King Philip who immediately returned it to the bishop as a *feudum oblatum* (fiefdom). Further bishoprics were established following the pattern of that in Riga, and so the following bishoprics sprang up: in Kurland with Piltene (Ger. Pilten) as its seat in 1219 (Weczerka 1962, 294); in Tartu (Dorpat) in 1225; in Ösel (Saaremaa) in 1228. Bishops were given the rank of Princes of the Empire, and the bishopric of Riga became a *Mark* of the Empire, that is a marquisate (Łowmiański 1973, 43). Establishing a Church state was always the underlying agenda of the crusades (Taube 1938, 21).

What did the Germans find there? At what level of organisation were those societies and of what ethnicity? The answers to these questions are inter-linked.

The most extreme answer to the first question was given by E. Dunsdorfs (an Australian exile). He followed the Latvian historians' of the 1930s, F. Balodis and A. Švābe, who said that Kukenois, Jersika, and Tālava were Old Latvian kingdoms. M. Hellmann alleges that their history writing was at the level of that of the Enlightenment, that is, at a level before history as a discipline (Hellmann 1954, 17). E. Dunsdorfs believed that at the time when the Germans appeared on the scene in the twelfth century there were no tribes there, rather "primitive states"—but they were still states. "Only after killing the kings, absorbing the nobility of the Latvian and the Estonian states, and liquidating the pagan and the Greek Orthodox faith was conquest finished... In fact, [accordingly], in the social structure of societies no great difference between the German and Danish invaders and the society they found in Latvia and Estonia respectively. The main difference in the initial stages of the conquest was in the technique of warfare; the Germans and the Danes had better armaments and better weapons" (Dunsdorfs 1970, 104).

In the ninth century 'king' meant a strong ruler, whereas after the tenth and twelfth centuries kings had to undergo a sacred (anointing) and a political (crowning) act conducted by the pope and/or Emperor. The rulers of the East Slavs were called *kn'yazъ*, which western sources translated in a range of phrases: Latin sources wrote *principes, duces, reguli, archontes, reges*, while German sources mentioned *Eldeste, kunige, die beste*. To exaggerate their power, some Grand Dukes were called kings in the East Slavic chronicles, but the only Slavic ruler in history who was indeed crowned a king was Danilo of Halicz in the mid-thirteenth century. Consequently, talk of kings before the Germans in Livonia is somewhat dubious.[23]

Dunsdorfs, though he compared social divisions, economies and ruling titles, missed the most important aspect: the cultural–ideological perspective. This is surprising given that the members of a society, which had had literary culture and converted to the Christian belief centuries before and was armed with an ideology, came to be superior to the pagans precisely because of their cultural and ideological superiority. This superiority explains why foreign conquest became partly inherent, "the secret behind the successes of a few thousand sword-bearing missionaries against more than a quarter of a million people, especially considering that they were constantly in the midst of fraught battles with the Russians and the Lithuanians, cannot be simply put down to a more developed technology of arms. It is only comprehensible if one observes the art of the immigrants with which they also won over many of the newly baptised people to the new lifestyle on offer. This is the only way it is possible for the majority of the subjugated (Estonians, Livonians, West Zemgalians, and Couronians), and those who willingly submitted themselves to conversion (Letgalians), to voluntarily comply with the new power structure in crisis situations, too" (Benninghoven 1965, 385).[24]

For this reason it is more acceptable to take the viewpoint in which the most the Livonian Dukes could have achieved before the Germans arrived was to make their power inheritable (Mugurēvičs 1965, 19). H. Łowmiański generalised this, stating that a process of state organisation or establishment had began in early thirteenth-century Lettenland, and also to a degree in Prussia, in order to influence the Lithuanian centres. This process was broken by the German invasion.[25] The Germans were able to interrupt it because the members of the military democracy

[23] Heinricus' sole mention of a king, "*rex Vetseke de Kukonoyse*," 'Vyachko, the King of Koknese', should not be overrated (Heinricus IX, 10). At that point the chronicler discusses the battles against the Livonians between 1207 and 1208, where the Latvian and Zemgalian nobles participated on the German side. Obviously the title of the Orthodox Christian Duke of Koknese, vassal of Polotsk, was exaggerated into kingship to emphasise the legality and righteousness of the fight against the pagans.

[24] Here are two quite significant examples that illustrate the disadvantages of paganism. The Balts had no calendar, which left them with the options of taking over either the western calendar, beginning at the birth of Christ, or that of the Orthodox church calculated from the creation of the world (in 5500 BC or 5508 BC). Otherwise they would have had to opt for no calendar at all which would have caused confusion in state administration (Jablonskis 1935–1942, 249). The lack of literacy posed a problem in foreign politics: in the Slavic world, in Rus' "in the eleventh, twelfth and the thirteenth centuries, and at times much later, too, all diplomatic negotiations were conducted orally, that is via the oral messages of delegates" (Likhachev 1947, 115).

[25] It may not be a forced analogy to apply L. Rowton's expression for this transitory state, a "dimorph" system of chieftains which was just as open toward tribalism as toward the state (cited in Simon 1983, 132).

of tribes or tribal federations were 'too equal'.[26] The society where no strong exploitative stratum had arisen was undivided, which from an ideo-cultural perspective corresponded to an impotence in internal and external communications springing from illiteracy. There is more than a simple difference of degree between societies with and without literacy, they belong to a different category qualitatively.[27] As a result the Livonian tribes were vulnerable to their conquerors.[28]

The social structure that the Germans found in Livonia is referred to by modern Anglo-Saxon research as a *chiefdom*, and by the German as *gentilic* (mostly after R. Wenskus). This describes a 'barbarian' structure, in the sense of social history, "which, from a socio-economic perspective, is characterised by a relatively strong division of wealth, and the elements of class relations (but not by a deeply divided class structure); in a political sense a simple ruling stratum (based on the chain of personal dependency and military escort rather than on territorial institutions); a primitive 'state'. If this structure is rooted in a more or less ethnically homogeneous (or at least dominantly determined by a certain ethnic element) social community, then we can talk about a 'gentilic' structure" (Szűcs 1992, 24).

5.5. *Drang nach Osten*

The German invasion can be evaluated in various ways. F. Benninghoven is the author of the most comprehensive work concerning the Order of the Brothers of the Sword. He believes, along with other German historians, that the German state established in Livonia protected it against the Russians and the Lithuanians for three hundred years (Benninghoven 1965, 383). [Although, like all patrons of the concept of '*Kulturträger*' (culture carrier), he put aside a small detail, no one had asked for protection several hundred kilometres from the

---

[26] Which does not mean that they were also free (in this way it is misleading to talk about them as free as we would today). I. D'yakonov rightly emphasised that "the concept of freedom of the individual is alien to this period in the history of humans, whereas the communal feeling was strong" (D'yakonov 1994, 23). As so often in the course of history, freedom and equality came into conflict: later the Germans could assimilate and break the Prussians by ensuring personal freedom for the nobility against the equality of the common people.

[27] To accept this, it is sufficient to highlight three characteristics of thought influenced by literacy: (a) people are liberated from memorisation through repetition, and mental energies can be exploited in more creative, and at the same time more abstract directions; (b) they are released from the context-bound nature of speech; (c) they are able to place themselves in various contexts in time and space distant from the here and now (Ong 1982). Members of 'oral societies' are provincial whereas members of 'literate societies' are universal.

[28] E. Gudavičius also explained the thirteenth-century defeats of the Lithuanian society, which was more developed (stronger), than Livonia (Gudavičius 1989, 168 ff.).

German borders.] H. Łowmiański was on the opposite side: "the German invasion disturbed the natural flow of history that would have led to Lithuania's unification with Polotsk and its Letgalian–Livonian regions, and subsequently to an expansion of the Lithuanian regimes onto the right bank of the Daugava. Through some extrapolation we can conclude that had it not been for the German conquest, a Baltic–Russian state might have emerged" (Łowmiański 1973, 77).

The *Drang nach Osten*, and in general any historical conquest or acquisition of any given territory can be evaluated from two perspectives: the rights of the conquering powers and those of the conquered people to self-determination. Of course, the latter is a relatively modern concept, which began to emerge with the Peace of Westphalia in 1648. In the Middle Ages there were only the rights of the conqueror, and the legal settlement of the conquered lands and the sanctioning of the Pope were, from the perspective of the conquered, always retrospective (for the legal aspects of the matter see Hough 1985, 303–351).

Nor could the rights of pagan tribes to self-determination have existed in the Early Middle Ages, for the reason that pagans had no rights at all. Nevertheless, the most important factor that had a decisive effect on the conversion of northern and eastern Europe in its entirety was that the Saxons, who conducted the conversions in the region and connected the rights of power to that of moral, that is divine rights. For them military victory proved the superiority of the new Christian god. Numerous examples can be drawn of that: to start with Rimbert who gave accounts of the Swedish military expeditions against the Couronians, where he wrote that the Christians conquered the pagans because, as if in a wrestling match, their god was the strongest (Rimbert, *Vita Anskari* 30); to end with Heinricus who derided the Orthodox Polotsk Dukes for putting the people to the yoke purely for taxes and money and not for any creed (Heinricus XVI, 2).

No matter how much I respect the great Polish historian H. Łowmiański I cannot see why or how a form of conquest could cause the natural flow of history and how another form of conquest would cause it to be unnatural. Evidently, the natural flow of history is what has happened. (Not to mention that, if through some further extrapolation we were to arrive at a Baltic–Russian state realised in the twentieth century and called the Soviet Union, the possibility does not seem so appealing any more...)

Why would the Lithuanian attacks of the latter part of the twelfth century, thanks to which whole Letgalian villages were exterminated, after which only a few scattered farms remained (Hellmann 1954, 62, 77), have been more natural than the conquests of the Danes or the Germans? Is it perhaps because once, half a millennium earlier, a Baltic language community existed? Something of the ilk is to be suspected behind the distinction, which E. Gudavičius uttered with particular clarity (perhaps following in the footsteps of H. Łowmiański whom he also held in high regard), "the missionary aggression interrupted the usual rhythm of life in the Baltic... [and broke] the flow of natural development... [which would have meant that Lithuania] would have joined the other Baltic tribes to hers" (Gudavičius 1989, 6, 26).[29] The last question is how far back in time one can or should go in the search for the 'natural own–unnatural alien' conflict? At one point the Baltic tribes had also broken the natural Venedic, Old European, or Finno-Ugric development, and since the Indo-Europeans—with the Balts amongst them—had stepped on European grounds from their Asian *Urheimat* the entire history of Europe has followed an unnatural path.[30]

The malleable nature of ethnic relations, so characteristic of the protracted establishment of the Baltic peoples, also gives rise to doubts about the existence of a pre-German Livonian state.

5.6. The East Balts

5.6.1. The Latvians

The ethnic synthesis of the Latvian people (Lat. *natio* 'nation') occurred during a period of German domination and only finished in the seventeenth century, yet we cannot talk about even the beginnings of a political nation before the last third

---

[29] M. Biskup, a former student of Łowmiański, likewise wrote that the Order State "interrupted, and ultimately distorted, the flow of history in the Baltic region, especially the free and natural process of the territories of Pomorze and Prussianland merging with the Polish state and its society, and the areas of Lithuania and Žemaitija with the coastal regions" (Biskup–Labuda 1986, 506). A familiar train of thoughts for the Hungarian ear, given that our conquering forefathers did nothing more than disturb the natural development of the Carpathian basin, for example concerning the Slovakian and Romanian peoples...

[30] The crux of the problem is not so much the moral undertones of the concepts of 'natural–unnatural', since the historian has to pass moral judgement over historical facts, but rather that they belong to the stock of concepts of another, later era. Of course, as a 'private individual' born after the Peace in Westphalia and appreciating peoples' rights to self-determination above all, I do not sympathise with the foreign subjugators of the Balts. However, censure of a period when the concept was non-existent would lead to questions beginning with 'what would have been if...' or 'how wonderful it would have been if...', which belong to chats over a cup of coffee around a white table and not to the circle of scholarship. Similarly, the image established of the history of the Balts in the Middle Ages is not altered by the recently launched news in which Pope John Paul II wished to make amends to the peoples who had suffered from the crusades on behalf of the Catholic Church, an act which would carry a current church political, or for believers, a current metaphysical significance, but no meaning for the discipline of history.

of the nineteenth century.[31] The noun *latvis* 'Latvian' first appeared in 1648 (Kabelka 1982, 86). Since then it has denoted the people with Latvian as their mother tongue as distinct from the other subordinates, all of whom (i.e. all the 'indigenous' Livonian peoples: Latvians, Estonians, Livians, Prussians, Couronians, Lithuanians, etc.) were referred to under the umbrella term of *Undeutsch*, that is non-German, in terms of their nationality up to the twentieth century.[32]

The change in burial customs, the most conservative trait of all, marks the expansiveness of gaining nationhood: the Latvians, growing together from various tribes such as the Latigalians, the Selonians, the Zemgalians, the Couronians, even the Livians, buried their dead in the Christian tradition by the seventeenth century, with their heads lying westwards, whereas earlier only women were buried in that way, while men were laid facing east—corresponding with the traditions of primitive tribes where men are buried facing the direction from where their tribes originated (Mugurēvičs 1981, 58). Nevertheless, even from the seventeenth century the term 'Latvian' referred to the language alone and not to territory. Only during the last third of the nineteenth century, at the dawning of national awareness, was the term *Latvija* 'Latvia' coined at the point when it became a burning issue that there was no territory inhabited by Latvians onto which the concept of 'homeland' could be projected. However, it was only in the twentieth century that the term gained general currency.

Use of the name 'Livonia–Livland' gradually spread from the thirteenth century and became exclusive by the fifteenth. In the founding charter of a trade guild in Riga in 1354, its inhabitants were first referred to as '*Undudisch*' = '*Undeutsch*'. There are two, quite different linguistic standpoints on the names used *before* these, that is the names that referred to the tribe(s) from which the Latvian people evolved, and to where its (their) settlement(s) had been.[33]

What do the sources say? At the same year, 1206, Heinricus wrote, "*Lethos, qui proprie dicuntur Lethigalli*" (Latvians who were properly called Letgalians[34]), and "*Letthi vel Letthigalli*" (Latvians, that is Letgalians), thus he identifies Latvians and Latland with Letgalians and Letgale (*letgals* 'the furthest edge of,

---

[31] Certain languages mark this difference with the word pair 'nation–nationality' (Ger. *Nation–Völkerschaft*, Russ. *narod–narodnost'*). In this sense "Latvian nationality (*narodnost*) evolved between the thirteenth and seventeenth centuries" (Sedov 1987, 379).

[32] It is also expressed in this way in the titles of the first Latvian books: Luther's *Enchiridion* was translated in 1586 "*aus dem Deutschen ins Undeutsche*" [from German to non-German], and the title of two collections of translations is *Undeutsche Psalmen und geistliche Lieder* and *Undeutsche Evangelia und Episteln.*

[33] Only linguistic standpoints, because there could not be an archaeological viewpoint, as "there is not a single find from the entire region of the Lower Daugava [the settlement of the Latvians—E. B.] from the eighth to tenth centuries" (Atgāzis 1980, 100).

[34] According to Bielenstein all this means is that the name 'Latvian' was more widespread than 'Letgalian' (Bielenstein 1892, 75).

the border of the Latvians') (Heinricus X, 3 and X, 15). The form 'Latvian' (*Lettos, Lette*, or *Lettia, Lettlandt, Lettlant, terra Letthorum, Letthorum provincia*) is customary usage in the western sources of Latin and German, and became exclusive after 1209. On the other hand the East Slavic sources talked solely about Lotgalians = Letgalians, and Lotgalia = Letgale. In the *Lavrentiy Compilation of Chronicles* there is *Lětьgola*, while *Lotьigola* appears in the *Chronicle of Novgorod*.

Consequently, western source materials that gave accounts of conquests starting out from the Gulf of Riga moving from the West to the East mentioned Latvians and Letgalians (the latter is only referred to at the outset of the conquests in the early period of becoming settled when news was probably passed on by word of mouth). The eastern sources catalogue conquests starting out from the Eastern Slavic settlements moving from the East to the West (reaching only Koknese on the Daugava, and perhaps never as far as the Gulf of Riga) and only mention the Letgalians.

One of the two interpretations analysing this data is represented by great linguists such as K. Būga or J. Endzelīns and has come close to canonisation due to the veritable esteem in which they are held (e.g. Būga 1923; Endzelīns 1913). They accepted Heinricus' identification of Latvian = Letgalian, and claimed that the ancestors of today's Latvians were exclusively the Letgalians who of course spoke Letgalian (sharing similar conclusions see also, for example, Balodis 1930; Gāters 1977, 10; Sedov 1987, 379). The excellent SSS extends as far as the thirteenth century, and offers no entry of 'Latvian', as if there had been no Latvians until that time, only Letgalians who must have turned into Latvians—who knows how or why?[35] [Political opposition to an awakening of Latgalian separatism at the beginning of the twentieth century can be suspected in this Latvian–Letgalian equation. To which J. Endzelīns' words resonate clearly, "the basis for today's meaning of the name 'Latgalian' is a purely cultural distinction, and not a linguistic, ethnic, or even religious difference... If that is the case, then it is not only scientifically but also politically dangerous to talk about Latvians *and* Latgalians" (Endzelīns 1913, 479). In other words, there is no distinction between the Latgalian and Latvian peoples today, nor were there in the tribal past. Endzelīns considered this thesis so important that he was willing to sacrifice the former existence of a separate Latvian tribe.]

This viewpoint encounters insoluble controversies, or at least inexplicable facts. Unification originating from the East among the Letgalians could not explain the word *Letgals* 'the end of the Latvians', because if there had been no Latvian tribe at that time, then at the end of, that is, the borderlands of what would the Letgalians have dwelled? In addition, if the Letgalian language from the East was the

---

[35] According to A. Erhart the term 'Latvian' "perhaps evolved from the abbreviation (sic!) of the earlier tribe name of the Letgalians" (Erhart 1984, 6).

assimilating actor, then how could the Middle Latvian dialect around Riga (Latv. *vidus izloksnes*) have been the basis of standard Latvian (see for example Endzelīns 1945, 402). Furthermore, why did later sources refer to the land, i.e. the *terra* as Lettenland and not as Letgale, as in, for example, the *Livonian Rhyming Chronicle "Da nach liet ein ander lant die sint Letten genant"* (*Livonian Rhyming Chronicle*, lines 341–342) "after that [the Selonians] stretches another land which is called Lettenland" (Latvijas 1937, 19). If it was not the Latvians who occupied the area of Riga, then who changed or assimilated the Letgalians who had advanced that far? Was it perhaps the (Finno-Ugric) Livians who also settled there? Or perhaps the presumably small number of Selonians who only periodically crop up in the sources? Or was it the Zemgalians? All nonsense.

The standpoint of Endzelīns' group was so rigid that even the idea of opposition was considered sacrilegious, an example being when S. F. Kolbuszewski raised the idea that the Latvian language might be an amalgam that emerged from the Riga area, a coalescence of the Letgalian, Couronian, Selonian, and Zemgalian languages built upon a Livian substratum (Kolbuszewski 1983). (Previously, only Gerullis represented this view—Gerullis 1924, 341.) However, in this hypothesis the Latvian language also constitutes a mixture of non-Latvian languages— Livian, Letgalian, Couronian, Selonian, Zemgalian—which came about by some miracle wherein the Latvian 'basic ingredient' is missing.

A logical conclusion is inherent in the sources: the western areas of the territory were occupied by the Latvians (as far west as the Couronians), while in the eastern parts lived the Letgalians; the latter must have emerged from the former and not the other way around, unless they were two separate tribes, which is highly unlikely. Alone, the ever sober and impartial Baltologist J. Kabelka put forward this carefully phrased theory, "it is possible that the Letgalians in the East were a part of the Latvians ... The almost unanimous statement that the language used in the whole of today's Latvia was Letgalian and not Latvian is highly doubtful" (Kabelka 1982, 88). Anyway, the difference between the stems *let-* and *lat-* can only be explained in this way, that is through a presumption of a Latvian tribe. There were Latvians in the Gulf of Riga which the Livonian word *lätt* (pronounce as [let] 'Latvian') also verifies. The Germans took over the *let-* form from the Livonians which, preceding a velar 't', transformed into *lat-* in the Slavic languages as it spread eastward. The ě > o(a) sound development is clearly visible in the references of East Slavic chronicles.

This sound development explains the form Latvi(j)a (Lettenland). This form is reflected back to a small rivulet (Latava/Latuva) on the right side of the River Šventojai on Lithuanian grounds(!) *solely* for the reason that the Baltic names for peoples usually developed from the names of territories which originally came from water names.

5.6.2. The Leitis

Another enigma lurks in the history of the Balts: not only the Latvian tribe, but also the Lithuanian is absent. The name *lietuvis* 'Lithuanian' is derived from the name of the state Litu(v)a 'Lithuania' (< *Liet-uva* < **Leit-uva*) extant from at least the tenth or eleventh centuries. However as a tribe or a tribal federation the Lithuanians are referred to either as *Aukštaitians* (*Aukštaičiai*) 'highlanders' or as *Žemaitians* (*Žemaičiai*) 'lowlanders', except for the *Povest' vremennyh let*, that is the *Nestor Chronicle*[36] that mentions the Lithuanians three times, always in the noun form '*Litva*' which, in the East Slavic Chronicles, meant both an area and its occupants. In the first two cases the word '*Litva*' is a *jazyk*. The first mention, which refers to the times before the amalgamation of peoples in Babel, denotes a clan (*Nestor Chronicle* 3). The second reference, which talks about times long after Babel, simply denotes a tribe. "Next to the Jafet settled the Rus', Chud, and all [kinds of][37] clans: Merya, Muroma, Ves, Mordva, Chud beyond the Volok, Perm, Pechera, Yam,[38] Ugra, Litva, Zimegola (Zemgale), Kors (Couronians), Lyatgola (Latgale), Lyub (Livias)... and there are other tribes who also paid tax to the Rus': Chyud, Merya, Ves, Muroma, Cheremis, Mordva, Perm, Pechera, Yam, Litva, Zimigola, Korsh, Neroma,[39] Lib" (*Nestor Chronicle* 10). We know that the third reference, "In the summer of 6548 [1040 AD] Jaroslav set out against Litva" (*Nestor Chronicle* 15) refers to a tribe because H. Łowmiański, and after him most recently E. Gudavičius prove, through a convincing analysis, that there could not be a Lithuanian state before the mid-thirteenth century that is before Mindaugas (Łowmiański 1931; Gudavičius 1998).

There is another conception which attempts to fill the dual hiatus of the absent Latvians and Lithuanians. It presumes a common Latvian–Lithuanian tribe which emerged from a common Latvian–Lithuanian '*Urheimat*', this time to be found in the Baltic region, and which later divided into Latvian (Latvian, Letgalian, and Zemgalian) and Lithuanian (Aukštaitian, Žemaitian, and Zemgalian). However, many of these points are supported by pure logic alone, and as such remain emphatically hypothetical. A contrasting *hypothesis* claims that the Zemgalian, Selonian, and Letgalian languages did not grow out of this East Baltic 'Proto-language' gradually, but departed from it one by one only to reunite in the Latvian and the Lithuanian languages (for example Plāķis 1930, 55). Moreover, some

---

[36] Apart from V. Sedov, who took the *Nestor Chronicle* as his starting point, and who, as far as I know, is the only scholar, who talks about a Lithuanian tribe with commendable consistency and clarity (Sedov 1987, 390).

[37] Another manuscript writes "the following clans".

[38] This refers to the Yam (Häm) people who belonged to the Votians, their name survived in the current town name Yamburg (Ammann 1936, 33).

[39] Cf. Part Two, Subchapter 4.2 on the Neuri.

linguists, such as V. Mažiulis or V. Dambe, believe that Selonian and Zemgalian are close to Couronian, in which case it is possible that these two languages, along with Couronian, broke away from the peripheral Proto-Baltic language very early (Eckert–Bukevičiūtė–Hinze 1994, 19).

K. Būga presumes that, due to pressure from the Slavs, the ancestors of the Balts migrated north and north-westwards from the Middle and Upper Dnieper (Būga 1924b, 551 ff.). This thought was uppermost for a long time before it was rejected. Nonetheless, it serves as the foundation for my hypothesis, with a modification in that the migration concerned the East Balts as the ancestors of the Latvians and Lithuanians, and not all the Balts.[40] These wanderings should be seen as a slow process (if for no other reason than the frequently mentioned terrain) that continues across several centuries. It must have been a movement rather like that of an accordion: a given extended clan or tribe settled somewhere for decades, their language unified, and then they set out again moving toward other dialects at which point, as a result of their convergence with the new ethnicity and language, the particular clan or tribe began to differ from its earlier configuration and to resemble the new one. R. Wenskus called this 'form of state' during migration a *Wanderband* 'bond of wandering' (Wenskus 1961, 46).

This periodic wandering was sometimes motivated by some other group of people applying military force—which does not contradict the previous argument. A. Myadvedzeu, the Belarusian archaeologist, is likely to be right when he says that in the sixth or seventh centuries, for example, when the Slavs appeared in Belarus territory they were the conquerors of the Balts, which provided the impetus for an extensive northward migration which started at that time (Myad-zvedzeu 1994, 37). However, there is no interruption in the archaeological finds which would signal that the Balts moving to the North would have chased away the Finnic peoples they found there, which proves that the Balto-Finn meeting involved peaceful assimilation. [Or otherwise that the encounter did not occur between current language families. Some representatives of molecular anthropology claim that genetically only the Lapps differ from the other European peoples, the Finns and Estonians do not. They arrived in the territories of today's Finland as Indo-Europeans, about four thousand years earlier and carried the knowledge of agriculture and animal husbandry with them from the South (Sajantila–Salem, et al. 1996, several authors of the volume edited by Kyösti Julku in 1997, e.g. the editor himself, then Ago Künnap, and Kalevi Wiik). The difference in the family trees based on genetics or language families can be explained in that the Finns, who were few in number, changed their original Indo-European language through Lapp influence (Sajantila–Pääbo 1995). However, more recently L. L. Cavalli–Sforza and other specialists in genetics also refute a Lapp separation (cf.

---

[40] Balts inhabited the Upper Dnieper region as late as the ninth century, together with the Slavs (the Krivichi) (Rüss 1981, 244).

Villems–Adojaan, et al. 1997), while M. Niskanen categorises them in a separate group between the Indo-Europeans and the Finns—Niskanen 1997.]

Even archaeology can hardly trace this several centuries long process, precisely because they deal with related ethnicities which only differ in minute details.[41] Nevertheless, it seems certain that during this staccato procession from south-east to north-west, the ancestors of the later Lithuanians were located at the southern end of this amalgam of tribes, while the predecessors of the later Latvians (Letgalians, Selonians, Latvians, Zemgalians) were in the northern areas. In this way, the ancestors of the Latvians were those who encountered foreign substrata: the Finnic tribes in the East (who, according to Zeps–Rosenschield occupied both the northern and the southern parts of Letgale around 500—Zeps–Rosenschield 1995, 350), then later the Polochans that is Krivichi; in the centre they met the Finno-Ugrian Livians, and perhaps the Venedi; the West Baltic Couronians in the West (who had moved westward about 500–1000 years earlier, and whose lands stretched as far as the Nemunas, and who were in contact with the West Baltic Prussians)[42].

The encounters with foreign languages would explain why the Latvian language has more neologised features than Lithuanian which has preserved its Baltic archaic character.

The time of this upwards migration or filtration is again a matter of conjecture. On the whole it is archaeologists and historians who estimate that it began during the early centuries AD, even earlier in the case of the Couronians and the Zemgalians, that is, during the Early Iron Age. [Although, Mugurēvičs and Tautavičius, the most respected Latvian and Lithuanian archaeologists, also acknowledge that "[fundamentally] the territories of tribes and tribal federations we know about from written sources of the ninth to fourteenth centuries, can only be demarcated from the mid- or late first millennium" (Mugurēvičs–Tautavičius 1980, 10)]. From the area of Vilnius the Selonians and the Letgalians would have reached the left and the right banks of the Daugava in the third or fourth century (Sedov 1985). From a possible Žemaitian–Zemgalian tribal federation between the first and the fourth centuries the Žemaitian federation became separated in the fourth to sixth centuries and remained extant until the thirteenth century, at which

---

[41] Some believe that the migration did not affect the East Baltic region. Others point out that the archaeological finds indicate alien conquerors along the coast and the Nemunas (perhaps the Goths–Alans–Heruli) (e.g. Šimėnas 1992, Myadzvedzeu 1994, 37). Or in another case: there is an undecided (or indeterminable) debate about finds in ninth- to eleventh-century burial sites in a rather large area, namely, whether graves that show burials with cremation should be connected to the Aukštaitians or the Žemaitians (Sedov 1987, 387).

[42] Certainly at the Courish Spit, but perhaps also because the Prussians lived along the Nemunas as far as Grodno (Lith. *Gardinas*) on the bank of the Nemunas, an area which the Lithuanians only invaded around 1400 (Gerullis 1924, 340).

point Mindaugas, the only Lithuanian king in history, hindered its endeavours to establish a state (Tautavičius 1981, 31).[43]

The other, better documented, theory was originally that of K. Būga and is accepted by linguists on the whole but has also recently been accredited by anthropologists and a few archaeologists (see e.g. Tautavičius 1980, 87 and *Myadzvedzeu* 1994, 37). According to this, a large group of Balts set out from the territory of Belarus towards the North and Northwest from the sixth or seventh century. Anthropological data underpins this. The Letgalians (Latvians) in the tenth to twelfth centuries, the Žemaitians in the ninth and tenth centuries, and the Smolensk Krivichi in the eleventh and twelfth centuries belong to the same anthropological type, which is explained by the fact that they came from Belarus (Denisova 1977, 125). There is an increase in graves found in the Latvian area from the seventh and eighth centuries to an extent which can only be explained by immigration and not through a natural demographic rise. The same is true of seventh-century Kurzeme in the period when the Couronians arrived, and in Letgale the phenomenon appears even later from the eighth century (Denisova 1977, 129–130).

From a craniological perspective the first millennium can be divided into two periods. In the first part, the West Baltic long-faced tribes wandered into the region of Lithuania and Latvia from the South and Southwest; in the second part, from the fourth and fifth centuries the wide-faced East Baltic tribes moved in from the East and Southeast. The wide-faced people appeared in larger numbers in Žemaitija and Zemgale only in the ninth century (Denisova 1989, 32).

The ancestors of the Latvians dwelt around Vilnius circa 550–650 (Būga 1924, 737 ff.), and Latvian began to be a separate language from the seventh century "when the Latvians crossed the Daugava, to reach Letgale" (Būga 1924b, 103). As a result of the several centuries long process, "phonetically the Latvian language of around 1200 does not differ from today's" (Būga 1920–22, 18). In the South their name also developed from various water names, at least according to theories accepted up to recent times: the names of the streams '*Leta*' or '*Lata*' (Būga 1923a, 629); from the name of the stream called 'Late' on the Lithuanian–Latvian border;[44] from the name of twenty-seven kilometre long the Leite stream running into the Rusne, a tributary of the Nemunas; or from the name 'Lietauka', an eleven kilometre long stream which flows into the Neris thirty kilometres from Kernavė (a probable seventh, eighth, or ninth-century(?) centre of the Lithuanian tribe, a little north-west of Vilnius (Kuzavinis 1964).

---

[43] The western border of the Žemaitian tribal federation was a coastal stretch of Lamatland mentioned in the thirteenth century. Its inhabitants were perhaps the same as the Germanic tribe, the *Lemovii* mentioned by Tacitus (Gudavičius 1981).

[44] This is connected to the IE. *lat- stem 'damp, watery swamp' (Laur 1972, 46), cf. with Old High German *lätto* 'clay' (Vasmer 1953–58/II, 19).

In the names of 'Leta', 'Lata', 'Late', 'Leite', and 'Lietauka' there are three variations of the stem: in the Lithuanian version there is a stem *liet-* (*Liet-uva* = Lithuania < *Liet-ava* < **Leit-ava*); in the Slavic version we can trace the stem *lit-* (*Litva* = Lithuania); and in the Latvian–Letgalian version the stem *lat-* can be seen (with an 'a' from 'e' after Slavic influence) (*Latvis* 'Latvian', **Latva* < *Latvija* = Lettenland, Latvia). All three variants go back to a form with the 'ei' diphthong, **Leita*, this includes all the names of the Latvians, Lettenland, Letgalians, Letgale, as well as the Lithuanians, and Lithuania. Ultimately this is connected to the IE. **lei* 'to flood' stem (compare with Lith. *lieti* 'to flood') (Fraenkel 1962/I, 368), and from this idea the original meaning could have been something like 'flooding river' or 'flooded area'.[45]

The research work of the linguist S. Karaliūnas and the historian A. Dubonis brought fundamentally new perspectives to the explanation of 'Lithuanian' and also to the etymology of the names of Baltic peoples in general (Karaliūnas 1995; Dubonis 1998). He claims that the word originates from the **leit-* 'go together, go with' stem instead of the **lei-* stem. As the OSlav. *Litva* emerging in the fifth or sixth century proves originally it meant 'the armed escort of the duke'. In this way it is related to Scandinavian–Germanic words like the Icelandic *lid* Old

---

[45] There were various attempts to explain Lithuania's name in the Middle Ages: < *L'Italia*; or < the Celtic *Letha* meaning the western coast of former Gallia; or < Latin *Litavia* 'coastal land'; or Lith. *lietus* 'rain' in which way Lithuania would be a 'rainy country'.

Chronicles from the Middle Ages strove to create an elegant past for the rulers of the Lithuanian Empire. One of these legends claims that the ancestors of the Lithuanian nobility were the Romans. Prince Palemon, being frightened of the tyranny of his relative the Emperor Nero, collected together all his beasts, assembled five hundred lords and an astrologer and escaped from Rome. The company sailed towards the sunset on the Mediterranean Sea, then onto the North Sea, and harbouring at the Nemunas estuary reached Žemaitija. Prince Kunas, Palemon's son, founded the town of Kaunas.

The sixteenth-century Michalo Lituanus, also believed to be of Roman origin, wrote in *De moribus tartarorum, lituanorum et moschorum* [On the customs of the Tartars, the Lithuanians, and the Moscowites], a sharply observant work, "the Russian language is alien to us Lithuanians, that is Italians, who spring from Italian blood. That it is so, is clear from our semi-Latin language and ancient Roman customs that have become extinct not so long ago" (Korsakas–Lebedys 1957, 27). According to Michael of Lithuania the predecessors of the Lithuanians were the soldiers of Julius Caesar who, whilst sailing to Britannia, fled before a tempest to the shores of the Baltic Sea. He enumerates several similarities in the Latin and Lithuanian vocabulary, as well as the cult of Aesculapius whom the Lithuanians respect in the form of a snake just as the Romans did.

One of Palemon's three sons settled on the bank of a river which his people named with the Latin *litus* 'bank', where they blew a tube made of oak. Connecting the two they called the locals *litusba* "which the simple people, speaking no Latin, pronounced as Lietuva". Well, some of the modern linguists actually also establish an etymological relationship between the Latin *litus* (< IE. **liet-*) and *Lietuva*...

Friesian *lid,* Middle Low German *leide* 'military escort, army'. Later the collective noun referring to a military escort was applied to a tribe (**Leita* > **leitis*). Similarly, the Viking name of the druzhina, the Slavs' military escort (*Rus*'), just like the name of the Franks' military escort *Deutsch,* became the name of a tribe or nation.

Then the name *leitis* (Lith. pl. *leičiai*) went through further shifts in meaning. As A. Dubonis demonstrated from fourteenth- to sixteenth-century documents, it denoted a privileged stratum in Lithuanian society, most likely the horsemen of the dukes. Both A. Dubonis and S. Karaliūnas consider the *Leitisi* to be the Lithuanians. However, I presume that **leitis* (pl. *leiši*) could have been the name of a common Lithuanian–Latvian tribe greatest in number. The name has meant 'Lithuanian' up to today (with a slightly sardonic undertone) in Latvian, and in the Lithuanian language a *leišis* is a person who speaks an Aukštaitian and not a Žemaitian dialect, that is a person from the original settlement of the Leitis tribe.

The tribe first formed between the Neris, Nemunas, and Merkys in the region of Vilnius and Kernavė, and from this Leita they pushed westwards while new Baltic peoples joined them as they arrived from the Southeast due to pressure from the Slavs.[46] They could have been the people of the Band ceramics culture usually identified with the ancestors of the Lithuanians (cf. Volkaitė-Kulikauskienė 1987, 185).

A burial rite spread from the Southeast which remained characteristic of the Balts until their conversion to Christianity, and to some extent much longer: the dead were cremated, the ashes were put in a grave with or without an urn, often their (live) horse was buried alongside the dead person. The cremation burial, which started in the fifth or sixth centuries, reached the north coast only in the tenth century (Volkaitė-Kulikauskienė 1987, 190).

The Leitis people moved directly northwards toward Riga (today's Vidzeme). K. Būga believes that in Vidzeme Lithuanians also lived amongst the Latvians, to which a number of place names attest with *leitis* in them (Būga 1923a, 612). When the *Nestor Chronicle* mysteriously mentions the Lithuanians, the Zemgalians, and the Couronians amongst the northern peoples who paid tax to Rus' (*Povest'*, 13), one can only assume that these were the Leitis people who paid tax to Polotsk. The tribal name of the Leitis group survived in the choice of word in western sources (starting from the thirteenth century), particularly in Heinricus: in the early thirteenth century King Mindaugas' title was *rex Lettowiae*; Gediminas' in the early fourteenth century was *rex letwinorum, letphinorum,* and in a German charter *koning van Lethoven, Lettowen.* Heinricus used three names for the area:

---

[46] The Slavonisation of those who stayed in the Dnieper region began in the eighth or ninth century (Sedov 1985).

Lettonia referred to the whole, including Lithuania[47] with its inhabitants the *lettonus* 'Lithuanians'; *Lettia* a smaller region of today's Vidzeme and the left banks of the Daugava's middle reaches with its settlers the *lettus* 'Latvian'; and finally *Lettigalia*, the eastern province of the *lettigals*.[48]

Naturally the language of this common Latvian–Lithuanian tribe was also common, "the only thing we know is that the Latvians settled in Tālava and Vidzeme when their language did not differ from the Lithuanian" (Būga 1923a, 630).

If interpreted well, A. Vasks' assumptions correlate beautifully with this picture. He believed that there were two migrations to the North: the Baltic wandering in the sixth century starting from Lithuania which resulted in the Letgalians of Vidzeme (whom I would term Latvians, that is Leitis); and a migration from Belarus from the eighth or ninth century which ended with the Letgalians of Letgale (Vasks 1992, 185). The two groups are not the same anthropologically: the Letgalians of Letgale resemble the Krivichi of Polotsk. The explanation is at hand: as Belarusian archaeologists claim (e.g. Duchyts 1995, 22) from the eighth or ninth century the Slavic tribe of the Krivichi reached the banks of the Upper Daugava (so, the second wandering northwards mentioned by Vasks was Slavic), and there they met and mixed with the Leitis people (by then Latvians) expanding from the West to the East. The Letgalians of Letgale emerged from this encounter, that is, the 'true' Letgalians who were therefore Slavs (Krivichi) who became Latvian–Leitis and spoke Latvian–Leitis.[49]

5.6.3. The Lithuanians (Žemaitians and Aukštaitians)

The Latvians preserved the once common name, and not only in their own name but also in the name of the Letgalians who migrated to the north-eastern periphery of their territory.

But not the Lithuanians. They had lost it, and doubly so, and because the Leitis people wandered not only towards the north-east and the north, but also in the directions of the West, the Southeast, and the Northwest.

[47] Bartholomaeus Anglicus, a thirteenth-century English Franciscan bishop wrote similarly in his world history, saying that Livonia is nothing but Lithuania's (*Lectonia*) continuum (cited in Gudavičius 1982, 43).

[48] In all these names 'e' most likely covers an 'ei' diphthong. In 1364 Philipp de Mezières referred to Lithuania as "*royaume de Layto*" (cited in Kiparsky 1940, 62), which in Gilbert de Lannoy's travel accounts from 1413–1414 could well have undergone a monophthongisation "*royaume de Letau*" (cited in Mortensen 1926, 73).

[49] R. Denisova talks about a precisely reversed exchange of languages: complying with the dominant Endzelīns theory she presumes an original Letgalian tribe, part of which—changing its own Letgalian language to Slavic—became Slavic (Krivichi) (Denisova 1989, 33).

Their western and south-western push ended between the Middle Nemunas and the Neris, which could be seen as the 'second *Urheimat*' of the Lithuanians. The debate about the location of the Lithuanian state established as 'the seed of Mindaugas' Lithuania' in the mid-thirteenth century has been going on for decades.[50] As J. Jurginis, one of the participants commented the debate "is explanation of an unknown through another unknown" (Jurginis–Merkys–Tautavičius 1968, 32). (Not to mention that if S. Karaliūnas is right, and he is, then the collocation does not refer to a place but denotes 'the military escort of Mindaugas'. Of course it is possible to debate where this and from this, the thirteenth-century state was established.) According to one argument the probable centres of the Lithuanian tribal federation of the late twelfth century were Kernavė and Vilnius. The viewpoint of the majority, posited by H. Łowmiański in 1931 and represented by, among others, Volkaitė-Kulikauskienė (Volkaitė-Kulikauskienė 1970, 271) and E. Gudavičius, places the centre between the Nemunas, Neris, and Merkys.

The two views are not irreconcilable. In the settlement around the first centre in Vilnius–Kernavė there could have been some kind of unification manifested in the Leitis tribe, which then disintegrated from the sixth or seventh centuries, and was followed by a new settlement perhaps in the seventh to ninth centuries that was more to the Southwest and became the new tribal centre—however, by then it was Lithuanian–Lietuvis.

In this way the name 'Leitis' was edged out by 'Lietuvis', however, the Lietuvis people called themselves that, i.e. Lithuanian, for only a short period of time. Later some of the Lietuvis people, that is the Lithuanians, moved to the Northwest, the uniform tribal name was exchanged for the Žemaitian = lowlander and Aukštaitian = highlander terms, while the county name Lietuva stayed except that it now meant 'Lithuanian' and not 'Lithuania' anymore (this territorial meaning, as opposed to an ethnic, gradually became richer with the strengthening of the Lithuanian state, and referred to more and more ethnicities). A proof of this are the separate references to Lithuania, Žemaitija, and Aukštaitija in a 1322 contract of Grand Duke Gediminas.

The latter two names were derived from the adjectives *žemas* 'low, small' and *aukštas* 'high, tall'. Grand Duke Vytautas explained in his letter to Emperor Sigismund in 1420, "terra Samaytarum [the land of the Žemaitians] is the same as Lithuania because it has the same language and the same inhabitants. Terra Samaytarum lies lower than Lithuania, therefore it is called Žemaitija (Szomoyth), which in Lithuanian means 'lower land'. The Žemaitians call the rest of Lithuania Aukštaitija (Auxstote) because that land lies higher than Žemaitija" (Vytautas in LIŠ/I, 92). The two concepts are indeed relative, since the highest point of Lithuania does not exceed three hundred metres. Moreover, Lithuania's rolling countryside is Žemaitija while the heart of the Aukštaitian Highlands is the Central

---

[50] For an objective account of the debate see Gudavičius 1983, 1983a, 1985, 1986.

Lithuanian plain. Consequently, the 'low–high' division must be highlighted differently.

According to K. Būga and A. Salys the name came from the valley of the Nevežis, on the border between the Žemaitians and the Aukštaitians–Lithuanians. H. Mortensen, H. Łowmiański and A. Šapoka derive the differentiation from the Lower and the Upper reaches of the Nemunas (Mortensen 1926, 83, and Łowmiański 1931, 36). Perhaps G. Gerullis' rationale is more logical in saying that when the Lithuanians (who, I presume, were called Leitis) on their way westwards reached the valley of the Nevežis then they found themselves there on the Central Lithuanian plains, in an area of lowlands and began to use the term highlanders for all the other Leitis people who stayed in the East and Southeast that is on the Vilnius–Ašmenai highlands (Gerullis 1924, 340). The occupants of the territory in the kernel of Lithuania were amongst the latter (whether it was their first or second *Urheimat*), who by then were referred to as Lietuvis. This would illuminate why the concepts of Aukštaitian and Aukštaitija gradually became identified with the concepts of the Lietuvis people and Lithuania, from which the also Lithuanian speaking Žemaitian and thus Žemaitija became remote.

Žemaitija was mentioned earlier in the sources (Lith. *Žemaičiai*, Russ. *Zhmud'*, Polish *Żmójdź*, *Żmudź*, Latin *Samogitia*, Ger. *Sameiten, Samaythen*, etc.), first in the Chronicle of Halicz–Volhynia at the year 1219 when the chronicler enumerated the participants of the peace talks, among them "Erdivil and Vikint Prince of Zhemotsk" (LIŠ/I, 34). The Lithuanian Aukštaitija (written in a number of ways in German and Latin sources: Austechia, Auxtote, Eustoythen, and so on) as the term for the south-eastern part of the country was in use from the late thirteenth century, with it first mention by Peter Dusburg as *Austechia*. The north-western Žemaitija separated from the Leitis group more and more, and with time stretched as far as the Baltic Sea, in the former Couronian territory.[51]

The basis of the division between the Lithuanian speaking Žemaitija and Lithuania is difficult to understand for the outsider. Several Lithuanian governors tried to explain it to the Pope. It is because Žemaitija at times belonged to Lithuania, and at others it did not, and only in 1413 did Grand Duke Vytautas succeed in joining it to the empire once and for all. While Lithuania–Aukštaitija became Christian in 1387, Lithuania–Žemaitija only in 1413, at which point it also received a bishopric separate from Vilnius. As the sixteenth-century chronicles show, it was referred to as the Duchy of Žemaitija even after 1569 (in this opposition, the Grand Duchy of Lithuania was called *Litwa za Niewiażą* 'Lithu-

---

[51] According to this view, which I see as the most acceptable, the Žemaitians came from the Southeast, and reached the coast only quite late, perhaps in the twelfth century. (Their first serious role came only in 1260, when they won a great victory against the crusaders—cf. Gudavičius 1987.) An opposite standpoint claims that the Žemaitians migrated there from the West, and much earlier (Vaitkauskienė 1990, 29).

ania beyond the Nevežis'—Jučas 1981, 39). The first Lithuanian poem written by
M. Mažvydas in 1547, entitled *The educational warning of the little book itself*
was still written for the Lithuanians and the Žemaitians, and even the nineteenth-
century S. Stanevičius called his poem *The glory of the Žemaitians* though it
trumpets the victorious past of the *whole* of Lithuania. Besides the two bishoprics,
another reason lies behind the differentiation of Žemaitija from Lithuania (essentially from Aukštaitija) was that in 1413 they were separate administrative units:
following the Polish pattern the former Duchies of Vilnius, Trakai, and Naugardukas became a voivode, while Žemaitija remained a Duchy with according
privileges from 1440. Up to the Modern Ages, perhaps even today, the characteristics of the two parts of the country remained different. Žemaitija became, so
to say, more 'local patriotic' or more Lithuanian than the other parts, which has
several reasons: the German attacks were principally and mostly targeted at
Žemaitija which left them to protect the Lithuanians there; feudal dependencies
were looser; greater equality, that is 'golden freedom' remained from the kin
society structure.

Besides this historical meaning, the word 'Žemaitis' carries a narrower sense,
too. Following the end of the Polish–Lithuanian state in 1795, it began to refer to
the Lithuanian dialect based on the Couronian and Zemgalian linguistic foundations of the western parts of Žemaitija with the centre of the town Telšiai, and on
the other hand all other Lithuanian dialects became Aukštaitian (Zinkevičius
1982).

Within Aukštaitija two separate areal and dialectical regions deserve mention.
One of these is Suvalkija, the south-western part of Lithuania, bordering Germany
and Poland, the land of the Suduvi mentioned by Ptolemy, the former Prussian
Suduva (which at times is also referred to as *Užnemunė* 'area beyond the Nemunas'), with Marijampolė as its centre. Linguists, historians, and most often politicians debate whether the territory inhabited by the Suduvi or Jatvingians belonged
to Lithuania or to Prussia = Germany. The area became uninhabited with the
disappearance of the indigenous Suduvi and a vast forest covered it. In the fifteenth
and more in the sixteenth centuries Lithuanians started to filter in again. Poland
kept in contact with the inland regions of Lithuania through this stretch and thus
in Polish it gained the name *Trakt Zapuszczański* 'track beyond the jungle'. In 1795,
when Lithuania was divided, this area belonged to Prussia which further induced
its separation, then later from 1807 to the Warsaw Principality created by Napoleon, then from 1815 along with the Principality to Russia. With Lithuania's
independence in 1918 a chunk of the territory became part of Poland with earlier
centres such as Augustow, Sejny, or Suwalki (which lent its name to the area as
in Suvalkija). The naming of the territory and its peoples had changed many times
with the turning wheel of history: the voivode, then governance of Augustow; the
Bishopric of Sejny; and so on. Most lately in 1939 Hitler and Stalin's secret pact
referred to it as the 'Lithuanian stretch' or the 'triangle of Suwalki', which meant

that the Soviet Union could invade the whole of Lithuania, except for this area which later, half a year before the German attack on the Soviet Union, it bought from Hitler for millions of dollars (Bojtár 1989, 49, 77, 256).

This changing of powers between Lithuania, Poland, Germany, and Russia evidently shaped the people of this region differently from the rest of the Lithuanians.

The other region within Aukštaitija is the South-eastern Dzūkija = Dzuks-land. Its inhabitants, the Dzuks received their name in the nineteenth century, as they pronounce a 'cz' and 'dz' instead of the literary 't' and 'd'.[52] The Dzuks show the most Slavic features among the Lithuanians. For this reason, or some other, they are seen, as similar to the 'crafty Transylvanians', as great rascals, drawn to dance and singing, and a hot-headed type. Their stubborn thirst for freedom was most notoriously obvious in 1918, when a small town of a thousand inhabitants called Perloja became bored with the perpetual raids of the Bolsheviks, Poles, Byelorussians, Ukrainians, and so on and they declared the independent Republic of Perloja.

5.6.4. The Zemgalians

The history of the tribe and territory of the Zemgalians is connected to the northern and north-western migration of the Leitis people. Their names crop up in various forms: Latv. *zemgaļi*,[53] Lith. *žiemgalai;* the *Zemgale* or *Žiemgala* place names occur in the sources as: Scandinavian *Seimgala,* Ger. *Semegallen, Semgallen,* Russ. *Zimgola*—they have two explanations. The second half of the compounding carries the meaning 'end, borderland' (familiar from the names of the Galindians and Letgalians), its first half '*ziem*' would be connected to the stem 'north', and thus the meaning of the name would be 'a person living on the northern ends'; or else it is connected to the stem '*zem*' 'low' in which case it would denote a person who lives on the plains of the Mūsa and Lielupe. Respected scholars like K. Būga, J. Endzelīns, or E. Fraenkel tend towards the first explanation.[54] From the earlier discussion, I consider the second etymology also plausible, which would place the Zemgalians to the borders of the Žemaitians.[55] Again, the two standpoints are

[52] Their territory is the same as the earlier Jatvingian Dainava.

[53] Unlike this, the inhabitants of Zemgale in today's Latvia are called *zemgalieši* which is different from this old name.

[54] "The Zemgalians emigrated from the lands of Vilnius in the sixth to seventh centuries" (Būga 1924, 267). The Zemgalians "could received their names from their current southern neighbours, the Lithuanians (the *Leiši*-Leitis)" (Endzelīns 1925, 420).

[55] The archaeologist is also of the opinion that based on the funeral customs and the finds of their graves "in the late first millennium the cultures of the Zemgalians and the Žemaitians were related. Later differences in their rituals increased: burial with cremation and equine inhumation spread among the Žemaitians" (Sedov 1987, 372).

not incompatible. It is very possible that the Leitis people from around Vilnius moved northwards just like fifty or a hundred years later the Žemaitians, and together they reached the coast, as Heinricus mentions the Zemgalian port (*portus Semigallorum*) at the year 1199 (Heinricus IV, 6). This port was for a long time marked on maps at the Lielupe estuary, but lately the view has been expanding that it was over the Daugava (cf. Mugurēvičs in Heinricus IV, 352). This would underpin a Zemgalian migration from the South, and that the Daugava was no obstacle for them, rather crossing it they advanced further to the North into Vidzeme—by then not as Zemgalians, but having been assimilated, as Latvians.

The Zemgalians are first mentioned in the thirteenth-century Danish chronicle the *Annales Ryenses* at the year 870. The Danish Vikings conquered the whole of Prussia, Zemgale (*Semigaliam*), the land of the Karelians, and many others. Three eleventh-century runiform stones also mention the Zemgalian region, but its rough whereabouts can only be deciphered from the thirteenth-century German sources (Atgāzis 1980, 89).

I am emphatically talking about the area. Unlike the region, the Zemgalian language had never become distinct in the decades-long wanderings and settling. Several items of evidence are at our disposal for this. One of these is the papal bull of Pope Gregory IX from 1234, reinforced in 1237, which demarcates the territories of the Zemgalian Bishopric between the Nemunas, Daugava, and Neris (Latvijas 1937–40/I, 197), in other words in the areas stretching from the starting to the end points of the migrations of the Leitis–Žemaitians–Zemgalians. The weightiest argument is the letter written a century later on May 26 1323 by Gediminas Lithuanian Grand Duke to the Minorites (Franciscans), in which "*Gedeminne, divina providentia lethpanorum ruthenorumque rex, princeps Semigalliae et dux*" requests four missionaries for the conversion of the still pagan inhabitants of the Grand Duchy of Lithuania who speak Polish, Zemgalian, and East Slavic ("*scientes polonicum, semigallicum ac ruthenicum*") (Gediminas, 51, 55). The Lithuanian, East Slavic and—by then already Latvian—Zemgalian parts of the empire are clearly divided in the title of the Grand Duke (not as a reality, because the Lithuanians could never completely conquer Zemgale, thus only in the form of a territorial demand.[56]) On the other side, the Zemgalian language is mentioned separately as the only Baltic language in a 'Baltic' empire—in precise order from the West to the East (Polish–Zemgalian–Ruthenian). This demon-

---

[56] After twenty-six years of independence the Zemgalian bishopric was joined to the Church district of Riga in 1251, which supports the assumption that Zemgale did not belong to Lithuania.

strates the stubborn persistence of the 'common Baltic' language: Zemgalian here means Lithuanian Žemaitian.[57]

In the fifteenth century the situation changed. Gilbert de Lannoy, a French knight, went to Livonia and Lithuania in 1413–1414 and he clearly differentiates between the Lithuanian language from the Livonians, among the latter the Couronian, Livian, and the Zemgalian which unambiguously equal Latvian.[58]

I believe that the Zemgalians, living in a separate region of Zemgale, did not speak a separate Zemgalian tongue. Dividing off the Žemaitians they spoke Lithuanian, and those who separated off from the Leitis group spoke Latvian. This would explain the strange fact that the northern Zemgalians became 'more Latvian than the Latvians', in other words that the middle dialect, basis of the standard Latvian language, is closest to the Zemgalian, and as Endzelīns put it, "earlier in the centre of Vidzeme lived the same tribe as in the basin of the Lielupe", that is,

---

[57] At this point V. Pašuta, the publisher of Gediminas' letters, mistranslated some words in his monograph, perhaps because he attached no great importance to the references to these languages: "Lithuanian, Polish, or Zemgalian" (Pašuta 1971, 322). S. C. Rowell again talks about three different languages: "Polish, Zemgalian, and Prussian" (Rowell 1994, 207 ff.). He claims that Polish was the language of "the Lithuanian slaves and to a smaller degree of diplomacy," while he explains Zemgalian—which he believes was different from Lithuanian, an individual language in itself—that Gediminas only intended to convert the population of Zemgale, which was in the hands of the Order of Knights, and left the Lithuanians alone. The latter may be plausible, but it is less believable that Gediminas would have exposed himself in that way in a letter to the Franciscans themselves. Another interpretation is also wide-spread—for example V. Pašuta and S. C. Rowell use it. It explains the request for Zemgalian speaking missionaries in that, after the Germans had won against the Zemgalians in 1289–1290 (as the last among the Livonian tribes) they fled southwards to Lithuania in their tens of thousands (according to a document from 1310, in which the Rigans denounce the Livonian Order of Knights to the Pope, a hundred thousand Zemgalians escaped their country). The number, in accordance with the 'genre' of denunciation, is certainly exaggerated. Careful calculations show that in the early thirteenth century the Zemgalians had a population of 17,000–24,500 people (Benninghoven 1965, 390). Their numbers aside, it is again hardly conceivable that the Grand Duke would have wished to convert them alone. As for the exchange of the 'East Slavs' (*ruthenicum*) with the 'Prussians' (*pruthenicum*) S. C. Rowell refers to the Berlin copy of Gediminas' letter, which says 'Prussian' (as opposed to the copy from Göttingen saying 'Ruthenian', which V. Pašuta took to be correct). Beyond this, S. C. Rowell argues *against* the East Slav version, by questioning that there would have been a need to convert the already Christian East Slavs (the counter-argument to which is that it is not at all certain that the Franciscans held Orthodoxy to be Christian, which the witty Gediminas, conducting pendulum-politics, must have very well known). On the other hand, S. C. Rowell has no arguments *for* the Prussian, which leaves us in a fog about why in the Grand Duchy of Lithuania Prussians had to be converted in 1323.

[58] For this reason the language has to be mentioned separately because its reference means more than "the Zemgalian language or dialect still existed then" (Kabelka 1982, 77).

the Zemgalians who, along with the Leitis–Latvians, were in the middle and thus the centre of the unification of the Latvian language (Endzelīns 1954, 480).[59]

The division of the territory and the language is also shown in an administrative document from 1426 which lists the Zemgalian districts that belonged to the Grand Duchy of Lithuania in the Lithuanian language (Zinkevičius 1984–94/II, 25), and from the mid-fifteenth century they are not mentioned as a separate group of people even in the North, yet the separate name of the territory remained: the official name of the Duchy of Courland established in 1561 was *Herzogthum Kurland und Semgallen* (Zeids 1980, 59).

The word *leitis* 'Lithuanian' which is preserved in several place names in this form with the 'ei' diphthong, and which can be found in both the Couronian and the Prussian languages refers to a further north-western and western advancement of the Leitis (Žemaitian–Zemgalian) tribe.[60]

5.6.5. The Selonians

The Selonians (Selians or Sels) are the only people who do not fit the centuries-long northward and north-westward push of the Leitis group or the map of the Latvian and Lithuanian territories that 'organically' evolved in the course of this migration and distancing.

East of the Zemgalians, on the left bank of the Daugava lived the Selonians, according to Heinricus, whose name is derived from river names that mean 'flow', 'trickle', 'stir up' (Latv. *sēļi*, Lith. *sēliai*, Lat. *Selones*, Ger. *Selen*).

Very little data survived about them, and what is most suspicious is that the chronicles of the East Slavs who lived near them do not mention them at all. "Is it perhaps because they did not differentiate them from the Latvians or the Lithuanians?" (Kabelka 1982, 82); a possibility that Bielenstein also considers (Bielenstein 1892, 171). They must have been few in number (about five to seven thousand people in the thirteenth century—Benninghoven 1965, 390), and by the early fourteenth century they must have assimilated into the Lithuanians or the

---

[59] The usual explanation for the 'Zemgalians being more Latvian than the Latvians' seems a little forced: the people of Zemgale fled from the German invasion, the area became uninhabited, repopulation beginning again as late as the fourteenth century. The much larger northern part was occupied by the Latvians, and the southern region by the Lithuanians. In the stead of the Zemgalians in the North, the 'true' Latvians arrived from the other side of the Daugava, from the centre of Vidzeme, and they would have brought the genuine indigenous Latvian dialect with them.

[60] Following J. Endzelīns the general viewpoint is that the leitis 'Lithuanian' is a Couronian loan word in the Latvian language (e.g. Kabelka 1982, 72 ff.). The opposite direction seems more logical to me: the Couronians borrowed the 'ei' diphthong from the Žemaitians. For the 'ei' diphthong in Prussian see Toporov 1975–90/V, 203.

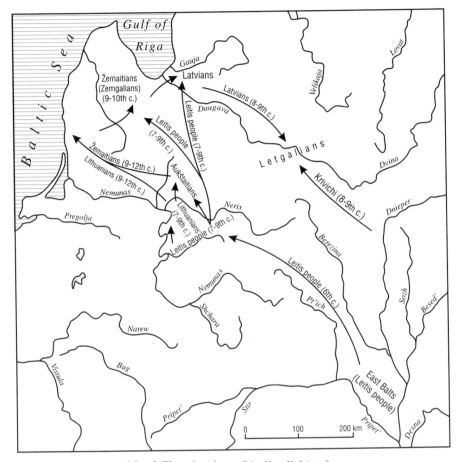

Map 5. The migrations of the East Baltic tribes

Latvians. Ultimately, it is more than doubtful whether they ever existed as an independent tribe, and Heinricus gave them a mention perhaps only because their fortress on the left bank of the Daugava (*castrum Selonum*, where the Latvian village near Jēkabpils is called Sēlpils to this day) served as a military base (*refugium*) for the Lithuanians in their attacks against the Livians, Letgalians, and the Estonians. (Bishop Albert disapproved of these and in 1208 lay siege to the fortress with his amassed army from the already converted Livians and Letgalians, and conquered the Selonians, who then also had to convert to Christianity.)

Another assumption, that of some archaeologists,[61] is that the Selonians constituted a separate tribe, even an anthropological type different from the Let-

---

[61] See Mugurēvičs in Heinricus 371.

galians, and moved to the banks of the Daugava as early as the first century BC. An archaeological and a linguistic fact's fitting into each other (or being fitted to each other) evidences this. Based on a solitary criterion the finds of the Kurgans between the second and the sixth centuries detaches from those of the Letgalians in the region where the Selonian dialect of the Latvian language is apparent (or the Selonian language itself, should it be viewed as an independent language). There the intonation is rising, as opposed to all other Latvian dialects.[62] In this case the statement of the *Tabula peutingeriana* would refer to them, *Caput Fluvii Selliani* 'the estuary of the river of the Selonians' which would be the Daugava. Accepting this, the Selonians would have had to be where they are mentioned in the sources for over a thousand years as some kind of an enclosure in alien surroundings (Who were their neighbours?), and so few of them survived because in the meantime they slowly vanished.

In one way or another, in the early thirteenth century the Selonians did not represent a significant power, which soon became apparent to the Germans. The bishopric of the land of the Selonians, established in 1218, was renamed in 1225 as the Zemgalian bishopric (Lit. E/XXXV, 306).

5.7. The West Balts

5.7.1. The Prussians

In the early thirteenth century, the Prussians occupied the area between the Lower Vistula and the Courish lagoon, on the left bank of the Middle and Lower Nemunas. The name, which seems to have replaced the 'Aesti' which vanished in the ninth century, presumably first represented a single West Baltic tribe (K. Būga believes that its centre was Truso in Pogezania). Only later did it come to mean all those living in this area, although the various other tribe names survived up to the ninth century.

The name itself occurs in the remnants of the Prussian language only as a singular accusative adjective (*prūsisken* 'Prussian'), and adverbial (*prūsiskai* 'in Prussian'). Even so, the substantival nominative forms (*prūsas—prūsai*) can be derived with absolute certainty (Latv. *prūsi*, Lith. *prūsai*).

Alongside the Geographus Bavarus the name (*Bruzi*) crops up (as *Brus*) in the Arabic writings of a Hispanic Jewish traveller, Ibrahim-ibn-Jakub. In 965 he visited the Slavic lands. He mentions the state of the Poles which bordered Rus' in the East, and the Burusi in the North. The latter lived on the shores of the Baltic

---

[62] For the Selonian question see Deņisova 1977, 156 ff.; Sedov 1987, 365.

Sea and their language was incomprehensible to their neighbours. Concerning the tenth–eleventh-century conversions the written Latin, Polish, and various other western European sources carry an increase in references to the Baltic peoples, for example *Pruzzi, Pruzos, Pruzorum, Prucorum, Pruzziae, Pruciam*, and others. As I mentioned before, *Borussi* was made up or neologised by Erasmus Stella, just as Prut + henus or Pruthenia was also a later creation.

Adam of Bremen was the first amongst the Germans to report on the Isle of Semland (Sembia) that borders the Russians and the Poles, where Sembians or Prussians live. They had blue eyes, red cheeks, and long hair and were "humane humans" (*homines humanissimi*) who offered help to the shipwrecked, or to those who were attacked by pirates. Their habitat was inaccessible because of the swamps and they would not tolerate rulers. The only problem with them was that they did not believe in Christ, and resolutely hunted down missionaries.

The East Slavic chronicles begin to refer to the Prusi at around the same time. As a people's name it must be relatively young because had it filtered into the Slavic languages in the sixth to eighth centuries it would be *prыsы* in Russian and *prysy* in Polish by today, because in these languages *ū* became -ы- and -y- (cf. Lith. *sūnus* with Russ. *sыn*).

There were numerous attempts to etymologise the word. It was connected to the Old Indic *purusas* 'human', or to the Lith. *prausti* 'to wash' and *prusti* 'grow, thrive' (from which the 'group of people, population' meaning would have evolved, like that of the Gothic *thiuda* 'a large group of people' > Old High German *diot*, Ger. *deutsch*, Flemish *dutch*); O. Trubachev relates it to the people's name 'Friesian', others to various water names. However, there are serious doubts concerning each of these explanations.

There is no data to indicate that any member of the Prussian tribal federation would have called themselves exclusively by this name, consequently from the etymologies based on such 'semantic fields' that of J. Okulicz seems the most convincing. He argues that their neighbours called them Prussians, which meant 'horse breeder, horse rider' (cf. Gothic *prus* 'horse', OSlav. *prusa* 'mare', because in the lives of the Prussians' horse breeding was of central economic significance (Okulicz 1973, 14). This is clearly supported by archaeological finds from the Early Iron Age to the Middle Ages. Prussian society can be considered to have been a settled community, still presumably for a long time animal husbandry played a more important role than agriculture.[63]

Nevertheless, the most plausible explanation, a 'geographical' one, is an idea from the seventeenth century that the Prussians (*porussi*) were people who lived next to (*po*) the Russians (*russi*). As J. Voigt reasons in detail, the name—though

---

[63] Wulfstan's description of a burial horse race, which will later be discussed in more detail, supports this. The survival of the custom is also known more recently among Lithuanians as late as in 1377; when Grand Duke Algirdas died his eighteen horses were cremated with him.

it represents a large tribe or tribal federation and did not crop up before the tenth century—was made up by the Poles for whom the area West of the Vistula was *Po-morze* 'sea-side' and East of it *Po-Rus* 'on the borders of the land of the Russians' (Voigt 1827–39/1, 299–307). (In the tenth–twelfth centuries foreign travellers generally thought of Lithuania, which fell between the Prussians and the Russians and was in the process of formation, as part of Rus'.)

The name 'Prussian' went through further shifts in meaning. It seems likely that first the Lithuanians started to call all inhabitants of the Prussian lands 'Prussian', including the invading Germans. Then, from the fourteenth century, the name meant only East Prussian Germans.[64] To avoid ambiguity in many languages the Balts are referred to as Old Prussians.

The rather tentative picture of Prussian society shows that in the ninth–twelfth centuries the Prussians formed a strong tribal federation, yet there was no 'Prussian consciousness' as such. There are no records of any incidents where the whole of the Prussian tribal federation would have acted as a single communal unit (see also Pašuta 1971, 211). The society was not stratified, there was a military democracy characteristic of tribal federations consisting practically only of freemen whose freedom meant military service, and among whom there was no leading stratum.[65] Anonim Gall, the Polish chronicler wrote that the early twelfth-century Prussians "lived without a king and law" (Book II, Chapter 42). Adam of Bremen made a similar observation, "these people, impossible to capture in the swamps, tolerate no rulers" (Book IV, Chapter 18). The reason behind it was that property (more precisely the property of the richer!) was not inherited. Wulfstan gave a detailed depiction of how the Aistii connected burials with horse races, and how the chattels of the deceased would be shared out in the form of prizes. This also explains the poverty of the graves found in the region from the Middle Ages, as opposed to those from the Roman times (Labuda 1972, 286). The institutions of the tribal federation, embracing several tribes, had a temporary character, and after a military expedition each tribe would remain separate (Odoj 1970, 62).

A common genesis myth, system of language, institution, and customs held a 'gentilic' kinship society together were not enough in themselves to found a state in the Middle Ages. However, as J. Szűcs points out, in central Europe the transition from gentilic societies into the formation of new states was much more continuous than in the western parts (Szűcs 1992, 40 ff.). Nonetheless beyond the ensemble of common *origo, lingua, instituta*, and *mores* another negative and a positive factor was needed to establish a state. The negative element was that there

---

[64] According to others for this reason it is misleading to use *'Preussen'* for the Baltic tribe, because it only means the Germans. L. Kilian suggests the word *'Prussen'* for the Prussians (Kilian 1982, 13).

[65] For this reason V. Kulakov's idea of putting even the commencement of the disintegration of the kinship society to the turn of the seventh and eighth centuries is without basis (Kulakov 1990).

should be no strong alien powers in proximity that would be able to conquer the people who were about to form a state. The positive component was that there should be neighbours whose threat could be contained only through the cohesiveness of a state proceeding from a looser community.[66]

The script, that is roughly the same in other places, for the founding of a Christian state did not actualise in the instance of the Prussians. According to P. Engel, "one of the pagan chieftains grabbed the initiative in his country, thrust his potential rivals aside, and at times eliminated them together with their families, then invited missionary priests from abroad to establish the organisational framework of the new religion. The prince's army would then ensure that this was convincing for everyone. Generally two generations were necessary to accomplish the work. The first carried out the destruction of the old system, the so-called 'dirty work', and the second one usually had the more rewarding task of 'building the new country'" (Engel 1990, 110).

This, however, is just one model for the adoption of Christianity. The other is when the pagans were converted by an external power through violence, as Charles the Great did with the Saxons, who then used the same methods to spread the word further to the East with the sword.[67] The Poles joined the Germans in converting the littoral West Slavs. Bolesław Krzywousty conducted mini crusades in 1147 and 1166 against the Pomeranians, and later his descendants against the Prussians.

In brief the difference between the two models is that the first, through which the given people were assimilated into Christian Europe, presumes a strong central power for the ruler supported by a military escort; while the second, which leads to isolation and ultimately to extinction, presumes some kind of democratic 'republic' where the tribal meeting of the nobility (*nobiles*) and religious leaders decide what is important (Mielczarski 1967, 62–63).[68]

This is what happened in the tenth–eleventh centuries in the "Vjelet tribal republic" in the region between the Middle Elbe and the Lower Oder where the Dukes were elected and at the point when it was already too late, and being pagans,

---

[66] F. Graus terms it as "nationalist feeling of the Middle Ages", an expression which is, in the case of the Balts (even the Lithuanians), probably too strong. The main criterion of its development is "the consciousness of an inner relatedness among the members of a tribe, and a sensitivity to their otherness to the aliens... as well as the evolution of a leading stratum that is capable of wording the feeling of this otherness" (Graus 1965, 60–61).

[67] Dörries also emphasises the essential similarity in the conversions of the Saxons and the Balts (Dörries 1956, 17). Evidently, the several centuries difference, belatedness if you like, changes many aspects of any type of essential sameness...

[68] As Saxo Grammaticus, the Danish Chronicler recounts, there was an even more rudimentary democracy among the Couronians who chose a temporal leader or a 'king' before an actual battle (Saxo Grammaticus, 3, 85).

they were forced to convert to Christianity (as the Danes coerced the Rugians, the last of the Slavic tribes, in 1168) or were assimilated, or exterminated (SSS, 6/430). From the twelfth century the desire to establish a state strengthened among the Prussians, however, as the contract of Chrystburg in 1249 demonstrates they "existed only as free individuals... and had not [already and still] constituted a co-operation capable of making a contract" (Patze 1958, 73). In K. Forstreuter's words, even their nobles "appeared as an anonymous group," consequently they were consumed by the wars among tribes and in the raids against the Poles (Forstreuter 1960, 264).[69] They had the strength to ward off the establishment of a missionary state, the attempt of the first early thirteenth-century missionaries, but it was not enough to stand up against the Teutonic Knights called in by their West Slavic (Polish) neighbours who were most threatened by the Prussian attacks. In this way, their political catastrophe was essentially built into the organisation of their 'over-democratic' society which was out-dated in comparison with that of their neighbours (see also Jażdżewski 1981, 629). The military democracy of the tribal federation did not transform into a military monarchy, unlike the Lithuanians'.

Magdeburg played some role in the conversion of the Prussians. Both bishops learnt there, as the *Chronicle* of Cosmas states, "in the region of the philosophers", and were killed by the Prussians: Adalbert, Bishop of Prague, baptised Vojtěch (ca. 956–997), perhaps the most significant Central European martyr, sprang from a Ducal Czech family and was active among the Czechs, the Poles, and the Hungarians;[70] and his fanatical follower, Bishop Bruno of Querfurt (Bonifac) (ca. 974–1009).[71]

Immediately after his death three biographies were written about Adalbert. Who the author of the first, *Vita s. Adalberti* from 999, might have been is debated. It was written by either Johannes Canaparius, Adalbert's fellow monk in the cloister of Saint Boniface and [Saint] Alexius on the Aventinus; or by Gaudentius (Radim), Adalbert's stepbrother who was with him in Prussia, witnessed his murder, and who in the year 1000, as the first Bishop of Gniezno, participated in the famous 'summit meeting' of Gniezno organised by Emperor Otto III. In any case, Bruno, also the member of the cloister on the Aventinus, originally from an aristocratic

---

[69] H. Łowmiański examined the reasons behind the Norman expansion from Scandinavia, and pointed out that 'adventuring' is a frequent phenomenon of still overly free early feudal societies. The ruling class, about to become separate, is not yet capable of covering its existential costs at the expense of the subordinate strata of its own society, therefore it is forced to embark upon raiding, conquests, and trade (Łowmiański 1957, 63).

[70] J. Hašek talked quite offensively about him: "Nothing has changed from the time when the robber Vojtěch, whom they nicknamed 'the Saint', operated with a sword in one hand and a cross in the other, murdering and exterminating the Baltic Slavs." (Hašek 1993, 136).

[71] M. Horváth embeds the mission of the two saints into the battle between Emperor Henry II and Pope John XVII (Horváth 1876, 241 ff.).

Saxon family, started to write the second history of his model Adalbert's life in 1004. By then he had to consider certain political aspects, too.[72]

The first biography demonstrates that conversion should not be envisaged as the cannibalistic natives automatically massacred the missionaries without a second thought. At first the Prussians simply told Adalbert and his armed escort to go home. However, the bishop demanded martyrdom. He stayed in a village quietly for five days with his two companions, then he began to preach again, and only then was he killed. Canaparius describes his death in the following passage, "The wrathful Sicco[73] leapt from the angry crowd and struck a great spear through his heart with a mighty blow. He was the priest of the idol worshippers and the leader of the alliance of the crowd, and therefore it was he who had to strike first. Then all of them ran to the spot and giving wounds they vented their rage... they left his body there but stuck his head upon a stake, and returned home celebrating their cruel deed with a mirthful song" (Canaparius in SRP/I, 230). This was no spontaneous murder, but the ritual enactment of a sentence at court: Adalbert had to die not because of the conversion, but because, most likely by accident, he had spent the night in a sacred pasture and thus committed sacrilege (his companions were left unharmed) (see also Mielczarski 1967, 127).

[72] The third biography was written around the year 1000. The author of the *Passio sancti Adalperti martiris* is unknown, it is attributed to a friend in the Cloister of Meseritz (Mannhardt 1936, 9–11). All three are published in SRP/I, 227–237.

[73] The author of the second biography Bruno of Querfurt describes Sicco as somebody taking revenge for his brother who was killed by the Poles.

The word 'Sicco' or at another place 'Siggo' is the first known Prussian word. It might be a proper noun, but perhaps A. Mierzyński is right in saying that it meant an office: *žigonutas* 'walking, stepping person', that is a wandering priest, a 'padre' (Mierzyński 1892–96/I, 41). Others also accept this solution, but they connect this priestly office with the meaning 'knowledgeable' (e.g. Būga 1908–1909, 172, and cf. Part Four, Subchapter 8.3.6). In the sixteenth century the word *signot* appeared for a Prussian pagan priest, which further derived became *sigonotta*, later connected with *sicco*. A. Bezzenberger says that *signot* < Pruss. *signat* means 'to bless' (Bezzenberger in Bertuleit 1924, 90).

Under the pen of Archbishop Thietmar the beheading of Adalbert became a literary motif. Thietmar was Bruno's fellow student in Magdeburg. He reported on Bruno's death as: "In the twelfth year of his busy, diligent monastic life he went to Prussianland (*ad Pruciam*) to fertilise its sterile soil with the divine seed; but the hard soil, in which only thistles grew, was not easily opened. When he preached at the borders of Russland (*Rusciae*), the locals at first protested, and as he carried on with the evangelism and the love of Christ who is the head of the Church, they beheaded him, along with his eighteen companions" (Thiemar 344). The *Annales Quedlinburgenses* mentions nothing about beheading: "In 1009, on the borders of Rus' (Rusciae) and Lithuania (*Lituae*), on February 23 the pagans beat the Bishop and Monk Saint Bruno, commonly called Bonifac, upon the head, and with his eighteen companions he flew into the sky" (SRP/I, 237).

Adalbert and Bruno's early mission in Prussia remained an isolated episode for nearly two hundred years. This gap was partly due to the difficulties involved in gaining access to the Prussians, and most of all the powers west and south of the Balts were occupied with the conversion of the West Slavic duchies and principalities, while the struggle for hegemony between Denmark and the German Reich was underway. Poland had a diminishing influence on the outcome of this struggle as it gradually crumbled into ever smaller states until it vanished altogether. (Without knowing details about it, the general picture that Anonim Gall painted seems trustworthy, "from the North Sea Poland is bordered by three wild and barbarous neighbouring pagan lands, these are Selentia,[74] Pomorze, and Prussianland. The Polish Duke vehemently fights to convert them. Nonetheless, it is impossible to tear their hearts from paganism with the sword of education, nor to completely wipe out these creatures with the sword of destruction. Though when the Polish Duke defeated them, their leaders often sought the shelter of the Cross, but as they pulled their strength together they denied the Christian religion once more, and picked up warfare against the Christians afresh"—Anonim Gall 9.)

Perhaps the most important point in this rivalry was the founding and consolidation of the Marquisate (*Mark*) of Brandenburg from the mid-twelfth century between the Elbe and the Oder. Henry the Lion established Lübeck in 1159, which was later to be the leading town in the Hanseatic League, which also traded with Livonia. Brandenburg conquered Denmark at the battle of Bornhöved in 1227, wresting not only the West Baltic region. Over time they gained Pomorze (*Pomerania*, Ger. *Pommern*) which had been conquered by the Poles, and finally in 1308–1309 (through the German Teutonic Order which had been established in the meantime), they took the so-called Pomorze Gdańskie, the coast of Gdańsk (Ger. *Pommerellen*), from Greater Poland (Ślaski 1969, 156 ff.).[75] Only the Land of the Estonians remained in the hands of Denmark between 1219 and 1346.

Corresponding to this situation the nine-volume *Gesta Danorum,* written by Saxo Grammaticus around 1200, gives a brief but tolerably authentic report on the Estonians, whilst indulging in fantasy about the other peoples and incorporating a number of sagas into the work.

Conversion also preceded the Crusades of the *Drang nach Osten* in Prussia.[76] The start of the Prussian mission is usually connected with the 1206 Papal Bull of Pope Innocent III (Labuda 1972, 425). A year later the Cistercians arrived in Prussian Land and conversion was so successful that in Rome the Pope appointed a Cistercian friar called Christian the first Bishop of Prussia in 1215–1216.

[74] It was an unknown territory, some believe that it stretched to the West of Pomorze, others identify it with the land of the Suduvi (Hellmann 1956, 161).

[75] Many scholars see this as the reason or excuse for the outbreak of the Second World War.

[76] From the vast amount of literature about the Eastern European crusades so decisively influential in the history of Europe most commendable is: Biskup–Labuda 1986; Łowmiański 1986, 1989; Urban 1975, 1980, 1981, 1989.

However, Christian's plans failed: in 1228, following his advice, the fifteen member Order of Knights of Dobrzyn (*Milites Chrysti, fratres de Dobrin*) was established, but in 1235, and without leaving any visible traces, it was assimilated into the Teutonic Order. The Bishop himself fell captive to the Prussians, and was only freed in 1238.[77]

The pagan Prussians were engaged in incessant battle with the various Polish and Pomoranian principalities and duchies, as well as with the Duchy of Vladimir-Halicz and other city-states of the Kievan Rus'. The Polish and Pomoranian Crusades in 1222–1223 did not succeed in overwhelming the pagan Prussians, and finally, with the intention of breaking them, Konrad invited the German Teutonic Knights into Prussian Land. (In the end, their southern tribe, the Jatvingians, were ground down by the East and West Slavs, and not by the Germans.)

In 1190, at the time of the siege of Akkon the citizens of Bremen and Lübeck established a German hospital under the name of the Hospital of Jerusalem, an Order which nursed the ill and became the German military Order in 1197–1198 when the town was invaded (*Der Deutsche Orden, Deutscher Ritterorden, Deutschherren, Kreuzritter, Ordo S. Mariae de domo Teutonica, Ordo Theutonicorum cruciferes, Ordo Equitum Teutonoricum*). The knights wore a black cross on their white robes. When Akkon fell in 1291 they transferred their centre of operations to Venice (Łowmiański 1973, 38). The Order of the Cross had vast amounts of property across the whole of Europe, and most of all in the German Reich. In 1211 András II, trying to create a buffer zone against the Kumans gave a vast tract of land to them in the Barcaland, a region in Transylvania, but fourteen years later they had to be driven out because of their depredations.

Konrad called them into Prussia from Transylvania, and offered them the land of Chełmno (archaic *Colmen*, Ger. *Kulm*). In the same year of 1226, through shrewd politics the Grand Master, Herman von Salza, obtained permission from the German Emperor Friedrich II in the famous Golden Bull of Rimini to establish the state of the Order under the Emperor's auspices and to launch a military expedition (for the text of the Bull see Hubatsch 1954, 46–53). However, in 1234 they forged a deed of gift from Konrad saying that the Duke of Mazovia relinquished all lands that were to be conquered in Prussian territories in the future. From that point on the Prussian Land formally became a *patrimonum sancti Petri*

---

[77] Konrad, the Duke of Mazovia, confiscated their lands and in 1237 sent them to the border town of Dobryczin against the Ruthenians (East Slavs) and the Prussians (Jatvingians). However, a year later the knights suffered defeat at the hands of Danilo, Duke of Halicz. They simply fled, reaching Mecklenburg in 1240 (Łowmiański 1973, 70).

(Labuda 1972, 770 ff.).[78] From there, in 1233, the Knights of the Cross established fortresses and towns, such as Elbing in 1237, and Königsberg (in the place of Tvankste the former Prussian village) in 1255 which by rare good fortune could develop peacefully, and during its history it was first ravaged only in 1944 by foreign (Soviet) troops. In this way, they enlarged their numbers not only with western European, mostly German, knights, but also through the immigration of peasants, and thus they built an independent state. Meanwhile they gradually conquered the Prussian tribes, who only lent their name to this state (Prussian Land, *Preussenland*). Finally in 1283 they reached the Lower Nemunas, with Lithuania on the other side.[79] In the meantime, in 1237 the Livonian Order of Knights (originally the Brothers of the Sword) became part of the German Order. (The actual territorial unification of Prussian Land and Livonia, the states of the two Orders, was hindered by the Lithuanian Žemaitians, for which reason their defeat became the principal aim of German politics for centuries to come.)

In delicately presenting the process M. Pollakówna emphasises that the disappearance of the Prussians did not exclusively, and not even primarily, mean extirpation (it is a twentieth-century invention) but mostly their assimilation, through "a loss of the elements of their difference, one by one" (Pollakówna 1958, 207). At first, their aristocracy sided with the Germans, later the peasants, left without the leading stratum responsible for culture, joined them, too (cf. Part Four, Subchapter 8.3.6). As H.-D. Kahl emphasises the German missions had two aims. A positive aim (*Christianisierung*, i.e. to lead the Prussian pagans to Christ), and a negative (*Entpaganisierung*, i.e. to annihilate the pagan belief system) (Kahl 1981, 125). This double aim very soon lost its ethnic character (German versus Prussian) and gained a sociological content. By the late thirteenth century the original Prussian nobility had been ranked into the powers of the Order State to the extent that the peasants of the uprising in 1295 first killed off their own nobles, and only after that did they turn against the Germans (Wenskus 1975, 421). As more recent research supports, "in the fourteenth century a lot of Prussians served as knight brothers, and on several occasions they themselves rose to the rank of the Komtur" (Wenskus 1975, 423).

---

[78] The Knights forged the deed of gift of Kruszwice themselves. It is evident from that that the, presumably Italian, composer of the document calls the Lithuanians 'Saracens', which would be unimaginable from anyone even faintly familiar with the local situation (Łowmiański 1973, 65).

[79] The German drive toward the East apparently collapsed four times because of native uprisings (in Livonia in 1236–1240 and 1260–1267, in Prussian Land in 1242–1249 and 1260–1274), but each time the Pope enlisted new forces. For those who enjoy meditating on predestination in history, the question of what would have happened if the Germans had been chased out of the East Baltic region in the thirteenth century rather than the twentieth is interesting. Could they really have been chased away? Or is 'historical predestination' such that the local rebels were *a priori* doomed to failure?

The most significant source for Prussian history and the activities of the Teutonic Knights is the *Chronica terrae Prussiae,* which knight brother Peter Dusburg wrote between 1324 and 1331 and in which he recounts the events between 1190 and 1326. Due to Nikolaus von Jeroschin, the chaplain of the Order the chronicle soon became a table book. Between 1335 and 1341 he translated Dusburg's Chronicle into German in 27,738 lines for the mostly illiterate Knights Templar who spoke very little or no Latin (*Kronike von Pruzinland*). It could only have an effect in this way, through Jeroschin's mediation. The *Chronicle* only survived in a few manuscripts, none from the Middle Ages, and was first published in print as late as in 1679 (Boockmann 1992, 24).

Peter Dusburg divided the Prussian territory into eleven parts:[80]

1. Kulm and Lubovia (Latin *Colmensis et Lubovia,* Polish *Chełmno* and *Lubawa,* Ger. *Löbau*), which the chronicler erroneously ranks among the Prussian lands, and which were in fact inhabited by Poles. At most there were a very few Balts in the almost uninhabited Lubovia.

2. Pomezania (Lith. *Pamedė,* Polish *Podlesie*), the name means 'forested area'. It was here that the Order began the conquest of Prussian Land in 1233. The local aristocrats sided with the Germans as early as 1249 (SSS, 4, 220).

3. Pogezania (Lith. *Pagudė* < Pruss. *pa-gud*) which the Germans only managed to occupy in 1275 before dividing it between the Marquisate of the Order of Elbing as well as the Polish bishopric duchy of Warmia (SSS, 4, 175).

4. Warmia (Polish and Latin *Warmia,* Latin *Warmienses, Warmi,* Ger. *Ermeland, Ermland,* Lith. *Varmė*) with the Warmi as its inhabitants.[81] The name is etymologised in two ways: Pruss. *wormyan* 'red'; and Lith. *varmas* 'mosquito' (cf. Latin *vermis,* Ger. *Wurm*). In the latter case the naming has a cultic background, as 'worms' are connected with fertility.[82] The Order conquered the land of the Warmi in 1249. Earlier in 1243 Wilhelm of Modena Papal Legate had established the Church Diocese of Warma. As opposed to the four bishoprics of Prussian Land (which formally belonged to the Church district of Riga) and the three other chapters of the cathedral (*Domkapitel*), the Order never managed to assimilate Warmia, and its inhabitants remained stoutly Catholic. The area was extant until the twentieth century (SSS, 6, 330–332).

5. Natanga or Notanga (Lith. *Natangai,* Lat. *Natania*) and its populace the Natangi or Notangi (a name derived from water names) were invaded by the

---

[80] The names mentioned by Dusburg were most completely reconstructed with a commentary by K. Būga and J. Endzelīns (Būga 1924, Endzelīns 1945).

[81] "It is difficult to determine whether this territorial division corresponds to some tribal division" (Sedov 1987, 398). Therefore it is possible that the Warmi (Pogezans, etc.) were a separate tribe, but it is also possible that the name simply indicates the inhabitants of the area.

[82] A. Brückner believes that the Polish *czerw* 'worm' > *czerwień* 'June' is the same type of naming, connected to beekeeping, because bees oviposit in June.

Germans in 1237–1242. Herkus Monte, the chief of the so-called Great Prussian Uprising in 1260, was also a Natangian.

6. Sembia (with Adam of Bremen: *Semland*, on a Swedish runiform script: *simskun, Sambia, Zambia, Samblandia, Semland, Samia*) its people were the Sembi or the Sambi (Lat. *Sambite*, Ger. *Semen, Samen*). The form without the 'b' is a Danish and German simplification. The 1400 km^2 peninsula stretching into the Baltic Sea lies between the Courish Lagoon and the Vistula Bay.[83] The etymology of the name is hazy. According to K. Būga it comes from < Pruss. *sembas* 'one of us' (cf. OSlav. *sebъ*), others believe it is connected to Pruss. *samb* 'corner, horn, cape' (cf. Lith. *žambas*, Polish *ząb* 'cape'); part of the area was called *Sudauischer Winkel* even in the twentieth century.

7. Nadrava, Nadruva or Nadruvia (*Nadrowia, Nadrawia, Nadrowen, Nadrua*) with the Nadruvi or Nadravi (Lat. *Nadrowite*). Its etymology is unclear but it is perhaps related to the Pruss. *druwis* 'carved out tree bark, swarm of bees'. Others believe that it means the banks of the Drava (*na-Drava*), where the Drava would be one of the tributaries of the Pregolja, which has vanished since then (Pėteraitis 1992, 54).

8. Skalva (in a thirteenth-century source *Liber Census Daniae: Scalewo*, Ger. *Schalowen, Schalmia, Schalow, Schalwen*, Lat. *terra Schalvensis*, Russ. *Skalva*) with the Skalvs. It is derived from the Skalve or Skalva (a dried-out tributary of the Nemunas) related to the Lith. *skalauti* 'to rinse, to wash' (Kuzavinis 1965, 87).

There are voices, most determinably represented by V. Sedov, that say that the Skalvs living on either banks of the Lower Nemunas constituted a separate West Baltic tribe with their own burial customs quite different from those seen from Prussian graves between the fifth and thirteenth centuries (Sedov 1987, 7, 409 ff.).

9. Suduva (Sudovia), its inhabitants are believed to be the Jatvingians, which is why it is discussed in the section dealing with them (cf. Part Two, Subchapter 5.7.2).

10. Galindia—its people were the Galindians discussed by Ptolemy. At the time of Dusburg only their name remained.

11. Barta Major and Minor (*major et minor Bartha, Barcia*, Ger. *Bartha, Barten*, Polish *Barcja*)—inhabited by the Barti (Russ. *Borty*). Its etymology is drawn from the name of the rivulet Barta coming from the IE. *bor-/ber-* 'damp place' stem (Pėteraitis 1992, 54). It is also connected to, which is more likely to be the case,

---

[83] The latter used to be Ger. *Frisches Haff* (Friesian Bay), Lith. *Aismares*, which probably carries Tacitus' *aesti* as the first half of its compounding; and also the *Estmere, Eastmere* mentioned by Wulfstan could have referred to the bay.

the Slavic *bartnik, bortnik* 'forest beekeeper' going back to the IE. *bher* 'to drill, to burrow out', in which way it would have the same meaning as '*nadruv*'.[84]

Other sources mention a few other regions: Sasna, a territory between Lubovia and Galindia which was always scarcely populated, and which the Poles and the Knights of the Cross divided between themselves after 1240 (Lith. *Sasna*, Ger. *Sassen*, Polish *ziemia sasińska* or *saska*, Latin *terra Sossinensia*, in other sources: *Sassin, Soysin, Sausyn, Sossen, Czossen, Czossin, Zossin*). All of these go back to a Pruss. *Sasno or *Sasna form related to the Pruss. *sasnis* 'rabbit' (SSS, 5, 75).

Pilsotas was a narrow stretch near the Klaipeda. Its first mention is from 1252 as *terra Pilsaten*. It is a compound from *pil* 'filled up moat' (Latin *pils*, Lith. *pilis*) + *sotas* (Couronian *sata, sats*) 'yard' (Pėteraitis 1992, 51).

5.7.2. The Jatvingians

The Jatvingians should be discussed together with the Prussians.[85] There are three viewpoints on their history: many scholars (mainly linguists) consider Jatvingian a dialect of Prussian; certain Soviet historians believe it to be West Lithuanian, i.e. a Lithuanian dialect, together with Skalvic and Nadruvian; recently some have held it to be a separate West Baltic language close to Prussian (for all this see Kabelka 1982, 36).

The names that Russian and Polish sources at the year 983 refer to as Jatvingian (Pruss. *jatvings*, Latv. *jatvings*, Lith. *jotvingis*, Polish *jaćwięg*, Russ. *yatvyag*, Latin *Jaczwingi, Jazuingi, Jathwingorum, Jatuiti, terra Gettarum, getharum*, etc.) crop up as Suduvian in German chronicles, and are identical with Ptolemy's Sudini (Lith. *suduvis*, Latin *Sudowite, Sudowenses, Sudowienses*, Ger. *Sudawen*; the name of the area is Lith. *Sudava*, Latin *Sudowia, Sudowen*, Ger. *Sudowen*, Polish *Sudwa*). Less frequently, from the thirteenth century the name *Dainava* (*terra Deynowe*) appears in Lithuanian deeds of gift, as synonymous to Jatvingia, Jatva, with the inhabitants called the Dainavi. Finally, Polish chroniclers used the name *polek-*

---

[84] The Hungarian words *barkács, barkácsol* 'handyman, to fix', which our etymological dictionary considers to be "a word family of unknown origin" (Benkő 1967, 251) come from the same stem. *Barkács*, in its first occurrence it meant 'honey trader' or 'forest beekeeper' (1402: *Paulus dictus Barkach*). In the Hungarian language the entire terminology associated with beekeeping is loaned from Slavic. The Slavic word *barcie* means 'artificial nook or churn carved or burnt out of a wood' and from that Hun. *barkács* is the 'person who drills and carves'. In this way, the meaning of the Hungarian word finds its Indo-European roots.

[85] The name is 'Jatving' or 'Jotving' depending on how the river name from which it comes from is reconstructed: *Jotva (K. Būga), or **Jat(u)va* (J. Otrębski, J. Ochmański) (Ochmański 1970, 204).

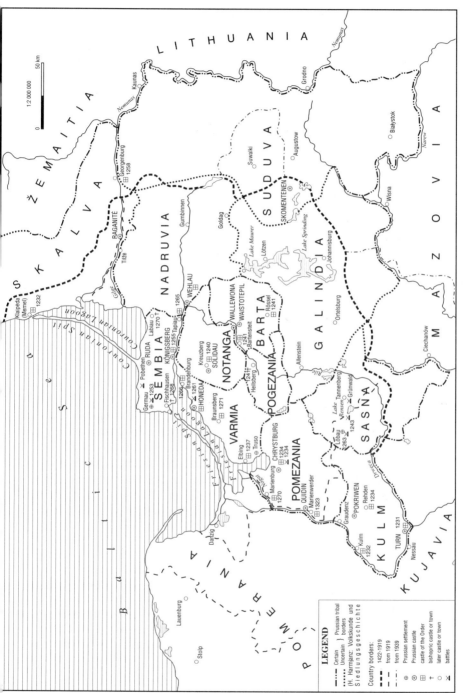

Map 6. Prussian lands in the thirteenth century

LITHUANIA

ŽEMAITIA

SKALVA

NADRUVIA

SUDUVA

SKOMENTENEN

GALINDIA

SEMBIA

NOTANGA

BARTA

WEHLAU

WALLEWONA

WAISTOTEPIL

POGEZANIA

VARMIA

CHRYSTBURG

SASNA

POMEZANIA

POKRIWEN

KULM

KUJAVIA

MAZOVIA

POMERANIA

Klaipėda
(Memel) 1232

Georgenburg
1258

RAGANITĖ
Tilžė

RUDA
Labau
1270

Pobethen

KÖNIGSBERG
Tapiau
1255

Germau 1253
Fischhausen
† 1288

HONEDA

Braunsberg
1271

Kreuzburg

SOLIDAU
1240

Brandenburg
1261

Bartenstein
1241

Rössel
1241

Hellsberg

Allenstein

Orteisburg

Johannisburg

Lötzen

Goldag

Gumbinnen

Suwalki

Augustow

Białystok

Wisna

Ciechanów

Grodno

Kaunas

Elbing

Trutso
1237

Marienburg

QUIDIN
1270

Marienwerder
1323

Graudenz

Rehden
1234

Kulm
1232

TURN 1231

Nessau

Löbau
1263

Tannenberg
Grünwald
1243

Lauenburg

Stolp

Datzig

Lake Sprinding

Lake Maurer

Lake Wenzen

Nemunas

Narew

Drweca

1265

1266

1261

1241

1243

LEGEND

Country borders:

Certain } Prussian tribal
Uncertain } borders

(H. Harmjanz: Volkskunde und
Siedlungsgeschichte

1422–1919
from 1919
from 1939

⊕ Prussian settlement
⊕ Prussian castle
⊞ castle of the Order
† bishopric castle or town
○ later castle or town
✕ battles

san[86] (Latin *Pollexiani*, Polish *Połeksanie*, the region is *Pollexia, Poleksia*). The name comes from the river name *Łek* (*Ełk*, Ger. *Lyck*),[87] just as the other three appellatves can be related to water names (Nalepa 1964).

All four names are at times used synonymously in some sources, and also as the names of different tribes. A document from Emperor Sigismund in 1420 says: "*terram vocatam Suderlant alias Jetuen*" (cited in Gerullis 1921, 44). The foreword of the first Prussian catechism differentiates between the Prussian (Jatvingian) and the Suduvian languages in saying that the language of the Suduvi whom the Teutonic Knights forced into Sembia is "somewhat simpler, yet still they understand the Prussian language of the catechism" (Mažiulis 1966–81/II, 67). S. Goebel, a doctor, wrote about the deported Suduvi in his work (Goebel, *Histori vnd Eigendlicher Bericht von Herkommen, vrsprung vnd vielfeltigem brauch des börnsteins*, 1566) that "their language is not totally alien from that of the Lithuanians... they live on the coast and that frosty place has left its mark upon them, a frostiness which the Holy Scriptures otherwise associate with the Jews. Therefore some are of the opinion that they actually are the people who, after the terrible destruction of Jerusalem when many Jews escaped by boat, the winds scattering them here and there, survived on this part of the Earth, and earn their living through fishing. Especially because in their ancient mourning songs they often repeat and wail the name Jeru, which is like Jerusalem" (Mannhardt 1936, 278–279).[88] A recently discovered thirteenth-century description (*Descriptiones terrarum*) mentions the Jatvingians as a separate tribe (*Jetwesia, Ituesi*) (Ochmański 1985, 108).

Consequently the term Jatvingian has a double meaning. In a narrow sense it means the Jatvingian tribe occupying the south-western part of the region, while in a wider sense it indicates "the entire tribal federation, including: the Suduvi, north of the Jatvingians; the Dainavi, to the East; and the Poleksanians along the River Ełk, to the Southwest" (Vanagas 1974, 20).

All this can be explained by the Polish and East Slavic expansion beginning in the tenth century as well as the expeditions of the German Knights which affected different groups among the Jatvingians. The East Slavs and the Poles first encountered the Jatvingian tribe in its narrower sense, so they extended that name to the entire tribal federation, while the Teutonic Knights coming from the North

---

[86] Most probably first to use it was W. Kadlubek, though as a result of a false comparison (*Historia Polonica*, Book IV, Chapter 19) (Łowmiański 1966, 89).

[87] The 'original' name of the river was *Łek* (< Baltic **lukas* 'waterlilly'), and due to an incorrect division syllabification it became *Ełk*: *we Łku* ('in *Łek*') > *w Ełku* > nom. *Ełk*.

[88] Several later German authors encountered the word 'jeru' in Latvian and Estonian songs. It transpired that it came from an Estonian love song, it has nothing to do with Jerusalem, and its correct form is *jörru* (Mannhardt 1936, 279).

came upon the Suduvi first and used their name for the whole area.[89] Meanwhile the tribal federation itself was at times looser at others times stronger.

Due to the incessant warring the territory was largely forsaken. This makes the distinction of the Jatvingian language almost impossible even among place names, because they are the same as either the Prussian or the Lithuanian, and in the latter instance whether or not it bears the influence of the later immigrating Lithuanians can hardly be determined.

The extinction of the Jatvingians—to which Poles, Lithuanians, and Germans all contributed, albeit unevenly—can be connected with an exact year (though, of course it was a process across a few decades at least). Skurda (*Scurdo capitaneus alterius partis Sudowiae*—cited in Kabelka 1982, 35) the last leader emigrated to Lithuania with his people in 1283 to escape from the Teutonic Knights. Smaller or larger groups had also emigrated before, which explains the place names around Vilnius beginning with the stem *dainas-*. Many were deported by the Germans, for example one thousand six hundred people to the north-western part of Sembia, where thus emerged the earlier mentioned 'Suduvian corner' (*Sudaischer Winkel*). The Suduvi had preserved the characteristic differences between their dialects, customs, and costumes and the other local inhabitants, even a hundred years later, so much so that they did not enter into marriage with them.

The southern part of the Jatvingian region was assimilated by the Poles. The language seems to have vanished completely in the sixteenth or seventeenth century, but a certain regional flavour remained for a long time. In the 1860 poll the southern region of the governance of Grodno, thirty thousand people who considered themselves Jatvingian were among those living in the swamp area and the depth of the forest region of Białowież—they were all Pravoslavs speaking their Belarusian mother tongue with a Lithuanian accent (Gaučas 1974).

The forest of Białowież had further surprises: it is possible that in 1983 Z. Zinkevičius came across the earliest written Jatvingian linguistic remnant, a Polish list of Jatvingian words with 215 items.[90] The professor of Vilnius very

---

[89] This type of naming was not uncommon. For example the insignificant Greek tribe could lend its name to the entire Hellas, because the Romans encountered them first. In the same way, the French name *'Allemagne'* signified the whole of Germany, though originally it referred to a small tribe, the Alemans, that is the Swabians (Nalepa 1964, 43).

[90] The couple of thin, hand written vocabulary books were attached to the end of a book in Latin. V. Zinov a certain young Belarusian man, an amateur archaeologist bought the book from some old man in a village in the forest of Białowież. The following is written on the front of the manuscript: *Pogańskie gwary z Narewa* (the regional pagan expressions of the Narewian dialect—The River Narew was the presumed southern border of Jatvingia). The young man copied the faded and washed away text into a note book, inasmuch as he could work it out. At which point he was conscripted into the army. His parents, who disapproved of their son's archaeological activities, threw the original into the bin. Consequently, the young man could only offer his own copy of the original to Z. Zinkevičius (Zinkevičius 1984).

cautiously declared that it was possibly Jatvingian rich in Lithuanian, but in the same way that it is Lithuanian built on a foundation of Jatvingian (Zinkevičius 1984–94/II, 53).

From this it seems the Jatvingian (Suduvian) tribal federation was one of the separate regions within Prussia. The other, economically and politically the strongest, was the area of the Sembians whose influence affected the Skalvs, the Nadruvians, and the Natangians. The Prussians of this area became Lithuanianised. After A. Bezzenberger Prussian and Lithuanian place names are generally differentiated on the basis of whether the Pruss. *ape, kaimis, garbis* 'river, farm, hillock' or the Lith. *upė, kiemas, kalnas* (with the same meaning) are apparent in them. It is practically impossible to draw a border between them because the regions that lost their population in the wars and epidemics (and which from the seventeenth century were called Lithuania Minor or Prussian Lithuania) were later occupied by Lithuanians, and it cannot be determined whether the Lithuanian place names are original or are the result of this more recent immigration.

The question is further complicated by the disagreement among historians even about the issue of whether there had indeed been Lithuanian immigration, or whether the Lithuanians had originally lived there on the lands of the Nadruvians and the Skalvs. The territory in question was of about thirty to forty thousand square kilometres, thought of as an uninhabited swamp region with vast dense forests, which Latin sources refer to as (*vasta*) *deserta*, (*magna*) *solitudo*, and German sources as *Wildnis*. There were no settlements there but there were nomadic people (*siedlungsleer, aber nicht menschenleer*). Whether these people were Skalvs, Nadruvians, or Lithuanians (or mixed) is difficult to decide because when the Order lost the Thirteen Year War in 1466, the region left in their possession was, for the most part, exactly this Wilderness. For this reason the last Grand Masters of the Order, and later the first rulers of the Duchy of Prussia, endeavoured to populate it, with Lithuanians amongst others. (For an excellent summary of the matter see Jakštas 1968.[91])

Presumably the Warmi, Pogezans, and Pomezans, and perhaps even the Barts who lived in the neighbourhood of the West Slavic Pomoranian and Mazurian people, formed a tribal federation. They were assimilated by the Poles in the same way as the Sembians were by the Lithuanians: firstly, before the Teutonic Knights arrived in 1230, the Poles had crossed the Vistula, the border between the Slavs and the Balts, then later from the fifteenth century as the population of the region

---

[91] In the 1930s the Prussian Lithuanian border of the Middle Ages became a hot political question, because what used to be Prussian was considered to be due to Germany, and what was Lithuanian to Lithuania. The question carries political overtones even in recent times. The contemporary Lithuanian historian disparaged the Lithuanian linguists from between the two World Wars who considered the Skalvs, the Nadruvians, and the Suduvians to be Prussians, saying that, "they had studied in Germany not so long before" (Merkys in Jablonskis 1979, 306) meaning that they had been infected by this anti-[Lithuanian] nationalist ideas.

became thinner 'thanks to' the German invasion Poles (Mazurians) were settled there.

Finally the last Prussian tribal unit was formed by the Galindians. Their extinction began earliest, having already commenced in the seventh century, and was accelerated by the expeditions of the eleventh and twelfth centuries, and most likely peaked in the Suduvian military campaign in the twelfth and thirteenth centuries. In any case, the Teutonic Knights did not have to subjugate the Galindians. Like the Wildnis, their huge forest area North of Mazovia was de-populated.

CHAPTER 6

THE BALTIC PEOPLES

6.1. The Prussians

The Prussian State, only loosely a dependency of the Pope and the Emperor (although it was formally a part of the Holy Roman Empire until 1701) conducted an aggressive foreign policy and was locked in continual warfare with the Lithuanians, the Poles, and the East Slavs. In the early fifteenth century it was inhabited by 140,000 Prussians, 140,000 Poles, and 200,000 Germans from among whom emerged a people attached to the new state with a 'New Prussian' consciousness. These were the *Preussen*.[1]

An increasingly secular society contributed greatly to the development of Prussian consciousness and the leader of this society was a Grand Master who moved from Venice to Marienburg (Polish Malbork) on the banks of the Nogat in 1309.[2] The high point of this process was the so-called Prussian Federation of the various orders delegated by earldoms and towns around the country in 1440. The Federation requested support from Poland against the Teutonic Order of Knights. In 1456, during the Thirteen Year War, the Grand Master was forced to transfer his seat to Königsberg. The War and its resolution in 1466 through the Peace of Toruń resulted in the division of Prussianland. Royal Prussia emerged (Ger. *Land Preussen Königlichen Antheils*, Polish *Prusy Królewskie*) as a part of the Polish Kingdom, along with Pomorze of Gdańsk which was conquered (or re-conquered) by the Germans in 1308, Kulmland, Warmia, and big cities like Gdańsk, Elbląg, and Toruń. The Prussianland of the Order, and following its secularisation the Duchy of Prussia (*Preussen Herzoglichen Antheils* or *Herzogthum Preussen*, Polish *Prusy Książęce*, Latin *Ducali Borussia* according to E. Stella's contemporaneously constructed word from Ptolemy's *Boruskoi*) became a vassal state of Poland.

---

[1] It is noteworthy that elsewhere the word means 'cockroach': Polish *Prusak*, Russ. *prusak*, Latv. *prusaks*, Lith. *prūsokas*.

[2] The Order had three types of member: knight brothers (due to celibacy their number went from one thousand to three hundred between the mid-fourteenth century and 1454) who constituted the army of the Order; priest brothers who were responsible for spiritual and political matters; servant brothers who were mostly from the middle classes.

For the best works on the development of Prussian consciousness see Maschke 1955, and Pollakówna 1958.

One very important factor is that throughout the sixteenth century the ideologists of both Prussian lands considered themselves to be Prussian, a unity further expressed in common parliamentary sessions. Clearly the Duchy of Prussia attempted to free itself from vassaldom, and when the war, instigated by the Grand Master Albrecht Hohenzollern, did not succeed it came to a watershed. Taking the advice of Martin Luther and the Poles into account, Albrecht linked the renewal of his oath of allegiance with the secularisation of the state thereby establishing the world's first Lutheran state. In 1525, as the first ruler of this state, he renewed his oath of fealty to his uncle, the Polish King Sigismund the Old, at the city square of Kraków, the Rynek.[3] During the Prussian surrender, renowned as *hold pruski* (painted by Matejko, it would later warm the hearts of many Poles) a symbolic incident occurred. An ageing lesser nobleman cut the Cross from a knight's robe—which of course now reminds us of the Soviet symbol cut from flags in the twentieth-century eastern European revolutions. Livonia, the other Order State, did not follow the example of Prince Albrecht (although Riga was the first town in the German Empire to be totally 'infected' by Lutheranism). The change would be instigated by Gotthard Kettler as late as 1561.[4]

The secularisation of the two Order States was inherent in their establishment. They came into being to baptise the pagans without anyone considering what the fate of these territories would be once all the pagans were baptised (Ivinskis 1933, 433).

The two parts of the Prussian *Doppelland* developed differently.[5] The royal territory grew ever closer to Poland, and the *Polak* and *Prusak* gradually came to be the same thing. Then in 1772 *Rzeczpospolita* was divided and the royal territory was rejoined to Prussia, which had in the meantime become powerful (Gdańsk and Toruń only joined in 1793). On the other hand, the territory of the Duchy strove towards its own independence, even though in 1626 its population was still fifty percent Polish. Albrecht made Königsberg, where he founded a university in 1544, its capital and enforced German immigration. A determining turning point came in 1563 when Albrecht, from the Ansbach branch of the Hohenzollerns, squeezed an assurance from Augustus Sigismund the Polish king, that if his line were to die out, the Brandenburg branch of the Hohenzollerns would inherit the throne. That is what happened in 1618, when Friedrich Wilhelm, Prince Elector of Brandenburg and of the House of Hohenzollern, which incidentally had become

---

[3] The first inter-state contract with a Lutheran state also indicates how much the division of the state and the church had widened. Jagello, the grandfather of Sigismund the Old, did not dare to accept the Czech crown from the heretic Hussites in the early fifteenth century, because he feared the Pope (Bogucka 1982, 102).

[4] There is a striking similarity between Prussia and Livonia, two states of the Order both vassal to the Polish–Lithuanian state. "A strong German state centre remained in both of them; like wealthy Danzig in the South, Riga in the North walked its own path" (Wittram 1954, 79).

[5] For more see Małłek 1987, 10–18.

Calvinist, succeeded to the throne. He linked Brandenburg with Berlin as its centre and Prussianland, and utilising the Swedish–Polish war (1655–1666), he renounced the oath of fealty to Poland. His son Friedrich had himself crowned in 1701—not yet as the King of Prussia, only as the King in Prussia "*in Preussen*". From that time on Prussianland was called Prussia, and after Königsberg, its capital was Berlin.

From 1772, when Prussia acquired Pomorze from the Polish–Lithuanian Republic which they called Western Prussia (although Prussians had never lived there), the remaining territory was Eastern Prussia from the Vistula to the Nemunas encompassing the former Duchy of Prussia and Warmia (Nitsch 1954, 313). (The north-eastern part of East Prussia where Lithuanian was spoken had been called Lithuania Minor or Prussian–Lithuania since the seventeenth century.) On this thirty-seven thousand square kilometre area lived the remaining indigenous Prussians, immigrant Lithuanians, Poles, and Germans. After the plague, which took more than a third of the six hundred thousand inhabitants between 1709 and 1711, the Protestants of Salzburg and the Huguenots of France arrived and were gradually Germanised.

Germanisation increased until the Second World War. There were two brief intermezzos, that of the so-called 'Polish corridor' of the First World War, as well as Klaipėda which the Lithuanians took in 1923. By the end of the Second World War the entire area became part of Germany which expansion was curtailed by its defeat in the War.

Schematically we can say that the history of Prussia was: Baltic Prussian until the appearance of the Crusaders; it was Polish and German from 1466 and through the entire sixteenth and seventeenth centuries; and from 1701 it was German (Małłek 1971).

As it turns out from W. Wippermann's comprehensive monograph, too, the evaluation of German state formations and the *Drang nach Osten* both corresponded to this historical schema (Wippermann 1979). In the Middle Ages, the German and Polish standpoints conflicted, ultimately the Poles were victorious because they won the fight for Western Prussia. Consequently, many historians, even those who were German, accepted the thesis that the Germans had had no right to initiate the crusades. This view strengthened after the peace of Westphalia, in itself a milestone in international law. The historians of the eighteenth-century enlightenment (Herder, for example) unambiguously opposed the crusades. As if to counterbalance this, the romantic nationalists (J. Voigt in particular) saw a Christian civilising mission in Germanisation from whence a straight road led to modern times, where the Soviet, East German, and (partly) the Polish historians viewed the Nazis as the direct (though opposite in values) cultural heirs of the Crusaders.

6.2. The Latvians

In the case of the Latvian people (Heinricus interchangeably uses the words *gens*, *populus*, or *nation*) German reign developed within the framework of the German state referred to as the Livonian Confederation. Two events determinably influenced the strengthening of this state. One was the victory of Alexander Nevsky, Prince of Novgorod, over the German Knights in 1242 on the ice of Lake Peipsi, which froze the north-eastern border between Germany and Russia until the end of the Second World War.

The other determining event was the battle near Saule[6] in 1236 when the Brothers of the Sword (with soldiers from Livonia, Letgalia, Estonia, and even Pskov) suffered a major defeat at the hands of the Žemaitian–Zemgalians. As a result, under the name Livonian Order of Knights, they were (at least formally) assimilated into the Teutonic Knights which had in the meantime been established in Prussianland.[7]

F. Benninghoven considers the battle at Saule to have been a "moment of world history..." "The dream of the Order's independence and of Livonia's hegemony went to the dogs. At the same time the opportunity of establishing a land bridge to Prussianland and the German Empire by merging with the Teutonic Order was lost. The Brothers of the Sword failed to achieve their great target. The history of the north-eastern region would have taken an utterly different direction had the outcome of the battle been different. Possible consequences might have been a single, uninterrupted state for the Order from the Vistula to the Narwa, an earlier, perhaps even a thirteenth-century end to the Crusades, or a strong Catholic Church influence on Russia by avoiding the West–East church division" (Benninghoven 1965, 346).

The defeat at Saule was not a military catastrophe for the Brothers of the Sword since they had already experienced and overcome a similar bloodbath in Estland in 1223. However, in 1236 the Teutonic Order was already in existence and leaching away the reserves of the German Reich. Consequently the Brothers of the Sword were no longer able to compensate for the losses.

The Brothers of the Sword and later the Livonian Order competed with the Order of Prussianland as well as with Riga. From 1226 the town received a third of the conquered territories, but in 1305 the Sword Bearers were forced to cede the castle of Riga to the archbishopric along with all their rights to it. From the

---

[6] Perhaps it is today's Šiauliai in Lithuania. For the question see Gudavičius 1988.

[7] H. Łowmiański believes that (from a German perspective) it had the advantage that "it made it easier to align aggression" (Łowmiański 1961, 145).

late thirteenth century the town became a member of the Hanseatic League which had total control over maritime trade.[8]

The Germans continued their conquests despite their defeat at Saule and within a century they created a state. In theory it was the fief of the German Emperor, but was in practice directed by the Grand Master whose seat was first at Riga and later in Cēsis.

The Livonian Confederation had five ecclesiastical mini-states: the German Order State of sixty-seven thousand square kilometres which was the leading force of the Confederation; the Archbishopric of Riga[9] (18,000 square km); the Bishopric of Kurzeme (4500 square km); the Estonian Bishoprics of Dorpat (Tartu) and of Saaremaa–Läänema (the latter from 1346 when the Order bought it from the Danes).

There was incessant warfare between the Order and the Bishop of Riga (who from 1243 oversaw not only the Livonian but the Prussian Church districts of Kulm, Pomezania, Warmia, and Sembia), and the increasingly powerful town of Riga, from 1282 a member of the Hanseatic League "almost free,... but where the Grand Master and the archbishop had their seats" (Mattiesen 1972, 50). From 1410, the time of the first *Landstag*, this conflict gained a parliamentary framework. The leading social stratum was the Brotherhood of Knights (*Ritterschaft*), which from the fifteenth century only nobles could enter and which at that time numbered four or five hundred. The *Landschaft* stratum encompassed the Lords, freemen, and craftsmen. The subjugated Undeutsch (non-German) constituted the strata of servants (*Knechtschaft*).

The question arises as to how, under German rule and influence, the Estonians and Latvians preserved their ethnic individuality, while the Prussians, seemingly in the same situation, were completely assimilated. The most plausible explanation is that German peasants arrived in Prussian territory very early, and, like the native inhabitants, lived as serfs from the mid sixteenth century, while in the eastern part of the Baltic area German peasants only began to appear from the

---

[8] The leading powers of the Hanseatic League which functioned between 1282 and 1669 were the Vend cities with Lübeck at the forefront (followed by Rostock, Wismar, Stralsund, Greifswald) which the Prussians joined (with Elbing-Elbląg, Thorn-Toruń, Königsberg, Bransberg, Kulm-Chelmno and later in the fourteenth century developed Danzig-Gdańsk) (cf. Schildhauer 1984). There were also dozens of other cities not on the Baltic Sea, the most westerly being Utrecht, the most easterly Tartu, and the most southern Erfurt. The League had a foreign representative office in several other places such as Bergen, London, Pskov, or Novgorod (D'yakonov 1994, 132).

[9] Once more, theoretically, the entire Confederation was under the Archbishopric of Riga, which of course was under Papal auspices, but the Roman Pope was just as distant as the German Emperor. "In the Middle Ages power was only effective in direct proximity, and the ruler had to continuously travel around his territories to show himself in each corner of it" (Schünemann 1937, 31).

eighteenth century. Latvian unification occurred earlier than the attempt to Germanise them. Consequently the lord–serf opposition took on a 'national' undertone. Although in serfdom, an ethnic identity was able to emerge from which a consciousness of national identity would develop by the late nineteenth century (Zeids 1980, 61). The collective name for the Livonians was 'Undeutsch' as opposed to the German town dwellers, thus implying 'village dweller'. In Pomerania and Prussianland, the two other territories of the Order, villages developed with German rights, whereas in Latvia they were *latifundium* (Hellmann 1954, 237).[10]

Hunfalvy establishes that in the last third of the nineteenth century among the inhabitants of the "three duchies, the Estonian, Livonian, and Couronian provinces" there were 200,000 Germans and "the other 1,650,000 were non-Germans that is Latvian, Estonian, and Livonian... [and, he warns] German here means lord" (Hunfalvy 1871/I, 57–58).

The Livonian Confederation existed until 1561, and so its territory was referred to as *Alt-Livland* (Old Livonia) until that year. At the end of the sixteenth century the area was rearranged as a result of the so-called Livonian War (that the Livonian Order of Knights lost and thus finally disappeared), the Reformation, the Counter Reformation, the destructive Russian intrusions, and the Polish–Lithuanian and Swedish interference. Its northern part became the Duchy of Estonia,[11] first under Swedish and then, from 1721, Russian rule. Its southern and western areas, that is from Zemgale and Kurland became the Duchy of Kurzeme and Zemgale. The central region that forms the southern part of today's Estonia, Latvian Vidzeme and Latgale retained the name Livonia, though officially it was called *Ducatus Transdunensis* 'Duchy beyond the Daugava'. The triad of the Baltic Sea provinces (*Ostseelande*) that is Livland, Estland, and Kurland began to replace the term Livonia used up to that point.

The Latvian people evolved from the various tribes by the seventeenth century. The most apparent signs of their appearance were the 'creation' of the term 'Latvian' for those who spoke the Latvian language, and also that the German priests had to establish their literacy in Latvian because of them. Perhaps the greatest obstacle in further development toward nationhood was that with the disintegration of Old Livland the Latvians and Letgalians, who thus far had lived under alien rule but were still in the same state, were pushed into three different state formations.

---

[10] Only the Latgalians, the largest tribe who were subjugated as late as the fourteenth century, had an individual name. The names of other smaller peoples that were later assimilated into Latvia were only references to geographical location, for example the term *Curonus* meant 'German in Kurzeme', or *Zemgale* meant 'German in Zemgale'.

[11] Here the term *Herzogtum* is always used to mean state-legislature.

6.2.1. Kurzeme

Kurland, or, to use its full title the Duchy of Kurzeme and Zemgale (1561–1795) was the vassal of Polish–Lithuanian *Rzeczpospolita*, but effectively an independent state which only required the consent of the Polish monarch to declare war or make peace.[12] In this way, their situation was similar to that of the Duchy of Prussia after 1525. Prince Albrecht's role was occupied by Gotthard Kettler, a Westphalian noble from the Ruhr region. He became the first secular ruler of the new state having been the last Grand Master of the Livonian Order of Knights, his subjects converting to Lutheranism alongside him. His dynasty ruled until its extinction in 1737. Thereafter, the family of Johann Biron (allegedly a former stable-boy) came to the throne of a republic noblesse and as the favourite of the Russians, an indication of the stronger Russian influence. To summarise the history of the principality concisely, the nobility, the infamous 'barons of Kurland' gradually took a hold on absolute power over their native subjects, a power which was not limited even after the area was formally joined to Russia in 1795[13] (its name became the governance of Kurzeme and its population were called *kurzem-nieks* 'the Kurzemes', including those who lived in Zemgale—Zeids 1992, 114).

6.2.2. The Duchy beyond the Daugava

The Duchy beyond the Daugava, also vassal to the Polish–Lithuanian state, Livonia in the strict sense of the word, did not remain intact for long. The Swedes declared war in 1600. At the close of the war the peace contracts of Altmark in 1629, and of Oliva in 1660 which reinforced Altmark, declared two thirds of the area, that is the southern part of Estonia and the whole of Vidzeme (*Liefland*) to be a Swedish protectorate. As an independent administrative unit the Duchy beyond the Daugava lived in peace for a mere twenty years of its sixty-eight-year existence. For the bulk of its life alien troops roamed the small state. In 1621 the Swedish King Gustavus Adolphus II occupied Riga, and in 1710 Czar Peter I triumphed over Charles XII. The ninety years of the 'Swedish era' was probably the brightest period in the history of Latvia, both in an economic and a cultural sense. In 1632 Gustavus Adolphus II turned the secondary school of Tartu into the *Academia Gustaviana*, thus establishing the first Lutheran university in the

---

[12] It was independent to the extent that it was the only coloniser of the Baltic region. In the mid-seventeenth century Kurland bought Tobago in Central America which it exchanged soon after for Gambia in West Africa.

[13] After the demise of Old Livonia, German privileges were established by the decree of Augustus Sigismund in a letter in 1561. Both the original and its official copy have now been lost and consequently whether it ever existed or not is debated (Zeids 1992, 95).

Baltic region. At the behest of the Swedish king E. Glück, a pastor from Saxony (1652–1705), learnt Latvian for over five years (1685–1689) and translated the entire *Bible*[14] which became the most important Latvian book for nearly two hundred years.[15]

When Czar Peter I took Vidzeme–Livonia into the Russian Empire in 1710, his troops ran amok and in the entire region only ninety thousand people survived. Even at this time the monopoly of the German nobility remained unchanged, because in the eighteenth century among the most influential actors in Russian major politics there were many Baltic Germans. In the 'Russian era' despite the 'second serfdom' the breeze of the enlightenment did reach Vidzeme with its gentler happier style similar to that of the Jacobite Enlightenment which had been brought about with the works of G. Merkel (1769–1850). This softer version was called *herrnhutism*[16] and won over the Latvian peasantry *en masse*. It was basically a much milder form of pietism than that of the original Hussitism. For example G. F. (Vecais–Elder) Stenders, a priest from the Netherlands (1714–1796) could also be viewed as pietist and founded Latvian literature, making up somewhat for the gap between generations. Alongside E. Glück he was to become a key figure in sustaining Latvian culture.

Although from 1795 all Latvian territory fell into the hands of the Russian Empire, German rule endured for a long time. "At the beginning of Alexander II's reign approximately 125,000 Germans completely dominated politically, economically, and culturally the nearly one million Latvians and Estonians of Livland, Estland, and Kurland" (Haltzel 1972, 143). The situation only changed after the abolition of serfdom in 1861 and even more so after the Polish–Lithuanian uprising of 1863–1864. The Czarist regime launched mass Russification.[17] The Slavophile J. Samarin's pamphlet of 1868 spectacularly documents the period and is an exemplar of Russian nationalist demagogy. C. Schirren, a professor at Dorpat replied on behalf of the Baltic Germans, still insisting on the autonomy of

---

[14] In the meantime the Latvian theologian and physician J. Reiter was forbidden to translate, because he had translated and published excerpts from the *Gospel according to Matthew* without the permission of the censors. In 1974 a single copy of Reiters' work was found in the Library of the University of Uppsala.

[15] J. Endzelīns believes that until 1860 literary language changed very little after Glück's translation (Endzelīns 1930, 59).

[16] On his land in Berthelsdorf in Saxony Baron Nikolaus von Zinzendorf of Vidzeme permitted the Moravian Brethren to build Herrnhut their model settlement, which lent its name to the movement. It found numerous followers not only in Livonia but also in Russia, North America, West Indies, and Greenland. For its Livonian history cf. Schaudinn 1937, 25 ff.

[17] Although the abolition of serfs occurred in 1817 and 1819, freedom was only nominal. The Latvians appropriately called the new situation a 'bird's freedom' (*putnu brīvība*), because while the bonds of the feudal peasant were lifted and they could go wherever they wished, the land remained in the hands of the earlier owners.

the *Ostseeprovinzen* and the German role of the '*Kulturträger*' which their historical rights sufficiently underpinned and sanctioned.

It was in this state of affairs, caught between two enemies, that the national awakening of the Latvians set out. It was the movement of the so-called 'young Latvians' which, in the last decades of the nineteenth century, became the 'new current' (*jaunā strāva*). Its minimal aim (and until 1917 its foremost aim) was to achieve autonomy for the territory occupied by Latvians, an area which they began to refer to as 'Latvija'. Due to its advanced industrial base, a characteristic feature of Latvian development was that the endeavours toward independence soon intertwined with the strong waves of socialism and the workers' movement (Riga was the third biggest industrial centre of the Russian Empire after Moscow and Petersburg). Germany and Russia lost a great deal of their lifeblood in the First World War and fell into the chaos of revolution. The Balts managed to get a toehold in the vacuum of power (or rather the narrow stretch) that emerged between the two countries, and thus, with this fortuitous situation on the international scene, an independent Latvia, Estonia, and Lithuania could emerge in 1918 [though it is true that the three states "had come into this world as more or less unwanted children" (Anderson 1974, 18)].

From 1934 the initial multi-party (too multi) democracy was changed to a moderate dictatorship established in a presidential putsch. The independence of the country was first ended in 1940 by the first Soviet invasion, then the 1941 German invasion, then second Soviet invasions in 1944, and was only regained in 1991.

6.2.3 Latgale

Under the *Rzeczpospolita*, what remained from Livonia in the strict sense was the eastern region of the river Aiviekste (*Livonia australis*). Until 1918, in the so-called Polish era of Latvia's history,[18] the region developed in a very different way from the other three territories occupied by Latvians, that is from Kurzeme, Zemgale, and Vidzeme. From the point of its division it was referred to by the Polish name of *Inflanty Polskie* (Lat. *Livonia Polonica*) or simply *Inflanty* (< sixteenth-century *Iflanty* < fifteenth-century *Liflanty* < *Liefland* < *Livland*). In the early twentieth century the words of the chronicles from the Middle Ages were

---

[18] The choice of words is not precise. More accurately it should be referred to as the Polish–Lithuanian era, because the territory was expressly a vassal dependency of Lithuania from 1561, and from 1569 to the common Polish–Lithuanian *Rzeczpospolita*. Of course the importance of the Lithuanians gradually diminished.

refreshed for the territory occupied by the Letgalian tribe,[19] and since then it has been called Latgale.

The differences in Latgale's development were evident from the outset as was first brought to light by M. Taube, and then in his footsteps the excellent B. Brežgo's first history of Latgale in the Latgalian language (Taube 1935, 1938; Brežgo, *Latgolas pagōtne*, – Latgale's past 1943). The Germans conquered the western Latvian region relatively quickly and easily,[20] whereas it was only in the fourteenth century that they managed a military occupation of the eastern parts where the Lithuanians had been lords in the thirteenth century. (In the meantime, Riga occasionally supported the Lithuanians and consequently there was almost civil war.) In this way Latgale "carried the signs of a strong Lithuanian blood link and East Slavic cultural influence very early on" (Hellmann 1954, 243).

The emergence of the Inflanty meant 'Polonisation' along with Catholicism, widening the gap between the already separate paths, and the region broke away from the other parts of Livonia for more than 350 years. From 1667 the public administrative unit called the Principality of Inflanty (*Księstwo Inflantskie*) was governed by the voivode who chaired in Daugavpils and was appointed by the Warsaw Sejm. It was the seat of the bishopric from 1685 and the Jesuites, the leading group of the Counter Reformation moved there from Swedish occupied Riga. In 1753 in Catholic Vilnius they printed the first Latgalian text, a translation of a collection of sermons (Gāters 1977, 12).

Polonisation meant a number of things: an established Polish aristocratic *latifundium* system; the institution of the serfdom as late as 1861; the consequent underdevelopment of economic and social systems; a crude barbarity compared with other Latvian areas (which is characterised in the Latgalians' Latvian slang-name *čangalieši* 'people from the forest's end'). Conditions sank further when in 1772 the Polish–Lithuanian state was first divided and Russia grabbed the territory. In 1802 it was ordered under the governance of Vitebsk. From 1863 it became part of the governance of Vilnius and was burdened with the same vindictive sanctions as the provinces inhabited by the Lithuanians: printing books using the Latin alphabet was outlawed until as late as 1904; the prosecution of the loathed Poles resulted in culture undergoing intense Russification; primary education was in Russian; the tens of thousands of peasants who left their Catholic religion and converted to the Pravoslav belief were offered land; and so on. In the last third of the nineteenth century the Latgalian renaissance movement began under such circumstances. It was initiated by G. Manteuffel (1832–1916) a liberal landlord

---

[19] As mentioned at the discussion of the Leitis people, in the opinion of the majority of J. Endzelīns and his followers the tribal territory was much bigger.

[20] Only Tālava remained a semi-dependency with Pskov to which it paid tax until 1285.

who started to publish popular educational calendars in 1863, and unveiled the cultural history of the Inflanty in several works in Polish and German.[21]

A movement with an ethnographic character evidently used the name 'Inflanty'. The words 'Latgale' and 'Latgalians' (Latv. *latgalieši,* in Latgalian *Latgola* and *lotgoliši*), renewed by the writer and poet F. Kemps (1876–1952) who graduated from St. Petersburg as an engineer, appeared on four postcards with Latgalian landscapes printed in 1900 (the use of these words was banned by the Czarist authorities). F. Kemps also published the first Latgalian language newspaper ("Gaisma" 'Light' in 1905–1906) and journal ("Austra" 'Dawn' in 1908). He wrote the first cultural history of Latgale (*Latgalieši* 'the Latgalians' in 1910). It is to his and the priest and politician F. Trasuns' (1864–1926) credit that the independence of Latgale and the issues around that slowly became known from the 1910s (an independence which had not consciously been acknowledged before, even by the Latvians).[22] In the last years of the First World War the establishment of an autonomous and independent Latvia was under negotiation. At that time the Latgalians voted for F. Trasuns' suggestion of unification with the future Latvia, and to discard F. Kemps' idea of Latgale autonomous within Russia.

After 1918 Catholic Latgale gained wide autonomy: the Latgalian language was officially acknowledged; freedom for Catholic religious practice was ensured; they could turn directly to Rome in matters of the Church; they gained extensive rights in local government; and much more. P. Zeile rightly called this period between the two World Wars the second Latgalian national awakening, after the first interval between 1904 and 1917 (Zeile 1992, 7). Initial steps were made to bring the territory together with the other parts of the country. This was necessary, because as a result of Catholicism population growth in Latgale was twice as fast as in Latvia, and on the other hand their economic and cultural underdevelopment was inversely proportionate. For example, literacy amongst the above ten-year-old group in 1930 was sixty-seven percent, while in 1920 it was only forty-nine percent (LKV/10, 20110). Following the Ulmanis putsch their rights to autonomy were strongly curtailed, which is understandable since the nationalist authoritarian system faced its greatest difficulties in Latgale. Even in 1930 of more than half a million people living on approximately fifteen thousand square kilometres only fifty-seven percent were Latgalian Latvians, while twenty-seven percent were Russian, six percent were Polish, four percent Belarusian, five percent Jewish,

---

[21] For an excellent overview on Manteuffel and in general on works dealing with Latgale culture up to 1945 see Počs–Poča 1993.

[22] The other two regions inhabited by Latvians, that is the German Lutheran led Vidzeme and Kurzeme, knew practically nothing about life in the Polish–Catholic and Russian–Orthodox Latgale. J. Čakste the State President was right when he said in eulogy of F. Trasuns who fought for the unity of Latvia, that he was the person who sewed the third star on the Latvian national flag. In the early twentieth century F. Trasuns wrote that "Latgola was equal to a second, newly discovered America" (cited in Bukšs 1972, 176).

and in the big cities where the Latgalian Latvians did not reach forty percent the proportion was even less 'nationalistic' (Lit. E./XIV, 208). It is a surprising fact that in 1939 only 109 people had a university degree among the Latgalians who constituted more than a third of the population of Latvia, as opposed to the 7504 Latvian graduates (cited in Škutāns 1978, 181).

After the Soviet invasion in 1940, and then again in 1944 almost every member of the Latgalian intellectual elite either became a captive in the Gulags, or emigrated. In Soviet Latvia Latgalian independence was silently opposed, then from 1956 it was officially outlawed. The last Soviet Latgalian papers were published in 1958 (Zeps 1978, 381). P. Zeile discusses how Latgalian culture suffered the heaviest Russification twice, firstly when the Empire opened a doorway onto Europe using the downtrodden Latgalians as a doorstep, first between 1864 and 1904, and secondly in 1959 after the infamous plenum of the Latvian Communist Party's Central Committee (Zeile 1992, 1). For this reason, the Latgalian Institute of Science was founded in Munich in 1960, and only moved home in the early 1990s, and re-launched their publication the "Acta Latgallica", which ran in Munich from 1965 to 1981 (besides the capital Daugavpils, Rēzekne was the other cultural centre of Latgale). This meant that Latgale arrived at the last moment when it could still be determined "whether Latgalian culture would survive" in the newly independent Latvia (Kursīte 1994, 149).

The demographic situation is foreboding, but not hopeless. After 1945 Latgale had the lowest population growth and the largest Russian immigration. However, in 1989 the inhabitants of the entire Latgalian area were 43 percent Russian, 42 percent Latgalian Latvian; in the capital 13 percent Latgalian Latvian, 13.1 percent Polish, and 70 percent Russian, Ukrainian and Belarusian (Zvidriņš–Krumiņš 1991).

V. Zeps created an excellent summarising chart of the Latgalian history described above:

"1750–1864: Religious literature under Polish guidance.

1865–1904: Manuscript literature during the First Prohibition of the Latin Alphabet.

1905–1934: Latgalian literature under Latgalian control.

1934–1943: Second (de facto) Prohibition during Ulmanis' rule and early the Second World War.

1943–1985: A brief flourishing at the end of the Second World War (1943–1944) Latgalian literature in exile (1945–1985) with a concurrent Third Prohibition in occupied Latvia.

1986–: End of Latgalian literature in emigration, renascence in the homeland" (Zeps 1993, 313).

What was Latvian history like? For the moment, let us be content with the seemingly simple answer: first it was East Slavic, then German, later Polish, Swedish, Russian, and finally a little bit Latvian...

6.3. The Lithuanians

In the annals for the year 1283 Peter of Dusburg wrote in capital letters, "the war against the Prussians has ended. The war against the Lithuanians has begun" (Dusburg in SRP/III, 221). In the North the Livonian Order had just conquered Zemgale on the right bank of the Nemunas. The Germans, however, could never conquer the Lithuanians who lay between the two battlegrounds as they did the Livonian tribes and the Prussians.

Among the Baltic tribes and peoples only the Lithuanians succeeded in establishing a state during the two centuries that followed their first recorded appearance in 1009. There is little precise data about the circumstances, consequently A. Mickiewicz's foreword to the work of Konrad Wallenrod published in 1827 (subtitled *A Historic Story from Lithuanian and Prussian History*) remained valid for a long time. "History has not as yet satisfactorily explained by what means a nation so weak, and so long tributary to foreigners, was able all at once to oppose and threaten all its enemies —on one side, carrying a constant and murderous war with the Teutonic Order, on the other, plundering Poland, exacting tribute from Great Novgorod, and pushing itself as far as the borders of the Volga and the Crimean peninsula" (Mickiewicz 1882, III).

Nonetheless, it is certain that in 1219 the Lithuanians made peace with the Halicz–Volhynian Principality as an independent country. There are three plausible reasons for the emergence of the Lithuanian state. Firstly, there was a genuine demographic explosion; secondly, the Polish and the East Slavic states broke up into smaller, often rival principalities and city-states, thus creating power vacuums; thirdly, perpetual warfare caused various alliances to spring up every few years between: the Germans and the Slavs, the Germans and the Lithuanians, the Lithuanians and the Slavs, and not least of all, the Lithuanians and the Lithuanians. In this situation with everyone pitted against each other or in alliance against the rest, the role of the military escorts to the dukes grew enormously. E. Gudavičius convincingly describes the process through detailed research, where from the early thirteenth century military escorts "grew to be a structure within a few decades, which the various political changes could no longer eradicate", and which became the state organisation itself (Gudavičius 1998, 106). The chronicler highlighted the five most distinguished nobles among the twenty Aukštaitian and Žemaitian dukes present at the peace agreement. Among them was Mindaugas,[23] who is rightly considered to have been the founder of the Lithuanian state. However, as E. Gudavičius correctly pointed out, he could be paralleled by Duke Géza or Mieszko I (Gudavičius 1998, 106) who, unfortunately for Lithuania, were

---

[23] In Slavic the name is most often Mendog. It has to be kept in mind that in the absence of literacy this name, like all other historical Baltic names in the Lithuanian and Latvian languages is the result of reconstruction.

Map 7. The partition of the Baltic in the fifteenth–eighteenth centuries

not followed by someone in the ilk of Hungary's St. István or Poland's Bolesław the Bold, but rather by the representatives of the pagan opposition (it was as if Mecwal had won in Poland, or Sámuel Aba in Hungary). His origins are unknown and the chroniclers later gave the name 'Rimgaudas' to his father. Nonetheless, it is a fact that around 1240 he overcame most of the smaller dukes through murder, warfare, promises, gifts, or by establishing kin relationships. He then took the title of Grand Duke of Aukštaitija and a part of Žemaitija, and instituted the hereditary title of Duke to benefit the children of the ruler. The former dukes were gradually demoted to Grand Lords (Lith. *bajoras*). By subjugating so-called Black-Russia, Mindaugas began to annex the East Slavic Duchies to his country. By the mid-fourteenth century, after conquering Polase, Polotsk, Minsk, Vitebsk, Volhynia, Kiev,[24] Chernigov and part of Podolia Lithuania's territory had grown to 650 thousand square kilometres. The empire expanded from Lithuania to Lithuania–Russia (East Slav) which "encompassed the basins of the Upper and Middle Daugava,[25] of the Nemunas, the South Bug, the Dnieper, and the Upper Oka which is today's Lithuania, Belarus, a large part of Ukraine, and a small area of Russia" (Lyubavskiy 1910, 32). Ethnographic Lithuania (ca. 70,000–80,000 km^2) always remained under the Grand Duke, who sent his relatives and supporters to the conquered duchies to govern alongside the local dukes. (This was to some extent similar, politically if not economically, to the western European vassal system.)

"Where Lithuania found the strength to do [these actions] remains unclear" (Hellmann 1956, 165). M. Lyubavskiy seems to be closest to the truth when he explains the successes through the multiplication of the Lithuanians themselves (Lyubavskiy 1910, 26). This is particularly valid for the last third of the thirteenth century when the danger of the Tartar attacks decreased due to the appearance of the Golden Horde. Against this, in the neighbouring duchies, particularly Lithuania's greatest rival the Duchy of Halicz-Volhynia, the Tartars, who took no male captives, greatly reduced the population. As a result, after 1349 Halicz became part of Poland and Volhynia a part of Lithuania, and the Grand Duke Algirdas was able to win a great victory over the Tartars at Sinyaya Voda in 1362 or 1363.[26]

Mindaugas' attempts at centralisation did not receive a unanimous welcome. Several individual opponents formed an alliance against him, including his nephew Tautvilas who made a claim on the throne and could rely upon Žemaitija

---

[24] Kiev was of course not *that* Kiev: following the Tartar destruction, in 1246 only two hundred houses remained in the once flourishing city seat (Lyubavskiy 1910, 23).

[25] However, it did not encompass the area of the Lower Daugava populated by Latvians, and it seems likely that this was what saved the Latvians from becoming Lithuanianised.

[26] There is an inconclusive debate about where it took place, whether at the meeting point of the Dnieper and the Southern Bug, or at a right tributary of the southern Bug (Batūra, 1975, 282 ff.).

which remained an independent duchy, the Duke of Halicz-Volhynia, Alexander Nevsky of Novgorod, or even the Bishop of Riga.

To neutralise his greatest enemy, the Livonian Order of Knights, Mindaugas decided on the determining step of undergoing baptism in 1251 along with his entire household and a number of *bajoras*, and in 1253 he had himself crowned with a crown he received from the Roman Pope Innocent IV. This was the first and last coronation in Lithuania's history. The king generously made a gift of Žemaitija, which he only partly and very conditionally owned, to the bishop and the Livonian Order.

(At the same time a similar event occurred in the neighbourhood of Lithuania. Danilo Romanovich, Duke of Halicz-Volhynia asked for western aid against the Tartar threat, and in 1253 at Drohiczyń on the Bug he received his crown, also from Pope Innocent IV who thus condoned a Latin and Eastern Church union. However, the process died away as did the unification of Halicz-Volhynia and Lithuania, in spite of Mindaugas' attempts to facilitate it by betrothing his daughter to Danilo's son Shvarn who ruled in Lithuania until his death in 1269 one short year later. Events swept away the union of both the two countries and the two Churches, and along with that the great opportunity of a 'Latin island' pushed into the East.)

Other developments also moved in this direction. Treniota, the Duke of Žemaitija rose up against the Knights of the Cross and in 1261 he offered Mindaugas unification with Lithuania, which by that time had been devastated by the Tartar invasion. Mindaugas accepted the offer without hesitation and in return had to end his alliance with the Crusaders and revert to the ancient pagan belief. In this way the genuine adoption of Christianity was fatally postponed by over a 120 years. Mindaugas was murdered at the height of his power by conspiring dukes. Among his descendants Vaišvilkas and the four talented brothers of the Traidenis converted to Orthodoxy. In spite of all this Christian Europe still (again) considered the Lithuanians to be pagan.

The name of the ruler of the Lithuanian Grand Duchy (1263–1569) is uncertain. Some of the scarce sources mention a Grand Duke, but that could simply reflect the late fourteenth-century situation when the title 'Lithuanian Grand Duchy' (*Lietuvos Didžioji Kunigaikštystė* [the LDK]) was officially established.

Most probably, an initial military democracy in a tribal federation, similar in form to that of the Prussians, gradually evolved into a military monarchy where the country's governing grand duke and his house shared an aim with the *bajoras*, that is, external conquest. It was the peace with Moscow in 1449 that finally ended Lithuania's piratical forays (Łowmiański 1934, 447), since the army was based on noble military obligation and had by then become completely ineffective, and there was no money for a mercenary army.

Two rulers are due credit for the development of the Grand Duchy of Lithuania.

Mindaugas was not able to secure his line's heredity to the throne because his sons were murdered, but Gediminas (1316–1341) succeeded in making his house the largest dynasty in Central and Eastern Europe through his grandson Jogaila (or as he is known to the Polish, Jagiełło; or to the Hungarians, Jagello). It produced a number of kings for the Poles, the Czechs, and the Hungarians (Ulászló I ruled in Hungary between 1440 and 1444, Ulászló II between 1490 and 1515, and Lajos II between 1516 and 1526).

Gediminas' foreign policy was two-sided. He strove to prevent the advancement of the Crusaders from the West: twice by converting the country to Christianity; the second attempt seems to have cost him his life when the 'pagan camp' poisoned him. At the same time, he successfully expanded the Lithuanian state borders towards the East, even though Ivan Kalita (deceased 1340) appeared on the scene. He was a Muscovite ruler who called himself the Grand Duke of all the Rus' and consciously aimed at unifying the Slavic lands, causing Moscow to become Lithuania's greatest enemy. Nevertheless, for the time being the city-states of Novgorod, Tver, Pskov, and some others sought Lithuania's protection against Moscow, and the Tartars in particular.[27] Gediminas went as far as establishing an Eastern Church bishopric in the centre of Black Russia in Naugardukas (Polish Nowogródek).

His actions within the country were significant, too. He made a trade contract with Riga, invited foreign tradesmen and craftsmen, and instigated the growth of the up to that point undeveloped town life. At the peak of his activities in this field he founded Vilnius, or at least he made it his new seat of power. Up to that point the status of 'capital' was transitory. Kernavė, Trakai, Vilnius, later Naugardukas, and Kaunas all served as capitals at one point or another.

Gediminas divided the country among his seven sons. The danger of Lithuania's fragmentation arose, but failed to occur because the attacks of the crusaders and the pressing need to conquer new eastern and southern territories (which provided the taxes necessary for warfare) made the unity of the country an imperative. After a brief interlude, this was aided by talented personalities like Gediminas' two sons Algirdas and Kęstutis who seized and shared power between 1345 and 1377. Algirdas made his Vilnius seat and bore the title of the Grand Duke. He was responsible for the eastern and southern conquests and the ever-greater rivalry with Poland. He achieved great successes: in 1363 he joined the reviving Kiev to the empire and, refreshing the earlier tradition, he set up an Eastern Church bishopric in 1375, and in 1368 and 1371 he besieged Moscow with his army. Kęstutis established himself in Trakai. He was a warrior figure with a straightforward heart, and undertook the fight against the crusaders and the protection of Žemaitija. This battle was a major undertaking; between 1345 and 1382 the knights encroached into Lithuanian territory precisely one hundred times, which warranted forty counter-expeditions. Catholic propaganda had its own separate

[27] In the thirteenth century the Tartars appointed the Grand Duke from among the rulers of Vladimir, Tver, or later Moscow.

term for these small crusades calling them '*Litauen-Reise*' (Lithuanian journey), not meaning a 'trip' but an expedition whose participants were recruited across the whole of western Europe.

Algirdas was succeeded by his first-born son Jogaila, and Kęstutis remained Duke of Trakai. Soon a power struggle broke out between them and included Vytautas, Kęstutis' son and Jogaila's cousin. Both parties allied at various times, either with the crusaders, or the Polish, or the East Slavic dukes. Kęstutis was the Grand Duke for a year before Jogaila murdered the stubborn pagan uncle in a quarrel at the end of 1382. Vytautas was only able to escape from prison dressed in female clothes to the crusaders to whom Jogaila had already promised both Žemaitija as well as to accept Christianity from their hands.

In the meantime, two important events took place close to Lithuania. In 1380 Dmitri, Duke of Moscow trounced the troops of Mamai Tartar Khan on the field of Kulikovo near the Don. With this he won the title *Donskoy* as well as the affection and trust of the East Slavs living under Lithuanian control. A year later the Archbishop of the Eastern Church moved his seat from Lithuanian Kiev to Moscow—this time once and for all. The possibility of converting to the Eastern Church and of allying with Moscow was open to Jogaila. His mother, from the ducal house of Vitebsk, mediated in the negotiations about Jogaila's marriage to Dmitri Donskoy's daughter which was aimed at protecting Lithuania from the constantly renewed attacks of the crusaders. This was yet another 'moment in world history'. Who knows what might have happened in Europe if this marriage had taken place and instead of Moscow, Vilnius would have become the 'third Rome'. However, neither party acted in haste. It was not in Moscow's interest to bolster its greatest rival, and for Lithuania a conversion to the Greek Orthodox Church would hardly have withdrawn the pretext for the attacks of the Crusaders, Rome considered the Eastern Churches to be semi-pagan. Neither would it have suited the Lithuanian lords to share the same empire, for the Slav duchies would have suddenly crowded around Moscow and caused an economic catastrophe because their biggest income came from these duchies.

In the end, Jogaila wedded elsewhere. In 1382 the Hungarian king Lajos the Great died and the Polish throne became vacant. To this day it is a mystery as to whose bold idea it was to crown Jadwiga (Hun. Hedvig), the younger daughter of Lajos, 'monarch' and marry her off to Jogaila who had in the meantime made peace with his cousin. Numerous Gordian knots were loosened by the act: the burdensome Hungarian–Polish personal union ended; Lithuania, until then a pagan enemy, became a Christian ally against the crusaders as well as against Moscow; and the Poles rid themselves of the Habsburg House because years earlier Jadwiga had been promised to Prince Wilhelm of Habsburg. What is more, *after* the agreement to the marriage of Jogaila in Krevo, a town in the area of today's Belarus, and before this news could have reached Poland, the Habsburg fiancé showed up in Kraków and married Jadwiga there and then, according to the rules and rituals.[28] The Poles soon chased Wilhelm away, and the agreement of Krevo came into force. In 1386 Jogaila marched into the Wawel, converted to Christianity and married Jadwiga. He was crowned Polish king as Władysław Jagiello, and remained a Lithuanian Grand Duke, too.

The agreement of Krevo prescribed Lithuania's conversion and in 1387 Jogaila returned to Lithuania and carried it out (Žemaitija, which was in the hands of the Order was only converted in 1413). Another point in the agreement was to regulate the relationship between Poland and Lithuania. In this matter the document applied the unfortunate term *"applicare"* which carries the meaning of joining, unification, and merging.

In any case, after 1385 Lithuania and Poland were two separate countries bound by a personal union. Soon even this bond was to break. The cousin, Vytautas, incited a civil war involving every potential foreign ally. Some strange situations emerged, for instance the German troops of Grand Master Konrad Wallenrod, sung about by Mickiewicz, and the Lithuanian troops of Vytautas together besieged Vilnius which was under the protection of Jogaila's Lithuanian, Russian, and Polish troops. The complications came to an end when in 1392 Jogaila became Jagiello once and for all, and occupied himself with the affairs of the Polish kingdom, leaving Lithuania to his cousin. He entered history with the name Vytautas the Great, and by his death in 1430 the Grand Duchy of Lithuania had reached its peak. At the time Lithuania, with a territory of a million square kilometres, was the largest state of the Europe of its day. Its southern borders stretched as far as the vast uninhabited steppes beyond the Black Sea, the eastern borders to within two hundred kilometres of Moscow, and had a narrow path to the Sea at Palanga. Its western neighbour was the alliance of the Polish and the Teutonic Order, which the united Polish and Lithuanian armies defeated at Grunwald in 1410 (Lith. *Žalgiris*) in one of the most fearsome battles of the Middle Ages. This was a decisive but not an annihilating defeat and similarly the peace of Melnas in 1422, which followed the battle of Grunwald eliminated the Lithuanian demands of the Teutonic Order but not their power.

Vytautas tried to make Lithuania completely independent of Poland. In 1398 the Lithuanian nobility declared him king, but the massive defeat at the hands of the Tartars at the River Vorska a year later dashed his hopes and he was forced to acknowledge that he was in thrall to Poland. In 1429 he once again asked for the crown from the German–Roman Emperor Sigismund of Luxemburg, however the Polish lords caught the delegates delivering the crown to him which led to much wrangling during which time Vytautas passed away.

The Grand Dukes attempted to ensure independence from the East (after Gediminas and Algirdas) by electing a Lithuanian archbishop. However, the

---

[28] Some rancorous Austrian chroniclers state that the marriage was also consummated, but it is highly unlikely since the young lady was not even twelve (Jogaila was thirty-five at the time).

leading body of the Eastern Church, the Synod of Czarigrad (Constantinople), voted against their elected representative and for the Muscovite archbishop.

Parallel with the struggle for Lithuania's independence, under Vytautas' rule a decisive step was made toward actual unification between Lithuania and Poland. The 1413 union of Horodle essentially established the Lithuanian nobility when forty-seven families were adopted into the older Polish nobility (Polish *szlachta*, Lith. *šlėkta*) to endow them with rights equal to them. The Polish families lent their coats of arms to the Lithuanian families who from then on could refer to themselves as nobles. At the same time, the union declared the perpetual rights to inherited lands, as well as the personal immunity of the nobles. The rights given to Catholic nobles in the union were soon expanded to the Orthodox aristocracy.

Nevertheless, they did not apply to the town-dwellers, even though under Vytautas both Vilnius, and later Kaunas became towns with Magdeburgian rights, that is to self-government and independence from any lordship (by the sixteenth century the number of these towns grew to forty).

The motivation behind the struggle for the throne after the cousins Jagiello (Władysław 1386–1434) and Vytautas was the strange nature of their personal union according to which the same ruler needed to be elected as both the Polish King and the Grand Duke of Lithuania, but separately. Until the extinction of the Gediminas (Jagiello) House in 1572 the list of rulers shows that the system did not work flawlessly.

POLISH KINGS	GRAND DUKES OF LITHUANIA
Władysław III (1434–1444)	Švitrigaila (1430–1432)
(also King of Hungary 1440–1444)	Zigmantas I (1432–1440)
Kazimierz IV (1447–1492) =	Kazimieras I (1440–1492)
Aleksander (1501–1506) =	Aleksandras (1492–1506)
Zygmunt Stary (the Elder) (1506–1548) =	Zigmantas II (1506–1548)
Zygmunt August (1548–1572) =	Zigmantas Augustas (1544–1572)

From the mid-sixteenth century Russia also entered into competition for *dominium maris Baltici* along with Sweden. The first peace contract between Lithuania and Moscow that acknowledges the two parties as equal is from 1449 (Šapoka 1936, 185). In 1480 Ivan III defeated the Golden Horde and married the last Byzantine Emperor's daughter Sofia (it was she who transferred the two-headed eagle from the Byzantine coat of arms onto the Russian coat of arms). From then on the ideology of 'Moscow the third Rome' gained ever greater weight in line with the idea that the ancient Rurik lands had to be regained from the Jagiellos (Łowmiański 1934, 448), which resulted in a growing Russian threat. For this reason the Lithuanians had to nurture a closer relationship with the Poles. In the negotiations around unification, the Poles, using the checkmate situation, simply detached Podlase, Volhynia, and Ukraine from Lithuania. In 1569 the Union of Lublin was signed which declared that "the Kingdom of Poland and the

Grand Duchy of Lithuania are now a united and undivided body, is one united Commonwealth (*Rzeczpospolita*)". Lithuania nominally kept its separation up until the disintegration of the Rzeczpospolita in 1795, yet the May 3, 1791 constitution (modern from a social perspective) did not even mention Lithuania. Consequently the Union of Lublin could rightly be seen as a final turning point toward the end of the Grand Duchy of Lithuania and the beginning of the loss of an independent state.[29]

Only the early fifteenth century offers a less disjointed account of the beginnings of Lithuania's history. Up to then scholars rely on the mentioned Livonian and Prussian chronicles, the fourteenth-century so-called 'Lithuanian journey accounts' (*litauische Wegeberichte*) documenting the 'travels' (expeditions) of the Order in the country, and the East Slav and Polish sources.[30] M. Hellmann warns that a source outlining the history of the Prussians cannot be directly referred to the Lithuanians on the grounds of 'this is Baltic so that is Baltic, too' as many historians from the Baltic region do (Hellmann 1989, 727).

The East Slavic chronicles describe the events with the bias of the dominant power (Likhachev 1958, 27). They survived not simply in various copies, but in a composition of copies with the most diverse modifications and additions, the so-called *svod* or chronicle compilations. These always reflect the power relations of the time and place of their collation.

The *Nestor Chronicle*, known to be the first East Slav chronicle and named after its author, presumably a monk born in the early twelfth century, remains only in various compositions from between the fourteenth and seventeenth centuries: the *Lavrentiy Compilation of Chronicles* compiled in 1377, and the *Ipatiy Compila-*

---

[29] The fundamental difference has only recently emerged with complete candor among the Poles, as to how the Poles and the Lithuanians experienced the Rzeczpospolita. The Poles felt and feel that, beyond the struggle against the Russians they, as *Kulturträger* the 'vectors of culture', lifted the barbarous Lithuanians up to their own European level, while the Lithuanians evaluated it as the loss of their freedom and independence. (To me it seems that, as usual, the feelings of the smaller, weaker party are closer to the truth...)

The two pictures of the Rzeczpospolita in public consciousness added to the tragedy between the two World Wars. J. Piłsudski, the Polish leader of Lithuanian origin, wanted to reconstitute the 'Republic of two nations' probably with the best of intentions because he believed that it (was) also good for the Lithuanians. Only when he failed did he have Vilnius and its surroundings stolen from the Lithuanians in 1920. This put an end to all cooperation and the relationship between Poland and Lithuania, which greatly contributed to Hitler and Stalin's division of Eastern Europe between themselves in 1939.

[30] The herald of the Prussian Order, Wigand von Marburg's *Chronica nova Prutenica* is a poetic work of great importance from the perspective of Lithuanian history. It is practically the only narrative source for the events between 1293 and 1394. Only about five hundred lines survived from the original circa 17,000 lines, but its entire Latin translation in prose remained intact which J. Długosz the Canon of Kraków, who spoke little German, had delegated (Dąbrowski in Długosz 1925, XI).

tion of Chronicles from 1425.[31] The latter is particularly significant in Lithuanian history because it contains the *Nestor Chronicle* (covering the period from 852 to 1117), as well as its continuation completed in 1200 (covering the period between 1118 and 1199), and its third part the *Chronicle of the Duchy of Halicz-Volhynia* (between 1199 and 1292). This last chronicle basically consists of the biographies of the dukes, and as such is not divided annually as is customary in chronicles. The dates were added by the composer of the *Ipatiy Compilation of Chronicles*, often in a rather clumsy way, and occasionally as much as four years out (Likhachev 1947, 433).

East Slavic chronicle compilations were written until the late sixteenth century, consequently they are entangled with the Polish chronicles[32] such as Anonim Gall's *Chronica Polonorum* (1112–1116), W. Kadlubek's *Historia Polonica* (1208–1218) and *Kronika polsko-śląska* (Polish–Silesian chronicle 1283–1285), the so-called *Mierzwa Compilation* (1306–1325), the *Kronika wielkopolska* (Grand Polish chronicle from the second half of the thirteenth century). Building on the scarce information in these works, J. Długosz (1415–1480) offers the most in terms of the history of the then new ally Lithuania in the twelve volume *Historia Polonica* (1455). As A. Shakhmatov demonstrated (cited in Mansikka 1922, 133) he relied largely upon the East Slavic chronicles and certain parts of the late sixteenth-century Russian annals borrowed from his work (Mansikka 1922, 113 ff.). Długosz' approach to the Lithuanians is shown in his comment at the year 1387 when they were converted to Christianity. "They are the most primitive of the European peoples, they had to serve and pay tax to the Ruthenes, so everyone was most surprised when they had the great fortune that, due to their courage or their neighbours weakening and laziness, came to rule the Ruthenes under whose rule they had lived as a horde of slaves for almost a thousand years" (Długosz at year 1387).

The Grand Duchy of Lithuania had its 'own' chronicles. In inverted commas, because neither the authors of these fragments of chronicles, nor the precise time and place of their recording are known. Although they seem to have been written around the end of the fourteenth and the fifteenth centuries from which three chronicle compilations were composed in the sixteenth century. For these reasons they evidently cannot be considered as falling under the umbrella of one common interest. Nonetheless, "based on their political and ideological characteristics they can certainly be considered Lithuanian" (Łowmiański 1961, 132).[33]

---

[31] The first one gained its name from a monk called Lavrentiy who led a group of copyists working on codices on behalf of the Duke of Suzdal. The second was named after the cloister of Ipatiy in Costroma where the manuscript was found.

[32] At least in their later period, because at the beginning they were of "Franco–German origin" (Tymieniecki 1948, 9).

[33] For the most detail on the Lithuanian chronicles see Jučas 1968. They were also called West Russian, Belarusian, and Belarusian–Lithuanian chronicles. They survived in twenty-three manuscripts with varying content and length, which were published in 1907 in one volume, volume XVII of *Polnoye sobraniye ruskih letopisey.*

So Lithuania's chronicle remained for posterity in three compilations. The first, the so-called brief redaction, was presumably compiled in Smolensk in 1446. The second, perhaps compiled in Vilnius in the early sixteenth century, carries the least Lithuanian interest. The third, the so-called Bykhovets Chronicle, was probably written in Luck around 1520 on behalf of the local magnates, the Goštautas.[34]

The Livonian chronicles, or Peter Dusburg's Chronicle of Prussianland concerned the conversion of the Baltic peoples and as such was about the battle between three powers, that is paganism, western Christianity, and eastern Christianity. All three parties were also inwardly divided which meant that various alliances were formed.

The forays of pagan tribes against one another are evident. The western world was divided by a rivalry between the Pope and the Emperor,[35] which left abiding vestiges in European history in the form of the Prussian state. Its birth was a result of the political swings between the two powers, which formally became independent first from the Pope during Reformation and later from the Emperor. There was a discrepancy between western and eastern Christianity, at least from 1054, the year of the Great Church schism. At times the distance was so small between

[34] The brief redaction consists of three parts: an extract from the Chronicle of Moscow; the annals of the Duchy of Smolensk 1395–1446; and 1341–1392. The basis for the latter was a two-page denunciation of Jogaila by Vytautas to the Germans, when Jogaila escaped to the Teutonic Order for the second time in 1392 (consequently its original German title is *Dis ist Witoldes Sache wedir Jagaln vnd Skargaln*—SRP, II/711–715; its Latin and Russian translations are *Origo regis Jagyelo et Witholdi ducum Lithuaniae* and *Litovskomu rodu pochinok*, or in another form *Rodstvo velikih knyazey litovskih*, the latter was entered into the brief redaction). The main characteristics of the middle compilation of chronicles (*Letopisec Velikogo Knyazhestva Litovskogo i Zhomoitskogo*) are its lack of dates and that, although the history of the Lithuanians is traced back to the Romans, Mindaugas is missing from it. The chronicle accounts for the events between 1446 and 1548. The longest chronicle is *Chronicle Bykhovtsa* which gained its name after a landlord called A. Bykhovets in whose household the manuscript was found in the nineteenth century. The beginning of the chronicle was never found, so its publisher T. Narbutt completed it using M. Stryjkowski's two-volume *Kronika polska, litewska, żmódska i wszystkiej Rusi* (The chronicle of Polish, Lithuanian, Žemaitian and all Russian lands) written in 1582. After Narbutt published it, the manuscript of the *Bykhovets Chronicle* was also lost, and for a long time many considered it another of the romantic Narbutt's forged works. However, the recent discovery of Narbutt's correspondence has proved that is in fact genuine (for example at the end of the 1930s K. Jablonskis considered it a forgery, but by 1958 he believed it to be genuine. For the history of the issue see Merkys in Jablonskis 1979, 231, 308–309). The *Bykhovets Chronicle* is also compiled of several parts: (a) the legend of the Lithuanians Roman origins, taken from the middle compilation of chronicles, extended with the events of the reign of Mindaugas extracted from the *Ipatiy Compilation of Chronicles*; (b) the somewhat extended brief redaction; (c) the events between 1446 and 1453.

[35] This is valid even though they organised the eastern European Crusades together with a certain division of labour: financial powers were given by the Reich, and the spiritual by Rome (Gudavičius 1989, 15).

them that a hybrid Church could emerge from the two, that is the Greek Orthodox Church, at other times it was so great, and that was more often, that the Latin Church considered the Orthodox people pagans. The characterisation *est Christianus, non Ruthenus* 'Christian, not Russian' was frequent in the fourteenth century (Winter 1960, 103). From the second half of the thirteenth century the West held the East Slavs, under Tartar rule at the time, to be the allies of the anti-Christian Tartars. Not only the thirteenth-century Livonian Chronicles, but also J. Renner (ca. 1525–1583) dubbed the Eastern Church *Unchristen* ('unchristian') in his work *Livländische Historien*. In his Papal Bull to the Teutonic Order Pope Alexander IV made his intention of using lands and goods to be reclaimed from the Tartars in Russia to convert the priests who "belong to the Greek schismatics who shamefully insist upon their rituals", saying that they could receive the aforementioned goods if they "return to the Holy Roman Mother Church faithfully and obediently" (Papal Bulls, 195). The other side was no better: the eleventh-century Feodosiy Pecherskiy considered the 'Latin belief' as more polluted than the Jewish faith. The "pagan Latins" or "pagan Germans" characterisation is frequent in the twelfth-century Chronicles of Pskov (Paszkiewicz 1954, 97–98). The assumptions are also not unfounded that Mindaugas was murdered by adherents of the Eastern Church, and that the second and final conversion of the Lithuanians (from Polish hands) saved them from Orthodoxy and not from paganism (Jurginis 1987, 117, 63).[36]

Between the ninth or tenth and the thirteenth or fourteenth centuries these three powers defined the area of power relations in which the history of the Baltic tribes ranged. The period can be described through the concept of 'political religiosity'.[37]

For Lithuania, as a consequence of its late conversion to Christianity, this period was fatally long. Lithuania was continually tossed about between these three powers, even when Vytautas was at the peak of his reign in the fifteenth century, and in the mid-sixteenth century when the country was weakened (although its territory was still 700,000 square kilometres with 3.5 million inhabitants, and there were a million Lithuanians amongst them). This tug-of-war, which finally tore the enormous country apart within two hundred years, was expressed by the absence of a personal consciousness based on a literary culture in their own language. It is because of this hiatus that the Pope could qualify Lithuania a *"terra nullius,"* a 'no-man's land', and a certain amount of sham and instability can be sensed in the institution of the Lithuanian state even in its heyday. All of this is the consequence of the late conversion to Christianity. Both the Emperor and the Pope were handing out rights during the conversion between the ninth and eleventh centuries, and the

---

[36] For a classical and fundamental work on the relations between the Eastern and the Western Churches see Halecki 1958. E. Winter's work also contains a lot of data, but his viewpoint is a 'pro-Soviet and 'anti-clerical reaction' (Winter 1960).

[37] K. Bosl cites F. Heer's fitting expression (Bosl 1971, 125).

new believers became equal members of the European community. Up to the eleventh century the Church disapproved of conversion by force (Benninghoven 1965). By the turn of the twelfth and thirteenth centuries the feudal system had been established in the Reich and the situation had completely changed because there were no more lands for potential fiefdoms. The Crusades departed for the no-man's land and whatever was grabbed belonged to whoever put their hands on it first. The population of no-man's land was pagan and therefore creatures without souls. From the thirteenth century the compromises between conquerors and conquered which had been the foundation of the ninth- to eleventh-century conversion politics of Northern and Central Europe were no longer possible. Pendulum politics was all that remained and even then only in Lithuania, as long as the military power held out.

Conversion to Christianity could have perhaps happened in time under Mindaugas. Having missed the last boat, or maybe the last but one, meant that the Lithuanians, whose culture was less developed, could not govern their empire which was continually expanding onto territories with non-Lithuanian Christian inhabitants.[38]

The point is not that the pagan culture would intrinsically have less value in itself than the Christian, but that paganism had a determining disadvantage: it was an oral culture as neither the size of the tribal society nor its structure demanded literacy. (The consequences of this were discussed in connection with the Livonian tribes.)

Evidently, written culture in the native language does not necessarily infer Lithuanian, but rather any language which the leading stratum of society that has culture-creating powers could identify with.[39] If Mindaugas' late conversion had proved to be permanent, then the Lithuanian culture would have been likely to have developed along the lines of the French,[40] Czech, Polish, Hungarian, etc. In the shadow of Latin culture the first pieces of a Lithuanian literacy could have emerged, but it did not happen that way. From the pagan times the only serious remnants in the Latin language are the six letters Gediminas sent to the West. However, at the time of the second and final conversion Lithuania was a multi-

[38] Not to mention that converting to the new religion in 1387 did not mean its instant spread and victory. The pagan way of thinking only slowly gave way, and for its eradication changes in the social structure were needed such as the emergence of a serf system initiated by the 1447 regulations decree of privileges by Grand Duke Kazimieras.

[39] Up to the twelfth century in the West almost everything was written in Latin, too. The king spoke the first English words to be heard in the English Parliament in 1399 (Curtius 1948, 43). Nonetheless, Latin became synonymous for literacy, and so the word 'littera' meant 'Latin language' and "only those who could read and write in Latin were able to note down the words, sentences, and poems of the people's language, on occasions" (Grundmann 1958, 4).

[40] "Latin education and poetry was at the forefront and French came after. Latin let the French tongue loose" (Curtius 1948, 388).

national empire with eight million Orthodox East Slavs among a population of nine million, and they had a literacy of their own, a language which developed into the literacy of Lithuania, too.

In this way Lithuania found itself between the mentioned three powers of political religiosity, that is, on no-man's land twice over. First when it was ruled by a pagan consciousness not in accordance with its own high level of social structure and its own strong state, and the second time when the western Christian ritual was coupled with eastern literacy.

The language of literacy was the East Slavic version of the Old Church Slavic. From its three types, the Church, popular–literary, and Chancery (Vinogradov 1956) it was the latter which was then further coloured by local linguistic influences. Initially a variant developed that could be identified with Ukrainian and later with Belarusian (Zinkevičius 1984–94/II, 133).[41] Through the work of the Lithuanian copiers, whose number increased in the late fifteenth century, more than three hundred Lithuanian words entered the texts (Jablonskis 1935–42, 224).

Not only the three mentioned compilations of chronicles, viewed as literature, were written in this language but also the documentation of the Chancery archives between the mid-fifteenth and eighteenth centuries called *Litovskaya Metrica*

---

[41] The name of this language has not yet been agreed upon in linguistic literature. Some linguists call it Old Belarusian, others West Russian, or Old Russian (Palionis 1979, 10). The inhabitants of today's in the fifteenth and sixteenth centuries in what is now Belarus and Ukraine, people felt that they were one group, so they unanimously called themselves 'Rusi' and others referred to them in the same way (Latin *Rutheni*, Ger. *Rut(h)enen*), even though they occupied three different regions: the Grand Duchy of Lithuania; the so-called Red Rus' belonging to Poland; and the Carpathians belonging to Hungary. They called the Slavs who fell under Moscow's auspices 'Muscovites' (Latin *moscali*, Polish *Moskali*). In this way the Old Russian people had two parts: Greater Russians, and West Russians. The latter only later divided further into Belarusian and Ukrainian, primarily after the Union of Lublin in 1569, when Belarus remained under Lithuanian control and the greater part of Ukraine fell under Poland.

During the Belarusian and Lithuanian political (territorial and border) debates following the disintegration of the Soviet Union, where evidently both parties refer to historical rights, the Lithuanian word, with which this language had been referred to thus far, underwent interesting shifts in meaning. *Gudas* (*Gudija*) thus far unambiguously meant Belarusian (Belarus) (e.g. Jablonskis 1979), which however would uphold Belarus' ancestral rights. Many Lithuanians, led by Z. Zinkevičius, the excellent linguistic historian of the greatest professional repute (a minister in the conservative government from 1996), deny this meaning as outrageous, and recently the word has come to mean all East Slavic inhabitants of the Grand Duchy of Lithuania, that is Belarusians, Ukrainians, and Russians.

(*Lithuanian Archives*),[42] the three statutes or constitutions of Lithuania (in 1529, 1566, 1588), and certain documents of the Lithuanian Catholic Church.[43] After the East Slavic territories had drawn together around Moscow the use of this language lost its purpose and Polish was adopted. In this way, apart from a momentum seen as a curiosity of Prussian history (see Part Two, Subchapter 6.3.1), the official beginning of a Lithuanian written culture in the Lithuanian language had to wait until 1918.

The Union of Lublin declared that Poles and Lithuanians should elect their king together who would then simultaneously become the Grand Duke. The ruler had formally also been elected before that, but since the throne was inherited, the election was a formality (not to mention that under the Jagiellos an actual election of the king would have meant giving up Lithuania, since that was the domain of the Jagiellos in perpetuity). However, the Union of Lublin happened almost simultaneously with the extinction of the Jagiellon House in 1572, from which point onwards the king was indeed elected. The free election of the king later served as an exemplar to the solution of any other matter in the country. At the same time it offered an opportunity for the emergence of the public spirit that can be characterised by saying that the seemingly democratic assertion of individual interests, primarily through the legal institution of *liberum veto*, led to a total destruction of public affairs, that is the Rzeczpospolita.

Lithuania's rapid Polonisation started with the Union of Lublin. Its history increasingly became equivalent to that of Poland. The strange Polish and Lithuanian relationship could be characterised by the Poles' desire to make the Lithuanians, who they held in the deepest contempt, Polish. On the other hand the Lithuanians tried for a while to keep, if not their independence, an approximate separation. In the seventeenth century the Lithuanian Parliament still came together from time to time, but hardly ever in the eighteenth century.

A new chapter also began in the development of 'Lithuanian consciousness'.

The eleventh- or twelfth-century tribal federation must already have had a certain amount of Lithuanian consciousness. There is no data about that, but the mere survival of the Lithuanians is evidence of it. Otherwise they would have been incapable of establishing a state that could resist all external enemies in the thirteenth century (see also Volkaitė-Kulikauskienė 1987, 174).

The self-consciousness that developed in the period between the two conversions to Christianity must have included the Lithuanian language and the pagan

---

[42] The *Lithuanian Archives* is a historical source of great value. In the First World War, a big section of the approximately six hundred volumes of documents, files, etc. was transported from Vilnius to the old Central State Archives in Moscow. The publication of the volumes is continuous.

[43] Contrary to this, the language of services in churches built on Slavic lands in the early fifteenth century was Polish, so that the local 'Belarusian' and 'Ukrainian' people would understand it.

religion. The only traces of this are the words of King Gediminas (after Długosz he is referred to as the Grand Duke) addressed to the Papal legate: "let the Christians respect their God according to their own beliefs, let the East Slavs (*Rutheni*) serve him in accordance with their own customs, the Poles also in their own ways, just as we also respect God following our own customs, and that all of us has one God" (Gediminas).[44]

A certain state patriotism emerged in the Grand Duchy of Lithuania that, however, due to the absence of a literary culture, could not develop into 'ethnic nationalism'. Lithuania's chronicles reflect this state patriotism, which focuses on the reigning Lithuanian family, and through that the origins of the Lithuanians.

State and nation were tragically divided, exactly at the time of the Reformation, which promoted a new concept of 'nation' based on a common culture and language.[45] In Lithuania this common language founding the new concept of 'nation' became the Polish. A striking example of this is that the formerly Orthodox aristocracy of Belarusian origin, who became Lutheran at the Reformation, then Catholic under the Counter Reformation, were consciously Lithuanian and spoke in Polish (Bumblauskas 1994, 74).

After the Union of Lublin, and mostly from the seventeenth century the nation-forming nobility, starting with the magnates became increasingly and rapidly Polish, to the extent that a nobleman soon was considered to be a Lithuanian Pole. Polonisation was swift. Although the first document in Polish is from 1523,[46] the state records office, and public records were kept in Polish immediately after the Union of Lublin, and from 1697 the state language of the Grand Duchy officially became Polish. In the early seventeenth century, when the necessity for church services being held in the mother language became apparent, the Jesuits, who had arrived there with the Union, decided after some debate that Polish was the local language in Lithuania. In the Jesuit College of Vilnius

---

[44] It is possible to come to the conclusion, as A. J. Greimas does, that the thirteenth- and fourteenth-century "Lithuanian imperialism had to be underpinned by a flourishing religious life, not only demographic and economic increase" (Greimas 1990, 17). Another conclusion could be that Gediminas, who tolerated the Orthodox Archbishop and the western orders, only wanted to appear to the Pope as an isolated believer to be in the right colours, and thus persuade him to deny his support to the crusaders, since he continues his words in this way: "what do you tell me about the Christians? Where is there greater injustice, inequity, discord, destruction, and exploitation than among the Christians, and especially among those who seem devout like the crusaders who conduct every possible evil?" (Gediminas 129).

[45] The state and a culture based on the national language are important for a group of people to survive. The historical fate of the Poles and the Lithuanians is an example that in some cases the latter is of greater significance. Nobody ever doubted the existence of a Polish nation, except for a few myopic Czarist clerks, even during its hundred and twenty years of abolition, while the Lithuanians achieved an outcome similar to the Latvians and Estonians who had never had an independent state.

[46] Russian files written in the Latin alphabet preceded this (Jablonskis 1935–42, 225).

(I. Báthory rose to the level of academic, that is, university status in 1579) the language of everyday communication was Polish, alongside Latin. Between 1575 and 1773 the Academic Printing House of Vilnius published 716 Polish, 820 Latin, and only 52 Lithuanian books.

Lithuanian areas became increasingly barbarous and depopulated. Between 1648 and 1667, due to the constant warring, famine, and the epidemics that followed them, the Grand Duchy of Lithuania lost 48 percent of its populace and cannibalism was not rare in the villages.

After the great eighteenth-century epidemics a real migration from the villages to the towns began. Slavs, mostly Belarusian swamped Vilnius, at the time. In 1737 Lithuanian sermons were stopped in the St. John's Church of the capital, because there was simply no one to preach to. According to statistics from 1770 a hundred and twenty priests spoke Lithuanian from a total of nine hundred and ten Lithuanian priests viewed as the guardians of culture.

The above illustrates that the development of 'consciousness of own' is not primarily obstructed by an alien language, but that Russian (East Slavic) and to some extent Polish were both the languages of other increasingly hostile states.

6.3.1. Lithuania Minor

The possibility of a 'self-consciousness' emerging had decreased to a minimum in a Lithuania that was slowly becoming Polish through the *Rzeczpospolita*. On the other hand Lithuania Minor belonged to the Duchy of Prussia of former Prussianland (so it was also called Prussian Lithuania or *Preussisch Litauen*). Some opportunity existed there to directly utilise the cultural movement of the Reformation in close connection with the development of a (new) Prussian consciousness.

The name *Kleinlittaw* crops up first in S. Grunau's work, evidently as a differentiation from Lithuania Major, that is Lithuania itself. The inhabitants of Lithuania were the *lietuvis* people, whereas those of Prussian Lithuania were called *lietuvininkas*.[47]

The greatest part of the region was the *Wildnis*, that is the enormous, unpopulated forest area left following the battles between the Germans, Couronians, Prussians, and Lithuanians. It consisted of various parts, which were named according to different ethnic, tribal, public administrative, political or linguistic variants, an entangled web that is practically imponderable. In 1890 about two million people lived on the approximately 37,000 square kilometres, among which almost 120,000 were Protestant Lithuanians.

---

[47] This had its German equivalent, too: *Litauer-Litthauer* (Hubatsch 1965, 659).

Lithuania Minor comprised the following parts: Klaipeda on the right bank of the Nemunas, north of the river (Ger. *Memel* < Nemunas) and its surroundings (2848 km^2); the territories south of the Nemunas inhabited by Lithuanians, which Peter Dusburg referred to as the Prussian Nadrava with a few important settlements such as Isrutsk (today: Chernakovsk), Gumbinė (today: Gusev), Stalupėnai (today: Nesterov); Skalva with its centre Tilžė (Ger. Tilsit, today: Sovietsk); Ragainė (today: Neman), and Lazdynai (today: Krasnoznamensk).[48] V. Pėteraitis also mentions Pilsotas, Königsberg (Lith. *Karaliaučius*) as part of the region, along with the once Prussian 'lands' around it, such as Sembia with its larger settlements Krantas (Zheleznodorozhniy), Labguva (Polesk), Žuvininkai (Primorsk); Warmia with Šventapilė (Mamonov); Natanga with Ylava (Bagrationovsk); and Barta (Pėteraitis 1992, 47–55).

To complicate things further, from the late eighteenth century Lithuania Minor was often referred to as East Prussia, or to differentiate it from Prussia which only came into existence in 1701 it was termed Old Prussia (*Altpreussen*). From the last third of the nineteenth century what the term 'Lithuania Minor' represented shrank. It referred to the north-eastern areas of East Prussia or Old Prussia inhabited by Lithuanian-speaking people and therefore as Germanisation progressed its borders were constricted and constantly challenged.

One of the most significant cultural novelties of the Reformation was that it gave local languages their due status against Latin. Priests were required to pass God's word directly to the Lithuanians of the Prussian Duchy in their mother tongue. Albrecht called pastors in from Lithuania, and granted scholarships to Lithuanian seminarians at the University of Königsberg, which he founded. Some humanists taught in its Lithuanian seminaries who had been chased away from Lithuania Major because of their Protestant beliefs, for example, A. Kulvietis who founded the first Protestant school in Vilnius in 1539, or S. Rapolionis.

Obviously, there were political reasons for supporting the Lithuanians. Albrecht also dreamt of the unification of the Duchy of Prussia and Livonia, compliance of the Grand Duchy of Lithuania. He did have some chance of achieving this as he was the cousin of the last of the Jagiellon house, Augustus Sigismund, and therefore theoretically in line for the throne of the Grand Duke after his death. To underpin his efforts he published several state orders and regulations in Lithuanian, thus making Lithuanian a state language for the first time in the history of the Duchy of Prussia (Budreckis 1976, 157). Albrecht was outlived by Augustus Sigismund and so his hopes died with him.

The Lithuanians' predicament worsened. In 1618 the Duchy of Prussia united with the Prince Electorate of Brandenburg, and the role of the Lietuvininkas

---

[48] On the maps from the sixteenth and seventeenth centuries, e.g. on the famous map of C. Hennenberger from 1576, Nadravia and Schalavonia is given instead of the whole of Lithuania Minor (Reklaitis 1976, 69).

diminished. In 1660 the capital moved from Königsberg to Berlin symbolic of the cessation of the vassal relationship of the Prussian state in the Rzeczpospolita, and Prussia's connection with Lithuania became much looser. As it had been for the Prussians during the period of the crusades when they were colonised and prohibited from moving to the towns and manufacturing, the Lithuanians were now denied the reductions in taxation and villeinage which the new settlers, the German *Junkers* enjoyed.

In the early eighteenth century the spirit of the Prussian–Lithuanian state was evoked once more, as Lutheran Prussia increasingly distanced itself from its Catholic neighbours, that is from Poland and the Habsburgs who were under strong papal influence at that time. The Pope did not acknowledge the rights of Lutheran heretics to the lands of the Catholic crusaders. For this reason they strove to appear as the heirs, not of the crusaders, but of the indigenous Prussians and their Lithuanian relatives. For example when in 1701 the Duchy became a kingdom, Friedrich Wilhelm I was crowned in Königsberg among decorations of Prussian motifs, and not in Berlin. This 'Prussian' spirit remained throughout the eighteenth century, and to some extent contributed to Lithuanian culture even if it seemed at times to be no more than a decoration alongside the social and economic measures aimed at achieving the precise opposite. The great cholera epidemic of 1709–1711 took fifty-three percent of the inhabitants of the Prussian Kingdom, mostly the Lithuanians who lived in miserable and impoverished conditions. Due to the influx of settlers Germanisation increased. To prevent 'dilution' by 'suspicious elements' a law was passed that banned any (Žemaitian) Lithuanian, Polish, or Jewish immigration.

K. Donelaitis (1714–1780), the founding father of Lithuanian literature and to this day the most acclaimed Lithuanian writer also internationally recognised, was born into such tangled and confused conditions. His main (and practically only) work was written between 1765 and 1775, although it was only published in 1818. The *Metai* (Seasons) is an idyll in four parts which has an aesthetic effect even for contemporary readers, which is largely because, as pointed out earlier, some Prussian–Lithuanian consciousness or spirit could emerge relatively freely in Lithuania Minor, but any demand for an independent state or even province was unconscionable. This total absence of a national image, exceptional in eastern Europe, did not interfere with the 'eternal human' endeavours of the writer.

Donelaitis and his publisher L. Rėza (1776–1840) can be seen as the last significant representatives of the literature of Lithuania Minor. In the course of the nineteenth century Lithuanian culture became increasingly stunted. The pinnacle of the effort to Germanise was reached in the state presidential decree of 1872, according to which only religious studies could be taught in Lithuanian, and even then only in the lower age groups. As a dialect and a culture Lithuania Minor can only be sensed in the twentieth century as a *couleur locale*, or 'local flavour' in the works of a few authors such as Vydūnas (1868–1953) or I. Simonaitytė

(1897–1978), and a handful of Germans like H. Sudermann (1857–1928) or J. Bobrowski (1917–1965).

The Reformation did not pass by the Grand Duchy of Lithuania, either. Evidently, it spread less extensively than in Lithuania Minor, but more than in Poland because that way the Lithuanians could escape the Polish Church and the Primate of Gniezno. Accordingly, first the nobility who would later oppose the Union of Lublin converted to the new religion, and on the principle of *cuius regio, eius religio* 'he who possesses the land, holds the religion' their adherents and serfs followed them. (Although from the sixteenth century there are numerous documented examples when, with the weakening of Catholicism, the peasants did not convert to the Reformist Church but reverted to paganism.)

The new education reached Lithuania from two directions. Calvinism from Poland spread among the nobility where, with Augustus Sigismund on the throne Protestantism was tolerated around 1542, and Lutheranism from Prussianland was popular among the common people. The difference had significance, the nobility did not push for the use of the Lithuanian language, whereas the latter group preferred it. For example Mikalojus Radvila (Radziwiłł) published the *Bible* in Polish. The Reformation also worked in favour of the Poles, since in Lithuania, where the inhabitants were mostly Ukrainian and Belarusian, using the mother tongue meant the Polish language that was related to theirs.

Protestantism in Lithuania was short lived. On the other hand, the Counter Reformation lead by the Jesuits who arrived in Lithuania in 1569 was more successful. Once again, re-conversion to Catholicism was initially targeted at the nobility, and was accomplished by the last third of the seventeenth century, but they went further and exceeded their aims. Many nobles and serfs who had previously been Orthodox became Catholic in this period (a process which was to have been institutionalised in the 1596 Church Union between the Pope and the Eastern Church, however, the resistance of the latter foiled the attempt).

Nonetheless, however brief it was the Reformation had a significant effect, from two perspectives in particular. Firstly, it rekindled an atmosphere of religious tolerance, which had last been felt in Lithuania under the pagan Gediminas. He had toyed with the idea of adopting both the Catholic and the Eastern Churches, a statement supported by several instances. When Henry Valois had the opportunity to gain the throne in 1572 the nobility of the Rzeczpospolita demanded his solemn promise to free religious practice. This was to ensure that the bloodbath of Saint Bartholomew's night in 'the educated West' would not be repeated there. The next king, István Báthory, was a Catholic yet chose an Arian Hungarian compatriot, Gáspár Békés, as his principal adviser and general. In spite of this, in less than a hundred years there was 'retrograde development' to the extent that in 1680 a young man was burnt at the stake for his ungodly views.

The other, more enduring effect of Protestantism was inherent in the raising and voicing of the demand for an education in the mother tongue. Its opposition, the

Catholic Counter Reformation, had to comply with that and sustain it. In these years two cultural centres emerged, one was the Jesuit College in Vilnius, the other was in Žemaitija where, at the instigation and support of a bishop with nationalist sentiments, M. Giedraitis, in 1595 M. Daukša (1527–1613) published the first Lithuanian book in Lithuanian, a translation of the catechism. Then the also Jesuit K. Širvydas (1580–1631) published the first dictionary, and in 1629 a collection of sermons which is considered to be the first original Lithuanian work.

Very generally speaking, both Reformation and Counter Reformation lost their power by the turn of the seventeenth and eighteenth centuries, and miserable circumstances made all forms of culture practically impossible. Nothing could stop the deterioration of the country. Austria, Prussia, and Russia dismantled the Rzeczpospolita in three attempts: in 1772, in 1793, and in 1795. After the third division Lithuania was given to Russia with the exception of Suvalkija which went to the Germans who named it New East Prussia (*Neu Ostpreussen*). Between 1807 and 1815 it belonged to the Grand Duchy of Warsaw, established by Napoleon and extant until his fall, after which it was joined to the so-called Congress Kingdom of Poland and with that it finally became a part of the Russian Empire in 1831. From that point on the term Russian Lithuania (*Russisch Litauen*) was used as opposed to Lithuania Minor which in contrast was narrowed to the Nemunas region, that is to *Memelland*.

The division extinguished the Grand Duchy of Lithuania completely. The nobility that formed the political nation had long since considered itself Polish (its form was *gente lituanus, sed natione polonus*) and they hardly spoke Lithuanian. For this reason M. Hellmann says that in the seventeenth or eighteenth century the history of the Grand Duchy of Lithuania "is no longer the history of the Lithuanian people" (Hellmann 1990, 87). In any event, the alleged political programme of Czarina Catherine II (of *depoloniser, decatholicisier, demoraliser*—that is to de-Polonise, de-Catholicise, and de-moralise) did not contain anything about *delithuaniser* 'to de-Lithuanianise'—there was no need. The Czarina and her grandson Czar Alexander I both declared on several occasions that in 1795 not a square inch of Polish (meaning Lithuanian) land was joined to Russia that had not always belonged there. The 'historical basis' for this statement was that, as seen, in the Grand Duchy of Lithuania Russian (East Slavic) was indeed the official language. Accordingly the title of the 'Czar' included the title of the 'Grand Duke of Lithuania' but not 'King of Poland'.

Poles played the leading roles on the stage of Lithuanian history exclusively until as late as 1864. It was they who fought against the Russians for the restoration of their homeland to its former, pre-1772 state. At best the Lithuanians could have fought for the sixteenth-century state before the Union of Lublin, but more appropriately for the era of Vytautas in the fifteenth century or even of the thirteenth-century Mindaugas. Nonetheless, it seems that historical memory, especially if it is as interrupted and embedded into foreign languages as is that of the Lithuanians, is unable to remember across such distances. Even in the last third of the nineteenth century the leaders of the—at that point indeed extant—Lithuanian nationalist awakening (for example the author of the national anthem V. Kudirka, or the linguist J. Jablonskis) were of the opinion that there was no need to be ashamed of their mother tongue, yet only madmen could imagine that the Lithuanian language could gain access to every area of life, that they could have their own journals, literature, Lithuanian Kraszewskis or Mickiewiczs.

Naturally, Lithuania also took part in the 1831 War of Independence, but not as Lithuania. To be liberated from Russia, the prison of the people, or to be free at all, meant being Polish.

To be able to belong to Poland once more was the goal that transformed the university town of Vilnius, a flourishing centre of Polish culture in the first two or three decades of the nineteenth century (of the other two towns which might have counted, Kraków belonged to Austrian Galicia, and Warsaw was given to the Prussians in 1795 to later become the centre of the Grand Duchy of Warsaw, and at the time it was an impoverished little town which was rapidly modernised from 1815). The great figures of Polish culture, such as Mickiewicz, J. Słowacki, Kraszewski, the historian J. Lelewel, numerous free-masons, various university student societies, the members of the Filarets and the Filomans were all, in some way, connected to Vilnius, a town with an intellectual world infused with the love of freedom. If a 'border fortress' intends to prove its place at the 'centre' or its equivalence to it, then it liberates such energies as could turn the border town itself into the 'centre'. This is what happened to Vilnius, and thus, from his own point of view Alexander I was justified when in 1819, removing the mask of the liberal ruler, he struck out first at the youth of Vilnius. His successor Nicholas I, the 'Czar with the Stick', was so irritated by the university, a 'nest of free thinking', that he had it closed down in 1832, and with the town as a whole he wanted to rename it *Chortovgrad*, 'Devil's town'. From 1840 any official reference to Lithuania or Belarusia was banned and instead the term 'the North-western Region' (including Latgale) was prescribed. In the same year, the 1588 statute or constitution that had been valid until that point, was exchanged for Russian jurisdiction.

Of course, it would be misleading to imagine that the Lithuanians were left unaffected by the ideals of the Enlightenment which spread ever wider as a result of the Napoleonic Wars, or by the struggles of the Polish national awakening (for example, during the 1812 Russian expeditions Napoleon established the temporary government of an independent Grand Duchy of Lithuania in Vilnius, though it existed only very briefly). However, it was all rather insubstantial and embryonic. It is characteristic that in his patriotic diligence the first Lithuanian history writer Simonas Daukantas (1793–1864) signed his various works for the enlightenment of everyday people with a different name on each occasion, thus trying to give the impression that the number of educated Lithuanians was increasing. Other writers, who were impoverished lesser nobles, all wrote in two languages: Polish and Lithuanian. The nature of the Lithuanian cultural awakening in the first six decades of the century was best represented by the *Baublys* of D. Poška. What was this *Baublys*? The poet felled a thousand-year-old oak tree on the verge of extinction. He sawed off a 9.2 metre piece at one end, hollowed out its centre, cut a door and a window into it, covered it with a roof, and thus ended up with a little hut with an interior diameter of two metres that most resembled the mushroom hut of the elves in the fairy tales.[49] The writer placed his collection of antiquities there: archaeological finds, old coins and money, arms and armour, his library of about two hundred books, and many other objects. He hung the portraits of scientists, philosophers, writers, and excerpts from his Polish and Lithuanian poems on the wall. *Baublys* became the first Lithuanian museum and became rapidly famous, it is still standing as a historic monument. It attracted visitors, even Mickiewicz sang about it in the *Pan Tadeusz*. Besides all its greatness the undertaking has a certain amateurish 'hobby' feel to it that characterised all the attempts to awaken a Lithuanian national past at the time.

One significant change was that after the 1863–1864 uprising of the nobility had been crushed by Czarist troops led by the Governor of Vilnius M. Muravyov (who earned the nickname 'the Hangman' because of his bloody methods), the Russians began the final solution of the Polish question. This solution was Russification and the enforcement of the Orthodox religion. The most important measure was that from 1864 Russian became the language of education even in primary schools. The secondary schools were closed (one solitary secondary institution was left in the whole of Žemaitija and that only, to use Muravjov's words, "to support Russian education"), and in Lithuania (and in Inflanty) "the printing of any publication written in any kind of Lithuanian or Zhmudyian dialect with the Latin–Polish alphabet" was banned. In other words Lithuanian books were only allowed to be published in the Cyrillic alphabet.[50] An individual Lithuanian with a university degree could not receive a settlement permit in the territory of Lithuania, with the exception of priests, lawyers, and doctors. This was one reason why there were no Lithuanian towns in 1876: the two biggest settlements, Vilnius and Kaunas were proportionally five-sixths Jewish, and one-sixth Polish, and the official language was Russian (Senn 1966, 29).

It should be emphasised that the Czarist authorities intended to eliminate Polish culture, with the idea that everything that was not Polish would automatically become Russian (that they were right is indicated by the regulation of the press

[49] The word itself comes from < *baubti* 'to buzz, roar'.

[50] Basically, the 'Latin–Polish' letter was simply Polish spelling. Lithuanian spelling at the time was not yet established. Some used the Polish, others the diacritical symbols borrowed from Czech, and yet others mixed the two in a 'Lithuanian way'. The Lithuanians protested against the press ban in various petitions throughout its existence. One of their arguments was that the books that were about to be printed were not of Latin–Polish, but Latin–Czech or Latin–Lithuanian letters.

that also applied in Inflanty under Polish cultural and intellectual influence, independent of that, the secondary victims of the law were the Latgalians). What referred to the Lithuanians was only that their Polonisation, supported until 1830 and silently tolerated afterwards, died away. Polonisation thus led as far as ignoring the Lithuanians and their culture.[51] Metaphorically the situation could be depicted as the Russians aiming at the Poles and also shooting the Lithuanians (and Latgalians) that were behind, or rather under them.[52]

The brightening of the dimly burning torch of Lithuanian culture began as the counter-measures of Russian anti-Polish politics. Since the most obvious attacks targeted the Church and publishing the response came from there, too.

In 1864 Muravyov, 'the Hangman', ordered that the art of sermonising in the seminaries for priests in Kaunas should be either taught in Russian or Lithuanian instead of Polish. The unsophisticated 'peasant's' Lithuanian was chosen in preference to the loathed Russian. The Czarist clerks turned the Catholic churches into Eastern churches, and by the end of the nineteenth century four Eastern Church bishoprics functioned in Lithuania. Religious books that were published or imported, not just after but even before 1864 were confiscated, and Catholic priests were hunted down. The sale of works in Cyrillic was encouraged. When they failed to sell for years at a time their distribution was entrusted to the local authorities and the police.

---

[51] A short-story by V. Krėvė sheds light on the extent of Polonisation. It is set late in the last century and depicts the linguistic relations of a Lithuanian village. "The parish was pure Lithuanian. A few squires of noble and city descent 'played Polish' at home, but even they understood and spoke Lithuanian well. Yet, in the church exclusively Polish words echoed. In his haste, the elderly priest Žemaitukas often did not even preach the Gospel in Lithuanian. This was the order that he found, when (as a young priest, many decades before) he arrived in the village. It did not even occur to him that it should be changed. Actually, he believed the noble Polish language would appeal more to God than the peasantish Lithuanian. He only chatted to the villagers in Lithuanian believing that Polish was only the due of the nobleman, and the servants of the Church, so he even Polonised the names of the organist and the sexton. Šakutis the organist was christened Sakiewicz, and Bolis the sexton to Boliński. 'God's servants cannot bear such peasant names.' A few times he had serious disputes with the villagers because of the language, some even complained to the bishop. But in vain, the priest was not willing to talk in Polish with them. 'You are peasants, not nobles, you just speak Lithuanian.' Ranking the Jews among the inferior people, he saw no need to talk to them in Polish either" (from the short-story Žemaitukas see Krėvė 1987, 218).

[52] In Prussian–Poland, especially under Bismarck's Polish-hating Chancellorhood, the same thing happened, only with German, Polish, and Lithuanian (lietuvininkas) actors.

The spiritual leader of the opposition was M. Valančius (1801–1875), a bishop from Žemaitija from a peasant background.[53] The Church could not do without the prayer books and hymnals. Lithuania Minor, and to some degree later the first emigrants who had obtained wealth in America, helped in circumventing the press ban. At the instigation of the bishop books were printed in Eastern Prussia and smuggled into Lithuania from there. 'Book carrier' became a profession with a separate word to denote it. Secret book distribution societies and centres emerged in the territory of Lithuania. The extent of 'culture smuggling' became significant, up to 1896 three million seven hundred books were printed in Lithuania Minor, mostly alphabet books, calendars, and religious literature. The first Lithuanian journal *Aušra* (Dawn, 1883–1886) was also published in East Prussia.

There was also another opportunity than in East Prussia to print Lithuanian publications. An addition to the censorship laws in 1880 permitted the distribution of scientific and scholarly works using the Latin alphabet—in areas inhabited by non-Lithuanians. Lithuanian intellectuals were driven to study elsewhere in the Empire by the lack of higher education in Lithuania, at universities in cities like Riga, St. Petersburg, or Moscow where they could utilise this opportunity. That is how a collection of *dainas* (folk-songs), a detailed map of Lithuania, and a volume of wedding songs came to be published in an obvious last-ditch attempt to save at least the traditional oral culture of a people destined for extinction.

The censorship failed not only because only fifty-eight books were published in Cyrillic during its operation (only one of which, a book on sewing, had a Lithuanian author), but also because it turned Lithuanian public opinion unanimously against the Russians.

Russification of education had a similar impact. The Lithuanians, in protest, simply did not send their children to school and education went on at home even though law prohibited it. The renowned statue by P. Rimša portrays the situation beautifully under the title *The Lithuanian school, 1864–1904:* a peasant woman sits at a loom teaching her son to write.

After 1918 both Estonia and Latvia found a place in the community of Europeans with little difficulty. Lithuania, on the other hand, dragged two heavy foreign political burdens, which had been (retrospectively) influencing the Lithuanian consciousness as well as their view of their history.

One of these was the question of Klaipeda and its surroundings. This harbour town, always free of ice, was connected to the Nemunas by a canal. Since its foundation in 1252 it had always been on the axis of the towns established in the

---

[53] The issue of national culture after 1864 no longer lay on the shoulders of the nobility, but of the priests of peasant origins who had by then emerged. Many of the nineteenth-century Lithuanian writers were priests, from A. Strazdas (1760–1833) the publisher of the first Lithuanian poetry book in 1814, through to A. Baranauskas (1835–1902), to the national figure of Maironis (1862–1932).

river estuaries of the Baltic Sea, that is Gdańsk on the Vistula, Königsberg on the Pregolja, and Riga on the Daugava. Lithuania Minor had always been dominated by Germany. Its urban populace was largely German (in Klaipeda over ninety percent), but its peasantry, though gradually assimilated, was mostly Lithuanian (in the 1925 polls many considered themselves neither one nor the other, but simply 'locals', i.e. Klaipedians. One often tires of History...). The peace settlement following the First World War gave the area to Lithuania, a decision that was difficult to realise because of opposition from the German public administration. At that point Lithuania launched into direct action leaving Germany with little option but to go along with them: in early 1923 the units of the Lithuanian army faked a rebellion and occupied Memelland. French troops had been stationed there since 1920 at the behest of Great Britain, Italy, France, and Japan the guarantors of the peace contract which had signed the so-called Convention of Klaipeda. The French troops did not resist, and when the League of Nations resigned themselves to the situation they left the region.

The area came under a special legal status whereby it was ruled by a government elected by the parliament of the province, whose president was appointed by Lithuania's governor. It became clear during the 1925 elections that the locals did not reciprocate the Lithuanians' desire to annex them to Lithuania. Although seventy-one thousand people considered themselves German and sixty-seven thousand Lithuanian, twenty-seven out of the twenty-nine representative seats were won by the United German Front.

The German Nazi party won the 1938 *Landtag* elections. After Hitler had taken power his slogan of uniting all German lands won over Memelland, too. It was only a matter of time before Germany would regain its 'rightful property' and the opportunity came in March 1939, one week after Czechoslovakia was invaded. Reacting to a German ultimatum, Lithuania 'voluntarily' handed over the territory to Germany—after the Second World War it was returned to be part of the Lithuanian Soviet Socialist Republic. The number of the Germans dwindled to a few thousand, and it seems that for the Lithuanians the German question was solved once and for all (?).

The other issue was the Polish question around Vilnius and its surroundings. At the end of the First World War only two percent of the one hundred and thirty thousand inhabitants of the ancient Lithuanian capital were Lithuanian, fifty percent were Polish, and forty-three percent were Jewish. The surrounding villages, also a debated area, were mainly occupied by people with Polish sympathies who considered themselves Polish but in fact spoke Belarusian (Gaučas 1989). All in all the issue affected about fourteen and a half thousand square kilometres and nearly half a million people.

After 1918 Vilnius was at times in the hands of the Poles, at others the Lithuanians, or the Red Army and a handful of Soviet–Lithuanians until 7 November 1920 when, under pressure from the League of Nations Poland renounced all rights to the city in the Agreement of Suwalk. The Poles had already broken the Agreement underhand by 9 November.[54] On that day General L. Želigowski 'rebelled' against the capitulatory behaviour of Piłsudski and his group and occupied Vilnius with his troops, declaring the so-called 'Central Lithuania' whose parliament voted to join Poland in early 1922. Hardly a year later, after the League of Nations had acceded to the reality of the situation (what else could it have done?), Piłsudski openly stated that the whole of Želigowski's rebellion was a previously agreed upon piece of theatre.

For the scholar examining the development of historic consciousness, the most interesting aspect of this act is that Želigowski named the established state Central Lithuania. J. Greimas' explanation for this is that the language was not identified with the country even at that time. Želigowski honestly believed that he was creating a Lithuania, only one where Polish was spoken (Greimas 1988). (There was a precedent in the Polish–Lithuanian Rzeczpospolita where the Lithuanian speaking populace were not counted as a part of the nation, nor the Belarusians—whose representatives Želigowski also invited to join the government.) J. Greimas called on Cz. Miłosz, among other examples, as somebody who was born in Lithuania, brought up in Vilnius, and is a Polish poet living in America; also the Jewish philosopher E. Levinas who writes in French, graduated in the Russian secondary school of Kaunas and lives in France. Both of them consider themselves Lithuanian, without actually speaking the language.

This mischief had serious consequences. Directly, there was a general cessation of all relations between Poland and Lithuania, from diplomatic connections to postal services, two countries that had been in a state federation for centuries.[55] Indirectly, uneasy relations between the two countries thwarted all attempts at alliance among other Baltic Sea nations, although such alliances could have constituted a counterbalance to both Germany and the Soviet Union.

The breach in the Lithuanian historical consciousness that developed with the detachment of Vilnius was patched by its Lithuanianisation after 1945. Nonethe-

---

[54] Later 9 October was declared a day of national mourning. The text of the broken agreement was exhibited in the Military Museum of Kaunas for twenty years to whip up anti-Polish feelings.

[55] There was barbed wire all along the nearly five hundred-kilometre border. Roads and railways abruptly stopped near the border, a few hundred metres from the guard towers on the Polish side and twenty kilometres on the Lithuanian side, running nowhere. Anti-Polish and anti-Lithuanian public feeling developed with some examples verging on the absurd, it can still be perceived today. In Lithuania Polish films were banned, along with those which had a Polish actor or actress in them. On the other side, Polonisation went on until there was not a single Lithuanian educator at the Sztefan Batori University of Wilno, and one solitary church gave sermons in the Lithuanian language. Lithuania considered itself to be practically in a state of war with Poland. It was stated in its constitution that Kaunas was only a temporary capital, the true one being Vilnius.

less, the question of whether the Vilnius region historically belonged to Poland or Lithuania between the two World Wars, places our enquiry in an even sharper light: what was Lithuanian history like? Despite its undoubted rise and prosperity before 1918 (between the tenth–thirteenth centuries) which is lost in the mists of time, has there ever been 'pure' Lithuanian history? At what point did it become Polish, and when Lithuanian once more?

The concluding chapter contains a detailed response to these questions, but that aside, it is certain that the history of the Baltic peoples developed in many diverse ways in spite of the great number of encounters, influences, and loans. Historians cannot even agree on whether the 'Baltic region' as a historical and political unit exists (cf. Loeber–Vardys–Kitching 1990). I believe that comparison must often show banal similarities and identicalness in order to better contrast unique features which inform us about what is truly interesting, and also about the 'moral' embedded in the history of every group of people. In other words, it pinpoints the values that the history of a people may carry for us. Almost every significant 'comparative historian' emphasises the uniqueness of historical events, something expressed most succinctly in the words of M. Bloch: "history is the discipline of changes, and, in many aspects, the study of differences" (Bloch 1937, 35).[56]

---

[56] Value and interest are connected in the, as far as I know, best definition of values, "value is any object of any interest" (Perry 1926, 116), where the word 'interest' carries the unity of value and interesting features.

PART THREE

BALTIC LANGUAGES AND DIALECTS

CHAPTER 1

COMMON BALTIC

There are three separate Baltic languages with written vestiges and some, as Palmaitis–Toporov termed them, toponomastic languages that have survived only in the names of places and people (Palmaitis–Toporov 1983, 36). These are the Selonian (Selian), Zemgalian, and Couronian languages which, because of the lack of data, can be characterised by a few features (not described) as transitions of and in relation to the three languages: i.e. western Prussian; and the eastern Latvian and Lithuanian languages as points on the widest possible axis. From these I would only consider Couronian to be a separate language, in the sense of what has been said about the Leitis (see Part Two, Subchapter 5.6.2). The other two could be dialects of Latvian and Lithuanian (to indicate this I will refer to them in parenthesis along with the problematic Latgalian).

The Baltic languages strongly resemble each other (although Latvians and Lithuanians cannot comprehend one another). The common features that constitute a kind of Common Baltic could be enumerated in a long list.[1] From among these the most important are the following: 1. There is a characteristic word stock, a large number of words which can only be found in these languages (Latv. *ozols*, Lith. *ažuolas*, Pruss. *ansonis* 'oak'; Latv. *logs*, Lith. *langas*, Pruss. *lanxto* 'window'; Latv. *lācis*, Lith. *lokys*, Pruss. *clokis* 'bear'; etc.) The same is true the other way round: five eighths of the basic word stock of Lithuanian originates from Indo-European vocabulary (Klimas 1969, 23). 2. The phonetic system is very rich and has an archaic totality, especially the consonants at word ends of the presumed Common Indo-European proto-language which have survived intact (Latv. *vilks*, Lith. *vilkas* 'wolf', as opposed to Ger. *Wolf*, Russ. *volk*). The 'n' vanished from the word ends, but it nasalised its preceding vowels which changed with the intonation: elongated under rising intonation (*circumflex*) ('ą', 'ę', 'į', 'ų'); while under falling intonation they shortened (*akut*). The only change in the system of vowels is that the IE. 'a' and 'o' both became 'a' (Latin *axis*, Latv. *ass*, Lith. *ašis*, Pruss. *assis* 'axis'; and Latin *oculus*, Latv. *acs*, Lith. *akis*, Pruss. *ackis* 'eye'). In

---

[1] For the most important summaries of the characterisation of Common Baltic see Kabelka 1982, Smoczyński 1988, Erhart 1984, Zinkevičius 1984–94/I, Eckert–Bukevičiūtė–Hinze 1994.

the various forms of the same words the stem vowel changes (*Ablaut*). The 'm' before a 'd' or a 't' did not disappear nor did it turn into an 'n' as it did elsewhere (Latv. *simts*, Lith. *šimtas* 'hundred', OSlav. *sъto*, Gothic *hund*, Latin *centum*, Tokharian *känt*). The system of consonants shows three characteristic neologisms: (IE. 'k', 'g', ('h') > 'š', 'ž' and 's', 'z'); the voiced aspirates merged with the non-aspirates: (IE. **dhumó* > **duma* > *dūmi, dumai, dumis* 'smoke'; and IE. **do-* > *dot, duoti, dat* 'to give'); the existence of the palatal (soft) and non-palatal (hard) sounds. 3. From morphology the following features are noteworthy: the dual verb form, i.e. the actions of two actors were retained in Lithuanian up to the twentieth century, along with the athematic verb, i.e. verbs connected to the stem without a linking vowel. The third person verb forms are the same in singular, dual, and plural. There is a simple future tense (derived by the 's' sound). A rich system of adjectival and adverbial participles developed. There is a locative derived without a preposition. 4. The syntax is the same as in the Slavic languages. There is no strict word order, its only characteristic feature is that in the genitive, unlike the Indo-European languages but similar to the Hungarian, the possessor comes before the possessed (*Latvju-gals* 'Latgale' is actually 'the border of the Latvians'). 5. Of course a modern Common Baltic spelling feature is to phonetically rewrite foreign words (Engl. lunch, Latv. *lenč*), just like proper nouns which also get their own ending to ease declination (Goethe = Lith. *Getė*).

To give a sense of the similarities, and as a textual example the oldest Baltic linguistic vestige is cited below. The so-called Prussian fragment of Basle from the fourteenth century is given with the presumed pronunciation of the two lines as well as their Latvian and Lithuanian translation:[2]

> Kayle rekyse. thoneaw labonache thewelyse,
> *Kails rikis. tu n'au labans tevelis
> Sveiks, kungs! Tu ne(esi) labs tevainis
> Sveikas, pone! Tu nebe geras dėdelis
> To your health, my lord! You (are) not a good friend,

> Eg koyte poyte nykoyte penega doyte.
> *ik koj-tu pót nikoj-tu penigan dót.
> ja gribi tu dzert, negribi tu naudu dot.
> jeigu nori tu gerti, (bet) nenori tu pinigą duoti.
> if you are willing to drink, (but) do not want to give money.

---

[2] V. Mažiulis considers the text a rhyming hexameter, whose transcript and interpretation I cited above (Mažiulis 1975, 125). C. McCluskey discovered it in 1973 in the University Library of Basle on a cover of a folio in Latin dated 1369. The handwritten text is presumed to have reached Basle from Prague through various intermediaries, and is nothing more than a witty little ditty to a fellow student by a Prussian student studying in Prague.

CHAPTER 2
WEST BALTIC LANGUAGES

2.1. The Prussian language

In the last twenty or thirty years the study of the Prussian language has grown into
a separate area within Baltology, and has been termed 'Prussistics'.[1] There are
some earlier works of great significance in the field, such as F. Nesselmann,
Thesaurus linguae prusicae, 1876; R. Trautmann, *Die altpreussischen Sprach-
denkmäler*, 1910; J. Endzelīns, *Senprūšu valoda* [Old Prussian Grammar], 1943,
and *Altpreussische Grammatik*, 1944. Recently three centres evolved, each around
an outstanding scholar: Vilnius (Mažiulis 1966–81), Moscow (Toporov), and
Pennsylvania (Schmalstieg 1974, 1976).[2]

[1] For a complete bibliography of preceding studies see Kubicka 1967.

[2] Currently there is an interesting attempt to revive the Prussian language and culture at two
independent locations. The *Tolkemita Preussen Freundeskreis* which has been functioning in
German Dieburg since 1980 (named after S. Grunau's birthplace). H. Gerlach's book gave the
initial inspiration for its founding (Gerlach 1978). The author discovered that his ancestors
were Prussians, and he wrote a history of the Prussians with a cordial Old Prussian bias. Many
of the members in the circle are of Prussian Baltic origin. They have published a series of books,
collected the remnants of Prussian culture, as well as tried to revive the Prussian language, for
example H. G. Podehl has already published poems written in New Prussian (Podehl 1985; cf.
also Hermann 1986, 11). Their motives differ: a search for an ancestry; nurturing of traditions;
respect for small cultures; some retrospective historic justice; and so on. G. Kraft-Skalwynas
has written a grammar of this New Prussian language, though the linguist M. L. Palmaitis
commented on this language fabricated by Latvian speaking amateurs, that it is less Prussian
than a "Baltic Esperanto" with Latvian foundations (Palmaitis 1989, 186). V. Toporov, one of
the greatest philologists of our time, is presumably drawn to publish works in New Prussian,
along with M. Palmaitis, by a playful experimental mood. He has published New Year's
greetings, grammar rules, dirges, and the *Lord's Prayer*. Three Old Prussian variants of the
Prayer were at their disposal, and I will enclose their version here, as a matter of interest:
*Nusan Tawa endangun, Swintints wirsei Twajs emmens, Peresiei Twajs riks, Twajs kwajts
audasei sin kagi endangun, tit digi nozemei. Nusan deininin geiten dais numans šandeinan be
etwerpeis numans nusan aušautins kaigi mes etwerpimai nusan aušautenikamans, be ni wedais
mans en baudasenin, sklait izrankais mans cze wargan* (Palmaitis–Toporov 1983, 57).
There is already a pun in the title of the article by the two linguists: 'recreation' as in
'amusement' and 're-create'. Their attempt is not without a precedent: in 1870 W. Pierson
published a Prussian dirge that survived in German which he 're-translated' into Prussian (in

There are written sources in the Prussian language noted down by Germans in 'German'. The 'ancestral' Prussian script had already been researched in the sixteenth century when, after the establishment of the Duchy of Prussia, a separate Prussian tradition was sought by all means available, and in consequence the slightest reference was latched onto. For example, from a single letter sent to the Aisti (cited earlier) by Theoderich the Great in the sixth century, an extensive Prussian and Gothic correspondence was assumed (Biržiška 1953, 39).[3]

E. Stella the chronicler of from Leipzig mentions the flag of Vidvutus (in its later Lithuanian form Vaidevutis), a precedent of forgery aimed at establishing a tradition.[4] S. Grunau continued to use this 'fact' from E. Stella in his own chronicle, which shall be discussed later. He colours it and adds to it.[5] Grunau's story is that in 500 the last Prussian ruler Widowuto and his elder brother the chief pagan priest Bruteni (*Prutenis* in Lithuanian) immolated themselves. A white flag—sheet of five ells in length and three ells in width remained after Widowuto, with a portrait of three Prussian gods and beneath it two white horses leaning on a coat of arms, with a script around the gods on the edge of the flag that resembles Cyrillic writing.[6]

Biržiška 1953, 82). After the 1989–1991 change the reconstruction of Prussian culture and language gained political meaning and significance. An idea cropped up that the possible future confederation of the three Baltic states (Estonia, Latvia, and Lithuania) could be joined by Sembia as a fourth member that had once been populated by the Prussians, the Kaliningrad area, currently in Russia (which is divided from the mother state by two independent states, that is Lithuania and Belarus). In this confederation New Prussian, alongside Russian, German (Polish?, and Lithuanian?) could be one of the official state languages of the 'canton' called Borussia. As T. Venclova remarks, "in eastern Europe even the wildest fantasies come true" (Venclova 1995, 13).

[3] The search for the ancestral Baltic script continues. Most recently, for example, a Lithuanian man living in Scotland has allegedly puzzled out the (undeciphered Linear A) script found on a fourteenth-century BC so-called Phaistos-disc found on the isle of Crete, based on Proto-Lithuanian script (Gustaitis 1992).

[4] Stella concocts his tales following the patterns in the Gothic chronicle of Jordanes. Jordanes used the *Vidivarii* name for a people, and Stella made the name of King Videvut (Jordanes 1960, 36; Mannhardt 1936, 183).

[5] A. Mierzyński posits that Grunau twisted the Prussian word out of the Polish wojewód 'voivoide, chief' (Mierzyński 1892–96/II, 183).

[6] Serious scholars tried to fathom it out (in 1903 even the young K. Būga, though toward the end of his life he qualified the obsession with the flag as 'daydreaming'), even though M. Perlbach who published Grunau wrote that "it is pointless to say that the flag and the script is exclusively based on Grunau's imagination. According to Dusburg (Chapter 5) the Prussians did not know how to write" (Perlbach in Grunau 1529/I, 78).

Dusburg indeed refutes that there was a Prussian (Baltic) script, "the Prussians did not know God. Being simple people their intellect did not reach Him, and since they had no writing they could not understand Him from writings, either. They were immensely surprised when they were told that humans are capable of passing on their will to another human who is not present, through writing" (Dusburg in SRP/III, 5).

The flag appears elsewhere, too, in the work of the historian and cartographer from Königsberg C. Hennenberger, for example (Hennenberger, *Prussiae, das ist des Landes zu Preussen wahrhaftliche Beschreibung*, with several publications after the first in 1576). M. Praetorius borrowed it from Hennenberger. In his history of Prussianland written in German he states that the script was borrowed not only by the Prussians, but also by the Lithuanians, the Couronians, and the Žemaitians from their close neighbours the Russians. He gives about thirty signs which allegedly decorated a Russian flag, and which have not yet been success-fully deciphered (Praetorius, *Deliciae Prussicae*, 1690).[7]

In the national Romanticism of the nineteenth century Grunau's flag came alive. It was published in print on numerous occasions, but even historians in our own century took it seriously. J. Basanavičius published it last in 1926 (Lit. E/XXXII, 439).[8]

Genuine written sources, besides the cited Basle fragment and four or five half sentence long fragments, are two handwritten German Prussian dictionaries, and three printed bilingual (German and Prussian) Lutheran catechisms. (These works are based on the repeated call of the Catholic Church, for example the Council of Basle in 1435, or the Synod of Warmia, for the priests to learn the local language, which the Protestants then made one of the fundamental tenets of their Church politics.) The authors of these works were exclusively German priests, who used the help of generally illiterate peasants for the translations. The sources of further mistakes were copying or printing errors. The uncertainties in the end results are well represented in the five different forms of the plural possessive of the word *grekas* 'sin' that can be encountered: *grikan, grijkan, grecon, griquan*, and *grecun* (Erhart 1984, 28).

The *Elbing German Prussian Dictionary* deserves a mention. A copy of it found in the library of Elbląg (Elbing) in Poland is from around 1400, the original may have come from around the turn of the thirteenth and fourteenth centuries. It contains 802 words, not in alphabetical order but according to concepts. As with all linguistic remnants, here too the problem is that the copier was hardly aware of the Prussian language, and wrote the, to him incomprehensible, words incor-rectly and inconsistently.[9] The dictionary was found among a wad of law-court

---

[7] The flag can be qualified as the imagination of the chronicler, but the script, resembling Cyrillic lettering, is more difficult to dismiss. Several deeds of gift in the German language survived from the sixteenth century from Prussianland and western Kurzeme, which were written in letters resembling Cyrillic. We know of no other explanation for the phenomenon than that the Cyrillic script used between the ninth and twelfth centuries under the rule of Polotsk lost its meaning, and became decoration or a 'series of patterns' (Malvess 1959, 557).

[8] Very recently the tale of the flag, along with so many others, has been re-vamped by neo-mythologists, principally V. Ivanov and V. Toporov (cf. Tokarev 1988/I, 380). Their followers from the Baltic region once more take it for granted (e.g. Iltnere 1993–94, 2/290), and 'historical' analyses of great expansion are built upon it (e.g. Beresnevičius 1989).

files in the early nineteenth century. Presumably it was intended for German judges, to help them in their contact with the Prussian peasants who spoke no German. The dictionary is based on the Pomezanian dialect, although words could have entered it from other dialects, too, because the German notary or copier had contacts with Prussians from different regions that moved around in order to escape the persistent wars.

The other dictionary is the *Simon Grunau's Dictionary* of about a hundred words. The monk from the Pogezanian Tolkiemyčiai (Ger. Tolkemit, today Polish Tolmickas) enclosed this vocabulary book with his chronicle written between 1517 and 1529, in trying to express that the indigenous people of Prussianland spoke some other language apart from German which the Poles did not understand at all, and the Lithuanians only a little. Although Grunau claims to have spoken some Prussian, rather like his other statements this should be queried. He often wrote words down without their endings, and mixed Polish and Lithuanian words into the text of an unsophisticated German style as if they were Prussian.

In his chronicle Grunau, whose trustworthiness is more than dubious, also published the *Lord's Prayer* in Prussian. Soon it turned out to contain perhaps two Prussian words (*nossen* 'our' *gaytkas* 'bread' instead of the Latv. *mūsų* and *maize*). In actual fact, as W. P. Schmid proved, it is either in Latvian with Couronian influences, or in Couronian with Latvian influences (Schmid 1983). Despite all this, even in 1948 there was a serious linguist (E. Hermann) who fought for the Prussian origins of this Prayer (Sabaliauskas 1986a, 100).

The three catechisms are all translations of Luther's so-called *Short Catechism* reflecting the Sembian dialect. It is highly likely that the Prussian language survived the longest on the out-of-the-way peninsula of Sembia protected by water, and the catechisms were also needed because there would have been many, as late as the Reformation, who did not understand the Gospels in German. Prince Albrecht, himself freshly Lutheran, had the matter of the new belief close to his heart.[10] Initially the German priests preached with the aid of local interpreters (the interpreter stood underneath the pulpit and translated sentence by sentence).

---

[9] "The German scribes copying down Old Prussian weren't even first year students of phonetics at a German university" (Schmalstieg 1973, 155).

[10] Of course, also in the case of the Prussians the problem was not with their knowledge of the language. In the foreword to the *Short Catechism* first published in 1529, Luther recounted his sad experiences during his Church visits (mostly among the Saxons): "Merciful God, what misery I have seen, the common people knowing nothing at all of Christian doctrine—especially in the villages!—and unfortunately many pastors are wellnigh unskilled and incapable of teaching, and though are called Christians and partake of the Holy Sacrament, they know neither the Lord's prayer, nor the Creed, nor the Ten Commandments, but live like the poor cattle and senseless swine" (Luther 1882–83, 359).

This was doubly true for the Prussians, among whom there were many untouched by Christian education, and who carried on living according to pagan beliefs.

However, this method proved to be ineffective, because the uneducated peasants twisted and distorted the words of the German priests, who were unable to check the translation. For this reason in 1544 Albrecht regulated the proceedings in a decree. Every Sunday the priests themselves had to give a sermon, without an interpreter. This is preserved in the foreword to the third catechism by the ruler himself (Mažiulis 1966–1981/II, 91–100). Therefore the catechisms were not for the believers but for the priests, which explains the low number of copies.

One hundred and ninety-seven copies of the first catechism were printed in Königsberg in 1545. It is the translation of Luther's *Short Catechism* published in Wittenberg in 1531. On the left hand side there is the German, and on the right the barely five and a half page-long Prussian text.

One hundred and ninety-two copies of the second catechism were published in the same year, the corrected version of the first and still containing many mistakes. As the foreword says, not only experienced translators but also people who spoke the language as their mother tongue were involved in the work.

The most extensive (54 pages of Prussian text) and most valuable Prussian linguistic vestige is the third catechism. An unknown number of copies were published in 1561. It is the translation of Luther's *Short Catechism* published in 1543 entitled the *Enchiridion*.[11] Contrary to the other two, its translator is known. He was a priest called Abel Will.[12] His greatest contribution was that he, albeit inconsistently, marked the stress, and even the intonation patterns of the diphthongs can be concluded upon.

To give a sense of the differences between the three catechisms, here is the *Lord's Prayer* according to the three Prussian catechisms,[13] as well as in today's Latvian, Latgalian and Lithuanian (after W. Smoczyński 1988, 900, 881, 867).

Thawe nuson kas thu asse andangon,
Thawe nouson kas thou aesse aendengon,
Tāwa Nouson kas tu essei Endangon,
Tēvs mūsu, kas esi debesīs,

[11] Luther's work echoes St. Augustine's handbook written in the fifth century (*Enchiridion*) in which the Bishop of Hippo summarised the fundamental principles of the Christian faith for the first time (Harmening 1979, 76).

[12] Although he spoke a little Prussian, A. Will was assisted by an 'official interpreter', a Prussian peasant called Paul Megott who worked beside the church. P. Megott spoke Couronian and Lithuanian, but was illiterate. A letter survived from both of them, which illustrates the struggle they had to go through during this work (for the letters see Mažiulis 1966–81/II, 241–249).

[13] The last sentence of the Prayer is missing from *The Gospel According to Luke* (11, 2–4), but is present in other versions ("For Thine is the kingdom, the power, and the glory, for ever. Amen.").

Taws myusu, kotrys essi Debbessis,
Teve mūsų, kurs esi danguje,
Our Father which art in heaven,

Swintints wirst twais emmens. Pergeis twais laeims,
Swyntints wirset tways emmens. Pareysey noumans twayia ryeky,
Swintints wīrst twais Emnes. Perēit twais Rijks,
svētīts lai top Tavs vārds, lai atnāk Tava valstība,
swetyts lay top tows Words, lay inok mums tawa Walstiba,
Teesie šventas Tavo vardas, teateinie Tavo karalystė,
Hallowed be thy name. Thy kingdom come.

Twais quaits audasseisin na semmey key andangon,
Tways quaits audaseysin nasemmiey kay endenga,
Twais Quāits Audāsin kaigi Endangon tijt dēigi nosemien,
Tavs prāts lai notiek kā debesīs, tā arī virs zemes,
tawa Wala lay nutik mums kay Debbessis, tay arydzam wersum zemes,
teesie Tavo valia, kaip danguje, taip ir ant žemės,
Thy will be done in earth, as it is in heaven.

Nusan deininan geittin dais numons schindeinan,
Nouson deyninan geytien days noumans schian deynan,
Nouson deinennin geitien dais noumans schian deinan,
Mūsu dieniško maizi dod mums šodien,
Muysu diniszku mayzi dud mums szudiń,
Kasdienės mūsų duonos duok mums šiandien,
Give us this day our daily bread.

Bha atwerpeis noumans nuson auschautins kay mas atwerpimay nuson auschautni-
kamans.
Bhae etwerpeis noumans nouson auschautins kay mes etwerpymay nouson auschau-
tenikamans.
Bhe etwerpeis noūmās nousons āuschautins kai mes etwērpimai noūsons auschau-
tenīkamans.
un piedod mums mūsu parādus, kā arī mēs piedodam saviem parādniekiem.
und atlayd mums musu parodus, kay un mes atlayzam sawim porodnikim.
ir atleisk mums mūsų kaltes, kaip ir mes atleidžiame savo kaltininkams.
And forgive us our trespasses, as we forgive those who trespass against us.

Bha ny wedais mans enperbandasnan. Sclait is rankeis mans assa wargan. Amen.
Bhae ni wedeys mans enperbandasnan. Slait isrankeis mans aesse wargan. Emmen.
Bhe ni weddeis mans emperbandāsnan. Schlāit isrankeis mans esse wissan wargan.
un neieved mūs kārdināšanā, bet atpestī mūs no ļauna.
und ne ijwed mums iksz kardinoszonas, bet atpesti mums nu launa.
ir nevesk mus į pagundą, bet gelbėk mus nuo pikto.
And lead us not into temptation, but deliver us from evil.

These linguistic vestiges contain around 2250 separate words all in all, from a variety of dialects and with an unknown proportion of distortion through copying. The lack of a complete paradigm increases the difficulties involved in reconstructing the language. For example fifty-seven percent of the remaining 280 verbs occur in one form only. Even the conjugation of the verb 'to be' is incomplete. A consequence of word for word translations is that hardly anything is known about the syntax. To fill in these gaps, place names and proper names are called upon, but also Prussianisms (Prutenisms) in German, Polish, and Lithuanian dialects in Prussianland, as well as Latvian and Lithuanian parallels.

Prussian was first to leave the Common Baltic language and then developed in isolation from Latvian and Lithuanian for a long while and is consequently more archaic than either of them. In addition there are signs of a strong Slavic (Polish and Kashubian) and especially strong Germanic influence.

The greater part of the leading stratum of Prussia fell in the battles of the so-called 'great Prussian uprising' of 1260. Then after the suppression of the persistently rekindled rebellions in 1295 the survivors fled to Lithuania or were Germanised or Polonised and Prussian finally degenerated to the level of a peasant language, a familiar phenomenon in the history of Central and Eastern Europe.

The further development of a Prussian literacy in the sixteenth century was hindered by all of these events. In the seventeenth century Prussian was still used in public discourse, then it gradually became a 'family language'. In the first decades of the eighteenth century it became extinct when the Seven-Year War and the outbreak of plague which followed it wiped out a great proportion of the inhabitants of East Prussia and new settlers from all over Europe came to fill their places. C. Hartknoch was a history writer of the Prussians, he discovered the *Dusburg Chronicle* and published it for the first time. In 1684 he wrote a work entitled *Altes und neues Preussen oder preussischer Historien zwei Teile*: "there was not a single village left where everybody would at least understand Old Prussian. There is the odd old man here and there who understands it". On the cover of the second catechism in St. Petersburg a note from 1700 says the same thing: "this old Prussian language has completely died out. Only one old man, who lived on the Courish Spit and knew it died anno 1677, though there could be some more" (cited in Endzelin 1944, 11–12). German also edged Prussian out of the sermons, or Lithuanian in Lithuania Minor where the Prussians lived together with the Lithuanians, whilst even earlier in the southern parts of the Prussian language area, Polish began to assimilate the language. The only writer who was possibly of Prussian origin was J. Bretkūnas (1536–1602) and he wrote in Lithuanian.

The following features can characterise the Prussian language, although these can only be viewed as probable for the reasons discussed above:

1. It has free stress. Its characteristic intonation shows similarities to the Latvian. It preserved the IE. 'ei', 'ai' ('oi') diphthongs, as opposed to the East Baltic where

the two developed into a further two 'ie/ei' and 'ie/ai' (IE. *deiuos* > Pruss. *deiw(a)s* 'god', but Latv. and Lith. *dievs, dievas*, and the archaic Lith. *deivė* 'goddess'). It retained the palatal 'k' and 'g' sounds like Lithuanian, and unlike Latvian 'c' and 'dz' (Pruss. *gemton*, Lith. *gimti*, Latv. *dzimt* 'be born').

2. It has neutral nouns, as opposed to the East Baltic where there are only feminine and masculine cases. There are various infinitive endings (*-t*, *-twei*, *-ton*, *-tun*). Five cases remained in substantive declination (nom., gen., dat., acc., voc.). Five stems are probable in noun declination (o, u, a, i, consonant), and three in adjective declination (o, i, u). Unlike the ordinal numbers, all the cardinal numbers are known from the *Ten Commandments* of the catechism. Among these the 'sixth' is more archaic (*usts, uschts, wuschts* < IE *uktos*) than those of the East Baltic (*sestais, šeštas*). There are three tenses in verb conjugation, and there is a separate desiderative mode besides the imperative and conditional modes.

2.2. The Jatvingian language

All in all, few features can be deciphered from place names. Like Prussian it preserved the IE. 'ie' diphthong. The Lith. š and ž are replaced by 's', and 'z'. Characteristic derivators are *-inge*, and *-ingis*. In the light of the earlier discussion, it is possible that even these, too, are simply dialectical particularities of Prussian.

CHAPTER 3

THE COURONIAN LANGUAGE

The Couronian language is a transition between the Prussian and the East Baltic which the following example demonstrates: As in Latvian, in Couronian the sounds 'k' and 'g' became 'c' and 'dz' before 'i', 'e', or 'ie', as opposed to Latvian and like Prussian (and Lithuanian) the 'an', 'en', 'in', and 'un' double sounds. In this way the first sound in the word *dzintars* 'amber' (which is considered to be a Couronian loan word in Latvian) is Latvian (cf. Lith. *gintaras*), while the other sounds are Prussian or Lithuanian (Sabaliauskas 1986, 90).

Contrary to the majority viewpoint, Couronian has more common features with Prussian than with Latvian, for example the kept 'u' preceding a 'v' or a 'b' as opposed to the Latvian 'i' (*zuve* 'fish', Lith. *žuvis*, but Latv. *zivs*) (Kabelka 1982, 73).

There are several written records of the language of those who lived on the Courish Spit. It was a dialect of the Latvian language with Couronian characteristics, or so-called 'Couronisms', also strongly affected by Lithuanian, and even more by German. Both A. Bezzenberger and J. Plāķis enclosed a few pages of sample texts in their monographs describing the language of the people of the Spit (Bezzenberger, *Über die Sprache der preussischen Letten*, 1988; Plāķis, *Kursenieku valoda* [The Couronian language], 1927). In 1931 P. Šmits published twenty-eight pages of folklore texts collected on the Spit (Šmits, *Kursu kapu folklora* [The folklore of the Courish Spit], 1931). There is a bilingual CouronianGerman book by a layman, R. Pietsch who considered himself Couronian and lived on the Courish Spit until the beginning of the Second World War. Born in 1915, his book, published in 1982, is only a curiosity compared to scholarly works, though a curiosity with much accurate data. R. Pietsch describes the villages of the Courish Spit, their material culture, customs, the names of the families living there, and so on. It is a last broadcast from a now extinct world, and of an extinct language (Pietsch, *Fischerleben auf der kurischen Nehrung*, 1982). R. Pietsch also published the collection of a priest P. Kwauka who also lived on the Spit (Kwauka, *Kurisches Wörterbuch* Berlin: 1977). As W. P. Schmid pointed out, the 'Couronian' term is incorrect in both cases, because the inhabitants of the Spit were likely not to have been the descendants of the Couronians, and certainly did not speak Couronian (Schmid 1983).

So, the Couronians were assimilated by the Latvians who were subjugated by the Germans, and not by the Germans themselves as the Prussians were. J. Endzelīns gives a number of explanations for this. Certain parts of Kurland were depopulated after the crushing of the thirteenth-century uprisings, and Zemgalians (Latvians) immigrated in the stead of the Couronians. The translations used for missions and later sermons were also made in a Latvian–Zemgalian dialect, which by then was probably not very different from Couronian. According to the sixteenth-century chronicler J. Reiter the Germans banned the use of the Couronian language, because of its 'unattractive' sound, and the Couronians adopted Latvian (cited in Kabelka 1982, 68).

CHAPTER 4

EAST BALTIC LANGUAGES

4.1. The Latvian language

The Latvian language broke away from the East Baltic unit, and separated from Lithuanian quite late in the sixth or seventh centuries, but some believe (including myself) the division only began in the ninth century. The encounter with the Finnic languages, especially Livian, had a determining impact which resulted in numerous neologisms in comparison to Lithuanian. This late Finnic influence is the main evidence that the Latvians arrived at their current linguistic location as late as the end of the first millennium AD. Those who believe that the Balts and the Finns were already neighbours from the second millennium BC cannot easily answer the question of why the 'disintegrating' effect of the Finnic languages started so late. V. Mažiulis, for example, believes that from the second half of the first millennium AD the web of territorial and tribal communities emerged from the earlier kinship societies (Mažiulis 1974, 122). This new type of organisation called for, and facilitated, more extensive 'international' relations, consequently the contacts along the Baltic–Finn border that had existed before, had a greater impact and spread across the whole language area.

The Finnic effect manifests in a few isoglosses: a consistent stress on the first syllable;[1] Baltic 'š', 'ž' > s, z (Latv. *zeme*, Lith. *žemė* 'earth'); Common Baltic soft 'k', 'g' > 'c', 'dz' (Latv. *dzimt*, Lith. *gimti* 'to be born');[2] the disappearance of the dual verb, already rare in sources from the sixteenth century; many Finn loan words (*māja* 'house' < Estonian, Finn *maja*; *vai* 'whether' < Livian, Estonian *voi*); in the possessive structure the possessor is in dative + verb 'to be' + possessed in nominative (*Man ir grāmata* 'I have a book'), as opposed to the Lithuanian or Old Latvian that expresses possession 'in the Indo-European way' with a verb (*es turu grāmatu* 'I own a book').

The Russian (East Slavic) loans are double layered, the first came with the appearance of the Germans before the thirteenth century (Pliskava < Russ. Pskov), then the second came when the Latvians came into contact with the Russians once

---

[1] Some explain this as a German influence. J. Endzelīns posits spontaneous Latvian development, the spread of which was influenced by East Finnic (Endzelīns in LE, 14/1340).

[2] J. Endzelīns also highlights these changes as an inner development which resulted from the more rapid speech of the temperamental Latvians [sic!] compared with that of the Balto–Finns (Endzelīns 1927, 693).

more after the eighteenth century (a sociologically characteristic loan with a shift in meaning is *strādāt* 'to work' < Russ. *stradat'* 'suffer').

Germanic (German) loans are also double layered. In the first layer, before the thirteenth century, there are few words (among them some refer to the early Scandinavian conquests and conversions: *kungs* 'lord' < OGer. *kunig*; *mūks* 'monk' < Danish, Swedish *munk*). On the other hand, the later German impact was very important because it influenced the development of the literary language in a determining way.

Latvian words and sentences first appear, apart from a few scattered words in Heinricus' chronicle, that is, in the founding charter of a guild of stevedores (*Losträgergilde*) from Riga in 1522. The first cohesive texts are the various sources of the *Lords Prayer* from the early sixteenth century, and the oldest book is a Catholic catechism from 1585 (which was instantly followed by the Lutheran catechisms). As mentioned earlier, E. Glück translated the *New Testament* by 1685 and the *Old Testament* by 1689. The first secular text, translated from the German, is the founding charter of the guild of flax weavers from 1625.

Latvian books were rarely published in the seventeenth and eighteenth centuries, among them the works of G. Manzel (1583–1654) and his student C. Fürecker (ca. 1615–1685) have to be mentioned. G. Manzel was a German priest and the rector of the University of Dorpat. He published his book the *Lang-gewünschte Lettische Postill* in 1654, a handbook of one thousand two hundred pages. Its sixth edition was published as late as the nineteenth century. C. Fürecker imposed rhymes on psalms that his master had translated and published them in 1685 as *Lettische geistliche Lieder und Collecten*, thus laying the foundations of Latvian poetry.

Until the second half of the nineteenth century the authors or translators of Latvian books were almost without exception German, and more often than not priests. (Many question whether they could be accepted as Latvian literature—see for example, Ozols 1965, 19.) Consequently the language of these works is often error-ridden and contains many Germanisms. This is true for the already mentioned works of Stender the Elder, the volumes with the first secular poems (Stenders, *Zingu lustes* [Joyful zings i.e. "ditties"], 1783–89), just like the second edition of the *Lettische Grammatik* of 1783 which is a grammar and also a spelling regulator, an ethnographical and folklore collection, and prosody and stylistics.[3]

---

[3] This is valid, even if Stenders learnt Latvian from a Latvian peasant, and even if, as he writes of himself, he "jotted down on a small board in his hands, each pronounced word, each unknown expression" (Stenders cited in Ozols 1965, 367).

The dual commitment of the German educators is well characterised in the example of Stenders the Elder who, by the end of his life, considered himself Latvian. His son A. J. Stenders the Junior wrote the first Latvian play, yet saw the end goal as total Germanisation. To that end he wrote the first German language book for Latvians in 1820, and he considered a culture in Latvian only necessary as a transitory period. In the foreword to a folklore collection he writes: "Oh, if only the Good Lord would let us experience the time when a single people,

The literary language created by German priests was not limited to that alone, but to deeper transformations of the language of the Latvian people [as the 1615 edition of the *Enchiridion* in Riga puts it "die Lieffländische Pawrsprach" (the Livonian peasant language)]. It was a consequence of the demands of Herrnhutism that the peasants learned to read and write, at least in Vidzeme where the Middle Latvian dialect formed the basis of the literary language and elementary education was of unprecedentedly wide ranging even by European standards (we could say that the Latvians caught up on the historical disadvantages springing from the absence of a state through the mass internalisation of literacy). The expansive second layer of German loan words came to the Latvian language at this time, among them (in an unusual way) the *un* 'and' conjunctive. This German influence had a strange stylistic consequence, too. Through translated literature, Germanisms, alien to the Latvian language, entered and in sermons and other church texts they are still in use today. They lent a certain pathos in the style (for example translating the definite article, absent in Latvian, with a demonstrative pronoun: Ger. *der Herr* Latv. *tas kungs* originally 'that lord', after the German influence 'the lord').[4]

A national renaissance similar to that of other Central and Eastern European peoples went alongside a trend of neologisation among the Latvians, too, that is, the creation of a codified and normalised (standard) literary language. Since alien influences, those already discussed and also because of the maritime relations of the country were very strong, they would later provoke an exaggerated puritan backlash. (The first English loan word is from the late eighteenth century, and in Lithuanian nearly a hundred years later, and there are around 2500 loan words from the Romance languages—Baldunčiks 1989.) Russification increased in the last third of the nineteenth century along with a slow proportional increase of Latvians in the evolving town culture, both of which hindered the evolving neologisation. In 1867 in Riga, of 102,066 people "47,479 were German, 25,670 were Russian, 23,718 were Latvian, 1,172 were Estonian, and 4,027 were from other nationalities" (Hunfalvy 1871/I, 29).

---

the single German language, and a single striving toward a respectable unified life ruled in Kurzeme and Vidzeme. Thus far do not scorn this small thing" (cited in Latviešu 1959, 566). A similar duality can be sensed later, practically throughout the entire nineteenth century, on the Baltic German side, too. For example A. Bielenstein (1826–1907) who is considered to have been the founder of Latvian philology, and who was the president of the 'Society of Friends of Latvia' for decades, at the same time writes in the foreword to the first scholarly grammar in 1863: "the Latvian people did not prove... that their place should be next to other cultural nations, even if a more fortunate destiny should slowly lift the Latvians to a higher social and intellectual level" (Bielenstein cited in Ozols 1965, 14).

[4] It is interesting that, independently of this, the same thing happened when R. Pietsch noted down the language of the fishermen on the Courish Spit. While taking his notes, its potential German translation was always in the back of his mind (Scholz in Pietsch 1982).

For that reason neologisation was much more prolonged than elsewhere, extending into the twentieth century. A literary language founded upon folk songs was established by a number of people. J. Rainis (1865–1929) was an emerging poet who produced world-class poetry. Other contributors were German philologists, for example the aforementioned A. Bielenstein, and two linguists K. Milenbahs (Müllenbach 1853–1916), and J. Endzelīns (1873–1961) who almost became a national institution during his long lifetime. Literary language was first set on paper in 1907, then in 1922 by J. Endzelīns in the thousand-page *Lettische Grammatik*. K. Milenbahs published a four-volume dictionary of definitions in 1923, which J. Endzelīns then expanded. Recently, there has been continual work on an 'academic' dictionary of definitions, and since 1972 eight volumes have been published.

Neologisers tried to use many different sources. In spelling, diacritical signs were adopted from the Czech language ('č', 'š', 'ž'), even though these could be employed after the First World War in the independent Latvia, as with other spelling and printing neologies, such as marking of long vowels and soft consonants, omitting double consonants, using antiqua instead of gothic letters, and so on (Rūķe-Draviņa 1990, 13). The prolonged process is well represented in that the palatal 'r' was dropped from the alphabet as late as in 1946, and 'ch' was only exchanged for 'h' in 1957 (Bergmane–Blinkena 1986), but that is only used in the country, the emigrants did not adopt the new trend (Fennel–Gelsen 1980, XXIII). The main resource for increasing vocabulary were regional dialects and related Baltic languages (for example *ķermenis* 'body' is a Prussian loan, *veikals* 'shop' is from Lithuanian). Linguists kept on trying to draw the two Baltic languages together as late as the thirties and forties.

In today's Latvian language there are three distinct dialects (*dialekts*), with several (around five hundred altogether!) sub-dialects (*izloksne*).[5]

1. Middle Latvian and its sub-dialects:
   (a) Livian Middle Latvian
   (b) Zemgalian Middle Latvian
   (c) Couronian Middle Latvian
   (d) Zemgalian–Couronian Middle Latvian
2. Tamnieks-Latvian[6] or Livian, with its sub-dialects:
   (a) Kurzemian Livian
   (b) Vidzemian Livian

[5] The evolution of the dialects in the place of the Livonian tribal languages and through their interaction is "not completely clear" (Plāķis 1930, 53). It is confused by the generally accepted theory of Endzelīns which has already been mentioned, that is, that the basis of the Latvian language was not Latvian (Leitis) but rather the language of the Letgalian tribe. No intellectual wizardry can explain how and when the Letgalian dialect spread to the territories occupied by the Livians, the Zemgalians, and most of all those of the Couronians.

[6] The meaning of the originally scornful naming is 'a person from there'.

3. High Latvian, with its dialects:
  (a) East High Latvian, which is spoken in Latgale and the northeastern
      region of Vidzeme (which I shall return to separately as the Latgalian
      language)
  (b) West High Livian or Selonian

The first and the second group of dialects is also called Low Latvian as opposed
to the third group's High Latvian (Gāters 1977, 13–14).

Today 1,690,000 people feel they speak Latvian as their mother tongue, that is
the state language of the Latvian Republic, and about another 115,000 people
abroad, mainly in the territories of the former Soviet Union, Canada, Sweden, the
USA, and Germany, and approximately 260,000 people in Latvia think of it as
their second language.

The language can be further characterised:[7]

1. Apart from a few exceptions there is, as well as the word stress on the first
syllable, a syllabic stress (or intonation) which is usually unmarked ("printing
technical reasons"—Rūķe-Draviņa 1990, 324), but marked in professional works.
It can take three forms depending on whether a syllable with a long vowel or one
or the other part of a syllable with a diphthong is stressed: rising (~), falling ('),
or interrupted (^). (In the majority of dialects there are only two intonations.) It
rarely has a meaning differentiating function, and then usually when it appears in
the first syllable of a word.

The length of the four simple vowels ('a', 'e', 'i', 'u') are marked and have a
meaning differentiating function (*upe* 'river', *upē* 'in the river'). The length of the
'o', which is apparent only in more recent loans, is unmarked, and in Latvian
words and older loans is pronounced [uo]. Only professional works and certain
dictionaries indicate perhaps the most characteristic feature of the Latvian language. That is that 'e' and ē express two different sounds: a closed and an open
sound (the sound nearer to 'a' is more open than the Hungarian 'e' is). This carries
a meaning differentiating function (*nesu* with a close 'e' 'I carried', *nesu* with an
open 'e' 'I carry'. Latvian is a harder sounding language than Lithuanian (or
Russian, for example), which is because the frontal vowels do not soften the
preceding consonant. The consonants 'h' and 'f' only come up in foreign words.
There are a number of diacritical consonants with the following pronunciations:
'č' = [ch], 'š' = [sh], 'ž' = [zh], 'ģ' = [dj], 'ķ' = [tj], 'ļ' = [lj], 'ņ' = [nj], 'ŗ' = [rj].
An important characteristic of Latvian tonality is that unvoiced consonants are

---

[7] Gāters 1977, Erhart 1984, Kabelka 1982, and Eckert–Bukevičiūtė–Hinze 1994 gave a
complete linguistic description; Endzelin in 1922 wrote a reader with a brief grammar;
Fennel–Gelsen in 1980 offered a detailed language book; whereas it is not my aim to do any
of these, therefore I shall only mention those interesting features that say something to those
without any knowledge of the language, and those which differentiate it from other Indo-European languages (in a few cases from the Hungarian).

pronounced long between two short vowels (*aka* 'well' pron: *akka*), but the conjunction of consonants are pronounced short: 'ts', 'ds' > [tz] (*galds* 'table' > [galtz]), or at word ends the 'zs' > [s], 'šs', 'žs' > [sh] (*biezs* 'dense' > [*biesh*], *mežs* 'forest' > [mesh]) and the 'v' > u at word ends (*nav* 'no' > [nau]).

2. From the seven cases of substantive declinations, there are practically only five-six in the language, since the sing. acc. and instr. and the pl. dat. and instr. suffixes are the same, and only nouns denoting a person have their own Voc. in sing. The sing. nom. suffixes give three masculine (-s or -š, -is, -us) and three feminine (-e, -a, -s) noun declinations, and there is one masculine (-s or -š) and one feminine (-a) adjective declination corresponding to that of the noun declination. (The so-called definite or pronominal adjectives have separate suffixes.)

The three verb conjugations are based on the differences in the stems of the present and past tenses, and the infinitive. Every verb tense and mode has an active and a passive voice, and can be derived as a simple, or a compounded form through a rich system of participles. Verbs without a prefix are continuous, those with a prefix are finished. There are two special verb modes in Latvian. The so-called *Debitivus* (obligatory) mode compounded from noun or pronouns in dat. + to be + jā and the verb in present tense, third person sing. (*man ir jādzied dziesma* 'I have to sing a song', or word by word: 'To me is must sing song'—as seen, the logical object is in nom.). The other one is the conjunctive mode derived with the aid of the adverbial participle, which I would term a 'putative mode' because it expresses the putative nature of an action (*Vecais barons ir laipns cilvēks* 'the old baron is a good man', *Vecais barons esot laipns cilvēks* 'the old baron being a good man' = 'the old baron is said to be a good man').

3. From syntax I mention only the so-called *dativus absolutus* (which is also present in Lithuanian). In a sub-clause expressing a previous action the predicate is an adverbial participle, and its subject is in dative (*saulei rietot, mes braucām mājās* 'after the sun had set...' word by word: 'to the sun setting, we set out for home').

4.2. The Latgalian language

The first printed Latgalian text is the so-called *Gospel of Asune*, a collection of excerpts from the *New Testament* translated from the German. It was published in 1753 in Vilnius, and several catechisms followed it. Secular texts are only from the very end of the nineteenth century (Gāters 1977, 12). Latgalian differs from the Latvian language mainly in its word stock and in its phonetics. From the latter the more important items are that in the place of the open 'e' there is an 'a', and in the stead of the 'a' there is an 'o'.

To illuminate the differences I enclose a poem by F. Kemps written in 1906 with a Latvian transcript (Kemps, *Latviešu* 1970–78/III, 337):

Tāvu zeme	*Tēvu zeme*	*Land of (our) fathers*
Tāvu zeme, võrgu zeme	Tēvu zeme, vergu zeme	Land of fathers, land of slaves,
Kō tu guli tymsumā?	Ko tu guli tumsumā?	Why sleepest thou in darkness?
Celīs, tovas dryvas, pļovas	Celies, tavas druvas, pļavas	Rise up, your lands and green pastures
Sābri kōjom samyna!	Sābri kājām samina!	Villainous hordes trample underfoot!
Tāvu zeme, paplēt acis,	Tēvu zeme, paplēt acis,	Land of fathers, open your eyes,
Verīs, gaismas saule lāc;	Veries, gaismas saule lec;	Look, for a day of sunlight is dawning;
Sābri pļaun jau zalta kvīrus,	Sābri pļaun jau zelta kvierus,	Villainous hordes already harvest
		the golden wheat,
Tovys teirums nav vēļ sāts.	Tavs tīīrums nav vēl sēts.	But still your lands are not sown.
Tāvu zeme, võrgu zeme,	Tēvu zeme, vergu zeme,	Land of fathers, land of slaves,
Celīs, sovus dālus sauc;	Celies, savus dēlus sauc;	Rise up, call upon your sons;
Verīs, cik vēļ dorba prikīā	Veries, cik vēl darba priekīā	Look, for much work lies before us
Un cik tōl jau sveři ļauds!	Un cik tālu jau sveři ļaudis!	And yet how far distant are
		the strangers!

As it can be seen, the difference between Latvian and Latgalian is not greater than between Czech and Slovakian (which are regarded as separate), and the differences are certainly slighter than between certain German dialects.

Is it then a separate language or a dialect? The question is burdened with political bias. V. Zeps answers soberly, "there is only one Latvian nation, one Latvian language, but there are two Latvian literary languages: one is based on the Lower Latvian dialect, the other on the High Latvian. These two literary languages are called Latvian and Latgalian" (Zeps–Rosenshield 1995, 313; see also Stafecka 1991).

4.3. The Lithuanian language

An initially misleading concept of the Lithuanian language emerged. In the Moscow Rus', in rivalry with Lithuania, the inhabitants and language of the Grand Duchy of Lithuania were universally dubbed Lithuanian without regard as to whether they were Lithuanians, Belarusians, or Ukrainians. This explains several unusual occurrences: Moscow, for example, indicated the official documents of the Grand Duchy of Lithuania written in the 'Ruthenian–Gudas' language as documents in Lithuanian; or there are several examples, even from the twentieth century, that late descendants of Russians, Ukrainians, or Belarusians originally from former Lithuania whose ancestors never spoke Lithuanian either, consider themselves to be Lithuanians (Biržiška 1952, 27).[8]

There are many Lithuanian words in the various documents, mostly proper and place names. Since the notaries were foreign, their value is rather doubtful. The *Chronicon Dubnicense* is a good example, where three words survived, known as the oath of Kęstutis. The unknown chronicler reports on the 1351 expeditions of Lajos the Great, which he launched at the behest of the cousin of the Hungarian King, the Polish King Kazimierz the Great, against the Lithuanians. The Lithuanian Grand Duke Kęstutis yielded to the united Polish and Hungarian armies without a battle, and, in accordance with pagan customs, at the peace contract he presented an ox as a sacrifice. He stabbed his knife, the *lituanicus* specially for this occasion, into the vein of the neck of the ox tied out on two stakes; he smeared the blood on his forehead and exclaimed in Lithuanian "*Rogachina roznenachy gospanany*". As A. Mierzyński pointed out, the sentence is not Lithuanian but actually East Slavic distorted in the process of writing it down. It means 'look at the ox, God is with us" (Mierzyński 1892–96/II, 78).[9] (This case also demonstrates that the state language in the Grand Duchy of Lithuania, at least on such official occasions, was East Slavic—in both its spoken and written forms.)[10]

Throughout its history the Lithuanian language remained in the shadow of East Slavic, Polish, and then Russian, up until 1918 it stayed a secondary, at times a forbidden 'peasant language'. In addition, due to the late Lithuanian conversion to Christianity many endowed the language itself with some pagan connotations.

The first cohesive Lithuanian text was found in 1962. It is a handwritten translation of the *Lords Prayer*, *Hail Mary*, and *Credo* from around 1515 in the

---

[8] As a matter of interest I include a similar current phenomenon: since the change in 1989–1991 the Society of Lithuanians speaking Slavic (!) established in Lithuania has encouraged the emergence of small local literary languages. They propagate, besides Lithuanian Polish and Belarusian based languages, a Lithuanian Slavic mixed language based on the *dzūkas* dialect (Dulichenko 1994, 83).

[9] In another translation "God look down on our souls and the ox" (Beresnevičius 1995, 174).

[10] Of course it is possible that S. C. Rowell, who summarises the debates around the oath, is right in writing that the pagan Kęstutis was tricking the other party of the contract (which is supported in that three days after he had set out with the troops to Buda, in accordance with the agreement, he simply fled home on hearing that the Lithuanian nobility who had been kept hostage were freed in accordance with the agreement); and so he pledged his oath in a foreign language, "*perhaps as a means of invalidating the oath from the beginning by using the 'wrong' language*" (Rowell 1994, 145). It is almost certain that it was also Kęstutis who a few years later in 1358 tricked Emperor Charles IV. After he had previously agreed with the Emperor that Lithuania would accept baptism from his hands, he simply failed to go to Breslau, the site of the baptism where the Emperor waited for him in vain (Boockmann 1992, 176).

last, empty page of a Latin book published in 1503, and contains ninety-four words (Naujokaitis 1973–78/I, 16).[11]

As mentioned earlier, Lithuanian culture was divided almost simultaneously with the appearance of Lithuanian book printing. Culture developed more dynamically in Lithuania Minor than in the Grand Duchy of Lithuania. In Königsberg in 1547 the novice M. Mažvydas (ca. 1520–1563) published the first book in Lithuanian and a translation of a catechism which has the first Lithuanian poem as a foreword or dedication. The first complete *Bible* translation was made in Königsberg, by J. Bretkūnas, but its publication is still awaited in the future. (The Protestant translation of the *New Testament* was published in 1701, the complete *Bible* translation, the work of a translation committee, in 1735; whereas the Catholic version came only in the mid-twentieth century and even then in England, in Lithuania it was as late as 1972.) D. Klein, the author of the first grammar book was from Prussia (*Grammatica Lituanica*, 1653), just like J. Šulcas who published the first Lithuanian book of literature in 1706. (The first text with a secular content is from 1589, a hexameter for greeting the King.) Later the emphasis was on Prussian–Lithuania, too, as far as the Enlightenment of the late eighteenth century, when 108 books were published in Lithuanian between 1578 and 1831, nearly twice as many as in Lithuania.

Lithuania only regained its leading role in the nineteenth century. With the suppression of the 1830 and 1863 uprisings the national renaissance movement died down twice at the point when it began to ignite. Neologism and the evocation of a literary language were also only accomplished by the twentieth century.[12]

Two personalities had significant roles in the codification and normalisation of the literary language based on the southwestern Aukštaitian dialect, which resembled Prussian–Lithuanian.[13] J. Jablonskis (1860–1930), this 'national awakener' published the first grammar book of modern Lithuanian under a pseudonym in Tilsit in 1901, its final version was completed in 1922. The 'Lithuanian Endzelīns', K. Būga (1879–1924) offered the theoretical and historical arguments.

[11] Several early nineteenth-century authors claim that around 1228, that is before Lithuania's conversion to Christianity, G. Mutinensis translated the grammar of a fourth-century Roman author, A. Donatus to Lithuanian at the behest of Wilhelm, Bishop of Modena, others believe it was to Latvian, Zemgalian, or Prussian. However, there are no traces of the translation, and it is completely improbable (Zinkevičius 1984–94/III, 16). On the other hand, the information from King Jagiello's chaplain from 1434 is more credible, according to which at the time of the baptism of the Lithuanians the King himself had translated the *Lords Prayer* from Polish to Lithuanian—true, this is lost without trace, too.

[12] The language of the *Aušra*, for example, changed with the dialect of the editor (Palionis 1979, 219).

[13] Next to Prussian–Lithuanian Z. Zinkevičius presumes two more "inter-dialects" or literary language variants within the Grand Duchy of Lithuania, however, as J. Palionis demonstrated, the presumption is forced [Zinkevičius (1984–94); Eckert–Bukevičiūtė–Hinze 1994, 57].

Even before the First World War Būga had begun to collect the complete word stock. The publication of his dictionary of definitions was interrupted by his untimely death. Still the 600,000 paper slips he collected were the foundations for the 'academic' complete dictionary that was initiated in 1968, which is approaching completion with its XVIth substantial volume; from the 1970s under the Soviet regime the collection of its data became a patriotic peoples' movement (Rinholm 1990, 295).

The Lithuanian language is divided into two big groups of dialects that are hardly comprehensible to one another, these are the Žemaitian and the Aukštaitian dialects. Each of them has at least three further sub-groups. As discussed earlier, their territories do not correspond to the administrative and political division of the Middle Ages, Žemaitija and Aukštaitija. The area of the Žemaitian dialect is considerably smaller than the former Žemaitija, and nearly three times smaller than the region of the other group of dialects.

There are totally contradictory viewpoints about the development of the Lithuanian dialects, centring on the break up of the East Baltic unit. Those who presume an early and separate migration of the given tribes (Selonian, Letgalian, Zemgalian, Lithuanian, and Žemaitian), which would have laid the basis for the later dialectical differences, refer to early differences which decreased with the later unification of the languages into two separate languages. On the other hand, those (myself included) who presume a late and gradual disintegration of the Common East Baltic tribe (the Leitis people) posit that the dialectical differences occurred later also within the already separate languages. For example, according to A. Salys the Žemaitian–Aukštaitian division began in the fifteenth century (cited in Kiparsky 1939, 56).

The Lithuanian language, which is the state language of the Lithuanian Republic is spoken by 2,900,000 people at home, approximately 100,000 in the successor states of the former Soviet Union (primarily in Belarus), 40,000 in Poland, and 3–400,000 in the USA (with Chicago as their centre).

In addition to those mentioned already, the following features characterise it:

1. Besides a free word stress, there is a syllabic stress, an intonation with a meaning differentiating function (*káltas* 'chisel', *kãltas* 'guilty'). Long vowels ('ą', 'ę', 'ė', 'o', 'į', 'y', 'ų', 'ū'), the six diphthongs, as well as the sixteen syllabic sound combinations ('al', 'am', 'an', 'ar', 'el', 'em', 'en', 'er', 'il', 'im', 'in', 'ir', 'ul', 'um', 'un', 'ur') can have falling (') or rising (~) intonation. There are no long consonants, and consonants shorten in foreign words, too (*kasa* '*cassa*'). Front vowels soften the preceding consonants, but to a lesser extent than in Russian.

2. There are five noun declinations according to endings (-as, -is, -ys; -us, -ius; and -uo masculine endings; -a, ė; -is feminine endings), and three adjective declinations (-as, -a; -us, -i; -is, -ė). Intonation, though unmarked, is so important in the Lithuanian language that the declination tables of the above are usually given according to the shift in stress in the seven cases, that is whether it stays on

the stem, or shifts to the ending. There is one more verb tense than in Latvian, the present, the finished past, the future, and a simple continuous past. Two adjectival participles can be derived from the latter, too, which (besides the rich intonation) gives the other special characteristic of the Lithuanian language, that is the great number of adjectival and adverbial participles. The thirteen participles allow subtle expression through compounded structures, among others, the conjunctive or 'putative mode'.

PART FOUR

BALTIC MYTHOLOGY

CHAPTER 1

PREHISTORY, FOLKLORE, MYTHOLOGY

There are cultures, for example that of the Balts, where due to the late development of literacy prehistory (or to use a more delicate expression as in the subtitle, 'antiquity') extended into recent times. Numerous fundamental difficulties can emerge in such circumstances if scholars use oral folklore and mythology to fill in for the absence of literacy in order concoct history from prehistory. In this chapter I shall highlight some of the pitfalls inherent in this problem.

The first questions concern whether or not there is any form of Baltic consciousness; and what meaning, if any, Baltic folklore and Baltic mythology carry.

There are Baltic languages whose current existence is undoubtedly rooted in a Common Proto-Baltic language that existed between 1800 BC and 500 AD. The reality and objectivity of the Common Baltic language and later offshoot languages, lends objectivity to the scholarship and sciences examining this language (or these languages), that is to Baltic studies in the narrow sense. This objectivity is not shaken by either the fact that the concept of 'Baltic languages' is a nineteenth-century theoretical construction, or by the lack of unanimous agreement about the number of extinct or even living Baltic languages. It is debatable whether, besides Lithuanian, only Latvian or also Latgalian (which is perhaps distant enough from Latvian to be more than a dialect) are to be considered as separate languages. Nonetheless severe doubt may surround the validity and explanatory value of Baltic Studies in its wider sense along with its subject, the other forms of 'Baltic' consciousness. These doubts do not concern the former existence or absence of these forms of consciousness since, I believe, it is correct to presume that the communities of prehistoric peoples had some form of folklore or mythology (religion) of their own, leaving little reason to doubt it in the case of the Balts. Instead, these doubts are focused on the issue of whether the former commonality, and the continuity of the language into today's Latvian and Lithuanian would offer sufficient grounds to presume the continuity and preservation of other forms of consciousness which in some ways rely upon language. (When Endzelīns calls for a third *Introduction* to follow the linguistic works of P. Šmits in 1936 and his own *Introduction to Baltic Philology* in 1945 which he states "should be written by a person who is knowledgeable in Lithuanian and Latvian literature and folklore", he essentially mechanically and without reflection transfers the linguistic concept onto literature and folklore—Endzelīns 1945, 352.) It is highly questionable as to whether other forms of consciousness can be parasitic upon, or to put it more delicately could take a share of the objective existence and continuity of a language. Whether the once common Baltic language is a sufficiently solid bonding material to sustain the unity of the other forms of consciousness over several thousand years, even when the community of these forms of consciousness has long since disintegrated, is uncertain. Another question concerns whether or not all language families *have* (and not only *had*) a family mythology, folklore, or perhaps even a literature, i.e. Finno-Ugric, Romance, Slavic, Germanic, etc. folklore and mythologies.[1]

A *common Baltic* literature, where literature is a form of consciousness at its most distant (and most unique) from Proto-Baltic (and the collectivity of language) has undoubtedly never existed. For this reason no one has, or could have written a history of Baltic literature.[2]

A common Baltic folklore would be equally problematic to demonstrate. P. Šmits posits that from among several hundred-thousand Latvian and Lithuanian *dainas* (folk-songs) thirty-seven resemble each other. This much similarity could certainly be found between the folklore of any European people (Šmits 1923, 8). (Similarly, J. Honti believes that ethnographical data is unsuitable for prehistoric comparison due to its lack of determinability or the international character of ethnic particularities—Honti 1935, 110.)

The scarcity of similarities in folklore is a decisive argument against the ancient nature of remnant folklore. As demonstrated earlier, the separation of Latvian and

---

[1] "The extent to which Balto–Finn folk mythology can be traced back to common Finno–Ugric predecessors is questionable. The existence of a pre-feudalist folk mythology can be assumed, but its particulars and ethno–local framework are not precisely known. Based on a correlation of names it later specified a singular god–sky god–air god, but at that point a still 'empty' god figure with undifferentiated features seems verifiable. The arrangement of the various gods into a particular system could only occur later during the independent existence of the various peoples. In this way, we cannot talk about a unified Balto–Finn folk mythology in the genetic sense" (Voigt 1967–68/4, 413).

[2] In A. Rubulis' book which, despite its rather misleading subtitle is a rather incidental anthology, the word 'Baltic' implies plurality and 'of the Baltic region', just as in R. Parolek, or F. Scholz, who included Estonian literature alongside Latvian and Lithuanian in their comparisons (Rubulis 1970, Parolek 1978, Scholz 1990), not to mention the volumes that do not even attempt to compare (e.g. *Die Osteuropäischen*, 1908; or Devoto 1963), but simply place separate national literary histories by different authors side by side (e.g. A. Bezzenberger and E. Wolter in the first volume, E. Blese and A. Senn in the second).

Evidently, comparisons based on either the typology or the relationship between Latvian and Lithuanian literatures do not operate with some form of common Baltic literature (for the most detailed work on the relationships see Nastopka 1971). What is more, the typological comparison can establish that Latvian literature shows more commonality and similarities with Estonian literature which is part of another language family than with Lithuanian which is related.

Lithuanian languages began during the sixth century and ended between the tenth–eleventh centuries. Given the several thousand years of their coexistence to that point, substantially more common or identical examples of folklore might be expected. Their absence illustrates that the vestigial folklore of today must have been generated after the tenth–twelfth centuries, that is, following the disintegration of the East Baltic (Latvian–Lithuanian) unit, and must have continued for several centuries, perhaps even into the nineteenth century. Their first recordings, both among the Latvians and the Lithuanians, were in the seventeenth century, and only more intensely from the nineteenth century.

Some scholars group folklore and mythology according to language families, these H. Łowmiański scornfully ranks among those working with ethnographic methodology (Łowmiański 1984, 661). Others see them as the representatives of cultural historical methodology, still others, mostly from America, with cultural or historical anthropological methods (cf. Klaniczay 1984). In any case, they identify certain forms of consciousness with each other (language with folklore, folklore with mythology, mythology with language, and so on, round and round) either unconsciously as self-evident or with a definite aim.[3] This is how a Latvian folk-song, the earliest record of which is at 1632, becomes "a peculiar reserve where many remnants of the Indo-European era are preserved with the greatest faith to the past, and without adulteration... it is more archaic than Ancient Greek or Old Indic poetry" (Toporov 1984, 37, 47).[4] "The old Lithuanian religion and mythology, archaic like the Lithuanian language, show a lot of common Indo-European features" (Vėlius 1995, 5). A. J. Greimas posits that mythology is identical with the entirety of social consciousness, that is with culture, and that the research of myths is a type of cultural anthropology (Greimas 1979, 18) because, as M. Gimbutienė writes, myths conserve very old poetic images "which go back not hundreds, but thousands of years, and some of their elements have been passed down over six thousand years" (Gimbutienė 1977, 204).

---

[3] H. Bausinger emphasises that "in most ethnographical concepts, ideological elements are inherent in the term for the subject area itself (*Volkskunde*). The customary topics, their customary division, and the customary stock of means for their discussion in ethnography are more heavily burdened with evaluations attached to them than those in other disciplines" (Bausinger, n. d., 9).

[4] The theory of the ancient nature of Baltic folklore, customs, beliefs, and so on, is dubious from the start because of the enormous pseudo-scientific fog around it. A small book published somewhere in the Western Hemisphere in 1977 by a certain Dr. A. Kauliņš claims that "Latvian is the oldest living tongue... [For which reason] the *original* Indo-European language can be reconstructed in *near* entirety from the current Latvian language... [For this reason] Sumerian is derived from Latvian, Latvian *dainas* are for the most part thousands of years old and are a uniquely ancient and copious record of earlier times" (Kauliņš, *The Baltic: Origin of the Indo-European Languages and Peoples*, 1977).

In this way, one of the sources of Baltic mythology is the 'eternal' and 'ancient' folklore. ("The main sources for reconstructing the characters of goddesses and gods are sagas, beliefs, mythological *dainas*, and especially the Latvian mythological dainas"—Gimbutienė 1984, 30.) The other source is directly *the* protolanguage, or the Indo-European Proto-language, which is of the same age since it is impossible to determine its age.[5]

These views go back to the Brothers Grimm. Those who believe in historical methods, as opposed to those above, emphasise the independence of the different forms of consciousness, based on the standpoint that distant societies on the same level of development necessarily construct similar ideological systems without necessarily being of the same origin (Renfrew 1987, 255 ff).[6] This is what inspires K. Kerényi to say that, "during a comparative examination of mythological material, it must be accepted as an axiom that no language relatedness should be presumed between peoples whose mythologies are being compared, neither should revealed mythological similarities lead us to such conclusions" (Kerényi 1939, 18). D. Čiževskij pinpoints the "internationalism" of folklore which stretches beyond language families when he criticises the theses of his early adulthood friend R. Jakobson, for presuming some kind of common Slavic literature that was realised through and embodied in a common Slavic folklore and based on the common origins of Slavic languages. "The commonality of folkloric pre-conditions connects not only the Slavs, but goes far beyond the borders of the families of Slavic peoples, and intertwining threads lead not only to other Indo-Germanic peoples, but also to the neighbours of the Slavs with completely different origins and languages, and even further to almost all the peoples of the world. Excellent examples can be taken from every work in the field of comparative research of tales and myths" (Čiževskij 1956, 2). Comparison through ethnographic methods is not true comparison because it can only ever demonstrate identical features, more precisely of the 'eternal' structures in the

---

[5] The Indo-European civilisation also has connections in other directions: typologically to the ancient eastern civilisations (Gamkrelidze–Ivanov 1984/II, 864). W. Schmidt posits that the two immigrant waves of the Indo-Europeans brought two types of religion to Europe, and A. Nehring also discusses the Indo-European religion as a mixture of the Caucasian and Ural beliefs (Schmidt 1949, 319; Nehring 1954, 400). The circle of comparison can be expanded with all these spaces...

[6] My emphasis is on the difference between methods, or even viewpoints, and not between subject areas or disciplines. The followers of the historical perspective are, by and large, but by no means without exception, historians. For example, the excellent ethnographic researcher J. Balys considers himself "of positivist inclinations", yet utilises strict historical perspectives in his examinations of folklore and mythology (Lit. E./XIX, 74); in Hungarian circles I. Györffy is a similar character. There are numerous examples from the opposing side, that is historians who have subjected themselves to ethnographic methods, who believe the values of folklore works without the application of source critique.

unfathomable distant common past. It leaves the developmental differences (most frequently uneven!) on separate paths after the once common road without remark (or even worse, at times it tries to create homogeneity by reflecting them back into the ancient and eternal commonality). Only the historical method can produce true comparison. As one of the greatest (if not the greatest) Hungarian philologists I. Goldziher put it: "The foundation of a *history of development*; and not the *a priori* construction of the history of development, or perhaps some kind of Hegelian synthesis, but a foundation derived from *facts* experienced in various circles of culture, that is if we presume that the religion of every race and people perceptible at any given historical point is the result of a necessarily long *evolution* or process of development. This foundation can form a sound basis for the characterisation of the '*comparative method*' precisely because it observes the steps of the history of development not in terms of race, but by the dimensions of the psychological and historical motions which have evoked development *in all humankind in the same manner*, and because where there seems to be a difference in relation to the majority of steps it then investigates the psychological and historical motions which lead to that divergence" (Goldziher 1878, 182).

The views of the two camps differ so fundamentally because they are based to a lesser extent on facts, and mostly on the beliefs of whoever wants or is willing to believe in what.[7] For this reason, in his fundamental study G. Komoróczy could state that: "Prehistory is always simply the historicalisation (or propagandistic historicalisation) of an ethnic or national consciousness of identity, that is the reflection of the family model and the tribal consciousness back into the timeless past. Prehistory is not a question of facts, of truth that can be uncovered, even if it has factual elements that can be examined through scientific methods.[8] It is, to put it coarsely, a matter of determination. Every nation chooses or writes a prehistory according to its will" (Komoróczy 1991, 20).

In connection with prehistory writing I have discussed the way historical facts are created, that the existence and cognizance of the various forms of consciousness are indivisible. Only that has existed which we know of, and what we know nothing of has at most existed in its irrelevant generality. It concerns the sources and their authenticity (cf. Part Two, Subchapter 1.1). (For example, Greek mythology exists because texts by Homer, Hesiod, and many other authors are at

---

[7] One of the major proponents of antiquity, N. Vėlius also acknowledged that "whatever someone is looking for in living traditions is almost always found" (Vėlius 1995, 19).

[8] In 1942 W. Wüst, professor of Indo-Germanic Studies at Munich, offered his collection of studies (*Indogermanische Bekenntnis* to Himmler, in which national-socialist ideology, "in a grotesque way, constantly becomes mixed with the particulars of professional knowledge" (See 1970, 98).

our disposal, there is a Jewish mythology because there is the *Old Testament*, and so on.)[9]

The supporters of ethnographic methods, having declared the various forms of consciousness identical, use these as sources for one or the other forms without

[9] Accident plays a large role because of the haphazard way in which written sources survive. "The review of *foreign* (German, Russian, Polish) demonstrated that we have to rely upon *contingent* sources, which offer contingent frames" (Ivinskis 1938–1939, 390). K. Kerényi is of a similar opinion: "In our narratives about the beginning of things three great goddesses play the role of the World Mother: Tethys the goddess of the sea; the goddess of the night; and mother earth. This trinity obviously came about by accident, since we know of only three such narratives" (Kerényi 1971, 36).

In the eyes of the historians, the survival of a source seems so important that they forget the decisive question of the authenticity of information in the source, that is its quality. For example Jordanes' work, which is no more than extracts from Senator Cassiodorus' twelve lost volumes, and was much quoted after Aeneas Silvius found and published it, became the basis for all kinds of theories. J. Voigt establishes that "he was the worst writer of the Early Middle Ages, in all aspects" (Voigt 1827–39/1, 94).

Of course, the authenticity of the sources is not a simple philological issue, but can have wide-ranging consequences. The 'Czech question' was decided by the outcome of the nine-teenth-twentieth-century debate over the so-called *Králodvorský* and *Zelenohorský Manu-scripts*, which proved to be forged. It decided what historical tradition (and conclusively what 'national character') the Czechs would accept as their own (cf. Havelka 1995).

In the history of Latvian and Lithuanian folklore there were no forgeries comparable to the *Manuscripts* or the *Ossian Songs*, still L. Rėza, the publisher of the first more serious collection of Lithuanian dainas also fabricated a few motifs into the folk-songs that are frequent in Latvian folk-songs (e.g. *dievo sunėliai* 'god's little sons', *dievo duktėlės* 'god's little daughters', *saules dukrytės* 'sun daughters') (Rėza 1825). (The Latvian motifs which were perhaps taken from Livian or Estonian cf. Balys 1977, 200.) These are vehemently cited as the heritage of a common Baltic antiquity. The mere occurrence of these motifs in Latvian folk-songs was sufficient for D. J. Ward to declare that "the Indo-European tradition of the twins is best preserved in the hymns of the *Rigveda*, in Greek mythology, and in the folk-songs of the Baltic area" (Ward 1970, 405). Although the latter were only collected in the nineteenth century, it is known (after A. Švābe) that the meter of many dainas had developed by the eighth century (Ward 1970, 418), and if nineteenth century were not old enough the eighth century must certainly be sufficiently ancient... (Independent of whether the term 'god's little sons' and 'sun daughters' are from the common Indo-European past, H. Biezais proved that there are no references to twins in Latvian folk-songs—Biezais 1972, 468.)

The Rėza collection also sheds some light on the extent to which folk art is the art of the 'folk'. From Rėza's correspondence it is clear that there was not a single 'son of the people', or peasant, among the eight people delivering the dainas for his collection, but all were learned people, and with one exception, all priests, just like Rėza the professor of theology (Naujokaitis 1973–78/I, 143). These dainas, among which there are obviously a number of German compositions, became popular and 'fell among the people', and a hundred years later, at the outset of the collection of folk-songs with scholarly methods, they could indeed have had a totally authentic, 'grassroots' feel.

hesitation. The other camp on the other hand, probably in a minority, accepts only written sources concurrent or close to a given period as authentic.[10]

Written Baltic sources, as shown earlier, are scarce and of highly questionable authenticity. Consequently, C. Lévi-Strauss' statement concerning cultures without literacy is valid for the 'ancient' Baltic culture, "our best efforts at understanding them can be no more than suppositions" (Lévi-Strauss 1952, 104).

The thought arises that perhaps, instead of contrasting historical and ethnographic methods, it would be better to use them together in a complementary way since, as A. J. Greimas believes, sources themselves are of two types: "The material to be studied for the mythology of the Lithuanian people is both historical and ethnographical. On the one hand there are the written sources: scarce thirteenth–fifteenth-century references about the religion of the neighbouring peoples; later from the Lithuanian annals and chronicles; then in the sixteenth–seventeenth centuries more extensive descriptions of the degraded religion, rituals, and customs. On the other hand there is detailed ethnographical collection pulled together carefully enough from the nineteenth century up to today, where

---

[10] Documents from the Middle Ages had already made this distinction among sources. For example in the *Chronica Bohemorum* Cosmas, 'the Czech Herodotus' (1045–1125) used two types of sources. (1) The fable-like reports of the elderly (*senum fabulosa relatio*), where the reader or listener has to decide(!) whether it is truth or fiction (*facta* versus *ficta*). (2) The true reports of trustworthy people (*vera fidelium relatio*), among which there are some where the chronicler was an eye-witness (and Cosmas places the written sources in this category!), and some that he had just heard of. This is noteworthy from the point of view of seeing how much significance was allotted to written sources, and that oral sources were differentiated from each other by the period of their recording—this has remained the main issue of debate up to the present day: whether the folklore and mythology of the Balts only say something valid about the time at which they were recorded, or also about a more distanced past, and consequently whether they are documents of the time of their recording or also of an earlier period. Of course, what is near to or distant from a given time primarily depends on the judgement of the historian. For example the *Edda Songs* of the ninth–twelfth centuries were recorded around 1200, and they are kept mostly in a hand written anthology, the *Codex Regius* (Balogh in *Edda* 1985, 496). The one hundred–three hundred years between its emergence and recording makes the authenticity of the *Epic Edda* debatable. "They knew no more about the events preceding the second half of the eleventh century than we" (Labuda 1960–75/II, 196). "They can only be used in comparison with other unquestionably authentic sources" (Łowmiański 1957, 85). "The question of whether the royal sagas are authentic is impossible to answer without ambiguity" (Gurevich 1972, 127).

Authenticity also depends on the genre and the style. The songs of the *skalds* survived in the prosaic sagas recorded in the twelfth–fourteenth centuries. It is likely that the historical data in the skald song of the manuscript is more authentic than the ones in the sagas because information is kept more securely in the binding form of poetry (cf. See 1981, 19). According to the poet J. Arany, genre, or "the poetic curve is what enables the traditional sagas to be handed down from generation to generation without the aid of literacy; without it the loose collection of pure facts would easily fall from the memory" (Arany 1860, 220).

the remnants of the old beliefs and customs are recognisable within the framework of the ruling Catholic religion" (Greimas 1979, 14). The problem is that these two types of sources for mythology are not of equal value. Ethnographic materials can conditionally verify authentic written sources, but the converse is not true. Folklore recorded in the nineteenth century only proves the authenticity of the data in a written source in the rarest of cases. The followers of the ethnographic method dismiss this aspect (for example A. J. Greimas, although he is aware of the dangers of doing so), and because folklore encompasses the entirety of the human world anything can be 'proven'.

What can historians do in such a situation? Either reconcile themselves to Wittgenstein's principle, "what can be said at all can be said clearly; and where of one cannot speak thereof one must be silent" (Wittgenstein 1998, 27), or accept the ethnographic method and give free rein to their imagination, since as A. Spekke lightheartedly comments on cosmography containing the tales of the eighth-century Aethicus Ister, "imagination is also a kind of source of knowledge" (Spekke 1938, 89).[11]

As mentioned earlier, without written sources language can only be used as a historical source to a minimal extent, if at all (cf. Part Two, Subchapter 1.1.3).

The same is true of works of folklore. What J. Grabowicz writes about Ukrainian folklore is valid for Latvian and Lithuanian folklore, too (but not the non-existent Baltic folklore), "one has no tools for dealing concretely with the problem of folklore, i.e. the creativity of the 'humble folk', the *narod*, prior to the eighteenth or at least the seventeenth century when the texts were first recorded" (Grabowicz 1981, 21).

For two reasons, whether folklore can be used as a historical source is more than questionable, the first of which is the problem of content. Folklore immobilises history as either 'eternally human' or an 'ancient' tale. "The more dynamic, individualised, and unrepeatable phenomena become [in popular culture] rela-

---

[11] However, this imagination is bound to facts and cannot fly liberally as artistic imagination does. "The writer's work begins where the *Tractatus* stops. Its first maxim is that 'what cannot be talked about is worthy of discussion'" (Farkas 1994, 147).

If artistic imagination is set into motion in science it always results in slippage and the distortion of reality, even if its subject or material is the same as in art. The best example of this is Bubilas (< *bub-* 'to buz') or Babilas (< *bab-* 'to thrash about'), which is the name of "the separate gods of bees and honey kept by the Old Balts (from Indo-European times)" (Gamkrelidze–Ivanov 1984/II, 607). They were created by 'scientists' of the fifteenth–sixteenth centuries, along with the other members of the Baltic Olympus. If a contemporary scholar takes them for gods, they make the mythological concept of god uninterpretably trivial. Nonetheless, significant Baltic writers created symbols and 'myths' of deep meaning by somehow connecting apiary and bees with death, through evoking the images of memory, childhood, and a formerly harmonic past (see the Latvian Virza 1933, 20; Miłosz 1953, 109; Kondrotas 1982, 20).

tively permanent, recurring, and in this sense, 'structures beyond time'" (Gurevics 1987, 381).[12]

It is difficult to say anything concrete about when a given work of folklore emerged. There was a debate about Latvian folk-songs between the two World Wars (Šmits 1923, 1932, 1937; Schmidt 1930; Švābe 1923). P. Šmits (Schmidt) at least tried to offer some definite historical time reference for the Latvian folk-songs, as opposed to generalities in the swirling mists of ancient times. The analysis of the content of the texts demonstrates a happy world which could only be imagined between the thirteenth and the sixteenth centuries because later, under the so-called Polish, Swedish, and particularly the Russian periods it seems to have been out of the question—which other sources about these later periods reveal. Latvian folk songs "are connected to the ideals of Christian belief, to German terminology, and the culture of the last seven hundred years" (Šmits 1923, 6). No one has found data in them, neither about Latvian heroes, rulers, dukes, the pagan priests nor magicians of pagan times, nor about the old Latvian tribes and settlements of long-gone times. There is no single cultic song among them. It cannot be declared that the Latvians in these folk-songs were not Christians. The two pagan gods, *Dievs*, meaning the celestial father [the Indo-European origins of the word are unquestionable—E.B.], and *Laima*, the goddess of happiness "had been completely assimilated by the Christian God, and Mary" (Šmits 1923, 24). Since then, E. Dunsdorfs, a historian living in Australia, posits that they are even more recent. On the basis of the types of currency in the folk-songs he concludes that "the flourishing of the dainas extant today, started in the sixteenth century" (Dunsdorfs 1973, 49).[13]

---

[12] The aforementioned first folk-song, recorded by F. Menius (Professor of History at Tartu) in *Syntagma de Origine Livonarum*, also contains the 'eternally human'. L. Bērziņš interprets it as 'sexually connotative', and it is indeed playful (Bērziņš 1930, 288). in Latvian / in English—Manne Balte Mamelyt, / My little white mother—Dod mann wene Kathenyt, / Give me a kitten,—Mann pelyte peejukus, / my little mouse took to—Py ta sweste bundeling. / the butter pot.

The first Lithuanian folklore texts were recorded by J. A. Brand in 1673–1674 during his journey to Moscow through Lithuania, and were published in print in 1702 (*Durch die Marck Brandenburg, Preussen, Churland, Liefland usw.*). Among these there are a mourning dirge, a 'drinking song' (daina), two proverbs, and descriptions of a Christening, a wedding, and funeral customs (Balys 1948, 207), but no 'history'. Goethe appreciated Latvian (Lithuanian) folk-songs, because "they move around in the most natural, most simple circles" (Goethe 1820, 346), and he believed that the dainas of the mentioned Rēza collection are commonly about "girls wishing to get married, and men of mounting horses" (Goethe 1828, 154).

[13] When H. Biezais declares that "professionals agree that Latvian folk-songs contain elements which come from before the ninth century or even earlier, although the majority of folk songs only emerged between the fifteenth–seventeenth centuries," unfortunately he fails to say who those concurring professionals are (Biezais 1954, 89).

J. Balys believes that from amongst the Lithuanian dainas "only the few dialogic songs (*sutartinė*) can have come from prehistoric times, the narrative types cannot be older than five hundred years" (Lit. E./XV, 479).

The other reason why using folklore as a source is questionable is formal–technical, that is the mode of handing down. How should 'from mouth to mouth' be interpreted, whose was the 'first mouth', how long does a folk-song survive, say, in the midst of wars, epidemics, or serfdom?

According to K. Jażdżewski examples stand as evidence that the "aristocracy preserved oral historical traditions more or less intact for as long as several centuries, because their political interests required it" (Jażdżewski 1963, 18). Yes, the aristocracy did, but because there was also some sort of literary tradition alongside the oral. (There was no aristocracy among the Balts, and in Lithuania they had a different mother tongue.) And what about the people? A. Funkenstein compares collective and individual memories to the language–speech (*langue–parole*) relationship. From this it becomes obvious why theorists studying oral handing down unanimously agree that "folk traditions do not live as a public property in the depths of the 'people's soul', but they depend much more on individual creativity. Each form of folkloric expression has active carriers and passive carriers, but these constitute only a numerically limited group within every community. What they pass on and how is rather accidental" (Dégh–Vázsonyi 1975, 109). For something to survive for several generations at least one institutional person is needed (some kind of permanent 'man of many songs' or 'teller of tales'), but there is no knowledge of anything of the kind.[14]

---

[14] O. Loorists, who studied Estonian popular belief, also states that when people with this type of social development find themselves in the European political, ideological and religious framework, then it emerges that "they have no leaders: priests or philosophers" (cited in Voigt 1994, 220). The lack of sources can encourage people to perform fantastic intellectual gymnastics, for example Gamkrelidze–Ivanov when they state that there is no common Indo-European word for the social function of the 'priest' and that this absence can be explained through the original word becoming taboo (Gamkrelidze–Ivanov 1984/II, 789). (The story comes to mind of the Soviet archaeologist who, having found telephone wires in a grave established that our ancestors were acquainted with the telegraph, and when there were no wires in the next grave the conclusion was ready that cordless telegraphs had been discovered.) On one occasion even the unsullied and soberly critical J. Balys explained 'the void' similarly: "It is unclear why written sources first mention Žemyna, Gabija, and Laima so late, but that does not mean that these goddesses were unknown before the sixteenth–seventeenth centuries. Gods are usually only known by the *initiated*, they do not appear to any outsider" (Balys 1966, 111). In the same way, H. Bertuleit posits that the Prussians had idols which chroniclers could not report on simply because the natives hid them from foreigners (Bertuleit 1924, 56). R. Rimantienė explains the controversy concerning the absence of any finds of amber ornaments in the territory of the Lithuania of the Bronze Ages, while in Europe amber was very much in fashion, by saying that "Europe did not like our ornamental forms" and not that there might not have been any amber craftsmanship in Lithuania at the time (Rimantienė 1995, 102).

Even when we have pieces of information, it is impossible to verify them. An ethnographer who studies shamanism reports that even today there are shamans in Siberia who know the names and knowledge of their predecessors of fifteen generations before (cited in Pentikäinen 1989, 98). Without writing, how do we know that the Soviet shaman did not only remember fourteen of his ancestors and lie? I give more credit to M. Finley who, in discussion of the concatenations of myth, memory, and history writes that 'oral' memory "is short-lived, going back to the third generation and, with the rarest of exceptions, no further. This is true even of genealogies... and without exception a few steps take them from human ancestors to gods or goddesses" (Finley 1975, 27). Finley emphasises the very important factor that memory here is not some accidental and spontaneous act of the consciousness, but always has an intention, and serves a purpose. In brief, only societies and groups within a society have an interest in preserving historical memories that have some degree of historical consciousness. For this reason H. Bausinger is right in positing that in ethnography "the category of duration is always of mythical nature" (cited in Ranke 1969, 102). In the unproblematic and unreflective view of handing down the question arises whether we are dealing with the remnants of the foggy ideas around the 'happy barbarian' or the 'happy ploughman'.

Scholars have choices between extremes, depending on their presumptions and prejudices, and according to their beliefs. The tale *Egle (Silver Pine) the Snake Goddess* exemplifies this. The rhyming-tale was written by the 'Lithuanian enthusiast' Polish romantic J. I. Kraszewski (1812–1887), as a song in the *Witolorauda* (Witolis' dirge) published in 1840, the first part of the three-volume, almost thousand-page historical narrative epic the *Anafielas*. K. Proniewska (Praniauskaitė) translated it to Lithuanian on a better level than her own dilettante Polish verses, and published it in an almanac in 1859. The tale had an unprecedented impact. As a fundamental work of Lithuanian high art even today, and practically the emblematic expression of the image the Lithuanians formed of themselves and of their 'Lithuanianness', it was reworked and reinterpreted in numerous forms, such as sculpture, painting, poetry, opera and ballet.[15] A contributor to its reception was that the story was also found in the form of a folk tale, first at the tail-end of the nineteenth century, then again in ever newer versions, they numbered eighty in 1981 at the Lithuanian Academy of Sciences.[16]

[15] As far as I know the most recent interpretation of the tale is K. Saja's short story, the first that has no 'Lithuanian' or 'national' aspect to it, only the 'eternally human'. Even so, it must be said that Saja continued the tale (for which the text did not have to be published again, since every Lithuanian knows it by heart) (Saja, *Po to, kai jie pavirto medžiais* [After they had turned into trees], 1976).

[16] As such it was added to the Aarne–Thompson international catalogue of folk-tales, categorised into the 'Amour and Psyche type number 425', but due to its uncategorisable uniqueness it alone constitutes the subgroup 'M' (in J. Balys' 1936 catalogue it is subgroup 'D').

J. I. Kraszewski was one of the most productive authors in the world with more than five hundred volumes-worth of novels, travel accounts, studies, and poems. The *Anafielas* is not the only work with a Lithuanian subject. He wrote a four-volume monograph about Wilno, the town of his university and later prison years, and a two-volume cultural history of Lithuania under the title *Litwa* that simultaneously filled the gap in the Lithuanian literature and historical research, barely extant at the time, and popularised them.[17] J. Kraszewski "who spoke Lithuanian to some extent" (Doveika 1962, 286), and drew his materials from the work of T. Narbutt who did not speak the language at all, and also from other also dubious sources; in any case, certainly not from the 'lips of the Lithuanian people'. In an article in 1940, J. Lebedys rightly said that "generally Kraszewski's historical material is not authentic", and he concluded that "Lithuania as described by Kraszewski cannot be considered ours any more" (Lebedys 1940, 354).

Nevertheless, in the nineteenth century the issue of authenticity did not disturb romantic patriots. A reviewer who signed his work with the initial 'M' in the first issue of Aušra, the first Lithuanian journal (the founder's name was J. Mikšys and the initial idea for the journal was Kraszewski's) in 1883 wrote of the now unreadable, out-dated, long-winded *Witolorauda* that "the *Witolorauda* is for us Lithuanians what the *Odyssey* and the *Iliad* are for the Greeks, the *Aeneis* is for the Romans, the *Old Testament* for the Jews, or the *New Testament* for the Christians". As late as 1924 Bishop J. Tumas-Vaižgantas, an influential person in the literary life of the day, called the work a "national epic", because Kraszewski, like Homer, Elias Lönnrot the Finn, or Dr. Kreuzwald the Estonian, "collected the mythological tales" of the Lithuanian people (cited in Doveika 1962, 292).

From all of this, two different conclusions can be derived. The historian considers the *Egle* an exemplar of the submerged cultural heritage theory of H. Naumann, as well as a rare moment when it is possible to trace how high art becomes folklore. The followers of the ethnographic method view it as a mythological folk-tale. A. Martinkus, living in France, devoted a whole book to the analysis of the *Egle*. (She is the daughter of A. J. Greimas who became world famous as the founder of structural semantics and who devoted the last twenty-five years of his life to Lithuanian mythology, finally becoming a leading light amongst the representatives of neo-comparativist mythological research.) She found a dozen Latvian variants, and although she mentions the possibility that these spread to Latvia from Lithuania through the bilingual border region, she does not exclude the possibility that the tale could be Proto-Baltic, "which unfortunately cannot be proven for the simple reason that no folklore material has survived in the third Baltic language, that is Prussian" (Martinkus 1989, 15). Nonetheless, the Lithuanian tale is ancient enough for her to see it as the cosmic tragedy of the clash

---

[17] To translate Kraszewski's works was a patriotic act in itself. A. Vistelis translated the *Witolorauda* under the pseudonym '*Lietuwis*' (Lithuanian).

between the two proto-elements Earth and Water, and thus making it a parallel to Greek mythology, and in particular to the story of the abduction of Persephone.

Handing down has another aspect to explain the survival of the several hundred thousand dainas, etc. over centuries, as if to verify the ancient nature of folklore. The memory of an 'oral person' functions differently from that of the 'literate person'. To use Gy. Király's precise description of the phenomenon, which was labelled 'hypercritical', the former has what is termed a *grand mémoire* which refers "to the extent and not the content" of the preserved data (Király 1921, 72).[18] This means that illiterate peasants (with the appropriate talent) who can remember several thousand four-lined, non-rhyming Latvian folk-songs in ninety percent trocheic (that is intonation following natural speech patterns) do not recall the same lines of verses, but through their talent know the technique for creating such lines by which they are capable of poeticizing infinitely.[19] "Orality (as opposed to the sense of time and history based on literacy) has a certain inherent societal amnesia which preserves the culture of the society in the linguistic memory of individuals, and remains in homeostasis while perpetually cleansing it and adjusting it to the present" (Szili 1993, 53).[20] Since this poetry-machine

[18] Its references are generally not the content. As discussed before, "'*grand mémoire*' maintained events of historic significance only for a few centuries with increasingly scanty contents, less trustworthy seeds of truth, and finally for the subject that lost its original composition to sink into obscurity for ever, or to gain a new life filled with a new content" (Kristó 1978, 57).

My intention is not to say that content has no influence on handing down. J. Horváth has already pointed out that in periods which perhaps stretch out over several centuries, when the two types of handing down co-exist oral handing down can overtake the aim of the written process, which is to preserve texts unchanged (Horváth 1980, 73). It is certain that some texts, fixed more in their theme or in their contents (e.g. oath, spell, etc.), lend themselves more readily to the process than those not connected to an occasion.

[19] In this way orality, memory, and poetry were already connected in Greece. "*Mnemosyne* or Memory is the mother of the goddesses of poetry, that is the Muse, not because the reciters of the song had to memorise it word for word, but because in remembering the memorised texts they created something new, recollection became versifying without being apparent" (Ritoók 1973, 27).

[20] Between the two World Wars M. Parry discovered the way '*grand mémoire*' functions. With the help of the newly created Serbian heroic epic of the 1920s, he believed he had proven that the several thousand line hexameters of Homer had survived for centuries from mouth to mouth without any recording of them because it mainly consisted of formulae and clichés, and is about a few cliché-like permanent events (Parry 1971). The rhapsodist Homer 'sewed together' songs from pre-manufactured units (Gr. *rhapsoidein* 'to sew together a song' < *rhaptein* 'to sew together' + *oide* 'song'—Ong 1982, 5). According to Zs. Ritoók 'threading' the song only means that the performers threaded their songs following each other, and "the rhapsodists were the performers following each other" (Ritoók 1973, 54 ff.)

can be set into motion at any time, its products are less suited to verifying historical facts.[21]

When identifying folklore and myths (more precisely scholarship about myths)[22] with language a timeless and never-ending cultural sphere emerges where everything is at once comparable to and verifiable with everything else.[23] Thinking in such an ahistorical cultural space is perhaps the most important common characteristic of the researchers whose work can be categorised under neo-comparativism or neo-mythology (e.g. K. Hauck, O. Höfler, F. R. Schröder, J. de Vries, etc.).

C. Lévi-Strauss laid down the theoretical foundations of structuralist research of myth. E. Meletinskiy rightly assails him because "he expands the analogy of the myths and natural languages as far as identifying them both with each other" (Meletinskiy in Propp 1995, 165). Besides C. Lévi-Strauss the most outstanding figure of neo-comparitivism and neo-mythology is G. Dumézil (see especially Dumézil 1952, 1968).[24] Members of these schools emphasise the role of the ritual and cultic archetypes based on a view that considers the perspective of time and space in ancient cultures as non-linear and circular, described in the category of

---

[21] P. Ruigys first published one of the most famous Lithuanian daina in 1747, Herder then published it in a German translation as a poem. "In its most beautiful form it was recorded in 1949–1950, without any signs of derivation of folk-songs (*Zersingen*)" (Lit. E./XV, 479).

[22] Mixing mythology (seen as myths in their entirety), and mythology (as a science about myths) can have dire consequences, because "the non-rationality of myth is its very essence, for religion requires a demonstration of faith by the suspension of critical doubts" (Leach 1969, 7), while science is perhaps founded upon exactly this critical doubt.

[23] Here are a few randomly chosen examples from among many for comparison of everything with everything. "It is not impossible to trace back a few images from Latvian dainas to the ancient Eastern examples which remained from the Indo-European *Urheimat*, for example in the image of the wise divine intellect" (Ivanov 1984, 28). Jonynas compares the 1249 peace contract between the Teutonic Order and the Prussians with a Lithuanian folk-song recorded in 1936 on the basis of a reference in both to a dead person who held a buzzard in their hands (Jonynas 1984, 29). Of course, this method is not only characteristic of Baltic studies. V. Diószegi, one of the most excellent researchers of pagan Hungarian beliefs, "draws parallels between the data of popular belief and customs of the Hungarian *táltos* (earliest references are from the eighteenth century) and Siberian data... he cites Siberian rock drawings from the Bronze Age in his Hungarian and recent Siberian research of popular beliefs" (Voigt 1977, 309). [The *táltos* is a type of Hungarian magician which some Hungarian researchers consider to be the successor of an assumed ancient Hungarian shaman that originated from the pre-Christian times and lived on until the Modern Age (Pócs, *Between the Living and the Dead*, 1997, 18). Translators' note]

[24] For a detailed, though enthusiastically one-sided account on Dumézil's work see Littleton 1966. It is characteristic of his bias that he belittles the 1939 book of the French researcher that deals with Germanic gods and is openly sympathetic to the Nazis (for this see Ginzburg 1989, 214). For the most recommended study on Dumézil see Momigliano 1984.

'ever returning'. One of the fundamental tenets of G. Dumézil's theory is that the similarities in the myths of the various Indo-European peoples are rooted in Indo-European prehistory, since "there is necessarily a genetic relationship between the ideologies of those who speak genetically related languages" (Littleton 1966, 204). From the common past Indo-Europeans inherited not only the language, the social structure and mythology but also "the epic themes, and more generally an Indo-European literature" (Dumézil 1968, 257), and even more generally "also narrative and prosodic schemata" (Rivière 1979, 98).[25] G. Dumézil built his theory upon Aryan, Romance, Celtic, and Germanic mythologies, which R. Jakobson, V. Ivanov, and V. Toporov strove to apply to Slavic material, and V. Toporov and J. Greimas to Baltic material.

G. Dumézil started out from Vedic poetry and described three groups of Indo-European gods based on the functions and tasks of the gods. The first is further divided into two. To this (or these) belong gods of magic, law, and contracts; the second group of gods oversee the functions of battle; the third control production. This would reflect the caste system of the ancient Indo-European society (which is the sociological foundation of Dumézil's theory!). The first function is carried out by the caste of the *Brahmin* (priests), the second the *kshátrija* (soldiers), and the third the *vaisiya* (workers).[26] The question arises as to why these three (which are actually four) are not five if we add the caste of the *śhudra* (slaves), or why not two in a division of producers and non-producers. Obviously it could be one or the other just as easily.[27]

[25] Of course this Indo-European *Urheimat* is not historically concrete, either. Dumézil and his followers "operate in a golden land of proto-Indo-European society and belief which is rooted neither in time nor in space" (Renfrew 1987, 286).

[26] It is not true that Dumézil, "starting from around 1950 changed his viewpoint, and the system of three functions from then on became an exclusively ideological structure without a realistic sociological basis for him" (Köves-Zulauf 1995, 35). As Momigliano pointed out, what Dumézil threw out of the door in the 1950s (in words), he brought back through the window in his book written in 1979 concerning Roman marriage and jurisdiction (Momigliano 1984, 317).

[27] The tripartite division is perhaps the reflection of the differentiation between the *oratores, bellatores,* and *laboratores* (priests, soldiers, workers). This division of the society does not originate from the ancient Indo-European mist, but more likely from the Middle Ages. It appeared in the late ninth century, spread in the eleventh, and became a commonplace in the twelfth century (Le Goff 1965, 63). G. Dumézil reflects this trinity back as far as the Scythians, and from there in all directions (Dumézil 1978, 178 ff.). Herodotus writes about the three tribes of the Scythians springing from three brothers, which in Dumézil's view corresponds with the three functions, so there would be the tribes of the priests, the soldiers, and the workers. However, Herodotus also recounts that the smallest brother Kolaxaias, who ruled over the royal Scythians, divided the country again into three parts. In this case the royal Scythians would have had to carry out the work of the soldiers, and workers as well (Herodotus IV, 5). Dumézil argues that this second division was not on a functional basis but was territorial and ethnic...

An important factor is that all the neo-comparativists are originally linguists who think in structures, or are straightforward structuralist linguists. G. Dumézil also emphasises that "in human representation everything, or at least everything important is: a system" (cited in Littleton 1966, 100). Let me add that it is a predetermined system or one that has filtered down from certain concrete historical material, into which every other later piece of data has to fit and in which there are no incidentals. (Incidentals which, for example, could come from the notary of a folk-song or a myth having had a foreign mother tongue, or were—God forgive me!—dumb, or lying.) When Dumézil discovers a fundamental myth of the Indians, Romans, Celts, and Germanic peoples which recounts the ancient

---

Furthermore, the social situation of the subjugated group of peoples is unexplained. As J. Harmatta comments, "we can see entire Scythian tribes or groups as the agricultural population subjugated by them" (Harmatta 1953, 37). Is it possible that the workers' tasks are usually carried out by subjugated tribes? The great number of unanswered questions arise in the absurdity of presuming the same system of castes in societies thousands of years apart from each other, unless starting out from the not very original wisdom that when more people come together, some sort of division of labour will necessarily emerge among them.

In any case, as J. Gonda demonstrated, the number 'three' did not enter into Vedic literature because of the structure of the Indo-European society, but because of its magical character (in Łowmiański 1984, 671). Of course, it also appears in the life of the Romans, but "bipartition was much more decisive: we need only think of patricians and plebeians, or of the two consuls" (Momigliano 1984, 328).

I cannot help quoting the caricature of the various structuralist divisions according to functions (tripartition, binary oppositions, etc.) which cuts to the quick because it calls upon the same references as structuralism, or this subject-free transcendentalism does, that is the eternal human structures, and their timeless movement creating ever newer formations. (J. Bell is right to state of the "idealist or high structuralism" of Lévi-Strauss that, according to this theory, it "assumes that universal patterns in human mentality are the primary levers in the formation of human social organization... and humans have no more control over those patterns than they do over economic forces". This is also a subject-free *transcendentalism* in the sense that "humans are viewed as pawns of forces which transcend their control"—Bell 1992, 34, and 53.) True, the following citation is from a novel, but the author of this theoretical novel is U. Eco who was himself a structuralist, and Greimas' fellow fighter on the barricades of structuralism in the 1960s. He gave his own views in the mouth of his characters, and according to my unverifiable conviction here he directly refers to the research of myths by Dumézil.

"We move on to the magic numbers your authors are so fond of. You are one and not two, your cock is one and my cunt is one, and we have one nose and one heart; so you see how many important things come in ones. But we have two eyes, two ears, two nostrils, my breasts, your balls, legs, arms, buttocks. Three is the most magical of all, because our body doesn't know that number; we don't have three of anything, and it should be a very mysterious number that we attribute to God, wherever we live. But if you think about it, I have one cunt and you have one cock—shut up and don't joke—and if we put these two together, a new thing is made, and we become three. So you don't have to be a university professor or use a computer to discover that all cultures on earth have ternary structures, trinities.

battle between the gods of the first two and the third functions, then the Slavist and Baltologist V. Ivanov and V. Toporov find this fundamental text, reconstruct it in Slavic mythology, largely from the building blocks of Belarusian folklore (Ivanov–Toporov 1974), and V. Toporov also reconstructs it in Baltic mythology from Latvian folk-songs.[28] (Behind the presumption of a fundamental myth lies the romantic idea, amongst others, that what is older is automatically more authentic and more complete than today's, and the text of the present is simply a corrupted version of the earlier perfect whole.)

"But two arms and two legs make four, and four is a beautiful number when you consider that animals have four legs and little children go on all fours, as the Sphinx knew. We hardly have to discuss five, the fingers of the hand, and then with both hands you get that other sacred number, ten. There have to be ten commandments because, if there were twelve, when the priest counts one, two, three, holding up his fingers, and comes to the last two, he'd have to borrow a hand from the sacristan.

"Now, if you take the body and count all the things that grow from the trunk, arms, legs, head, and cock, you get six; but for women it's seven. For this reason, it seems to me that among your authors six is never taken seriously, except as the double of three, because it's familiar to the males, who don't have any seven. So when the males rule, they prefer to see seven as the mysterious sacred number, forgetting about women's tits, but what the hell.

"Eight ...eight...give me a minute... If arms and legs don't count a one apiece but two, because of elbows and knees. You have eight parts that move; add the torso and you have nine, add the head and you have ten. Just sticking with the body, you can get all the numbers you want. The orifices, for example."

"The orifices?"

"Yes. How many holes does the body have?"

I counted. "Eyes, nostrils, ears, mouth, ass: eight"

"You see? Another reason eight is a beautiful number. But I have nine!" (Eco 1989, 363–64).

[28] "The so-called 'fundamental myth' is about the battle between the Thunderer (Perkūnas) and his enemy, encrypted with the *Vel- stem as a taboo name. This was preceded by a 'celestial wedding feast', which provoked the ill feeling, and to which other characters are also connected (Jānis, Mara, Laima, etc.). All this can be seen in the Latvian dainas, but not the Lithuanian, therefore Latvian is evidently more complete than the Old Indic" (Toporov 1984, 48–49). (Obviously, my suspicious nature is at fault, but to me the celestial wedding is reminiscent of the wedding at Pohjola in the *Kalevala* that stretches over five-songs, songs which V. Kaukonen proved to be those which Lönnrot had fabricated as a part of the Finn national epic poem, and there is no trace of a wedding at Pohjola in the epic folk songs that allegedly constitute the basis for the *Kalevala*—Kaukonen 1954, 28.)

We are offered a jocular answer to the question, from what aspect is this myth fundamental? (perhaps in time? or in its lexis?). "The fundamental text is connected to the most important parameters of the cultural and material life of the old Slavs" (Ivanov–Toporov 1974, 3). The "most important parameters" (Who determines which these are?) again refer to the infinity of cultural space.

The reproaches of the representatives of neo-comparativism are justified because of the arbitrariness with which structuralism shuns the accidental and packs everything into systems, as well as the arbitrariness of the ethnographic method through which folklore texts and mythology are identified at least with the Indo-European proto-language, and thus create a practically boundless cultural space.[29]

The spread and rule of the neo-comparativist view had a root in the history of sciences. By the 1960s the potential of traditional philology relying on written materials seemed to have been exhausted, at the same time archaeology, anthropology, mythological research, and ethnography gathered up a lot of new knowledge. To summarise or even just to have an overview of these one needed to be a true polymath (Labuda 1960–75/III, 39). This is how these great structuralist polymaths came directly to be the heirs of the nineteenth-century positivist philologists.[30] E. H. Carr's biting comment is valid in respect of most of their works: "When I am tempted, as I sometimes am, to envy the extreme competence of colleagues engaged in writing ancient or mediaeval history, I find consolation in the reflection that they are so competent mainly because they are so ignorant about their subject" (Carr 1962, 9). St. Urbańczyk's words about R. Jakobson

[29] "The structures of the neo-mythologists do not stand the trial of source critique at a number of points" (Gurevich 1979, 12). "V. Ivanov and V. Toporov take all information in the sources at face value" (Urbańczyk in Brückner 1980, 24)."The dangers of the 'structuralist revolution' (or 'counterrevolution') are apparent in being anti-historical, and in the dismissal of careful philological work, sometimes ungrateful, but always indispensable. This characterises C. Lévi-Strauss' thought provoking and motivating global constructions which could not undergo the counter-probe of falsification (in the Popperian sense), just as G. Dumézil's all-embracing 'tripartitioned' Indo-European ideology theory, or more precisely, hypothesis" (Lehrmann–Venclova 1981, 254). The endeavours of R. Jakobson and M. Gimbutas "in connecting the gods that appear in Baltic beliefs to Dumézil's schemata have to be seen as the fruit of creative fantasy which has little to do with historical reality... [Certain works of V. Toporov and V. Ivanov] are more or less witty constructions without a foundation of true fact" (Biezais 1990, 24). It is not surprising either, when E. Leach calls the views of Dumézil and his followers "enthusiastic fantasies" (1990, 238).

A. J. Greimas cleverly fends off any criticism. He, who began his career as a campaigner for the exactitudes of the humanities in the last part of his life dealt with mythology as a poet, as a subjective philosopher, since "the subject of mythology is not the world and its trappings, but what humans think about the world, its trappings, and themselves" (Greimas 1990, 29). The thought, independent of its quality, cannot be questioned from the perspective of authenticity (Beliauskas 1992, 230). Of course, this is true, but it makes a difference if a thought was generated three thousand or thirty years ago.

[30] The same characterises them as in what H. Bausinger says of the antiquarian–positivist view of history. "It surpasses the question of the truly memorable, without which history cannot be described in a sensible manner, nor be understood... [consequently it commits itself to ever changing conceptions, and from these] the mythologising view of history is the closest" (Bausinger 1970, 32).

could be said of all of the best neo-comparativists: "The width of their scholarly perspectives, the material of their knowledge is intimidating, at the same time it makes one suspicious" (cited in Brückner 1980, 24).

In one case V. Toporov compares the Aestii (Prussian?) and Greek customs of connecting burials and horse races, and reiterates the common Indo-European origins of the tradition with an Old Indic parallel (Toporov 1990). This astounding study is a striking example of the amount of illuminating detail, which rarely gives rise to suspicion in the majority of neo-comparitivist works. At the same time, due to the almost superhuman material knowledge contained in them they are practically impossible to refute and all criticism can appear to be unfair, petty, and envious nit-picking against them (just like the nagging feeling that 'something is not right in the whole of this').

Wulfstan, the ninth-century Anglo-Saxon traveller, reported that the Ests sometimes did not bury their dead for months, and he carries on: "On the very day on which they intend to carry the dead man to the pyre, they divide his property—whatever is left of it after the drinking and gambling—into five or six portions, sometimes more, depending on how much there is. They place the biggest portion about a mile from the settlement, then the second, then the third, until it is all distributed within the mile, so that the smallest portion is closest to the place where the dead man lies. All the men who have the swiftest horses in the country are assembled at a point about five or six miles from the property and then they all gallop towards it. The man who has the fastest horse comes to the first portion (which is the largest) and then one after another until it has all been taken. He has the smallest portion who gets his ride the one nearest to the settlement" (Wulfstan 1984, 186).[31] V. Toporov goes into a deep elaboration to demonstrate that burial and competition are both rooted in the 'pre-sport' and 'pre-religious' ritual when the dead are, in a sense, 'played over' to the otherworld. He then continues: "[in Wulfstan] the formulae 'five or six' is repeated twice... a repetition which can hardly be accidental" (Toporov 1990, 23–24). It is not accidental, because Toporov sees the five or six division of the belongings and the

---

[31] V. Toporov published not only the original but also V. I. Matuzova's Russian translation, which (at least this section) differs from Mierzyński's Polish translation in only a few small details (Mierzyński 1892–96/I, 31–32). The most important is the word *tune* that comes up three times and that I translate as 'camp' ('two camps' in the sense of 'two sides'), Matuzova as *gorod* 'settlement, town' (but Toporov adds in brackets at the last occurrence *dom* 'house', thus supposing (probably rightly) that the pyre was next to the house), while Mierzyński uses three different words: *miasto* 'town', *miejsce* 'place' and *dwór* 'yard, land'. The description is misleading because the same two words mean the same place (*tune*), and because scattering the belongings before the competition is in opposition to the competition itself. The dead are in the goal, the organisers set out from there (together with the competitors) to share out the belongings by the mile, and when they reach the start line five–six miles away, the competition starts—backwards.

five or six miles distance of the competition not as a cause and result relationship. (So, not as, I believe, Wulfstan thought, i.e. that it depends on the quantity of belongings as to how many parts it is divided into—it could be seven or eight, and the competitors measure out the same number of miles, accordingly.) For a structuralist, there are no accidents. The Proto-Slavic name for funeral feast *trizna* can be connected to a competition with three events, a kind of triathlon fashionable at burials, the five division horse race of the Prussian funeral feast can be connected to the pentathlon of the Olympic games sung of by Pindaros. (In the meantime, the number 'six' mentioned by Wulfstan disappeared from the scene...)

Another Greek parallel to Wulfstan is the twenty-third song of the *Iliad* where sports events are played at Patrocles' burial.[32] Indeed, there is a horse race among them (more precisely a carriage race, or trotting race), but also eight other types of sport: boxing, wrestling, running, fencing, shot putting, archery, and javelin throwing. I wonder which Indo-European structure carries the number eight?[33]

[32] The rituals of the Est and the parallel of the *Iliad* cropped up years earlier in Žiemys 1984.

[33] The question here is rhetorical, though many have posed it seriously, too. For example in a popular dictionary of symbols it says: "In Christian symbolism 'eight' stands for the 'eight days of creation', that is for the renewal of humankind. 'Eight' also symbolises Christ's ascension (*Agnus Dei*) and the hope of all humankind of going to heaven" (*Lexicon Symbole* 1978, 9).

Comparing numbers in themselves offers no information, since they form systems within cultures (cf. Curtius 1948, 493 ff.). For example Pindaros, mentioned by Toporov, is barely comprehensible without the mysticism or symbolism of numbers by Pythagoras a hundred years earlier.

CHAPTER 2

HOW FAR BACK DOES BALTIC
ANTIQUITY REACH?

I reckon the most accurate answer is paradoxical: until the point when it began, that is the fifteenth–sixteenth centuries, and often even longer, until the very end of the nineteenth century, or even the beginning of the twentieth. Before that, that is before the development of a Latvian and Lithuanian consciousness, the Latvians and Lithuanians existed and were a reality only in a natural and not a historical sense.[1] Historically only that exists which can be fixed in time and, because words disappear this is only possible through literacy: historically only that exists about which there is a written source, or that which can be connected to some written source. (The expression 'written source' is almost a pleonasm.) This is why everybody, from G. Childe to C. Kluckhohn, agrees that among the very few (two or three) features that differentiate between 'natural' 'pre-historical' peoples and 'civilised' 'historical' peoples, the most important one is probably that the latter were literate and the former were not (Daniel 1972, 13).[2] W. J. Ong is ashamed of the belittling inherent in the differentiation in use ('primitive', 'barbarous', 'peripheral' peoples, etc.), and even considers C. Lévi-Strauss' exchange of these for 'without literacy' negative.[3] He suggests the conceptual couple 'oral–written' (Ong 1982, 188). The development of literacy is of decisive significance, not only

---

[1] Of course in an everyday sense this statement is absurd. It only makes sense philosophically in the context of the philosophy that peaked with Hegel, and which F. Engels summarises as "according to Hegel, reality is, however, in no way an attribute predictable of any given state of affairs, social or political, in all circumstances and at all times" (Engels 1888, 358).

[2] The historian of scripts talks about "tribes of people without a script, and therefore a history" (Jensen 1969, 11). O. Szemerényi believes that the decoding of the linear B-script from the fourteenth–thirteenth centuries BC created history from five hundred years of Greek pre-history (Szemerényi 1971–82/II, 116).

[3] Here is another thought to add to the feeling of shame of the western 'white people' also characteristic of C. Lévi-Strauss. "Recent anthropology has rightly rejected the categorical distinctions between the thinking of 'primitive' and 'civilised' peoples, between 'mythopoeic' and 'logico-empirical' modes of thought. But the reaction has been pushed too far: diffuse relativism and sentimental egalitarianism combine to turn a blind eye on some of the most basic problems of human history" (Goody–Watt 1963, 344). If 'pre-historic' means the same as 'pre-literate' then the expression does not only denote time, but inevitably also a level of social development.

because the people of the past began to communicate to us, their descendants, through writing, but also because "they began to communicate with themselves through it, too" (Vogt 1949, 333). K. Jaspers phrases this as humans who "were liberated from the sphere of the present" through literacy (Jaspers cited in Köhler 1961, 307).

The classical wording of the division of peoples as 'pre-historic' and 'historic' comes from Hegel: "Those periods—whether we estimate them in centuries or millennia—which elapsed in the life of nations before history came to be written, and which may well have been filled with revolutions, migrations, and the most violent changes, have no objective history precisely because they have no subjective history, i.e. no historical narratives. It is not that the records of such periods have simply perished by chance; on the contrary, the reason why we have no records of them is that no such records were possible" (Hegel 1840, 136).

During the act of recording (which is never neutral, often even copying is not) the recorder creates a historical fact from natural data. There are numerous peoples from Antiquity, and even the Middle Ages (for instance the Balto-Finn Karelian, Izhor, Ves (Vesp, Vepse), Votian—Shaskolskiy 1976) whose true names are also uncertain and change with the sources; for example some Slavic chronicles referred to the Vepse as Chud (Domokos 1985, 78).[4] In catalogues of peoples where only names are given the factors of categorisation are mixed: "...after their families, after their tongues, in their lands, after their nations" (Genesis 10, 31). The sources allocated various characteristics (geographical, racial, religious,

---

[4] Historical facts about which just one, or only a few written sources have survived, are dependent on their notaries. The existence of the Scythians is reinforced by several sources, but that they were seen as a people who believed that golden objects could fall from the sky can be attributed to Herodotus (Herodotus IV, 5). Although there could well have been 'atheists' doubting the tale of the plough, yoke, battle axe, and beaker coming from the sky (since Herodotus, who was at the level of the era, did not believe in them either), still descendants only have the right to assume 'believer' Scythians. (Unless we think that the Scythians were at the initial level of creating myths and folk poetry when "all individuals are still ruled by a practically total intellectual uniformity... the particular individual could not create anything that would have differed from that of another individual"—Goldziher 1876, 73).

The researcher of Antiquity is also prone to polyhistoricism because of the scarcity of facts, and to exaggerate the little that the skies gave: they need to squeeze an explanation out of every letter of every word. Only one example of this is that, according to Pytheas of Massilia, the islanders burnt amber instead of wood. If we had more data we could obviously easily shrug our shoulders: Pytheas again, as usual, prevaricates. However, we know that the Greek oracles used amber for their rituals. The great nineteenth-century historian J. Voigt therefore interprets Pytheas' data as correct, that the inhabitants of the island Abalus (perhaps the ancestors of the Prussians) did indeed set fire to amber because they fed the eternal flame at the sacrificial altar, consequently there was possibly a Prussian cult in the fourth century BC that resembled that of the Greeks (Voigt 1827–39/1, 27).

political, etc.) to a name that denotes a group of people.[5] These characteristics constitute the basis for the communal consciousness of any given group of people who thus feel different from others.

The characteristics determining a communal consciousness create a complex web that changes in time. In the case of the Balts, for a long period language was missing from the characteristics that ensured self-identification. (It was also absent in the case of the East Slavs, probably closest to the Balts in their social organisation. As H. Paszkiewicz convincingly pointed out, it is a fundamental misunderstanding to imagine a homogeneous Russian national community in the vast territory stretching between the North Sea and the Black Sea, the Carpathian mountains to the Oka and Volga regions on the grounds that sources talk about 'Rusland' and 'jazyk'. The latter term has only come to mean 'language' today and at that time meant the Orthodox 'belief' which was common in the lands of Rus', as opposed to the Latin (Catholic) jazyk.[6]] Language became the most important determiner of a common national consciousness from as late as the nineteenth–twentieth centuries.[7]

---

[5] It has to be emphasised that, whether concurrent or later sources suggest that the names of many peoples "actually do not denote a people, but are only symbols of research technology", which foreigners often give to a particular people (Wenskus 1961, 89). The picture is more muddled because "the peoples of Europe in the Middle Ages learned to believe in fictitious 'prehistoric peoples' whom literate people constructed for them from the historical, geographical, and ethnographical knowledge of Antiquity remnant in the Middle Ages" (Szűcs 1985, 31).

[6] The Chant of Prince Igor uses the expressions Rus' and ruskaya zemlya 'Russian land' in an ethnic and 'national' sense, and that is one of the strongest pieces of evidence that the authenticity of the only manuscript of the Chant of Prince Igor, that survived until the eighteenth century and was burnt in the 1812 war, is doubtful, or at least there are certain retrospective adages in it because it reflects late eighteenth-century use of concepts back to the time of the event which was in 1185 (Paszkiewicz 1954, 348).

[7] In East Prussia in the early sixteenth century the 'nations' of the 'French' (émigrés from France) and 'Pomoranians' (émigrés from Pomorze) existed, which of course did not mean those speaking French or Pomoranian (Pomoranian had by then died out); a person was characterised by the region they came from, by their religion, and by the social stratum they belonged to (Falkenhahn 1941, 148).

Identification of language with nation occurred in the nineteenth century, especially in Eastern and Central Europe where there could be no fully-fledged nations only, to use Novalis' term from 1798, nationalities (Nationalität), that is peoples that did not have their own states. A striking example of the shift in meaning of the word is that in S. Linde's Polish dictionary from 1809 narodowość still means "the collection of features that differentiate one nation from another", while in a dictionary from 1904 it also denotes "the collection of people who speak the same language, independent of their political status, and the area inhabited by them" (Zientara 1977, 291).

The seeds of unification through community, nation, and language were latent earlier, too, in places where language that became written met with some kind of state organisational structure.[8] With conversion to Western Christianity the dead Latin language acted as an obstacle to this potential,[9] and with the late Middle Ages and then after the set-back in the fourteenth century with the Renaissance, the Reformation, and the Counter Reformation that established literacy in the national language, it very slowly became a reality, but even then a reality with many gaps.[10] In Eastern Christianity the situation was different. Contrary to the western tradition every language was considered equal to the three sacred languages of the Cross, that is to Hebrew, Greek, and Latin (Borst 1957–63/I, 320). Consequently, in the Kievan Rus' conversion to Christianity automatically instigated the emergence and development of 'national' literacy. The Tartar invasion

---

[8] R. Wenskus calls social and political faiths (*Schicksale*), faith formations what I refer to as state organisational structures, and emphasises that these have a greater role in the development of the consciousness of an ethnicity than common language and culture do (Wenskus 1961, 93). From the eighteenth century the general view was, as A. L. Schlözer (1735–1809) put it, "while the Lithuanians [meaning Balts] had no state, they had no history either. They belonged to the history of nature and not of society" (cited in Šimėnas 1994, 19).

[9] The seventh-century Izidor of Seville believes that Latin, being the absolute language, has a metaphysical priority over other languages, because only Latin signifies things with their true and natural names (cited in Curtius 1948, 33).

[10] As, mainly, J. Szűcs convincingly demonstrated, before the eighteenth century there could hardly have been a continuous Hungarian consciousness (Szűcs 1992). M. Havelka discusses a national consciousness of Czech identity at a 'lesser degree' in the nineteenth century, which was the mirrored concurrent Czech national society whose division had gaps.

The concept of 'continuity', which has a special role within the discipline of history (Bausinger 1969, 9), was questioned by German historiography. After both the First, and then again the Second World War it was lifted out of its everyday self-evidence when it contrasted a view of history (which presumed an unbroken continuity from the Indo-Germanic primordial fog, through the Germanic tribes of the Early Middle Ages, to the German nation) with the challenge that "continuity only realises itself through minor fractures and shifts in functions, and is often concerned with external permanence while undergoing strong internal changes" (Bausinger n. d., 75).

Continuity has a major role in the development of communal consciousness, since as De Vos puts it "ethnicity... is in its narrowest sense a feeling of continuity with the past" (cited in Keyes 1981, 9). A feeling, and a feeling of long-gone people: this poses practically unanswerable questions (for example how Germanic and German consciousness were connected to each other). Still, perhaps it makes more sense to emphasise the differences between the various periods and social structures than the continuity itself; for example, to underline the basic difference between 'nationalism' after the eighteenth century and the 'national consciousness of the Middle Ages', otherwise "we could start talking about the 'nationalism' of Red Indian or African tribes" (Szűcs 1992, 83).

put a stop to this and lent an Asian flavour to Russian history, which is still apparent today.[11]

The Latvians were subjugated by the Order of the Sword Bearers as a parallel to their conversion. In their case it was the missing state which hindered them from becoming a 'state forming factor'. As mentioned earlier, the noun *latvis* 'a Latvian' was only created in the seventeenth century in order to separate the Latvian speakers from the Livonian 'natives', the *Undeutsch*. It is likely that Latvian self awareness only awoke with the primary education of the Latvian peasants from the 'Swedish times', that is when language generally became written allowing a differentiation between 'us' and 'them' (see also Hroch 1985, 107).[12] What J. Horváth emphasised in Hungary "about the national language creeping into literacy" is also valid for the Latvians. This is deeply significant because it "creates two educational classes" among a circle of people sharing the same language, that is Latvian orality, and Latvian literacy (Horváth 1980, 82 ff.).

The Lithuanian case is more complicated. To summarise the history discussed above (cf. Part Two, Subchapter 6.3): a consequence of their late, twofold conversion to Christianity was that in Lithuania first East Slavic, then Polish became the languages of literacy. Consequently in the Polish–Lithuanian state, a strange personal union, Lithuanian remained the language of the lower classes that were marginalised within the 'nation'. The noun *Litva*, which the East Slavic chronicles applied to Lithuania and its inhabitants, became an adjective in the early fourteenth century (*litovskoy*) (Rowell 1994, 302), but it meant 'of Lithuania' and not 'Lithuanian'! The 'Lithuanian person, as a speaker of Lithuanian' was dissolved into the concept of a 'Lithuanian', 'inhabitant of the Grand Duchy of Lithuania'. It is evident from the way outsiders referred to the populace and language of the Grand Duchy of Lithuania as 'Lithuanians', whether Polish, Lithuanians, Belarusians, Ukrainians, Rus' (as the Ukrainians under Polish rule

---

[11] For this reason D. Likhachev's patriotic trumpeting has some basis: "Russian literature is all but a thousand years old. It is one of Europe's oldest literatures. It is older than the French, the English, or the German. Its beginnings stretch back to the second half of the tenth century" (Likhacheva–Likhachev 1971, 52). That it only has a marginal basis in reality is because "what Rus' received, in fact, was a vast number of medieval *Reader's Digests*, various compilations, condensations, mythologies and selections" through Christianity from Byzantine literature (Grabowicz 1981, 23). It was not so much because, as I. Ševčenko puts it, "on the whole, barbaric nations, as opposed to individual barbarians, were too despised to be genuinely accepted into the community of Byzantine civilisation, even after they had accepted baptism" (Ševčenko 1964, 226), but more because high Byzantine culture had no market or audience at the time.

[12] The Estonians were in the same situation as the Latvians, yet, according to E. Hobsbawm, even in the nineteenth century "there is no evidence that the Estonian peasants thought in such national terms. In the first place they do not appear to have seen themselves as an ethnic–linguistic group. The word 'Estonian' came into use only in the 1860s" (Hobsbawm 1990, 48).

were referred to). In his chronicle from the late sixteenth century M. Stryjkowski mentions "the victorious Lithuanian [that is] Russian and Žemaitian nation", where 'Lithuanian' means 'of Lithuania' including those speaking Russian and Lithuanian (Žemaitian) (Stryjkowski I/27).

As 'Latvian' had to be extracted from the Livonian collective concept of the *Undeutsch*, so did the concept of 'Lithuanian' from 'of Lithuania'. The first secular Lithuanian book, a selection of Aesop's fables, was published in 1706 in J. Šulcas' (Schultzen) translation in Königsberg. P. Ruigys (Ruhig) added an ode in German as a foreword to the volume praising the translator for the "joy of looking into the future with gleaming eyes, because the *linguistic Babel was over* [author's italics][13] and then Gumbinė [the capital of the province, where Šulcas was a priest, today in the Kaliningrad area and named Gusev] became the centre of the righteous movement, and for the Lithuanians turned into what Orléans, Rome, Athens, and Breslau [the last is now Wrocław where a university was established in 1702] mean to their respective countries" (Ruigys 1745, 373).

When in the mid-late sixteenth-century Latvian and Lithuanian literacy was born, it could only be categorised as part of the Latvian and Lithuanian consciousness with the hindsight of later events. At the point of its inception and long afterwards, it contributed much more to the development of a Catholic and Protestant consciousness.[14] The Latvian and Lithuanian languages were themselves first given credence only in the late seventeenth century, then more strongly through the influence of the eighteenth-century Enlightenment—but still only as a natural phenomenon. The texts of Latvian and Lithuanian folklore, like other Baltic languages prone to extinction, were collected like butterflies. As late as 1881, at the Synod of Kurland a German priest called the Latvians and the Estonians 'people-crumbs', who can be termed people only in an ethnic sense, just as babies, blind, invalid, or mentally handicapped people are called humans (cited by Rudzītis in Pumpurs n.d., 20).

That even in the nineteenth century the works of the Balts were treated exclusively as ethnographic peculiarity, purely as objects of the former existence of a race of people about to become extinct, is most apparent in the case of K. Donelaitis. In 1818 L. Rėza published the descriptive poem in four parts by the priest–poet from Prussia. The work, *Seasons* is perhaps the most outstanding work from eighteenth-century Central and Eastern European literature, which retains an aesthetic vitality even for today's reader. L. Rėza immediately enclosed a German translation of it, and the German press of the day gave it almost its due

---

[13] J. Jurginis considers this, mistakenly, a purist comment (in Ruigys 1745, 477).

[14] This can be said of every multilingual country, therefore also of Hungary, because "preceding the emergence of bourgeois nations, the frameworks of the social strata, politics, state, or the Church were stronger factors in the formation of a society than ethnic and linguistic conditions" (Klaniczay 1966, 22).

credit. From the 1820s onwards lively interest arose in Prussia for the native populace of the country, the Prussians and their related tribe, the Lithuanians, as a part of the establishment of Prussian patriotism. The *Preussische Provinzial Blätter* (1829–1866) was one of the main instigators and forums for this interest where everything that was Prussian was discussed, and almost everything Lithuanian, too. However, at the same time, even Donelaitis' name was hardly mentioned. The explanation for this was that, because of the Rėza publication, he had already found his way into the museum storeroom, there was no reason to read, re-read, or interpret him, "so there was no sense in bringing up his name again" (Gineitis 1991, 76).[15]

The genuine beginnings of a Lithuanian consciousness can only be considered from the late eighteenth century when the Lithuanian peasants started to go to school to learn how to read and write—the same thing happened much earlier for a wider band of Latvians—through which some positive feeling of togetherness emerged (Gudavičius 1993, 69). The peasantry that remained Lithuanian and newly encountered literacy were able to counterbalance the nobility's loss of its nationality, a process also finalised by the late eighteenth century.

In 1918 the main issue in the freshly established Latvian and Lithuanian Republics was not that their languages were acknowledged for the first time in history as state languages, but rather that, with their independence, the process in which the linguistic community changed from natural to historical in just a few decades was officially sanctioned.

This turn was facilitated by the dual nature of language: natural and historical (social). (Natural people also have a language.)[16] Since language was the only element that was always on the surface, the false illusion easily emerged where according to Montesquieu's there-favoured sentence, "the language is the nation".[17] From the moment at which this belief took root it became inconceivable that this would not have been true from the outset, and thus that whoever had spoken Indo-European (Finno-Ugrian), then common Baltic, then East Baltic (Ugrian), and so on thousands of years earlier would not necessarily have become

---

[15] In the minds of the Polish, Lithuania existed as a nature reserve until as late as in the twentieth century, "a whole hunting literature existed which limited itself to Lithuania" (Miłosz 1988, 150).

[16] They only lack literacy, "while language is the common treasure of humanity from which each nation get its share, script is a different matter. Writing expands the temporal and spatial borders of language" (Jensen 1969, 9).

[17] *"La langue, c'est la nation."* What the identification of language with nation served is exemplified in the words of I. Széchenyi in the introduction to his book *Hitel* [Credit] published in 1830 "a healthy nationality's... principle escort is the national language, because as long as it lives, the nation lives, too" (cited in Faragó 1991, 11). Evidently this is true, because every nation has a language. However, the reverse is not true, which could be one of the suggestions of the statement "the language is the nation", meaning that every ethnicity which speaks is a nation.

Latvian, Lithuanian (Hungarian), and so forth. Since language came to be a determining part of national consciousness this has not only become inconceivable (for many even today), but also intolerable. Consequently, the manufacture of the past began, a series of forgeries, along with the reflection of historical consciousness back into the past along language. It seems as if language would be allocated ever newer forms of national consciousness (Latvian folk-songs from Antiquity, Lithuanian myths from Indo-European times, etc.) as an acknowledgement of its contributions to the survival of the nation. The process is conducted along language because it can contain elements that point forward (once it has become written, and only then!); it is most frequently borrowed, or more rarely is the creation of an extraordinary genius.

These elements can then play the role of way-markers or handrails for this reflection. (Hegel's beautiful expression *"die Voreiligkeit der Sprache"* refers to this—Hegel 1840, 125.) Due to its inherent feature of naturalness language can be reflected back infinitely, or at least as far as the appearance of human speech.[18] Therefore through the identification of the history of language with that of people the potential lays open for the presumption of three thousand years of Hungarian, or six thousand years of Baltic history.[19] Through the retrospective identification of language with national community, and thus the denotation of natural to historical existence, a past can be created which is basically as old (and of course victorious) as one wishes.[20]

[18] O. Szemerényi also believes that linguistic historians, sooner or later, always reach a point "where explanation ends in statement" (Szemerényi 1971–82/II, 2).

[19] L. Kilian goes back from the Middle Ages to the Neolithic period when he calls the so-called Rzucewo archaeological culture Prussian from the second half of the third millennium BC to the beginning of the second millennium BC.

[20] At times this is achievable by taking possession of a slice of a period from somewhere else, or more often from a common victorious past. The 'theoretical' grounds for this process is always that since Hungarians, Latvians, Lithuanians, etc. existed, there has always been a continually homogeneous Hungarian, Latvian, Lithuanian, etc. consciousness. This is how the Belarusians do it: In 1993 the representatives of the independent Belarus were seeking a document from the U.N. stating that the Grand Duchy of Lithuania had been a Belarusian state. This is what the Russians do: they join the history of the Kievan Rus' to patch up the white blotch on the history of Russia with Moscow at its centre (i.e. Moskovskaya Rus'), based on linguistic equivalence or at least similarity. (It is as if the grafted branch that ultimately became the strongest would appropriate the stronger roots of the stock, even from the times when this branch itself had been a young shoot on a different trunk, in this case the Balto-Finno-Ugric tribe. The first reference to Moscow is from 1147. Its name means 'a smelly little village': < Baltic = Golyad' *Mask-(u)va* 'stinking boggy swamp' < *mask/mazg* 'swamp'—Toporov 1981, 29; popular language referred to the River Moscow as Smorodinka even in the eighteenth century, which is either a translation of Moscow or the Russified version of the Baltic *smard-iu* 'stinking place'—Toporov 1982b, 266.) It turns out in K. See's excellent summary that from the late eighteenth century the Germans 'borrowed' their national past and the national cultural

The reflection of the view that almost identifies language with nation in the most modern times is aided by three circumstances.[21] One is the coneology, meaning that we can only talk about change in time or history as the changing of some unit or entity in time, and we would be worse off with an entity other than language (territory, state, religion, culture), since none of those have a natural side.[22] The other is that the coherence of language and nation seems terribly

---

consciousness from the Scandinavians (See 1970, 36). Slovakian historians act similarly, unanimously choosing the words of V. Mináč as the motto of the two-volume history of Slovakia. The motto invokes the special history, a history of a small peaceful people, following the logic that today's Slovakian nation consists of Slovakian speaking people who obviously had parents and ancestors, and that whoever speaks Slovakian had parents who spoke Slovakian, too. "If history is the story of kings, emperors, generals, and princes, of victories, and conquered lands, and if history means the story of violence, robbery, and exploitation, then we have no history. But if history is the story of civilisation, labour, interrupted but always winning constructions, then that is ours, too. Since we are a nation of builders, and not only in the metaphysical sense of the word, but also in its real one: we built up Vienna and Pest as brick layers, masters, and unskilled labourers, we were there at the building of many other foreign towns, and destroyed none. I know that our historical heritage is humble but if once the history of civilisation will be measured justly, by the labour carried out, then we shall have nothing to fear, either: we have probably done even more than our due tasks. So, there is no reason for us to hanker or harness sorrow after the so-called 'great' history: that is the history of great robbers" (*Dějiny Slovenska slovom i obrazom* [Slovakia's history in words and pictures], 1973; cited in Szarka 1992, 9).

It would be easy to employ, yet not worth the effort of irony for this boastful demagogy, because a serious issue lies behind it: what history is it all about? When M. Hellmann posits that "in large areas Lithuanian people and Lithuania's history do not cover each other" (Hellmann 1990, 17), then what are we supposed to understand under 'Lithuanian people'? The concepts of 'Lithuanian' and 'Lithuania' were not the same in the thirteenth century (Gudavičius 1989, 167). At which point did they merge? And what about the relation between the concepts of 'Latvian' and the 'Latvia' born at the very end of the nineteenth century?

This is not only the problem of the Balts, since "around the year 1000 AD it is only right to say 'the French' or 'the Germans' because of terminological ease, but for example 'the Italians' or 'the English' are even with that justification more problematic" (Szűcs 1992, 15). The problems are the 'when?' because of the late development of Latvian and Lithuanian consciousness, and that in their case a consciousness of the Modern Age attempts to create a continuity with Antiquity.

[21] W. H. McNeill believes that in the history of humanity the ethnically, or linguistically homogeneous nation state was only an ideal social organisational model between the period of 1750 and 1920 (cited in Hofer 1991, 228). Not only did the period not end around 1920, it is unfortunately still apparent today. Its beginnings, however, were indeed somewhere in the eighteenth century: the most obvious borderline is the French Revolution.

[22] We have strong memories of those bulky volumes which commenced the history of the various Soviet Socialist Republics with the Ice Age (and finished it with the Khrushchevian thaw...). Is it much more sensible to discuss Lithuanian Antiquity than the Lithuanian Ice Age?

natural, since language with its natural character "has always been there!"[23] The third and most important circumstance is that once something has emerged during history, for example the concept of a Lithuanian person being the same as the person speaking Lithuanian, it lends clarity to any elements and seeds of the past that point towards this something, even if in its own time that certain element was a part of another whole. Therefore, I intentionally exaggerate when I say that no Latvians or Lithuanians existed before the eleventh century. The Latvian language existed, the people existed, so the two can be connected. Indeed the present creates the facts of the past from the data of the past.[24] Would this mean that all reflection is legitimate after all? Not at all. What decides on legitimacy or arbitrariness is once more the existence or absence of sources.[25] To stick to our examples, both sources of the 'Latvian speaking person' 'are there'.[26] Its history will correlate to how much can be deciphered from these two sources, that is, very little. In the cases of the other forms of consciousness also, only that can be reflected back which has at least some elements or seeds in (written) sources. Therefore, it is not a complete nonsense to talk about Latvian or Lithuanian folklore because there are sources about it ('only' their age is questionable), but for the same reason it is absurd to be talking about Latvian mythology with no Latvian myth at our disposal, or of Lithuanian mythology with one solitary Lithuanian myth fragment.

It could be posited that the various forms of consciousness could fill in the gaps between each other, so for example, myths could be concluded from the fragments of myths that survived in folk-tales.[27] That much is tru. However, a limitation is that the product of at least one of the forms of consciousness should be determinable in time, otherwise one unknown is explained through another. The inde-

---

[23] Similarly, we do not want to believe what Marx and Engels declared, that love is the invention of the class society of the Middle Ages since love's natural, physical part 'has always been there'... (in more detail see Engels 1884, 139–140)

[24] Its acknowledgement is inherent in one of P. Esterházy's characterisations, "he is looking into a victorious past" (Esterházy 1979, 375).

[25] In his colossal monograph H. Łowmiański warns that "expanding the history of the Slavs back in time depends on the character and the condition of the sources at our disposal" (Łowmiański 1963–70/I, 2).

[26] This is why language is used as a leading thread: it is 'always there', and it is the most natural means of deciding who is 'ours' and who is 'alien', to the extent that 'aliens' are considered handicapped in comparison with one's self, e.g. Czech *Němec* 'German' < *němý* 'dumb'; or the Krivichi people (an East Slavic tribe constituting the foundations of the Belarusian people) who were named by their neighbours from *krivoy* 'fake, treacherous' (> current Latv. *krievu* 'Russian'); or the Russian dialectical word *latyshit'* ('to latvian') 'to talk nonsense' (Vasmer 1953–58/II, 19).

[27] An example of when history is concluded from a myth: among the trends of myth research G. J. Larson mentions the so-called 'cultural circle theory' of the Viennese school which attempts to use "myth as impartial evidence for piecing together the history of preliterate cultures" (Larson 1974, 8).

pendence of forms of consciousness is injured even through the most careful transmission of one into another, meaning that, for example, a folk-tale was not told in order to say something about the pagan gods. J. Balys, the most knowledge-able person on Lithuanian folklore emphasises that "a folk-song is primarily poetry, and has to be seen as such" (Balys 1953, 8). M. Finley declares that "the epic *was not history*" (Finley 1975, 14), or as J. Hampl puts it in the title of a study *"The Iliad is not a history book"* (Hampl 1975). Of course debate can be circum-vented with a theoretical refutation of the independence of the various forms of consciousness by, for instance, stating that this independence did not exist in the olden days (how olden?). As does the archaeologist, "in the Neolithic period art did not yet serve beauty. Artistic creations (figural, human and animal images, symbols) were made with interest towards determined aims" (Kalicz 1985, 72). What can be said about this? It is just as indisputable as its opposite, "in the Upper Paleolithic period... an aesthetic sense emerged" (Anisimov 1981, 297), and prehistoric people drew some of the cave drawings just letting their playful and artistic instinct run free. The renowned Latvian archaeologist I. Loze devoted a small book to the art of the Stone Age, in which he discusses stylistic features that differentiate East Baltic art from other *artistic* trends.

I believe that every form of consciousness has its own structure, meaning, and value system, and any comparison between them should be undertaken with the greatest care.[28] Consequently the strongest objection against neo-comparativism is precisely that in all the infinity of cultural space where, through transmission of the forms of consciousness to one another, for example Homer's *Iliad* and Wulfstan's travel account can arise together, values are washed away and finally disappear, the leading principle of (historical) scholarship vanishes, that is the demand for truth (*Wahrheitsanspruch*). To use R. Wittram's words "it steps over the simple factography and is not exhausted in the proof of the true value of facts and their statement, but it also encompasses the category of meaning, and an evaluation of views corresponding to this is its aim" (Wittram 1971, 601). If the discipline of history loses its guiding star from before its eyes it becomes a collection of free associations—that could just as well be connected to facts as not.

Neo-comparativists deny that historical facts are unique and unrepeatable, or are valuable and disclosing in that uniqueness, and in the spirit of structuralist inter-textuality imagine history to be ultimately a puzzle of units, or as C. Geertz says of Lévi-Strauss, "a trim world of transposable forms, a disheveled one of coincident discourses" (Geertz 1985, 259).

---

[28] When A. Švābe tries to conclude the legal relations among Latvian peasants pre-thirteenth century from folk-songs, M. Hellmann warns that the procedure will remain questionable until "the age, authenticity (*Überlieferungstreue*), and contents of the folk-song is examined in the finest detail" (Hellmann 1954, 240).

Once again the best example of this is what is perhaps V. Toporov's most excellent study, a matchless pinnacle of achievement in the neo-comparativist school. It dazzles us with a whole series of associations (philologically almost always indisputable) which illuminate one another, a chain from the proto-pattern of the 'sinful town' *topos* Babylon to the founding legends of Vilnius, from the poems of Rilke and Goethe to references to Dickens and Dostoyevsky. It finally culminates, by expanding Vilnius' prehistory onto the history of the Balts, in a mystifying view of "mythologised history... [and] almost indivisible historicised mythology" (Toporov 1980, 90). In the case of Vilnius and partially in that of Lithuania it would be justified by that "in Vilnius itself, from as early as the first half of the fourteenth century when the town's name is first mentioned in trustworthy sources, various (Lithuanian, Slavic, and later Jewish) cultural–linguistic elements are present" (Toporov 1980, 10–11).

I do not believe that the gaps in and the uncertain ontological status of Baltic history, and consequently Latvian and Lithuanian communal consciousness, would justify such conclusions.

Vilnius, where according to V. Toporov Lithuanians and Slavic Krivichi lived together long before its fourteenth-century establishment (Toporov 1980, 68–69),[29] underwent heavy Polonisation from the fifteenth century, then strong Russification from 1831, and in the early twentieth century it became Vilnius. From 1920 it became Wilno once more, and from September 1939 Vilnius once again; all this with corresponding linguistic, religious, and ethnic changes occurring within its walls. Still, Vilnius had been a historical fact all along, and its faith, reflected in the changes in its name, has to be uncovered and described as historical fact.

Archaeologists posit that the settlement, inhabited from the fifth–eighth centuries, emerged on the 'cape' at the meeting of the River Neris and the Rivulet Vilnia.[30] It was likely to have developed into a town during the thirteenth-century

---

[29] R. Batūra qualifies this as an unfounded presumption (in Dusburg 1985, 357).

[30] Neris in Slavic (Polish, Russian, and Belarusian) is *Wilia, Vilija*. Since this was easily mistaken for Vilnia it was later given a diminutive form and became *Wilenka* in Polish, and from that in Lithuanian *Vilnelė*, Belarusian and Russian *Vilija* (Jurginis–Merkys–Tautavičius 1968, 19). In an early work K. Būga believed that the stem of *Vilija* was the same as the stem of Vilna, he later refuted this thought. M. Vasmer adopted the mistake which is why it is still in use (Vasmer 1953–58/I, 200). V. Toporov, although aware of it, dismisses the rebuttal, and with a neat trick he pretends that the respected American-Lithuanian linguist P. Skardžius, who actually opposed the early Būga–Vasmer thesis, would be on his side. Toporov re-mythologises the *vil-* stem: he says that the *vel-* stem (from whence *vil-* really comes) means 'soul of the dead', which he amplifies in the 'death' meaning when he connects the Lithuanian name of the river Neris (< Lith. *nerti* 'to sink', etc.) with the mythological underworld (Toporov 1980, 57). In fact, as A. Salys points out, "Vilnius' name has nothing to do with *Vilija*," the latter is mentioned in the Ipatiy Compilation of Chronicles in 1232 as Vel'ya, which comes from the *veliya* 'big' adjective: when the Slavs reached the Vilnius region around the sixth century, they simply named the Neris, the widest there, the Big river (Lit. E./XXXIV, 213–214).

establishment of the state, during which time three castles were built on its territory: the Upper and Lower castles of stone, and the so-called Crooked Castle (*curvum castrum*) of wood which in 1390 the Crusaders razed to the ground without trace. We have several trustworthy sources of information that Mindaugas raised a Catholic cathedral in the town connected to the bishopric (for example the Procurator of the crusaders talked about this at the Ecumenical Council of Constance in 1414–1418 that refers to it).

Nevertheless, the town is mentioned by name only late, first in 1323, then again in 1324 when the Grand Duke Gediminas mentions it with two endings in his Latin letters (*in ciuitate nostra Vilna, Datum Wilno*), and in a German letter with a third ending (*de Vilne*) (Gediminas 1966, 31, 171, 75).[31] The name, looking at its origins is, so to say, ethnically indifferent: it is a simple transmission of the river name *Vilna* or rather *Vil'na* to the settlement on its bank; and the etymology of the water name is also clear: < East Lith. *vilnia*, West Lith. and literary *vilnis* 'wave' (cf. Latv. *vilnis*, Slavic *vilna*, Ger. *Welle* 'wave'), which is compounded from the Lith. *velti, valstyti, valyt'* 'to roll, to mill' verbs stem (cf. Russ. *vali'*) and the +*ni, nja* derivator, so it referred to the rapid flow of the small river.[32]

There was nothing mythical in its name, establishment, or ancient history, nor in its modern faith. There is nothing mythical in that in 1920 General Żeligowski occupied the town through an infamous trick and turned it into Wilno, or that in 1939 first Hitler and then Stalin tried to motivate the Lithuanians to give up their neutrality by handing the town back to them. It can also be explained rationally that, so to say, a time section is missing from the entire nineteenth-century Lithuanian consciousness, and that is the present, because fighting against Russian oppression for their current freedom was equal to fighting for the re-establishment

[31] V. Toporov convincingly refutes its earlier alleged references, like the Anglo-Saxon *Widsith* (The traveller), a 'heroic legend' from the tenth century; the Icelandic Snorri Sturluson's work the *Heimskringla* (Globe) from the twelfth century; or the Russian *Voskresenskiy Compilation of Chronicles* starting from the twelfth century (Toporov 1980, 11).

[32] This original feminine form 'Vilna' remained in several (Hungarian, Russian, and a few western European) languages. The Polish and sometimes Russian neutral 'Wilno' adjusted to place names such as Grodno, Berezno, Rybno, etc. There is a reference to the Lithuanian masculine 'Vilnius' only from the sixteenth century, although most likely it had been in use earlier in this form, too, which is demonstrated by that in the fifteenth century J. Długosz created a certain Prince Vilius as the Roman founder and namesake of the town with this masculine ending, although obviously he must have known that the town and the river were called by the same name in Latin and in Russian (Jurginis–Merkys–Tautavičius 1968, 36). The 'Vilnius' form came about through a process, where in the Baltic languages the possessive structures common in place names (*Vilnios upė > miestas* 'Vilna's river' > 'Vilna's town') the qualifier in gen. (*Vilnios*) was transmitted to the masculine ones with the -*ju* stem (for more examples of similar transmissions see Lit. E./XXXIV, 212). This is supported by that one of the qualified words (rivulet) has a masculine and a feminine form in Lithuanian (*upelis, upelė*), and the other qualified word (*miestas* 'town') is masculine.

of Polish freedom—while Poland did not exist! Lithuanians had only a past. This is connected to the topic of Vilnius in that when at the turn of the nineteenth and twentieth centuries the issue arose as to what the capital of Lithuania, which had obtained some autonomy, should be, then among the six towns at stake, only Vilnius could seem irrationally mystical because only one argument was for it, and that was that it *had been* once Lithuania's capital—though at the time only two percent of its populace was Lithuanian.

Nonetheless, all this simply means that the facts of Baltic history lend themselves to being connected to legends or 'myths', this should not, however, hinder the historian in separating historical facts from among the avalanche of data and differentiating them from myths.

CHAPTER 3

MYTHS AND SYSTEMS OF MYTHS

If, after this long introduction, I finally pose the question of what constitutes Baltic mythology, or indeed if there is no such thing and only "out-dated romanticism presumes it" (Šmits 1926, 4), then what constitutes Latvian, Lithuanian, and Prussian mythology, the straight answer can only be: 'it depends'. It depends on who considers what to be mythology. S. Urbańczyk, one of the most reliable experts on Slavic mythology, posits that 'mythology' has a dual meaning. On the one hand it denotes the assortment of myths (and since there are no Slavic myths, then there is no Slavic mythology in this sense either). On the other hand the collection of what has been thought or written about the myths (and in this sense, several libraries worth of material has been heaped up about the aforementioned nothing) (SSS/3, 266).

There is little value in pondering long on a definition of the basic unit, the myth. L. Honko analyses eleven different definitions (social, psychological, metaphysical, etc.) (Honko 1972, 12–14). Here, the minimum that is unanimously acceptable is sufficient: myth "is a narrative concerning anthropomorphised gods, their origins, relationships, creative deeds, battles, and passions. Therefore the content of myths (theogony, cosmogony, anthropogony) is in general the beginning of everything that exists" (SSS/3, 265–266).

Contrary to I. Goldziher's belief that mythology continues in religion (Goldziher 1876), I do not find it necessary to differentiate between the two, because of a characteristic Baltic development where an 'own' mythology was replaced by an 'alien' religion (Christianity). Unlike L. Schroeder, who declares myths to be narratives about religion (Schroeder 1914–16/I, 28), I do not consider 'narrativity' to be a decisive feature since myths, "tales (fables) about gods, semi-gods, and other supernatural beings and powers from preliterate times were handed down not only in the form of narratives but also of rituals" (Markiewicz 1987, 155). Narrated myth and acted out myth are two aspects of the same phenomenon,[1] consequently, in a discussion of the mythology of the Balts, sources relating to rituals or cults have to be taken into consideration just as much as narrated myths.

---

[1] E. Meletinskiy rightly compares the question of which instigated which to the 'hen and egg' dilemma (Meletinskiy 1986, 15).

In the first sense, Baltic mythology is barely extant: as we shall see it amounts to the names of a few gods or words referring to cults with a generally impenetrable etymology, and a solitary Lithuanian mythological narrative (in Russian). However, in the second sense everything belongs to Baltic mythology that anyone has mentioned, even in passing, since Wulfstan, Tacitus about the Aestii, or even Herodotus about the Slavic Neuri. The result is a busy Baltic Olympus laid out before us in the works of the neo-mythologists. In their imposing mythological encyclopaedia V. Ivanov and V. Toporov devote separate entries to seven common Baltic, five Latvian, thirteen Lithuanian, and eighteen Prussian gods, discounting some more minor mythological characters (Tokarev 1988). In a section of the most recent mythological encyclopaedia partly written, partly compiled by Latvian researchers there is no entry for 'Baltic mythology', yet some of the six Latvian, twelve Lithuanian, and sixteen Prussian gods are discussed as being common Baltic (Iltnere 1993–94).[2]

There is another very important difference between mythology seen as the collection of myths and that viewed as a reflection on or scholarship about myths which has grown to an impenetrable quantity. Naturally there is little Common Baltic in the first category since, following the disintegration of the Proto-Baltic unit, the West Baltic Prussians and the East Baltic Latvians–Lithuanians lived separately for perhaps as long as a thousand years. Their fresh encounter only resulted in a neighbourhood relation instead of the resurrection of the former unity. Consequently, in Baltic culture common features only came about with Christianity, this is amplified by the fact that pagan Baltic culture had to define itself communally in opposition to Christianity, and also that exclusively Christian accounts report on these common features, often homogenising or stereotyping them into a Common Baltic (or even more widely to pagan).

In the other sense of mythology the culture of Prussian, Lithuanian, Livonian (Latvian) territories qualify as common without hesitation, and any of these pasts can be pushed behind either of the presents. It has not always been like this. Firstly, in the late sixteenth century, M. Stryjkowski inserted the (forged) Prussian gods into Lithuanian mythology. Later in the nineteenth century, T. Narbutt augmented it by amalgamating them as Baltic. On the Latvian side in the late eighteenth century, Stenders the Elder (in *Lettische Grammatik nebst Lexicon*, 1861), J. Lange (*Vollständiges deutsch–lettisches und lettisch–deutsches Lexicon*, 1777), then Stender the Elder (who added a chapter Lettische Mythologie, 1783 to the later work which he re-published and expanded) carried out this work, and in the late nineteenth century in the *Lāčplēsis* the 'national epic' by A. Pumpurs (which

---

[2] The entries of the volume were written by work groups. The author of the 'Latvian mythology' can be established because the entry is the same, almost word for word, as one of I. Kokare's summarising studies (Kokare 1991).

became compulsory reading in schools) Common Baltic already seemed to be self-evident.

I do not intend to detail from start to finish the road that led from 'hardly anything' to 'mesmerising wealth', or from one meaning of mythology to the other; for this route see the works of the two nineteenth-century scholars, the Polish A. Mierzyński (1829–1907) and the German W. Mannhardt (1831–1880) working in Gdańsk. A. Mierzyński published the sources of Baltic mythology in two widely annotated volumes, from Tacitus to the mid-fifteenth century.[3] W. Mannhardt added many others to roughly the same sources with substantial and trustworthy commentaries, up to Kotzebue, known as a dramatist from the early nineteenth century. The anthology of the German scholar had a troubled life. It was already complete in 1870, but was stranded for various periods on K. Müllenhoff's desk in Berlin, A. Bezzenberger's in Königsberg, and A. Bielenstein's in Riga, and it took decades for it to be finally published in Riga in 1936; from a number of contributors the anthology owes the most to T. Doebner, the president of *Lettisch–Literarische Gesellschaft* in Riga, who edited and professionally annotated Mannhardt's commentaries. After T. Doebner's death in 1919, the collection went to G. Gerullis in Leipzig, then back to Riga to P. Šmits and N. Busch, and gained its final shape from A. Bauer. The circumstances of its publication show how the vast amount of material discovered and collected by Mannhardt came to be widely known during its sixty-six years of wandering from place to place. Baltic mythology was evidently also incorporated into W. Mannhardt's work,[4] and through that into the context of European scholarship, primarily with the inter-mediation of the monumental work by L. Schroeder along the line of Mannhardt's views (Schroeder 1914–16).

The Polish and the German scholars were similar from a number of aspects. They did not speak 'Baltic' well,[5] so they had to rely on the help of linguists. Their major virtues were shared, too: positivist meticulousness; precision; a critical spirit as a counter-reaction to the previous romantic school, in filtering the Baltic Olympus; they were also aided by their view that the religion of the Balts was an animistic belief system where personal gods played no roles. Currently, many (mostly the representatives of the ethnographic method) qualify this critical spirit as exaggeration, for example, J. Puhvel states that "the ancient traditions of the Old Prussians, Lithuanians, and Latvians are waiting to be rehabilitated from their Mannhardtian put down as just another instalment of rustic European *Wald- und Feldkulte*" (Puhvel 1974, 75). Of course nothing has cropped up that would justify such a rehabilitation.) Without the chrestomathies of A. Mierzyński and

---

[3] For an objectively Lithuanian evaluation of the work of the Polish scholar who refuted and unveiled the romantic 'Lithuanomania' see Ivinskis 1938–39, 361 ff.

[4] For this cf. Scherer in Mannhardt 1884.

[5] Mannhardt "was not adequately in possession of the language" (Usener 1896, 84).

W. Mannhardt research of Baltic mythology would be unimaginable. Unfortunately, they have only one follower, the Lithuanian N. Vėlius (1937–1996) who planned to publish the sources of Lithuanian and Baltic mythologies in separate volumes. Due to his painfully early death, only the first volume of the Lithuanian series was published in his lifetime, which follows on from where Mannhardt left off. It encompasses the writings on nineteenth-century Lithuanian mythology (and evidently contains many Common Baltic references), up to A. Brückner in the early twentieth century (Vėlius 1995). The second volume of the Lithuanian sources was published in 1997, and the third and last volume is underway. The first of the planned four volumes of the *Baltų religijos ir mitologijos šaltiniai* [The sources of Baltic religion and mythology] was published in 1996; in essence these are the Mierzyński–Mannhardt work carried forward into the twentieth century and annotated. (Unfortunately I was only able to look into these after the completion of this book.)

For these reasons I shall restrict myself to little more detail about the 'hardly anything' that can be tied to assured sources, and I will only outline modern myth-creation at its major conjunctions.

CHAPTER 4

THE THEORY OF SOCIAL FORMATION

Perhaps the main difference between the historical and the ethnographic viewpoints is that the latter sees belief systems as timeless, while the former considers them to be historical formations which follow changes in social structure, therefore a certain form of social organisation attracts a certain mythological and religious system. This view reached its zenith in the Marxist theory of social formation (from Marx to Stalin), and for many it lost its credibility once and for all simply because of this association.

The strictly dogmatic view of the theory of social formation states that, subject to forces, history proceeds through the same stages everywhere (class-free prehistoric community, class societies of slave-holding societies, feudalism, then capitalism, and finally to a once again class-free communism), becoming increasingly perfect towards its one and only purpose. Indeed, contrary to this dogmatic theory (or indeed any dogmatic theory) numerous objections can be raised. These can be summarised in that the theory of social formation "in all cases prescribes a fixed course to history, is in all cases teleological" (Komoróczy 1986, 387), and in that it superimposes the scheme of European, or even western European social development onto the history of humankind in its entirety, thus turning "history into a moral success story... If history is the working out of moral purpose in time, then those who lay claim to that purpose are by that fact the predilect agents of history. The scheme misleads in a second sense as well. If history is but a tale of unfolding moral purpose, then each link in the genealogy, each runner in the race is only a precursor of the final apotheosis and not a manifold of social and cultural processes at work in their own time and place" (Wolf 1982, 5).

Indeed we would not get far with the purist theory of social formation for several reasons.[1]

---

[1] Marx himself protested, on numerous occasions, against "metamorphosing my historical sketch of the genesis of capitalism in Western Europe into a historico-philosophical theory of general development, imposed by fate on all peoples, whatever the historical circumstances in which they are placed..." (Marx 1877, 200).

For the "immanent problematics" of the theory of social formation see the various writings of R. Simon, e.g. 1996, 109–128, 130–158.

One of these is that the various formations modify and transform according to the local geographical and climatic factors (which is how the 'third, fourth, and umpteenth paths' can come about). It can be stated that regular formation only exists as a working hypothesis and that in reality there are only its variations. The emergence of variations, for example the northern and southern variations of Europe, can already be detected at the very beginnings: the Neolithic revolution occurred only partly in the northern forested zone (in the area of ceramics and development of stone tools), and with a shift in phase it stretched into the Bronze Age; in the millennium following the revolution in the North, the typical economic activities were not in the field of agriculture but still in animal husbandry and "Mesolithic fishing, hunting, and gathering" (Okulicz 1973, 61 ff.).

[Due to the shift in phases as a result of some societies 'walking on the spot' sometimes even across millennia, the phenomena of vast distances in time could come under the same social formation umbrella which questions the sense of comparisons based on formations. I do not believe we become much wiser if we establish that the Vedic hymns of the first millennium BC and Homer's epic works from the eighth–seventh centuries BC reflect the same chiefdom–gentilic formation that is apparent in the pre-ninth-century Anglo-Saxon or the pre-twelfth-century Scandinavian and Slavic states (D'yakonov 1994, 38), or that this realisation would alleviate the task of seeking and explaining the differences and signs of otherness that disappear in the background of typological equations.]

Furthermore, the clarity of the picture is also clouded in that the same society does not proceed at all times in a straight line from one social formation to the next, but can occasionally regress, make detours, or stiffen into a set frame. H. Moora made a singularly important observation when stating that the herders, and agriculturists, i.e. the tribes of the Battle axe culture who populated the East Baltic from the South returned to a fishing and hunting lifestyle in adjusting to the colder northern conditions (Moora 1956, 73). It can be assumed that the achievements of a previous formation will rapidly disappear in the economic 'basis', as opposed to the superstructure where the new system never entirely ends the previous system but rather builds upon in. Thus unclear formations of consciousness emerge, for example in Baltic mythology where, as we shall see, several remnants are layered on top of each other: the memory of Indo-European antiquity squeezed into the shape of folklore or the guise of a 'redundant god' (*deus otiosus*); preceding it traces of the matriarchy of the 'Vened period'; the shamanism of the forest zone; the natural belief system of the tribal period; and Christianity which moulded and subdued all of these.

A further, and perhaps the principal weakness of the dogmatic view of the theory of social formation, and for which in its purest form, it must be rejected, is that it sees the various social formations following each other as development toward a goal of perfection, and because it presumes value differences between these formations. G. Childe's words suggest something similar: "At the beginning of the Bronze Age Central Europe was not only behind Hither Asia, but separated therefrom by a regular series of descending grades of culture" (Childe 1950, 122).

Is capitalism more valuable than feudalism? To me it is not just an acquiescent response, but the question itself which is absurd since the concept of value can always only be connected to the individual, the subject, and expands only over a human lifetime, that is, it is not historical. The question attempts to connect this concept with the concept of formation that is only applicable to a group of people or a society. [The absurdity of the question is even more apparent if it is twice re-phrased. On the one hand if it refers to the value of an individual life which is customarily marked by the word 'happiness', and in this way the question would be whether an individual living under capitalism is happier than one under feudalism. On the other hand it can be expanded to some (non-existent) collective subject, in which case it would decide whether the nation that had gone through a 'higher degree of development' had also become more valuable by it. There would consequently be good and bad nations.]

There is only one aspect in which it makes sense to differentiate between values, at least among formations of consciousness, that is the 'superstructures' of certain formations, and the extent to which they are sufficient to their own 'basis' and constitute a useful whole together from their own perspective. In this sense it is perhaps justified to think of Christianity based on literacy, on the written Gospel rather than the oral paganism at the point when, for example, Lithuanian society reached the degree of development, i.e. a state organisation, in which it would have required literacy.[2]

However, the objections against the theory of social formation dissipate if one considers it only as a very general frame which barely tries to state more than human societies consist of periods that grow out of one another, and that human-kind went through the stages of gathering, fishing, hunting, husbandry, agriculture, manufacturing, and their more or less concordant intellectual counterparts where each section invoked a practically infinite number of variations. Accordingly, if we wish to be precise, plural forms have to be used, as in agricultures, feudalisms, polytheisms, and so on.[3]

If this scheme is used only to reveal the past without wishing to point towards the future in the way that Marx, Engels, Lenin, Stalin, etc. did, then so little te-

---

[2] G. Childe says that the development of "the Indo-European languages might be regarded as the consequence of adapting a series of savage dialects to be a means of intercourse in pastoral, warlike, and patriarchal societies with new interests, material and social" (Childe 1950, 175). If I really wanted to I could conclude that for G. Childe there is a value difference even in the various formations of language.

[3] For an interesting attempt at a 'normal' refreshment of the theory of social formation free of ideological and political overtones, see I. D'yakonov's mini world history published in 1994, in which the author differentiates eight formations in the history of humanity, instead of the previous five (D'yakonov 1994).

leology remains in the concept that is apparent in any theory of history, i.e. as much as the historian brings to it.[4]

The nineteenth-century comparative school of the history of religions, with A. Kuhn and M. Müller in the lead represented the principles of the theory of social formation, or as they called it, the principle of the graduality of progress. I. Goldziher considered himself a follower of this school who amalgamated the linguistic basis with social history, and Steinthal's 'folk psychology' into an individual and *moderate* synthesis. Goldziher believes that mythology continues in religion, and accordingly comparative myth research continues in the comparative history of religions. He gave a brief summary of this view: "The tasks of comparative mythology are to study the way the names emerged that carry the myths of humans, the stories that are connected to these names as the contents of the myths; how the mentioned names transformed into proper nouns; what supported the process of personalisation and the individualisation which led to the names of natural phenomena becoming proper nouns; how natural legends turned into national sagas, and the solar and lunar heroes into national heroes. The tasks of the comparative history of religions are to demonstrate how those elements of myths which did not become part of narratives with a historical undertone changed into religious concepts; how the individualised *nomen apellativums* of natural phenomena became the names of gods, and how these *nomen apellativums* developed into polytheistic groups; through what process polytheism condensed into dualism or henotheism, and in what way and under what psychological laws it moved towards the direction of monotheism; during this long process, where the first foundation and starting point was a motion in the realm of linguistic history and how the ethical elements connected to the theistic ideals; where and in what direction these degrees of progress show in the forms of religions demonstrable in history, and what the relation between the individual *ingenium* of the various individuals (so-called creators of religions) to the necessary influence of this developmental march" (Goldziher 1878, 176).

---

[4] G. Komoróczy basically comes to the same final conclusion, when he sees the importance of K. Polányi in that "he conducted typological analyses, at times with only ad hoc generalisations, and did not expand the validity of typology without moderation" (Komoróczy 1986, 387). It is indeed true that there is no better recipe for a historian than moderation.

CHAPTER 5

POLYDOXY, PROTOTHEISM, POLYTHEISM

I believe that there is no more valid system of development of myths and religions than the one that emerged out of socio-history, linguistic history, and psychology than that depicted by I. Goldziher here and elsewhere (natural religion > polytheism > dualism [henotheism] > monotheism). Even so, I shall take H. Łowmiański's scheme which is very similar to that of Goldziher's and is in fact in some points the same, as the basis for my presentation of the Baltic belief system. H. Łowmiański applied his system of the pagan Slavic religion between the sixth–twelfth centuries, and due to the historical semblance of the Slavic and Baltic material, his general theoretical concepts are also easier to adjust (see especially Łowmiański 1979).

The Polish scholar differentiates between two fundamental religious systems: polydoxy characteristic of class free and preliterate societies; and the polytheism of class societies organised into a state.

Polydoxy is a system preceding the development of 'personal gods' where the human calls the most varied phenomena of the world surrounding him, that is nature, *sacrum* 'sacred' or 'god', therefore the circle of gods is boundless and their numbers are practically infinite.

Polydoxy comprises four basic forms: magic; belief in life after death and in the soul after death; belief in various natural phenomena, and their cults; and demonology, or belief in the 'unclean' soul' which in Christian religions emerges as idolatry.

Prototheism constitutes a transition between polydoxy and polytheism. It is the belief in the physical sky (in every religion the physical sky is first to become personalised or anthropomorphised among the momentary and transitory gods). This turns into the belief in the sky god. Polydoxy survived in certain areas of life for a long time (for example in superstitions, or beliefs even today), even after the system of polytheism was layered onto it, or when the highest form of religion, monotheism emerged, which, as opposed to the polydoxy of a group (tribal) religion, is "universal and beyond groups, and necessarily takes over the ethical control of the believers from the group, and develops an eschatological conception" (Łowmiański 1979, 398).

CHAPTER 6

SHAMANISM

The 'polydoxy–prototheism–polytheism–monotheism' developmental series has to be widened by an element that presumably played an important role in the Baltic belief system, and that is shamanism.[1]

It is debatable whether shamanism, as the 'generalists' claim, is a definite degree (the first) of the general development of religion, and consequently an independent belief system; or, as the 'regionalists' posit, it is simply a localised phenomenon spread only in northern Russia, Lapland, and Mongolia (Hultkranz 1989, 43–44), and as such it is an incomplete form of polydoxy since it contains only a few of its elements. The question is practically unanswerable, because shaman belief in all aspects is very likely to be the most ancient and as such constitutes a religion–non-religion leaving the least of traces behind. Its monographers, M. Eliade and H. Findeisen both posit its beginnings at the Early Paleolithic Age of prehistory (Eliade 1994–96/III, 14; Findeisen 1957, 7). Alongside its great distance in time, its social distance contributes to the scant vestiges it has left. I. D'yakonov connects shamanism to the primary degree of human social organisation (D'yakonov 1994, 22), A. Hultkranz posits that "shamanism is the heritage from the ancient *hunting* culture" (Hultkranz 1989, 47). Similarly V. Voigt considers it characteristic of "forest hunting people" living in kinship, or a kinship society on the verge of disintegration. For this reason "shamanism has no words or place in a tribal or more highly organised social unit... its tasks usually do not spread beyond the kinship society and its settlement" (Voigt 1965, 381). Of course this does not stop elements of it living on in other belief systems that follow or oust it, even more so, because shamanism is the most ancient from a phenomenological perspective, too, since its initial seed is that from whence all religions, and in general *the* religion spring: the answer to the only inexplicable

[1] The '-isms' that follow each other in regular sequence give the totally false impression that it only concerns strict religious–dogmatic systems. In fact, at the outset only local cults at most could have existed, along with slowly developing religious images always mixing with other belief images. In the case of the Balts, 'outset' quite probably meant 'all along, until the victory of Christianity'. This definition is even more appropriate in the case of shamanism, which V. Voigt rightly declares (if anything can be rightly declared about it) that "shamanism, in the strict sense, is not yet a religion" (Voigt 1975, 212).

mystery of human life, the mystery of death and the dead.[2] The basic purpose of the shaman falling into a trance is to gain entry to the empire of the dead, and to be able to guide others there as a soul-guide. This time M. Eliade can rightly say that the "shaman ascending to the skies is a primary phenomenon (*un phénomène originaire*), it belongs to the human being as such in its integrity and not so much to the human as a historical being," although in general I do not accept his opposition of "the human as such" and "the human as a historical being" (Eliade 1951, 10). That shamanism constitutes the universally valid (first) stage, of the development of religion and society, can perhaps be supported by all the places its traces are thought to have been discovered from Siberia to Oceania (cf. Eliade 1951).

The Balts, pressing eastward and northward, could have encountered shamanism from two directions, that is from the North and the South. V. Diószegi's research reveals how important a role shamanism must have played in the proto-religion of the Ugrian Hungarians (e.g. Diószegi 1954). According to J. Pentikäinen "the ancient Finnish religion seems to be an indistinguishable part of Arctic shamanism" (Pentikäinen 1989, 98), what is more, "the remnants of ancient shamanism can be suspected in several ecstatic customs of the old protestant sects among the Lapps, or even the Swedes and Finns, not so long ago" (Voigt 1975, 207).

From the South the Scythians were the intermediaries who handed over shamanism (that preceded the Scythian tribal federation and nomadic state) to the Greeks on the Pontus in the seventh century BC (which is why "some scholars think... that shamanism brought about the idealistic philosophy of Pythagoras and Plato"—Hultkranz 1989, 48); and, either directly or through the Slavs, to the Balts.[3]

---

[2] This is the reason why "funeral customs represent the beginnings and essential kernel of religion" (Greimas 1990, 365).

[3] For a convincing analysis of the clear signs of shamanism in Scythian mythology see M. Eliade 1951, 354 ff. The Romanian scholar already accepts G. Dumézil's thesis about a uniform mythology in the Indo-European period, and he claims that "the Indo-Europeans [like this, the Indo-Europeans *en bloc*—E. B.] preserved traces of a shaman ideology and techniques", still he gives no mention to either Slavic nor Baltic (Indo-Europeans after all) shamanism (Eliade 1951, 338).

CHAPTER 7

BALTIC MYTHOLOGICAL SYSTEMS

The majority of scholars who study Baltic mythology either (independent of any system) accept the data from ethnic religion (*Volksreligion*) recorded in the modern age as the historical source of former pagan mythology (and thus presume a multitude of deities to be self-evident), or as the heritage of Indo-European polytheism. Those who are more moderate, such as H. Bertuleit, believe that "beside the polytheism that developed to a notable degree, a deep rooted animism is also apparent" (Bertuleit 1924, 66). As for myself, I shall possibly disregard the data of 'ethnic religion' and consider the minimalist view to be tenable after a thorough examination of the historical sources detached from ethnic religions, a perspective which was predominant in the nineteenth century, but has become only a minority view, hopefully temporarily. In this it is posited that the Balts, in a series of religious and mythological systems loosely following and intertwining with one another, were at the level of polydoxy at the time when they encountered Christianity and consequently appear in the sources. Full credit should be given to H. Lowmiański's synopsis in which he stated that, "the first elements of polytheism reached the Indo-European peoples through their contact with the countries of the 'fertile crescent', however, this form only became general from the Mediterranean Sea to India in the second and first millennia BC;[1] it only reached the Germanic peoples in the first century AD through their contacts with the Romans; and it began to emerge among the Slavs as late as the tenth century AD, perhaps remaining completely unknown to the Balts" (Lowmiański 1979, 398).

7.1. Baltic prototheism

At the point when Baltic polydoxy could have developed into polytheism, Christianity came along and consequently only prototheism could evolve. It is expedient to introduce a presentation of Baltic mythology at this highest level: two

---

[1] According to the mythologists such as H. J. Rose and H. Wagenvoort, whom Dumézil contemptuously terms 'primitivists', Roman personal deities are also late developments from a primitive impersonality (cf. Momigliano 1984, 319).

(names of) chief gods enter the picture and offer a clear example of the fundamental contradiction between the archaic nature of language and the not necessarily archaic features of mythological characters.

7.1.1. *Deivas

The Baltic word (Latv. *dievs*, Lith. *dievas*, Pruss. *deywis*) denoted the physical sky and later the Christian God.[2] That the word first meant 'sky' is evident in its survival in (East) Lithuanian, and Latvian in particular, to the present day,[3] and that it was passed on in this meaning: Finn. *taivas*, Estonian *taevas*, Livonian *tövas* 'sky'. A number of signs show the sky becoming 'divine': Debess tēvs 'Father of sky' (which can be of course also the mirror translation of the Latin *pater coeli*) is frequent as the synonym for the Christian god and the pagan thunder god Pērkons in the Latvian folk-songs; and the Lithuanian superstition according to which, if one points at the sky[4] one's finger will shrivel up (Lit. E./IV, 390).

As P. Skardžius thoroughly presented, the Baltic word goes back to the IE. adjective *deiwos* 'celestial', where the *dei*- stem means 'to light, glitter, shine', and the same stem is apparent in the Baltic *deina* 'day(time)', too (Latv. and Lith. *diena*, Pruss. sing. acc. *dienan*) which correlates with the IE. *din* (OInd. *dinam* 'daytime', Latin *nundinae* 'market at every ninth day', OSlav. *dьnь*, Czech *den*, Croatian *dan* 'daytime', etc.).

It is likely that besides *deiwos* there was a *djeus* root noun (*Wurzelnomen*), which presumably has traces neither in Baltic nor in Slavic languages, even though great linguists such as Trubetzkoy or Vaillant attempt to explain the Russ. *dozhdь*, Polish *deszcz* 'rain' from here, as IE. *dus* 'bad' + *djeus* > *djus* 'gone wrong, overcast sky'.

The original meaning of the 'sky > personalised sky > chief god, father god' shifts in meaning has only survived in the Baltic, in other languages it only reached various degrees in the shift of meaning. The original word itself can be found in almost all Indo-European languages, but not in the meaning of 'sky', but of deities 'at various levels': OInd. *devas*, OLat. *deivos*, Germanic *Tiwaz* > Old High German *Ziu*, *Zio*, Old Nordic *Tyr*, *Thor*, etc. According to Gamkrelidze–Ivanov the shift had occurred already in the Indo-European period: from the *t'ieu-/t'iu-

---

[2] Besides the Prussian, the Lith. *deivė* 'goddess' points to the original -ei- diphthong, a goddess which can be discerned in a 'witch, idol, carved picture' meaning only from the sixteenth century.

[3] Lith. *Dievu trobas dengta* means 'hut covered with dievas, i.e. sky (that is a hut with a hole in the roof)', Latv. *saule noiet dievā* means 'the sun goes down in the sky', in a folk-song *nav saulite dievā gajsi* means 'the little sun did not go down in the sky' (Skardžius 1963, 256).

[4] In Lithuanian they point at the cloud, because in that language *debesis* survived in the meaning 'cloud', as opposed to the Latvian where *debesis* is 'cloud', and *debess* is 'sky'.

'sky' which had already become the sun god–father god at that point (*t'$ieu(s)$-$p(h)Ht(h)er$, OInd. *Dyaus pita*, Greek *Zeu pater*, Latin *Diespiter, Jupiter* < *$djeu$-$pater$* where *Ju*- is the vocative, Umbrian *Jupater*, Hitt. *šiu* 'god', Luwiyan *Tiuat* 'sun god', whose children are the divine twins (Gamkrelidze–Ivanov 1984/II, 475, 777). V. Toporov also writes about a direct Baltic heritage for the Indo-European concept of 'god', based on Dumézil's thesis, saying that the pagan deities of Antiquity and the Middle Ages are the descendants of the Indo-European period ("the Balts and the Inds retained the meaning of 'god' as the continuum of the IE. *$deiuo$-s") (Toporov 1975–90/I, 324). In this case it ought to be presumed that the concept of 'god' was 'secularised', among the Balts alone, that is it degraded to apply to the notion of the physical sky, for which process there is no other example anywhere.[5]

H. Biezais cites the *only* data for the existence of Dievs as a Baltic (Latvian) god from Bishop Valenti's reports in Italian from 1604: *Tebo Deves*, which is claimed to be "undoubtedly the erroneous form (*korrumpierte Form*) of *Debess Dievs* 'the God of the Heavens'" (Biezais 1975, 323), although it is undoubtedly the amalgam of *debess dievs* 'heavenly god' and *debess tēvs* 'heavenly father'.

The diminutive form of the word (Latv. *dieviņš*, Lith. *dievaitis*) is used for pagan gods, primarily for the thunder god.[6]

---

[5] Although it was probably possible to transgress the semantic border between 'sky' and 'sky god', I would explain the 'd' in *debesis*, as opposed to an 'n', through the impact of *$deivas$ (cf. Old Slavic and Russ. *nebo*, Old Indic *nabhnas*, Avestan *nabah*, Latin *nebula* 'sky, cloud'), which according to Fraenkel is "unclear" (Fraenkel 1962, 1965, 1, 85).

The intervening stage between 'sky > chief god' can be seen only in one reference, and that is Germanic. Tacitus wrote about the sacred grove of a Suebian tribe, the Semnon, which "is regarded as the cradle of the race and the dwelling place of the supreme god *regnator omnium deus* to whom all things are subject and obedient" (Tacitus 39). I. Borzsák translates *regnator omnium deus*, as "god ruling over all," accepting R. Pettazoni's position that here *deus* is simply "an undefined supernatural power, a *numen*" (Pettazoni, "*Regnator omnium deus*" in *Essays on History of Religions*, 1951). The majority, both before and after the R. Pettazoni study claim that the phrase refers, although non-specifically, to the personal god of the Germanic people, i.e. to *Tiwaz*, so its correct translation is "the almighty god" (see e.g. the latest Heidelberg edition of Tacitus, 1967). Here Tacitus only used the somewhat modified formulae which the Romans applied to Jupiter. "He [Tacitus] hesitated to impose Jupiter's name on the barbarous divinity, and he limited it to quote it as a permanent attribute... The turn that Tacitus described concerning the personalisation of the sky must have occurred through the influence of Rome in Gallia following its annexation to Rome, that is from the second half of the first century BC" (for the issue in general see Łowmiański 1976a, 357).

[6] So much so, that H. Biezais identifies the two, i.e. the little god and Pērkons (Biezais 1961, 51 ff., 1972, 106 ff.), which is not justified, since Lithuanian dainas refer to other pagan deities such as the moon, as 'little gods'. K. Būga believes that idols are also referred to in that way (Būga 1908–09, 145). However, contrary to the opinion of many, this is not a minor pagan sky god, who existed before the Christian god, but the result of becoming a taboo twice over.

'Dievs', derived from the minor god of Latvian folk-songs, and the Indo-European origin of the actual *word* were reason enough to presume a pagan Baltic father god, which then "transformed into meaning the Christian god in the language of all three Baltic peoples'" (Šmits 1926, 15). P. Šmits explains this process, "when the first Christian missionaries reached the Prussians, Latvians, and Lithuanians the neighbouring Germans, Poles, and Russians had already been baptised. Since the missionaries heard the Balts mention a celestial 'Dievs' which strongly reminded them of the Latin *deus*, they believed that this must have been a misheard version of the Christian God" (Šmits 1930a, 195). To see Dievs as a pagan god became so deeply rooted with Latvian mythologists that it was entered into the most recent mythological encyclopaedia, and as is customary in such cases the total absence of data matters not one jot (Iltnere 1993–94/2, 171). Even the author of the entry is obliged to admit that there is no trustworthy information concerning the cult of Dievs, his temples, priests, sanctuaries, sacrifices, prayers expressly for him in Latvian folklore or historical sources.[7]

In actual fact, the meaning 'sky' could have directly become 'God' in the Christian times. Plausible circumstances for the shift in meaning can easily be depicted: when the Christian missionaries tried to explain the concept of the heavenly Father, this was naturally associated with the word meaning 'sky' in the pagan mind.

Corresponding to the level of prototheism there is not much data for the existence of the personalised sky god *Deivas as an intermediary between the two meanings. There is one other solitary source, often viewed with skepticism, for Dievas–Dievs which often come up in folk-songs together with Perkūnas–Pērkons, who is undoubtedly a sky god. The additions to the *Malalas Chronicle* in 1262, and to the *Halicz-Volhynian Chronicle* in 1252, and 1258 (to be discussed later) mention the names of seven or eight Lithuanian deities. Among these are Perkūnas, and three others that contain the *diev-* 'god' stem (Andaj, Nunadjev, Diverikz/Diviriks). These are names of deities who are equal in rank to Perkūnas (Diverikz), or even superior to him (the other two). It would be lengthy to

---

J. Balys discusses how the name of Perkūnas, the thunder god, was not permitted utterance, and instead *dievaitis* was used (Balys in Lit. E./IV, 542). The taboo was evidently valid the other way round, too: the name of God = Deivas was also not to be mentioned under the same breath as the objects of a pagan cult, which could at best be minor gods.

[7] Let me call attention to the cunning nature of such statements, so very frequent in myth research. By saying that 'Dievs' temple does not exist' the existence of Dievs appears to be evident.

Latvian mythologists succeeded in making others believe in the existence of Dievs. The Dievs-believers, after regaining independence, established a pagan religion and Church, which in 1996 the Latvian Parliament accepted as an official religion acknowledged by the state and granted rights equal with the traditional great religions.

enumerate the attempts to derive these. V. Toporov's suggestion is the most acceptable of the reconstructions of the first two in the forms *An(t)deiv- and *No-(an)-deiv-, Nu-(an)-deiv-, and all he says concerning their meaning is that the *na-, an-* derivators appear in the names of other Baltic deities. V. Toporov gives an example from a Latvian folk-song to demonstrate that both of them could denote the physical sky: *saulite iet nodievā* 'the little sun rises into the sky', and their father–god status (Zeus), superior to that of Perkūnas (Jupiter) is only supported inasmuch as they precede Perkūnas in all three additions (most likely by the same author) (Toporov 1970, 535; 1972, 311).[8] There are two interesting interpretative standpoints on the third name. According to the first the primary meaning is *Dievų rykis* 'lord of the Gods' (again represented from A. Mierzyński 1892–96/I, 142 to J. Greimas 1990, 390). The second one posits *Dievo-rykštė* 'rainbow' (word for word 'God's lash') (from A. Brückner 1904, 72 to V. Toporov 1972, 311). The second argument is utterly convincing, but it still only demonstrates the personalisation of the physical sky under various names.

7.1.2. Perkūnas (Pērkons)

It seems that Christianity took the name for its concept of God exactly at the point when *deivas* could have become personalised, that is in the centuries when kinship society was disintegrating and a tribal or tribal federation society was about to evolve. In this way, *deivas* for the Balts became God, instead of Zeus or Jupiter.

However, there is another common Baltic word, Latv. pērkons, Lith. perkūnis, Pruss. percunis which was personalised into a god (the only pagan god!), but only for the East Balts, and definitely only for the Lithuanians where Perkūnas became a god carrying out the Zeus–Jupiter functions of thunder and lightening. H. Usener establishes the same: "Only one single Lithuanian god-name, Perkūnas stretches back as far as the Indo-Germanic prehistoric times," and this is why the German

---

[8] It was V. Toporov who discovered the *deiv-* stem in the name Andaj. The name had previously been either presumed to be unknown, or the most amazing origins were posited. In the nineteenth century E. Wolter created a kind of snake god from the southwestern Lithuanian local word *angis* 'snake'. A. J. Greimas, as a result, of "a dawn enlightenment after a beautiful night spent awake" came to a Lithuanian Neptune, a sea god from the Lith. *vanduo* 'water', through far-fetched associations (Greimas 1990, 388). The *deiv-* stem in the other name did not cause any problems for scholars from A. Mierzyński to Greimas, who explain the first part of the name differently: *namo dievas* 'house god', that is the house god of the ruling dynasty, which is again a non-contextual explanation (Mierzyński 1892–96/I, 141; Greimas 1990, 389).

scholar excluded *deivas from his list of about two hundred Baltic mythological figures, despite its Indo-European roots (Usener 1896, 109).[9]

The addition of the *Malalas Chronicle* first mentions Perkūnas as a god in 1262, and similarly the *Livonian Rhyming Chronicle* around 1290. Its unknown author writes about an attack on Livonia in 1219: *"Zu swurben vuren sie ubir se,/ Das ist genant das osterhap,/ Als es perkune, ir apgot gap,/ Das nimmer so hart gevros"* [They reached Swurben by crossing the sea that was called Osterhaff, and which thanks to their pagan god (*Abgott*) Perkune has never been so frozen] (*Livonian Rhyming Chronicle* ca. 1290, line 1434 in Mierzyński 1892–96/I, 116).

The word itself existed in Prussian, too, but no trustworthy source mentions it as a deity. Neither the 1249 peace contract of Chrystburg, nor P. Dusburg. The latter, and after him Nikolaus von Jeroschin include thunder (*tonitrua, donre*) among his enumeration of creatures and phenomena that the pagans adored instead of the Creator, such as: Sun, Moon, stars, birds, four-legged animals, and even reptiles and insects (Mannhardt 1936, 107). As a god he is a secondary, literary invention. The forger S. Grunau introduced him into Prussian 'mythology' in the early sixteenth century. Whether he lifted the name of the Lithuanian god from previous chronicles or from the 'Prussian lips' where "it existed due to either the thirteenth-century subjugation of the Jatvingians, or the fifteenth-century Lithuanian colonisation" is uncertain (Łowmiański 1976, 149).

The Livonian sources on Pērkons would refer to some interim stage between the Prussian *percunis* and the Lithuanian Perkūnas. It is mentioned by the name quite late, first in the chronicle of the Catholic D. Fabricius written after 1610 and of dubious authenticity (*Livonicae historiae compendiosa series*, cf. Mannhardt 1936, 457–458). Until then, like the Prussians, there are only references to the sinful pagan custom of respecting thunder as a god. The first example of that is a 1428 decision of the Synod of Riga which says that the pagans have to be forced to "leave the phenomena of nature and the lowly creatures behind, such as thunder which they pray to as their god, snakes, reptiles and insects, and trees that they believe in" (Mannhardt 1936, 156). This god-concept is only marginally more personal than that of P. Dusburg's. An Estonian word borrowed from Latvian and

---

[9] Unconditional 'Dumézilists' like A. Gieysztor believe it to be the exact reverse: "The god name did not ... emerge from the common noun of 'thunder', but the other way round. The former god name underwent secularisation and served to describe the phenomenon of the atmosphere" (Gieysztor 1982, 46). Contrary to this, I. Goldziher posits that "on the one hand, the area of mythology is not about handing down ancient revelations guarded by priestly castes from people to people, but myths that reveal common utterances reaching back into the most ancient times of peoples, the time of the evolution of language. On the other hand, the contents of mythology are not filled with the symbolic expression of deep philosophy of a religion, but the simplest element of human images are expressed in the simplest language" (Goldziher 1881, 23).

recorded in 1660 unambiguously denotes lightening (*perckun nohl*), and not god (Mägiste 1982, 1996). Evidently the way *pērkons* crops up in place names (first in a charter from 1291, *Percunecalve*—Biezais 1972, 152) does not prove anything, because a place name can originate from a common noun just as easily as from a proper (god) name, so *Percunecalve* could have meant the Isle of Pērkons or the Isle of Lightening. In the latter case the name would refer to a place that was struck by a lightening, that is a place where some supernatural power had given a sign, but that is not necessarily a personal power (see also Łowmiański 1979, 219). Based on a mere name without a local legend connected to the act of the name giving it is impossible to decide whether lightening or the god of lightening was the inspiration behind the name.

Two circumstances motivated the process of *perkūnas* 'thunder' becoming Perkūnas a pagan god, unlike *deivas* 'sky'. One of these is that the Christian god took on the name of 'sky', leaving the other phenomenon of the physical sky, i.e. thunder, to develop in its own way as it became superfluous. The other decisive factor was that Perkūnas had its Slavic correspondent in the person of Perun, which the Lithuanians did not simply borrow, but sensed as an example which appeared for them exactly at the time when the creation of a sky god was about to occur through a shift in meaning of the same word 'thunder' > 'thunder god'.

This shift in meaning had happened much earlier among the Slavs, or rather had been fully used as a mirror-word, and thus Christianity did not confuse its usage as much as with the Balts where *interpretatio christiana* kept on pushing the personalised god on the brink of emergence back among the 'idols' of creatures and the phenomena of nature.

Perun was first mentioned (without a name) in the sixth-century Byzantine chronicle by Prokopios of Caesarea the *De bello Gothico* reporting on the customs of the Slavs (Ants and Sklavens), "one god, the creator of lightening is held to be the only lord of the universe!" (Prokopios III, 14, 22 in Mansikka 1922, 381). It crops up by name in the ninth-century peace contract between the Byzantium and the Kievan Rus', first in the contract of 902 then in 945 as the pagan chief god, equal to the Christian God, "he who broke his oath be cursed by God and Perun" (in *Povest' vremennykh let*, 25, 39). H. Łowmiański gave details that 'Perun' was a god for the East and the South Slavs, but not the West Slavs where the word has survived in the meaning of 'thunder' to the present day, just as with the West Balts, the Prussians (cf. Polish *piorun*).

The etymology of the Slavic and Baltic words has been the subject of heated debates over the last century because on the basis of the shared meaning (thunder–god) and the shared derivation (*per-, perk- + un*) the etymologisers tried to explain the two words from each other, at times as a Baltic and at other times as a Slavic loan. (Or else, completely without foundation they would demonstrate a Germanic loan < Gothic *Fairhuns* 'range of hill covered with oak'—for this cf. Biezais 1972, 96.) The difficulty lies in that despite the same meaning and derivation the phonetic forms of the two stems are different. The Slavic word is a so-called *nomen agentis*, its stem is the IE., Slavic, and Baltic *per-* 'to strike, to hit' (cf. Proto-Slavic **perti-*, Latv. *pert,* Lith. *perti* 'to strike, to hit'), and from that *perun–Perun* 'that which—who strikes, hits', which is the same as the noun from the permanent attribute of Zeus *Keraunos* 'the striking, the thundering'. The trouble is that the *perk-* stem as the basis of the Lith. Perkūnas is only apparent in this one word, and otherwise is absent in the Baltic and the Slavic languages. In this way, nothing deters the connection of the two stems (*perk-* and *per-*), and indeed the most striking of etymologies sprang up. The word was associated with words meaning 'oak', 'oak wood' > 'oak god' [Latin *quercus*, Old High German *forha* (once) 'pine', (today) 'oak', Old Nordic *Fjorgynn* 'oak god, the mother of the god Thor', Celtic *Hercynia silva* the collective expression for the 'chain of hills from the Danube's source to Dacia', originally 'oak (pine) forest', etc.]. The idea of connecting the thunder god with the oak god springs from the unreliable E. Stella and S. Grunau. Their identification reached only as far as Perkūnas the god of thunder living in an oak tree, so the pagans would also adore the tree as a sacred being. Many modern linguists go further, starting with H. Hirt in the nineteenth century. Lightening would sanctify the object it hit, and because this was often an oak on a mountain peak, or the peak itself, rock, thunder, and oak as well as their deities came to be identified, and that, of course, already happened in the ancient Indo-European period (Gamkrelidze–Ivanov 1984/II, 615). (The rock comes into the picture in that the *per-* stem expanded not only with a 'k' but also a 'g', and thus the Hittite names *perunaš* 'rock', 'goddess', Sanskrit *Parjányas* 'thunder god', < **perg* 'mountain', Перынь mentioned in a chronicle of Novgorod, an Old Russian place name for a mountain area (*Pregын*), and a Polish village name *Przeginia*—for all of this cf. S. Urbańczyk's sober summary in SSS/4, 69.)

A. Brückner represents the most extreme wing of the 'oak party', because he stands out for the view that denies all connections with the *per-* 'strike' stem, and who speaks of the secularisation of the name, like many neo-mythologists, but at least he puts forward linguistic arguments for examination (Brückner 1918, 107). According to the Polish scholar the word has no connections to the 'strike' stem, but denotes a Lithuanian–Slavic oak god.[10] The Perkūnas which survives today had its regular Slavic correspondence: **Perkyn* (of course both < IE. **perkus*

---

[10] A. Brückner's statement only a few years later demonstrates how hopelessly tangled the question is (and of course that he also often voiced indulgently provocative views in his demythologising upheaval—itself usually justified) "there is not the slightest linguistic connection between Perun and Perkūnas; 'the striking' and 'the one with the oak' are only related as objects (*sachlich*); there is no 'Lithuanian–Slavic' divinity. The mythology of the two peoples are completely different and do not share any points of contact with one another" (Brückner 1926, 345).

'oak'), from which -k- was dropped because of the *perti* 'hit, strike' verb: *Perkyn pere* 'Perkyn strikes' > *Peryn pere* > *Perun pere*. "The name Perun, as a god's name for the Slavs gave its place to others, but as a place name remained, but then not in a cultic but instead referring to a natural phenomenon." The reflex counter-argument arises as to how the Perun *god* came to be in the Kievan court, Brückner's answer is that "it 'revived' with the influence of the Norman Thor" (Brückner 1918, 111).

It is evident there are no comfortable solutions for the twofold (Slavic and Baltic) stem. The most obvious is to accept the *per-* stem as a starting point, as did A. Fraenkel and after him P. Skardžius in positing that *perk-* emerged with its expansion to which P. Skardžius believes there are other Lithuanian examples (and which of course is a magic word that explains nothing, yet there is no better one) (Fraenkel 1962, 1965/I, 575; Skardžius 1963, 318, 313). Whether this expansion occurred during the Indo-European unity or after its disintegration is a question of imagination and belief (if the latter was the case then the resemblance to the stems *perk-* 'oak' and even more *perg-* 'cliff' are completely accidental, just as the meanings of 'oak', 'cliff', and 'lightening' would have come closer to each other quite late in the second millennium AD, probably through the endeavours of the myth creating chroniclers and modern linguists).

I see the first, down-to-earth solution as the most sensible, and one which also corresponds to the nature of the creation of god names. In this way, the Slavic *perun-* stem served as a starting point, and its expansion resulted in *perkūnas* meaning 'thunder'. H. Łowmiański's enlightening hypothesis points out that as a result of the influence of, or following the example of the Scythians the Slavs, on the level of prototheism, mirror translated the Greek *keraunos* as *perun*, first as the attribute of Svarog chief god (sun god), which became a noun at the turn of the third–second centuries BC when the Scythian Empire collapsed under the Sarma-tian attacks. At that time the Slavs of the so-called Zarubinetzkaya Culture (divis-ible between the second century BC to the fourth–fifth centuries AD at the Upper and Middle Dnieper, in the basin of the southern Pripet and the Desna) entered Kievan lands where they came into contact with the Scythians and left after the Sarmatian invasion. (The Slavic *bog* initially 'wealth' 'success', then 'tax of wealth', finally 'god' springs from this Iranian–Slavic contact, since it is the trans-mission, or at least shows the influence of the Old Persian *baga* 'supernatural be-ing'.) The Slavs handed down not the name, but the technique of creating god names from this area of the Zarubinetzkaya Culture to the Balts, or more precisely the 'Proto-Lithuanians' of the southern wing of the East Balts (the Leitis group), based on *perkūnas*, a Baltic word corresponding to *perun*. (They had no contact with the

West Balts or the West Slavs, in which cases Perun could not edge out Svarog, which had been more deeply rooted due to an 'Old-European' substratum.)[11] The Lithuanian Perkūnas slowly spread further northward among the Latvians, too.[12] The Latvian place names containing Pērkons, which J. Endzelīns published in 1922, show this south–north movement, nineteen come from Kurzeme and Zemgale, eight from Vidzeme, and one from Latgale (cited in Biezais 1972, 153). The density of place names in general only points to the direction of diffusion, but not the time, so in this case it could equally have begun in the tenth–eleventh centuries or centuries later.

[11] A. Brückner produced the only counter-argument to this idea that is worth mentioning. He explains that the Lithuanian *perk-* stem is a thousand years older than the Slavic *per-* stem, which is proven in that the Proto-Finnish (*prafiński*) borrowed the Lithuanian word *Perken* 'devil' around the time of Christ (Brückner 1918, 104). This argument would not be credible even if A. Brückner gave the source of his data, since if an oak god is borrowed in the meaning of 'devil' then that could, at best, prove that the transmission occurred in a late period when the Baltic god degenerated to a place among the Finn demons. As for the place and the time, this could be matched to historical facts, although evidently not to a Finn and Lithuanian, or rather a Finn and Latvian encounter. (The Finns could hardly have met the Lithuanians, but especially not around the time of Christ.)

However, semantically and mythologically it is utterly impossible that a thunder god, still less an oak god would become a devil. And not even a devil, since the word in Finnish actually means 'hell'. What is A. Brückner actually talking about? M. Agricola, a sixteenth-century parson, was the 'discoverer' of Finn mythology, who mentions *perkele* (or *perchele*). A word with an unknown etymology, and of which the modern Finn etymological dictionary, seemingly without any basis, declares that it "most likely originates from the Lithuanian perkūnas" (Toivonen 1955–62/I, 523). The word crops up in other related languages as well, for example the Votyak *peri*, *päri* 'devil, elf, bad spirit' (Munkácsi 1890–96, 550), or the Estonian *pergel* > *porgel* > *porgu* 'hell'. At least the Estonian etymological dictionary keeps quiet about the origin of the word, thus presuming it as unknown, and does not drag up any kind of examples of *perkūnas* (Mägiste 1982, 2289). Voilà! This is the 'Proto-Finn' proof for the Lithuanian *perk-* being a thousand years older than *per-*...

This is connected to what emerges as a self-evident fact, even in the work by the painstaking and scholarly H. Łowmiański. Perkūnas was further borrowed from the Lithuanians by the Mordvins: *purgine* 'thunder' > *Purgine-pas* 'thunder god' (Łowmiański 1979, 221). As to where and when the exchange between the Lithuanians and the Mordvins could have occurred, J. Balys posits as "circa 2000 years BC on the southern Russian steppes, near the Middle Volga where the Mordvins lived and still live" (Balys 1966, 112), and in this way it is proven that Perkūnas was already a Lithuanian god by then. The source for the Mordvin 'data' is U. Harva who simply announces that the Mordvin word "was borrowed from the Lithuanians (cf. Finn. *perkule*, *perkele*)" (Harva 1952, 158), from which it is obvious that the Mordvin word is connected to the Finn-Permian word for 'hell', but not really to the Lithuanian.

[12] H. Biezais 'argues' against a Lithuanian origin for the Latvian Pērkons cult that "Pērkons is the old god of the Baltic peoples" (Biezais 1972, 153). Perhaps this implies that all three Baltic peoples received the god simultaneously at some point in the good old days.

The following scheme shows the trend discussed above:

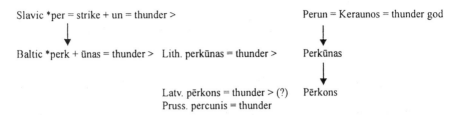

Slavic *per = strike + un = thunder >   Perun = Keraunos = thunder god

Baltic *perk + ūnas = thunder >   Lith. perkūnas = thunder >   Perkūnas

                     Latv. pērkons = thunder > (?)   Pērkons
                     Pruss. percunis = thunder

These complex processes of loans and shifts in meaning were crossed by the concurrent centuries-long development of the other sky god deivas becoming a personal god, and also the appearance of the Christian God. It has to be seen in such a way that, for the Balts the Zeus Keraunos = Deivas Perkūnas did not refer to one person, but to the qualitative structure divided into two separate nouns, and then into deities (that is a Christian and a pagan god), but because both of them came from the meaning 'sky' (the first from a clear, the second from a cloudy, stormy sky) there remained some connection in meaning between them, even if only partial.

The uncertainty around the functions and divine nature of Perkūnas springs from all this. It is difficult to judge whether or not the thunder god was a chief god at the same time[13] and as such took on additional functions (as a few 'Dumézilists' would like to see it) and thus could be seen as a god similar to the military Indic Indra or Scandinavian Thor, or a god of justice (possessing the second Dumézilian function). It seems certain that its original meaning was 'thunder', and other meanings coloured this and survived in popular belief for centuries. In 1768 S. Rostowski wrote about "the simple people of Lithuania, Žemaitija, and Zemgale" who during the Reformation returned to the forests and there "prayed according to the pagan customs of their ancestors to their oak trees, and Jupiter the lightening-caster whom their parents' parents called Perkūnas" (Rostowski cited in Ivinskis 1938–39, 406).

It is a late, secondary, and as G. Komoróczy points out in his analysis of the Mesopotamian Pantheon, a necessary and regular development that the chief god, independent of and alongside its original features should become a fertility god in the local cult (and as we shall see Perkūnas is the only pagan god that had a demonstrable cult). "This is natural, since its main aim and task is to ensure the

---

[13] According to V. J. Mansikka a Germanic–Scandinavian influence motivated the thunder god's promotion to chief god (Mansikka 1922, 381).

country's fertility and well-being by winning over the irrational powers" (Komoróczy 1975, 24). This is what happened with Perkūnas–Pērkons.[14]

Obviously the Christian God = Dievas, Dievs alone adopted all these functions from Perkūnas (and in general all the functions of the pagan gods), who in this way often emerge as the heir of Perkūnas, or together with it.[15]

Another circumstance could play a role in the moulding of the concept of sky god, or chief god. I. Goldziher discusses that the night sky stood in the foreground of the myths of nomadic societies, and the cult of the daytime sky and the sun, characteristic of the next developmental stage, that is of agriculture, edged out and re-interpreted (but did not annihilate!) this. (Goldziher 1876, 72 ff.) During their thousand-year wanderings the Balts are likely to have undergone both of these stages, consequently 'popular memory' could preserve the remnants of both myth types. Belief respecting the sun and the moon in the physical sky could have undergone another transformation when the Balts, having occupied their historic territories, at least partly accommodated to a hunting and fishing lifestyle again. There is no data at our disposal about the economic or technical nature of this adjustment. Nonetheless it seems probable that agriculture carried out on the forested steppes differs from that occurring in a purely forest zone, and the value system expressed in myths could change accordingly. To a nomad the night sky that brings relief is of a higher value, whereas for the farmer it is the sun that encourages vegetation, while for the forest dweller both are important. Perhaps this is what the washed-together manifold functions of Perkūnas–Deivas expresses. (Of course all of this is purely an exercising of the imagination.)

7.2. Baltic polydoxy

What was the common Baltic belief system from which the sky god arose and which was the same in Livonia, Lithuania, and even Prussianland?

Z. Ivinskis, the greatest Lithuanian historian who lived in Rome after the Second World War, had the most extensive knowledge of the sources and applied a strictly critical methodology. In several of his works he described this belief system as a natural religion which, however, "was not some form of unsophisticated fetishism, but manifested itself in animism and a particular concept of pantheism of various natural objects" (Ivinskis 1938–39, 389). There was no distinct borderline between human beings, seen as a part of nature, and animals, plants, or rock. A mysterious energy was believed to be flowing through the universe which could

---

[14] So much so, that on the basis of Latvian folk-songs H. Biezais discusses a god who played a lead role in peasant life, which, to me, only indicates that the folk-songs in question are late (Biezais 1961, 75; 1972, 179; 1975, 346).

[15] H. Biezais cites several examples for this from Latvian folk-songs (Biezais 1961, 107 ff.).

concentrate in some objects, lending them power, which were then seen as sacred and the spirit of good (meaning useful) would occupy them. Among trees: oak, lime, pine, and maple were thought to possess extraordinary powers, and amongst animals: bulls, horses, and cockerels. Fire was the most effective force against evil in the battle between good and evil in the universe. There was no belief in resurrection, but there was a conception of life after death as a continuation of terrestrial life. The dead were cremated in order to liberate them from their bodies so that their souls could make contact with both the purely spiritual sky god and other human souls. Archaeological findings indicate that horses buried beside the dead were not cremated but were either strangled or placed alive into the graves and stoned to death because animals only possess bodies. Nature and the life of people "was inter-woven with innumerable *material gods* who had *neither anthropomorphic existence nor proper names.* The names of these smaller, not yet anthropomorphised gods show that, together with different natural objects and phenomena and a variety of places (sacred rivers, hills, and rocks), events of everyday life *were animised* too" (Ivinskis 1937, 465).

The sources of all three Baltic areas describe this process of creating gods and correlating levels of religion, which is widely known and is evident among other peoples, too.

The earliest source is from Prussianland. The first is the biography of Adalbert by Canaparius, which mentions the sacred grove of the Prussians that Adalbert desecrated, for which act he paid with his life. Adam of Bremen also mentions forests and springs which it was forbidden to approach because the pagans who protected them believed that Christians would "pollute them simply by drawing near" (Adam Bremensis IV, 18). Oliverius Scholasticus, the Bishop of Cologne and later of Paderborn, wrote a book on the Holy Land (*Historia regum Terre sancte*, ca. 1220) and the habits of the newly converted peoples through leaflets and letters circulating amongst the crusaders. He exploits the concepts of Greek mythology, "Liv (meaning Livonian), Estonian, and Prussian tribes worshipped the forest spirits–gods (*dryad, amadryad*), the mountains spirits (*oread*), the valleys (*napea*), the water spirits (*naiad*), the field spirits (*satire*) and the forest spirits (*faun*). They expected help from forests untouched by the axe in which they worshipped springs, trees, mountains, hills, sheer cliffs and gentle slopes as if they could find strength and power from them" (Mierzyński 1892–96/I, 51). Documents, in particular 'travel accounts' from Prussian and Lithuanian territories from the late thirteenth century until the early fifteenth century, mention numerous 'sacred' place names of this type.

P. Dusburg (who moved to Königsberg) gives authentic descriptions of the Prussian natural religion. He devoted a short chapter of his chronicle to "idolatry, rituals, and customs of Prussians". It is significant that there is no reference to any names of personal gods. "As Prussians do not know God, it is understandable that they worship different phenomena such as the sun, the moon, and the stars, thunder, birds, quadrupeds, even creeping things. They have sacred copses, groves, and waters where no one would dare to cut a tree, till the soil or fish... They worship the eternal flame as was the custom in olden times" (Dusburg III, 5 in SRP).

The earliest such reports from Livonia (most likely not referring to the Latvian–Leitis people but the Livs) is from the 1199 Papal Bull of Innocent III in which he calls for a crusade against the pagans who, obviously on the basis of Bishop Meinhard's information, "worshipped dumb animals, gnarled trees, clear waters, rich grass, and unchaste spirits with respect that is owed to God" (Papal Bulls, 25).

Aeneas Sylvius Piccolomini (1405–1464), from 1458 Pope Pious II, summarises all of this, and his work about the Lithuanians remained the main source for theories on Baltic beliefs for many centuries.[16]

Aeneas came from Siena and spent 24 years of his adult life in German lands, and his "notorious pro-German bias... helped stimulate a sense of national consciousness" (Knoll 1991, 14). These nationalistic prejudices emerged during the interrupted Synod of Basle (1431–1443) where he also participated in the struggles between the different factions within the papacy: between the Pope and the Emperor; between the papacy and heretical movements; and between the papacy and widespread paganism.[17] His prejudices were further entrenched when he became the Chancellor (emissary) of Emperor Friedrich III and as such travelled around Europe as well as becoming acquainted with the case between Lithuania and the Teutonic Order. This was taken to the Synod and led to a war in 1453 in which he took the side of the Order. Before he was ordained as a priest in 1447, this knowledgeable and brilliant stylist earned great respect as a poet, a historian, and a geographer and maintained his good name as a cardinal, and received high praise as one of the so-called Renaissance popes.

He dealt with Baltic peoples in four of his works. When Aeneas found the manuscripts of *Getica* by Jordanes in the monastery of Gottweig he published a part of it, filling and interpreting any gaps with his own ideas and information garnered from elsewhere based on the assumption that the old Prussians were actually Goths. (E. Stella adopted this concept from him and enlarged upon it as the basis of his 'Borussia theory'.) This is how the *De pruthenorum origine* (1453) was created. His other three works appeared in print only in 1551 under the title *De Europa*, but some chapters of his weighty tome *De Livonia* (partly about Livonia and partly about Prussianland), *De Polonia,* and *De Lithuania* had been widely known from copies. Out of these three areas the would-be pope only visited Prussianland personally in 1457 when the Pope made him the Bishop of Warmia, an area populated by the Prussians and the Poles, to reward him for his services

---

[16] For Aeneas Sylvius see primarily the brief monograph of A. Janulaitis, which discusses the previous professional works, among them G. Voigt's great work (Janulaitis 1928).

[17] For all this see Gergely 1982, 172–183.

despite the opposition of the Poles. He only had second-hand information about the other two territories and he mentions only one of his living, non-literary sources who offered him information about Lithuania about whose customs and pagan beliefs he describes alongside its history and concurrent politics.

This source of information was Jerome of Prague (Jeronym Pražský, Hyeronymus von Prag, his real name was Jan Munscheck, 1369–1440) a Czech priest who worked in the court of Jagiello in Kraków, until the king suggested that he moved to his cousin, the Grand Duke Vytautas, in Lithuania. From 1401 or 1406 he worked unsuccessfully as a missionary in Žemaitija for three years, before returning via Poland to Italy where he became a monk. (The area that Jerome visited in Lithuania is still debated. W. Mannhardt and Z. Ivinskis following G. Voigt posit that it was Žemaitija, officially converted only years later in 1413—Mannhardt 1936, 133; Ivinskis 1938, 380; Voigt 1856, 63.) A. Janulaitis believes it was eastern Lithuania, that is the border of Lithuania and Belarus (Janulaitis 1928, 49).[18] These two men, Jerome of Prague and Aeneas met in Basle, "at the Synod of Basle they told adventurous, and often miraculous stories about the converted Lithuanians. Jerome of Prague, the monk of Camaldul, himself an apostle of this pagan nation... spread these wonders. Aeneas wished to be convinced of their truth and he visited the monk in the Carthusian monastery over the Rhine with some of his company. Jerome retold what he knew of the Lithuanians with an honest and open face, bracing his words with an oath, which Aeneas recorded and thus preserved for us. 'As I heard, so I speak, yet responsibility for it I deny. Nonetheless, I went with my company to ascertain the truth of his words'" (Pór 1880, 358).

What did Aeneas learn of the paganism of the Lithuanians? He writes of four types of cult, which according to Z. Ivinskis would mean that Jerome visited four different regions of Lithuania, each with its own distinct belief system (Ivinskis 1938–39, 381).

"The first Lithuanian people I met worshipped snakes. Every householder kept a snake lying mutely in the corner of the house, which he fed and to which he sacrificed. Jerome ordered them all to be beaten to death and burnt in public on the square. There was one bigger than the others which could not be burnt although it was put on the fire several times" (SRP/IV, 238; Jurginis–Šidlauskas 1983, 42).

This snake is the first description of the cult held as characteristic of the Balts (the snake was certainly not venomous, but a grass snake, Latin *Tropodonotus natrix* or often some other type of reptile). It was followed by a number of similar

[18] The Catholic priest, who was not a scholar, and never wrote anything, is not to be mistaken for the other Jerome of Prague, the Hussite polemic who, like John Hus was burnt at the stake in Konstanz in 1416 for his heretic teaching. Although, this Jerome also allegedly visited the courts of both Jagiello and Vytautas. Lithuania and the Hussites are known to have had a good relationship in general, they even offered the Czech crown to Vytautas, and at the University of Prague, Queen Jadwiga established a Lithuanian college (for this see Svatoš 1981).

descriptions of both the Lithuanian and Latvian peoples. Practically everyone writing about folk customs presents it.[19] I shall mention just two very influential works as examples.

S. von Herberstein, the Austrian diplomat, stopped in Lithuania while returning from Moscow in 1517. His book *Commentarii Rerum Moscovitarum* was first published in 1549, and by 1600 it was republished seven more times. It was translated into German, and in the eighteenth century into Russian. In his description of Žemaitija he claims that there were many fetishists who kept fat, black, four-legged animals that were bigger than a lizard, longer than three elbows, and were fed like babies. They were called *Givuoites* (Lith. *gyvatė* 'snake') (Mannhardt 1936, 307 ff.).

In Livonia S. Henning, the advisor of the ruler of Kurzeme G. Kettler, writes in his report published in 1587 (later used by J. Lange and Stenders the Elder) that the pagan *Undeutsch* "worship the sun, stars, moon, fire, water, rivers and in general all kinds of creatures. They consider snakes and all forms of ugly creeping things as their gods. These are, as I myself saw, fat and bloated to the extent that if thrown to the ground or beaten to death a little milk trickles from their bodies. At this the wailing old witches (*Breckin* perhaps from Latv. *brēkt* 'to cry'; from which later J. Lange concluded that *brēkiņa* was the protector of house-snakes and creeping things among the old Latvians—cf. Šmits 1926, 40) gather and wail, making *malefactum*: *Man pene Math, Man pene Math* 'Oh, my milk mother, oh, my milk mother'. These wailers often changed into wolves" (Mannhardt 1936, 412–414). Here the snake is identical to 'milk mother', the patron saint of cattle which is common in Latvian folklore, just as it is common (as E. Liparte demonstrated with rich documentation—Liparte 1993) that the snake at times appears as a useful and at other times as a malevolent 'god'.[20]

However, I doubt that this general spread would prove the existence of some type of snake god. A. Warburg's illuminating study examines the snake cult among the North-American Pueblo Indians from "the development from primitive paganism, through the paganism of classical antiquity to modern man" (Warburg 1923, 4). This characterisation of the snake as a dual (good and bad) being can be found in European tradition as well as in the rituals of Native Americans at the turn of the twentieth century. [The snake of Eden is the origin of sin and it is a privilege of the apostles to "take up serpents" (Mark 16, 18), which symbolises

[19] J. Balys follows the reports on snake cults in Lithuanian traditions up to the early twentieth century (see Balys 1948/II, 65–76).

[20] To me it also seems likely that J. I. Kraszewski's tale of Egle entered Lithuanian folklore so quickly, because the snake cult already constituted a widespread popular belief.

V. Toporov accounts for its further survival up to the late twentieth century. In 1956 on the bank of the Nemunas in Belarus he met an old Lithuanian woman who regularly went to the forest to commune with the snakes, and took milk for them. "There was something wonderfully intimate, familiar, and gentle in her relationship with snakes" (Toporov 1980, 53).

their immunity to sin because they can have contact with the snake. Nonetheless, Moses had commanded the Israelites in the wilderness to heal snakebites by setting up a brazen serpent for devotion on God's advice. This was in spite of the prophets' and later apostles' fight against fetishism: Isaiah had the idol of the brazen serpent pulled down; apostle Paul burnt the viper that bit him without dying of the bite, from which time Maltese pagans saw him as an invincible saint. Even so, the miracle of the brazen serpent "was reinforced in a passage of the *Gospel According to John* in *the New Testament*. The imagery of the serpent cult was typologically compared with the crucifixion" (Warburg 1923, 18). In Lithuanian the word 'snake' (*gyvatė*) has the same stem as 'life' (*gyvata*) and 'cattle' (*gyvuliai*). A. Warburg poses the question, "through which qualities does the serpent appear in literature and art as a usurping imposter? (ein verdrängender Vergleicher)?" His answer, taking into consideration primitive and European traditions is this: "1. It experiences through the course of a year the full life cycle from the deepest, deathlike sleep to utmost vitality; 2. It changes its slough and remains the same; 3. It is not capable of walking on feet and remains capable nonetheless of propelling itself with great speed, armed with the absolutely deadly weapon of its poisonous tooth; 4. It is minimally visible to the eye, especially when its colour acts according to the desert's laws of mimicry, or when it shoots out from its secret holes in the earth; 5. Phallus. These are qualities which render the serpent unforgettable as a threatening symbol of the ambivalent in nature: death and life, visible and invisible, without prior warning and deadly on sight" (Warburg 1923, 55).]

From the perspective of Baltic research it can perhaps be concluded that in their snake cult the ancestral or the 'universal human' amalgamated with the Christian tradition of the notaries of the cult, and that neither of these think in terms of the concept of snake god corresponding to polytheism.

Let us go back to the report of Jerome–Aeneas. Apart from snakes, Lithuanians worship the eternal fire. The priests of the sanctuaries (*sacerdotes*) protect it from extinction. With the help of the fire these priests can tell whether a sick individual will recover or die. If they can see the shadow (spirit?) of the sick person facing the fire, then they will recover, if their back is to the fire they will die. Jerome explained to them that this was trickery and put the fire out, and destroyed the sanctuary (*templo*). As he travelled inland he encountered a tribe which worshipped the Sun and connected to it, a huge iron hammer. The priests said that once, a long time before they could not see the Sun for many months for it had been captured by a powerful king and enclosed in an enormous tower. The signs of the Zodiac helped the Sun, shattering the tower with this hammer and returning the Sun to the people. Jerome described this as a ridiculous tale. Going further at last he met a tribe which worshipped the grove, the home of the spirits. After days of persuasion, he himself began to cut down the most sacred forest, after which the pagans, who had not dared to touch the trees until then, followed his example. In the middle of the forest there stood an ancient oak, the most sacred amongst all trees, the home of the gods. One of the pagans with great reluctance he brought himself to cut it, but as he swung his two-bladed axe against it, he cut into his own leg and fell to the ground semi-conscious. The crowd standing around him started to cry and wail and accuse Jerome, but Jerome calmed them by saying it was all an evil trick. He commanded the man who had fallen down to stand up and he showed that there was no injury on his leg, then they cut the forest along with the giant oak (Mannhardt 1936, 135–136; Jurginis–Šidlauskas 1983, 43).

The Jerome–Aeneas report is especially valuable and interesting not only because its effect lasted for centuries, but because it gives a good example of the extent to which the image it offers can be considered authentic. The aspects that decide the degree of authenticity in this particular case, *mutatis mutandis* can be applied in general on the reports of the thirteenth–fifteenth centuries mentioned earlier. To wit:

(A) The circumstances of the recording. Jerome did not know the language of the 'natives' (so Aeneas said that Lithuanian was a Slavic language), and what he heard in this unknown language, evidently through an interpreter, he later reinterpreted and discussed in the court of Vytautas; some 20–25 years later it was told to Aeneas, who allegedly recorded it at the time, but only put it into a literary form (seasoned with some doubt) after another 20–25 years.

(B) The prejudices coming from the personal lives and historical position of the authors of the sources. The hostile attitude toward Lithuanians, detectable in both men, in the case of Jerome obviously springs from a delegation of women who complained to Grand Duke Vytautas about Jerome's drive to destroy the sacred groves, saying that felling the forests would leave no place for their gods to dwell. Their husbands declaring that if it continued they would sooner leave the lands of their birth and emigrate amplified this. After this the Grand Duke revoked their conversion to Christianity, at least for them, and expelled Jerome from the country. Apart from writing this down with malicious glee Aeneas says, on the basis of other unnamed sources, that Lithuanians living in the depth of swamps and frosty forests are the descendants of the Tartars. Vytautas is a barbarian tyrant who rides about with bow bent, and simply kills those who act against his will with his arrow, or has them sewn into bearskin and torn to pieces by bears. When he decided to distinguish himself from his subjects even by appearance, and his order for all men to shave their beards was not complied with (because a Lithuanian man would sooner lose his head than his beard), the Grand Duke shaved his head, sentencing to death anybody who dared to follow his example (Janulaitis 1928, 58).

(C) The (entertaining) nature of the sources. Although there are two sides to practically every sentence Aeneas wrote, both true and false, G. Voigt is right in stating that the historic works of Aeneas were led by one intention: to entertain and to give aesthetic pleasure to the reader (*ästhetisch zu erfreuen*) (Voigt 1856–63/II, 317). We should not forget that this was common. The chronicles of the Middle Ages fulfilled a literary function, and the Renaissance only strengthened this characteristic of historical narratives. The intent to entertain colours all of Aeneas' descriptions to a greater or lesser extent. The bizarre cult of the giant hammer is evidently a tale invented by him, which is clearly a mythological *hapax legomenon*, a story that never appears anywhere else. It could be connected in a forced and indirect way to the few cases when some chroniclers, like the copier of the *Ipatiy Compilation of Chronicles*, and J. Długosz tried to translate the name of Hephaistos–Vulcan the smith god into Lithuanian.

7.2.1. *Interpretatio christiana*

(D) The most important circumstance against authenticity, but paradoxically also for it, is the general Christian bias which drove the authors to be interested in the pagans from only one aspect, that is what kind of sins they committed in their ignorance that could serve as an excuse for (generally violent) conversion. The literary name and the means of manifestation for this Christian bias is the Christian interpretation of events that is *interpretatio christiana*. This is no more than a net of concepts that homogenises or more precisely 'dualises' anything that it is thrown onto, i.e. it divides the world into two parts according to the Augustinian duality, *civitas Dei–civitas diaboli*. The emergence and mechanisms of this world interpretation from late Antiquity until the flourishing Middle Ages were comprehensively described by D. Harmening at least in the Germanic–German tradition (Harmening 1979).

The central concept of the Christian interpretation was *superstitio* that emerged under the Roman Empire denoting any non-Roman religious phenomena. Christians applied it to any non-Christian, that is pagan religion (Harmening 1979, 41). This meant a range of things: superstition, idolatry, fetishism, magic or wizardry, witchcraft, and all the morally, spiritually, and religiously unacceptable ways of 'other thinking', which compared with the pure and single divine truth contain some kind of exaggeration, addition, superfluity (*super*) (Harmening 1979, 41). Although the concept is of Roman origin, its Christian scope and systemic organisation was obviously influenced by the *Old Testament*, which was completed with the addition of the *New Testament* at this time,[21] which carries a number of examples for the condemnation of *superstitio*. (Moses militates against the enemies of Israel with the following words: "Ye shall destroy their altars, and break down their images, and cut down their groves, and burn their graven images with fire"—Moses V. 7, 5.) However, the theoretical basis of the *interpretatio christiana*, the fight against *superstitio* was put by the Apostle Paul condemning the pagans with the following words: "[they] changed the glory of the uncorruptible God into an image

---

[21] "Christianity became the religion of the two Testaments between 150 and 250 AD" (Pelikan 1971–78/I, 226).

made like corruptible man, and to birds, and fourfooted beasts, and creeping things, [...] changed the truth of God into a lie, and worshipped and served the creature more than the Creator, who is blessed forever" (Romans 1, 23–25).

As a result of this system the reports from the Middle Ages on paganism "are only rarely referred to contemporaneous circumstances, rather they are mostly connected with a scholarly tradition" (Harmening 1979, 318). On close examination a literary pattern can be discovered behind most sentences.[22]

If everything is literature, then where is the authentic reality, and how can it be deciphered? I believe the only way to proceed is to determine the probability of authenticity in information forced into literary–theological schemata on the basis of the degree of social and intellectual development, as well as assuming that a given literary web was applied in order to best suit the reality in question. This means assuming that what covers also uncovers—and this is the paradox to which I refer, because *interpretatio christiana* basically emerged against polydoxy, so we have good reasons to infer polydoxy wherever it is applied. In practice this implies that although we are well aware that we receive all information through alien schemata developed over centuries, in the absence of an alternative we accept it as authentic. However, this is limited to information that recurs frequently and consistently over a long period (which of course carries the danger of automatically excluding anything unique, any *hapax legomenon*, for example the great hammer of Aeneas), and which is supported by data from subsequent centuries.

Although we have to be careful with the sources from the subsequent centuries, i.e. post fifteenth century, because in these many different factors interfered with the homogeneous cleanliness of *interpretatio christiana*. It was primarily the Reformation which, with the appearance of priests preaching in national languages could have brought a deeper knowledge and understanding of the belief world of lay people and yet like the Catholic Church ignored it (see also Ivinskis 1938–39, 367). Instead the protestants concentrated on demonstrating how carelessly the Catholics carried out their mission, and on pointing out the sinful paganism which the people were left in, which was actually true. To support this, they created pagan gods by expanding *interpretatio christiana*. Similarly, the Catholic Counter Reformation, which drove the priests to mingle with the people for the first time (which is why the mass disappearance of paganism can only be seen from the sixteenth century) created a rich pagan mythology to demonstrate the importance of its own activities and the vast extent of the work to be done.

---

[22] All this is of course true, not only of the Baltic but also the Hungarian situation. For example the so-called First Decree of the King St László describes that there are some who give sacrifices to wells, trees, springs, or stones as well as to pagan gods, and they are punished with an ox. It is unlikely that this concerns some ancient Hungarian religion, since "neither the examined Latin sources, nor the Hungarian Statutes give further details which would lead to the assumption of some custom. This fact reinforces the presumption that it concerns a topos and not a genuine ritual" (Voigt 1994, 237).

This was not difficult because there was a virtually unrestricted passage between the ritual and cult of Catholicism (e.g. patron saints) and pagan polydoxy, Christian patron saints becoming pagan gods is only one of the many examples of this. Based on the reports of Aeneas and others, it can be assumed that the Balts worshipped fire (but not a fire god!). This is supported by expressions such as *"Oho! moy myle schwante Panicke"* 'Oh! My dear little sacred fire' which is quoted in the work of H. Maletius from the latter part of the sixteenth century (*panicke < panno* 'fire', cf. Būga 1908–09, 154), or Latv. *ugunsmāte* 'fire mother', *dimspats* 'lord of smoke'. All this in Lithuanian would correspond to a fire god named Gabija, first and last mentioned/invented in Jan Łasicki's work in the late sixteenth century (*De Diis Samagitarum*) which is basically the transmission of the name of the Orthodox patron saint of fire, St. Agatha, Russ. Gafiya (Brückner 1926, 336).

The inseparability of the 'original' reality of pagan belief and the literary style of Christian reports is increased by the well-known psychological circumstance that Christian prohibitions and stigmatising restrictions not only reflected, but also created reality.[23] Pagan polydoxy, about which we have information exclusively through the forming-deforming filter of Christianity, could itself have been malleable, that is, in the phase when having just reached prototheism it could have developed into some form of a polytheism. This transitory stage of the procedure of creating gods is well expressed by the two *terminus technicus* that were coined by H. Usener from Roman, and specifically Lithuanian and Latvian mythology and is applied to them: 'momentary gods' (*Augenblicksgötter*) are born in a way that a qualifier sanctifies the attributed word through becoming a symbolic noun only once; while 'occasional gods' (*Sondergötter*) are the attachment of these momentary gods to recurring occasions, times, and places.[24] (For example the momentary god of 'the last sheaf' can become set as the occasional god of 'harvest' from whom some Demeter-like personal 'cultivation-goddess' could emerge in a polytheistic system.)

---

[23] D. Harmening's fierce bluntness about the Germanic–German belief system seems to be true of the Balts, too. "If almost the entirety of the cited evidence, which goes back to Caesarius of Arles, were left without any attention as sources for German and Germanic beliefs and customs, then, the whole cloud of the literary and Church legislation accounts (J. M. Heer) would deteriorate into what they really are, that is into a fog... All the messages that our sources carry about their subject are that they reflect condemned superstitions or exclusively the Celtic–Roman relation, or else that they were spread across the entire western hemisphere, or, what is also possible is that Christian criticism of superstitions spread them. However, they shed no light on whether or not the Germanic people had a similar cult. Many factors point towards their familiarity with it, but the Church evidence alone cannot be taken as sufficient proof of a Germanic or German cult" (Harmening 1979, 73, 75).

[24] For a comparison between the Roman gods known as *indigitamentae, dii indigetes* (which H. Usener claims to have sprung from poetry) and the gods of Latvian folk-songs, see Biezais 1993.

A striking example of reports filtered through *interpretatio christiana*, positing the sky god, and assuming the existence of momentary and occasional gods in a Christian transcript, is the Latin preface to the first Lithuanian book printed in Königsberg in 1547. "I ask you to dwell upon how terrible it is not to know God, what a horrid plague of the soul is idolatry, how Satan rejoices in stealthily spreading new idolatry and false beliefs [a swipe at Catholics in the spirit of Luther—E.B.]. Furthermore, and to mention this not without pain, compared with other peoples how uncivilised and dark is ours, how little it knows of piety and Christian religion, how few are such people amongst the masses who, dare I say, correctly know the whole lesson of the catechism, but are able to remember even the first word of the Lord's Prayer. Moreover, and it pains me more to hear it, that there are many who practice idolatry before others, and do confess it freely. Some worship trees and rivers, others worship snakes, and still others worship objects as their gods. There are some who swear oaths to Perkūnas, some worship *Laukosargas (Laucosargus)* for the grain, and *žemepatis (Semepates)* for the animals, some turn their souls to evil and hold *aitvaras* and *kaukas* as their gods."

Beside the objects of natural religion (trees, rivers) there is Perkūnas the sky god and there are two typical momentary or at most occasional 'gods' *lauko + sargas* 'field + its protector', *žemė + patis* 'earth + its lord', and two lesser demons the *aitvaras*[25] and the *kaukas*.[26] The last two were mentioned by the Lutheran priest M. Mažvydas, who came from the area of Klaipeda and later worked in East Prussia, in his preface, following the Latin foreword, which is a verse to the common people of Lithuania, "reject *kaukas*, *žemepatis* and *laukosargas*, and leave behind all kinds of evil creatures and idols (*deives*)" (Mažvydas 92, 100). It is evident that the report of the priest talking about the pagan belief system in the national language, for the first time among the Balts, differs from accounts of foreigners only in not adulterating the names, however the content remains the same.[27]

---

[25] A. Brückner demonstrates the chain of < Old Polish *oćwiara* 'ghost, demon', though it is strongly debated (Brückner 1904, 56 and 215–216).

[26] Most likely it is < Pruss. *kauks* (*cawx*) 'devil', originally 'house elf' (Toporov 1975–90/III, 293).

[27] Although precisely these names carry ambiguity in their grammar. The Latin foreword, written in the first person singular, is also attributed to the German Rector of the University of Königsberg who spoke Lithuanian, which perhaps explains the phrase "our Lithuanian language" (cf. Zinkevičius 1984–94/III, 25). It is also likely because the Lithuanian names come up in their Latinised forms in the text, e.g. *laucosargus* instead of the Lith. *laukosargas*, or *semepates* instead of the Lith. *žemepatis* (both in nom. sing.). As opposed to the singular forms of the Latin text, in the Lithuanian poem by Mažvydas the same names are in the plural. 'Nitpicking' is perhaps appropriate, because it could prove that in the mid-sixteenth century the Lithuanians were in a transitional period when they no longer thought in terms of pagan gods but rather in terms of spirit creatures emerging from anthropomorphised natural phenomena, without any personal names allocated to them.

LATVIAN 'GODS'. Of the belief systems of the three Baltic nations, that of the Latvians (excluding the barely discernable sky god Pērkons) is within the system of polydoxy and consequently be described using its concepts.

It is different in character from the other two and from all other polydoxy as a result of two factors. Firstly, that it has an ancient layer; and secondly, that it was inseparably and indistinguishably interwoven with Catholicism.

(a) *Latvian 'mothers': a Venedic heritage?*

There is a mythological group that falls between the natural objects of 'pure' natural religion and the personified figures of prototheism–polytheism that is only apparent in Latvian folklore. That is, the group of various mothers (*māte*): field-mother, forest-mother, earth-mother, sea-mother, garden-mother, wind-mother, dung-mother [sic!], Riga-mother, etc.; up to such neo-formations as money-mother. Approximately 70 such mothers were counted in Latvian folk-songs (Biezais 1975, 368). They are first mentioned in the work *Wiederlegunge der Abgötterey* written in 1627 by P. Einhorn (deceased 1655) who spoke excellent Latvian. Two other sources refer to them, which repeat the sections concerning the religious life of the Latvians (*Reformatio gentis Letticae* and *Historia Lettica*). We are indebted to him for the first detailed and authentic description of Latvian customs in general. P. Einhorn, like his grandfather A. Einhorn, was a superinten-dent and inspector general of the Evangelical Church. Both of them worked in the same historical context, they wanted to clean up the mess left there by the papists. The grandfather, following the orders of the ruler, G. Keller, took part in the visits to the church districts where they had to estimate to what extent and in what forms paganism lived on among the *Undeutsch* after the four hundred years of Catholic activity. The grandson, who obviously inherited his grandfather's notes concern-ing these visits, did the same following the Catholic Counter Reformation, during the 'Swedish times' of counter-Counter Reformation.[28] They both equally con-demned pagan and Catholic idolatry in their stubborn Lutheranism.

From where did these many Latvian mother-figures emerge? And why are they absent among the Prussians and Lithuanians (or why are the 'gods' at a similar degree of development masculine among the latter: Žemepatis, Laukopatis, etc.) and why do they exist among the Livians and the Estonians? J. Balys posits that it is simply a question of the Finnic influence. P. Šmits' explanation seems more convincing to me. He considers the numerous mother figures to be a new for-mation among Latvians as well as the Finnic peoples which, however, could not have emerged without a common ancestor. He fails to name this common an-cestor who lived in Livonia before the Latvians, Estonians, and Livians at around the time of Christ. Their mother figures arose because of their matrilineal marriage and inheritance system similar to that of the Germanic peoples and the Basques

[28] For the two Einhorns and their historical background see Mannhardt 1936, 420 ff.; 459 ff.

(Šmits 1926, 86 ff.). In the sense of the above (cf. Part Two, Chapter 3) I would identify this with the non-Indo-European, or the non-Finno-Ugric Veneds. Tacitus' sentence (cited several times) about the Aestii (who were doubtlessly in connection with the Veneds, and either assimilated them and/or replaced them in their homeland) seems to refer to this, "they worship the mother of gods" (Tacitus 45).

The most striking characteristic of Latvian popular belief system, that is, its impressively beautiful feminine features can be attributed to this (naturally unverifiable) Venedic matrilineal heritage, the preservation and spread of which were evidently nurtured through the later mother-god cult (note that Livonia was 'officially' the country of Mary).

This delicate femininity is manifested not only in the great number of mothers, but for example in the three 'fate goddesses' that appear in Latvian folk-songs, too, Laima, Kārta and Dēkla.

Laima is a goddess of happiness and fortune common with the Lithuanians, a simple personification of 'fortune and happiness' *laime* (< *lam-*, cf. Latv. *lemt*, Lith. *lemti* 'to determine fate').

The name of Kārta who determines the course of life is a verbal noun formed either from the verb *kārt* 'to determine, to levy, to suspend', or from *kārtot* 'to settle, arrange something'. The goddess holds the thread of life in her hand.

The third, Dēkla, often interchanged with Laima emerged from the Catholic St Theresa through folk etymology (see also Biezias 1975, 366). However, since in folk-songs Dēkla holds the fate of children in her hands and Laima is connected with mothers, many mythologists derive the name from *dēht* 'to protect, to take care of', *Puppi dēht* 'to breast feed', which in this way is related to the Sanskrit *dha-* and IE. **dhe-* stems, from which Latv. *dēt* 'to have something made, to breast feed, to lay eggs, etc.' (Iltnere 1993–94/2, 172).

Perhaps it is unnecessary to mention that many scholars consider the Laima–Kārta–Dēkla trio to be the direct descendants of the three Fates.[29]

(b) The Latvian 'mixed Pantheon'

The mixture of the characters of natural religion and Christianity occurred most completely among the Latvians, because there it started very early. The (ancestors of) the Latvians must have first encountered orthodoxy, but no traces of this remained except for a few loan words from Russian. Catholicism had a greater effect because in one way or another it began to edge out or mould pagan religious images fifty to one hundred years earlier than among the Prussians and two hundred years earlier than among the Lithuanians.

How successful it was is unclear, that is, what sort of pagan characters existed before the figures of Catholic mythology because all our information comes

[29] Laima "phenomenologically belongs to the circle of fate gods known in the Indo-European religions" (Biezais 1975, 365).

through the filter of the ultimately victorious Reformation in Livonia. As I mentioned earlier with regard to the two Einhorns, *Undeutsch* paganism and Catholic idolatry were considered to be the same sin. The eighteenth-century creators of Latvian mythology—J. Lange, another clerical superintendent, Stenders the Elder a Lutheran priest—and their descendants up to the twentieth century adopted this identification implicitly or explicitly. Thus the most varied figures of the Catholic religion (Mary, St. John and several other saints) became the characters of 'ancient' pagan mythology. This identification, which could well be called the Latvian Protestant variation of *interpretatio christiana* masks the true and original features of mythical characters, possibly preserved in folk-songs. That is why P. Šmits is absolutely right to say we know nothing of the genealogy of the Latvian gods at different levels of personification, which means that anyone might imagine any of them to be as ancient as they wish (Šmits 1926, 79).

The character of Mara, apart from the three Fate goddesses, exemplifies this. She, according to the most convenient explanation, is the folklore version of the virgin Mary (e.g. Šmits 1926, 33). Her most important function is, like her companion Maršava in many of the folk-songs, to be the benefactor of cattle. However, many people believe that they are both pagan goddesses from Indo-European times. The name can be explained from the stem **mr-*, which has a dual connection, with death (Latin *mors*, OSlav. *sъ-mrьtь*) and the death gods (OInd. *mrtyu*, Slavic *Morena, Marena*); or with water (Lith. *marios* 'lagoon', Ger. *Meer*, Russ. *more* 'sea') (Iltnere 1993–94/2, 172). The question remains of how the goddess of death or the sea could become the benefactor of cows. Examples could be found for each shade of meaning among the several hundred thousand four-lined dainas and there must be a high probability of lines that mention Mary together with death or water.

The pinnacle of Latvian *interpretatio christiana* is the work of the twentieth-century scholarly mythologists, especially the works of H. Biezais, a priest living in Sweden. They conjure a whole family of 'major gods' based on the rare reports starting with that of P. Einhorn and especially on folk-songs. It is done by personalising natural phenomena, simply spelling their names with a capital initial: Sun, Moon, Pērkons, Morning Star. The four-lined lyrical songs (as is customary in folk-songs, these are mostly concerned with natural phenomena) contain the completeness of human life. So nothing could be easier than making up 'ancient myths' from their motifs: the wedding or the hostility of the Sun and the Moon; about the sons of the Elder God; about the daughters of the Sun; about the duo of the Pērkons and the Elder God; about the marriage of the Sun and the Morning Star; and so on. The characters of this world of gods, composed from the motifs of folk-songs, are qualified as ancient (not only Old Latvian, but Proto-Baltic, and Indo-European) on the basis of the theory that governed the process of declaring the characters of Catholic religion ancient, which I have discussed a number of times. This was based on the thesis that claims folk poetry, mythology, and language to be the same age. If a major share of the basic vocabulary of the Latvian language can be derived from Indo-European, then the gods created from these words (Sun, Moon, etc.) are of Indo-European origin, too. Latvian folk-songs recorded mostly in the nineteenth century, and the Sanskrit names of gods could shed light on each other without difficulty, because the archaic nature of the Latvian language guarantees the archaic nature of the folk-song.[30] H. Biezais who described this 'daina Olympus' in full detail in three of his books, characterises the Indo-European sky god on the basis of the Dievs figure of the dainas (Biezais 1955, 1961, 1972). "The heavenly farmer of the dainas could also be called the sacred peasant" (Biezais 1961, 57), consequently, the Indo-European was also the god of agriculture and the main function of the Balto–Slavic thunder god was to increase fertility as the function of Pērkons in the folk-songs was the same (Biezais 1961, 87).

The identification of folk poetry with mythology of course works in the opposite direction as well. Paradoxically, precisely H. Biezais proves, through an exemplary and fastidious analysis, that some neo-mythologists were wrong on the grounds that what did not survive in Baltic folklore, could not have existed in mythology either. The Slavic Volos–Veles god and his Baltic connections deserve a mention because they offer a fine example of the almost boundless 'possibilities' springing from the identification of the Indo-European language family with the mythological family. It is also questionable in itself as to whether the god of cattle, Volos, mentioned at the same rank with Perun in the contract between the Kievan Rus' and Byzantium in 972, is identical with the later Veles, or is a translation of Christian St. Vlasiy, the patron saint of herds (cf. Schütz 1967, 90). The function of Volos–Veles is even more debatable. He has been thought of as a number of gods: the god of the dead, the Slavic Pluto (A. Brückner); the patron god of shepherds and poets (D. Likhachev); the patron of traders (B. Unbegaun); or the god of magic (A. Gieysztor). The words Latv. velis, Lith. vėlė 'the spirit of the dead, living dead' and derived from that the Latv. velns, Lith. velnias 'devil' were connected to this dubious Slavic god simply because of phonological similarity. From this connection R. Jakobson, then M. Gimbutas in his footsteps created a

---

[30] The paradoxical impression that the strictest philological analyses clash with fundamental logic comes from the basic fault in identification between language, mythology, and folklore. The linguistic disclosure of the Indo-European connections of god names resembles the evidence brought up by 'Sumerologists' believing in a Hungarian–Sumerian linguistic relationship, or the 'great Soviet scholar' Marr, who deduced all the languages of the world from four one-unit element.

However, not only the language but all phenomena of popular life becomes 'trans-mythicised': folklore, the most insignificant customs, costumes, eating habits, etc. All carry ancient mythological content. An aphorism by S. J. Lec says: "When gossip ages it becomes myth" (Lec 1991, 26). Our mythologists seem to think it the other way round, and they find myth in every piece of gossip.

Baltic Devil, a god of the underworld and the dead who is the third member of the godly trio accompanying Dievas–Dievs, and Perkūnas–Pērkons. As H. Biezias demonstrated, this transmitted an error of Stenders the Elder (Gimbutas 1985, 170; Biezais 1961, 13).

The contradictory feature of the Latvian Pantheon, linguistically demonstrable but mythologically unsound, is only amplified by the group of gods which were familiarised by J. Lange and Stenders the Elder, and most mythologists believe it to be a 'pseudo-Olympus', a fabrication (e.g. Kokare 1991). It is seen as a group of gods taken from Prussian, and (to lesser extent) from Lithuanian. Although they were fitted into Latvian mythology on the basis of the same principle of language = mythology just as in the case of the earlier gods that were accepted as genuinely Latvian. P. Šmits offers an example of a 'god' on the Prussian 'pseudo-Olympus' called Potrimpus, whose name is Latvianised into Patrimpus by J. Lange and which then means 'the one under Trimpus' (*pa* 'under'), from which it could be logically inferred that there was a god called Trimpus, a Latvian Bacchus, because his name is related to *thriambos* in Greek. Stenders the Elder adopts this god from J. Lange, but explains the name from Latvian as *tīrum–pus* 'plough land–half', because the Latvians customarily drink half of the harvest (of the plough land) away. Trimpus has two drinking chums, Antrimpus, the god of the sea (*ant* 'onto') and Potrimpus, the god of the rivers, and they are his friends, because water is also needed to produce drink...[31]

7.2.2. Interpretatio classica (Romana, Graeca)

The *interpretatio christiana*, dominating the sources of the thirteenth–fifteenth centuries with its both concealing and revealing features, is an adequate interpretative principle for polydoxy. The same is not true of *interpretatio classica* that distorts and falsifies the Baltic reality that had just reached the level of prototheism, by superimposing Graeco-Roman polytheism on it. (Naturally, *interpretatio christiana* also had a side that attacked the faith of the non-Jewish peoples of the *Old Testament*. Nonetheless, the polytheism of the *Old Testament* cannot be compared with the wonderfully elaborate system of Graeco-Roman mythology. Consequently, with some simplification I shall treat *interpretatio christiana* as the

---

[31] The explanation of current philologists like V. Ivanov and V. Toporov is that "Trimps is a fertility god in Prussian mythology. His name **Trimp(a)s* is reconstructed from the god names of Autrimps and Potrimps (where *au-* and *pr-* are prefixes). Ideas about this probably emerged through the doubling of T. (perhaps an outside influence). Etymologically T.'s name is connected to the Lith. *trempti* 'tred, trample'. Trampling on the earth is characteristic of the mythological figures with the function of fertility (Tokarev 1988/I, 378).

As seen, the eighteenth-century and the twentieth-century explanations both operate with indisputable evidence...

explanation of polydoxy, while *interpretatio classica* as the exegesis of polytheism.)

As I. Goldziher writes, "since mankind connects the concept of god with the attributes of power and sovereignty... the perspective that has been acquired through the experience of the power of secular rulers could easily be applied to gods, and their power is conceptualised with the same qualities that are perceived in their secular rulers day by day" (Goldziher 1876, 320). This implies that polytheism, which is (also) a complex power system, could only develop in a society with a complex power structure. H. Łowmiański expresses this as, "the great gods are historical categories that appear in a predetermined phase that is in a phase of statehood, or in extraordinary historical circumstances, under the influence of the pantheon of neighbouring state organisations" (Łowmiański 1979, 53).

The 'phase of statehood' is completely absent for the Latvians because their situation was determined very early on by the German conquest. Establishing a Latvian (Latgalian or any other) state was out of the question and so there are no personal Latvian gods either.[32] This imbalance between the Latvian and the Prussian–Lithuanian Grand Duchies was further intensified by the fact that the Latvian (Livonian) polydoxy was a great deal weaker, and there is much less data about it than in the other two cases. The simple explanation for this is that when Western Christianity reached them in the late twelfth century the Latvians were already Christians, albeit Orthodox, and in the eyes of the 'Latin Church' their paganism less extreme than the true, unadulterated paganism of the Prussians and the Lithuanians. On examination of the Latvian religious terminology it seems improbable that a people which had converted to Christianity centuries earlier would have practised natural religion with the same intensity as those who had been left undisturbed. This would have been the case even if the Latvians periodically reverted to paganism when their ties with the Duchy of Polotsk were loosened.

The personal gods of the *interpretatio classica* appear among the Prussians and the Lithuanians at the point when the state was (about to be) established, or the position or character of the existing state became uncertain. This first occurred in the mid-thirteenth century which, although Europe paid no attention to it, was a highly significant moment in world history. This was not simply because the process of forcing the Prussians into Europe and preventing them from establishing their own state was underway, but also that, for a short time, there were two fiercely competitive 'Latin' kingdoms, the Lithuanian and the Halicz–Volhynian, trying to join Europe. The second such occasion was at the turn of the fourteenth and fifteenth centuries when it was decided that the Lithuanians would

---

[32] Accordingly, V. Toporov's study, although its title indicates Baltic mythology, discusses only Prussian and Lithuanian gods (Toporov 1972).

join Western Christianity and accordingly Moscow began its rise as the central power in Eastern Europe. The next occasion was at the turn of the fifteenth and sixteenth centuries when the opposition between the Poles and the Germans (Prussians), which increasingly manifested as Catholic–Protestant antagonism, determined events in the region and the world's first Protestant state was born.

All this was followed by ideological struggles concerning the origins of the reigning dynasties and, consequently, the extraction of their people. One illuminating example of this from the mid-thirteenth century is that the Halicz–Volhynian annals deems the baptism of Mindaugas to have been disingenuous. However, in a letter written in 1268 to the Czech King Otto II the Pope Clement IV depicts Mindaugas as 'a glorious memory' (clare memorie Mindota), even five years after the king's assassination when the court must have learned of Mindaugas' apostasy (Ivinskis 1951, 43). In the fifteenth century, when the uncomfortable personal union between Poland and Lithuania was emerging, two 'theories' were born concerning the origins of the Lithuanians who had just joined the community of European nations and so felt compelled to prove their ancient origins. One of these, which was constructed by J. Długosz, the 'father of Polish history writing', originates them from the Romans.[33] The other source is Aeneas, who dubs the Prussians as Gothic an idea to which E. Stella later adds historical 'precision' by saying that the predecessors of the Prussians and the Lithuanians were two Gothic tribes, the Heruli and the Alans (lital-alan 'littoral Alan' > Lithuanian).[34] The legend of Roman origin was also aimed against the Russians, as a response to the slander of the lowly origins of the Grand Duke Gediminas, the establisher of the dynasty that sprang from the Russian annals. Simultaneously, the Russians were anxious to prove their own Roman extraction through the Prussians, po + rus 'neighbour to a Russian' (Jučas 1993).[35]

---

[33] The idea can be used any time in the future, too. It can be found for example in the Stryjkowski Chronicle in the late sixteenth century since, while writing his work, the author enjoyed the support of the separatist bishop M. Giedrelis who wanted to re-establish the Union of Lublin, a Lithuania independent of Poland, and for that he needed a historical argument: the Lithuanian nobility is older than the Polish.

[34] The Scandinavian people of the Heruli and the Iranian people of the Alans migrated together with the Goths. A. Gvagnini adopted the idea to derive the Lithuanians from the Heruli and the Alans from E. Stella, a view which had followers even in the twentieth century, along with the great 'national awakener' J. Basanavičius. Gvagnini simply plagiarised the Stryjkowski Chronicle, and modified the theory by saying that the nobility is of Roman, the common people of Gothic origin (for all this see Jurginis 1981).

[35] The ancient origin of the Russians was expressed in the "Moscow, the third Rome" thesis. Only under Ivan IV in the sixteenth century did it become connected to a Biblical origin which is widespread in the Russian Chronicles (Borst 1957–63/I, 322). In the West, the two origins were connected much earlier: on the crown of the Empire (today exhibited in Vienna) with which Otto I was crowned German–Roman Emperor in 962, King David's picture also features.

I shall end the list here because *interpretatio classica*, which although it infrequently appears in the sources from the thirteenth–fifteenth centuries does so with an almost spectral regularity (thus denying the accidental survival of sources) and always at times when, at the mentioned crossroads, power struggles intensify. *Interpretatio classica* was first linked with *interpretatio christiana* in those chapters of *Historia Polonica* which concern the conversion of Lithuania and Žemaitija by J. Długosz, who never set foot in Lithuania. It became dominant from the sixteenth century and at the same time was turned into a self-perpetuating *literature*. The various catalogues of gods following the Graeco-Roman tradition were adopted, extended, and passed from hand to hand among the humanists of the Renaissance. These catalogues, at best, were connected to 'ancient' pagan mythology through fragments surviving in popular beliefs, but probably had less and less to do even with contemporaneous ideological struggles. For this reason Z. Ivinskis is right to consider the account of Jerome of Prague and Aeneas to be the last authentic description of Lithuanian religious customs (despite its qualities, as discussed) because it cannot have been distorted by the 'reality-alien' system of *interpretatio classica* (Ivinskis 1938–39, 381).[36]

7.3. Baltic 'polytheism'

The dittos are to signal that, in the sense of what has been said so far, there is no Baltic polytheism. Apart from Perkūnas and Pērkons and the Christian God (Dievas–Dievs) there are no gods, they are the inventions of mythologists who handed down and gradually populated the Baltic pantheon across the centuries. I classify the chroniclers who covered whatever remnants of pagan beliefs they found with the net of *interpretatio romana* as mythologists as well. The conceptual net perhaps more closely resembles a grid of iron bars which, should we want to match it to the much smaller area underneath, will continually slip and accidentally cover one area or another. In this way the gods of the ancient world are linked with this or that accidentally heard or misheard Baltic word or concept. Consequently, even the Baltic 'gods' coming from an otherwise reliable source should be considered the results of *interpretatio romana* and, to a lesser extent, of *interpretatio christiana* and as such a well intentioned misunderstanding. This is especially true of the sources that start in the fifteenth century and last until the nineteenth-twentieth centuries when the desire to create gods is evident.

[36] The two different interpretations continued into the nineteenth and even the twentieth centuries. The romantics identified Lithuanian paganism with the polytheism of antiquity, while the positivists with pantheism. I consider the modern neo-mythologists the late employers of *interpretatio romana*. The representatives of the historical viewpoint rightly rely upon the traditions of *interpretatio christiana*, in preference.

7.3.1. The Prussian 'gods' of reliable sources

In actual fact there is not one such god, but in the eyes of certain mythologists the authenticity of the sources lends them a god-like quality.

There are only two such sources. One of them is the Peace Treaty of Chrystburg.[37] The relevant part states that the Prussian pagans "promise that they will not offer sacrifices either to the idol (*ydolo*) to which they used to make and erect (*confingere*) once a year at harvest time and worship as a god, and which was given the name of *Curche*, or to other gods who created neither the sky nor the earth".

The etymology of the name is as yet unsolved. A. Brückner identifies it with the Slavic *korčij* 'blacksmith', E. Fraenkel with *kurklys* 'creator' in the meaning of the blacksmith god, the Slavic Svarog and Hephaestus (Brückner 1918, 131; Fraenkel 1962, 1965/1, 316). Others link this form to Cerera, the Roman harvest goddess. Cz. Kudzinowski posits that it is the adaptation of the Finn. *kurko* 'evil spirit' "from the time of the Volga Finno-Baltic unit" (Kudzinowski in SSS/2, 59). The majority of Finnish linguists believe that it happened the other way round and that it is a Baltic loan word in Finnish. Analogous to the theory in which Churcho is a West Baltic sky god–chief god, i.e. the Creator corresponding to the East Baltic Perkūnas, H. Łowmiański forms a connection with the Lith. verb *kurti* 'to create' (Łowmiański 1976, 148; 1979, 553).[38]

In fact the text is clearly about an idol that was only honoured as god by the uneducated pagans. It is also evident that according to the pagans themselves they did not have even a single sky god who would have created the sky and the earth. It seems that the name, which cannot be found in other reliable sources, was only mentioned here by chance. However, the custom, which is described here, is well known, the Balts, the Slavs, and the Finnic peoples all made a corn-dolly from the last sheaf of straw at harvest.

The other document, the *Collatio Episcopi Varmiensis*, is a memorandum written by the Bishopric of Warmia to the Pope in 1418. It is part of the dispute between the Teutonic Order and Poland following the battle of Grunwald in which the Pope acted as an arbitrator. In the memorandum J. Abezier, the Bishop of Warmia, lists the merits of the Order at the request of the Grandmaster. The knights earned these merits in the conversion of the pagans who "honour such horrible demons as *patollu Natrimpe* and other horrific beasts, *alia ignominiosa fantasmata*" (Mierzyński 1892–96/II, 144). How many of these randomly mentioned demons there are is debatable, as well as whether the word *patollus* is an adjective

---

[37] For more details on the contract see Part Four, Subchapter 8.3.2. For the complete text see Toporov 1975–90/V, 227; in Lithuanian Pakarklis 1948, 240; in German Voigt 1827–39/2, 621, and Hubatsch 1954, 80–99.

[38] For the various hypotheses see Biskup–Labuda 1986, 64; Toporov 1975–90/IV, 309.

describing Natrimpus, who was probably a kind of fertility 'god' similar to Churche (see Part Four, Subchapter 7.2.1), or, as is assumed by almost everybody, was another 'god'.[39] Regardless of the number, these demons cum idols were only transformed into gods by later sources.

7.3.2. The Lithuanian 'gods' of reliable sources

There are three different sources, all most likely written by the same author. One of them is an insertion into the *Malalas Chronicle* quoted above, in which the chronicler mentions the following "horrible gods": Andaj (original sing. dat. Andaevi); Perkun the thunderer; Zhvoruna the bitch (Zhvorune); Teljavel the blacksmith, who forged the sun that shines upon the earth and threw it into the sky (Teljaevi).

The other sources are the two additions to the *Chronicle of Halicz-Volhynia* which are ironically hostile towards the Lithuanians. The first one, from 1252 states:

"Mindaugas has sent to the Pope and converted to Catholicism. His baptism was disingenuous and he continued to sacrifice to his gods in secret, firstly to Nunadjev (again in sing. dat. form) and to Teljavel and Diverikz (Diverikьzu), to the Rabbit-god, and to Mendeina (Mendeine). When he was riding in the fields and a rabbit ran across [in front of him] he did not go deep into the forest, nor did he dare to break a branch. He offered a sacrifice to his gods, and burnt the bodies of the dead, and he openly admitted to being a pagan." The number of gods that are mentioned here depends on whether we treat the rabbit-god as an independent god or as an apposition of Diverikz–Medeina which precedes and follows it before and after the word. I think it is justified to consider it an independent form that is used by the chronicler to poke fun at Mindaugas' superstition: the sovereign honours a rabbit-god and is so superstitious that he is scared of a rabbit that ran across in front of him as of a bad omen.

---

[39] *Patollu* had become *Patollus* in the writing of sixteenth-century mythologists, which were then mixed with the Pecullus and Picullus versions. These are connected to the words Polish *piekło* > Pruss. *pyculs* 'hell', and Lith. *piktas* 'angry, evil', *pikulas*, Latv. *pikals* 'evil demon' inter-effecting each other (Fraenkel 1962, 1965/I, 589). *Patollu Natrimpe* means 'evil (hellish) Natrimpe'. Others believe that Pykuls, Pykullos, Pecullus, Pecols, Pocols 'devil, hell creature' were confused with the name Patollus who was the god of the dead for the Prussians, due to their phonological similarity (see e.g. Bertuleit 1924, 50). Some posit that the compounding hides the same stem with the meaning 'many' as in *tuliss* (e.g. Biskup–Labuda 1986, 66), others believe that the name denotes the god of the underworld because the second part of *pa + tula* means 'earth' (from Būga 1920–22, 78, through Toporov 1972, 299, to Vėlius who gives a summary of viewpoints in 1987, 254–256).

The story of the 1258 addition is that the Duchy/Kingdom of Halicz–Volhynia and Lithuania were allies at that moment, King Danilo and his son Roman who was the ruler of Nowogródek in the Grand Duchy of Lithuania, agreed to meet together with their troops and lay siege to the Castle of Vozglavl'. However, Roman and the Lithuanian troops arrived late by which time Danilo's troops had already captured, looted, and torched the castle. "When Roman and the Lithuanians reached the castle and the Lithuanians rushed in, they did not understand (see) anything, only fires (burning) and dogs running (everywhere) and [the Lithuanians] just spat morosely and exclaimed in their language 'janda!', calling upon their gods, Andaj and Diviriks and enumerated all their gods, that is devils" (Mierzyński 1892–96/I, 138–139).

Altogether seven names are mentioned in the three texts. One of them, Diverikz–Diviriks, is referred to twice and another one three times, that is if the curse janda 'for god's sake!' is counted as 'Andaj'. There are several theories that attempt to explain these words from the most conservative who say that Perkūnas is the only authentic name among these (Balys in Lit.E./XIX, 68), to the most permissive 'Dumézilists'. The representatives of the latter categorise the gods, who are believed to be authentic, complying with the Dumézilian triple function (Toporov 1966, 1970, 1972; Greimas 1990; Vėlius 1990; Beresnevičius 1995). Both these theories contain brilliant ideas, notwithstanding the fact that, as a result of the general attitude of their authors to Baltic mythology, the theses are perhaps fundamentally different.[40]

The majority of scholars turn to two more sources for help. One of them is an additional insertion in the Russian translation of the *Malalas Chronicle* whose author is presumably the same as the author of the three additions mentioned previously, or at least comes from the same circles at the Court of Halicz. This source mentions two Slavic gods, Svarog and Dazhbog the first of which the chronicler identifies with Hephaestus the blacksmith god ("After the death of Hephaestus, who is also called Svarog...").

The other one is the *Długosz Chronicle*, whose writer probably knew and used the *Malalas Chronicle* and the *Chronicle of Halicz–Volhynia*. In this chronicle the Lithuanian gods are translated into 'Roman': Perkūnas is referred to once as Jupiter and at other times as Vulcan (the Roman equivalent of Hephaestus); Aesculapius the house god; Diana the god of the moon and hunting; and Silvanus, the god of the forests.

Including these 'alien' sources is even more justified in that the most important factor in the appearance of some of the Lithuanian gods (or at least some of them) was probably the 'translation' itself. The chronicler probably had some Lithuanian informant who could supply him with the names of Lithuanian gods, and tell him the approximate Lithuanian translation of the 'classical' gods.

---

[40] For a most comprehensive report on the standpoints so far see Vėlius 1990.

The gods of the physical sky, Perkūnas, Andaj, Nunadjev, and Diverikz, whose names contain the *deiv-* stem as mentioned earlier (Part Four, Subchapter 7.1.1), belong to the first group among the gods that were mentioned voluntarily, as it were, by the Lithuanian informant.

Among the gods that were translated cum interpreted into Lithuanian on the basis of the chronicler's 'intentional questioning' there are three gods that belong to the second group. Two of these gods are also connected to the physical sky and one of them is a personified natural phenomenon corresponding to the level of polydoxy. Albeit surprising, Zhvoruna the bitch can be linked to the physical sky (cf. Lith. *žvėris* 'wild animal', *žvėrynas* 'a large group of animals'. The name is the Lithuanian translation of Diana–Artemis, and the classical goddess was not only the goddess of hunting but also of the moon.[41] The 'bitch' apposition calls our attention to the fact that the name is not connected to the moon but, as A. Mierzyński discovered, to Syrius the Evening Star, which belongs to the configuration of stars called 'the Dog' (*Canis*) (Mierzyński 1892–96/I, 46).

The mysterious 'Teljavel the blacksmith', who is the equivalent of Hephaestus–Vulcan, also belongs to the sky. What makes him mysterious is not the name, which, as in the previous case, is the translation of the Greek god's qualifier, it goes back to the form *kalevelis* (Lith. *kalvis* 'blacksmith').[42] In this case, however, the chronicler not only translated the name, but also adopted the particular local characterisation of the god from his informant. As H. Łowmiański pointed out following A. Brückner, neither the Graeco–Roman nor the Slavic Hephaestus–Vulcan–Svarog myth contain the motif of the blacksmith forging the sun, which was, however, known among the Latvians and the Lithuanians (Brückner 1904, 75; Łowmiański 1979, 98). A. Mierzyński cites a Latvian folk-song in which the blacksmith works on the coast where the sky and the earth meet in the red light of the Morning Star which is his workshop, the embers falling to the ground following each of his blows (Mierzyński I, 150). This motif was known in the Finnish 'popular religion' as well. Ilmarinen the blacksmith of the *Kalevala* says

---

[41] Many fail to take into account exactly this. H. Łowmiański for example superficially considers Zhvoruna a demon "the patron of hunting dogs, praised by the social elite", whom Mindaugas would have respected as a god along with the rabbit demon and the forest demon because he was a passionate hunter (Łowmiański 1976, 151–152).

[42] K. Būga is of the opinion that *kalevelis* became *Telavel(is)* through *kal-* > with an umlaut *kel-* and the palatal Lithuanian 'k' sounded like a 't' to the Slavic ear. J. Jaskanis offers an even simpler explanation, a feature of the dzūkas dialect is a 't' instead of the literary 'k', and thus the 'literary' Kelavel became Teljavel, which means that the informer of the chronicler spoke with a dzūkas dialect (in Brückner 1904, 223).

This completely sensible and clear etymology does not satisfy those for whom the concept of a blacksmith god does not fit. For example N. Vėlius presumes a compounded word of Tel(ja) + velj, where the first part would be connected to the Latin *Tellus mater* 'mother earth', while the second is to the Lith. *velnias, vėlė* 'devil', 'the soul of the dead' (Vėlius 1995, 535).

of himself: "I'm working a moon in gold, in silver a sun / for heaven's top up yonder to go on the six bright lids" (the *Kalevala*, Song 49).

Finally, the name of Mendeina was a simple translation (< Lith. *medis* 'tree') and in the knowledge of the worship of the sacred groves it was easy to translate the name of Silvanus into Lithuanian.

Six out of the seven Lithuanian 'gods' reflect the transition from polydoxy into prototheism, 'the agonies of birth' of the rise of the sky god.

7.3.3. The Prussian 'Pantheon'

In essence, the history of Baltic mythology could end here: what actually existed, what could exist, is this much. Everything that is added to it, Baltic polytheism, was formed from the end of the fifteenth century and especially from the beginning of the sixteenth. This is not related to the Baltic religion of Antiquity, but rather is connected to and can be explained by the era of its inception. The reason why people have believed in it for centuries until the present (I would like to emphasise once more that it is a matter of faith); why it has been kept, nurtured, cultivated and embellished; and why it is probably impossible to eradicate, is that the *fallacies* (that is the national and religious biases and the vainglorious exhibition-istic writers and scholars) that brought it into existence were in force as eternally human characteristics, are still in force, and will remain in force in the future.

One person is credited (unfortunately undiminishingly) for the development of the Prussian and the Baltic pantheon in general. That person is the often criticised S. Grunau (deceased 1529) who wrote and expanded his own Prussian chronicle from 1517 until his death. M. Perlbach began to publish this in small notebooks in 1875 (as an exhortation!). This amounts to three substantial volumes which every later chronicler used as their principle source (after the chronicles of P. Dusburg and S. Grunau), even M. Praetorius the author of the third Prussian chronicle from 1690). According to W. Mannhardt even in the last century, "in every village school the heads of the young were filled with his narratives, richly imaginative, concerning the respect for the Gods of the old Prussians" (Mannhardt 1936, 190).

S. Grunau, who came from the area of Gdańsk, lived at the time when the struggle between Polish Catholicism and (German) Protestantism became really fierce and resulted in the division of Prussianland into the Kingdom of Prussia which belonged to Poland, and the Duchy of Prussia which was only a vassal state of Poland and became the world's first Lutheran state in 1525. These two worlds were also in conflict in S. Grunau's mind.

On the one hand he was a Catholic, what is more a Dominican monk, and the Dominicans were always the enemies of the Teutonic Order, even more so when the whole Order converted to Lutheranism. S. Grunau lived his whole life in

Warmia of the Royal Prussianland, always supporting the Polish. papists and boasting about the fact that he knew both the Pope and the Polish king personally, and he despised the Teutonic Order. This motivated him to emphasise the non-German origin of the Prussians. According to his theory, the Prussian people were a mixed people, the result of the amalgam of Kimbers driven away by the Goths from Denmark and the Ulmingans or Culmingans autochthon in Sembia. He adopted these non-existent tribe names from E. Stella and distorted the imaginary names even further.

On the other hand this pro-Polish Catholic was of German-Prussian origin, and as we know, the ideologists of both Prussianland areas were working on the re-unification of Prussianland and the shaping of a correspondingly uniform 'new-Prussian' identity throughout this period. These ideologists only used, though manipulated, reinterpreted, and falsified, the traditions of the Baltic Old Prussians to achieve this aim. It is absurd to expect authenticity from such people: they were not interested in the real religion and the customs of the Baltic Prussians, all this was only required for their own ideological purposes. The people who later showed real interest in the second half of the 17th century, like M. Praetorius and K. Hartknoch, found only an almost extinct language and ethnographic data which were inseparable from the lies of the chroniclers such as S. Grunau. The common aim of creating the new-Prussian identity resulted in the seemingly incongruous phenomenon of S. Grunau adopting much from E. Stella who served Prince Albrecht, on the other hand the Protestant David Lucas (1503–1583), the third Prussian chronicler of the sixteenth century, adapts and expands almost everything from S. Grunau.[43]

To describe Prussian ancient prehistory S. Grunau came up with the greatest prevarication of his career: he created an entire ancient chronicle, which included

---

[43] In a strange way Grunau's Catholic religion only backfired later when there was no need to emphasise Prussian unity any more, because a German–Prussian Protestant consciousness existed. J. Voigt was the first to make a critical attack on Grunau, in the meantime praising David Lucas, who merely repeated Grunau in his description of the prehistory of Prussianland, as a serious scholar, thus "letting Grunau in through the backdoor" (Bertuleit 1924, 36). In the end Töppen gave the final word on this source on ancient sin, when in a long chapter he uncovered Grunau's tricks as he went from line to line (Töppen 1853, 122 ff.). W. Mannhardt gave the last stab: "What has remained of the manifold legends about the origins and religion of the Prussians, which a monk from Tolkem had allegedly pulled into a system? Less than nothing, a piece of cloth torn out from the works of earlier writers' and sewn into a glaringly obvious piece of stitch work" (Mannhardt 1936, 207–227). Given all this, it is at least strange that G. Beresnevičius urges a revision of Grunau, because "the Prussian chronicle did not undergo a special historical examination" (Beresnevičius 1995, 78). There is no need for a more specialist historical study than those of Töppen and Mannhardt, the last word has been uttered there, and until new data comes up there is no need for a 'post script'.

two others.[44] The author of the ancient chronicle was allegedly a real person, Christian the first Prussian Bishop. The manuscript which had not been seen by anybody for three hundred years before S. Grunau discovered it, and which disappeared again mysteriously after he had taken notes, this time permanently, was called *Liber filiorum Belial*. S. Grunau borrowed this title from P. Dusburg who called the pagan Prussians the sons of Belial several times. Apart from his own observations Christian used two other chronicles as well, a historical book written by his friend, Jaroslav the parish priest of Plock, and the notes of a certain naturalist called Dywonys. Together with his companions Dywonys arrived in the grim North from a town called Salura which was probably located in the more tropical India, at the time of Emperor Augustus to find out if people could live under the seventh and the eighth circles of the sky. He was the only surviving member of the expedition which arrived in the lands of Prussia by accident and who kept a diary in Russian using the Greek alphabet. This diary had been left lying unnoticed for 1200 years until Christian discovered and utilised it. It is probably apparent that S. Grunau's tales might well be entertaining had he not been such a poor writer and a bit of a know-it-all. S. Grunau tells the ancient prehistory of the Prussians in the words of Dywonys and then Christian up to the sixth-century Videvuto–Bruteni, the *Krive* ruling pair. Finally he describes Romove–Rickoyoto, where the sacred oak tree grew with the three gods inside: the old bearded Patollo, the god of the under-world and the night; the beardless young and cheerful Potrimpo, the god of cereal crops; and the middle-aged Perkuno, the god of lightning and thunder. S. Grunau could have arrived at the first two names from *Collatio* ('patollu Natrimpe'), and as M. Töppen and H. Bertuleit demonstrated, the whole triad of gods was taken from the chronicle of Adam of Bremen, where the Thor–Wodin–Fricco triad of gods are enthroned in a sanctuary in Uppsala (Töppen 1853, 190; Bertuleit 1924, 41). S. Grunau also names three minor gods: Vursajto (cf. Lith. *viršaitis* 'the highest judge', *krivulė*) Svajbrotto (cf. Pruss. *swais brati* 'his own brother') are the embodiments of Videvuto and Bruteni, while Churche, the 'Mazurian god' obviously appears from the Treaty of Chrystburg.

As can be seen, S. Grunau collected everything that he could find from Adam of Bremen to P. Dusburg, from the Treaty of Chrystburg to the chronicle of Maciej z Miechowa which abstracted from Długosz, amalgamating it with the concurrent folklore, unscrupulously recasting and expanding to suit his own imagination.

---

[44] According to U. Arnold's summarising opinion "in any case it seems certain that the *Christian Chronicle* did not exist", although earlier (I believe with an unjustified care) he leaves leeway, even though it is only in the form of a question, for the possibility that the so-called *Die ältere Chronik von Oliva* from the mid-fourteenth century had assimilated the *Christian Chronicle* (Arnold 1967, 116, 16).

The words of A. J. Greimas are unfortunately true: "According to general opinion the pantheon of Prussian gods in S. Grunau's chronicle is the basic source of Baltic mythology" (Greimas 1990, 380). An opinion Greimas himself shares. One of the secrets behind S. Grunau's success is that his catalogue of gods soon received the seal of approval from the other, Protestant, side. The first religious meeting called by the Protestant bishops assessed the situation left after the Catholics and established that, just as in Livonia, the Prussians had kept their pagan gods under Catholic rule. The book of ceremonies, the *Constitutiones Synodales*, which was published in 1530 by the synod, immediately lists ten of these pagan gods together with their classical equivalents: Pruss. *Occopirmus* 'the first'–Saturn; Pruss. *Suaixtix* 'bright'–Sol; Ausschauts–Aesculapius; Autrympus–Castor; Potrympus–Pollux; Bardoyats–Neptune; Piluuytus–Ceres; Parcuns–Jupiter; Pecols and Pocols–Furiea (Mannhardt 1936, 235).

It is easy to recognise that two sources, the *Collatio* and S. Grunau were the starting points. Aside from Perkūnas, they simply doubled the patollu Natrimpe, following Grunau's recipe (Antrimpus–Potrympus, Pecols–Pocols). The other names are better or worse hasty translations of the names of the classical gods (or their qualifiers) according to the dual, anti-Catholic and anti-pagan ideological needs of the twofold new state. A. Brückner is absolutely justified in saying that the respectable body "simply invented the whole list", like H. Łowmiański whose verdict was that the list of gods "should be rejected as an absolute forgery" (Brückner 1918, 66; Łowmiański 1979, 50).

However, it was not rejected, on the contrary, treating the Baltic–Prussian past as easy prey it was incorporated into the German, Polish, and then into the Lithuanian and Latvian past and present with varying emphasis.[45] This tendency became really strong in the nineteenth century. As only a German state existed at the time the Prussian tradition was particularly affected, there are countless books propagating Prussian mythology, of course mostly that of S. Grunau's, in the form of tales and legends. The last book of this kind that I know of is Hinze–Diederichs,

---

[45] One of the first to apply and add to it was the German Protestant priest of Polish origin J. Malecki (Maletius), who added a few names to the inventory of gods by *Constitutiones* in his private letter in Latin written after 1545 and published several times. J. Malecki's son H. Malecki translated the letter into German, further added to it and distorted it, and published it in 1561 (Malecki, *Wahrhafftige Beschreibung der Sudawen auf Samlandt, sambt jhren Bockheyligen vnd Ceremonien*, in brief *Sudauerbüchlein*, 1961). This again served as a source for further adapters, the majority of whom spoke no Baltic, and often added and distorted during copying. This resulted in the majority of the mythological figures appearing in multiple versions, and in deciphering them, the interpreter can select from them according to their general conceptions...

published in 1983. In this publication the reader finds the authentic historical facts hopelessly entangled with the tales of the chroniclers, as well as the real and unrecognisably distorted Prussian and Slavic words and expressions.[46]

7.3.4. The Lithuanian 'pantheon'

The Lithuanian 'pantheon' was created in the same way as the Prussian. It was initiated by J. Długosz and first completed by M. Stryjkowski (1547–1593) who, in the two weighty volumes of his chronicle used all the sources mentioned and not mentioned above: the Lithuanian, Polish, and Prussian chronicles, scholarly books and the folk customs he experienced. He sewed it all together at times in prose at others in verse, but he was not talented in organising the materials along a thread. As he was aware of this, writing his chronicle made him ill and probably caused his death.[47] Stryjkowski was a Polish nobleman who was widely travelled, was incredibly hard working, and even learned some Lithuanian. He was interested in trying to prove that the Lithuanian aristocracy and thus its mythology,

[46] It is amusing to see that not only mythology as the collection of myths, but also mythology as a scholarship about myths became a descended 'cultural possession' (gesunkenes Kulturgut). In their brief explanatory notes the co-authors continually talk about the three categories of Prussian gods (three gods each would belong to the first and the second categories, and twelve to the third), without imparting the basis of the categorisation (e.g. Hinze–Diederichs 1983, 298) which is evidently (?) the Dumézilian triple function.

[47] Although it is of incomparably less importance, the Protestant Polish nobleman J. Łasicki (Lasicius) who spoke no Lithuanian should be mentioned. He wrote his work around 1580 and it was published in 1615 in Basle. All in all, it is eighteen pages long, yet this is the first enumeration of the pagan gods of Žemaitija, about eighty in all. The author gives his source, too, which is his friend J. Laskowski, a Polish lesser noble who spoke no Lithuanian either, who worked as a royal land surveyor, and gathered his information from the peasants there. "The notes of Laskowski and the brief work of Łasicki had a dual purpose: to provide the world with interesting ethnographic and antiquarian information from a forgotten corner of Europe, and to show that if amazing wonders can be told about Prussian (as Malecki did) then twice that much can be found among the Žemaitians (besides this, Łasicki intended to ridicule the Catholic cult of the saints by showing it through a distorted mirror" (Brückner 1904, 106). According Z. Ivinskis the mythology offered by the two Polish noblemen "seems to be a joke that later generations took too seriously for a long time" (Lit. E./XIV, 184). Indeed, many used the work uncritically, but it also underwent numerous critical analyses. S. Stanevičius the poet was the first, who generally speaking was the only sober critic of Baltic mythology among the Lithuanians throughout the nineteenth century (Stanevičius 1838). (Perhaps it is not by accident that his work remained as a manuscript until 1967.) W. C. Jaskiewicz, a Catholic priest living in America, was the last and the most thorough in his analysis of Łasecki's gods, and he did it with philological care. He found only three to be authentic: Perkūnas, Žemyna the mother earth, and Medeina the patron of the forests. The Marxist J. Jurginis responded to his work, "the author is the frantic apologist of the Catholic Church, and being a propagator of Catholicism, he cannot forgive one fatal sin of Łasecki and Laskowski: that they were protestants" (in Stanevičius 1967, 68).

was of Roman origin because his patron, Prince M. Giedraitis, the Bishop of Žemaitija, was trying to achieve Lithuania's independence from Poland. He thought that it was both possible and necessary to undo the 1569 Union of Lublin.[48]

He generalised the ten Prussian gods mentioned in the *Sudauerbüchlein* as Baltic, "Lithuanian, Žemaitian, Sembian, Latvian, and Prussian" gods and supplemented them with sixteen additional Lithuanian and Žemaitian gods. Among these some, for example Chaurirari, the horse-god, whose origins no one as yet has even tried to guess. On the whole, J. I. Kraszewski's characterisation is valid: "Stryjkowski's chronicle is a monstrous compilation full of falsification, imagination, artistry, and anachronism" (Kraszewski 1847–50/II, IV).[49]

The other person to contribute to the completion of Lithuanian mythology is T. Narbutt, the nineteenth-century Polish romantic historian, who dedicated the first gargantuan tome from his nine-volume work on the history of Lithuania to Lithuanian (Baltic) mythology. T. Narbutt's attitude towards history was based on the principle that the subject of history is not humanity but the 'soul of the nation'. The other two representatives of the school of historical rights, J. Kraszewski, who wrote in Polish and could not even speak Lithuanian properly, and the Lithuanian S. Daukantas shared this attitude. The most characteristic manifestation of the soul of the nation is its mythology. Therefore, the search for this mythology and, if none exists, its creation even at the cost of falsification, is the most important duty of the patriot.[50] T. Narbutt was a typical *gente lituanus, natione polonus* (Berenis in Narbutt 1992, 11) and as such, apart from real scholarly investigation also created myths. The only difference is that he did not plant Graeco-Roman gods into Baltic soil, but, complying with contemporary fashion, the gods of India. Therefore, J. Kraszewski, who otherwise used T. Narbutt's work extensively, is right to observe that, "the way Mr. Narbutt examines history is inspired by patriotism to such an extent he is impervious to facts and their true nature" (Kraszewski 1847–50/II, VI).

However, T. Narbutt was the last to enrich the Lithuanian–Baltic pantheon with new figures. His successors, including contemporary mythologists only use the material supplied.

[48] At the same time M. Stryjkowski was also a Polish patriot, what is more, the ideologist of the Polish centred Slavic–Baltic 'Sarmatian' empire. Consequently both Lithuanian and Polish voices claimed he was a traitor (for all this see Kuolys 1992, 105 ff.).

[49] Its effect was enormous. The Rector of the College of Vilnius, the Jesuit Vijūkas-Kojalavičius published it in an abbreviated version in Latin, which G. Merkel then used in establishing Latvian mythology (cf. Jurginis in Vijūkas-Kojelavičius 1987, 386). L. Schlözer found all information about Lithuania in Stryjkowski (Schlözer, *Geschichte von Littauen, Kurland und Liefland*, 1785).

[50] In the nineteenth-century Polish Romanticism generally connected patriotism with an enthusiasm for myths about untouched ancient Lithuania. For example the members of the student society of Free Masons founded in Vilnius in 1817, the *Towarzystwo subrawców* chose the names of Lithuanian gods as pseudonyms.

CHAPTER 8

BALTIC CULTS

It is rather difficult to answer the question of whether or not the Balts had a cult. The three aspects of a cult that need to be examined are priests, idols, and temples. What makes the question problematic, besides scarce sources, is that very often even the same source looks at the problem through two different filters, that of *interpretatio christiana* and *interpretatio classica*, often resulting in uncritical homogenisation of data.[1]

8.1. Idols

The discussion of the existence of cults needs to begin with the examination of the existence of idols, as pagan religions in general are often referred to as idolatry (Latin *idolatria,* Ger. *Abgötterei*).

Idolatry was first mentioned in the first biography of Adalbert, written in 999, "*Sicco, sacerdos idolorum*" [*Sicco* the priest of idols]; *sicco* in all lower case denotes 'a man of knowledge'. Here and in other sources the word *idolum* can be interpreted as idol, a carved image but also as a spirit or demon. The former interpretation is connected with an idolatry that is similar to the Catholic cult while

---

[1] This currently rather foggy sentence will hopefully be clear later, and is only intended to point out that if a source in the spirit of, say, *interpretatio christiana*, claims that the Prussians had priests, which is almost certainly the case, then the statement of the source, in the sense of *interpretatio classica*, that they also had a lot of gods is not automatically true.

As far as possible I shall disregard views coloured by nationalist fallacy which (who consider even the raising of the issue a sacrilege) reject a natural religion lacking sanctuaries and an expanded priestly hierarchy as a barbarous uncivilised culture that would have been entirely uncharacteristic of the Balts. Typical outrage which was voiced even by the young K. Būga, followed the criticisms of the Polish A. Mierzyński and A. Brückner when, in the late nineteenth century, they were the first to refute the romantic fantasies woven around the cult. The Lithuanians simply called those who denied the cult, though only in private correspondence, 'anti-Lithuania fanatics' (cf. Balys 1929/8, 33 ff.). Slowly, things calmed down, in part due to K. Būga's moderate philological analyses. However, once again at a time of renaissance for nationalism political and ideological battles seem to interfere in the discussion of the issue.

the latter implies a cult of natural religion that does not need idols as its cultic objects can be found in the natural environment.[2]

Tacitus defines the slight difference between 'pure' natural religion not tied to location, and idolatry, which perhaps represents a more advanced degree of development and is connected to places and objects. He writes of the Suebi: "They consider it incompatible with the grandeur of those in the sky to force their gods among walls or to mold them into the attributes characteristic of humans, they respect groves and copses as sacred places, and call those mysterious phenomena they only experience in pious contemplation by the names of gods" (Tacitus, 9).

8.2. Sanctuaries

Another problem is deciding where religious celebrations were held. We know of 'open air services', for example the Prussians promised to make their new Catholic churches majestic and magnificent because "they wanted to experience greater joy praying and sacrificing in these buildings than in the forest". This probably only meant that certain natural places were segregated and designated as sacred. To the question of whether any services and idolatry took place, and if so, in what form, the only answers are the usual Christian commonplaces, such as an eternal fire, a sacred grove, and so on.

The existence of megaliths (Latv. *pēdakmeņi*), which are 1–1.5 metres high and the same diameter, point to some kind of cultic activity. There are 104 such stones known in Latvia (Iltnere 1993–94/2, 215), and about 250 in Lithuania (Lit. E./I, 73). The stones are decorated with different motifs, such as palm-imprints (the 'devil's footprints'). However, these stones are not significant in a special Baltic religion because they originate either from the Neolithic era, or from the early 'metal ages', and thus the Baltic people could only have inherited them from the people who populated this area earlier. Another factor that proves their insignificance is that these stones can be found a long way from Baltic settlements, usually in the depths of the forest. On the other hand, the large number of place names with *alk-, *elk-* stems around earth castles points to the existence of Baltic cultic places. Probably the words *alka(s)* and *elka* originally meant 'sacred grove' and were later transferred to other natural objects (Pruss. *Alkayne*, Lith. *Alkokalnis*

---

[2] The double meaning of the concept is apparent even when other sources use other words (Ger. *Götze*, Polish *bałwan*, Latv. *elks* = Lith. *alka[s]*, Latv. *stabs* = Lith. *stabas*—the latter's meaning of 'idol' also slipped into the Pruss. *stabis* 'stone' in error) (cf. Balys 1929/10, 41). For this reason the young K. Būga's argument is untenable, when he states that there must have been idol worship among the Lithuanians, because there are more than ten words in Lithuanian for expressing the concept *idolum* (Būga 1908–09, 148). All these words could have meant two things.

'sacred mount', *Alkupis* 'sacred stream', *Alkgiris* 'sacred forest', Latv. *Elkazeme* 'sacred land', *Elkezers* 'sacred lake', and from secondary derivation > Latv. *elks* 'idol') or the other way round, the original meaning of the word was 'idol' and that became 'the place for worshipping idols'.[3]

8.2.1. Romova

The fact that the Latvians and even the Prussians, who were at the level of polydoxy, did not require real sanctuaries and temples is neatly demonstrated by the reliable P. Dusburg who describes a religious centre where, however, the temple is an oak tree: "Among these disingenuous people [Prussians] there was a place in Nadruva called Romow [in Nikolaus von Jeroschin who versified Dusburg it is Romowe], which was named after Rome, and there lived a man called *Criwe*, who was respected as the Pope is. As the Pope reigns over the whole church of the believers, not only these tribes, but also the Lithuanians and other peoples of Livonia obey this man's will and orders. He is held in such great respect that whenever he, his relatives, or even his messengers travel across the land of these heathens carrying his staff *(baculum)* or other well known symbols they are treated respectfully by the princes, aristocrats, and laymen alike" (Dusburg III, 5 in SRP).

The idea of a Prussian Rome became very popular in the following centuries.[4] What was probably just a simile used by the chronicler to give an explanation for the German occupation (i.e. the children of Belial are so well organised that they even have a Rome and a Pope), was first coloured and expanded by S. Grunau (Grunau 1529/I, 62 ff.). S. Grunau himself did not (or not always) adopt the name Romava from P. Dusburg, because in an attempt to make his readers believe he spoke Prussian he pretentiously translated it as Rickoyto–Rikoyoto (< Pr. *rijki* 'empire', *rikijs* 'ruler' + *-ote* place name derivator). There is a magnificent evergreen oak tree in the centre of Rickoyto. The trunk is divided into three equal parts and the idols of the three gods, Patollo, Patrimpo, and Perkuno look out from them.

---

[3] Etymologically it is usually brought into contact with the words for 'temple' OEng. *ealk*, Old Saxon *alhs* (cf. Ger. Allstedt, Alsberg, Alsfeld, Alsheim). V. Toporov ventures an interesting assumption when he discovers the 'crooked, curvy' meaning in the names of natural objects and magical symbols (cf. Pruss. *alkunis*, Lith. *alkūnė* 'elbow', Latv. *elks* 'bend') for which there are also other examples among which the best known is *krive* 'pagan priest' < *kreivs* 'crooked' (Toporov 1975–90/I, 74 and II, 24).

[4] In Lithuanian it comes up in the forms of Romuva, Romove, Romava. Some attempt to bring the name in connection with the Latv. *rams*, Lith. *romus* 'gentle, peaceful', even though P. Dusburg clearly stated that he created the name to resemble the pattern of 'Rome' (Bertuleit 1924, 67).

S. Grunau's tale was polished further in the late sixteenth century by M. Stryjkowski, who interpreted the name Romove as 'new Rome' (*nowy Rzym = Romnowe*) just like Constantine the Great who renamed Byzantium as *Roma nova* (Stryjkowski 1582/I, 49).

The Dusburg–Stryjkowski name and the Grunau–Stryjkowski imagery lived on in the works of Vijūkas-Kojelavičius (Vijūkas-Kojalavičius 1650–1669, 60), and then in the works of the romantic writers of the nineteenth century. Romava–Romova–Romuva thus became an integral part of the archaised Prussian tradition, and especially the Lithuanian 'national' tradition which was blended with Prussian traditions without any compunction whatsoever, only to enter the twentieth-century encyclopaedias and textbooks.

The search for Romova, which mainly involved attempts to find place names close to each other and with the stems *ram-, rom-,* and *kriv-* began as early as the sixteenth century. Despite great efforts, nothing was found between Nadruva and Warmia, or Natanga and Sembia.[5]

8.2.2. The sanctuary of Vilnius
(The legends of Šventaragis and Gediminas)

It is natural that Romova cannot be found, since it is difficult to imagine that the Prussians living in a loose tribal federation of freemen would have needed an ideological centre. The Lithuanians on the other hand, working towards the foundation of a state, did need such a centre, thus it is hardly surprising that probably the only pagan sanctuary of the Balts was in Vilnius.[6]

Raising temples is not typical of polydoxy which characterises all three Baltic peoples. Latvians, Prussians, and Lithuanians fitted into the mediaeval world order in different ways and they progressed in different directions, latest from the twelfth–thirteenth centuries, so different things would be found in each case.

---

[5] For this cf. R. Batūra in P. Dusburg 1985, 355 ff. In 1994 in our last conversation, my friend N. Vėlius explained this with the unverifiable suspicion that, similarly to the case of the Lithuanian Grand Dukes' seat not being determined until the legendary foundation of Vilnius in 1323 (and even a bit afterwards), Romova was also a wandering sanctuary. It developed somewhere in Scandinavia, then drew south- and westward, expanding to be a religious centre of ever varying settlements. Of course nothing remained of it since it was built of wood (a circumstance which indeed one must never forget) (discussed at J. Voigt 1827–39/1, 705; also elaborated in Vėlius 1983, 223).

[6] Of course, not as the Lithuanian 'counterpart' of the West Baltic Romova, as G. Beresnevičius believes when trying to give everybody their fair share (Beresnevičius 1996, 122). (But then where are the poor Latvians? Do they get no sanctuary? Or should they be happy with their 6000 year old folk-songs?)

THE LEGENDS OF ŠVENTARAGIS AND GEDIMINAS. The statement that the sanctuary in Vilnius existed can be based on, among other things, the two intertwined legends of the founding and early history of the town. Both legends were compiled, and were probably conceived in the sixteenth century. They appeared in Western Russian (Lithuanian) yearbooks,[7] and in their most comprehensive form in the Stryjkowski Chronicle (Stryjkowski 1582/I, 308–311, 369–373).

The culture-hero of the first cycle is the Grand Duke Šventaragis (Svintorog, Swintoroh)[8] who, according to the chronicles, died in 1271. The prince ordered his son Gerimundas (Skirmont, Germont) to cremate him on the 'cape' where the small river Vilnia (Vilna, Wilna) meets the river Neris (Velja, Wilia), where from then on all princes were to be cremated and not in the place of their death. His wish was fulfilled (although that we only know from Stryjkowski), and Gerimundas cremated his father on a pyre at the desired spot (which was then named Šventaragis valley), armed and attired in his finest regalia, along with his dogs, hawks, hunting eagles, horses, and his favourite servant or lover. During the ceremony the noblemen and young herdsmen threw claws of bears and lynx into the fire so that the deceased could use them on judgement day to help him on the steep path to the top of the mountain where god sits on his throne. Germont raised a pagan sanctuary in this place, where the fire was fed by oak and kept lit all the time by priests and seers, *kapłani i worożbity*, in honour of Perkūnas, 'the god of thunder, lightning, and fire'. This necropolis was used until the Jagiello period when the Lithuanians converted to Christianity.

The Grand Duke Gediminas, the hero of the other related legend, is a historical figure. Once, after he had moved from Kernavė to Trakai, the new capital he had founded, he went hunting. At nightfall he fell asleep in the Šventaragis Field and dreamt he saw an enormous wolf dressed in armour standing in the place where the rivers Vilnia and Neris meet in the Crooked Valley (*Krzywa dolina*, the same stem as *krive*, the name of the pagan priest). A hundred wolves were howling inside the big wolf. The Grand Duke's pagan bishop, Lizdeika or in other words his 'Krive Krywejta', interpreted the dream as: "The iron wolf means that an enormous castle, your capital will stand here. The hundred wolves mean that it will be famous all over the world." The next day Gediminas began to raise two castles, the Lower Castle in the Šventaragis Field and one on the Crooked Hill, and called them both Vilnius. According to V. Toporov, the hill is a Krive hill (Toporov

---

[7] For the Russian original with variations see Toporov 1980, 16, 40). For their summary in the *Bykhovets Chronicle* see Lithuania's Chronicles 60, 71.

[8] I shall give the personal and place names translated into Lithuanian, and their Russian and Polish originals in parentheses.

1980).[9] Lizdeika was the son of a *krive krivaitis*. In another version of the legend he was an abandoned baby found by Gediminas in an eagle's nest in the forest, hence the name, Lith. *lizdas* 'nest'.

Apart from the two legends there are other documents of a more historical kind that prove the existence of sanctuary(-ies) in Vilnius.

Two sacred houses, *domos sacras*, are mentioned by Wigand von Marburg who took part in the German crusaders' campaign against Vilnius in 1394 (Mierzyński 1892–96/II, 117). One of the houses protected the sacred fire from the rain, snow and other elements, the other served as the priest's house.

The most detailed description comes from J. Długosz, who gave an account, almost a hundred years after the event, of how the new Polish King Władysław Jagiello converted Lithuania. He adopts the description of the pagan beliefs from Aeneas Silvius Piccolomini: "The reluctant barbarians claimed that it would be not only evil and pointless to deny their gods (the most important of which are fire, believed to be eternal and kept alive by their priests day and night, the forests, which were believed to be particularly sacred, and vipers and other snakes), but it would also bring destruction on them. In Vilnius, the most important city of this nation, King Władysław ordered the eternal fire (kept alive by a priest, called a *znicz* in their own language, who gives mendacious answers received from the gods to those who turn to him about their future), to be extinguished in front of the eyes of barbarians. He also ordered the temples and altars where the barbarians placed their sacrifices to be destroyed, and all the snakes and other crawling creatures that used to serve as protecting gods in every home to be killed... King Władysław erected a church in honour of the Holy Trinity and named it after Stanisław, the famous bishop and martyr... and he erected the great altar in the place where the pagans' eternal fire had burnt before, so that everyone could see the sins of the pagans." J. Długosz also reports on the Papal Bull of Pope Urban VI issued in the same year in which the Pope thanks the king, "in destroying the sanctuaries of the demons that misled their poor souls you have erected the Almighty's sanctuaries in their place".

In the next chapter, where he writes about the Lithuanians' Roman origin, J. Długosz superimposes the typical *interpretatio classica* onto the typical *inter-*

---

[9] In his study, referred to several times, V. Toporov considers the Šventaragis legend a link in the chain between the mythologised history of Lithuania and its 'historical history'. Šventaragis ('sacred cape, horn') is connected to Perkūnas "whose attribute was the horn [cf. Perkūnas with a horn, the horned beasts of Perkūnas, or place names of the Perkūnragis 'Perkūnas cape, horn' type]. It can be presumed that there is a connection between Šventaragis as the founder of terrestrial traditions (below, in the valley) and Perkūnas above (in the mountain or in the sky), and that Šventaragis is similar to Perkūnas or serves the lightening thrower. The buzzard, horse, and dog cremated together with him are the determiners of the three zones of the cosmos (sky, earth, underworld), zones which became accessible for Šventaragis after his death" (Tokarev 1988/I, 378).

pretatio christiana. "Worshipping the same gods and carrying out the same
ceremonies as the Romans did when they lived in the sins of paganism, they
worship *Vulcan* in the fire, *Jupiter* in the thunderbolt, *Diana* in the forests and
Aesculapius in the vipers and other snakes. In their principal towns (*in civitatibus
principalibus,* that is in more than one place!) they keep the fire alive... Worshipping Jupiter in the form of thunder they call him Perkūnas the Striker in their
own language." (For the Latin text, including the Lithuanian translation, see
Dainauskas 1991, 144–160.)[10]

The name of Perkūnas and the pagan temple in Vilnius were explicitly linked for
the first time a hundred years later by M. Stryjkowski. He heaped together all the
sources and non-sources (including Długosz), and gave the legends of Šventaragis
and the town founder Gediminas a literary form (or rather invented it himself).

The next stage was a compilation written in German. T. Narbutt, the great forger
(1835, 208 ff.), first published the part on the sanctuary of Perkūnas in Polish. He
was the person who, on the basis of the initials J. F. R. on the manuscript attributed
it to J. F. Rivius (1673–1730/37) who graduated from the University of Tartu.
Rivius 'translated' the lost sixteenth-century history of Lithuania by A. (Miele-
sius) Rotundus from Vilnius from the original Latin into German.[11] According to
Rivius-Rotundus, the stone-built, square, towered sanctuary with the statue of
Perkūnas was founded in 1285. However, the nineteenth-century historians,
T. Narbutt, S. Daukantas, and J. Kraszewski, dated it 20 years earlier. The earlier
date is more probable because it allows a link between the foundation of the temple
and the apostasy of Mindaugas (1261). The temple could have been built by the
king himself or, following his assassination in 1263, by his pagan opposition. In
either case the new temple was built on the foundations of the original Catholic
Church built by Mindaugas at the time of his baptism. The earlier date is also
easier to accept as it explains why it was necessary to establish a religious centre
in the second half of the thirteenth century. At that time the only possible reason
was negative and external, as a bastion *against* Christianity. Contrary to the
opinion of the majority of Baltic mythologists, there could not have been a positive
and internal motive rising at the level of polydoxy–prototheism. What happened
here is very similar to the situation of the Slavs living in the region of northern
Elbe and in Western Pomerania. They accepted Christianity very early, the first
Obodrit princes were baptised in 821 (Herrmann 1972, 254). Even so, the exten-

---

[10] The Polish chronicler not only had no idea about the Lithuanian gods, but as A. Brückner
and H. Łowmiański proved, point by point, the Polish pantheon was also an invention of his
based on raw materials gathered from here and there (Brückner, 1918, 83–84; 1924, 223 ff.;
Łowmiański 1979, 214 ff.; 1984, 677).

[11] The manuscript of the work is not Narbutt's creation, it is still in the Academic Library
of Vilnius (Kitkauskas 1989, 16). More recently Dubonis proved beyond doubt that J. F. Rivius
did not exist, the figure is Narbutt's invention, along with his biography and it is almost certain
that the manuscript is also the result of his patriotic enthusiasm (Dubonis 1997).

sive polytheism and the corresponding cult only appeared later (unlike the temples of Svantevit in Radogost and Arkona, demolished by the Danish in 1186) from the second half of the tenth century, and especially in the eleventh–twelfth centuries. They were formed secondarily to counter the threat of German Christianity.[12] Similarly, the temple of Perkūnas in Vilnius was built as a reaction to the existence of Christian churches, both Catholic and Orthodox, certainly by the late thirteenth century.[13]

I would like to refer back to the neatly compiled explanation of V. Toporov (and in general other mythologists) which relates dry facts to mythical ancient times. The facts state that King Mindaugas founded a Catholic church in the mid-thirteenth century which was later converted into a temple to Perkūnas, either by Mindaugas himself, or by one of his successors. These events were commemorated in two legends from the late sixteenth century. The historical event of founding the church was the consequence of concurrent sociological factors, i.e. the chroniclers of the sixteenth century wanted to prove the aristocratic origins of Lithuanian kings and that Vilnius was not only an ancient political, but also a religious centre. Instead V. Toporov links it with the fundamental myth of the fight between Perkūnas ("according to Dumézil's theory Gediminas was his epic form") and death (represented by the snake). This myth goes back to the ancient Indo-European times and worked as a script across the centuries (Toporov 1980, 45).

One example that illustrates the difference between historical and mythological explanations is that of Šventaragis. The culture-hero first appears in the sixteenth-century western Russian chronicles already mentioned. From this V. Toporov concludes that the origin of the name (and the whole legend) was Šventaragis Valley, which never appeared again under this name (Toporov 1980, 28). Why would a part of the future Vilnius region be called the Sacred Cape? V. Toporov explains that the pagan Lithuanians called it that because the temple of Perkūnas stood there (or the other way round, they erected the temple here because it was a sacred place). The only problem is that 'sacred' is a word created by Christianity. The word sanctus (which is of course equivalent to all the following: first, in the late sixteenth century, Lith. šventas, Latv. svinīgs 'festive', Pruss. swent, Polish święty, Russ. svyatoy 'sacred', and so on) was originally used to describe a place reserved for gods which was free of profane sanctio 'sanctions' (Pauly–Wissowa's..., 1920/II/2, 2247). We cannot determine when the word took on its Christian meaning even in the case of the Romans. We have no way of answering the question of what the pagan Lithuanians called the things that were later referred to as sacred by the Christians, or if the same things were treated as sacred.

[12] For more details see Łowmiański 1976, 1979, 166–202, 399–401.

[13] For this reason it is unjustified, or rather is only justified through an, otherwise fair, bias towards Gediminas, that S. C. Rowell puts the time of the reversion from this Christian church to pagan temple to the era of the Grand Duke, that is the early fourteenth century.

A more down-to-earth view explains that the name Šventaragis (of both the prince and the valley), which constitutes the basis of the whole pagan cult, was invented, or rather translated by the sixteenth-century chroniclers. They translated it either from the legends of the foundation of Rome, or from Russian following the pattern of the numerous *Svyatoy Nos* 'sacred cape' place names (cf. Vasmer 1953–58/II, 598).

Although a lighthearted handling of facts was not alien to either Długosz or Narbutt, in 1984–1985 their accounts of the temple of Perkūnas proved indisputably true, when archaeologists started to uncover the remains of a temple, built in 1387 and burnt down in 1419, under and around an eighteenth-century cathedral. The ruins of an open, square-shaped pagan temple with a sacrificial altar in the centre was found first. Underneath that lay the remains of a three winged mid-thirteenth-century transitional Romanesque–Gothic style church which had been ruined by fire.[14]

8.3. Priests

In contrast to the carved images and especially in the sanctuaries which depended on the economic and technical background, 'priests' or some kind of spiritual leaders can presumably be found in every human society. The question is what role they played in the life of the Baltic societies. The sources give a great deal of information regarding this matter.

8.3.1. Sicco

The definition of the word *sicco*, first mentioned in the Adalbert biographies, which offer some information about the religious life of the Prussians, is revealing. It could be a proper name, however, it is more likely to refer to a position, either of a travelling priest or, more probably, a man of knowledge. In the biography

[14] N. Kitkauskas, one of the leaders of the excavations, gave accounts of all this in his professional and richly illustrated book (see Kitkauskas 1989). M. Gimbutienė's account presents a striking example of how much the information filtered through the enthusiasm of the arche-mythologist patriot can differ from the dry and factual description of the archaeologist. Gimbutienė spent five days in Vilnius in 1986 and visited the excavations. On her return to Chicago she told the Chicago Lithuanians that "among the Stone Age settlements and later temples there is a cultural stratum with early Lithuanian origins from the Iron Ages with characteristic Corded-Ware Pottery. Then begin the pagan sanctuaries, one on top of the other... On the site of today's cathedral there has been a religious centre for several hundred centuries, at least from the ninth century if not earlier. Beside that was the sacred grove, the grove of Šventaragis" [and so on and so forth] (Gimbutas 1987).

written by Canaparius he is *"sacerdos idolorum et dux conjuratae cohortis"* [the priest of idols (demons) and the leader of the raging masses]. In Bruno of Querfurt's version the sicco is described as *"dux et magister nefariae cohortis"*, [the leader and teacher of the unholy masses] (Mierzyński 1892–96/I, 40, 43). It is obvious that around 1000 AD the secular and religious powers were not yet separated in Prussian society. Consequently, Z. Ritoók's definition of the *demiurgos* fits the sicco as well: "Originally they were the chiefs of the clans that pursued specialised occupations and sought special knowledge. These occupations were therefore connected with the cult or at least possessed cultic undertones" (Ritoók 1973, 74).

8.3.2. The tuliss and the ligash

The indisputably authentic document from 250 years later offers the first detailed account of Prussian life and draws a picture of a more sophisticated division of power. In 1249, one year after the first great Prussian uprising, a peace treaty was signed in Chrystburg (today's Polish Dzierzgoń) by the Teutonic Order and the Prussians, mediated by J. von Lüttich the papal legate. It stated that "the newly baptised idol worshippers (*neophytes*) promise God, the Roman Church and the brothers that neither they nor their children shall conduct the following pagan customs: they shall not cremate nor bury their dead together with their horses, people, arms, clothes or any other treasures. On the contrary, they promise that according to Christian customs they will bury the dead in the cemetery and not in any place outside. They also promise not to offer sacrifices to the idol Churche that they were accustomed to make and erect and worship as a god once a year at the harvest time. Similarly, they will not sacrifice to any other gods, as those created neither the sky nor the earth. Instead they shall remain in the faith of Our Lord Jesus Christ and the Catholic Church, and shall act in humble obedience to the Roman Church. They promise to keep neither tulisses nor ligashes any more." The pl. nom. *-ones* ending is obviously the Latinised version of the original Baltic words: *non habebunt de cetero Tulissones vel Ligaschones*. Furthermore, "as they (the tuliss and ligash) are well known lying hypocrites (*histriones*[15]) and fully

---

[15] The Prussian priests emerged in connection with burial customs, therefore the *histriones* could be those actors, barnstormers, and tricksters who took part in the pagan death rituals of the Middle Ages, even conducted them, or played a lead role. For example the Czech Cosmas reports in the *Chronica Bohemorum* that the Czech Duke Břetislav banned pagan rites when he came to power, among others those "which semi-pagan villagers held on Pentecost Tuesday or Wednesday, when in a pagan way they organised *scenas* (*scenae*) on double or triple cross roads for the rest of the souls, etc." The various translators and interpreters explained the *scena* in different ways: Ger. *feierliche Aufzüge, theatrum* (L. Niederle); Czech *tryzna* 'death feast', *hry* 'plays'; Polish *korowody* 'line dance', *widowisko* 'spectacle', *igrzyska* 'plays'. A. Brück-

deserve the agonies of hell as punishment for their sins. They act as pagan priests at funerals (*quasi gentilium sacerdotes in exequiis*), they predict the good and the bad,[16] and praise the deceased for the theft, robbery and other trespasses and sins committed in their lifetimes. They turn their eyes to the sky and screech their lies, and claim that they see the deceased flying in the sky on horseback adorned in shining armour, with a hunting eagle on their arm, galloping to the other world in the company of great horde."

These two names appear again in a slightly distorted form in another German source, *Preussische Schaubühne oder Deliciae Prussicae*. It was finished in 1703 by M. Praetorius, originally a Lutheran priest from Lithuania Minor who later converted to Catholicism, creating a major scandal. He mentions the following different kinds of Prussian priests (*Scribenten*): "*Weydenlutt* [also known as *vajdelot*, to be discussed later], *Priestern-Zygenotten, Tillusseji* or *Tillusunei, Lingussunei, Wurszkaitei, Burtonei*" (Mannhardt 1936, 549).

A. Mierzyński considers the tuliss and ligash to have been a priest with the same function. The dual naming springs from the Prussians who signed the Peace Treaty representing various regions, such as Pomezania, Warmia, and Natanga, where "the priests were called tuliss by some and ligash by others" (Mierzyński 1892–96/I, 96).[17] Their function was to see the soul of the dead and thus report to the relatives if the soul had easily left the body. To prove this, A. Mierzyński cites P. Dusburg who reports that when the krive (the Prussian chief priest) was asked by the relatives of the dead "if he had seen anybody visiting their house that night, the priest described in detail the clothes, the arms, the horses and the company (*familia*) of the deceased without any hesitation, and for greater certainty he showed the relatives the marks left on the doorframe by the spear or other weapon of the deceased" (Dusburg III, 5). This report, as well as the description of the

---

ner, following L. Niederle, writes that there was a play during the death feast which had symbolic characters playing, and the heart of which was a battle scene, the actual *tryzna* which, for this reason, V. Toporov rightly connects to the Czech word *trýzeň* 'agony' (Toporov 1990, 41). In the light of the *histriones* of the peace contract of Chrystburg these translations connecting the burial with a play are justified, and S. Urbańczyk seems not to be right in his otherwise very appealing down-to-earth anti-fraud stance, when he tries to translate the above cited passage as "scenes were made up" where *scenae budki* would be 'store, shed, barn'.

Wulfstan's cited account is evidence for the intertwining of burial and plays about the horse races for distributing the inheritance as if they were legal acts that occurred at burials of the Esti who by then certainly had become Prussian.

[16] E. Šturms and P. Pakarklis give an unjustified translation of this as "bad is said to be good" (Šturms 1938, 104; Pakarklis 1948, 240).

[17] W. Mannhardt also considers the two words to be the same, but in different languages. The First one is Vend (i.e. Slavic) and would correspond to the Polish *tuliczyna* 'dirge' (< *tolić*, *tulić* 'to give a big hug, to comfort'), while the second would mean the same in Prussian (Mannhardt 1936, 45).

priests who could see the dead while in trance in the Treaty of Chrystburg a century earlier, reminds M. Eliade, with good reason, of the shamans of Asia, "the 'visionary' bards who led the souls of the dead to the other world at the end of the funeral 'banquet'" (Eliade 1994–96/III, 36).

The survival of the elements of shamanism is crucial as another pagan priest, Lizdeika, from the legend of the foundation of Vilnius, can be characterised with shamanistic motifs, "being an outcast, the future shaman is sitting in an eagle's nest in the shaman tree, falling into a trance, and especially has the ability to read dreams" (Toporov 1980, 62).

The widely debated etymology of the two names also supports the theory that these people were not priests in the Catholic sense of the word, i.e. sacrificing to the gods in the temple, but the successors of those shamans who were much more concerned with the dead, the cremation, and the afterworld. Therefore they were only 'quasi-priests'. So much so, that the document does not mention them in connection with Churche or other gods which further on, in dealing with the baptism of the pagans, explicitly states that the Prussians "did not have priests or temples for a long time". That is, the tuliss and ligash are not categorised as priests!

The meaning of tuliss was probably 'dirge, singer, poet', hence the Latin expression *histriones*, cf. Pruss. *tuldisnan* 'joy', Old Icelandic *tulr* 'poet', and OEngl. *tyle* 'orator at festivities'. The last word can be related to the Slavic *tьlk*, the Russ. *tolk* 'meaning, opinion', from which > Latv. *tulks*, Lith. *tulkas* 'interpreter' (Būga, 1920–22, 92; 1918, 633–634). Although A. Brückner incorrectly derives the name from the Pruss. *tulan* 'many' still he reaches the same, correct, conclusion: *tuliss* refers to the singer who performs at the burial feasts, thus spreading and multiplying the fame of the deceased (Brückner 1904, 44).

V. Toporov writes of the second type of priests: "As a result of the 1249 Peace Treaty the Prussians accepted a local version of the Christianised legal and judicial system. It proscribed who was innocent and who was guilty, what was right and wrong, and replaced the ligash who had been entrusted with this function and had practised it at least at funerals until the Treaty, and to some extent afterwards as well. Consequently the ligash could be seen as a kind of judge-priest, who determined the status of the deceased in the after-world according to his position on the scale of right and wrong. They took part in the rituals only after the tuliss had performed his duties." In accordance with this it is connected with the following words: Pruss. *ligint, leygenton, liginton* 'foretell, determine somebody's fate', *lijgan* 'sentence' and *ligan* 'court' which, according to K. Būga, all go back to the Common Baltic stem **ligas* which means 'equal' (Būga 1907–10, 111).[18]

___

[18] Other suggestions were made, among which the Lith. *liga* 'illness' > *ligas* 'spell caster, sorcerer' (e.g. Bertuleit 1924, 92), but that does not fit the context: a doctor to the dead is like an enema. The Estonian liga 'illness' word could as rightfully be connected here, since the Prussians are the inheritors of the mixed tribe of the Aestii (Venedic, Germanic, Baltic, Finnic groups).

8.3.3. The sovij
(an addition to the *Malalas Chronicle*)

This story, conceived at almost the same time as the Treaty of Chrystburg is the only myth, or mythical story of the Baltic people. Not only does it describe a type of burial, popular among the Lithuanians, which is similar to the burials of the Prussians, but it also describes its origin and the culture-hero who first introduced it.

The story is an addition to *Chronographia* by I. Malalas of Antioch (ca. 491–578) translated from the Syrian into Church Slavic. The original *Chronographia*, a chronicle of the world, is the first and one of the most influential products of popular Byzantine history writing. It sets out from the creation of the world and continues with the stories of Adam, Jesus, the Romans, Ancient Greece and Alexander the Great, and finishes with the account of Byzantine history until 565 AD at the death of Emperor Justinian, the time when it was written (Hadzisz 1974, 34).[19]

The Slavic translation, which remained only in a later fragmented Russian translated edition, was written in the tenth–twelfth century, possibly in Western Russia. M. Weingart, who has carried out the most detailed research into it, suggests that the Slavic translation was made in Bulgaria and was extremely popular among the Bulgars, Serbs, and East Slavs, and was likely to have influenced the author of the *Nestor Chronicle* (Weingart 1922, 42).

Either the original Church Slavic text, or a copy of the Russian translation was translated (copied) into Russian and a story was inserted into the text by the translator (copier), many think in 1261. M. Weingart posits, in my view correctly, that the translation originated in Lithuania in 1262 (however, it is demonstrable that this took place in the Duchy of Halicz–Volhynia, which at that time was briefly a kingdom). Like the Syrian chronicle and the Church Slavic–Russian translation, the manuscript of this addition (and perhaps also the insertion concerning Slavic gods written concurrently or somewhat earlier) was also lost and there are only two copies extant: a shorter version kept in Moscow known as the Muscovite or archival manuscript, which was probably written in Southern Russia, possibly in Halicz–Volhynia, in the early fifteenth century, and the longer version, the so-called Vilnius manuscript (originating from the monastery of Suprasl), which the majority of scholars believe to have been composed in sixteenth-century Lithu-

---

[19] The eighteen-volume work by Malalas did not survive, only one single complete manuscript remained of a shortened extract, from the eleventh century (Moravcsik 1938, 191).
The Chronographia was a sort of *Reader's Digest* in the Middle Ages. For Malalas "the past is an anecdote grab-bag, where Paris is a scholar and a panegyrist to Venus" (Grabowicz 1981, 23).

ania. M. Weingart, however, dates it to the thirteenth century along with the original (Weingart 1922, 29).[20]

The archival manuscript describes the story as *An account of the straying of the pagans who called Sovij a god*. The title of the Vilnius manuscript is *About the straying of the pagans in our country: A story told about pagans straying as it happened in our Lithuania*. The copier's distance from the story indicates that the original comes from another country. On the margin there is another note written in the sixteenth century, or even later by another person: "This is how the pagans stray in our Lithuania, too. This evil went on until Vytautas, because his wife was cremated in Iryakola and after that they gave up the custom of cremation."

"Sovij was (a) man. He killed a (magic) boar. [The words *diviy vepr* could as easily refer to a wild boar as a magic boar.] He took out the boar's nine spleens and gave them to the ones who were born to him to roast them. [In the Vilnius version, which often interprets the text, the part "to the ones born to him" reads as "to his children"]. When they ate them, [Sovij] became angry with the ones who were born to him. He tried to go down into hell. He could not pass the eight gates but at the ninth he achieved what he wanted with some help from the one who was born to him, that is his son. [Here the Vilnius version adds, "who showed him the way."] When his brothers got angry with him [the son], he asked their permission to leave and went to look for his father and he went down to hell. After he and his father had dinner, he prepared the bedding for his father and buried him in the ground. In the morning when he [the father] woke up he [the son] asked him if he had rested well. The father sighed, oh! worms and crawling creatures (toads) nibbled me. The following day he made dinner for his father once more, prepared his bedding in a tree (in the trunk of a tree) and put him to sleep. Next day he asked him again if he had slept well and the father answered, it felt as if a lot of bees and mosquitoes bit me, oh! I had slept so badly. The following day he [the son] lit a fire and threw him [the father] into it. Next day he asked him if he had slept well. He answered that he had slept as soundly as a child in the cot.

Oh, great evil straying that was brought to the Lithuanian, the Jatvingian, the Prussian, the Jem [häme, a Balto–Finn tribe], the Liv and many other tongues [tribes] which are called Sovitsa who, believing that Sovij, who lived at the time of Abimelek leads their souls to hell, and they burn the bodies of their dead on the pyre like Achilles, Eant, and other Hellens.

This straying was introduced to them by Sovij. [In the Vilnius version it reads as "This straying of Sovij was introduced" (*Siyu prelestъ Sovii*, the possessive adjectival structure is in the accusative. This is the most significant difference between the two versions.] He ordered them to offer sacrifices to the loathsome

---

[20] For its original and Polish translation see Mierzyński 1892–96/I, 127 ff., for German see Mannhardt 1936, 57 ff., for the Lithuanian translation see Greimas 1990, 355 ff. (from the ink of B. Savukynas and J. Tumelis).

(false) gods, Andaj and Perkun, that is to the thunder and Zhvoruna the bitch and to Teljavel the blacksmith who forged the sun that shines on the earth and threw it into the sky. This loathsome straying came to them from the Hellens. It had been 3000 and 400 and 40 and 6 years from the time of the Abimelek and of the several clans of the loathsome Sovij till the year when I started writing this book."

What is the most striking about the story when reading it for the first time is just how badly it is told, verging on the incomprehensible. So it is probably not pointless to summarise, starting at the end, what it is about.

Essentially, it describes the origin of cremation among the peoples referred to under the term of Sovitsa. This word was derived in a similar way to *cirillitsa*, which in Rowell's words, "this Sovitsa or 'Sovidom' is almost the inverse of Christendom" (Rowell 1994, 130). Based on the phrase in the Vilnius version "straying of Sovij" I venture to translate it as 'Sovij-people', 'Sovij-clans'. Sovij lived at the time of Abimelek[21] and he served as the leader of souls in the Sovij tribes. These tribes still cremate their dead in a sinful and loathsome way and offer sacrifices to their gods, listed above.[22] They adopted their sinful customs from the Hellens. (In Byzantium the naming of the Hellens "equalled 'pagans' in the Christian era"—Moravcsik 1966, 44. It also meant 'barbarian, pagan, Tartar' besides 'Greek' in the Church Slavic–Old Russian–Vasmer 1953–58/I, 397.)[23]

The first part of the story tells us that this sinful tradition started when the sons of a man (called Sovij, a lost and/or ambitious generation) disturbed the accustomed order and ate the funeral feast, the nine spleens of the wild boar, which are essential for passing through the nine gates of hell. As a result of this, the soul leading father could only rely on one of his sons for help (who might have been the youngest and most beloved in accordance with the rules of folk-tales) to enter the other world (which the chronicler refers to as hell because it concerned pagans). The son who followed his father tried to bury him three times. First in the ground.[24] Secondly he hung him on a tree, but the father did not like it. He only found peace when his son threw him onto the fire and burnt his body.

---

[21] The Philistine king of the Old Testament was the contemporary of Abraham the patriarch (cf. Genesis, 20–26).

[22] For the issue of the god names along with the Churche of the Treaty of Chrystburg see Part Four, Subchapter 7.3.2.

[23] The 1262 anthology could mark the pagans collectively as Hellens, because the Greek word also had a meaning of 'Jewish, a Jew speaking Greek' (Chantraine 1968, 340), and the entire *Malalas Chronicle* concerns Jewish history (hence the Old Testament calendar). It was even referred to as Y*udeyskiy khronograf XIII veka* [A thirteenth-century Jewish chronograph] (Weingart 1922, 43).

[24] This is the point where a number of authorities refer to Tacitus who wrote that the Suebi "worship the mother of the gods; as an emblem of that superstition they wear the figures of wild boars" (Tacitus 45): nineteenth-century comparative historians of religion and myth researchers; modern neo-comparativists and neo-mythologists, for example V. Toporov who

If we examine the text on its own we find several contradictions. The most important of these is that Sovij, the father, the leader of souls, in spite of living at the time of Abimelek (if we accept the above mentioned possessive adjectival structure, which is not in nominative in the Vilnius version) he did not do anything. Everything was done to him, he was a passive rather than active, that is only the object and not the subject of these events, although he was a soul leader he did not lead. The person who reforms the burial customs is the son who crosses the border between this and the other world as if he was a leader of souls, just like his father. But even if we consider the son(s) as the follower(s) of the new customs and the father as the follower of the old, then why did the father reject the first two funeral rites.

There are two explanations to resolve these contradictions that do not exclude one another.

One, already implied, is that not only Sovitsa, but also Sovij, must be regarded as a collective noun and not a personal name. They are names of the clan of soul leaders where both the father and his sons belong, where there was religious reform, but they were not named after this reform, or the cremation. There is a hint as to what or who they were named after, the title that is not connected to the story that follows it, since the story is not about the fact that Sovij was called god. But it is easy to imagine that the clan doing the special duties of soul leading was named after a god called Sovij mentioned in the title (for which there are numerous examples, e.g. the Levites of *The Old Testament*). The author of the insertion reacts to this with the first sentence, stating the 'ideologically correct view' "Sovij was (a) man."[25]

The etymology of the name has been widely examined since the nineteenth century. It was originated from the southern Arabic word *Sobi*, from the Arameus *Sabis* (since Malalas was Syrian) and naturally, mostly from the Lithuanian. V. Toporov first derived it from the IE. *saue- 'sun' stem (linking it with Svarog, the Slavic sun god) (Toporov 1966, 148). Later (following A. J. Greimas' view, published in 1979 connecting Sabis, the god of fire worshippers, still extant in Iran, to the word šova 'hearth'), V. Toporov traced it to *šovej(a)s, sovej(a)s 'pushing, moving' which is < šauti 'to put something (a corpse, bread) to a certain place (fire, hearth) (Toporov 1984a; Greimas 1990, 369). N. Vėlius derives it from the sav- 'own' stem, and from the compound word sav + ejis 'self-moving,

---

believes in the preconception of Indo-European origin of myths (Toporov 1966); following him G. Beresnevičius who offers many excellent observations and analyses among the furor of comparing everything with everything (Beresnevičius 1990, 1992, 1995), claiming that the "wild boar belongs to the semantic field of Mother Earth" (Beresnevičius 1990, 79), and of course burial in the ground even more so.

[25] A. J. Greimas, while unjustifiably pointing out that Sovij was a god, overexalts the thought and posits that "he was not only a soul leader but also a religious reformer, the Lithuanian Zoroaster" (Greimas 1990, 375).

self-walking' connected to it, because "Sovij found the way to the other world by himself" [sic!] (Vėlius 1986, 20; Beresnevičius 1990, 75). In one of his later books Beresnevičius reverted to the explanation that was first raised by A. Mierzyński. This explanation supported by historical facts, seems most plausible. In his chronicle of Poland, Bogufal, the Bishop of Poznań mentions a tribe that is likely to be Lithuanian, the *Scovitas* or *Scovas* between the Jatvingians and the Prussians, neighbouring the Polish and the Russians. The name of this clan of the Sovij soul leaders or believers in the god Sovij the Russians transferred, albeit temporarily, to other tribes (Beresnevičius 1995, 52; Mierzyński 1892–96/I, 134).

The other, simpler solution to the above mentioned contradictions is to identify the whole story with the initiation ceremony of the shamans. During this ceremony the prospective shaman dies a ritual death, descends to the underworld, to hell where he takes part in his own dismemberment, witnesses the demons decapitating him, gouge out his eyes, and so forth (Eliade 1994–96/III, 14–15). The tree burial, which the copier was so unfamiliar with that he corrected tree to a wooden trunk, i.e. coffin in the Vilnius version, though it is well known in shamanism. "A famous shaman is not buried in the ground but hung on a wooden frame called an *aranga*. When the *aranga* decays and collapses three multiplied by three, six, or nine new shamans are incarnated from his bones over time" (Findeisen 1957, 98). Nonetheless, it was also common to hang the corpse not only on an aranga but also in a hollow in a tree or on its branches. It was widespread not only among the Siberian tribes but also among the Lithuanians, as G. Beresnevičius proves with certain motifs found in Lithuanian folk-tales (Beresnevičius 1990, 81). The confusion between the functions of father and sons also loses its significance if we interpret the Sovij story as a shaman initiation ceremony: either because the shaman's qualities can be inherited from father to son, or because the shaman normally takes eight helpers with him when he descends into the nine underworlds.

Whatever the result of a 'close' examination of the Sovij name and story might be (which only appears on this one solitary occasion) it must be treated with skepticism. Its author was neither a pre-historian nor a mythologist, and what is more, not even motivated by the desire to entertain, as was Malalas, the author of the main body of the text, the chronograph anthology. For this reason it is easy to imagine that he made a connection between a name that he came across by accident and a well known shaman initiation ritual. His motivation was not to tell a nice (Lithuanian) myth, but on the contrary, to give anti-Lithuanian ideological fuel to contemporary power struggles.

Events of global significance were taking place in the region at the time (the emergence of German domination in Eastern Europe due to the two Orders; the Tartar threat; the Baltic tribes becoming nations or their assimilation or disappearance, and so on). Some of these were concerning the Duchy of Halicz–Volhynia.

The rise of the area that Hungary and Poland also desired at the beginning of the thirteenth century was the result of Danilo's activities. He was the Prince of

Halicz (deceased 1264) who annexed Volhynia to Halicz in 1245. He converted from Orthodox to Catholic and received a crown from the Pope in 1253, a year earlier than Mindaugas. However, he returned to the Eastern Catholic Church soon afterwards. Lithuania was a rising power at this time and Mindaugas was converted from paganism to Catholicism and then reverted again. To say that Danilo had an ambivalent relationship with Mindaugas' Lithuania is an understatement. The military campaigns alternated against and alongside each other and similarly, intermarriage was followed by massacres of the other's family. Danilo's two sons, Shvarn and Lev (after whom Lwów–L'viv was named), also became Mindaugas' sons-in-law, the former even rose to the throne of Lithuania for a short time. It is very likely that Danilo was involved in the assassination of Mindaugas, and it is definitely true that the people of Halicz, either Lev or Danilo's brother Vasilka, murdered Mindaugas' son, Vaišvilkas in 1267. It was not simply one murder among many but, according to the *Bykhovets Chronicle*, the termination of the Lithuanian dynasty that went back to Palemon the Roman Prince (*The Chronicle of Lithuania*, 59). The periodically antagonistic or cooperative rivalry was accompanied by religious apostasies which often appeared in the guise of inter-generational conflict because it was common that the children of pagan fathers married into Catholic or Orthodox families, or the other way round.

The factors of foreign policy were paralleled by complex internal politics; the best possible example to illustrate this is when Mindaugas was 'appointed' king in 1251. His nephew, Tautvilas (who probably played the chief role in the later assassination of the king and one of whose sisters married Alexander Nevsky of Novgorod and the other Danilo), was the Bishop of Riga, and thus the head of the diocese to which Lithuania belonged. The Pope had to specifically issue a bull to end this connection and the independent Lithuanian diocese was established under the leadership of Bishop Christian who was loyal to Mindaugas (Ivinskis 1956, 50; 1970, 169).

I believe that this is the real context of the Sovij-story (the apostasies that manifested themselves in burial customs, and the conflicts between fathers and sons) and not the Iranian fire worshippers. Furthermore, as the author of the 1262 insertion is almost certainly the same person who wrote two other insertions about Mindaugas' disingenuousness which interrupt Danilo's biography in the *Chronicle of Halicz–Volhynia* (part of the *Ipatiy Compilation of Chronicles*) in 1252 and in 1258. These insertions were written, to put it mildly, under the influence of the leader of Halicz–Volhynia. This can probably be said of the Sovij-story as well.[26]

---

[26] The possibility that the author of the three adages could be the same was already raised in the nineteenth century, and I believe that V. J. Mansikka proved it with indisputable arguments that all three of them sprang from somewhere in Western Russia (Mansikka 1922, 66 ff.). In presenting the history of the debate H. Łowmiański's arguments that express doubt seem forced (Łowmiański 1979, 93).

(The story of a minstrel called Mitus illustrates how strong this influence could be. Mitus refused to sing in praise of Danilo when he occupied Peremisl in 1244. To which Danilo responded by having him quartered between horses—Likhachev 1947, 257.)

Whoever the author of the insertions might be, it is obvious that the Sovij-story is told by an orthodox outsider hostile towards the pagan Lithuanians and the Sovij peoples and definitely not an attempt to create a mythical Lithuanian tradition, as is supposed by our mythologists.

In the ideological struggle between the pagans and the Christians burial versus cremation became the most important criterion. The Sovij-story, the Treaty of Chrystburg, as well as *all* the Christian documents of this era consider cremation to be the greatest pagan sin. The 1252 addition states that "Mindaugas' baptism was disingenuous" because in secret he still sacrificed to his former gods and "burnt the bodies of the dead" (Mierzyński 1892–96/I, 138). Heinricus reports an occasion in 1222 when, after regaining an area from the Germans and the Danes, the Estonians recovered and cremated their dead that had been previously buried in accordance with the Christian customs (Heinricus XXVI, 8).

As V. J. Mansikka emphasises, the two types of funeral themselves are not antagonistic, for centuries the Slavs practised both. Each expresses the ambivalent attitudes of the living towards the dead, the fear and the affection. It is necessary to cremate the body to make sure that it is destroyed, so that it cannot return, but at the same time the 'soul' was kept in an urn. Similarly, the body was put under the ground so that it could not return, which can be ensured by positioning the grave in the midst of water or at crossroads, and by piling earth on top of it, but at the same time food was put on the grave viewed as the home of the deceased.

These two methods probably come into conflict when two cultures meet because burial rituals are the most fundamental cultural tradition of humans and prone to polarisation, i.e. a right and a wrong method. Thus the contrast between the meeting cultures is clearly apparent.[27]

After the encounter between Baltic pagans and Christianity the two funeral rites fell into opposition by the late thirteenth century. "Presumably, some kind of discussion took place about the issues of pagan beliefs and the ideas concerning pagan funeral rites regained their strength" (Toporov 1980, 36). Of course, it can be presumed although it is unlikely that pagan ideologists initiated the discussion.

---

[27] Where Christianity spread sooner, conflict arose sooner, too. A bizarre example for the ideological battles around this issue is the record of an Arabic diplomat from 922. According to which, in the Kievan court a Russian person defended cremation with the following words: "Oh, how stupid you are, you Arabs! You take the person closest to your hearts and put them in the ground, where dust, rotting, and the worms devour them. We, on the other hand, burn them in a trice, and they can reach paradise instantly" (cited in Rybakov 1981, 275).

During the Christian conquests and the crusades beginning with the tenth and eleventh centuries the Baltic peoples encountered situations when people were burnt alive in castles and fortresses for the first time. On the other hand, the inquisition, first aimed at pagan, heretic Cathars and later, from the 1229 Synod of Toulouse widely adopted against all pagans, instituted the jurisdiction of the stake. This way the contrast between pagan and the Christian times and world views gradually boiled down to the cremation–burial opposition. In the words of V. Toporov before the appearance of the Christians the pagans cremated their dead to enable them to resurrect but afterwards they burnt the strangers alive to destroy them for good (Toporov 1990, 40).

Cremation persisted longest among the pagan Lithuanians but it was viewed decreasingly negatively in proportion with the expansion of Christianity. The copier of the Vilnius version of the Sovij-story felt the need to distance himself from it, "in our Lithuania... used to be". What the author of the insertion considered outrageous in 1262 was stated as a matter-of-fact by M. Stryjkowski. "The Lithuanians knew the custom and the method of cremation instead of burial from Palemon and the other Romans who came here... The Romans and others from Italy adopted and preserved it from Aeneas of Troy" (Stryjkowski 1582/II, 311).

8.3.4. Krive

About a hundred years after the Treaty of Chrystburg, P. Dusburg also mentions a Prussian priest, the *krive* who governed from Romova like a pope. A. Mierzyński believed krive to be a proper name, but his theory was convincingly refuted by K. Būga who at the same time agreed with all his other ideas concerning the name (Mierzyński 1892–96/II, 34; Būga 1908–09, 171). His position is that the krive had primarily judicial functions like the tuliss. In the words of Nikolaus von Jeroschin he was *der obriste ewarte*, 'the highest judge' (Jeroschin line 4023).[28] In P. Dusburg the high priest gained his name from the crooked stick that the chronicler mentioned as the most important symbol of his power, and which is still called *krivulė* in Lithuanian (Toporov 1975–90/IV, 196). The etymology of the name is clear: Latv. *krievs*, Lith. *kreivas*, Russ. *krivoy*,[29] Latin *curvus* 'curved, crooked' and Latv. *kreiss*, Lith. *kairus* 'left' (Vasmer 1953–58/I, 663). It is easy to imagine the situation in which the name was given: a Prussian authority in Königsberg is

---

[28] Perhaps it is a coincidence, but perhaps the word is etymologically connected to the Goth *crewe*. About this J. Voigt says that "in the Scandinavian North and everywhere where there were Goths, the word denoted the judge or the person responsible for justice (*den Pfleger der Gerechtigkeit*)" (Voigt 1827–39/1, 152).

[29] The Russian word > *krivich* 'mendacious person' became a tribal name, and from that came the Latv. *krievisks* 'Russian person' (Endzelīns 1899, 81).

trying to explain to P. Dusburg, who does not speak Prussian, who or what this person is, that the Christians in P. Dusburg call 'a pastor and possessing a crosier'.[30]

From P. Dusburg the word was adopted by S. Grunau (who spelt it in various ways: *criwe, criwen, kirwayt, kyrwait, krywo*) and 'improved' using the Greek *kyrie* 'our lord after God, Lord'. According to K. Būga he left out the link word from the expression *crywe adir kyrwaide*, 'krive that is kirvaite' and in this way gained a double name, which was obviously supposed to mean the 'krive of the krives', *sanctus sanctissimus* or *judex judicum* (Grunau 1529/I, 62; Būga 1908–09, 173). Correctly it is Pruss. *criwan/criwon criwo*, Lith. *krivų krivaitis*. This double name was distorted in most varied ways and there were several interpretations in the following centuries. M. Stryjkowski for example reverted it to 'the original Greek' and he got *kyrie kyrieito* (Stryjkowski 1582/I, 49). Using the biblical pattern 'the God of gods' S. Daukantas created *kurėjų kurėjas* 'creator of creators' (Daukantas 1845, 562). V. Toporov posits that the second part of the double name *krive krivaitis* is the diminutive form of the first part, and like the Romulus–Remus pair, krive referred to the high priest who founded the city (cf. *curvum castrum* in Vilnius, which does not mean 'crooked castle' but rather 'krive castle'), while *krivatis* denoted the ruler (Toporov 1980, 63 ff.). V. Toporov extends this analogy to the tale of Stella–Grunau which concerns Widowuto, the last Prussian ruler who reigned in 500 AD and his brother, Bruteni the chief pagan priest. This version was further developed by G. Beresnevičius who thinks that not only the two sixth-century culture heroes Bruteni and Widowuto, but also Gediminas and Lizdeika are pagan priests in the legend of the foundation of Vilnius. Some of the Lithuanian rulers from the thirteenth century onwards who reigned in pairs were the embodiments of the mythological 'divine twins', the Sanskrit Ashvin and the Greek Dioscuros.

Viewing timeless mythological structures as scripts of and explanations for processes leading to a division and centralisation of historically concrete secular and religious powers is reflected in the double name. These flamboyant hypotheses merge and homogenise the history of the eighth-century Latin–Etruscan, thirteenth-sixteenth-century Prussian, and thirteenth-fourteenth-century Lithuanian societies. It is exactly the names that show how extensive the differences were even between the last two.

As for the *krive krivaitis*, invented by S. Grunau, some remnants of the double function of priests were probably still extant in the sixteenth century. S. Grunau belonged to that most dangerous kind of prevaricator who often tells the truth as well. He was familiar with the everyday life of the people and he blended elements

---

[30] The tradition of the shepherd's stick is extant. The provost summons the village by sending out the stick of a crooked oak tree (the *krivulė*) to each house, and in the regions beyond the Nemunas, every gathering called together with an official summons is called a *krivulė* (Toporov 1980, 66).

of it, customs, legends, tales, with data obtained and from the scientific literature that he uninhibitedly distorted.

At the time of the Treaty of Chrystburg the ligash and the tuliss were the only leaders of Prussian society and probably not only spiritual leaders. As the duality of the names suggests, some kind of division of labour already existed between them. The further division of labour, the crystallisation of secular power was brought to a halt because of the German conquest. Prussian development continued on the path of the Germans. It explains why the Teutonic Order focussed on the ideological struggle in the Treaty and only named the tuliss and ligash, as those who were most in the way, and insisted on their elimination. It was difficult to find one well defined and named representative of secular power among the many free peoples. The Treaty ambiguously says that only those youths who had been converted to the Catholic belief and came or would come from a noble family, could put on the soldiers' sash.[31] It can be interpreted in two ways: some form of nobility already existed or would emerge from the converted descendants of the old nobility. (As everywhere in world history it was obviously the nobility who led the way in the process of becoming German Prussians from Baltic Prussians, through the 'betrayal of the nation'. The consciousness of Prussian unity persisted longest among the masses and for this reason the 1295 uprising in Sembia was not only against the Order but also against the German–Prussian 'new nobility'—Pollakówna 1958, 175.)[32]

Thanks to the activity of the German knights, i.e. they sacrificed the Prussians, the tuliss and ligash had already disappeared by P. Dusburg's time. What was left was the krive, some kind of town crier whom the chronicler stylised as a pope.

8.3.5. Kunigas

The situation in Lithuania was different. The military monarchy that existed here was a strong secular power, unlike the Prussian military democracy. Latv. *kungs*, Lith. *kunigas* 'lord, sovereign', is a loan word from around 1200 (< Old High German *kunig* < Germanic *kuningaz* > with a typical semantic shift, OSlav.

[31] *Accingi cingulo militari*—it is difficult to decide whether it concerns the knights sash, or simply a young soldier becoming suitable for service (Voigt 1827–39/2, 624).

[32] R. Trautmann's collection of Prussian names gathered from the thirteenth–fifteenth-century documents do not contain any names in which *tuliss* or *ligash* could be discovered (Trautmann 1925). A. Brückner also wrote about the thirteenth–fifteenth-century Mazovian Prussian lesser nobles (*Witingen* < Old Polish *wiciędz, wicięg*), and could mention only one personal name with *ligash* (Ligaso from 1398), but *tuliss* only crops up in place names, most likely even in those not from the Prussian priest's reference, but rather from the word *tulan* 'many', and there are many personal names coming from that in Trautmann's collection as well (Brückner 1929, 57).

kъnędz, Czech *kněz* 'priest' and the Russ. *knjazъ* 'prince'—Būga 1920–22, 91).
In Latvian the word avoided semantic shifts, because the hierarchical structure
(German lords and Livonian subjects) that emerged after the German occupation
stabilised, and thus the word retained the meaning, 'lord' to this day. In Lithuanian,
the diminutive form *kunigaikštis* kept the meaning 'duke', with the difference that
it denoted a lesser duke subordinate to the grand duke. However, the word kunigas
shifted to its current meaning 'priest', parallel to the ruler seizing all power,
including spiritual power as he became a (high) priest. In the absence of Lithuanian
literacy there is no data about this shift until the seventeenth century, but it must
have taken place during the thirteenth century. In the early fourteenth century
Gediminas wrote his letters to westerners as the head of the pagan church. In 1351
Prince Kęstutis sacrificed animals in the role of the priest, even if he was talking
gibberish. At the end of the century, when Jagiello baptised the Lithuanians he did
not require the services of a pagan high priest, nothing of the sort was mentioned.[33]

The unusually high incidence of joint sovereignty in Lithuanian history from
the latter half of the thirteenth century (which left its mark on the relationship
between Jagello governing Poland and Vytautas governing Lithuania, and in
general on the peculiar Polish–Lithuanian personal union) demonstrates the kind
of struggles surrounding this shift, and also that the normal succession-dynastic
conflicts were possibly influenced by the duality of religious and secular power
(for a thorough analysis of dual sovereignty this see A. Nikžentaitis 1989, 12 ff.).

8.3.6. Žynys, waidelott, Wisten, mācītājs

Religious and secular power was concentrated in the hands of the Lithuanian
sovereign, which makes it conceivable that there were lower ranking priests who
carried out ceremonies, since there must have been a need for them. According to
J. Długosz these priests who were keepers of the eternal fire "were called *Zincz*
in their language" (Mannhardt 1936, 139). K. Būga first reconstructed the word
in Lithuanian as *žynys*, later as *žinčius* 'the wise, sapientem, Russ. znakhorъ' (cf.
Lith. *žinoti*, Latv. *zinat* 'to know', Latv. *zintēt* 'to foretell' and *apzintēt* 'enchant';
its variants in Długosz are Zyncz, Znicz, Zinze) (Būga 1908–09, 180; 1920–
22, 33).[34]

---

[33] E. Fraenkel posits that the Lithuanian kunigas–kunigaikštis developed following the
pattern of the Polish ksiądz–książę 'priest'–'duke' pair. This unusual presumption is not
underpinned by anything, and is semantically completely unjustified.

[34] S. Daukantas, the first nineteenth-century romantic historian who spoke Lithuanian,
further derived the word in the žinyčia 'pagan sanctuary' meaning, which had never come up
in even the most dubious sources.

The Livonian Rhyming Chronicle of 1259 mentions a pagan priest among the Žemaitians, too (*The Livonian Rhyming Chronicle,* line 4680). Before their next campaign against the Crusaders "their *Blutekirl* foretold the future and without a moment's delay sacrificed a live animal in front of the gathered crowd, because he knew well how to do this (*als er wol wiste*)" (Mierzyński 1892–96/I, 118). 'Knowledge' is also among the criteria of the OGer. *blutekirl,* 'a priest sacrificing animals and people to the gods' (< Goth. *blotan* 'sacrifice to the gods').

Possibly there was a priest with a similar function among the Prussians as well. Although the *waidelotts* first appear in S. Grunau there is no reason to doubt their existence (Grunau 1529/I, 62). There are also female *Waidelinns* that feature alongside the male Waidelottes, but they are obviously the result of the chronicler's effort to try transport the Vesta priestesses from the Roman sanctuaries onto the Prussian lands. The word was adopted into other languages (Lith. *vaidelis, vaidelotis,* Ger. *Waidler* 'pagan priest', from Lithuanian Polish *wajdelota, wajdelotka* through the works of the Romantics, especially A. Mickiewicz 'bard, minstrel'), probably via the literary transmissions carried in later chronicles which used Grunau's work as a source (e.g. M. Praetorius, M. Stryjkowski, etc.). This can be explained by the fact that there was already a form in Lithuanian, *vaidila,* which denoted the priest acting out ceremonies, but also meant 'actor' (cf. contemporary Lith. *vaidila* 'actor', *vaidmuo* 'role') and the person in authority over an area, e.g. a village (cf. Part Four, Subchapter 8.3.2 on *histriones*). All these meanings are explained by the etymology of the word which, through the works of J. Voigt and later K. Būga are clear: Pr. **waidils* 'the wise, the seer, the one who knows' (diminutive > **waidiluttis*) can be reconstructed < Pruss. **waida* 'knowledge, experience, science' (cf. Sanskrit *veda,* Russ. *veda* 'knowledge', etc.), < Pruss. **waist-/waid-* 'to know, to (fore)see, to sense' (cf. Slavic *věděti* 'to know', Polish *wiedma* 'fortune teller' and Russ. *vedьma* 'witch'), from which only one form survived in the 1561 Enchiridion-translation in first person plural, present tense conjunctive: *waidleimai '(dass) wir zaubern',* which, here explaining the second commandment, means 'Do not conjure, charm, or bewitch with or in the name of God (Voigt 1827–39/I, 606; Būga 1908–09, 183; Mažiulis 1966–81/II, 108).[35]

This meaning of the role of the priest is further strengthened by *The Livonian Rhyming Chronicle,* line 3872: in the description of the 1253 battle of Sembia the pagan priests are called *die wisten* 'the wise' which according to A. Mierzyński is the literal translation of *waidelott* (Mierzyński 1892–96/I, 122).

---

[35] To originate the word from the *vid-* 'to see' stem with an ablaut is not controversial with originating it from the *věd-* 'knowledge' stem (cf. Latv. *veids* 'looks, form', Lith. *veidas* 'face', Slavic *viděti* 'to see'), as Mannhardt does it, thus allocating the seer (*Seher*) meaning to it (Mannhardt, 1936, 213).

It seems more convenient to assume a literal Latvian translation of the Latvian word *mācītājs* 'priest' literal meaning 'teacher, wise' (cf. *mācīt* 'to teach', *mācēt* 'to know') and not of the Prussian word. *Mācītājs* belongs to the group of words that emphasise the spiritual power of the priest (sicco, ligash, žynys, and waidelott), contrary to those focusing on the secular power of priests (sicco, tuliss, krive, kunigas). It was translated as *Wisten* instead of the customary *Priester*, which shows that the origins of the word still lingered.[36]

Corresponding to the three different areas of the cult there are three different answers to the initial question about the existence of a cult among the Balts.[37]

During the transition from polydoxy to prototheism the worshipping of natural objects could transform into a form of anthropomorphic idolatry, in the words of J. Balys, "into idolatry at a certain degree" (Balys 1929/10, 45). Paradoxically, this was further entrenched by Catholic idolatry eager to eradicate it.

The existence of a pagan temple can only be assumed in Lithuania and even then in a later period as a counter-reaction to Christianity.

There were priests but their existence was different in the three areas inhabited by Baltic peoples. Sicco points to a common starting point, as the distant successor of clan heads, the community judges who knew the law, and the shaman-like guard of the sacred grove. Later, this shared function was divided. Among the Prussians the division of spiritual and secular power remained at a 'local level' and was limited to problems concerning funerals and inheritance, as well as judicial matters (waidelott, ligash, as well as tuliss and krive), while among the Latvians the foreign conquerors carried out these duties (kungs, mācītājs), and among the Lithuanians the kunigas exercised spiritual as well as secular power.

---

[36] According to E. Fraenkel the Latv. *mācēt*, Lith. *mokėti*, Pruss. *mukint* 'to know, to teach' words go back to the **makh-* stem, and, for phonological reasons, not to the more obvious *magh, magh-* 'to know, to be able to' stem carrying the 'knowledge is power' semantic cohesion. (Cf. Goth. *maht*, Russ. *moch*, 'power' < Proto-Slavic **mokt* 'to know, to be able to' > Czech, Polish *moc* 'many'—Vasmer 1953–58/II, 167.) Contrary to all my respect for phonetic laws I would uphold the possibility of a common origin for the mācītājs and Ger. *Macht*. Semantic laws are worth as much as phonetic laws (even J. Pokorny the linguist, a devotee of phonetic laws, also leaves a small window open: "In case Fraenkel is right..."—Pokorny 1959–69/II, 695).

[37] Just like A. Mažiulis, the editor in chief of the ethnographic material of the thirty-seven volume Lithuanian encyclopaedia published in the USA, who says that there can be no doubt about the existence of the *krive*. However, written sources or archaeological finds hardly underpin the existence of idols, and their existence is refuted by "the entire ancient Lithuanian belief system". Romova should at most be imagined as a local sacrificial place that became renowned and not as some pagan Rome (Lit. E./XIII, 165; XXVIII, 397; XXV, 504).

PART FIVE

CONCLUSION

OWN AND ALIEN IN HISTORY

The picture traced here can lead to numerous conclusions, from which I shall only touch upon one, and that from only one perspective: how the amalgam customarily referred to as (national) consciousness emerges from historical events, language, mythology, and various nondescript remnants in Central and Eastern Europe.

A plenitude of historical facts with uncertain states of existence, amazingly frequent and rapid changes in viewpoints when creating these facts are together responsible for the illusion that there is a third group alongside the groups of prehistoric peoples (*praehistoria, Vorgeschichte*) without written traditions and historic peoples with written records. Only sources put down by outsiders are left behind concerning this third group (Tymieniecki 1963, 264). In the course of their history, the Baltic peoples evidently fall into this category.[1]

At first glance this categorisation seems self-evident. Nevertheless, it raises problematics which are barely soluble and superfluous for many people: that is, the definition of what is 'alien' and what is 'own' in history.

The answer is ambiguous, even if we accept the contemporary viewpoint that identifies language with nation, because language does not constitute national (community) consciousness completely even today. What is 'alien' and what is 'own' is always determined by the component parts of a community's consciousness, as well as their role in establishing and shaping it. In the nineteenth century many considered the works of J. Kraszewski, or even A. Mickiewicz (of Lithuanian origin), which contain Lithuanian subject matter, as contributors to Lithuanian culture. Their writing carried a strongly pro-Lithuanian ideology which helped overcome the fact that not a single line was written in the Lithuanian language. Furthermore, Lithuanian consciousness itself was barely palpable when they wrote and so in order to create it, the main aim of the 'national awaken-

[1] This is why P. Einhorn could write with extreme honesty: "Small peoples have no history of their own" (cited in Zeids 1992, 137).

ing', even 'alien' material came to be admissible to the cannon of Lithuanian literature.[2]

G. Merkel's works (1769–1850) were used in the same way for the later
development of national consciousness. He was a Jacobean influenced by the
so-called 'Prophets' Club', a workshop of *Sturm und Drang* in Riga (cf. Rauch
1982). He wrote exclusively in German, for example *Die Letten, vorzüglich in
Liefland, am Ende des philosophischen Jahrhunderts*, 1796; an exemplary romantic Latvian and Estonian prehistory, *Die Vorzeit Lieflands* I–II, 1798–1799; or the
'Latvian legend' that was the foundation for Latvian national romanticism, *Van-
nem Ymanta*, 1802. These works are now all part of both Latvian and German
histories of literature, with a greater emphasis in the first. A. Johansons, an
otherwise excellent historian living in Sweden, has recently urged their abandonment as Latvian works (as if a writer could not contribute to more than one nation's
literature). His justifications are that the foggy concept of a 'Latvian mentality'
should not be sufficient to include G. Merkel as a contributor to Latvian literature,
and that although his works had an effect on it, it is only to the extent that any
other work by a foreign writer might (a statement which is of course easily
refutable) (Johansons 1975, 445).

Latvian culture in particular has a high incidence of examples of transfer from
alien to own which can be fixed to a precise point in time. Two almost miraculous
incidents can certainly be seen as having determined Latvian literacy and perhaps
even Latvian existence. The first one concerned E. Glück who translated the *Bible*,
and the other was Stenders the Elder who had the following text inscribed on his
gravestone: "Here lies G. F. Stenders. The Latvian."[3]

However, as far back in the past as the Latin Middle Ages linguistic aspects
perhaps played no role in national consciousness whatsoever. Who the author of
the first Polish chronicle (1112–1116) was remains unsure; he is referred to as
Anonim Gall although he must have been a foreigner (he possibly came from
Provence through Hungary) and wrote his work in Latin. Nonetheless, *Historia
Polonorum* is considered to be the first work of Polish national literature. Whether
the unknown author of the *Livonian Chronicle*, named Heinricus de Lettis, was
German or Latvian (Henry from Latvia or Latvian Henry) is essentially insignifi-

---

[2] For the indivisibility of own and alien, an anecdotal example is the difficulty in determining
where 'the greatest Polish poet' A. Mickiewicz was baptised (who had never been to either
Warsaw or Kraków). The small town where he was christened is called Navahrudak in
Byelorussian, Novogrudok in Russian, Navaredok in Yiddish, Naugardukas in Lithuanian,
Novogrudok in German, and Nowogródek in Polish (Grudzińska Gross 1995, 296).

[3] The two examples also demonstrate how language becomes an increasingly decisive factor
in communal consciousness in the formation of cultures in a separate national language, to the
extent that the precondition for entering a culture is to learn its language. The French poet
O. Milosz, a typical *gente lituanus, natione polonus*, for example, having accepted the foreign
representation of Lithuania in France in 1920 started to learn Lithuanian.

cant. It is obvious from the text that the chronicler knew the local languages (both Latvian and Livian), but it also becomes clear that he was unequivocally loyal to Albert the Bishop of Riga who spread Christianity militantly and violently among the Livonian peoples. Consequently, the chronicler can be regarded as alien if the own are seen as the pagans.

Anybody who would unhistorically reflect the absolutism of the linguistic factor in a community's identity back into times when there was no extant Latvian or Lithuanian identity, will face irresolvable antagonisms. V. Vīķis-Freibergs lives in Canada and changed disciplines from psychology to research of myths. As one of the leading figures of 'pan-folklorism', she identifies 'own' with the Latvian speaking pagans who handed down dainas orally. Compared to them, every "alien observer is hostile because their accounts are colored with their own religious and ideological prejudices" (Vīķis-Freibergs 1989a, 93). Following this logic apologising for paganism, the history of Latvian existence was interrupted from the moment an alien German Christianity was taken on, until their independence in 1918.[4]

[4] The real root of the issue is that universal Christianity can hardly be matched to nationalist ideology. The propagators of Christianity had always been opposed to ethnic separation from the very beginning, but especially during the Reformation, and thus everything that was connected to ethnicity or nationhood (folklore, mythology) was automatically pagan. (The situation is further complicated by the fact that in many places it was the Reformation that formed the grounds of national separation and literacy in a national language. Additionally, there were significant differences between the factions of the Reformation on this matter, for example between nationalist Calvinism and the more international Lutheranism.)

For this reason the concept of 'national Christianity' (e.g. 'Polish, Lithuanian Catholicism', or 'Hungarian Protestantism'), which emerged later is paradoxical (unless it is a purely objective denotation), just as much as from the perspective of Christianity as nationhood (cf. Maceina 1987, 34–41).

This is the fundamental dilemma of A. Pumpurs' *Lāčplēsis*. The national epic (or as A. Pumpurs called it 'epic song') came about through the influence of the *Kalevala*, of the *Kalevipoeg* and the Serbian heroic songs, and most of all against the theory of the German W. Jordan (1819–1904) who rewrote the *Nibelungenlied* and who claimed that only the Indians, the Persians, the Greeks, and the Germanic people were capable of creating a national epic. Thus the *Lāčplēsis* would have been a compensation for the lost 'national epic' (some believe it fulfilled its function with success: the author's name was 'omitted' from the title page of the Moscow edition in Russian, an exemplary introductory study and notes are included by J. Rudzītis, thus creating a suitable folklore work in the series of Turkmen, Uzbek, Altaian, Adigian and Kazah 'adventure' and 'heroic' epics.)

A. Pumpurs illustrates the battle between the German knights and the Latvian people in the form of a tale, but because in the end the Latvians took on Christianity, he makes peace between the ancient Latvian pagan gods and Christ in a confusing manner on a theoretical basis in the prologue of the first song. All the way through the tale describes the way the new belief, Christianity, emerged to eliminate the Baltic people honouring Pērkons (lines 552–583). In the first song the old gods gather in Pērkon's palace in the sky where the chief god Liktentēvs

Instead of this rigid opposition between alien and own (alien often being identified with the enemy), I would rather adopt C. Renfrew's wording, "ethnicity is a matter of degree" (Renfrew 1987, 217). Consequently, I would sooner talk about the shifting proportion of alien–own as dependant on history, where the own cannot dwindle to zero because of the preserved language. If it does settle to zero, which would mean a group of people and their language becoming lost without trace, there is nothing to debate. However, historical circumstances determined that a Latvian and Lithuanian national identity developed late due to the absence of a literary foundation. As a result, the majority of sources are alien, as if others had always been talking about the Balts. This is the other main characteristic of their history, alongside their geographical isolation.[5]

The Balts were pushed onto the periphery of Europe because of these two factors, and stayed there all throughout apart from a few exceptional historical moments such as their 1989–1991 independence from the Soviet Union. In 1413, a delegate of the Livonian Order of Knights had to draw a map of Livonia for the Pope in Rome, even though it formally and legally fell under his authority, because the enemies of the Order were trying to prove that the Bishopric of Dorpat (Tartu) was to be found in Sweden (Zeids 1992, 7). L. Arbusow was also forced to realise that the East-Baltic peoples remained almost completely unfamiliar to the West, as the "ignorance [of another Pope, Pius II] and the silence of almost every chronicler of the late Middle Ages proved" (Arbusow 1939, 203).

('Father of fate' its basis—*liktenis* 'fate', is a neologism, a totally unknown word in the Latvian folk tongue) announces to the crowd that magic has occurred and that Christ is born, but the people turn his words to evil. The solution is this: "Christian belief / must be introduced to Latvia, too, / however the gods can shape the human mind to their moods!" So, the people turned the good words of Christ to evil, but the Latvians, with the help of the pagan gods, can return to the untarnished good. Pērkons, who was moved to speak like the Prime Minister after the President, reinforces: "I promise that I shall keep the Latvian nation with me. / I shall permit the good teachings." Moreover, he adds an argument for the Latvians being the elected people: "Christ's teachings are not new, / their foundations came from the East." This implies that A. Pumpurs shared the view, widespread at the time, that the Latvians moved northwards from the shores of the Ganges in India, the cradle of mankind, and could consequently have already been familiar with Christ's words in their original, and true form.

The motif also crops up in the 'Lithuanian national epic' of the *Witolorauda* by J. Kraszewski: "Hear the song! This song has arisen from the grave / It tells you the story of your past; / it saw your ancestral fathers in the Eastern world / and talks to their sons through their voices" (Kraszewski 1846, verse V).

[5] The two are evidently closely related and, in fact, emerge from each other. All three of the scripts of the Germanic people could emerge because they were in contact with the Mediterranean world. The Runic script of the first centuries BC developed from a northern Italian alphabet, Bishop Wulfila's Gothic script of the fourth century emerged from the Greek and Latin alphabets, while from the sixth century recorded texts in the various Germanic folk languages were noted down in the Latin script (Sonderegger 1964, 706).

These two factors are also responsible for the length of time the Balts remained in a state of natural existence, and that a tale like J. Kraszewski's *Egle* (Silver Fir), *the Snake Queen* could become Lithuania's 'own' and the expression of its 'soul'. The story concerns the youngest of a fisherman's three daughters who married Žilvinas, the Snake King of the Sea. They lived happily together in the palace in the sea and the queen gave birth to two sons and a daughter. Until one day the woman visited her home with her children. The queen's twelve brothers wanted to discover the Snake King's name. They tortured their two nephews in vain, for they would not give away their father's name, but their niece did. When the Snake King came from the sea at the brothers' call they beat him to death with a hoe and scythe. His wife turned herself into a silver fir, changed one of her sons into an oak tree and the other into a maple tree, and the treacherous girl into a poplar tree. The usual interpretation of this tale is that the most important Lithuanian national characteristic is faith, which is a possible reading. However, to me the tale is more general, it presents the Balts as forest dwellers who saw words, represented by the name, as a means of betrayal, furthermore, having failed to coexist with the aliens they saw their only option out in withdrawing into a silent natural phenomenon, as Egle the Silver Fir.

The destiny of the Lithuanians was ultimately similar, as illiterate natural beings they remained on the periphery of history. In German history the continuity between Antiquity and the Middle Ages is a principal issue (Bausinger 1969, 10). In the case of the Balts (apart from a brief Lithuanian interlude in the Middle Ages) Antiquity, the period where the prehistoric age, ancient times, and the Middle Ages all melt into one another, is continued into the Modern Age. In Greece, the historically important cultural shift when orality transferred into literacy occurred in the sixth century BC. In the Baltic region it only really came about in the eighteenth–nineteenth centuries in close connection with the emergence of nationhood. The foundation of Vilnius, mirroring that of Rome, occurred in the thirteenth century, and the Lithuanian version of the Romulus–Remus legend appeared in the sixteenth century. Elsewhere in Europe, the phenomenon of the extinction of entire ethnicities was a part of the prehistoric ages, ancient times, or latest in the Middle Ages. In the Baltic there were precedents in the Early Modern and Modern Ages, and was a genuine danger until 1991.

The division between the 'western' and the 'eastern' parts of Europe does not lie between paganism and Christianity, but rather in the time (delay!) in how and when conversion took place.[6] In the first three hundred years of Christianity, in the West baptism was only possible on an individual basis following one of the

---

[6] The quotation marks denote that initially the 'western' did not mean the West, nor even Europe, since the centres of Latin Christianity were in Antioch, and mostly in northern Africa—just think of St. Augustine, Bishop of Hippo. Rome only won its leading role after the Vandal attacks on Africa in 426 AD and finally the seventh-century Arabic conquests.

fundamental principles of baptism: "He that believeth and is baptised shall be saved; but he that believeth not shall be damned" (Mark 16, 16). Conversion was always preceded by a certain period of the catechumenate, or being 'prepared for Christianity', which was a regular 'pedagogical system' (Hernegger 1963, 374). This is emphasised in another basic tenet of Christianity: "go ye therefore, and teach all nations, baptising them in the name of Father, and of the Son, and of the Holy Ghost: teaching them to observe all things whatsoever I have commanded you" (Matthew 28, 19–20). During the three years, a person had to learn the doctrines of Christ, participate in charitable work, experience asceticism through prayers and fasting, and if necessary they even had to change professions. People became Christians at their own request. This ceased in 380 when Christianity became a state religion, and under Constantine the Great the punishment for non-Christians was death in the Byzantine period. At that time—and not at the time of Protestantism—entire tribes and groups of people were converted to Christianity on the new principle of *cuius regio, eius religio* 'He who has power rules religion'. Nonetheless, the previous three hundred years had not passed by without trace. An enormous difference exists between the Germanic barbarians who stepped smoothly into the heritage of Rome from the fifth–sixth centuries, and the new barbarians of the ninth–tenth centuries, who were forced to join Europe, and the even newer Baltic barbarians of the thirteenth century.[7] In Eastern Europe, only the ruler received individual preparation before he converted the people *en masse*. Vladimir, the Prince of Kiev did it in this way. One day he destroyed the huge statue of the pagan God Perun, and the next day he had his people driven into the river Dnieper for baptism. Jogaila (Jagiello) the Polish King also acted similarly in 1387 and allocated the same names to some large groups of people in baptism.[8] Taking on Christianity this way is a little contradictory since, as the doctrine of individual redemption, it promised entry on an individual

---

[7] J. Szűcs described very precisely how the 'fictive dualism' (*civitas Dei, civitas terrena*) of St. Augustine became 'real dualism' twice over. First Germanic tribes opposed Christian Rome (and consequently, in a simplified way at least the seeds of Central Europe as a historical region emerged), then the new and the newer barbarians who created Eastern Europe followed them in the role. In the latter case, the fundamental Augustine principle that only people who are convinced should be baptised was frequently dismissed (Szűcs 1992, 71 ff. and 107 ff.) Although, it should be mentioned that another thesis of St. Augustine which entered the 'constitution' of the Catholic Church, i.e. the cannon, contradicts this previous principle. It declares that what matters is not that a person is forced, but what he is forced into, good or bad. Of course in examining the emergence of the eastern and western regions of Europe it has to be noted that the Roman Empire disintegrated under the attacks of already settled tribes, while Eastern Europe was attacked by nomadic robbers throughout.

[8] As many have pointed out, this information, exclusively drawn from J. Długosz, is more than doubtful because the frozen river in February would not have been suitable for the action (e.g. Jurginis 1987, 154; or Dainauskas 1991, 166).

basis into the empire of freedom, and liberation from the captivity of ones sins.[9] This was also its attraction, it declared the individual equal to all others in this liberation from sins, as the words of the 1249 Treaty of Chrystburg illustrate (note the theological and philosophical arguments in a peace contract!): "As long as no sin has been committed every individual is equal, and only sin subjugates a person and makes them miserable. And in the same way, each individual, let them be as free as ever, becomes the slave of sin if they commit a crime" (Mannhardt 1936, 41). Of course, in this way, the baptised Prussians individually became members of the Order State, and a Prussian community was out of the question (cf. Patze 1958, 73).

This fundamental difference in the manner of baptism is evidently rooted in the entanglement of a thousand threads of Jewish–Greek–Roman 'paganism' with Christianity. For example, Plato probably knew the Old Testament, and according to the Church Fathers who put together the Christian doctrines "not only Moses but Socrates had been both fulfilled and superseded by the coming of Jesus" (Pelikan 1971–78/I, 63). For this reason Christian converts had to accept as much from pagan religions as possible, and put forward the teachings of Jesus as the rectification and simultaneous completion of a given pagan religion. Dismissing the impatient hurry of the fourth and fifth centuries Christianity created a continuity in the thinking of the 'educated world'. As Justinian wrote, "whatever things were rightly said among all men... are the property of us Christians as the correction and fulfilment" (in Pelikan 1971–78/I, 62).[10] However, the Balts said

---

[9] Perhaps Martin Luther's words (The Freedom of a Christian, 1520) express this the most concisely: "I will therefore give myself, as a sort of Christ, to my neighbour, as Christ has given himself to me, and will do nothing in this life what I see will be needful, advantageous and wholesome for my neighbour, since by faith I should abound in all good things in Christ" (Luther, 1882–83, 54).

[10] The Apostle Paul gave the theoretical basis for a continuity: "But before faith came, we were kept under the law [= Old Testament], shut up unto the faith which should afterwards be revealed" (Galatians 3, 23). Dante considers himself the honoured follower of five great non-Christian poets—Homer, Horace, Ovid, Lukanus, and the master Virgil—whose only fault, but not sin, was that they were born before Christianity. They consequently found themselves in the first circle of hell (The Inferno, IV. lines 31–102). There were even some (such as Adam, Eve, Abel, Noah, Moses, David, Israel, Rachel) for whom Jesus 'the Almighty' descended into hell and took them into 'grace'.

The Middle Ages were 'middle' (medium aevum as the historian from Halle, C. Keller (Cellarius) first put it in 1688 in his history text book the Historia antiqua, historia medii aevi, historia nova) that is, between Antiquity and Modernity, "the years between Constantine [deceased 337] and the fall of Constantinople [1453]". The struggle of the Renaissance in the Caroling period and of the twelfth–thirteenth-century theologists to bring the dogmas of religious life into harmony with Aristotelian logic and dialectics (Breisach 1983, 139), as well as the thirteenth–sixteenth-century Humanism and Renaissance (primarily through the disciplines of studia humanitatis and artes liberales) all constructed a bridge between paganism and

nothing. They remained mute and were accordingly treated as pagans of 'nature' and not of 'history'. I am not sure if anyone who tried to intermingle these differences would not be doing a great mis-service to these peoples, as well as falsifying the past. That is, if they attempted to present it as though there had been more than just a pure natural existence, that is a historical existence complete with its own mythology and folklore (its symbols dominant in today's Latvian and Lithuanian intellectual and everyday life) and equal to the alien historical reality brought to them on the edge of the sword. To this 'never-have-been state' it would probably be possible to return from the horrible, modern 'Americanised' world.[11]

I offer only one reference to illustrate what the golden age was or might have been. The excavations of a fourth-century Suduvian settlement, in all probability the biggest, showed that the average life span of men was thirty, of women twenty-five years. Only one man was found in a grave described as 'princely' who had lived, almost miraculously, until fifty-five years of age (Antoniewicz 1962, 8). Perhaps a brief 'historico-philosophical' comment from an amateur could be risked here: a general controversy lies between the increase of human population and the decrease in their quality of life. Every form of social organisation can support greater numbers of people than the previous one, but in more difficult

---

Christianity (see Knoll 1991). (The handbook of the seven free arts was created by the African Martianus Capella as early as the fifth century, and remained the most decisive book of Christian education until the Reformation—Curtius 1948, 30.)

[11] Of course, instead of becoming 'Americanised' the precise expression would be 'Sovietised', and that is the root of the problem. Modernisation, as A. Šliogeris pointed out in his delicate analysis, was carried out by the Soviet system, "while the Bolsheviks modernised the material life of Lithuania, Lithuanian intellectuals and the entire culture were pushed towards conservatism" (Šliogeris 1994, 15).

A. Šliogeris also stated in an interview in 1991, that the anti-Soviet attitude and the national character of the Lithuanian opposition at the end of the sixties and beginning of the seventies developed in two directions (the third comprised the 'cosmopolitan'–liberal T. Venclova alone). One was connected to the Catholic Church at an insignificant intellectual level, the other one was connected to the Ramuva Society, extant for a few years from 1969 and named after P. Dusburg's Romova, comprising the cream of the intellectuals. It folded partly at its own behest, and partly because of the police ban under Brezhnev. The 'Ramuvians' attempted to awaken the pagan past: they organised ethnographic expeditions, sang dainas, and formed small folk groups. The story of the Society, which became official after independence, is interesting. The former members by that time had gone their separate ways. The new members, who carried on the old name, degraded the programme, actually rather unclear, to serve their own political purposes. They tried to have the Society accepted as a pagan church to obtain financial support from the state. However, the Parliament, with the socialists in majority, rejected their inauguration as an official religion in 1996. It is certain that they will make further attempts through the recently formed conservative government, and perhaps one day there will be another Baltic 'neo-pagan church' after the Latvian Dievs believers.

circumstances. According to C. Renfrew's calculations, the agriculture of prehistoric Europe fed fifty times more people, in percentage terms five thousand times more than a fishing–hunting–gathering lifestyle, but not with an improvement in their lives (peasants were constantly on the verge of starvation), and through more and harder work (Renfrew 1987, 125). Societies changing from agriculture to industry show the same tendency.[12] That is without mentioning that castles and towns in Eastern Europe can thank their emergence to wars that became a constant feature. The previous easier lifestyle inevitably gives rise to the myth of a golden age.

C. Lévi-Strauss differentiated between two types of culture, "a progressive acquisitive type ... and another type, lacking the gift of synthesis which is the hallmark of the first", the precondition for the first is literacy (Lévi-Strauss 1952, 107). "The unrecorded work can never be as solid a foundation for progress as a written work that has gained stability through its recording and thus cries out to be understood always in its original form, communicating unchanged to the reader or listener in the most distant eras. Folk poetry can always move just one step forward at a time and can be consciously connected only to its direct predecessor. It is an inherent part of its nature that if it does not generate instant repercussions it vanishes without a trace. The whole of world literature stands behind a work recorded in writing and its foretelling and effects are limitless." Pointing at the essence of the two types of cultures J. Gy. Szilágyi continues, "Written work presumes a creative individual and the demand and presence of a message for which the creative work of an individual who is incapable of dissolving into a community is needed. The emergence of this demand is not incidental but a historical necessity in the same sense as the emergence of writing" (Szilágyi 1957, 418, 421).

People have and may observe the past from two different perspectives, from history and from nature. Historically, events are believed to move forward towards some target, as Hegel and Marxism (which, rooted in Hegel, ruled the thinking of the entire twentieth century) imagined: "The history of the world accordingly represents the successive stages in the development of that principle whose substantial content is the consciousness of freedom" (Hegel 1840, 129). From the perspective of nature, the events of human existence are believed to move in an

---

[12] Praising the actually rather poor and miserable life of the peasantry as opposed to that of the urban society "hardly had anything to do with ethnographic reality" (Chirot 1996, 2). As for the future, "mankind is irreversibly committed to industrial society, and therefore to a society whose productive system is based on cumulative science and technology. This alone can sustain anything like the present and anticipated number of inhabitants of the planet... Agrarian society is no longer an option for its restoration would simply condemn the great majority of mankind to death by starvation" (Gellner 1983, 39).

endless cycle abiding by the rules of nature and the universe.[13] For the former history is progression, often towards perfection. For the latter this is not the case.[14] Humankind lost its way when it forgot the order of nature and dirtied the universe, a process the beginning of which is posited by some as the twentieth century, by others at the Enlightenment, by still others at the Middle Ages.[15]

Everyone can opt for one or the other as they see fit. However, one thing must be avoided: a mixing of the two, for there lies the cliché of turning the wheels of history backwards. In the words of J. Vogt, if one intends to make history out of prehistory, "if one invokes the phenomena of pre-literate times as facts of historical existence then another danger arises that historical perspective and judgement will be disturbed" (Vogt 1949, 339). Again, and again: in a mythicised history where everything is compared with everything values intermingle, including the most important values of all, those ones constituting the uniqueness of a given people's history.[16] "Perhaps a future generation will come to recognise that the most misguided, though well intentioned, feature of our present age was that, having discovered by the methods of genuine science that man is a single zoological species and thus a unity in his *physical* nature, we tried, by political coercion and propaganda, to impose on man, as a cultural moral being, a comparable sense of unity which contradicts the very essence of our *human* nature" (Leach 1982, 85).

The emergence of various fallacies discloses the confusion of different values. We have talked about the most important, nationalist 'slippage' (cf. Part One,

---

[13] This duality that stretches across European culture springs from the Jewish and Greek concepts of time. The first is linear, envisaging a one-off creation and that history will at some point end; the second sees an eternal cycle (Grierson 1975, 228 ff.). Consequently, in Antiquity only the Jews were interested in history that is, "the story of the unfolding of God's will from the Creation to the final triumph in the future" (Finley 1975, 24). Greek myths moved about in the eternal present.

[14] "It would be a real misunderstanding to think that we are at a higher level of human development than the hunters of the Stone Age. Homo sapiens were just as well developed physically, psychologically, and emotionally thirty-five thousand years ago as we are" (Rimantienė 1995, 11), she bases this opinion on prehistoric man's ability to preserve the balance of nature, while today's humans are incapable of doing so.

[15] The origins of this worldview are probably the Zoroastrian system, where "each age was of three thousand years, and in each law and morality declined by one-forth" (Finley 1956, 27).

[16] Concerning one of the most influential comparisons by O. Spengler, R. Musil wrote, with well-placed irony, that "there are yellow butterflies and there are yellow Chinese. So in a certain sense we can say the butterfly is the Eastern European dwarf Chinese with wings. It is known that butterflies, just like the Chinese, are the symbols of joy. This is where the thought first occurred that the fauna of the lepidoptera and the great period of Chinese culture resemble each other in an earlier never suspected manner. And that butterflies have wings, and the Chinese do not, is only a superficial phenomenon" (cited by Csejtei in Spengler 1994/II, 750).

Chapter 4). Another example linked to this, which could be called the misconception of scholarly attitudes, arises when unverifiable data, or perhaps data supported by a single authority, is treated as a fact simply for the sake of roundness and the appeal of the argument.[17]

Slippage in scholarship was exaggerated by the dominant trend in comparative research of myths in the field of Baltic Antiquity, structuralism, which was seen as a moral and political category under the Soviet regime. At first structuralists were labelled 'anti-Soviet' and were barely tolerated. They were the real scholars, the scholars who carried out real scholarship, as opposed to the pseudo-scholars manipulated by Soviet ideologies.

Thus the—from the aspect of nationalism–patriotism and structuralism—morally and politically unimpeachable fallacies hampered the works of the enumerated great scholars of neo-comparativism, as well as the new generation who followed in their footsteps. They became the cultural anthropologist researchers of myths who speak several languages, are open to the world, and practised real scholarly work all the way through the difficult times of the Soviet system, that is structuralist Baltology. G. Komoróczy's concise characterisation, given for the Hungarian version of the Soviet *Mifi narodov mira* (1980–1982) [Mythological encyclopaedia] (1988) is valid in regard to their work, "structuralist in its contents, nationalist in its form" (Komoróczy 1990).

After the revolutionary changes in 1989, and now that the Baltic States have won back their independence, finally the potential has opened up for scholarly

---

[17] E. Leach calls this misconception an "intellectual inertia", implying an intellectual inactivity and sloth at the same time. One of V. Pisani's studies is a good example of this. The excellent linguist posits that Indo-European unity stretched between Scandinavia and the Volga, developed under the rule of the conquerors from the Southeast whose language he call "Proto-Sanskrit", and culture "Proto-Brahmin", because "they were best preserved in Sanskrit and the Brahmin culture of the Vedic times" (Pisani 1968, 16). The only problem is, as E. Leach points out, that "There is no genuine evidence that the text of the Rig Veda existed in its present form before about 400 BC, but no contemporary Indo-European scholar will admit as much. If you ask such a scholar for his or her evidence (as I have done on several occasions), you will find that the answer is simply a slightly tidied up version of what Max Müller said in 1878" (Leach 1990, 233). Pisani, then supports his definition of the time of the Vedic period, which came from the nineteenth century and has since then hardened into a dogma, with a "Proto-Brahmin" argument. Not only the tribal federation of Indo-European conquerors was led by warriors and priests or Brahmins but also the institution of the Brahmin, the chief priest, the Roman *Pontifex Maximus* survived among the Prussians in the Middle Ages which the Romova mentioned by P. Dusburg and the krive respected as a 'Pope' supports (how much this is worth we have seen already). A few paragraphs later Pisani handles these two in themselves highly dubious statements connected together as proven facts, "such a 'Pope' among the Indians is missing: perhaps this figure of the ancient 'Proto-Brahmin' priesthood only emerged in Europe" (Pisani 1968, 16).

work free of all kinds of outside and, so to say, preformed misconceptions. It is rather doubtful that this generation of scholars would wish, or would be able to change their direction.[18]

As J. Gy. Szilágyi warned us, philology can mean the collection of things worth knowing, or just as easily the discipline of those which are not. At times like ours when the moral and ideological external support collapses, there is only one thing to do, call for help from our original internal support, that is curiosity, the thirst for knowledge. With that, the search for truth becomes the only sufficient moral reason. I, by no means, wish to take up the ridiculous banner of the champion of truth, nor become the captive of the fallacy caricatured by O. Szemerényi, "everything that is not completely scholarly is *ipso facto* totally unscholarly, and therefore without legitimacy" (Szemerényi 1961, 5).

I understand that it is not at all easy to practice philology in the absence of any external moral encouragement. No matter how long I ponder over my reason for writing this book, I can only say that it has satisfied my own and perhaps my Readers' curiosity.

*1986–1997**

---

[18] Inertia in both its senses is a hard taskmaster. According to J. Boissevain's parable, science is like a big hole at the bottom of which people are digging, and whoever digs deepest receives praise. If somebody discovers that a few metres from the hole there is a place where much more ore could be found, the people will not leave the hole for they are so wonderfully deep down there, and even if they dig on a couple of shovels more, they will once more be ten centimetres deeper (cited in Hofer 1994, 83).

*Throughout the past eleven years, I have enjoyed the benefits of the understanding, patience, and support of my workplace, the Institute for Literary Studies of the Hungarian Academy of Sciences, as well as the institutions founded by George Soros: the Soros Foundation, and the Central European University. I thank them for it.

BIBLIOGRAPHY[1]

Actes 1966: *Actes du VII-e Congrès International des Sciences Préhistoriques et Protohistoriques 1,* Prague.

Adam Bremensis*: "Gesta Hammaburgensis Ecclesiae Pontificum," (annotations, ed., Werner, T.) in *Quellen 1961,* 136–503.

Adamovičs, F. 1931: "Kurzer Überblick über die Geographie Lettlands," in Schmidt 1930, 7–48.

Adamovičs, L. 1930: "Die Letten und die katholische Kirche," in Schmidt 1930, 215–239.

— 1937: *Senlatviešu religija vēlajā dzelzs laikmetā* [Old Lettish religion in Late Iron Age], Riga: 115.

Aeneas Sylvius Piccolomini: "Preussen betreffende Schriften," in SRP/IV: 212–239. Extracts in Lithuanian: Jurginis–Šidlauskas 1983, 42–44, and in Janulaitis 1928, 55–63.

Alekseyev, L. V. 1966: *Polotskaya zemlya v IX–XIII vv.* Moscow: 295.

— 1980: *Smolenskaya zemlya v IX–XIII vv.* Moscow: 261.

Ammann, A. M. 1936: *Kirchenpolitische Wandlungen im Ostbaltikum,* Rome: 314.

Ancitis, K.–Jansons, A. 1962: "Nekotoryye voprosy etnicheskoy istorii drevnikh selov," *Sovetskaya Etnografiya,* 1962/6, 92–104.

Anderson, E. 1974: "Military policies and plans of the Baltic states on the eve of World War Two," *Lituanus,* 1974/2, 15–34.

Anderson, P. 1974: *Passages from Antiquity to Feudalism,* London: 304.

[1] The title 'referred literature' would be more precise because in this bibliograpy I only enumerate works which I actually refer to or quote from among those which I am familiar with and use. I opted for this solution because I managed to obtain the majority of the works in this bibliography during the preparation and writing of this book. They are available to anyone in Budapest, either from my private library or, foremost, from the Central European University Library.

I would hereby like to thank M. Karčiauskas of Vilnius, D. Preimane of Riga, J. Snopek of Warsaw for their indispensable help in the difficult task of finding books; and last but not least M. Szlatky, Director of the CEU Library.

* Bilingual.

Anisimov, A. F. 1981: *Az ősközösségi társadalom szellemi élete* (*Dukhovnaya zhizn' pervobitnogo obshchestva*), 1966 and *Istoricheskiye osobennosti pervobitnogo mishleniya*, 1971. Budapest: 370.

Anonim Gall: *Kronika polska,* [Polish Chronicle], (annotations, transl., M. Plezia), Wrocław etc.: LXXXIII+176.

Anthony, D. W. 1991: "The archaeology of Indo-European origins," *The Journal of Indoeuropean Studies*, 1991, 193–222.

Antoniewicz, J. 1962: *The Sudovians,* Białystok: 20+XXIV.

— 1964: "Tribal territories of the Baltic peoples in the Hallstatt–La Tène and Roman periods in the light of archaeology and toponomy," *Acta Baltico-Slavica*, 1964/4, 7–27.

Arany, János 1860: "Naiv eposzunk" [Our naive epic], in 1975, 217–229.

— 1975: *Prózai művek* [Works of prose], Budapest: 1184.

Arbusow, L. 1939: "Die mittelalterliche Schriftüberlieferung als Quelle für die Frühgeschichte der ostbaltischen Völker," in Engel 1939, 167–203.

Arnold, U. 1967: *Studien zur preussischen Historiographie des 16. Jahrhunderts.* Bonn: 249.

Arnold, U.–Biskup, M. (eds.) 1982: *Der Deutschordensstaat Preussen in der polnischen Geschichtsschreibung der Gegenwart*, Marburg: 278.

Ars historica 1975: *Ars Historica. Księga pamiątkowa G. Labudy* [Festschrift in honour of G. Labuda], Poznań.

Atgāzis, M. 1980: "Voprosy etnicheskoy istorii zemgalov," in Mugurēvičs 1980, 89–101.

Baldunčiks, J. 1989: "West Europe and the Baltic: Types of language contacts and lexical borrowings," *Baltistica*, 1989/III(1), 5–11.

Balodis, A. 1991: *Latvijas un latviešu tautas vēsture* (*Lettlands och det lettiska folkets historia*, 1990) [The history of Latvia and the Latvian people], Riga: 430.

Balodis, F. 1930: "Lettische Vorgeschichte," in Schmidt 1930, 89–139.

Balodis, F. – Šmits, P.–Tentelis, A. (eds) 1932: *Latvieši* [The Latvians] Riga: 511.

Baltic 1973: *Baltic Literature and Linguistics,* Columbus: 251.

Baltiyskiye 1973: *Baltiyskiye yazyki i ikh vzaimosvyazi so slavyanskimi, finno-ugorskimi i germanskimi yazykami.* Riga: 130.

Balto-slavyanskiy 1972: *Balto-slavyanskiy sbornik.* Moscow: 360.

Balys, J. 1929: "Ar senovės lietuviai turėjo stabų?" [Did the old Lithuanians have idols?], *Jaunoji Lietuva*, 1929/8–9–10, 33–37, 44–46, 40–45.

— 1948: *Lietuvių tautosakos skaitymai* [Lithuanian ethnographic lectures], I–II, Tübingen: 243, 270.

— 1949: "Latvian folklore," in *Funk–Wagnalls Standard* 1949/II, 606–607.

— 1953: "Parallels and differences in Lithuanian and Latvian mythology," in *Spiritus* 1953, 5–11.

— 1966: *Lietuvių liaudies pasaulėjauta tikėjimų ir papročių šviesoje* [World conception in Lithuanian folklore in the light of superstitions and customs], Chicago: 119.

— 1977: "Mitologija ir poezija" [Mythology and poetry], *Metmenys*, 1977 (33), 200–202.

— 1987: "Lietuviško velnio istorija" [The story of the Lithuanian devil], *Varpas,* (Chicago): 1987/22, 128–136.

Bartha, A.–Czeglédy, K.–Róna-Tas, A. (eds.) 1977: *Magyar őstörténeti tanulmányok* [Hungarian prehistoric studies], Budapest: 342.

Batūra, R. 1975: *Lietuva tautų kovoje prieš Aukso Ordą* [Lithuania in the people's battle against the Golden Horde], Vilnius: 383.

Bausinger, H. n.d.: *Volkskunde*. Berlin–Darmstadt: 303.

— 1969: "Zur Algebra der Kontinuität," in Bausinger–Brückner 1969, 9–30.

— 1970: "denkwürdig," in Harmening–Lutz–Schemmel–Wimmer 1970, 27–33.

Bausinger, H. – Brückner, W. (ed.) 1969: *Kontinuität?* Berlin: 187.

Beck, C. W. 1982: "Der Bernsteinhandel: naturwissenschaftliche Gesichtspunkte," *Savaria*, 1982 (16), 11–24.

— 1985: "The role of the scientist: the amber trade, the chemical analysis of amber, and the determination of Baltic provenience," *Journal of Baltic Studies*, 1985/3, 191–199.

— 1985a: "Criteria for 'amber trade': the evidence in the Eastern European Neolithic," *Journal of Baltic Studies*, 1985/3, 200–209.

Beck, H. 1973: *Geographie*, Freiburg–Munich: 510.

Bednarczuk, L. 1977: "Finno-Ugric Loans in Baltic," *Journal of Baltic Studies*, 1977/2, 99–104.

— 1982: "Onomastyka bałtycka w źródłach antycznych" [Baltic place names in sources from Antiquity], *Acta Baltico-Slavica*, 1982, 49–66.

— 1984: "Wokół etnogenezy Białorusinów" [On the ethnogenesis of the Byelorussians], *Acta Baltico-Slavica*, 1984, 33–47.

— (ed.) 1988: *Języki indoeuropejskie* [Indo-European languages], Warszawa: 487.

Beliauskas, Ž. 1992: "Lietuvių mitologijos rekonstrukcija A. J. Greimo darbuose" [The reconstruction of Lithuanian mythology in the works of A. J. Greimas], in Gaižutis 1992, 218–232.

Bell, J. 1992: "On capturing agency in theories about prehistory," in Gardin–Peebles 1992, 30–55.

Benac, A. (ed.) 1964: *Simpozijum o teritorjalnom i hronološkom razgraničenju Ilira u praistorijsko doba* [Symposium on the distancing of the Illyrians in time and space in prehistoric times], Sarajevo: 293.

Ben-Amos, D.–Goldstein, S. K. 1975: *Folklore. Performance and Communication,* The Hague–Paris: 308.

Benkő, L. (ed.) 1967: *A magyar nyelv történeti-etimológiai szótára* [The historical-etymological dictionary of the Hungarian language], Budapest: 1142.

Benninghoven, F. 1965: *Der Orden der Schwertbrüder.* Köln–Graz: 525.

Beresnevičius, G. 1989: "Prūsų pagonybės reforma: Videvutis ir Brutenis" [The reform of Prussian paganism: Videvutis and Brutenis], *Sietynas*, 1989, 72–93.

— 1990: *Dausos* [Paradise], Klaipėda: 214.

— 1992: "Sovijaus mitas kaip senosios baltiškos kultūros šifras" [The Sovij myth, as the key symbol of ancient Baltic culture], in Gaižutis 1992, 88–107.

— 1995: *Baltų religinės reformos* [The religious reform of the Balts], Vilnius: 221.

— 1996: "Baltų religijų metmenys" [The foundations of Baltic religions], *Metai*, 1996/8–9, 112- 125.

Berger, H. 1880: *Die geographischen Fragmente des Eratosthenes*, Leipzig: 393.

Bergmane, A.–Blinkena, A. 1986: *Latviešu rakstības attīstība* [The development of Latvian spelling], Riga: 434.

Berichte 1973: *Berichte über den II. Internationalen Kongress für slavische Archaelogie, I–II.* Berlin: 483.

Bertuleit, H. 1924: "Das Religionswesen der alten Preussen mit litauisch–lettischen Paralellen," *Sitzungsberichte der Altertumsgesellschaft Prussia*, Königsberg: 113.

Bērziņš, L. 1930: "Über das lettische Volkslied," in Schmidt 1930, 284–309.

Bielenstein, A. 1892: *Die Grenzen des lettischen Volksstammes und der lettischen Sprache in der Gegenwart und im 13. Jahrhundert*, St. Petersburg: 548.

Biezais, H. 1954: *Die Religionsquellen der baltischen Völker und die Ergebnisse der bisherigen Forschungen*, Uppsala: 128.

— 1955: *Die Hauptgöttinnen der alten Letten*, Uppsala: 320.

— 1961: *Die Gottesgestalt der lettischen Volksreligion*, Stockholm etc.: 267.

— 1972: *Die himmlische Götterfamilie der alten Letten*, Uppsala: 593.

— (ed.) 1972a: *The Myth of the State*, Stockholm: 188.

— 1975: "Baltische Religion," in Ström–Biezais 1975, 307–391.

— 1990: "Vēsture un struktūra baltu un slāvu folkloras un reliģijas pētniecībā" [History and structure in the research of Baltic and Slavic folklore and religion], *Zinātņu Akadēmijas Vēstis*, 1990/10, 7–28.

— 1993: "Romiešu un latviešu īpašo dievu problēma" [The problem of the separate gods of the Romans and the Latvians] *Latvijas Zinātņu Akadēmijas Vēstis,* 1993/10, 32–37.

Bilmanis, A. 1951: *A History of Latvia*, Princeton: 441.

Birnbaum, H. 1970: "Four Approaches to Balto-Slavic," in Rūķe–Draviņa 1970, 69–76.

— 1987: *Praslavyanskiy yazyk*, (*Common Slavic*, 1973–1983) (introduction, transl., V.A. Dybo, conclusion, V. K. Zhuravlev) Moscow: 512.

Birnbaum, H. – Puhvel, J. (eds.) 1966: *Ancient Indo-European Dialects,* Berkeley–Los Angeles: 247.

Biržiška, M. 1919: *Lietuvių dainų literatūros istorija* [The history of the literature about the Lithuanian dainas], Vilnius: 116.

— 1952: *Lietuvių tautos kelias į naująjį gyvenimą* [The road of the Lithuanian people into the new life], Los Angeles: 240.

Biržiška, V. 1953: *Senųjų lietuviškų knygų istorija* [The history of old Lithuanain books], I. Chicago: 208.

Biskup, M.–Labuda, G. 1986: *Dzieje Zakonu Krzyżackiego w Prusach* [The history of the Order of the Crusaders in Prussianland], Gdańsk: 624.

Blacker, C.–Loewe, M. (eds.) 1975: *Ancient Cosmologies,* London: 270.

Blese, (Blesse) E. 1930: "Die Entwicklungsphasen der lettischen Sprache," in Schmidt 1930, 61–70.

— 1930a: "Die Kuren und ihre sprachliche Stellung im Kreise der baltischen Volksstämme," in *Congressus* 1931, 293–312.

— 1937: "Seno kuršu etniskā piederība" [The ethnic belonging of the old Couronians], *Senatne un Māksla,* 1937/2, 65–78.

Bloch, M. 1937: "Mit várjunk a történelemtől?" (Que demander à l'histoire), (transl., Kosáry, D.) in 1974, 29–65.

— 1974: *A történelem védelmében,* (annotations, ed., Kosáry, D.; conclusion, Benda, Gy.) Budapest: 326.

Bobrowski, J. 1966: *Litauische Klaviere,* Berlin, 1966: 171.

Bogolyubova, N. D.–Jakubaitis, T. A. 1959: "Istoriya razrabotki voprosa o balto-slavyanskikh yazykovykh otnosheniyakh," in Sokols 1959, 331–375.

Bogucka, M. 1982: *Hold pruski* [Prussian submission], Warszawa: 203.

Bohnsack, D.–Follmann, A. B. 1976: "Bernstein und Bernsteinhandel," in Hoops 1976, 288–298.

Boiko, K. (ed.) 1994: *Lībieši* [The Livians], Riga: 319.

Bojtár, E. 1985: *Kevés szóval litvánul* [With a few words in Lithuanian], Budapest: 311.

— 1989: *Európa megrablása* [The ride-rape of Europe], Budapest: 334.

— 1990: *Litván kalauz* [Lithuanian guide], Budapest: 130.

Bóna, I. 1974: *A középkor hajnala: A gepidák és a langobardok a Kárpát-medencében* [The dawn of the Middle Ages: The Gepides and the Langobards in the Carpathian Basin], Budapest: 176.

Bonfante, G. 1935–36: "'Arcaico' e 'conservativo' nel gruppo baltico," *Studi Baltici,* 5, 30–37.

— 1985: "The Word for Amber in Baltic, Latin, Germanic, and Greek", *Journal of Baltic Studies,* 1985/3, 316–319.

Bonfante, L. 1985: "Amber woman and situla art," *Journal of Baltic Studies,* 1985/3, 276–291.

Boockmann, H. 1992: *Deutsche Geschichte im Osten Europas. Ostpreussen und Westpreussen*, Berlin: 479.

Borst, A. 1957–63: *Der Turmbau von Babel* I–IV, Stuttgart: 2320.

Bosch-Gimpera, P. 1968: "Discussion sur le problème indo-européen," in Jażdżewski 1968, 57–67.

Bosl, K. 1971: "Adalbert von Prag – Heiliger an einer europäischen Zeitwende," in 1976, 125–136.

— 1976: *Böhmen und seine Nachbarn*, München–Wien: 346.

Bosse, H. 1986: "Die Einkünfte kurländischer Literaten am Ende des 18. Jahrhunderts," *Zeitschrift für Ostforschung*, 1986/4, 516–594.

Brakas, M. (ed.) 1976: *Lithuania Minor*, New York: 304.

Brandenstein, W. 1962: "Das Indogermanenproblem," in Scherer 1968, 523–537.

Breisach, E. 1983: *Ancient, Medieval, and Modern*, Chicago–London: 487.

Brückner, A. 1904: *Starożytna Litwa* (Old Lithuania) (introduction, annotations, J. Jaskanis), Olsztyn, 1985: XVII+243.

— 1918: "Mitologia słowiańska" [Slavic mythology], in 1980, 65–218.

— 1924: "Mitologia polska" [Polish mythology], in 1980, 219–326.

— 1926: "Tezy mitologiczne" [Mythological theses], in 1980, 327–350.

— 1929: "Preussen, Polen, Witingen," *Zeitschrift für slavische Philologie*, 1929, 56–66.

— 1980: *Mitologia słowiańska i polska* [Slavic and Polish mythology], (introduction, annotations, S. Urbańczyk), Warszawa: 383.

Budreckis, A. 1976: "The Lithuanian language decrees and proclamations of the Prussian Kings," in Brakas 1976, 151–213.

Būga, K. 1907–10: "Kalbos dalykai" [Linguistic matters], in 1958–61/I, 101–139.

— 1908–09: "Medžiaga lietuvių, latvių ir prūsų mitologijai" [Addenda to Lithuanian, Latvian and Prussian mythology], in 1958–61/I, 143–189.

— 1918: "Zamechaniya i dopolneniya k etimologicheskomu slovaryu russkogo yazyka A. Preobrazhenskogo," in 1958–61/II, 499–694.

— 1920–22: "Kalba ir senovė" [Language and antiquity], in 1958–61/II, 7–328.

— 1923: Prof. P. Šmidta Lekcijų konspekts Ievads baltu filoloģijā [Lecture notes of Prof. P. Šmits on Introduction to Baltic philology], in 1958–61/III, 660–662.

— 1923a: "Latvijas vietu vārdi" [Place names of Latvia], in 1958–61/III, 612–648.

— 1923b: "Aistiškos kilmės Gudijos vietovardžiai" [Baltic place names in Belarus], in 1958–61/III, 518–550.

— 1924: "Lietuvių tauta ir kalba bei jos artimieji giminaičiai" [The Lithuanian people and language, and the closest relatives], in 1958–61/III, 85–282.

— 1924a: "Aisčių praeitis vietų vardų šviesoje" [The past of the Balts in the light of place names], in 1958–61/III, 728–742.

— 1924b: "Lietuvių įsikūrimas šių dienų Lietuvoje" [The settling of the Lithuanians in today's Lithuania] in 1958–61/III, 551–583.

— 1958–61: *Rinktiniai raštai* [Selected writings], I–III. Vilnius.

Bukšs, M. 1972: "Die Rolle Trasuns bei der Vereinigung Lettlands," in Ziedonis–Winter–Valgemäe 1974, 175–187.

Bumblauskas, A. 1994: "Apie Lietuvos baroko epochą barokiškai" [On the Baroque period of the Lithuanians in a Baroque style], *Kultūros Barai*, 1994/5, 68–74.

— 1994a: "Dėl Lietuvos DK civilizacijos pobīdžio" [On the nature of the civilization in the Grand Duchy of Lithuania], *Kultūros Barai*, 1994/10, 63–70.

Butrimas, H. (ed.) 1990: *Žemaičių praeitis* [Žemaitija's past], Vilnius: 243.

Butrimas, H.–Girininkas, A. 1990: "Staryye mestnyye i novyye pogrebal'nyye obryady v neolite Litvy," in Ivanov–Nevskaya 1990, 7–157.

Cantor, N. F.–Werthman, M. S. 1972: *Ancient Civilization: 4000 B. C. – 400 A. D.*, New York: 278.

Cardona, G.–Hoenigswald, H. M.–Senn, A. (eds.) 1970: *Indo-European and Indo- Europeans*, Philadelphia: 440.

Carr, E. H. 1962: *What is History?* London: 155.

Cassiodorus: "Cassiodori Senatoris Variae," in *Monumenta Germaniae Historica*, XII. Berlin, 1854: 597.

Caune, A. 1992: "Rīgas varda izcelsmes skaidrojumi un to atbilstība arheoloģiskajām liecībam" [The explanations of the name 'Riga' and their correlations in archaeological finds], *Latvijas Zinātṇu Akadēmijas Vēstis*, 1992/6, 35–41.

Cavalli-Sforza, L. L.–Cavalli-Sforza, F. 1995: *The Great Human Diasporas (Chi siamo)*, (transl., S. Thorne) Reading: 300.

Čepėnas, P. 1977–86: *Naujųjų laikų Lietuvos istorija* [The history of Modern Lithuania] I–II. Chicago: 543, 840.

Chantraine, P. 1968: *Dictionnaire étymologique de la langue grecque*. II. Paris.

Chatterji, S. K. 1968: *Balts and Aryans in their Indo-European Background*. Simla: XX+180.

Childe, G. 1950: *The Dawn of European Civilization*, London: XIX+362.

— 1958: *The Prehistory of European Society*, 1958, London: 182.

Chirot, D. 1996: "Herder's multicultural theory of nationalism and its consequences," *East European Politics and Societies*, 1996/1, 1–15.

Christiansen, E. 1980: *The Northern Crusades. (The Baltic and the Catholic Frontier. 1100–1525)*, London–Basingstoke: 273.

Cipolla, C. M. 1969: *Literacy and Development in the West*, London: 144.

Čiževskij, D. 1956: "Einige Probleme aus der vergleichenden Geschichte der slavischen Literaturen," in 1956a, 1–16.

— 1956a: *Aus zwei Welten*,'s-Gravenhage: 358.

Congressus 1931: *Congressus Secundus Archaeologorum Balticorum Rigae*, 19.–23. VIII. 1930. Riga: 495.

Cosmas: *Cosmas Pragensis: Chronica Bohemorum*. (introduction, annotations, B. Bretholz) Berlin: 1923, 295.

Cultus 1976: *Cultus et Cognitio*, Warszawa: 685.

Curtius, E. R. 1948: *Europäische Literatur und lateinisches Mittelalter,* Bern: 601.

Dainauskas, J. 1991: *Lietuvos bei lietuvių krikštas ir 1387-ji metai* [The conversion of Lithuania and the Lithuanians, and the year 1387], Chicago: 352.

Dambe, V. 1990: "Par Rīgas vārda izcelsmi" [On the origins of the name 'Riga'], in Laumane 1990, 5–20.

Daniel, G. 1972: "The advent of civilization," in Cantor–Werthman 1972, 4–31.

Das heidnische 1969–70: *Das heidnische und christliche Slaventum, Acta II. Congressus internationales historiae Slavicae,* Wiesbaden, I-II.

Daukantas, S. 1845: "Būdas senovės lietuvių, kalnėnų ir žemaičių" [The customs of the ancient Lithuanians, Aukštaitians, and Žemaitians], in 1976/I, 403–654.

— 1976: *Raštai* [His writings], I–II. (selected, introduction, annotations, V. Merkys), Vilnius.

Dégh, L.–Vázsonyi, A. 1975: "The hypothesis of multi-conduit transmission in folklore," in Ben-Amos–Goldstein 1975, 207–252.

Deksnys, B. (ed.) 1986: *Krikščionybė ir jos socialinis vaidmuo Lietuvoje* [Christianity and its social function in Lithuania], Vilnius: 318.

Deņisova, R. 1975: *Antropologiya drevnikh baltov.* Riga: 403.

— 1977: *Etnogenezis latyshey (po dannym kraniologii).* Riga: 360.

— 1989: "Baltu cilšu etniskās vēstures procesi m. ē. 1. gadu tūkstotī [The processes of the history of Baltic tribes in the first millennium AD], *Latvijas Zinātņu Akadēmijas Vēstis,* 1989/12, 20–36.

— 1991: "Austrumbaltu ciltis agrajā dzelzs laikmetā" [East Baltic tribes in the early Iron Age], *Latvijas Vēsture,* 1991/1, 7–14.

— 1991a: "Baltu ciltis Baltijas somu teritorijā" [Baltic tribes in the Finnish area of the Baltic region], *Latvijas Vēsture,* 1991/2, 7–11.

Devoto, G. (ed.) 1963[2]: *Storia delle letterature baltiche,* Milano: 451.

De Vries, J. 1961: *Forschungsgeschichte der Mythologie,* Freiburg–München: 381.

Die osteuropäischen 1908: *Die osteuropäischen Literaturen und die slavischen Sprachen,* Berlin–Leipzig: 396.

Die Sorben 1970: *Die Sorben,* Bautzen: 248.

Diószegi, V. 1954: "A honfoglaló magyar nép hitvilága kutatásának néhány kérdéséhez [A few issues on the research of the belief system of the Hungarian people at the time of their settlement], *Ethnographia,* 1954/1–2, 20–68.

— 1967: *A pogány magyarok hitvilága,* [The belief system of the pagan Hungarians], Budapest: 142.

Długosz, J. 1925: *Bitwa Grunwaldzka* [The battle at Grunwald] (introduction, annotations, J. Dąbrowski), Kraków: LXIV+112.

Dobiáš, J. 1964: *Dějiny československého území před vystoupením Slovanů* [The history of Czechoslovak lands before the appearance of the Slavs], Praha: 475.

Dolukhanov, P. M. 1989: "Etnolingvisticheskie protsessy na territorii Vostochnoy Pribaltiki po dannym arkheologii i smezhnykh nauk," *Baltistica* 1989, III (1), 50–63.

Domokos, P. 1985: *A kisebb uráli népek irodalmának kialakulása* [The emergence of the literature of minor Uralian peoples], Budapest: 354.

Dörries, H. 1956: "Fragen der Schwertmission," in Wittram 1956, 17–25.

Doveika, K. 1962: J. "Kraševskio ryšiai su Lietuva ir lietuvių literatūra" [J. Kraszewski's relationship to Lithuania and Lithuanian literature], in Korsakas 1962, 266–301.

Dubonis, A. 1997: "Rivijaus kronikos byla" [The trial of the Chronicle by Rivius], *Lituanistica*, 1997/4, 3–12.

— 1998: *Lietuvos didžiojo kunigaikščio leičiai* [The Leitis of the Grand Duke of Lithuania], Vilnius: 169.

Duchyts, L. 1995: "Balty i slavyane na Belarusi u pachatku II tysyachagodz'dzya [Balts and Slavs in the territories of Belarus at the beginning of the second millennium]," *Belaruski Gistarychny Aglyad* 1995/1, 15–30.

Dulichenko, A. D. 1994: "Fenomen literaturnykh mikroyazykov v sovremennom slavyanskom yazykovom mire," *Bibliotheca Slavica Savariensis*, 1994/II, 76–84.

Dumézil, G. 1952: *Les Dieux des Indoeuropéens*, Paris: 267.

— 1968: *Mythe et Épopée*, I. Paris: 653.

— 1978: *Romans de Scythie et d'alentour*, Paris: 380.

Dundulis, B. 1985: *Lietuvos kovos dėl Baltijos jūros* [Lithuania's battles for the Baltic Sea], Vilnius: 142.

Dunsdorfs, E. 1970: "Did Latvians live in tribal societies in the twelfth and thirteenth centuries?" in Rūķe-Draviņa 1970, 96–106.

— 1973: "Dainologija" [Dainalogy], *Archivs* (Australia), 1973/IV, 41–52.

Duridanov, I. 1969: *Thrakisch–dakische Studien. I. Die thrakisch- und dakisch-baltischen Sprachbeziehungen*, Sofia: 103.

Dusburg: Petri de Dusburg: "Chronicon Terrae Prussiae," in SRP/I: 3–219.

— 1985: Petras Dusburgietis: *Prūsijos žemės kronika*, (transl., L. Valkūnas; introduction, annotations, R. Batūra), Vilnius 1985: 497.

Dvornik, F. 1949: *The Making of Central and Eastern Europe*, London: 350.

D'yakonov, I. M. 1982: "O prarodine nositeley indoevropeyskikh dialektov," *Vestnik Drevney Istorii* 1982/3, 3–30, 4, 11–25.

— 1994: *Puti istorii. Ot drevneyshego cheloveka do nashikh dney.* Moscow: 383.

Ebert, M. (ed.) 1924: *Reallexikon der Vorgeschichte.* 4/1. Berlin: 581.

Eckert, R.–Bukevičiūtė, E. J.–Hinze, F. 1994: *Die baltischen Sprachen*, Leipzig etc.: 416.

Eco, U. 1989: *Foucault's Pendulum* (*Il pendolo di Foucault, 1980*) (transl., Weawer, W.), London: 946.

Edda, 1985 (introduction, annotations, Balogh, N. A.), Budapest: 506.

Eichel, H. M. 1978: "The new geography and the ancient Balts," *Journal of Baltic Studies,*" 1978/4, 315–325.

Einhard (Éginhard)*: *Vita Karoli Magni Imperatoris* (transl., introduction, ed. L. Halphen), Paris, 1967: 128.

Eliade, M. 1951: *Le chamanisme et les techniques archaïque de l'extase,* Paris: 447.

— 1987: *A szent és a profán* (*Das Heilige und das Profane,*1957), Budapest: 231.

— 1994–96: *Vallási hiedelmek és eszmék története.* (*Histoire des croyances et des idées religieuses, 1976–83*) I–III. (transl., Saly, N.; conclusion, Simon, R.), Budapest.

Ellis Davidson, H. R. 1976: *The Viking Road to Byzantium,* London: 341.

Endzelīns, (Endzelin) J. 1899: "Latyshskye zaimstvovaniya iz slavyanskikh jazykov," in 1972–81/I, 80–113.

— 1911: "Ventas vārds un kīru tautība" [The name of Venta and the ethnicity of the Couronians], in 1971–1982/II, 357–359.

— 1912: "Über die Nationalität und Sprache der Kuren," in 1971–1982/II, 440–453.

— 1913: "Latvieši un latgalieši [Latvians and Latgalians], in 1971–1982/II, 477–479.

— 1922: "Lettisches Lesebuch," in 1971–1982/III/1, 176–349.

— 1925: "Piezīmes par zemgaļu vārdu un dialektu" [Notes on the name of the Zemgalians and their dialect], in 1971–1982/III/1, 419–421.

— 1927: "Indogermanische Grammatik von H. Hirt," in 1971–1982/III/1, 688–695.

— 1930: "Die Letten und ihre Sprache," in Schmidt 1930, 56–60.

— 1944: *Altpreussische Grammatik,* Hildesheim–New York: 202.

— 1945: "Ievads baltu filoloģijā" [Introduction to Baltic philology], in 1971–1982/IV/2, 352–410.

— 1954: "Latviešu valoda Vidzemē" [The Latvian language in Vidzeme], in 1971–1982/III/2, 478–491.

— 1971–82: *Darbu izlase* [Selected works], I–IV. Riga.

Engel, C. (ed.) 1939: *Ostbaltische Frühzeit,* Leipzig: 498.

Engel, P. 1990: Beilleszkedés Európába, a kezdetektől 1440-ig [Adjusting to Europe from the beginnings to 1440], Budapest: 388.

Engels, F. 1884: *The Origin of the Family, Private Property and the State* (Der Ursprung der Familie, des Privateigentums und des Staats), (transl., West, A.), London: 1981.

— 1888: "Ludwig Feuerbach and the End of the Classical German Philosophy" ("Ludwig Feuerbach und der Ausgang der klassischen deutschen Philosophie"), in Marx–Engels 1989/26.

Erhart, A. 1984: *Baltské jazyky* [Baltic languages], Praha: 199.

Esterházy, P. 1979: *Termelési regény (kisssregény)*, [A novel of production], Budapest: 473.

Ethnic 1981: *Ethnic Changes*, (ed., C. F. Keyes), Seattle–London: 331.

Etnograficheskiye 1980: *Etnograficheskiye i lingvisticheskiye aspekty etnicheskoy istorii baltskikh narodov*. Riga: 1980.

Falkenhahn, V. 1941: *Der Übersetzer der litauischen Bibel Johannes Bretke und seine Helfer*, Königsberg–Berlin: 487.

Faragó, J. 1991: "Nyelvében él a nemzet," [In its language lives the nation], *Élet és Irodalom*, 27 September 1991, 11.

Farkas Zs. 1994: *Mindentől ugyanannyira*, [The same distance from all], Budapest: 211.

Fennel, T.–Gelsen, H. 1980: *A Grammar of Modern Latvian*, I–III, The Hague etc.: 1368.

Findeisen, H. 1957: *Schamanentum*, Stuttgart: 240.

Finley, M. I. 1956: *The World of Odysseus*, London: 202.

— 1972: "The Greek City-State," in Cantor–Werthman 1972, 62–95..

— 1974: "Schliemann's Troy – one hundred years after," *Proceedings of the British Academy*, 1974, 393–412.

— 1975: *The Use and Abuse of History*, London: 254.

— 1991: *The Ancient Greeks*, London: 204.

Finno-ugry 1979: *Finno-ugry i slavyane*. Leningrad: 175.

Fischer, D. H. 1970: *Historians' Fallacies. Toward a Logic of Historical Thought*, London: 338.

Fodor, I. 1961: "A glottokronológia érvényessége a szláv nyelvek anyaga alapján" [The validity of glottochronology on the basis of the material on Slavic languages], *Nyelvtudományi Közlemények*, 1961, 308–344.

Fodor, I. – Hagège, C. (ed.) 1990: *Language Reform*, Vol. V. Hamburg: 802.

Fortstreuter, K. 1960: "Fragen der Mission in Preussen von 1245 bis 1260," *Zeitschrift für Ostforschung*, 1960, 250–268.

Fraenkel, E. 1950: *Die baltischen Sprachen: Ihre Beziehungen zu einander und zu den indogermanischen Schwesteridiomen als Einführung in die baltische Sprachwissenschaft*, Heidelberg: 126.

— *Litauisches etymologisches Wörterbuch*, I–II, Heidelberg: 1962; Göttingen: 1965.

Funk–Wagnalls Standard 1949: *Dictionary of Folklore, Mythology and Legend*, I–II, New York.

Funkenstein, Amos 1989: "Collective memory and historical consciousness," *History and Memory*, 1989/1, 5 –26.

Gábori, M. 1977: "Közép- és Kelet-Európa benépesedése," [The population of Central and Eastern Europe], *Századok*, 1977/1, 11–47.

Gaižutis, A. (ed.) 1992: *Ikikrikščioniškosios Lietuvos kultūra*, [Lithuania's pre-Christian culture], Vilnius: 245.

Gamkrelidze, T. V.–Ivanov, V. V. 1980: "Drevnyaya Perednyaya Aziya i indo-
    evropeyskaya problema," *Vestnik Drevney Istorii*, 1980/3, 3–27.
— 1981: "Migratsii plemen–nositeley indoevropeyskikh dialektov–s pervon-
    achal'noy territorii rasseleniya na Blizhnem Vostoke v istoricheskiye mesta
    ikh obitaniya v Evraziyu," *Vestnik Drevney Istorii*, 1981/2, 11–33.
— 1984: *Indoevropeyskiy yazyk i istoriko-tipologicheskiy analiz prayazyka i
    protokul'tury*, Tbilisi, 1–2: XCVI+428, 1328.
— 1985: "The problem of the original homeland of the speakers of Indo-European
    Languages (In response to I. M. Diakonoff's articles)", *The Journal of In-
    doeuropean Studies*, 1985,175–184.
Gardin, J.-C.–Peebles, C. S. (ed.) 1992: *Representations in Archaeology*, Bloom-
    ington–Indianapolis: 395.
Gāters, A. 1954: "Osti und Ostsee," *Beiträge zur Namenforschung*, 1954, 244–
    248.
— 1977: *Die lettische Sprache und ihre Dialekte*, The Hague etc.: 187.
Gaučas P. 1974: "Jotvingiai XIX a. ?!" [Jatvingians in the nineteenth century?!],
    Mokslas ir Gyvenimas, 1974/2, 21–24.
— 1989: "Lietuvių kalba Vilniaus krašte" [Lithuanian language in the Vilnius
    region], *Pergalė*, 1989/6, 148–167.
Gediminas*: *Gedimino laiškai* [Gediminas's letters] (ed., annotations, V. Pašuta,
    I. Štal), Vilnius: 1966, 199.
Geertz, C. 1985: "The uses of diversity," in Mc Murrin 1986, 251–275.
Gellner, E. 1983: *Nations and Nationalism*, Oxford: 150.
Gergely, J. 1982: *A pápaság története*, [Papal history], Budapest: 457.
Gerlach, H. 1978: *Nur der Name blieb. Glanz und Untergang der alten Preussen*,
    München–Zürich: 205.
Gerullis, G. 1921: "Zur Sprache der Sudauer–Jatwinger", in *Festschrift Adalbert
    Bezzenberger*, Göttingen, 44–51.
— 1924: "Baltische Völker," in Ebert 1924, 335–342.
Geschichte 1964: *Geschichte der Textüberlieferung der antiken und mittelalter-
    lichen Literatur*, I–II, Zürich: 1121.
Gieysztor, A. 1982: *Mitologia Słowian* [Mythology of the Slavs], Warszawa: 271.
Gimbutas, (Gimbutienė) M. 1956: *The Prehistory of Eastern Europe*, 1, Cam-
    bridge (Mass.): IX+241.
— 1958: *Ancient Symbolism in Lithuanian Folk Art*, Philadelphia: 148.
— 1966: "The Kurgan culture," in Actes 1966, 483–487.
— 1966a: "Europos civilizacijos pradžia ir indo-europiečių antplūdis" [The be-
    ginning of European civilization and the migration of the Indo-Europeans],
    Metmenys, 1966/11, 107–115.
— 1970: "Proto-Indo-European Culture: The Kurgan culture during the fifth,
    fourth, and third millennia BC" in Cardona–Hoenigswald–Senn 1970, 155–
    197.

— 1971: "Indoeuropiečių protėvynė" [The *Urheimat* of the Indo-Europeans], *Metmenys*, 1971/22, 67–94.

— 1974: *The Gods and Goddesses of Old -Europe*, Berkeley–Los Angeles: 303.

— 1977: "Apie lietuvių mitologijos populiarizacijos reikalą bei šaltinius baltų mitologijai atkurti" [On the popularization of Lithuanian mythology and the sources for the reconstruction of Baltic mythology], *Metmenys*, 1977/33, 203–206.

— 1984: "Senosios Europos deivės ir dievai lietuvių mitologijoje" [Old-Europe's goddesses and gods in Lithuanian mythology], *Metmenys*, 1984/4, 28–57.

— 1985: *Baltai priešistoriniais laikais*. (*The Balts*, 1963) [The prehistoric Balts], Vilnius: 191.

— 1985a: "East Baltic amber in the fourth and third millennia B.C.," *Journal of Baltic Studies*, 1985/3, 231–256.

— 1985b: "Primary and secondary homeland of the Indo-Europeans: Comments on Gamkrelidze–Ivanov articles," *The Journal of Indoeuropean Studies*, 1985, 185–202.

— 1987: "Pasikalbėjimas apie Kernavės miestą, Vilniaus katedras ir Perkūno šventyklą" [A talk on the town Kernavė, the cathedrals of Vilnius, and the temple of Perkūnas], *Draugas*, 1987/66, 1–2.

— 1989: *The Language of the Goddess*, (introd., J. Campbell), London: XXIII+ 388.

— 1991: *The Civilization of the Goddess*, San Francisco: 529.

Gineitis, L. 1991: "Prīsiškasis vėlyvojo etapo patriotizmas ir lituanistika" [A late period of Prussian patriotism and Lithuanian Studies], *Lituanistica*, 1991/4, 64–85.

Ginzburg, C. 1984: "Germanic Mythology and Nazism: Thoughts on an Old Book by Georges Dumézil," in 1989, 126–145.

— 1989: *Clues, Myths, and the Historical Method*. (*Miti emblemi spie: morfologia e storia*), Baltimore–London: 231.

Girininkas, A. 1992: "Rytų baltū kultūros kilmės ypatybės" [The characteristics of the origins of East Baltic culture], in Milius 1992, 5–12.

Goethe, J. W. 1820: "Annalen," in MDCXL/30, 120.

— 1826: "Kurze Anzeigen," in MDCXL/38, 48–55.

— 1828: "Nationelle Dichtkunst," in MDCXL/38, 142–154.

— MDCXL: *Sämtliche Werke*, Stuttgart–Berlin 1–40.

Gołąb, Z. 1982: "Kiedy nastąpiło rozszczepienie językowe Bałtów i Słowian?" [When did the Baltic–Slavic linguistic division occur?], *Acta Baltico-Slavica*, 1982, 121–133.

Goldziher, I. 1876: *Der Mythos bei den Hebräern und seine geschichtliche Entwickelung*, Leipzig: 402.

— 1878: "Az összehasonlító vallástudomány módszeréről" [On the methodology of comparative studies of religion], *Magyar Tanügy*, 171–186.

— 1881: "Az összehasonlító mythologia fejlődése" [The development of comparative mythology], *Budapesti Szemle*, 1881/28, 1–35.

Goody, J. 1959: "Indoeuropean society," *Past and Present*, 1959/16, 88–91.

Goody, J.–Watt, I. 1963: "The consequences of literacy," *Comparative Studies in Society and History*, 1963/3, 304–345.

Górski, K. 1946: *Państwo Krzyżackie w Prusach* [The state of the crusaders in Prussianland], Gdańsk–Bydgoszcz: 295.

Grabowicz, G. 1981: *Toward a History of Ukrainian Literature*, Cambridge (Mass.): 103.

Graudonis, J. 1967: *Latviya v epokhe pozdney bronzy i rannego zheleza*. Riga: 164+XLII.

— 1990: "Pogrebal'nyye obryady na territorii Latvii v epokhe pozdney bronzy i rannego zheleza," in Ivanov–Nevskaya 1990, 157–163.

Graus, F. 1965: "Die Entstehung der mittelalterlichen Staaten in Mitteleuropa," *Historica*, 1965(10), 5–65.

Grāvere, R. 1990: "Latviešu etnoģenēzes antropoloģiskais aspekts" [The anthropological aspect of Latvian ethnogenesis], *Latvijas Zinātņu Akadēmijas Vēstis*, 1990/12: 8–17.

Greimas, A. J. 1970: Apie folklorą, religiją ir istoriją [On folklore, religion, and history], *Metmenys*, 1970, 32–51.

— 1979: "Apie dievus ir žmones" [On gods and people], in 1990, 5–342.

— 1988: "Antanas Smetona ir kas toliau" [Antanas Smetona and what is next], *Naujoji Viltis*, (Chicago), 1988/21, 32–40.

— 1990: *Tautos atminties beieškant,* [Examining the memory of a nation], (concl., B. Savukynas),Vilnius–Chicago: 526.

— 1990a: "Europa be europiečių" [Europe without the Europeans], *Metmenys*, 1990, 157–161.

Grierson, P. 1975: "The European heritage," in Blacker–Loewe 1975, 225–258.

Grudzińska Gross, I. 1995: "Adam Mickiewicz: A European from Nowogródek," *East European Politics and Societies*, 1995/2, 295–316.

Grunau, S. 1529: *Preussische Chronik* (ed. introd., M. Perlbach, R. Philippi, P. Wagner), I–III, Leipzig: 1876–96, 755, 786, 440.

Grundmann, H.: "Litteratus–illiteratus," in *Archiv für Kulturgeschichte*, 1958, 1–65.

Gudavičius, E. 1981: "Lemoviai". ("Lemovii"), in Volkaitė-Kulikauskienė 1981, 75–83.

— 1981a: "Naujausi duomenys apie gotų santykių su baltais ir slavais prielaidas" [Most recent data for the preconditions of a relationship of the Goths with the Baltic and Slavic peoples], *Lietuvos TSR Mokslų Akademijos Darbai. A serija*, 1981/3, 103–112.

— 1982: "1219 metų sutarties dalyviai ir jų vaidmuo suvienijant Lietuvą" [The participants at the 1219 Treaty and their role in the unification of Lithuania], *Istorija*, 1982, 33–46.

— 1983: " 'Lietuvos' vardas XI a.–XII a. I pusės šaltiniuose" [The name 'Lithuania' in sources from the eleventh and early twelfth centuries], *Lietuvos Mokslų Akademijos Darbai. A serija*, 1983/3, 79–86.

— 1983a: "Dėl Lietuvos valstybės kūrimosi centro ir laiko" [On the center and time of the emergence of the Lithuanian state], *Lietuvos Mokslų Akademijos Darbai. A serija*, 1983/2, 61–70.

— 1984: "Dėl lietuvių žemių konfederacijos susidarymo laiko" [On the time of the emergence of the confederation of Lithuanian lands], *Istorija*, 1984 (XXIV), 12–28.

— 1985: "Litva Mindovga," in Volkaitė-Kulikauskenė 1985, 212–227.

— 1986: "Dar kartą dėl Lietuvos valstybės kūrimosi centro ir laiko" [Once more on the center and time of the emergence of the Lithuanian state], *Lietuvos Mokslų Akademijos Darbai. A serija*, 1986/2, 53–60.

— 1987: "Kas kovėsi Durbės mūšyje?" [Who fought in the battle at Durbe?], *Istorija*, 1987, 3–21.

— 1988: "Saulės mūšio (1236 m.) vietos problematika" [The problem of the location of the 1236 battle at Saule], *Lietuvos Mokslų Akademijos Darbai. A serija*, 1988/4, 64–72.

— 1988a: "Lietuvos krikščionybės priėmimo politinė problema" [The political question of Lithuania's conversion to Christianity], *Lietuvos istorijos metraštis*, 1988, 14–22.

— 1989: *Kryžiaus karai Pabaltijoje ir Lietuva XIII amžiuje*, [The Crusades in the Baltic region and thirteenth-century Lithuania], Vilnius: 191.

— 1992: W. Urban: "The Samogitian Crusade," *Lietuvos istorijos metraštis*,1992, 182–186.

— 1993: "Kas sava ir kas skolinta mūsų kultūroje" [What is own and what is borrowed in our culture?], *Kultūros Barai*, 1993/11, 66–69.

— 1994: "Lietuvių tautos ankstyvieji amžiai: laimėjimai ir praradimai" [The early centuries of the Lithuanian nation: gains and losses], *Kultūros Barai*, 1994/5, 57–60.

— 1998: *Mindaugas*, Vilnius: 359.

Gurevich, A. 1966: *Pokhody vikingov*. Moscow: 152.

— 1972: *Istoriya i saga*. Moscow: 197.

— 1979: *Edda i saga*. Moscow: 191.

— 1987: *A középkori népi kultúra* [Mediaeval folk culture] (*Problemy srednevekovoy narodnoy kultury*, 1981), Budapest: 441.

Gustafsson, B. 1972: "Durkheim on Power and Holiness," in Biezais 1972a, 20–30.

Gustaitis, A. 1992: "Lietuvių genčių senojo rašto ieškojimas" [A search for the old script of Lithuanian tribes], *Pasaulio Lietuvis*, 1992/2, 14–15.

Haarmann, H. 1994: "Contact linguistics, archaeology and ethnogenetics: an interdisciplinary approach to the Indo-European homeland problem," *The Journal of Indoeuropean Studies*, 1994, 265–288.

Hadzisz, D. (ed., introd., annot.) 1974: *A bizánci irodalom kistükre* [Anthology of the Byzantine literature], Budapest: 843.

Haeseler, A.–Sajantila, A.–Pääbo, S. 1996: "The genetical archaeology of the human genome," *Nature Genetics*, 1996 October, 135–140.

Halecki, O. 1958: *From Florence to Brest: 1453–1596*, New York: 463.

— 1993: Európa millenniuma [The millennium of Europe, 1963] (transl., Bérczes, T.), Budapest: 370.

— 1995: *A nyugati civilizáció peremén* [On the borderlands of Western civilization 1952], (transl., Szilágyi, T.), Budapest: 352.

Haltzel, M. H. 1972: "The Russification of the Baltic Germans: a dysfunctional aspect of imperial modernization," in Ziedonis–Winter–Valgemäe 1974, 143–152.

Hamp, E. P. 1959: "Venetic isoglosses," *American Journal of Philology*, 1959/318, 179–184.

Hampl, J. 1955: "Beiträge zur Beurteilung des Historikers Tacitus," in 1975/III, 267–294.

— 1967: "Gedanken zur Diskussion über die Grenzscheide zwischen Altertum und Mittelalter," in 1975/II, 305–316.

— 1975: *Geschichte als kritische Wissenschaft*, I–III, Darmstadt.

— 1975a: "Universalgeschichte am Beispiel der Diffusionstheorie," in 1975/I, 182–236.

— 1975b: "Die 'Ilias' ist kein Geschichtsbuch," in 1975/II, 51–99.

Harmatta, J. 1949: "Mitikus orientáció nyomai a görög földrajzi világképben" [The traces of mythical orientation in the Greek geographical world view], *Antiquitas Hungarica*, 1949/12, 1–4.

— 1953: *A kimmer kérdés* [The Cimerian question], Budapest: 76.

— 1954: "Egy finnugor nép az antik irodalmi hagyományban" [A Finno-Ugric people in the literary traditions of Antiquity], *MTA Nyelv- és Irodalomtudományok Osztályának Közleményei*, 1954/3–4, 341–351.

— 1964: "Das Pelasgische und die alten Balkanensprachen," *Linguistique Balkanique*, 1964/1, 41–47.

— 1965: "Pelasgok, görögök, hettiták" [The Pelasg, Greeks, Hittites], *Antik Tanulmányok*, 1965, 77–81.

— 1966: "Az indoeurópai őshaza problémája és az őskorkutatás" [The problem of the Indo-European *Urheimat*, and the research of prehistory], *Antik Tanulmányok*, 1966, 246–248.

— 1966a: "Kimmerek és szkíták" [Cimerians and Scythians], *Antik Tanulmányok,* 1966, 107–116.

— 1967: "Régészet, nyelvtudomány és őstörténet" [Archaeology, linguistics, and prehistory], *Archeológiai Értesítő,* 1967: 215- 216.

— 1967a: "Zum Illyrischen," *Acta Antiqua Academiae Scientiarum Hungaricae,* 1967/1–4, 231–234.

— 1972: "Az indoeurópai népek régi településterületei és vándorlásai [Ancient settlements and wanderings of Indo-European peoples], *MTA Nyelv- és Irodalomtudományok Osztályának Közleményei,* 1972/3–4, 309–324.

— 1972a: "Európa nyelvei és népessége a középső paleolithikumban" [Europe's languages and population in the Middle Paleolithic], *Antik Tanulmányok,* 1985–86/2, 244–248.

— 1977: "Irániak és finnugorok, irániak és magyarok [Iranians and Finno-Ugrians, Iranians and Hungarians], in Bartha–Czeglédy–Róna-Tas 1977, 167–182.

— 1985–86: "Venetica I.," *Antik Tanulmányok,* 1985–1986/2,187–201.

— 1989–90: "Eltűnt nyelvek és írások nyomában [On the search for vanished languages and scripts], *Antik Tanulmányok,* 1989–90, 110–118.

— 1990: "A magyarság őstörténete" [The prehistory of the Hungarians], *Magyar Tudomány,* 1990/3, 243–261.

Harmening, D. 1979: *Superstitio. Überlieferungs- und theoriegeschichtliche Untersuchungen zur kirchlich-theologischen Aberglaubensliteratur des Mittelalters,* Berlin: 379.

Harmening, D.–Lutz, G.–Schemmel, B.–Wimmer, E. (eds.) 1970: *Volkskultur und Geschichte,* Berlin: XIX+694.

Harva, U. 1952: *Die religiösen Vorstellungen der Mordwinen,* Helsinki: 454.

Hašek, J. 1993: *The Good Soldier Švejk and His Fortunes in the World War* (transl., Parrott, C.) London.

Häusler, A. 1997: "Überlegungen zum Ursprung der Indogermanen," in Julku–Wiik 1998, 36–52.

Havelka, M. (ed., introd.) 1995: *Spor o smysl českých dějin. 1895–1938* (Debate over the sense of Czech history], Praha: 867.

Hegel, G. W. F. 1840: *Lectures on the Philosophy of World History* (*Vorlesungen über die Philosophie der Weltgeschichte*) (transl., Nisbet, H. B., introd. Forbes, D.), Cambridge: 1975.

Heinricus*: *Heinrici Chronicon–Indriķa Hronika.* (transl., A. Feldkuns; introd., annot., Ē. Mugurēvičs), 1993, Riga: 451.

Hellmann, M. 1954: *Das Lettenland im Mittelalter,* Münster–Köln: 264.

— 1956: "Anfänge des litauischen Reiches," *Jahrbücher für Geschichte Osteuropas,* 1956, 159–165.

— (ed.) 1981–89: *Handbuch der Geschichte Russlands,* 1–2. Stuttgart: 1089.

— 1989: "Das Grossfürstentum Litauen bis 1569", in 1981–89/2, 717–851.

— 1990: *Grundzüge der Geschichte Litauens und des litauischen Volkes*, Darmstadt: 179.

Hennig, R. 1944: *Terrae Incognitae. Eine Zusammenstellung und kritische Bewertung der wichtigsten vorkolumbischen Entdeckungsreisen an Hand der darüber vorliegenden Originalberichte*, I, Leiden: 462.

Hensel, W. 1988[3]: *Polska starożytna*, [The ancient Poland], Wrocław etc.: 721.

Hermann, A. 1986: "Mirusiųjų prisikėlimas" [The resurrection of the dead], *Akiračiai*, 1986/3, 11.

Hernegger, R. 1963: *Macht ohne Auftrag. Die Entstehung der Staats- und Volkskirche*, Freiburg: 478.

Herodotus*: *The Histories (Historiae)* (transl., Sélincourt, A., rev. with intr., notes Burn, A. R.) New York, 1972.

Herrmann, J. (ed.) 1972: *Die Slawen in Deutschland*, Berlin: 530.

Hettner, A. 1929: *Der Gang der Kultur über die Erde*, Leipzig–Berlin: 164.

Hinze, Ch. – Diederichs, U. 1983: *Ostpreussische Sagen*, Köln: 304.

Hobsbawm, E. 1990: *Nations and Nationalism Since 1780*, Cambridge: 191.

Hodder, I. 1991: *Reading the Past*, Cambridge: 221.

Hofer, T. (ed.) 1984: *Történeti antropológia* [Historical anthropology], Budapest: 366.

— 1991: "Kulturális pluralizmus," [Cultural pluralism], *Ethnographia*, 1991/3–4, 225–230.

— 1994: "Interjú," (Interview) *Buksz*, 1994/spring, 76–86.

Honko, L. 1972: "The problem of defining myth," in Biezais 1972a, 7–19.

Honti, J. 1935: "Mesetudomány és vallástörténet" [Science of tales and the history of religions], *Népünk és Nyelvünk*, 1935/VII, 107–124.

Hoops, J. (ed.) 1976[2]: *Reallexikon der germanischen Altertumskunde*, 1–7. Berlin–New York.

Hoppál, M.–Istvánovits, M. (eds.) 1978: *Mítosz és történelem*, [Myth and History], Budapest: 401.

Hoppál, M. – Sadovszky, O. (ed.) 1989: *Shamanism: Past and Present*, 1–2, Budapest–Los Angeles.

Horváth, J. 1980: *A magyar irodalom fejlődéstörténete*, [The history of the development of Hungarian literature], Budapest: 373.

Horváth, M. 1876: *A kereszténység első százada Magyarországon*, [The first century of Christianity in Hungary], Budapest: 476.

Hough, W. J. H. III 1985: "The annexation of the Baltic States and its effect on the development of law prohibiting forcible seizure of territory," *New York Law School Journal of International and Comparative Law*, vol. 6/2, 301–533.

Hroch, M. 1985: *Social Preconditions of National Revival in Europe*, (transl. B. Fowkes), Cambridge: 220.

Hubatsch, W. (ed.) 1954*: *Quellen zur Geschichte des Deutschen Ordens*, Göttingen etc.: 204.

— 1965: "Masuren und Preussisch–Litauen in der Nationalitätenpolitik Preussens 1870–1920," *Zeitschrift für Ostforschung*, 1965/4, 641–670.

— 1966: "Politische Gestaltung im nordostdeutschen Raum vom Mittelalter bis zur Mitte des 18. Jahrhunderts," *Zeitschrift für Ostforschung*, 1966/2, 201–231.

Hughes-Brock, H. 1985: "Amber and the Mycenaeans," *Journal of Baltic Studies*, 1985/3, 256–267.

Hultkranz, A. 1989: "The place of shamanism in the history of religion," in Hoppál–Sadovszky 1989/1, 43–52.

Hunfalvy, P. 1871: *Utazás a Balt-tenger vidékein* [Travels around the regions of the Baltic Sea], 1–2, Pest.

Iglói, E. 1988: *Az orosz irodalmi múlt* [Russian literary past], Budapest: 316.

Iltnere, A. (ed.) 1993–1994: *Mitologijas enciklopēdija* [Mythological Encyclopedia], 1–2, Riga: 316, 414.

Inno, K. 1979: "Mare Balticum and Balticum," *Journal of Baltic Studies*, 1979/2, 135–147.

Ivanov, V. V. 1984: "O mifopoeticheskikh osnovakh latishskikh dayn," *Balto–Slavyanskiye Issledovaniya*, 1986, 3–28.

Ivanov, V. V.–Nevskaya, L. G. 1990: *Issledovaniya v oblasti balto-slavyanskoy dukhovnoy kul'tury. Pogrebal'nyy obryad*. Moscow: 256.

Ivanov, V. V.–Toporov, V. N. 1961: "K postanovke voprosa o drevneyshikh otnosheniyakh baltiyskikh i slavyanskikh narodov," in Tolstoy 1961, 273–303.

Ivanov, V. V. – Toporov, V. N. 1974: *Issledovaniya v oblasti slavyanskikh drevnostey*, Moscow: 341.

Ivinskis, Z. 1933: "Krikščioniškosios Vakarų Europos santykiai su pagoniškąja Lietuva" [The connections of Christian Western Europe with pagan Lithuania], in 1978–1989/II, 432–442.

— 1936: "Eiliuotinė Livonijos Kronika ir jos autentiškumas" [The Livonian Rhyming Chronicle and its authenticity], in 1978–1989/II, 51–63.

— 1937: "Senosios lietuvių kultūros problemos pagal rašytus šaltinius [The question of old Lithuanian culture based on written sources], in 1978–1989/II, 457–469.

— 1938: "Senovės lietuvių religijos bibliografija" [A bibliography of old Lithuanian religion], in 1978–89/II, 471–630.

— 1938 –39: "Medžių kultas lietuvių religijoje" [The tree cult in Lithuanian religion], in 1978–89/II, 348–408.

— 1944: "Senasis lietuvių tikėjimas" [Ancient Lithuanian belief system], in 1978–89/II, 326–347.

— 1951: "Mindaugo krikštas ir Lietuvos bažnytinės provincijos įsteigimas" [Mindaugas' conversion and the establishing of the Church district of Lithuania], in 1978–89/IV, 38–50.

— 1955: "Lietuvių tautos santykiai su krikščionybe iki XVI amžiaus pradžios [The Lithuanian people's connection to Christianity until the early sixteenth century], in 1978–89/IV, 185–210.

— 1956: "Popiežius Inocentas IV ir Lietuva" [Pope Innocent IV and Lithuania], in 1978–1989/IV, 50–52.

— 1961: "Rytprusiai" [East Prussia], in 1978–1989/II, 288–293.

— 1970: "Lietuvos istorija iki Vytauto Didžiojo mirties" [Lithuania's history until the death of Vytautas the Great], in 1978–1989/I, 1–411.

— 1978–89: Rinktiniai raštai. [Collected works], I–IV, Rome.

— 1986: "Istorinius šaltinius tyrinėjant [Researching historical sources], in 1978–1989/II, 1–114.

Jablonskis, K. 1935: "Ar Mažosios Lietuvos lietuviai autochtonai?" [Are the Lithuanians of Lithuania Minor autochthonous?], in 1979, 131–139.

— 1935–42: "Lietuvos rusiškųjų aktų diplomatika" [The diplomatics of Lithuania's Russian documents], in 1979, 219–296.

— 1940–60: "Lietuvos valstybės ir teisės istorija iki XVI a. vidurio" [Lithuania's state and legal history until the mid-sixteenth century], in 1979, 140–218.

— 1979: Istorija ir jos šaltiniai [History and its sources], (ed., annot., V. Merkys), Vilnius: 327.

Jakštas, J. 1968: "Žvilgsnis į Mažosios Lietuvos istoriografiją" [A glance at Lithuania Minor's historiography], Lietuvių Katalikų Mokslo Akademijos Metraštis, IV, Roma: 1–49.

James, P. 1993: Centuries of Darkness, (introd., C. Renfrew), New Brunswick–New Jersey: XV+434.

Janulaitis, A. 1928: Enejus Silvius Piccolomini bei Jeronimas Pragiškis [Aeneas Sylvius Piccolomini and Jerome of Prague], Kaunas: 63.

Janūnaitė, M. 1981: "Nekotorye zamechaniya ob indoevropeyskoy prarodine," Baltistica, XVII (1), 66–76.

Jaskiewicz, W. C. 1952: "A study in Lithuanian mythology: Jan Lasicki's treatise on the Samogitian gods," Studi Baltici, 1952, 65–106.

Jażdżewski, K. 1963: "O trwałości i wiarogodności ustnej tradycji historycznej" [On the endurance and reliability of oral historical traditions], in Munera 1963: 7–19.

— (ed.) 1968: Liber Josepho Kostrzewski octogenario a veneratoribus dicatus, Wrocław etc.: 641.

— 1981: Pradzieje Europy środkowej, [Prehistory of Central Europe], Wrocław etc.: 711.

Jensen, H. 1969: Die Schrift in Vergangenheit und Gegenwart, Berlin: 608.

Johansen, P. 1939: "Kurlands Bewohner zum Anfang der historischen Zeit," in Engel 1939, 263–306.

Johansons, A. 1975: Latvijas kultūras vēsture 1710–1800 [Latvia's cultural history], Stockholm: 647.

Jonynas, A. 1984: *Lietuvių folkloristika*, [Lithuanian folklore studies], Vilnius: 373.

Jordanes* 1960: *Getica–O proishozhdenii i deyaniyah getov*, (transl., introd., annot.,: E. Skrzhinskaya, Moscow: 433.

Jučas, M. 1968: *Lietuvos metraščiai*, [Lithuania's chronicles], Vilnius: 186.

— 1981: "Dėl vakarinių ir šiaurinių Žemaičių ribų" [On the western and northern borders of the Žemaitians], in Volkaitė–Kulikauskienė 1981, 36–46.

— 1993: "Apie romėniškosios lietuvių kilmės legendą [On the legend of the Roman origins of the Lithuanians], *Kultūros Barai*, 1993/1, 72–74.

Julku, K. (ed.) 1997: *Itämerensuomi–eurooppalainen maa*, Oulu: 293.

Julku, K.–Wiik, K. (eds.) 1998: *The Roots of Peoples and Languages of Northern Eurasia*, Turku: 200.

Jurginis, J. 1971: *Legendos apie lietuvių kilmę* [Legends about the origins of the Lithuanians], Vilnius: 198.

— 1976: *Pagonybės ir krikščionybės santykiai Lietuvoje*, [The connections between paganism and Christianity in Lithuania], Vilnius: 126.

— 1981: "Lietuvių kildinimas iš alanų ir herulų" [Origination of the Lithuanians from the Alans and the Heruli], in Volkaitė-Kulikauskienė 1981, 84–92.

— 1987: *Lietuvos krikštas* [Lithuania's conversion], Vilnius: 333.

Jurginis, J.–Lukšaitė, J. 1981: *Lietuvos kultūros istorijos bruožai* [An outline of Lithuania's cultural history], Vilnius: 344.

Jurginis, J.–Merkys, V.–Tautavičius, A. 1968: *Vilniaus miesto istorija nuo seniausių laikų iki Spalio revoliucijos*, [The history of the town Vilnius from the most ancient times to the October Revolution], Vilnius: 395.

Jurginis, J.–Šidlauskas, A. (select., annot.,) 1983: *Kraštas ir žmonės. Lietuvos geografiniai ir etnografiniai aprašymai. XIV–XIX. a* [Regions and people: Lithuania's geographical and ethnographic descriptions, fourteenth–eighteenth centuries], Vilnius: 224.

Juška, A.–Mališauskas, J.–Pupšys, V. 1994: *Lietuvininkų žemė* [The land of the Lietuvininkas], Kaunas: 173.

Kabelka, J. 1982: *Baltų filologijos įvadas*, [Introduction to Baltic philology], Vilnius: 147.

Kadlubek, W.: *Kronika Polska* [Polish Chronicle], (introd., transl., B. Kürbis), Warszawa: 253.

Kahl, H.-D. 1981: "Zur Problematik der mittelalterlichen Vorstellung von 'Christianisierung'," in Nowak 1983, 125–128.

Kahle, W. 1986: "Die Christianisierung im baltischen Raum," in Kahle 1991, 13–26.

— 1991: *Symbiose und Spannung*, Erlangen: 410.

Kalevala: The Kalevala. An Epic Poem after Oral Tradition by Elias Lönnrot (transl., introd., notes Bosley, K., foreword, Lord, A. B.), Oxford, 1989.

Kalicz, N. 1970: *Agyag istenek: A neolitikum és a rézkor emlékei Magyarországon,* [Clay gods: The memories of the Neolithic and the Bronze Ages in Hungary], Budapest: 84+73.

— 1985: *Kőkori falu Aszódon,* [A Stone Age village in Aszód], Aszód: 195.

Karaliūnas, S. 1968: "Kai kurie baltų ir slavų kalbų seniausiųjų santykių klausimai" [A few questions around the oldest connections between the Baltic and Slavic languages], in Sabaliauskas 1968, 7–100.

— 1987: *Baltų kalbų struktūrų bendrybės ir jų kilmė,* [The commonality in the structure of the Baltic languages, and their origins], Vilnius: 258.

— 1995: "Lietuvos vardo kilmė" [The origin of Lithuania's name], *Lietuvių kalbotyros klausimai,* 1995 (XXXV), 55–91.

Karma, T. 1994: "Vai libiešu valoda ir jau gatava?" [Is the Livonian language over?], *Latvijas Zinātņu Akadēmijas Vēstis,* 1994/11, 12–46.

— 1994a: "The Livonian language – past and present," in Pusztay 1994a, 22–27.

Katičić, R. 1964: "Suvremena istraživanja o jeziku starosjedilaca ilirskih provincija" [Current research on the language of the autochthon people of Illyrian provinces], in Benac 1964, 9–58.

Katinas, V. 1983: *Baltijos gintaras,* [Amber of the Baltic Sea], Vilnius: 110.

Katonova, E. M. 1985: "Balto-slavyanskiye kontakty i problemy etimologii gidronimov," in Volkaitė-Kulikauskienė 1985, 211–218.

Kaukonen, V. 1954: "A Kalevala és alapjai" [The Kalevala and its bases], *MTA I. Osztály Közleményei,* 1954, 1–4, 1–57.

Kavass, I. I. – Sprudzs, A. (eds.) 1972: *Baltic States: A Study of their Origin and National Development: Their Seizure and Incorporation Into the U.S.S.R,* Buffalo–New York: 537.

Kazlauskas, J. 1968: "Dėl kursių vardo etimologijos" [To the etymology of the 'Kurs' name], *Baltistica,* 1968/1, 59–63.

Keppen, P. 1827: *O proiskhozhdenii yazyka i literatury litovskikh narodov,* Sankt-Petersburg: 327.

Kerényi, K. 1939: "Was ist Mythologie?," in 1971, 13–34.

— 1971: *Antike Religion,* München–Wien: 309.

Keyes, C. F. 1981: "The Dialectics of Ethnic Change," in *Ethnic* 1981, 4–30.

Kilian, L. 1955: *Haffküstenkultur und Ursprung der Balten,* Bonn: 320.

— 1982: *Zur Herkunft und Sprache der Prussen,* Bonn: 177.

Kiparsky, V. 1939: "Baltische Sprachen und Völker," in Engel 1939, 48–59.

— 1939a: *Die Kurenfrage,* Helsinki: 469.

— 1939b: "Die Ostseefinnen im Baltikum," in Engel 1939, 36–47.

— 1940: "Philippe de Mézières sur les rives de la Baltique," *Neuphilologische Mitteilungen,* 1940/1–2, 61–67.

Király Gy. 1921: *A magyar ősköltészet* [Hungarian prehistoric poetry], Budapest: 135.

Kiš, D. 1997: *The Encyclopedia of the Dead* (*Enciklopedija mrtvih*, 1983) (transl., Heim, M. H.), Evanston.

Kiss, L. 1978: *Földrajzi nevek etimológiai szótára* [Etymological dictionary of geographical names], Budapest: 726.

Kitkauskas, N. 1989: *Vilniaus pilys* [The castles of Vilnius], Vilnius: 231.

Klaniczay, G. 1984: "A történeti antropológia tárgya, módszerei és első eredményei" [The subject, methodology, and first results of historical anthropology], in Hofer 1984, 23–60.

Klaniczay, T. 1966: "Az írók nemzeti hovartozása" [On the nationality of the authors], in 1973, 19–31.

— 1973: *A múlt nagy korszakai* [The great periods of the past], Budapest: 525.

Klimas, A. 1969: "The importance of Lithuanian for Indo-European linguistics," *Lituanus*, 1969/3, 10–24.

— 1979: "Iš užkampio į sostą" [From a forgotten corner to the throne], in *Lituanistikos Instituto 1977 metų suvažiavimo darbai,* Chicago: 1979: 151–160.

— 1988: "Sukilimas indoeuropiečių kalbotyroje" [Revolution in Indo-European linguistics], *Draugas*, 1988/15.

Knoll, P. 1991: "The european context of 16th century Prussian humanism," *Journal of Baltic Studies*, 1991/1, 5–28.

Köhler, O. 1961: "Die Historiker und die Kulturmorphologen," *Saeculum*, 1961, 306–318.

Kokare, E. 1991: "Ieskats latviešu mitoloģisko tēlu sistēmas pamatstrukturā" [An overview of the fundamental structure of the system of concepts of Latvian mythology], *Latvijas Zinātņu Akademijas Vēstis*, 1991/9, 20–39.

Kolbuszewski, S. F. 1983: "Zu den Grundproblemen der lettischen Philologie," *Acta Baltico-Slavica*, 1983, 271–281.

Komoróczy,G. 1975: "Az istenek összessége" [All the divinities], *Világosság*, 1975/1, 23–26.

— 1976: "A sumer nyelv rejtélye mint őstörténeti probléma" [The mystery of the Sumerian language as a problem in prehistory], *Valóság*, 1976/10, 102–107.

— 1986: "Polányi Károly történeti utópiája" (K. Polányi's utopia of history) in 1992, 383–389.

— 1990: "Tartalmában strukturalista, formájában nemzeti" [Structuralist in its contents, nationalist in its form], *Buksz*, 1990/summer,164–175.

— 1991: "Meddig él egy nemzet?" [How long does a nation live for?], *2000*, 1991/9, 13–25.

— 1992: *Bezárkózás a nemzeti hagyományba* [Confined in national tradition], Budapest: 404.

Kondrotas, S. T. 1982: *Žalčio žvilgsnis*, (The glare of the snake), Vilnius: 352.

Kontakty 1977: *Kontakty latyshskogo yazyka.* Riga: 341.

Korsakas, K. (ed.) 1962: *Kalba ir Literatura* [Language and literature], Vilnius: 494.

Korsakas, K. – Lebedys, J. (ed.) 1957: *Lietuvių literatūros istorijos chrestomatija* (Lithuanian textbook of literary texts], Vilnius: 527.

Kortlandt, F. 1990: "The spread of the Indoeuropeans," *The Journal of Indoeuropean Studies*, 1990, 131–140.

Kosman, M. 1979: *Historia Białorusi* [The history of Belarus], Wrocław etc.: 397.

Kostrzewski, J. 1967: "Über den gegenwärtigen Stand der Erforschung der Ethnogenese der Slaven in archäologischer Sicht," in *Das heidnische* 1969-1970/I, 11–25.

Köves-Zulauf, T. n.d.: *Bevezetés a római vallás és monda történetébe* [Introduction to the history of Roman religion and legends], Budapest: 254.

Krahe, H. 1938: *Die sprachliche Stellung des Illyrischen,* Pécs: 24.

— 1950: "Das Venetische," *Sitzungsberichte der Heidelberger Akademie der Wissenschaften*, 1950/3, 1–37.

— 1957: "Indogermanisch und Alteuropäisch," in Scherer 1968, 426–454.

— 1962: "Die Struktur der alteuropäischen Hydronymie," *Abhandlungen der Geistes- und Sozialwissenschaftlichen Klasse*, 1962/5, 285–341.

— 1964: *Unsere älteste Flussnamen,* Wiesbaden: 123.

Kraszewski, J. I. 1846: *Witolorauda,* Wilno: 284.

— 1847–50: *Litwa* [Lithuania], I–II, Warszawa.

Krek, G. 1887: *Einleitung in die slavische Literaturgeschichte,* Graz: 887.

Krėvė, V. 1987: *Dangaus ir žemės sūnus* [The son of the sky and the earth], Vilnius: 302.

Kristó, Gy. 1978: "Volt-e a magyaroknak ősi hunn hagyományuk?" [Did the Hungarians have an ancient Hunnish tradition?], in Hoppál–Istvánovits 1978, 55–64.

Krompacher, B. 1935: "A Kalevala keletkezése" [The origins of the *Kalevala*], *Budapesti Szemle*, 1935/dec., 256–285.

Kronasser, H. 1959: "Vorgeschichte und Indogermanistik," in Scherer 1968, 478–509.

Kruopas, J. (ed.) 1966: *Lietuvių kalbos leksikos raida* [The development of the Lithuanian vocabulary], Vilnius: 240.

Kubicka, W. 1967: "Bibliografia języka staropruskiego do 1965. r." [The bibliography of the Old-Prussian language until 1965], *Acta Baltico-Slavica*, 1967, 257–296.

Kulakov, V. I. 1990: "Pogrebal'nyy obryad prussov v epokhe rannego srednevekov'ya," in Ivanov–Nevskaya 1990, 182–196.

Kuolys, D. 1992: *Asmuo, tauta, valstybė Lietuvos Didžiosios Kunigaikštystės istorinėje literaturoje* [Personality, nation, state in the historical literature of the Grand Duchy of Lithuania], Vilnius: 286.

Kuper, L. (ed.) 1975: *Race, Science and Society,* London–Paris: 370.

Kursīte, J. 1994: "Latgaliešu literatūra — kas tu esi?" [Latgalian literature — what are you?], *Karogs*, 1994/2, 143–149.

Kuzavinis, K. 1964: "Lietuvos vardo kilmė" [The origins of the name 'Lithuania'], *Kalbotyra*, 1964, 5–18.

— 1965: "Skalva," *Baltistica*, 1965/6.

Laakmann, H. 1939: "Die Gründungsgeschichte Rigas," in Engel 1939, 350–354.

La Baume, W. 1952: "Sprache und Heimat der Prussen," *Zeitschrift für Ostforschung*, 1952/4, 591–594.

Labuda, G. (ed.) 1958: *Pomorze średniowieczne* [Pomorze in the Middle Ages], Warszawa: 527.

— 1960: *Źródła, sagi i legendy do najdawniejszych dziejów Polski* [Sources, sagas, and legends for the most ancient history of Poland], Warszawa: 346.

— 1960–75: *Fragmenty dziejów Słowiańszczyzny zachodniej* [Some questions on the history of the West Slavs], I–III, Poznań.

— (ed.) 1963: *Wschodnia ekspansja Niemiec w Europie Środkowej* [Germany's eastward expansion in Eastern Europe], Poznań: 321.

— 1963a: "Historiograficzna analiza tzw. niemieckiego 'naporu na wschód' [The historiographical analysis of the so-called 'Drang nach Osten'], in Labuda 1963, 14–56.

— 1968: "O wędrówce Gotów i Gepidów" (On the migration of the Goths and Gepids], in Jażdżewski 1968, 213–236.

— (ed.) 1971: *Węzlowe problemy dziejów Prus XVII–XX. wieku* [The crucial issues of seventeenth–twentieth-century Prussia's history], Poznań: 215.

— (ed.) 1972: *Historia Pomorza* [Pomorze's history], I. (1–2) Poznań.

Labuda, G. – Tabaczyński, S. 1987: *Studia nad etnogenezą Słowian i kulturą Europy średniowiecznej* [Studies on the ethnogenesis of the Slavs and the culture of Europe in the Middle Ages], I–II., Wrocław etc.

Lakatos, P. 1973: *Quellenbuch zur Geschichte der Gepiden*, Szeged: 135.

— 1978: *Quellenbuch zur Geschichte der Heruler,* Szeged: 118.

Lambertz, M. 1949: "Die Albaner, ihre Sprache und ihre Kultur," *Blick nach Osten*, 1949/1–2, 21.

Larson, G. J. 1974: "Introduction: the study of mythology and comparative mythology," in Larson 1974a, 1–16.

— (ed.) 1974a: *Myth in Indo-European Antiquity*, Berkeley etc.: 197.

Łasicki (Lasicius) J.*: *De Diis Samagitarum Caeterorumque Sarmatarum et Falsorum Christianorum. (Apie Žemaičių, kitų sarmatų bei netikrų krikščionių dievus* [On the Žemaitian and other fake Sarmatian gods], (transl., annot., concl., J. Jurginis) Vilnius: 1969, 101.

László, Gy. 1987: *Őstörténetünk* [Our prehistory], Budapest, 173.

Latviešu 1959: *Latviešu literatūras vēsture* [The history of Latvian literature], I, Riga: 642.

— 1970–78: *Latviešu dzejas antoloģija* [The anthology of Latvian poetry], I–VIII, Riga.

Latvijas 1937–40: *Latvijas vēstures avoti* [The sources for the history of Latvia], I–II, Riga.

— 1974: *Latvijas PSR arheoloģija* [The archaeology of the Latvian SSR], Riga: 374–80.

Laumane, B. (ed.) 1990: *Onomastica Lettica*, Riga: 300.

Laur, W. 1972: "Baltisch und Balten," *Beiträge zur Namenforschung*, 1972, 45–72.

Lautenbakh, J. 1915: *Ocherki iz' istorii litovsko-latyshskago narodnago tvorchestva. Yur'ev'*: 415.

LE: Latvju Enciklopēdija [Latvian Encyclopaedia], Ed. A. Švābe, 1–4, 1950–62, Stockholm.

Leach, E. 1966: "Virgin Birth," in 1969, 85–122.

— 1969: *Genesis as Myth*, London: 124.

— 1982: *Social Anthropology*, London: 254.

— 1990: "Aryan Invasions over four millennia," in Ohnuki-Tierney 1990, 227–245.

Lebedys, J. 1940: "Kraševskio lietuviškoji trilogija šimto metų perspektyvoj" [Kraszewski's Lithuanian trilogy with a hundred years of hindsight], in 1972/I, 339–355.

— 1972: *Lituanistikos baruose* [In the workshop of Lithuanian studies], I–II, Vilnius.

Lec, S. J. 1991: *Mysli nieuczesane* [Incombed reflections], Warszawa: 270.

Le Goff, J. 1965: "Note sur société tripartie, idéologie monarchique et renoveau économique dans la chrétienté du IXe au XIIe siècle," in *L'Europe* 1968, 63–71.

L'Europe 1968: *L'Europe aux IXe – XIe si ècles*, Varsovie: 527.

Lehrmann, A.–Venclova, T. 1981: "Algirdo J. Greimo mitologinių studijų klausimu" [Issues around A. J. Greimas' mythological studies], in Užgiris 1985, 243–259.

Lehr-Spławiński, T. 1959: "Czy Słowianie przyszli ze wschodu?" [Did the Slavs come from the East?], in 1961, 7–18.

— 1961: *Od piętnastu wieków* [Fifteen centuries ago], Warszawa: 181.

Lévi-Strauss, C. 1952: "Race and history," in Kuper 1975, 95–134.

Lexikon Symbole 1978: *Herder Lexikon Symbole*, Freiburg: 171.

Likhachev, D. S. 1947: *Russkiye letopisi i ikh kul'turno-istoricheskoye znacheniye*. Moscow–Leningrad: 499.

— 1958: *Chelovek v literature Drevney Rusi*. Moscow–Leningrad: 185.

Likhacheva, V. D.–Likhachev, D. S. 1971: *Khudozhestvennoye naslediye Drevney Rusi i sovremennost'*. Leningrad: 120.

Liparte, E. 1993: "Labā un ļaunā čūska latviešu folklorā" [The good and the bad snake in Latvian folklore], *Latvijas Zinātņu Aakademijas Vēstis*, 1993/4, 32–36.

Liš: *Lietuvos TSR istorijos* šaltiniai [Sources of the history of the Lithuanian SSR] I–V., 1955.

Lit. E.: *Lietuvių Enciklopedija* [Lithuanian Encyclopedia] I–XXXVII, Boston, 1953-85.

Lithuania's chronicles: *Lietuvos metraštis* (transl., introd., annot., R. Jasas), 1971, Vilnius: 397.

Littleton, C. S. 1966: *The New Comparative Mythology. An Anthropological Assessment of the Theories of George Dumézil*, Berkeley–Los Angeles: 242.

Livonia's chronicles: *Livonijos kronikos: Heinricus de Lettis, Hermann de Wartberge* (transl. into Lithuanian, introd., annot., J. Jurginis), Vilnius: 1991, 223.

— *The Livonian Rhymed Chronicle (Die livländische Reimchronik)* (transl., introd., annot., J. C. Smith–W. L. Urban), Bloomington 1977: XXVII+150.

LKV.: *Latviešu Konversācijas Vārdnīca* [Stock of Latvian popular knowledge] ed. A. Švābe, 1–21, Riga, 1927–40.

Loeber, D. A.–Vardys, V. S.–Kitching, L. P. A. (eds.) 1990: *Regional Identity under Soviet Rule: the Case of the Baltic States,* Hackettstown: 470.

Łowmiański, H. 1931: "Studia nad początkami społeczeństwa i państwa litewskiego" [Studies on the beginnings of the Lithuanian state and society], in 1983, 11–347.

— 1932: "Geografia polityczna Bałtów w dobie plemiennej" [The political geography of the Balts in the tribal period], *Lituano-Slavica Posnaniensia*, 1985/I, 1–105.

— 1934: "Uwagi w sprawie podłoża społecznego i gospodarczego unii jagiełłońskiej" [Notes on the social and economic basis of Jagiello's union], in 1983, 365–454.

— 1935: *Prusy pogańskie* [The pagan Prussianland], Poznań: 56.

— 1935a: "Zagadnienie feudalizmu w Wielkim Księstwie Litewskim" [The issue of feudalism in the Grand Duchy of Lithuania], in 1986, 610–617.

— 1949 "Z zagadnień spornych społeczeństwa litewskiego" [From the debated questions of the Lithuanian society], *Przegląd Historyczny*, 1950, 96–127.

— 1954: "Agresja Krzyżaków na Litwę w XII-XV w." [The aggression of the Crusaders against Lithuania in the twelfth–fifteenth centuries], *Przegląd Historyczny*, 1954, 338–371.

— 1957: *Zagadnienie roli Normanów w genezie państw słowiańskich* [The question of the role of the Normans in the emergence of Salvic states], Warszawa: 202.

— 1961: "Uwagi o genezie państwa litewskiego" [Notes on the emergence of the Lithuanian state], *Przegląd Historyczny*, 127–146.

— 1963–70: *Początki Polski* [The beginnings of Poland], I–IV, Warszawa.

— 1964: "Zagadnienie słowiańskich i bałtyjskich nazw plemiennych w Sarmacji Europiejskiej Ptolemeusza" [The question of the Slavic and Baltic tribal names in Ptolemy's European Sarmatia], *Acta Baltico-Slavica*, 1964/1, 37–47.

— 1966: "Pogranicze słowiańsko-jaćwieskie" [Slavic–Jatvingian borderlands], *Acta Baltico-Slavica*, 1966/3, 89–98.

— 1966a: "Słoweni nadilmeńscy i początki Nowogrodu" [The Slovenians of the Ilmen banks and the beginnings of Novgorod], *Zapiski Historyczne*, 1966/2, 7–41.

— 1972: "Russko-litovskiye otnosheniya v XIV–XV. vv," in Pashuto 1972, 269–275.

— 1973: "Anfänge und politische Rolle der Ritterorden an der Ostsee im 13. und 14. Jahrhundert," in Arnold – Biskup 1982, 36–85.

— 1976: "Elementy indoeuropiejskie w religii Bałtów" [Indo-European elements in the religion of the Balts], in Ars historica 1976, 145–153.

— 1976a: "Rodzime i obce elementy w religii Germanów według danych Tacyta" [Local and alien elements in the religion of the Germanic people based on Tacitus' data], in Cultus 1976, 353–363.

— 1976b: "Trzy koncepcje feudalizmu w historiografii polskiej do roku 1939" [The three conceptions of feudalism in Polish historiography until 1939], in 1986, 582–594.

— 1979: *Religia Słowian i jej upadek (w. VI–XII)* [The religion of the Slavs and its decline: sixth–twelfth centuries], Warszawa: 431.

— 1983: *Studia nad dziejami Wielkiego Księstwa Litewskiego* [Studies from the history of the Grand Duchy of Lithuania], Poznań: 579.

— 1984: "Zagadnienie politeizmu słowiańskiego" [The question of Slavic polytheism], *Przegląd Historyczny*, 1984, 655–693.

— 1986: *Studia nad dziejami Słowiańszczyzny, Polski i Rusi w wiekach średnich* [Studies on the history of the Slavic peoples, Poland, and Rus' in the Middle Ages], Poznań: 686.

— 1989: *Prusy–Litwa–Krzyżacy* [Prussianland–Lithuania–Crusaders], Warszawa: 481.

Loze, I. A. 1969: "Novyy tsentr obrabotki yantarya epokhi neolita v Vostochnoy Pribaltike," *Sovetskaya Arkheologiya* 1969/3, 124–134.

— 1979: *Pozdniy neolit i rannyaya bronza Lubanskoy ravniny*. Riga: 204.

— 1980: "Voprosy kartografirovaniya nakhodok yantarya epokhi neolita na evropeyskoy chasti SSSR," *Latvijas Zinātņu Akadēmijas Vēstis* 1980/9, 73–86.

— 1983: *Akmens laikmeta māksla Austrumbaltijā* [Arts in Stone Age in the East Baltic region], Riga: 127.

Lukinich, F. 1935: *A lívföld és népe* [The Livonian land and its people], Budapest: 96.

Luther, M. 1882–83: 'Short catechism' (Catechismus minor, 1529) in Jacobs, H. E. *The Book of Concord.* Philadelphia 1970: 'The Freedom of a Christian' (Von der Freiheit eines Christenmenschen, 1520) in E. G. Rupp and B. Orerrery (eds.): *Martin Luther*, London: 140.

Lyubavskiy, M. K. 1910: *Ocherk istorii litovsko-russkago gosudarstva do Lublinskoy unii vklyuchatel'no.* 1966, The Hague (Russian Reprint Series XIV.): 378.

Maceina, A. 1987: *Ora et labora*, Perugia: 215.

Maciej z Miechowa: *Opis Sarmacji Azjatyckiej i Europiejskiej. (Tractatus de duabus Sarmatiis, Asiana et Europiana)* (transl., annot., T. Bieńkowski, introd., H. Barycz, concl., W. Voisé), Wrocław 1972: 96.

Maciūnas, V. (ed.) 1973: *Lituanistikos darbai* [Works in Lithuanian studies], III, New York: 216.

Mägiste, J. 1982: *Estnisches etymologisches Wörterbuch* I–XII, Helsinki.

Makkay, J. 1982: *A magyarországi neolitikum kutatásának új eredményei* [Recent results of research in Neolithic Hungary], Budapest: 182.

— 1991: *Az indoeurópai népek őstörténete* [The prehistory of Indo-European peoples], Budapest: 315.

Malinowski, T. 1982: "L'ambre jaune baltique et le problème de son exportation pendant les premières périodes de l'age du fer," *Savaria*, 1989/16, 113–123.

Małłek, J. 1971: "Przedmiot dziejów Prus w XVI–XVIII w." [The subject of the history of Prussianland in the sixteenth–eighteenth centuries], in Labuda 1971, 128–130.

— 1987: *Dwie części Prus* [Two parts of Prussianland], Olsztyn: 220.

Mallory, J. P. 1989: *In Search of the Indo-Europeans,* London: 288.

Malvess, R. 1959: "Jautājums par raksta lietošanu Latvijas territorijā līdz XII beigām" [The question of the use of writing in the areas of Latvia until the late twelfth century], in Sokols 1959, 555–566.

Mańczak, W. 1984: "Sur l'habitat primitif des indo-européens," *Baltistica,* 1984/XX(1), 23–29.

Mannhardt, W. 1884: *Mythologische Forschungen,* (introd., K. Müllenhoff, W. Scherer), Strassburg–Leipzig: 382.

— 1936: *Letto-preussische Götterlehre,* (introd., A. Bauer), Riga: IX+674.

Mansikka, V. J. 1922: *Die Religion der Ostslaven,* Helsinki: 405.

Marić, Z. 1964: "Problem sjevernog graničnog područja Ilira" [The question of the northern border of the territory of the Illyrian settlement], in Benac 1964, 177–214.

Markiewicz, H. 1987: "Literatura a mity" [Literature and myths], *Twórczość,* 1987/10, 55–70.

Marstrander, S. 1957: "Die Urheimat der Indoeuropäer," in Scherer 1968, 417–425.

Martinkus, A. 1989: *Eglé, la reine des serpents,* Paris: 290.

Marx, K. 1877: "Letter to Otechestvenniye Zapiski", in Marx–Engels 1989–90/24.

Marx, K. – Engels, F. 1989–90: *Collected Works*, Moscow.

Maschke, E. 1955: "Preussen. Das Werden eines deutschen Stammesnamens," in Maschke 1970, 158–187.

— 1970: *Domus Hospitalis Theutonicorum*, Bonn–Godesberg: 198.

Mattiesen, H. 1972: "Gotthard Kettler und die Entstehung des Herzogtums Kurland", in Ziedonis–Winter–Valgemäe 1974, 49–59.

Matuzova, V. I. 1982: "Ideyno-teologicheskaya osnova 'Khroniki zemli prusskoy' Petra iz Dusburga," in Pashuto 1984, 152–169.

Mayer, A. 1957–59: *Die Sprache der alten Illyrier*, I–II, Wien: 364, 263.

Mayer, H. E. 1995: "Slavic Archaic/Baltic Archaic," *Lituanus*, 1995/2, 67–72.

Mažiulis, A. 1965: "Vaidevutis" ("Waidelott"), in Lit. E./XXXII, 439.

Mažiulis, V. 1966–81: *Prūsų kalbos paminklai* [The Prussian linguistic records], I–II, Vilnius: 251, 394.

— 1973: "Otnositel'no konservativnogo kharaktera baltiyskikh yazykov," in Baltiyskiye 1973, 28–29.

— 1974: "Sotsiolingvisticheskiye zametki k arkhaichnomu kharaktery yazyka (Baltiyskiye yazyki)," *Baltistica*, 1974/X (2), 119–127.

— 1975: "Seniausias baltų rašto paminklas" [The oldest Baltic written remnant], *Baltistica*, 1975/XI(2), 125–131.

— 1981: "Apie senovės vakarų baltus bei jų santykius su slavais, ilirais ir germanais" [On the old West Balts, and their contacts with Slavic, Illyrian, and Germanic peoples], in Volkaitė–Kulikauskienė 1981, 5–11.

— 1984: "Westbaltische und Slawische," *Zeitschrift für Slawistik*, 1984/29, 166–167.

Mažvydas, M.: *Pirmoji lietuviška knyga* [The first Lithuanian book], (transl., introd., annot., M. Ročka), Vilnius 1974: 347.

Mc Murrin–Sterling M. (eds.) 1986: *The Tanner Lectures on Human Values*, Salt Lake City–Cambridge: 288.

Meletinskiy, E. M. 1986: *Vvedeniye v istoricheskuyu poetiku eposa i romana*. Moscow: 319.

Mel'nikova, E. A. 1977: *Skandinavskiye runicheskiye nadpisi*, Moscow: 275.

Merlingen, W. 1955–66: "Zum Ausgangsgebiet der indogermanischen Sprachen," in Scherer 1968, 409–413.

Meyer, E. 1946: "Die Indogermanenfrage," in Scherer 1968, 256–287.

Mickiewicz, A. 1827: *Konrad Wallenrod* (transl. Ashurst Biggs, M.), London: 1882.

Mielczarski, S. 1967: *Misja pruska Świętego Wojciecha* [St. Adalbert's Prussian mission], Gdańsk: 165.

Mierzyński, A. 1892–96: *Źródła do mytologii litewskiej* [The sources of Lithuanian mythology], I–II. Warszawa.

Mikkola, J. J. 1938: "Einiges über den eurasischen Bernsteinhandel," *Senatne un Māksla*, 1938/1, 33–37.

Milius, V. (ed.) 1992: *Rytų Lietuva* [East Lithuania], Vilnius: 240.

Miłosz, Cz. 1953: *Dolina Issy*, [The Issa valley], Paris, 1980: 267.

— 1988: *Autoportret przekorny* [Humble self-portrait], Kraków: 350.

Misiūnas, R.–Taagepera, R. 1983: *The Baltic States*, Berkeley–Los Angeles: 333, in Hungarian in Rauch–Misiūnas–Taagepera 1994, 161–467.

Molino, J. 1992: "Archaeology and symbol systems," in Gardin–Peebles 1992, 15–29.

Momigliano, A. 1984: "Georges Dumézil and the trifunctional approach to Roman civilization," *History and Theory*, 1984, 312–330.

Moora, A. 1956: "Voprosy slozheniya estonskogo naroda i nekotorykh sosednikh narodov v svete dannykh arkheologii," in 1956, 49–141.

— (red.) 1956a: *Voprosy etnicheskoy istorii estonskogo naroda.* Tallinn: 328.

Moora, H. 1964: *Zur Frage nach der Entstehung des ostbaltischen historischen Kulturgebietes*, Tallinn: 9.

Moora, H. – Ligi, H. 1970: *Wirtschaft und Gesellschaftsordnung der Völker des Baltikums zu Anfang des 13. Jahrhunderts*, Tallinn: 99.

Moravcsik, Gy. 1938: "A honfoglalás előtti magyarság és a kereszténység" [The Magyars and Christianity before the Conquest], in Serédi 1938, 171–212.

— 1966: *Bevezetés a bizantinológiába*, [Introduction to Byzantology], Budapest: 164.

Mortensen, H. 1926: *Litauen: Grundzüge einer Landeskunde*, Hamburg: 321.

Mugurēvičs, Ē. 1965: *Vostochnaya Latviya i sosedniye zemli v X–XIII. vv.* Riga: 144+ XXXII.

— 1970: "Problema vendov v period rannego feodalizma v Latvii," in Berichte 1973, 291–299.

— (ed.) 1980: *Iz drevneyshey istorii baltiyskikh narodov po dannym arkheologii i antropologii.* Riga: 139.

— 1981: "Problema formirovaniya latishskoy narodnosti v srednevekovye po dannym arkheologii", in Volkaitė-Kulikauskienė 1981a, 56–66.

— 1993: "Archaeological science in the Baltic States," *Journal of Baltic Studies,* 1993/3, 281–294.

Mugurēvičs, Ē.–Tautavičius, A. 1980: "Sostoyaniye i zadachi arkheologichesk-ogo izucheniya etnogeneza baltskikh narodov," in Mugurēvičs 1980, 7–13.

Munera 1963: *Munera Archaeologica Josepho Kostrzewski*, Poznań: 426.

Munkácsi, B. 1890–96: *Votják szótár* [Dictionary of the Votyak language], Budapest: 835.

Myadzvedzeu, A. 1994: "Nasel'nitstva Belarusi u zhaleznnya veku (VIII st. da n. e.–VIII st. n. e)" [The populace of Belarus in the Iron Ages: eighth century B.C. to eighth century A.D.], *Belaruski Gistarychny Aglyad"* 1944/1, 15–37.

Nadeschdin, N. 1841: "Mundarten der russischen Sprache," *Jahrbücher der Literatur*, 1841, 181–240.

Nagy, F. 1932: "Északi nyelvrokonaink Tacitusnál" [Our related languages in the North in Tacitus], *Egyetemes Philológiai Közlöny*, 1932/56, 99–108, 169–175.

Nalepa, J. 1964: *Jaćwięgowie* [The Jatvingians], Białystok: 60.

Narbutt: Narbutas, T. 1992: *Lietuvių tautos istorija* (*Dzieje starożytnego narodu Litewskiego*, 1835) [The history of the ancient Lithuanian nation], (transl., R. Jasas., introd., V. Berenis, N. Vėlius), Vilnius: 1992, 392.

Narr, K. J. 1981: "Urgeschichte," in Hellmann 1981, 71–101.

Nastopka, K. 1971: *Lietuvių ir latvių literatūrų ryšiai* [The connections between Lithuanian and Latvian literature], Vilnius: 414.

Naujokaitis, P. 1973–78: *Lietuvių literatūros istorija* [The history of Lithuanian literature], I–IV. n.p.

Neckel, G. 1944: "Die Frage nach der Urheimat der Indogermanen," in Scherer 1968, 158–175.

Nehring, A. 1954: "Die Problematik der Indogermanenforschung," in Scherer 1968, 385–408.

Nestor: *Die Nestor-Chronik,* (introd., annot., D. Tschižewskij), Wiesbaden, 1969: 325.

Niederle, L. 1902–11.: *Slovanské starožitnosti* [Slavic Antiquity studies], 1–3, Praha.

Nikolaus von Jeroschin: "Di Kronike von Pruzinlant," in SRP/I, 291–624.

Nikžentaitis, A 1989.: *Gediminas.* Vilnius: 218

Niskanen, M. 1997: "Itämerensuomalaisten alkuperä fyysisen antropologian näkökulmasta" ("The origin of Baltic-Finns from the physical anthropological viewpoint"), in Julku 1997, 104–118.

Nitsch, K. 1954: "O nazwach: *Pomorze* i *Prusy* [About the names 'Pomorze' and 'Prussianland'], *Język Polski*, 1954/4, 312–313.

Nowak, Z. H. 1983 (ed.): *Die Rolle der Ritterorden in der Christianisierung und Kolonisierung des Ostseegebietes*, Toruń: 139.

Ochmański, J. 1966: "Weneckie początki Litwy [Lithuania's Venedic beginnings], *Acta Baltico-Slavica*, 1966/3, 151–158.

— 1970: "Nazwa Jaćwięgów" [The name of the Jatvingians], in *L'Europe* 1968, 197–204.

— 1985: "Nieznany autor 'Opisu krajów' z drugiej polowy XIII wieku i jego wiadomości o Bałtach" [The thirteenth-century anonymous author of the 'Descriptiones terrarum' and his knowledge about the Balts], *Lituano-Slavica Posnaniensia*, 1985/I, 107–114.

— 1990[3]: *Historia Litwy* [Lithuania's history], Wrocław etc.: 395.

Odoj, R. 1970: "Dzieje Prusów do czasów krzyżackich" [The history of Prussianland until the period of the Crusaders], *Komunikaty Mazursko-Warmińskie*, 1970/1, 51–63.

Oesterley, H. 1883: *Historisch-geographisches Wörterbuch des deutschen Mittelalters*, Gotha: 806.

O'Flaherty, W. 1981: "The Indo-European Mare and the King," in Segal 1981, 23–33.

Ohnuki-Tierney, E. (ed.) 1990: *Culture through Time*, Stanford: 342.

Okulicz, J. 1973: *Pradzieje ziem pruskich od późnego paleolitu do VII w. n. e.* [The prehistory of Prussian lands from the late Paleolithic to the seventh century B.C.], Wrocław etc.: 588.

Olender, M. 1992: *The Languages of Paradise*, Cambridge–London: 193.

Ong, Walter J. 1982: *Orality and Literacy: The Technologizing of the Word*, London– New York: 201.

Otkupshchikov, Yu. V. 1984: "O mnimykh slavizmakh v baltiyskikh yazykakh," *Balto-Slavyanskiye Issledovaniya*, 1986, 89–102.

Ovid (Ovidius), P. N.: *Metamorphoses* (transl., Melville, A. D.), Oxford–New York, 1986.

Ozols, A. 1965: *Veclatviešu rakstu valoda* [The language of Old Latvian literacy], Riga: 626.

Pääbo, S. 1995: "The Y chromosome and the origin of all of us (men)," *Science*, 1995 May 26, 1141–1142.

Pakarklis, P. 1948: *Kryžiuočių valstybės santvarkos bruožai* [The characteristics of the state structure of the Crusaders], Vilnius: 267.

Palionis, J. 1979: *Lietuvių literaturinės kalbos istorija* [The history of the Lithuanian literary language], Vilnius: 317.

Palmaitis, M. L. 1989: "Kraft Skalwynas G.: Grammatika prūsiskas kalbas, pobānda swaises ernausnas. Für Freunde in der Tolkemita," Dieburg, 1982: 425. *Baltistica*, XXV/2, 179–187.

Palmaitis, M. L.–Toporov, V. N. 1983: "Ot rekonstruktsii staroprusskogo k rekreatsii novoprusskogo," *Balto-Slavyanskiye Issledovaniya*, 1984, 36–63.

Papal Bulls*: *Popiežų bulės dėl kryžiaus žygių prieš prūsus ir lietuvius XIII a.* [Papal Bulls in the matter of the thirteenth-century Crusades against the Prussians and Lithuanians], (select., P. Pakarklis, annot., E. Gudavičius, A. Nikžentaitis), Vilnius 1987: 309.

Parolek, R. 1978: *Srovnávací dějiny baltických literatur* [The comparative history of Baltic literatures], Praha: 126.

Parry, M. 1971: *The Making of Homeric Verse*, Oxford: 483.

Pashuto, V. T. (ed.) 1984: *Drevneyshie gosudarstva na territorii SSSR*, Moscow.

Pasquinucci, M. 1982: "Aquileia and the amber trade," *Savaria*, 1982, 273–281.

Pašuta, V. 1971: *Lietuvos valstybės susidarymas* [The emergence of the Lithuanain state], Vilnius: 424.

Paszkiewicz, H. 1954: *The Origin of Russia*, London: 556.

Patze, H. 1958: "Der Frieden von Christburg vom Jahre 1249," *Jahrbuch für die Geschichte Mittel- und Ostdeutschlands*, 1958/VII, 39–91.

Pauly–Wissowa's 1920, 1955: *Real-Encyclopädie der classischen Altertumswissenschaft*, Stuttgart.

Pelikan, J. 1971–78: *The Christian Tradition*, 1–5, Chicago–London.

Pentikäinen, J. 1989: "The Shamanic poems of the Kalevala and their Northern Eurasian background," in Hoppál–Sadovszky 1989/1, 97–102.

Perry, R. B. 1926: *A General Theory of Value*, New York: 426.

Péteraitis, V. 1992: *Mažoji Lietuva ir Tvanksta* [Lithuania Minor and Tuvangste], Vilnius: 454.

Petr, J.–Řeháček, L. (eds.) 1981: *Praha–Vilnius*, Praha: 125.

Pietsch, R. 1982: *Fischerleben auf der kurischen Nehrung,* (introd., F. Scholz), Berlin: 323.

Piggott, S. 1965: *Ancient Europe from the Beginnings of Agriculture to Classical Antiquity*, Edinburgh: 343.

Pisani, V. 1968: "Rom und die Balten," *Baltistica*, 1968/1, 7–21.

Pistohlkors, G. (ed.) 1994: *Deutsche Geschichte im Osten Europas: Baltische Länder*, Berlin: 607.

Plāķis, J. 1930: "Die baltischen Völker und Stämme," in Schmidt 1930, 49–55.

Plinius, Caius Secundus: Pliny: *Natural history (Naturalis historia),* I–X. (transl., Rackham, H. and Eichholz, D. E.) 1958–62, Cambridge–London.

Počs, K.–Poča, I. 1993: *Ieskats Latgales vēstures historiogrāfijā* [A glance into the historiography of Latgale's history], Rēzekne: 40.

Podehl, H. G. 1985: "Was ist das, Prussisch?" *Baltisches Jahrbuch,* 1985, 162–164.

Pokorny, J. 1936: "Substrattheorie und Urheimat der Indogermanen," in Scherer 1968, 176–213.

— 1959–69: *Indogermanisches etymologisches Wörterbuch,* I–II, Bern–München.

Pollakówna, M. 1958: "Zanik ludności pruskiej" [The extinction of the Prussian populace] in Labuda 1958, 160–207.

Pór, A. 1880: *Aeneas Sylvius (Pius II. pápa)* [Aeneas Sylvius (Pope Pius II), Budapest: 384.

Povest' vremennykh let. Red.: D. S. Likhachev. (Introd., D. V. Likhachev, V. A. Romanov.) 1950, Moscow–Leningrad: 405.

Powierski, J. 1981: "Wybuch II powstania pruskiego a stosunki między Zakonem Krzyżackim i książętami polskimi: 1260–1261 [The eruption of the second Prussian uprising, and the relation between the Order of the Crusaders and the Polish Princes], *Komunikaty Mazursko–Warmińskie*, 1981/3, 298–332.

Pritsak, O. 1982: "The perspective of the Slavs, Finns and Balts," *Journal of Baltic Studies*, 1982/3, 185–201.

Pritzwald, K. S. 1952: "Das baltische Deutsch als Standessprache," *Zeitschrift für Ostforschung*, 1952/3, 407–422.

Propp, V. J.: *A mese morfológiája* [Morphology of tales] (*Morfologiya skazki*, 1928) (transl., Soproni, A., concl., J. M. Meletinskiy), Budapest: 1995, 214.

Prūsijos 1994: *Prūsijos kultūra* [The culture of Prussianland], Vilnius: 267.

Ptolemy (Ptolemaios), C.: *The Geography (Geographia)* (transl., Stevenson, E. L., introd., Fischer, J.), New York, 1991.

Puhvel, J. 1974: "Indoeuropean Structure of the Baltic Pantheon," in Larson 1974a, 75–85.

Pulgram, E. 1958: "Indoeuropäisch und 'Indoeuropäer'," in Scherer 1968, 455–477.

Pumpurs, A.: *Lāčplēsis,* Riga, n.d.: 156. In Russian: (ed. introd., L. Rudzītis.) Moscow: 1975, 350.

Pushkin, A.: *Selected Verse* (prose transl., Fennell, J.), Bristol, 1964.

Pusztay, J. 1994: "Das sprachliche Bild der Bernsteinstrasse-Region," in Pusztay 1994a, 68–76.

— (ed.)1994a: *Das sprachliche Bild der Bernsteinstrasse-Region,* Szombathely: 132.

— (ed.) 1996: *SCLOMB und Mittel-Europa,* Szombathely: 114.

Quellen 1961: *Quellen des 9. und 11. Jahrhunderts zur Geschichte der hamburgischen Kirche und des Reiches,* Berlin: 751.

Ranke, K. 1969: "Orale und literale Kontinuität," in Bausinger–Brückner 1969, 102–116.

Rauch, G. 1970: *Geschichte der baltischen Staaten,* Stuttgart etc.: 265, in Hungarian in Rauch–Misiūnas–Taagepera, 5–159.

— 1982: "Der Rigaer Prophetenclub", *in Mittel- und Osteuropa im 18. und 19. Jahrhundert,* Berlin: 233–242.

Rauch, G. – Misiūnas, R.–Taagepera, R. 1994: *A balti államok története* [History of the Baltic States], (transl., Pálvölgyi, E., Bojtár, P.), Budapest: 467.

Reklaitis, P. 1976: "Kleinlitauen in der Kartographie Preussens," in Brakas 1976, 67–119.

Renfrew, C. 1972: *The Emergence of Civilization: the Cyclades and the Aegean in the Third Millenium,* London: XXVIII+595.

— 1973: *Before Civilization,* London: 292.

— 1979: *Problems in European Prehistory,* Edinburgh: 405.

— 1987: *Archaeology and Language. The Puzzle of Indo-European Origins,* London: 346.

— 1989: "Change in language and culture," *Transactions of the Philological Society,* 1989/2, 103–155.

— 1989a: "The Origins of Indo-European Languages," *Scientific American,* 1989/October, 82–90.

— 1990: "Foreword," in James 1993, XIII-XV.

— 1991: *Archaeology,* London: 543.

Révész, G. 1942: "Das Problem des Ursprungs der Sprache," reprinted from *Proceedings* Vol. XLV, Nos. 1, 2, 3 and 4, 1942, 1–28, Nederl. Akademie van Wetenschappen.

— 1946: *Ursprung und Vorgeschichte der Sprache*, Bern: 279.

Rimantienė, R. 1973: "Lietuvos akmens amžiaus šukinė puodų ornamentika ir finougrų klausimas [Lithuania's comb marked ceramics of the Stone Ages and the Finno-Ugrian question], *Lietuvos istorijos metraštis*, 1973, 5–26.

— 1985: "Rol' nemanskoy kul'tury v obrazovanii baltov," in Volkaitė-Kulikauskienė 1981a, 7–11.

— 1995: *Lietuva iki Kristaus* [Lithuania before Christ], Vilnius: 199.

Rimbert: *"Vita Anskarii," (ed., annot., W. Trillmich), in Quellen 1961, 1–135.

Rinholm, H. D. 1990: "Continuity and change in the Lithuanian standard language," in Fodor–Hagège 1990, 269–300.

Ritoók, Zs. 1973: *A görög énekmondók* [The Greek minstrels], Budapest: 147.

Rivière, J.-C. 1979: *Georges Dumézil à la découverte des Indo-Européens*, Paris: 271.

Róna-Tas, A. 1978: *A nyelvrokonság* [Linguistic kinship], Budapest: 487.

— 1983: "A nomád életforma geneziséhez" [On the genesis of nomadic life style], in Tőkei 1983, 51–65.

— 1989: "Nép és nemzet" [People and nation], *Valóság*, 1989/6, 1–13.

Rowell, S. C. 1994: *Lithuania ascending: A pagan empire within East-Central Europe, 1295–1345*, Cambridge: 375.

Rubulis, A. 1970: *Baltic Literature: A Survey of Finnish, Estonian, Latvian and Lithuanian Literatures*, Notre-Dame–London: XII+215.

Ruigys, P.* 1745: *Lietuvių kalbos kilmės, budo ir savybių tyrinėjimas (Betrachtung der litauischen Sprache, in ihrem Ursprunge, Wesen und Eigenschaften)* (transl., annot., V. Jurginis, introd., V. Mažiulis), Vilnius: 1986, 485.

Rūķe-Draviņa, V. (ed.) 1970: *Donum Balticum*, Stockholm: XIV+598.

— 1977: *The Standardization Process in Latvian*, Stockholm: 130.

— 1990: "Entstehung und Normierung der lettischen Nationalsprache," in Fodor–Hagège 1990, 1–27.

Rüss, H. 1981: "Das Reich von Kiev," in Hellmann 1981–89/1, 199–429.

Rybakov, B. A. 1963: *Drevnyaya Rus'*. Moscow: 359.

— 1979: *Gerodotova Skifiya*. Moscow: 245.

— 1981: *Yazychestvo drevnikh slavyan*. Moscow: 608.

Sabaliauskas, A. 1966: "Lietuvių kalbos leksikos raida" [The development of the wordstock of the Lithuanian language], in Kruopas 1966, 5–141.

— (ed.)1968: *Baltų ir slavų kalbų ryšiai* [The connections between Baltic and Slavic languages], Vilnius: 283.

— 1979–82: *Lietuvių kalbos tyrinėjimo istorija* [The history of the research of the Lithuanian language], I–II, Vilnius: 254, 268.

— 1984: *Kaip tyrinėta lietuvių kalba* [How was the Lithuanian language researched], Kaunas: 133.

— 1985: "Baltų pavadinimo kilmė" [The origins of the name 'Baltic'], *Baltija*, 1985, 51–54.

— 1986: *Mes baltai* [We Balts], Kaunas: 141.

— 1986a: *Baltų kalbų tyrinėjimai 1945–1985* [The research of the Baltic language: 1945–1985], Vilnius: 122.

Safarewicz, J. 1964: "Przedhistoryczne związki językowe italsko-słowiańskie" [Prehistoric Italic–Slavic language connections], *Rocznik Sławistyczny*, 1964/1, 19–25.

Šafařík, P. J. 1837: *Slovanské starožitnosti* [Slavic antiquity], Praha I–II: 1005.

Sajantila, A.–Pääbo, S. 1995: "Language replacement in Scandinavia," *Nature Genetics*, 1995/December, 359–360.

Sajantila, A.–Salem, A H.–Savolainen, P.–Bauer, K.–Gierig, C.–Pääbo, S. 1996: "Paternal and maternal DNA lineages reveal a bottleneck in the founding of the Finnish population," *Proceedings of the National Academy of Sciences of the United States of America*, 1966/ October 15, 12035–12039.

Salys, A. 1958: "Kuršiai" [The Couronians], in Lit. E./XIII, 418–426.

Šapoka, A. (ed.) 1936: *Lietuvos istorija* [Lithuania's history], Kaunas: 687.

Saxo Grammaticus: *The History of the Danes*, I–II, (transl., P. Fischer, annot., H. Ellis Davidson), Suffolk: 297, 209.

Schaudinn, H. 1937: *Deutsche Bildungsarbeit am lettischen Volkstum des 18. Jahrhunderts*, München: 167.

Scherer, Anton 1950: "Das Problem der indogermanischen Urheimat vom Standpunkt der Sprachwissenschaft," in Scherer 1968, 288–304.

— (ed.) 1968: *Die Urheimat der Indogermanen*, Darmstadt: 571.

Schildhauer, J. 1984: *Die Hanse: Geschichte und Kultur*, Stuttgart: 246.

Schlesinger, W. (ed.) 1975: *Die deutsche Ostsiedlung des Mittelalters als Problem der europäischen Geschichte*, Sigmaringen: 809.

Schmalstieg, W. R. 1973: "Several Studies on Old Prussian," in Maciūnas 1973, 153–170.

— 1974: *An Old Prussian Grammar*, University Park–London: 174.

— 1976: *Studies in Old Prussian*, University Park–London: 232.

Schmid, W. P. 1966: *Alteuropa und der Osten im Spiegel der Sprachgeschichte*, Innsbruck: 150.

— 1976: "Baltisch und Indogermanisch," *Baltistica*, 1976/12(2), 115–122.

— 1978: "Indogermanistische Modelle und osteuropäische Frühgeschichte," *Abhandlungen der Geistes- und Sozialwissenschaftlichen Klasse*, Mainz: 1978/1.

— 1981: "Die Ausbildung der Sprachgemeinschaften in Osteuropa," in Hellmann 1981–89, 102–121.

— 1983: "Zum baltischen Dialekt der Kurischen Nehrung," *Indogermanische Forschungen*, 1983/88, 257–268.

Schmidt, L. 1941: *Geschichte der deutschen Stämme*, München: 653.

Schmidt, (Šmits) P. (ed.) 1930: *Die Letten*, Riga: 472.

— 1930a: "Die Mythologie der Letten," in Schmidt 1930, 192–214.

— 1930b: "Das lettische Volkslied," in Schmidt 1930, 310–332.

Schmidt, W. 1949: "Die Herkunft der Indogermanen und ihr erstes Auftreten in Europa," in Scherer 1968, 312–323.

Schmitt, R. (ed.) 1968: *Indogermanische Dichtersprache*, Darmstadt: 343.

Scholl, U. 1959: *Die Sprachen der vorkeltischen Indogermanen Hispaniens und das Keltiberische*, Wiesbaden: 233.

Scholz, F. 1990: *Die Literaturen des Baltikums*, Opladen: 356.

Schrader, O. 1883: *Sprachvergleichung und Urgeschichte*, Jena: 490.

Schroeder, L. 1914–16: *Arische Religion*, I–II, Leipzig.

Schumacher, B. 19583: *Geschichte Ost- und Westpreussens*, Würzburg: 402.

Schünemann, K. 1937: "Ostpolitik und Kriegführung im deutschen Mittelalter," *Ungarische Jahrbücher*, 1937/XVII, 31–56.

Schuster-Šewc, H. 1970: "Über die sorbische Sprache," in Die Sorben,125–133.

Schütz, J. 1967: "Denkform und Sinngehalt ostslavischer Götternamen," in Das Heidnische, 1969–70/II, 86–93.

Schwarz, E. 1956: "Das Vordringen der Slawen nach Westen," *Südost-Forschungen*, 1956, 86–108.

Sedlar, J. W. 1994: East Central Europe in the Midlle Ages, 1000–1500, Seattle–London: XIII+556.

Sedov, V. V. 1970: "Slavyane i plemena yugo-vostochnogo regiona baltiyskogo morya," Berichte 1973/I, 11–23.

— 1980: "Balty i slavyane v drevnosti po dannym arkheologii," in Mugurēvičs 1980, 14–21.

— 1985: "Dneprovskiye balty," in Volkaitė-Kulikauskienė 1981a, 20–30.

— (ed.) 1987: *Finno-ugry i balty v epokhe srednevekov'ya*. Moscow: 510.

See, K. 1970: *Deutsche Germanen-Ideologie*, Frankfurt: 105.

— (ed.) 1978: *Europäische Heldendichtung*, Darmstadt: 463.

— 1978a: "Was ist Heldendichtung?" in See 1978, 1–38.

— 1981: *Edda, Saga, Skaldendichtung*, Heidelberg: 539.

Segal, D. (ed.) 1981: Slavica Hierosolymitana V–VI, Jerusalem: 641.

Seibt, F. 1983: "Zwischen Ost und West," in Seibt 1983a, 1–16.

— (ed.) 1983a: *Die böhmischen Länder zwischen Ost und West*, München–Wien: 382.

Semyonova, M. F. 1977: "Iz istorii yazykovykh vzaimootnosheniy v gorode Rige," in Kontakty 1977, 32–47.

Senn, A. 1966: "The relationships of Baltic and Slavic," in Birnbaum–Puhvel 1966, 139–151.

— 1966a: *Handbuch der litauischen Sprache*, I, Heidelberg: 495.

— 1970: "Slavic and Baltic linguistic relations," in R ūķe–Draviņa 1970, 33–47.

Serédi, J. (ed.) 1938: *Emlékkönyv Szent István király halálának kilencszázadik évfordulóján* [A book of remembrance for the nine hundredth anniversary of the death of King Stephen], Budapest: 602.

Setälä, E. 1889: "A lív nép és nyelve" [The Livonian people and their language], *Nyelvtudományi Közlemények*, 1889/XXI, 241–264.

Ševčenko, I. 1964: "Three paradoxes of the Cyrillo-Methodian mission," in 1982, IV.

— 1982: *Ideology, Letters and Culture in the Byzantine World*, London: 368.

Shaskolskiy, I. P. 1976: "Problemy etnogeneza pribaltiysko-finnskikh plemen yugo- vostochnoy Pribaltiki v svete dannykh sovremennoy nauki," in Finno-ugry 1979, 41–48.

Silzemnieks, E. 1928: *Latvijas atdzimšana* [Latvia's renaissance], Riga: 141.

Šimek, E. 1930–53: *Velká Germanie Klaudia Ptolemaia* [Claudios Ptolemy's Great Germania], I–IV, Praha.

Šimėnas, V. 1992: "Nauji V a. pab.-VI a. pr. laidojimo papročiai Nemuno že-mupyje [New burial rites at the Lower Nemunas at the turn of the fifth and sixth centuries], in Gaižutis 1992, 23–35.

— 1994: "Legenda apie Videvutį ir Brutenį" [The Videvutis and the Brutenis legends], in Prūsijos 1994, 18–63.

Simon, R. 1983: "Nomádok és letelepedettek szimbiózisa" [The symbiosis of the nomads and the settled], in Tőkei 1983, 123–143.

— 1990: "Kelet és Nyugat: a ciklikus és a lineáris történelmi reflexió elágazásai. Az ó-görög és az arab út egybevetése" [East and West: the differences between the cyclical and linear historical reflexion. A comparison between the Ancient Greek and the Arabic paths], *Keletkutatás*, 1990/spring, 23–29.

— 1996: *Orientalista Kelet-Közép-Európában* [Orientalist in Eastern and Central Europe], Szombathely: 424.

Skardžius, P. 1963: "Dievas ir Perkūnas" [Dievas and Perkūnas], *Aidai*, 1963/6–7, 253–57, 311–318.

Škutāns, S. 1978: "*M. Bukšs: Latgaļu atmūda*" [M. Bukšs: The national awaken-ing of the Latgalians], *Journal of Baltic Studies*, 1978/2, 180–182.

Ślaski, K. 1969: *Słowiane Zachodni na Bałtyku w VII–XIII wieku* [West Slavs in the Baltic region in the seventh–thirteenth centuries], Gdańsk: 200.

Šliogeris, A. 1993: "Pokalbis" [Interview], *Akiračiai*, 1993/February, 8.

— 1994: "A Nyugat és Litvánia kultúrája" [The cultures of the West and Lithu-ania], *2000*, 1994, February 13–16.

Šmits, (Schmidt) P. 1923: "Par mūsu tautas dziesmu vecumu" [About the age of our folksongs], in 1923a, 3–25.

— 1923a: *Etnogrāfisku rakstu krājums* [Ethnographic studies], II, Riga: 140.

— 1926: *Latviešu mitoloģija* [Latvian mythology], Riga: 151.

— 1928: "Latviešu tautas dvēsele" [Latvian 'folk-soul'], *Daugava*, 1928/1, 81–88.

— 1932: "Dažādi laikmeti tautas dziesmās" [Various ages in folksongs], in Balodis–Šmits–Tentelis 1932, 7–14.

— 1936: *Ievads baltu filoloģijā* [Introduction to Baltic philology], Riga: 147.

— 1937: "Vēstures nedrošība [The uncertainty of history], in 1937a, 27–39.

— 1937a: *Vēsturiski un etnogrāfiski raksti* [Historical and ethnographic writings], Riga: 186.

Smoczyński, W. 1988: "Języky bałtyckie" [Baltic languages], in Bednarczuk 1988, 818–905.

Šnore, E. 1985: "K voprosu etnogeneza latgalov," in Volkaitė-Kulikauskienė 1981a, 39–47.

Sokols, E. (ed.) 1959: *Rakstu krājums* [A collection of studies], Riga: 736.

Solta, G. 1952: "Gedanken zum Indogermanenproblem," in Scherer 1968, 324–345.

Sonderegger, S. 1964: "Überlieferungsgeschichte der frühgermanischen und altnordischen Literatur," in Geschichte 1964/II, 703–761.

Spekke, A. 1938: "Senas ģeografiskas legendas par Baltijas jūras zemēm. Aethicus Ister" [Old geographical legends about the countries of the Baltic Sea], *Senatne un Māksla*, 1938/1, 86–94.

— 1957: *The Ancient Amber Routes and the Geographical Discovery of the Eastern Baltic,* Stockholm: 120.

Spengler, O. 1994: *A Nyugat alkonya (Der Untergang des Abendlandes,* 1918–22), I–II, (transl., concl., Csejtei, D.), Budapest.

Spiritus 1953: *Spiritus et Veritas (Festschrift für K. Kundziņš),* Eutin: XIV+190.

SRP: *Scriptores Rerum Prussicarum.* I–V (ed., introd., annot., T. Hirsch, M. Toeppen, E. Strehlke), Leipzig: 1861–1874.

SSS Słownik starożytności słowiańskich [Dictionary of Slavic Antiquity] 1–7, Wrocław–Warszawa–Kraków–Gdańsk–Łódź, 1961–82.

Stafecka, A. 1991: "Trīs posmi latgaliešu rakstu valodas vēsturē" [The three stages of the history of the Latgalian written language], *Latvijas Zinatņu Akadēmijas Vēstis,* 1991/1, 45–56.

Staknienė, A. 1994: "Marija Gimbutienė: prie giliųjų Europos šaknų". [Marija Gimbutienė: At Europe's deep roots], *Metmenys,* 1994/67, 161–167.

Stanevičius, (Staniewicz) S. 1838: "Wyjaśnienie mythologii litewskiej" [The explanation of Lithuanian mythology], in 1967, 216–302.

— 1967: *Raštai* [Collected works] (introd., annot., J. Lebedys), Vilnius, 655.

Stang, Ch. S. 1966: *Vergleichende Grammatik der baltischen Sprachen,* Oslo: 356.

Starodubets, P. A. 1955: "Knyazhestvo Kokneze v bor'be s nemetskimi zakhvatchikamu v Vostochnoy Pribaltike v nachale XIII veka," *Srednie veka* 1955/7, 199–216.

Strabo (Strabon): *Geography (Geographika),* 1–8. (transl., Jones, H. L.), London, 1. vol., 1917.

Ström, A. V.–Biezais, H. 1975: *Germanische und Baltische Religion,* Stuttgart: 391.

Stryjkowski, M. 1582: *Kronika polska, litewska, żmódzka i wszystkiej Rusi* [The chronicle of the Polish, Lithuanian, Žemaitian, and all the Russian lands], I–II. (introd., M. Malinowski, J. Danilowicz), 1846, Warszawa: 63+XVII+392, 572.

Studien 1985: *Studien zur Ethnogenese*. Opladen: 208.

Šturms, E. 1930: "Die bronzezeitlichen Funde in Lettland," in Congressus 1931, 103–139.

— 1936: *Die ältere Bronzezeit im Ostbaltikum*, Berlin–Leipzig: 155+34.

— 1938: "Chroniku un senrakstu ziņas par baltu tautu bēru parašām 13. un 14. g. s. [Chronicles and information of old scripts about the burial rites of the Baltic peoples in the thirteenth–fourteenth centuries], in Tautas 1938, 84–110.

Sudnik, T. M. (ed.) 1980: *Balto-slavyanskiye etnoyazykovyye kontakty*, Moscow: 339.

Sulimirski, T. 1933: "Die schnurkeramischen Kulturen," in Scherer 1968, 117–140.

— 1970: "Die Veneti-Venedae und deren Verhältnis zu den Slawen, Berichte 1973/II, 381–387.

Sužiedėlis S. 1989: "The Molotov–Ribbentrop Pact and the Baltic States: an introduction and interpretation," *Lituanus*, 1989/1, 8–46.

Švābe, A. 1923: "Latvju dainu vecums" [The age of the Latvian dainas], *Latvju Grāmata*, 1923/9–10, 13–19, 117–22.

— 1938: "Kas bij Latviešu Indriķis?" [Who was Heinricus de Lettis?], *Senatne un Māksla*, 1938/4, 11–38.

Svatoš, M. 1981: "Litevská kolej pražské university. 1397–1622" [The Lithuanian college of the Prague university. 1397–1622], in Petr–Řeháček 1981, 19–32.

Szarka, L. 1992: "A történeti Magyarország a szlovák történetírás tükrében [Historical Hungary in the mirror of Slovakian history writing], *Világtörténet*, 1992/autumn–winter, 8–23.

Szemerényi, O. 1948: "Sur l'unité linguistique balto-slave," *Études slaves et roumaines*, 1948, 65–85, 159–173.

— 1957: "The Problem of Balto-Slav Unity," *Kratylos*, 1957/2, 97–123.

— 1961: *Trends and Tasks in Comparative Philology*, London: 21.

— 1971–82: *Richtungen der modernen Sprachwissenschaft*, I–II. Heidelberg:148, 318.

Szilágyi, J. Gy. 1957: "A görög irodalom kezdetei" [The beginnings of Greek literature], *MTA Nyelv- és Irodalomtudományok Osztályának Közleményei*, 1957 (X), 415–450.

— 1969–79: "Kerényi Károly emlékezete" [Károly Kerényi's memory], in 1982a, 237–272.

— 1982: "Mi, filológusok" [We, philologists], *Antik Tanulmányok*, 1984/31, 167–197.

— 1982a: *Paradigmák*, (Paradigms), Budapest: 340.

— 1994: "Szolgáló tudomány" [Serving science], *Buksz*, 1994/spring, 69–75.

Szili, J. 1993: *Az irodalomfogalmak rendszere* [The system of literary concepts], Budapest: 227.

Szűcs, J. 1970: "A nemzet historikuma és a történetszemlélet nemzeti látószöge" [The historicum of the nation, and the national perspective of the view of history], in 1984, 11–188.

— 1974: "Teoretikus elemek Kézai *Gesta Hungarorum* -ában" [Theoretical elements in Kézai's *Gesta Hungarorum*], *Valóság*, 1974/8, 1–24.

— 1984^2: *Nemzet és történelem* [Nation and history], Budapest: 669.

— 1985: "Történeti 'eredet'-kérdések és nemzeti tudat" [Historical questions of 'origin' and national consciousness], *Valóság*, 1985/3, 31–49.

— 1992: *A magyar nemzeti tudat kialakulása* [The emergence of Hungarian national consciousness], Szeged: 330.

Tacitus: "Germania" (transl., Hutton, M.), in *Tacitus in Five Volumes*, I, London–Cambridge, Mass., 1970, 116–215.

Taube, M. 1935: "Russische und litauische Fürsten an der Düna zur Zeit der deutschen Eroberung Livlands. XII. und XIII. Jahrhundert," *Jahrbücher für Kultur und Geschichte der Slaven*, 1935/XI, 367–502.

— 1938: "Internationale und kirchenpolitische Wandlungen im Ostbaltikum und Russland zur Zeit der deutschen Eroberung Livlands. 12. und 13. Jahrhundert," *Jahrbücher für Geschichte Osteuropas*, 1938/3, 11–46.

Tautas 1938: *Tautas vēsturei* [To national history], Riga: 643.

Tautavičius, A. 1980: "Baltskiye plemena na territorii Litvy v I. tysyachel. n. e.," in Mugurēvičs 1980, 80–88.

— 1981: "Žemaičių etnogenezė" [The ethnogenesis of the Žemaitians], in Volkaitė–Kulikauskienė 1981, 27–35.

— 1986: "M. Gimbutienė: Baltai," *Literatura ir Menas*, 1986. October 4.

Tentelis, A 1930: "Die Letten in der Ordenszeit," in Schmidt 1930, 140–163.

The Bible. (British and Foreign Bible Society), Oxford, 1960.

Thietmar von Merseburg: *Chronik* (transl., annot., W. Trillmach), Berlin, n.d.: 516.

Todd, J. M. 1976: "New evidence of Baltic–Adriatic amber trade," *Journal of Baltic Studies*, 1976/4, 330–342.

— 1985: "Baltic amber in the ancient Near East: A preliminary investigation," *Journal of Baltic Studies*, 1985/3, 292–301.

Todd, J. M.–Eichel, M. H. 1974: "A reappraisal of the prehistoric and classical amber trade in the light of new evidence," *Journal of Baltic Studies*, 1974/4, 295–314.

Toivonen, Y. H. 1955–62: *Suomen kielen etymologinen sanakrija* [Finnish etymological dictionary], I–III. Helsinki.

Tokarev, S. A. (ed.) 1980–82: *Mify narodov mira* . I–II. Moscow: 671, 718.

— 1988: *Mitológiai enciklopédia* [Mythological encyclopedia] (*Mify narodov mira*, 1980–82), I–II. Budapest.

Tőkei, F. (ed.) 1983: *Nomád társadalmak és államalakulatok*, [Nomadic society and state organization], Budapest, 391.

Tolstoy, N. I. (red.) 1961: *Issledovaniya po slavyanskomu yazykoznaniyu*. Moscow: 323.

Toporov, V. N. 1975–90: *Prusskiy yazyk*. I–V. Moscow.

— 1966: "Yatvyazhskaya mifologema," *Acta Baltico-Slavica*, 1966/3, 143–149.

— 1970 "K balto-skandinavskim mifologicheskim svyazyam", in Rūķe-Draviņa 1970, 534–543.

— 1972: "Zametki po baltiyskoy mifologii," in Balto-slavyanskiy 1972, 289–314.

— 1980: "Vilnius, Wilno, Vil'na: gorod i mif," in Sudnik 1980, 3–71.

— 1980a: Γαλινδαι–Galindite–Golyad' in Etnograficheskiye 1980, 124–136.

— 1981: "Drevnyaya Moskva v baltiyskoy perspektive," *Balto-Slavyanskiye Issledovaniya*, 1982, 3–61.

— 1982a: "Galindy v zapadnoy Evrope," *Balto-Slavyanskiye Issledovaniya*, 1983, 129–140.

— 1982b: "Baltiyskiy gorizont drevney Moskvy," *Acta Baltico-Slavica*, 1982, 259–272.

— 1982c: "Novyye raboty o sledakh prebyvaniya prussov k zapadu ot Visly," *Balto-Slavyanskiye Issledovaniya*, 1983, 263–273.

— 1984: "K rekonstruktsii odnogo tsikla arkhaichnykh mifopoeticheskikh predstavleniy v svete 'Latvju dainas'," *Balto-Slavyanskiye Issledovaniya*, 1986, 29–59.

— 1984a: "Indoevropeyskiy ritual'nyy termin souh-, etro- (-etlo-, -edhlo-)," *Balto-Slavyanskiye Issledovaniya*, 1986, 81–89.

— 1990: "Konnyye sostyazaniya na pokhoronakh," in Ivanov–Nevskaya 1990, 12–47.

Toporov, V. N.–Trubachev, O. N. 1962: *Lingvisticheskiy analiz gidronimov Verkhnego Podneprov'ya*. Moscow: 267+13.

Töppen, M. 1853: *Geschichte der preussischen Historiographie von P. v. Dusburg bis auf K. Schütz*, Berlin: 290.

Tovar, A. 1977: "Krahe's alteuropäische Hydronymie und die westindogermanischen Sprachen". *Sitzungsberichte der Heidelberger Akademie der Wissenschaften*, 1977/2, 1–42.

Trautmann, R. 1923: *Baltisch–Slavisches Wörterbuch*, Göttingen: 382.

— 1925: *Die altpreussische Personennamen*, Göttingen: 204.

Tret'yakov, P. N. 1962: "Etnicheskiy protsess i arkheologiya," *Sovetskaya Arkheologiya*, 1962/4, 3–16.

— 1966: *Finno-ugry, balty i slavyane na Dnepre i Volge,* Moscow–Leningrad: 307.

Trubachev, O. N. 1968: *Nazvaniya rek Pravoberezhnoy Ukrainy*, Moscow: 289.

— 1980: "Replika po balto-slavyanskomu voprosu," *Balto-Slavyanskie Issledovaniya*, 1981: 3–6.

— 1982: "Yazykoznaniye i etnogenez slavyan," *Voprosy Yazykoznaniya'*, 1982/4, 10–26, 1982/5, 3–17.

Trubetzkoy, N. S. 1939: "Gedanken über das Indogermanenproblem," in Scherer 1968, 214–223.

Tymieniecki, K. 1948: *Zarys dziejów historiografii polskiej* [The outline of Polish history writing], Kraków:141.

— 1963: "Problem tzw. północnych Ilirów" [The question of the so-called northern Illyrians], in Munera 1963, 261–284.

— 1968: "W okresie wenedzkim" [In the Venedic period], in Jażdżewski 1968, 199–212.

Ucko, P. J. 1962: "The interpretation of prehistoric anthropomorphic figurines," *The Journal of the Royal Anthropological Institute of Great Britain and Ireland*, 1962, 38–54.

— 1968: *Anthropomorphic Figurines of Predynastic Egypt and Neolithic Crete with Comparative Material from the Prehistoric Near East and Mainland Greece*, London: 530.

Untermann, J. 1983: "Ursprache und historische Realität. Der Beitrag der Indogermanistik zu Fragen der Ethnogenese," in Studien 1985, 133–164.

Urban, W. 1975: *The Baltic Crusade*, De Kalb: 296.

— 1980: *The Prussian Crusade*, Lanham etc.: 457.

— 1981: *The Livonian Crusade*, Washington: 562.

— 1989: *The Samogitian Crusade*, Chicago: IX+303.

— 1991: "Renaissance humanism in Prussia: Early humanism in Prussia," *Journal of Baltic Studies*, 1991/1, 29–72.

— 1991a: "Renaissance humanism in Prussia: Copernicus, humanist politician," *Journal of Baltic Studies*, 1991/3, 195–232.

Urbańczyk, S. 1985: "Aus den Studien über die alte Religion der Slawen," *Slavica Hierosolymitana*, 1985/VII, 241–244.

Urtāns, V. 1977: *Senākie depozīti Latvijā, līdz 1200 g* [The oldest archaeological sites in Latvia, until 1200], Riga: 283.

Usener, H. 1896: *Götternamen*, Bonn: 1929², 391.

Užgiris, Č. I. (ed.) 1985: *Proceedings of the Institute of Lithuanian Studies 1981*, Chicago: 391.

Vaitkauskienė, L. 1990: "Dėl žemaičių kilmės" [On the origins of the Žemaitians] in Butrimas 1990, 26–41.

— 1992: "Gintaras senovės baltų mene ir tikėjimuose" [Amber in ancient Baltic arts and beliefs], in Gaižutis 1992, 36–49.

Vanagas, A. 1974: "Jotvingiai" [The Jatvingians], *Mokslas ir Gyvenimas*, 1974/2, 19–21.

— (ed.) 1981: *Lietuvių onomastikos tyrinėjimai* [Lithuanian onomastic studies], Vilnius, 215.

— 1981a: "Lietuvių hidronimų semantika" [The semantics of Lithuanian water names] in Vanagas 1981, 4–153.

Vasks, A. 1992: "Sedovs, V.: Balti senatnē" [Sedovs, V.: Balts in Antiquity], *Latvijas Vēstures Institīta žurnals*, 1992/3, 181–186.

Vasmer, M. 1913: "Kritisches und Antikritisches zur neueren slavischen Etymologie," in 1971/I, 3–30.

— 1929: "Beiträge zur slavischen Altertumskunde," *Zeitschrift für slavische Philologie*, 1929, 145–204.

— 1929a: "Beiträge zur alten Geographie der Gebiete zwischen Elbe und Weichsel," in 1971/II, 540–547.

— 1930: "E. Kucharskis baltische Theorie," in 1971/I, 210–214.

— 1941: "Die alten Bevölkerungsverhältnisse Russlands im Lichte der Sprachforschung," in 1971/I, 80–99.

— 1953–58: *Russisches etymologisches Wörterbuch* I–III. Heidelberg.

— 1971: *Schriften zur slavischen Altertumskunde und Namenkunde* I–II. Berlin: 1033.

Vekerdi, L. 1976: "Újrégészet" [New archaeology], *Valóság*, 1976/11, 26–41.

Vėlius, N. 1983: *Senovės baltų pasaulėžiūra* [The world view of the ancient Balts], Vilnius, 309.

— 1986: "Senoji lietuvių religija ir pasaulėžiūra [The ancient Lithuanian religion and world view], in Deksnys 1986, 9–42.

— 1987: *Chtoniškasis lietuvių mitologijos pasaulis* [The chthonic world of Lithuanian mythology], Vilnius: 318.

— 1988: "Baltų religijos ir mitologijos šaltiniai" [The sources of Baltic religion and mythology], *Mokslas ir Gyvenimas*, 1988/1–2, 22–23, 10–11.

— 1990: "Lietuvių mitologijos rekonstrukcija" [The reconstruction of Lithuanian mythology], *Mokslas ir Gyvenimas*, 1990/11–12, 13–15., 18–22.

— (ed., introd., annot.) 1995: *Lietuvių mitologija 1* [Lithuanian mythology], Vilnius: 603.

Venclova, T. 1995: "Borusija – ketvirtoji Baltijos respublika?" [Borussia – the fourth Baltic republic?] *Akiračiai*, 1995/1, 1–13.

Viitso, T.-R. 1994: "Possible reflections of the prehistoric amber way in modern languages," in Pusztay 1994a, 104–110.

Vijūkas-Kojalavičius, A. (Wiiuk Koialowicz): *Lietuvos istorija* (Historia Lituana, 1650–69) 1–2. (introd., annot., J. Jurginis), Vilnius: 1987, 818.

Vīķe-Freiberga, (Vīķis-Freibergs) V. 1993[2]: *Dzintara kalnā* [On the amber mountain], Riga: 178.

— (ed.) 1989: *Linguistics and Poetics of Latvian Folk Songs*, Kingston–Montréal: 371.

— 1989a: "The major gods and goddesses of ancient Latvian mythology," in Vīķis-Freibergs 1989, 91–112.

Vilinbakhov, V. B. 1967: "Kilka słów o migracji Słowian bałtyckich na wschód" [A few words about the eastward migration of the Baltic Slavs], Zapiski Historyczne, 1967/3, 50–60.

Vilinbakhov, V. B.–Engovatov, N. V. 1963: Predvaritel'nyye zamechaniya o zapadnykh galindakh," Slavia Occidentalis 1963/23, 233–269.

Viliūnas, G. 1994: "Lituanistai nebebus patriotai profesionalai?" [Will the Lithuanianists never be professional patriots again?], Šiaurės Atėnai, 1994/46.

Villems, R.–Adojaan, M.–Kivisild, T.–Metspalu, E.–Parik, J.–Pielberg, G.–Rootsi, S.–Tambets, K.–Tolk, H.-Viivi 1997: "Reconstruction of maternal lineages of Finno-Ugric speaking people and some remarks on their paternal inheritance," in Julku–Wiik 1998, 180–200.

Vinogradov, V. V. 1956: "Voprosy obrazovaniya russkogo natsional'nogo literaturnogo yazyka," Voprosy Yazykoznaniya, 1956/1, 3–25.

Virza, E. 1933: Straumeni (introd., I. Ziedonis, concl., V. Vecgrāvis),1989, Riga: 252.

Vogt, J. 1949: "Geschichte und Vorgeschichte. Die Bedeutung der Schrift," in 1960, 327–339.

— 1960: Orbis, Freiburg etc.: 400.

Voigt, G. 1856–63: Enea Silvio de Piccolomini, als Papst Pius der Zweite und sein Zeitalter, I–III, Berlin.

Voigt, J. 1827–39: Geschichte Preussens, von den ältesten Zeiten bis zum Untergange der Herrschaft des deutschen Ordens 1–9, Königsberg.

Voigt, V. 1965: "A sámánizmus mint etnológiai kutatási probléma" [Shamanism as an ethnological research problem], Nyelvtudományi Közlemények, 1965, 379–390.

— 1967–68: "A balti finn népek folklórja mint az európai folklór része" [The folklore of the Balto-Finnic peoples, as part of European folklore] Ethnográfia, 1967/1, 406–437, 1968/1, 37–61.

— 1971: "Hungaro-Baltic preliminaria," Acta Linguistica Academiae Scientiarum Hungaricae, 1971/3–4, 391–400.

— 1975: "A szibériai sámánizmus," [Shamanism in Siberia], Nyelvtudományi Közlemények, 1975/1, 207–214.

— 1977: "Folklorisztika és őstörténet," [Folkloristics and prehistory], in Bartha–Czeglédy–Róna-Tas 1977, 305–318.

— 1978: "A folklór történeti kutatásának eredményei," [Results in historic research of folklore], Világosság, 1978, 382–386.

— 1980: "On Baltic and Hungarian Prehistoric Contacts," Journal of Baltic Studies, 1980/1, 78–83.

— 1994: *A balti finn népek folklórja, mint az európai folklór része* [The folklore of Balto-Finnic peoples as part of European folklore], Budapest (dissertation in manuscript format): 276.

Volkaitė-Kulikauskienė, R. 1970: *Lietuviai IX–XII amžiais* [Lithuanians in the ninth–twelfth centuries], Vilnius: 296.

— (ed.) 1981: *Iš lietuvių etnogenezės* [On Lithuanian ethnogenesis], Vilnius: 117.

— (ed.) 1981a: *Problemy etnogeneza i etnicheskoy istorii baltov.* Vilnius: 156.

— (ed.) 1987: *Lietuvių etnogenezė* [The ethnogenesis of the Lithuanians], Vilnius: 254.

Wahle, E. 1952: *Deutsche Vorzeit*, Basel: XII+358.

Warburg, Aby M. 1923: *Images from the Region of the Pueblo Indians of North America (Schlangenritual)* (transl., introd., Steinberg, M. P.), Ithaca– London, 1995: XIII+114.

Ward, D. J. 1970: "An Indo-European mythological theme in Germanic tradition," in Cardona–Hoenigswald–Senn 1970, 405–420.

Wartberge, H.: *Chronicon Livoniae,* in SRP/II: 9–178, Lithuanian in Livonia's chronicles.

Wattenbach, W.–Lewison, W. 1952–63: *Deutschlands Geschichtsquellen im Mittelalter*, 1–5, Weimar.

Weczerka, H. 1962: "Kartographische Beiträge zur kirchlichen Gliederung Ost-Mitteleuropas," *Zeitschrift für Ostforschung*, 1962, 292–323.

Weingart, M. 1922: "Byzantské kroniky v literatuře církevně–slovanské" [Byzantine chronicles in Church Slavic literature], Bratislava: 360.

Wenskus, R. 1961: *Stammesbildung und Verfassung*, Köln–Graz: 656.

— 1975: "Der deutsche Orden und die nichtdeutsche Bevölkerung des Preussenlandes mit besonderer Berücksichtigung der Siedlung", in Schlesinger 1975, 417–438.

Wermke, E. 1958–63: *Bibliographie der Geschichte von Ost- und Westpreussen*, I–II, Marburg: 256, 377.

Werner, R. 1981: "Die Frühzeit Osteuropas," in Hellmann 1981–89/1, 122–198.

Wielowiejski, J. 1982: "Politische und siedlungswirtschaftliche Voraussetzungen der Verschiebung nach Osten des Hauptbernsteinweges im dritten Viertel des 1. Jh. u. Z.," *Savaria*, 1982/16, 265–272.

Wigand von Marburg: *Chronica Nova Prutenica,* in SRP/II, 429–662.

Winter, E. 1960: *Russland und das Papsttum*, I, Berlin: 375.

Wippermann, W. 1979: *Der Ordenstaat als Ideologie*, Berlin: 456.

Wittgenstein, L. 1998: **Tractatus logico-philosophicus*, 1921 (transl., Ogden, C. K., introd., B. Russell), London–New York.

Wittram, R. 1954[2]: *Baltische Geschichte. Die Ostseelande Livland, Estland, Kurland 1180–1918*, München: 323.

— (ed.) 1956: *Baltische Kirchengeschichte*, Göttingen: 347.

— 1971: "Methodologische und geschichtstheoretische Überlegungen zu Proble- men der baltischen Geschichtsforschung," *Zeitschrift für Ostforschung*, 1971/, 601–640.

Wolf, E. R. 1982: *Europe and the people without history*, London.

Wulfstan: SRP/I: 732–5. and in *Two Voyagers at the Court of King Alfred, the ventures of Ohthere and Wulfstan Together with the Description of Northern Europe from the Old English Orosius*, (ed., Lund, N., transl., Fell, Ch. E., introd., Crumlin-Pedersen, O.), York, 1984: 71.

Wyka, K. 1946: "Sprawa Sienkiewicza" [The Sienkiewicz question], in 1956, 113–140.

— 1956: *Szkice literackie i artystyczne* [Literary and artistic sketches], I–II, Kraków: 330, 354.

Zeids, T. 1980: "Obrazovaniye latyshkoy narodnosti v otobrazhenii pismennykh istochnikov," in: Etnograficheskiye 1980, 55–63.

— 1992: *Senākie rakstītie Latvijas vēstures avoti* [Ancient written sources of Latvia's history], Riga: 216.

Zeile, P. 1992: "Latgales kultūras vēstures pamatmeti" [The bases of Latgale's cultural history], *Latvijas Zinātņu Akadēmijas Vēstis*, 1992/2, 1–9.

Zeps, J. V. 1962: *Latvian and Finnic Linguistic Convergences*, Bloomington: 228.

— 1978: "Velta Rūķe-Draviņa: The standardization process in Latvian," *Journal of Baltic Studies*, 1978/4, 380–382.

— 1993: "Latgalian literature in exile," *Journal of Baltic Studies*, 1993/4, 313–328.

Zeps-Rosenshield, J. 1995: "Pre-Latgalian hydronyms in East Latvia," *Journal of Baltic Studies*, 1995/4, 345–352.

Ziedonis, A.–Winter, W. L.–Valgemäe, M. (eds.) 1974: *Baltic History*, Columbus: 340.

Žiemys, E. 1984: "Galima prūsų *Ligaschones* reikšmė" [The possible meaning of the Prussian *Ligaschones*], *Mūsų kalba*, 1984/4, 47–48.

Zientara, B. 1977: "Struktury narodowe średniowieczne" [The national structures of the Middle Ages], *Kwartalnik Historyczny*, 1977/2, 287–311.

Zinkevičius, Z. 1982: "K voprosu o proiskhozhdenii zhemaytskogo dialekta," *Balto-Slavyanskiye Issledovaniya*, 1983, 113–119.

— 1984: "Jotvingių kalbos žodynėlis?" [A Jatvingian vocabulary book?], *Mokslas ir Gyvenimas*, 1984/5, 22–23.

— 1984–94: *Lietuvių kalbos istorija* [The history of the Lithuanian language], I–VI, Vilnius.

Zutis, J. 1949: *Ocherki po istoriografii Latvii. I. Pribaltiysko-nemetskaya isto- riografiya*, Riga: 259.

Zvidriņš, P.—Krumiņš, J. 1991: "Demograficheskaya situatsiya v vostochnoy chasti Latvii," *Latvijas Zinātņu Akadēmijas Vēstis*, 1991/1, 37–44.

INDEX

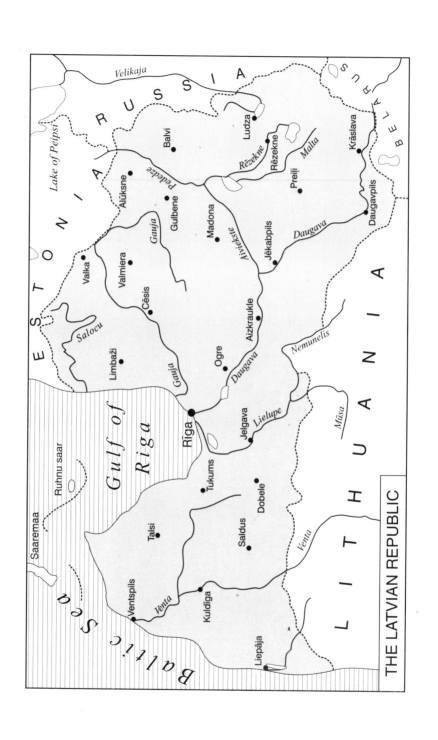

THE LATVIAN REPUBLIC